"**I did like** [the avatars] **because they helped me to understand** [the material] **better. Thank you for finding ways to help those of us who need a little extra help.**"

—LaTricia Scott, Central Texas College

Scott is single and in his mid-thirties. He is taking care of his father, who was diagnosed with lung cancer. Scott is taking prerequisite classes for a radiologic technology program. In his spare time, Scott enjoys BMX racing.

Scott

Vickie is in her mid-fifties, and is returning to school to earn a counseling degree so that she can work as a substance abuse counselor. She is outgoing and enjoys volunteering, such as delivering meals to the elderly and working with at-risk teens.

Vickie

Zach is a recent high school graduate, and is very much a skater. He's always listening to his iPod, with his skateboard by his side. He is a first-year college student and is still exploring his options.

Zach

"**I liked them all.** [The avatars] **make work more fun and engaging.**"

—Zuzana Melnova, Montgomery College

"**The** characters **are helpful; they show me when I'm doing well.**"

—Paula Ray, Delgado Community College

mhconnectwriting.com

English Skills
with Reading

Eighth Edition

English Skills
with Readings

John Langan
Atlantic Cape Community College

McGraw Hill

Connect
Learn
Succeed™

Connect
Learn
Succeed™

Published by McGraw-Hill, an imprint of The McGraw-Hill Companies, Inc., 1221 Avenue of the Americas, New York, NY 10020. Copyright © 2012, 2008, 2006, 2002, 1999, 1995, 1991, 1988. All rights reserved. No part of this publication may be reproduced or distributed in any form or by any means, or stored in a database or retrieval system, without the prior written consent of The McGraw-Hill Companies, Inc., including, but not limited to, in any network or other electronic storage or transmission, or broadcast for distance learning.

This book is printed on acid-free paper.

3 4 5 6 7 8 9 0 DOC / DOC 1 0 9 8 7 6 5 4 3 2

Student Edition:

ISBN: 978-0-07-337168-9
MHID: 0-07-337168-8

Instructor's Edition

ISBN: 978-0-07-740420-8
MHID: 0-07-740420-3

Vice President and   gn Manager and Cover Designer:
Publisher: *David*   *reston Thomas*
Senior Sponsoring   o Researcher: *Emily Tietz*
Director of Devel   *r: Tandra Jorgensen*
Developmental Ed   tal Product Manager: *Janet Smith*
Senior Marketing   ia Project Managers: *Bethuel Jabez and*
Editorial Coordina   *aria Betancourt*
Production Editors   position: *11/13 Times by Aptara®, Inc.*
  Brett Coker   ing: *45# New Era Thin by R.R. Donnelley*
Production Service   *Sons*

Credits: The credit   779 and is considered an extension of the copyright page.

Library of Congress Cataloging-in-Publication Data

Langan, John, 1942–
    English skills with readings / John Langan.—8th ed.
      p. cm.
    Includes bibliographical references and index.
    ISBN-13: 978-0-07-337168-9 (acid-free paper)
    ISBN-10: 0-07-337168-8 (acid-free paper) 1. English language—Rhetoric. 2. English language—Grammar. 3. College readers. I. Title.
    PE1408.L3182 2011
    808'.0427—dc22

2010048315

The Internet addresses listed in the text were accurate at the time of publication. The inclusion of a Web site does not indicate an endorsement by the authors or McGraw-Hill, and McGraw-Hill does not guarantee the accuracy of the information presented at these sites.

Contents

PART 1:   Basic Principles of Effective Writing   1

PART 5:   Handbook of Sentence Skills   411

Readings Listed by Rhetorical Mode

Note: Some selections are listed more than once because they illustrate more than one rhetorical method of development.

NARRATION

ARGUMENT

Behind every McGraw-Hill education product is research.

Thousands of instructors participate in our course surveys every year, providing McGraw-Hill with longitudinal information on the trends and challenges in your courses. That research, along with reviews, focus groups analyses, and ethnographic studies of both instructor and student workflow, provides the intensive feedback that our authors use to ensure that our revisions continue to provide everything you need to reach your course goals and outcomes.

Some KEY FINDINGS from our Developmental Writing Course Survey

50% of Developmental English instructors say they require lab component each week. **85%** of these respondents say they use the lab to teach grammar and punctuation.

> Connect Writing is built around the five core skill areas instructors say they want addressed. Students will see these five areas in all three levels of Connect Writing.

> With Langan, *English Skills with Readings*, 8e students get an individualized learning plan when they take the diagnostic test in Connect Writing. This individualized instruction makes sure that all students get the practice they need to improve their grammar and punctuation skills.

51% of instructors say that they choose their text on the basis of how the pedagogy supports student learning.

79% say that the text they choose must have worthwhile activities and writing assignments.

FOUR BASES Checklist for Cause and Effect

About *Unity*

☑ Have I introduced my essay with a clearly stated thesis and plan of development?

About *Support*

☑ Is each of my main points supported by solid, specific details?

About *Coherence*

☑ Have I used transition words such as *first, another, in addition*, and *also*?

About *Sentence Skills*

☑ Have I used a consistent point of view throughout my essay?

☑ Have I used specific rather than general words?

☑ Have I avoided wordiness and used concise wording?

☑ Are my sentences varied?

☑ Have I checked my writing for spelling and other sentence skills, as listed on the inside back cover of the book?

> Langan's Four Bases checklists serve to remind students of the core areas they need to address in their writing.

Is the United States a health-conscious nation? Look at this photograph and write a paragraph in which you answer that question. Use examples found in the media, in the photograph, or in your own daily observations to support your point.

> Students are introduced to writing from the beginning as each assignment chapter starts with a photo and a writing task.

If you would like to participate in any of the McGraw-Hill research initiatives, please contact us at **www.mhhe.com/faculty-research.**

Preface

English Skills with Readings will help students learn and apply the basic principles of effective composition. It will also help them master essential reading skills. It is a nuts-and-bolts approach based on a number of assumptions or beliefs about the writing process:

Keys to Effective Writing

- *English Skills with Readings* **assumes that four principles in particular are keys to effective writing:** *unity, support, coherence,* **and** *sentence skills.* These four principles are highlighted on the inside back cover and reinforced throughout the book.

    ✓ Part One focuses on the first three principles and to some extent on sentence skills; Part Five serves as a concise handbook of sentence skills.

    ✓ The four principles are applied in different types of paragraph development (Part Two) and in several-paragraph essays (Part Three).

    ✓ Part Four discusses research skills.

    ✓ Part Six presents seventeen reading selections.

> ## FOUR BASES Checklist for Argument
>
> **About** *Unity*
>
> ☑ Imagine that your audience is a jury who will ultimately render a verdict on your argument. Have you presented a convincing case? If you were on the jury, would you both understand and be favorably impressed by this argument?
>
> ☑ Does every one of your supporting points help prove the argument stated in your topic sentence?
>
> **About** *Support*
>
> ☑ Have you backed up your points of support with specific details?
>
> ☑ Have you appealed to your readers' senses with these details?
>
> **About** *Coherence*
>
> ☑ Have you used emphatic order in your paragraph, saving the most important, strongest detail for last?
>
> **About** *Sentence Skills*
>
> ☑ Have you used strong verbs (rather than *is* and *to be*) throughout?
>
> ☑ Have you written your argument in the active, rather than passive, voice?
>
> ☑ Have you checked your paper for sentence-skills mistakes, including spelling? Use the checklist on the inside back cover of this book.

The ongoing success of *English Skills with Readings* is evidence that the four principles are easily grasped, remembered, and followed by students.

- *English Skills with Readings* **also reflects a belief that, in addition to these four principles, there are other important factors in writing effectively.** The second chapter discusses *prewriting, rewriting, and editing.*

Besides encouraging students to see *writing as a process,* the chapter asks students to examine their *attitude toward writing,* to *write on what they know* about or can learn about, to consider keeping a *writing journal,* and to make *outlining* a part of the writing process.

- *English Skills with Readings* **assumes that the best way to begin writing is with personal experience.** After students have learned to support a point by providing material from their own experience, they are ready to develop an idea by drawing on their own reasoning abilities and on information in reports, articles, and books. In Parts Two and Three, students are asked to write on *both experiential and objective topics.*

Connect Writing

Connect Writing is a course enhancement that prepares students for success in college and beyond. *Connect Writing* teaches students to be more effective writers in the kinds of writing that are crucial to their success—college essays, business letters, memos, and more.

With *English Skills with Readings,* students gets an individualized learning plan when they take the diagnostic test in *Connect Writing.* This individualized instruction makes sure that all students get the specific practice they need to improve their grammar and punctuation skills. *Connect Writing* also uses avatars to present a variety of writing scenarios where clear writing means effective communication for different purposes and audiences. The avatars act as guides as students work through each writing scenario.

Realistic Models

- *English Skills with Readings* **also assumes that beginning writers are more likely to learn composition skills through lively, engaging, and realistic models than through materials remote from the common experiences that are part of everyday life.** For example, when a writer argues that proms should be banned, or catalogs ways to harass an instructor, or talks about why some teenagers take drugs, students will be more apt to remember and follow the writing principles that are involved.

- **A related assumption is that students are especially interested in and challenged by the writing of their peers.** After reading vigorous papers composed by other students and understanding the power that good writing can have, students will be more encouraged to aim for similar honesty, realism, and detail in their own work.

- **Another premise of *English Skills with Readings* is that mastery of the paragraph should precede work on the several-paragraph essay.** Thus Part One illustrates the basic principles of composition writing using paragraph models, and the assignments in Part Two aim at developing the ability to support ideas within a variety of paragraph forms. The essential principles of paragraph writing are then applied to the several-paragraph essays in Part Three.

- **The grammar, punctuation, and usage skills that make up Part Five are explained clearly and directly, without unnecessary technical terms.** Here, as elsewhere, *abundant exercise material* is provided, especially for the mistakes that are most likely to interfere with clear communication.

- **A final assumption is that, since no two people will use an English text in exactly the same way, the material should be organized in a highly accessible manner.** Because each of the six parts of the book deals with a distinct area of writing, instructors can turn quickly and easily to the skills they want to present. At the same time, ideas for sequencing material are provided in a section titled "Using This Text" at the end of Chapter 1. And a detailed syllabus is provided in the Instructor's Manual.

I am very grateful for the ongoing popularity of *English Skills with Readings*. Instructors continue to say that the four bases really do help students learn to write effectively. And they continue to comment that students find the activities, assignments, model passages, and reading selections especially interesting and worthwhile.

The Readings

The seventeen selections in Part Six have been chosen for their content as much as for rhetorical mode. The Readings are organized thematically into three groups: "Goals and Values," "Education and Self-Improvement," and "Human Groups and Society." Some selections reflect important contemporary concerns: for instance, "Let's Really Reform Our Schools," "'Extra Large,' Please," and "What Good Families Are Doing Right." Some provide information many students may find helpful: examples are "Anxiety: Challenge by Another Name,"

Group Pressure
Rodney Stark

PREVIEW

We've all experienced group pressure at one time or another, but how much do we really know about how that phenomenon affects us? The following selection from the college textbook *Sociology*, Third Edition, by Rodney Stark, will give you a fascinating view of this common behavioral situation.

It is self-evident that people tend to conform to the expectations and reactions 1 of others around them. But what are the limits of group pressure? Can group pressure cause us to deny the obvious, even physical evidence?

Over thirty-five years ago, Solomon Asch performed the most famous exper- 2 imental test of the power of group pressure to produce conformity. Since then his study has been repeated many times, with many variations confirming his original results. Perhaps the best way to understand what Asch discovered is to pretend that you are a subject in his experiment.

You have agreed to take part in an experiment on visual perception. Upon 3 arriving at the laboratory, you are given the seventh in a line of eight chairs. Other students taking part in the experiment sit in each of the other chairs. At the front of the room the experimenter stands by a covered easel. He explains that he wants you to judge the length of lines in a series of comparisons. He will place two decks of large cards upon the easel. One card will display a single vertical line. The other card will display three vertical lines, each of a different length. He wants each of you to decide which of the three lines on one card is the same length as the single line on the other card. To prepare you for the task, he displays a practice card. You see the correct line easily, for the other lines are noticeably different from the comparison line.

The experiment begins. The first comparison is just as easy as the practice 4 comparison. One of the three lines is obviously the same length as the comparison line, while the other two are very different. Each of the eight persons answers in turn, with you answering seventh. Everyone answers correctly. On the second pair of cards, the right answer is just as easy to spot, and again all eight subjects are correct. You begin to suspect that the experiment is going to be a big bore.

Then comes the third pair. The judgment is just as easy as before. But the 5 first person somehow picks a line that is obviously wrong. You smile. Then the second person also picks the same obviously wrong line. What's going on? Then

"How They Get You to Do That," and "Group Pressure." Some recount profoundly human experiences: "All the Good Things," "From Father to Son, Last Words to Live by," "Joe Davis: A Cool Man," and "A Drunken Ride, a Tragic Aftermath." (A list on pages xv–xvii presents the readings by rhetorical mode.)

- Each reading begins with a preview that supplies background information where needed and stimulates interest in the piece.

- The ten reading comprehension questions that follow each selection give students practice in five key skills: understanding vocabulary in context, summarizing (often by choosing an alternative title), determining the main idea, recognizing key supporting details, and making inferences. Reading educators agree that these are among the most crucial comprehension skills.

- Discussion questions following the reading comprehension questions deal with matters of content as well as aspects of structure, style, and tone. Through the questions on structure in particular, students will see that professional authors practice some of the same basic composing techniques (such as the use of transitions and emphatic order to achieve coherence) that they have been asked to practice in their own writing.

- Finally, two paragraph writing assignments and one essay writing assignment follow the discussion questions. The assignments range from personal narratives to expository and persuasive essays about issues in the world at large. Many assignments provide guidelines on how to proceed, including sample topic sentences or thesis statements and appropriate methods of development. In addition, the final selection features a fourth writing assignment requiring some simple online research.

When assigning a selection, instructors may find it helpful to ask students to read the preview as well as to answer the reading comprehension and discussion questions that follow the selection. Answers can then be gone over quickly in class. Through these activities, a writing instructor can contribute to the improvement of students' reading skills.

Changes in the Eighth Edition

Here is a list of what is new in the eighth edition of *English Skills with Readings:*

- The discussion of both purpose and audience in relation to the writing of paragraphs and essays has been extended.

- Coverage of the writing process has been expanded and revised.

- More writing samples illustrating expository and argumentative approaches have been included.

- Several of the writing assignments at the end of the chapters in Parts 1, 2, and 3 ask students to discuss issues beyond those that are purely personal in nature.

- The chapter covering the writing of a full essay has been expanded to stress the importance of audience analysis.

- The chapter on using the library and Internet has been updated and expanded, especially in terms of evaluating both print and electronic sources.

- The discussion of the principles of researching and notetaking has been expanded. It also provides extensive coverage of ways to spot and avoid unintentional plagiarism.

- The explanations of how to include and cite researched materials have been expanded, and the text has been revised to include the most recent changes in MLA documentation style.

- The sample research paper has been updated to reflect students' more frequent use of electronic sources and to reflect the new MLA documentation formats. In addition, the section entitled "Model Entries for a List of *Works Cited*" has been expanded and updated.

- In Part 5, "Handbook of Sentence Skills," many of the in-text examples as well as the activity and review-test items use materials from a variety of academic disciplines as their subjects. The same is true for several of the paragraph-length samples and editing assignments.

Instructor and Student Supplements

- An *Annotated Instructor's Edition* consists of the student text complete with answers to all activities and tests, followed by an Instructor's Guide featuring teaching suggestions and a model syllabus.

- An *Online Learning Center* (**www.mhhe.com/langan**) offers a host of instructional aids and additional resources for instructors, including a comprehensive computerized test bank, the downloadable *Instructor's Manual and Test Bank,* online resources for writing instructors, and more.

- An *Online Learning Center* (**www.mhhe.com/langan**) offers a host of instructional aids and additional resources for students, including self-correcting exercises, writing activities for additional practice, guides to doing research on the Internet and avoiding plagiarism, useful Web links, and more. The site is powered by Catalyst, McGraw-Hill's innovative writing and research resource.

You can contact your local McGraw-Hill representative or consult McGraw-Hill's Web site at **www.mhhe.com/english** for more information on the supplements that accompany *English Skills with Readings,* Eighth Edition.

Acknowledgments

A special thanks to reviewers who have contributed to the eighth edition, as well as the sixth and seventh editions:

Spencer Belgarian, Fashion Institute of Design and Merchandising
Vivian Brown-Carman, Bergen Community College
Sylvia Boyd, Phillips Community College of the University of Arkansas
Cedric Burden, Lawson State Community College
Jacintha Burke, Kings's College
Margie Campbell, Montgomery College
Anne J. Chamberlain, Community College of Baltimore County
Neeta Chandra, Cuyahoga Community College
Terry Clark, Kennedy-King College
Gladys Clay, Edward Walters College
Giono Cromley, Kennedy-King College
Maureen Eggert, Central Community College
Molly Emmons, College of the Redwoods – Del Norte
Rita Fork, El Camino College
Mib Garrard, Grayson County College
Jeanne Grandchamp, Bristol Community College
Shelly Godwin, South Georgia Technical College
Anneliese Homan, State Fair Community College
Peggy F. Hopper, Walters State Community College
Christy Hughes, Orangeburg-Calhoun Technical College
Patsy Krech, University of Memphis
Irmagard Langmia, Bowie State University
Jennifer Leamy, Wake Technical Community College
Candace C. Mesa, Dixie College
Robert Miller, Terra Community College

Ron Reed, Kentucky Community and Technical College System

Mark Ristroph, Augusta Technical College

Bernd Sauermann, Hopkinsville Community College

Su Senapati, Abraham Baldwin Agricultural College

Kathleen Shaw, Montgomery County Community College

Elizabeth W. Smith, Manatee Community College

Pam Smith, Copper Mountain College

Sean Smith, Montgomery College

Rachel Sosta, Riverside Community College

Loretta S. Stribling, Whatcom Community College

Judy Stockstill, Central Christian College

Mary McCaslin Thompson, Anoka-Ramsey Community College

Starlette Vaughn, Sacramento City College

Felisa Williams, Bladen Community College

I am also grateful for the talented support of my McGraw-Hill editors, John Kindler, Linda Stern, and Jesse Hassenger. Many thanks to the skilled production and design team, including Brett Coker and Aaron Downey.

Joyce Stern, Assistant Professor at Nassau Community College, contributed the ESL Tips to the *Annotated Instructor's Edition* of *English Skills with Readings.* Professor Stern is also Assistant to the Chair in the Department of Reading and Basic Education at Nassau Community College. An educator for over thirty years, she holds an advanced degree in TESOL from Hunter College, as well as a New York State Teaching Certificate in TESOL. She is currently coordinating the design, implementation, and recruitment of learning communities for both ESL and developmental students at Nassau Community College and has been recognized by the college's Center for Students with Disabilities for her dedication to student learning.

Donna T. Matsumoto, Assistant Professor of English and the Writing Discipline Coordinator at Leeward Community College in Hawaii (Pearl City), wrote the Teaching Tips for the *Annotated Instructor's Edition* of *English Skills with Readings.* Professor Matsumoto has taught writing, women's studies, and American studies for a number of years through the University of Hawaii system, at Hawaii Pacific University, and in community schools for adults. She received a 2005 WebCT Exemplary Course Project award for her online writing course and is the author of McGraw-Hill's *The Virtual Workbook,* an online workbook featuring interactive activities and exercises.

John Langan

About the Author

John Langan has taught reading and writing at Atlantic Cape Community College near Atlantic City, New Jersey, for more than twenty-five years. The author of a popular series of college textbooks on both writing and reading, John enjoys the challenge of developing materials that teach skills in an especially clear and lively way. Before teaching, he earned advanced degrees in writing at Rutgers University and in reading at Rowan University. He also spent a year writing fiction that, he says, "is now at the back of a drawer waiting to be discovered and acclaimed posthumously." While in school, he supported himself by working as a truck driver, a machinist, a battery assembler, a hospital attendant, and an apple packer. John now lives with his wife, Judith Nadell, near Philadelphia. In addition to his wife and Philly sports teams, his passions include reading and turning on nonreaders to the pleasure and power of books. Through Townsend Press, his educational publishing company, he has developed the nonprofit "Townsend Library"—a collection of more than fifty new and classic stories that appeal to readers of any age.

English Skills
with Reading

Basic Principles of Effective Writing

PREVIEW

College offers many different challenges for students. Knowing your individual strengths and weaknesses can help you be a successful student. Take a few minutes to think about your strengths and weaknesses as a student. How can you use this information to be a better student?

1

An Introduction to Writing

Though some of us may stumble upon the job of our dreams, many of us have also had a job that seemed more like a nightmare. In this chapter you will read a student's paragraph about his worst job. Think about the best or worst job you have ever had. Later in the chapter you will be asked to write a paragraph of your own on this topic.

This book grows out of experiences I had when learning how to write. My early memories of writing in school are not pleasant. In middle school, I remember getting back paper after paper on which the only comment was "Handwriting very poor." In high school, the night before a book report was due, I would work anxiously at a card table in my bedroom. I was nervous and sweaty because I felt out of my element, like a person who knows only how to open a can of soup being asked to cook a five-course meal. The act of writing was hard enough, and my feeling that I wasn't any good at it made me hate the process all the more.

Luckily, in college I had an instructor who changed my negative attitude about writing. During my first semester in composition, I realized that my instructor repeatedly asked two questions about any paper I wrote: "What is your point?" and "What is your support for that point?" I learned that sound writing consists basically of making a point and then providing evidence to support or develop that point. As I understood, practiced, and mastered these and other principles, I began to write effective papers. By the end of the semester, much of my uneasiness and bad feelings about writing had disappeared. I knew that competent writing is a skill that I or anyone can learn with practice. It is a nuts-and-bolts process consisting of a number of principles and techniques that can be studied and mastered. Further, I learned that while there is no alternative to the work required for competent writing, there is satisfaction to be gained through such work. I no longer feared or hated writing, for I knew I could work at it and be good at it.

English Skills explains in a clear and direct way the four basic principles you must learn to write effectively:

1. Start with a clearly stated point.
2. Provide logical, detailed support for your point.
3. Organize and connect your supporting material.
4. Revise and edit so that your sentences are effective and error-free.

Part One of this book explains each of these steps in detail and provides many practice materials to help you master them.

Understanding Point and Support

An Important Difference between Writing and Talking

In everyday conversation, you make all kinds of points, or assertions. You say, for example, "I hate my job"; "Sue's a really generous person"; or "That exam was unfair." The points that you make concern such personal matters as well as, at times, larger issues: "A lot of doctors are arrogant"; "The death penalty should exist for certain crimes"; "Tobacco and marijuana are equally dangerous."

The people you are talking with do not always challenge you to give reasons for your statements. They may know why you feel as you do, or they may already agree with you, or they simply may not want to put you on the spot; so they do not always ask "Why?" But the people who *read* what you write may not know you, agree with you, or feel in any way obliged to you. If you want to communicate effectively with readers, you must provide solid evidence for any point you make. An important difference, then, between writing and talking is this: *In writing, any idea that you advance must be supported with specific reasons or details.*

Think of your readers as reasonable people. They will not take your views on faith, but they *are* willing to consider what you say as long as you support it. Therefore, remember to support with specific evidence any statement that you make.

Point and Support in Two Cartoons

The following two *Peanuts* cartoons will show you quickly and clearly what you need to write effectively. You need to know how to (1) make a point and (2) support the point.

Look for a moment at the following cartoon:

Peanuts © United Feature Syndicate, Inc.

See if you can answer the following questions:

- What is Snoopy's point in his paper?

  Your answer: His point is that _____

- What is his support for his point?

  Your answer: _____

Snoopy's point, of course, is that dogs are superior to cats. But he offers no support whatsoever to back up his point. There are two jokes here. First, Snoopy is a dog, so he is naturally going to believe that dogs are superior. The other joke is that his evidence ("They just are, and that's all there is to it!") is no more than empty words. His somewhat guilty look in the last panel suggests that he knows he has not proved his point. To write effectively, you must provide *real* support for your points and opinions.

Now look at this other cartoon about Snoopy as a writer.

See if you can answer the following questions:

- What is Snoopy's point about the hero in his writing?

  Your answer: His point is that _____

- What is his support for his point?

  Your answer: _____

Snoopy's point is that the hero's life has been a disaster. This time, Snoopy has an abundance of support for his point: The hapless hero never had any luck, money, friends, love, laughter, applause, fame, or answers. But the flaw in

Snoopy's composition is that he does not use enough supporting *details* to really prove his point. Instead, he plays the opposites game with his support ("He wanted to be loved. He died unloved.") As readers, we wonder who the hero wanted to be loved by: his mother? a heroine? a beagle? To sympathize with the hero and understand the nature of his disastrous life, we need more specifics. In the final panel of the cartoon, Snoopy has that guilty expression again. Why might he have a hard time ending this paragraph?

Point and Support in a Paragraph

Suppose you and a friend are talking about jobs you have had. You might say about a particular job, "That was the worst one I ever had. A lot of hard work and not much money." For your friend, that might be enough to make your point, and you would not really have to explain your statement. But in writing, your point would have to be backed up with specific reasons and details.

Below is a paragraph, written by a student named Gene Hert, about his worst job. A *paragraph* is a short paper of 150 to 200 words. It usually consists of an opening point called a *topic sentence* followed by a series of sentences supporting that point.

My Job in an Apple Plant

Working in an apple plant was the worst job I ever had. First of all, the work was physically hard. For ten hours a night, I took cartons that rolled down a metal track and stacked them onto wooden skids in a tractor trailer. Each carton contained twenty-five pounds of bottled apple juice, and they came down the track almost nonstop. The second bad feature of the job was the pay. I was getting the minimum wage at that time, $3.65 an hour, plus a quarter extra for working the night shift. I had to work over sixty hours a week to get decent take-home pay. Finally, I hated the working conditions. We were limited to two ten-minute breaks and an unpaid half hour for lunch. Most of my time was spent outside on the loading dock in near-zero-degree temperatures. I was very lonely on the job because I had no interests in common with the other truck loaders. I felt this isolation especially when the production line shut down for the night, and I spent two hours by myself cleaning the apple vats. The vats were an ugly place to be on a cold morning, and the job was a bitter one to have.

Notice what the details in this paragraph do. They provide you, the reader, with a basis for understanding *why* the writer makes the point that is made. Through this specific evidence, the writer has explained and successfully communicated the idea that this job was his worst one.

The evidence that supports the point in a paragraph often consists of a series of reasons followed by examples and details that support the reasons. That is true of the paragraph above: Three reasons are provided, with examples and details that back up those reasons. Supporting evidence in a paper can also consist of anecdotes, personal experiences, facts, studies, statistics, and the opinions of experts.

The paragraph on the apple plant, like almost any piece of effective writing, has two essential parts: (1) a point is advanced, and (2) that point is then supported. Taking a minute to outline the paragraph will help you understand these basic parts clearly. Add the words needed to complete the outline.

Activity 1

Point: Working in an apple plant is the worst job I ever had.

Reason 1: _____

    a. Loaded cartons onto skids for ten hours a night

    b. _____

Reason 2: _____

    a. _____

    b. Had to work sixty hours for decent take-home pay

Reason 3: _____

    a. Two ten-minute breaks and an unpaid lunch

    b. _____

    c. Loneliness on job

        (1) No interests in common with other workers

        (2) By myself for two hours cleaning the apple vats

See if you can complete the statements below.

Activity 2

1. An important difference between writing and talking is that in writing we absolutely must _____ any statement we make.

2. A _____ is made up of a point and a collection of specifics that support the point.

An excellent way to get a feel for the paragraph is to write one. Your instructor may ask you to do that now. The only guidelines you need to follow are the ones described here. There is an advantage to writing a paragraph right away, at a point where you have had almost no instruction. This first paragraph will give a

Activity 3

quick sense of your needs as a writer and will provide a baseline—a standard of comparison that you and your instructor can use to measure your writing progress during the semester.

Here, then, is your topic: Write a paragraph on the best or worst job you have ever had. Provide three reasons why your job was the best or the worst, and give plenty of details to develop each of your three reasons.

Notice that the sample paragraph, "My Job in an Apple Plant," has the same format your paragraph should have. You should do what this author has done:

- State a point in the first sentence.
- Give three reasons to support the point.
- Introduce each reason clearly with signal words (such as *First of all, Second,* and *Finally*).
- Provide details that develop each of the three reasons.

Write your paragraph on a separate sheet of paper. After completing the paragraph, hand it in to your instructor.

Benefits of Paragraph Writing

Paragraph writing offers three benefits. First, mastering the structure of paragraphs will make you a better writer. For other courses, you'll often write pieces that are variations on the paragraph—for example, exam answers, summaries, response papers, and brief reports. In addition, paragraphs serve as the basic building blocks of essays, the most common form of college writing.

Second, writing paragraphs strengthens your skills as a reader and listener. You'll become more aware of the ideas of other writers and speakers and the evidence they provide—or fail to provide—to support those ideas.

Most important, paragraph writing will make you a stronger thinker. Writing a solidly reasoned paragraph requires mental discipline. Creating a paragraph with an overall topic sentence supported by well-reasoned, convincing evidence is more challenging than writing a free-form or expressive paper. Such a paragraph requires you to sort out, think through, and organize ideas carefully.

Writing as a Skill

A sure way not to learn how to write competently is to believe that writing is a "natural gift" rather than a learned skill. People who think this way feel that everyone else finds writing easy and that they're "just not good at it." This attitude makes them try to avoid writing and, when they do write, to do less than their best. Their attitude becomes a self-fulfilling prophecy: Their writing fails chiefly because they have brainwashed themselves into thinking that they don't have the "natural talent" needed to write.

But writing is a skill, and like most other skills, such as typing, driving, or cooking, it can be learned. If you have the determination to learn, this book will give you the practice you need to develop good writing skills.

Of course, it's frightening to sit down before a blank sheet of paper or computer screen and know that, an hour later, you may not have written a lot worth keeping. Transforming thoughts from one's head into words on a sheet of paper can be a challenge, and at times it can be frustrating. But writing is not an automatic process—we will not get something for nothing, and we shouldn't expect to. For almost everyone, competent writing comes only from plain hard work—determination and sweat. It is a head-on battle. The good news is that you can do it if you are ready to work hard.

Activity

4

To get a sense of just how you regard writing, read the following statements. Put a check (✓) beside those statements with which you agree. This activity is not a test, so try to be as honest as possible.

_____   1. A good writer should be able to sit down and write a paper straight through without stopping.

_____   2. Writing is a skill that anyone can learn with practice.

_____   3. I'll never be good at writing because I make too many mistakes in spelling, grammar, and punctuation.

_____   4. Because I dislike writing, I always start a paper at the last possible minute.

_____   5. I've always done poorly in English, and I don't expect that to change.

Now read the following comments about the five statements. The comments will help you see if your attitude is hurting or helping your efforts to become a better writer.

Comments

- Statement 1: *"A good writer should be able to sit down and write a paper straight through without stopping."*

  Statement 1 is not true. Writing is, in fact, a process. It is done not in one easy step but in a series of steps, and seldom at one sitting. If you cannot do a paper all at once, that simply means you are like most of the other people on the planet. It is harmful to carry around the false idea that writing should be easy.

- Statement 2: *"Writing is a skill that anyone can learn with practice."*

  Statement 2 is absolutely true. Writing is a skill, like driving or word processing, that you can master with hard work. If you want to learn to write, you can. It is as simple as that. If you believe this, you are ready to learn how to become a competent writer.

  Some people hold the false belief that writing is a natural gift that some have and others do not. Because of this belief, they never make a truly honest effort to learn to write—so they never learn.

- Statement 3: *"I'll never be good at writing because I make too many mistakes in spelling, grammar, and punctuation."*

  The first concern in good writing should be content—what you have to say. Your ideas and feelings are what matter most. You should not worry about spelling, grammar, or punctuation while working on content.

  Unfortunately, some people are so self-conscious about making mistakes that they do not focus on what they want to say. They need to realize that a paper is best done in stages, and that applying the rules can and should wait until a later stage in the writing process. Through review and practice, you will eventually learn how to follow the rules with confidence.

- Statement 4: *"Because I dislike writing, I always start a paper at the last possible minute."*

  This habit is all too common. You feel you are going to do poorly, and then you behave in a way that ensures you *will* do poorly! Your attitude is so negative that you defeat yourself—not even allowing enough time to really try.

  Again, what you need to realize is that writing is a process. Because it is done in steps, you don't have to get it right all at once. If you allow yourself enough time, you'll find a way to make a paper come together.

- Statement 5: *"I've always done poorly in English, and I don't expect that to change."*

  Even if you did poorly in English in high school, it is in your power to make English one of your best subjects in college. If you believe writing can be learned, work hard at it! You *will* become a better writer!

  Your attitude is crucial. If you continue to believe you will never be a good writer, chances are good that you will not improve. If you start believing that you *can improve*, chances are excellent that you *will improve*.

Writing as a Process of Discovery

In addition to believing that writing is a natural gift, many people believe, mistakenly, that writing should flow in a simple, straight line from the writer's head onto the page. But writing is seldom an easy, one-step journey in which a finished paper comes out in a first draft. The truth is that *writing is a process of discovery* that involves a series of steps, and those steps are very often a zigzag journey. Look at the following illustrations of the writing process:

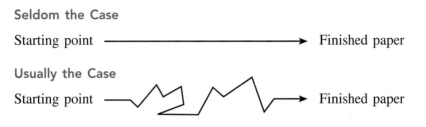

Seldom the Case

Starting point ⟶ Finished paper

Usually the Case

Starting point ⟶ Finished paper

Very often, writers do not discover exactly what they want to write about until they explore their thoughts in writing. For example, Gene Hert had been asked to write about a best or worst job. Only after he did some freewriting on good and bad jobs did he realize that the most interesting details centered on his job at an apple plant. He discovered his subject in the course of writing.

Another student, Rhonda, talking afterward about a paper she wrote, explained that at first her topic was how she relaxed with her children. But as she accumulated details, she realized after a page of writing that the words *relax* and *children* simply did not go together. Her details were really examples of how she *enjoyed* her children, not how she *relaxed* with them. She sensed that the real focus of her writing should be what she did by herself to relax, and then she thought suddenly that the best time of her week was Thursday after school. "A light clicked on in my head," she explained. "I knew I had my paper." Then it was a matter of detailing exactly what she did to relax on Thursday evenings. Her paper, "How I Relax," is on page 87.

The point is that writing is often a process of continuing discovery. As you write, you may suddenly switch direction or double back. You may be working on a topic sentence and realize suddenly that it could be your concluding thought. Or you may be developing a supporting idea and then decide that it should be the main point of your paper. Chapter 2 treats the writing process directly. What is important to remember here is that writers frequently do not know their exact destination as they begin to write. Very often they discover the direction and shape of a paper during the process of writing.

Keeping a Journal

Because writing is a skill, it makes sense that the more you practice writing, the better you will write. One excellent way to get practice in writing, even before you begin composing formal paragraphs, is to keep a daily or almost daily journal. Writing a journal will help you develop the habit of thinking on paper and will show you how ideas can be discovered in the process of writing. A journal can make writing a familiar part of your life and can serve as a continuing source of ideas for papers.

At some point during the day—perhaps during a study period after your last class of the day, or right before dinner, or right before going to bed—spend fifteen minutes or so writing in your journal. Keep in mind that you do not have to plan what to write about, or be in the mood to write, or worry about making mistakes as you write; just write down whatever words come out. You should write at least one page in each session.

You may want to use a notebook that you can easily carry with you for on-the-spot writing. Or you may decide to write on loose-leaf paper that can be transferred later to a journal folder on your desk. Many students choose to keep

electronic journals on their computers or online through livejournal.com or a similar Web site. No matter how you proceed, be sure to date all entries.

Your instructor may ask you to make journal entries a specific number of times a week, for a specific number of weeks. He or she may have you turn in your journal every so often for review and feedback. If you are keeping the journal on your own, try to make entries three to five times a week every week of the semester. Your journal can serve as a sourcebook of ideas for possible papers. More important, keeping a journal will help you develop the habit of thinking on paper, and it can help you make writing a familiar part of your life.

Activity 5

Following is an excerpt from one student's journal. (Sentence-skills mistakes have been corrected to improve readability.) As you read, look for a general point and for supporting material that could be the basis for an interesting paper.

October 6

Today a woman came into our department at the store and wanted to know if we had any scrap lumber ten feet long. Ten feet!
"Lady," I said, "anything we have that's ten feet long sure as heck

continued

isn't scrap." When the boss heard me say that, he almost canned me. My boss is a company man, down to his toe tips. He wants to make a big impression on his bosses, and he'll run us around like mad all night to make himself look good. He's the most ambitious man I've ever met. If I don't transfer out of Hardware soon, I'm going to go crazy on this job. I'm not ready to quit, though. The time is not right. I want to be here for a year and have another job lined up and have other things right before I quit. It's good the boss wasn't around tonight when another customer wanted me to carry a bookcase he had bought out to his car. He didn't ask me to help him—he _expected_ me to help him. I hate that kind of "You're my servant" attitude, and I told him that carrying stuff out to cars wasn't my job. Ordinarily I go out of my way to give people a hand, but not guys like him. . . .

- If the writer of this journal is looking for an idea for a paper, he can probably find several in this single entry. For example, he might write a narrative supporting the point that "In my sales job I have to deal with some irritating customers." See if you can find another idea in this entry that might be the basis for an interesting paragraph. Write your point in the space below.

  _____

- Take fifteen minutes to prepare a journal entry right now on this day in your life. On a separate sheet of paper, just start writing about anything that you have said, heard, thought, or felt, and let your thoughts take you where they may.

Using This Text

Here is a suggested sequence for using this book if you are working on your own.

1. After completing this introduction, read the remaining five chapters in Part One and work through as many of the activities as you need to master the ideas in these chapters. By the end of Part One, you will have covered all the basic theory needed to write effective papers.

2. Turn to Part Five and take the diagnostic test. The test will help you determine what sentence skills you need to review. Study those skills one or two at a time while you continue to work on other parts of the book. These skills will help you write effective, error-free sentences.

3. What you do next depends on course requirements, individual needs, or both. You will want to practice at least several different kinds of paragraph development in Part Two. If your time is limited, be sure to include "Exemplification" (pages 180–195), "Process" (pages 196–211), "Comparison or Contrast" (pages 226–246), and "Argument" (pages 307–322).

4. After you develop skill in writing effective paragraphs, go on to practice writing one or more of the several-paragraph essays described in Part Three.

5. Turn to Part Four as needed for help with projects that involve research.

Remember that, for your convenience, the book includes the following:

- On the inside back cover, there is a checklist of the four basic steps in effective writing.
- On page 633, there is a list of commonly used correction symbols.

Get into the habit of referring to these guides on a regular basis; they'll help you produce clearly thought-out, well-written papers.

English Skills will help you learn, practice, and apply the thinking and writing skills you need to communicate effectively. But the starting point must be your determination to do the work needed to become a strong writer. The ability to express yourself clearly and logically can open doors of opportunity for you, both in school and in your career. If you decide—*and only you can decide*—that you want such language power, this book will help you reach that goal.

The Writing Process

2

This chapter will explain and illustrate

- the sequence of steps in writing an effective paragraph
- prewriting
- revising
- editing

Getting started is often the hardest part of writing. You may have looked and felt like the student pictured here many times when working on a writing assignment. What could this student do to help get ideas flowing? As you will learn in this chapter, using various prewriting techniques can help make the writing process a lot easier.

Chapter 1 introduced you to the paragraph form and some basics of writing. This chapter explains and illustrates the sequence of steps in writing an effective paragraph. In particular, the chapter focuses on prewriting and revising—strategies that can help with every paragraph that you write.

For many people, writing is a process that involves the following steps.

1. **Discovering a point—often through prewriting.**
2. **Developing solid support for the point—often through more prewriting.**
3. **Organizing the supporting material and writing it out in a first draft.**
4. **Revising and then editing carefully to ensure an effective, error-free paper.**

Learning this sequence will help give you confidence when the time comes to write. You'll know that you can use prewriting as a way to think on paper (or at the keyboard) and to discover gradually what ideas you want to develop. You'll understand that there are four clear-cut goals to aim for in your writing—unity, support, organization, and error-free sentences. You'll realize that you can use revising to rework a paragraph until it is strong and effective. And you'll be able to edit a paragraph so that your sentences are clear and error-free.

Prewriting

If you are like many people, you may have trouble getting started writing. A mental block may develop when you sit down before a blank sheet of paper or a blank screen. You may not be able to think of an interesting topic or a point to make about your topic. Or you may have trouble coming up with specific details to support your point. And even after starting a paragraph, you may hit snags—moments when you wonder "What else can I say?" or "Where do I go next?"

The following pages describe 5 techniques that will help you think about and develop a topic and get words on paper: (1) freewriting, (2) questioning, (3) making a list, (4) clustering, and (5) summarizing. These prewriting techniques help you think about and create material, and they are a central part of the writing process.

www.mhhe.com/langan

Technique 1: Freewriting

When you do not know what to write about a subject or when you are blocked in writing, freewriting sometimes helps. In *freewriting,* you write on your topic for ten minutes. You do not worry about spelling or punctuating correctly, about erasing mistakes, about organizing material, or about finding exact words. You just write without stopping. If you get stuck for words, you write "I am looking for something to say" or repeat words until you think of something. There is no need to feel inhibited, since mistakes *do not count* and you do not have to hand in your paper.

Freewriting will limber up your writing muscles and make you familiar with the act of writing. It is a way to break through mental blocks about writing. Since you do not have to worry about mistakes, you can focus on discovering what you want to say about a subject. Your initial ideas and impressions will often become clearer after you have gotten them down on paper, and they may lead to other impressions and ideas. Through continued practice in freewriting, you will develop the habit of thinking as you write. And you will learn a technique that is a helpful way to get started on almost any paragraph.

Freewriting: A Student Model

Gene Hert's paragraph "My Job in an Apple Plant" on page 6 was written in response to an assignment to write a paragraph on the best or worst job he ever had. Gene began by doing some general freewriting and thinking about his jobs. Here is his freewriting:

> I have had good and bad jobs, that's for sure. It was great earning money for the first time. I shoveled snow for my neighber, a friend of mine and I did the work and had snowball fights along the way. I remember my neighber reaching into his pocket and pulling out several dollars and handing us the money, it was like magic. Then there was the lawnmowing, which was also a good job. I mowed my aunts lawn while she was away at work. Then I'd go sit by myself in her cool living room and have a coke she left in the refrigarator for me. And look through all her magazines. Then there was the apple plant job I had after high school. That was a worst job that left me totaly wiped out at the end of my shift. Lifting cartons and cartons of apple juice for bosses that treated us

continued

> like slaves. The cartons coming and coming all night long. I
> started early in the evening and finished the next morning. I still
> remember how tired I was. Driving back home the first time. That
> was a lonely job and a hard job and I don't eat apples anymore.

At this point, Gene read over his notes, and as he later commented, "I realized that I had several potential topics. I said to myself, 'What point can I make that I can cover in a paragraph? What do I have the most information about?' I decided to narrow my topic down to my awful job at the apple plant. I figured I would have lots of interesting details for that topic." Gene then did a more focused freewriting to accumulate details for a paragraph on his bad job:

> The job I remember most is the worst job I ever had. I worked
> in an apple plant, I put in very long hours and would be totaly
> beat after ten hours of work. All the time lifting cartons of apple
> juice which would come racing down a metal track. The guy with
> me was a bit lazy at times, and I would be one man doing a
> two-man job. The cartons would go into a tracter trailer, we would
> have to throw down wooden skids to put the cartons on, then wed
> have to move the metal track as we filled up the truck. There is
> no other job I have had that even compares to this job, it was a
> lot worse than it seems. The bosses treated us like slaves and the
> company paid us like slaves. I would work all night from 7 P.M.
> and drive home in the morning at 5 A.M. and be bone tired. I
> remember my arms and sholders were so tired after the first
> night. I had trouble turning the steering wheel of my father's car.

Notice that there are problems with spelling, grammar, and punctuation in Gene's freewriting. Gene was not worried about such matters, nor should he have been. At this stage, he just wanted to do some thinking on paper and get some material down on the page. He knew that this was a good first step, a good way of getting started, and that he would then be able to go on to shape that material.

You should take the same approach when freewriting: Explore your topic without worrying at all about being "correct." Figuring out what you want to say and getting raw material down on the page should have all of your attention at this early stage of the writing process.

To get a sense of the freewriting process, take a sheet of paper and freewrite about different jobs you have had and what you liked or did not like about them. See how much material you can accumulate in ten minutes. And remember not to worry about "mistakes"; you're just thinking on paper.

Activity

1

Technique 2: Questioning

In *questioning,* you generate ideas and details by asking as many questions as you can think of about your subject. Such questions include *Why? When? Where? Who? How? In what ways?*

Here are questions that Gene Hert asked while further developing his paragraph.

Questioning: A Student Model

www.mhhe.com/langan

Questions	Answers
What did I hate about the job?	Very hard work. Poor pay. Mean bosses.
How was the work hard?	Nonstop cartons of apple juice. Cartons became very heavy.
Why was pay poor?	$3.65 an hour (minimum wage at the time). Only a quarter more for working the second shift. Only good money was in overtime—where you got time-and-a-half. No double time.
How were the bosses mean?	Yelled at some workers. Showed no appreciation. Created bad working conditions.

continued

> In what ways were
> working conditions bad?
>
> Unheated truck in zero-degree weather.
> Floor of tractor trailer was cold steel.
> Breaks were limited—only two of
> them. Lonely job.

Asking questions can be an effective way of getting yourself to think about a topic from different angles. The questions can help you generate details about a topic and get ideas on how to organize those details. Notice how asking questions gives Gene a better sense of the different reasons why he hated the job.

Activity

2

To get a feel for the questioning process, use a sheet of paper to ask yourself a series of questions about your best and worst jobs. See how many details you can accumulate in ten minutes. And remember again not to be concerned about "mistakes," because you are just thinking on paper.

Technique 3: Making a List

www.mhhe.com/langan

In *making a list,* also known as *brainstorming,* you create a list of ideas and details that relate to your subject. Pile these items up, one after another, without trying to sort out major details from minor ones, or trying to put the details in any special order, or even trying to spell words correctly. Your goal is to accumulate raw material by making up a list of everything about your subject that occurs to you.

After freewriting and questioning, Gene made up the following list of details.

Making a List: A Student Model

> Apple factory job—worst one I ever had
> Bosses were mean
> Working conditions were poor
> Went to work at 5 P.M., got back at 7 A.M.
> Lifted cartons of apple juice for ten hours
> Cartons were heavy

continued

Only two ten-minute breaks a night

Pay was only $3.65 an hour

Just quarter extra for night shift

Cost of gas money to and from work

No pay for lunch break

Had to work 60 hours for good take-home pay

Loaded onto wooden skids in a truck

Bosses yelled at some workers

Temperature zero outside

Floors of trucks ice-cold metal

Nonstop pace

Had to clean apple vats after work

Slept, ate, and worked—no social life

No real friends at work

One detail led to another as Gene expanded his list. Slowly but surely, more details emerged, some of which he could use in developing his paragraph. By the time he had finished his list, he was ready to plan an outline of his paragraph and then to write his first draft.

To get a sense of making a list, use a sheet of paper to list a series of details about one of the best or worst jobs you ever had. Don't worry about deciding whether the details are major or minor; instead, just get down as many details as you can think of in five or ten minutes.

Activity

3

Technique 4: Clustering

Clustering, also known as *diagramming* or *mapping,* is another strategy that can be used to generate material for a paragraph. This method is helpful for people who like to think in a visual way. In clustering, you use lines, boxes, arrows, and circles to show relationships among the ideas and details that occur to you.

www.mhhe.com/langan

    Begin by stating your subject in a few words in the center of a blank sheet of paper. Then, as ideas and details occur to you, put them in boxes or circles around the subject and draw lines to connect them to each other and to the subject. Put minor ideas or details in smaller boxes or circles, and use connecting lines to show how they relate as well.

Keep in mind that there is no right or wrong way of clustering. It is a way to think on paper about how various ideas and details relate to one another. Below is an example of what Gene might have done to develop his ideas:

Clustering: A Student Model

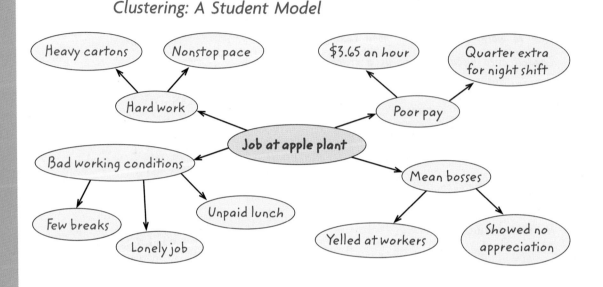

TIP: In addition to helping generate material, clustering often suggests ways to organize ideas and details.

Activity

4

Use clustering or another type of diagramming to organize the details about a best or worst job that you created for the previous activity (page 21).

Technique 5: Summarizing

Often, you can gather ideas and details about your topic in the work of other writers. When you *summarize* someone else's work, you condense that person's ideas and put them into your own words. Always shorter than the original, a summary is an effective way to combine new information with what you already know.

Always make sure to use your own words throughout the summary. Also, give the source of your information credit by identifying the author. For example, you might write, "Dr. Henry Davison claims that eating a lot of fiber is important to good digestion." You can learn more about summarizing and identifying sources in Chapter 20.

Writing a Topic Sentence and Preparing a Scratch Outline

After reading over the information you have gathered through one of the prewriting techniques just discussed, write a working topic sentence. A topic sentence expresses the *point* you want to make about the *subject* of your paragraph. This point, discussed further in Chapter 3, should be clearly stated and narrow, and it should be drawn from the ideas you have recorded in your prewriting.

In Chapter 1, you read Gene Hert's paragraph entitled "My Job in an Apple Plant," which responds to an assignment that asked students to discuss their best or worst jobs. Look back to Gene's freewriting (pages 17–18); you'll notice that he rewrote his first attempt, narrowing his focus to only one job in the second version. His working topic sentence emerged when he wrote his second version: "The job I remember most was the worst job I ever had." As with any other aspect of writing, however, a working topic sentence can and often should be revised for clarity and exactness. Gene revised his topic sentence in the final version of his paragraph (page 6): "Working in an apple plant was the worst job I ever had."

Once you have composed a topic sentence, you should prepare a scratch outline, which can be the *single most helpful technique* for writing a good paragraph. Though a scratch outline usually comes after you have written a working topic sentence, it may even emerge as you complete your freewriting, questioning, or other type of prewriting activity.

Making a scratch outline is part of prewriting because it is a good way to see if you need to gather more information for your paragraph. If you cannot come up with a solid outline, then you know you need to do more prewriting to clarify your main point and provide more support.

In a scratch outline, you think carefully about the point you are making, the supporting items for that point, and the order in which you will arrange those items. The scratch outline is a plan or blueprint to help you achieve a unified, supported, and well-organized paragraph.

Scratch Outline: A Student Model

In Gene's case, as he was working on his list of details, he suddenly realized what the plan of his paragraph could be. He could organize many of his details into one of three supporting groups: (1) the job itself, (2) the pay, and (3) the working conditions. He then went back to the list, crossed out items that he now saw did not fit, and numbered the items according to the group where they fit. The illustration on the next page shows what Gene did with the list he had created.

Apple factory job—worst one I ever had

~~Bosses were mean~~

3 Working conditions were poor

~~Went to work at 5 P.M., got back at 7 A.M.~~

1 Lifted cartons of apple juice for ten hours

1 Cartons were heavy

3 Only two ten-minute breaks a night

2 Pay was only $3.65 an hour

2 Just quarter extra for night shift

~~Cost of gas money to and from work~~

3 No pay for lunch break

2 Had to work 60 hours for good take-home pay

1 Loaded onto wooden skids in a truck

~~Bosses yelled at some workers~~

3 Temperature zero outside

~~Floors of trucks ice-cold metal~~

1 Nonstop pace

3 Had to clean apple vats after work

~~Slept, ate, and worked—no social life~~

3 No real friends at work

Under the list, Gene was now able to prepare his scratch outline:

The apple plant was my worst job.

1. Hard work

2. Poor pay

3. Poor working conditions

After all his prewriting, Gene was pleased. He knew that he had a promising paragraph—one with a clear point and solid support. He saw that he could organize the material into a paragraph with a topic sentence, supporting points, and vivid details. He was now ready to write the first draft of his paragraph, using his outline as a guide.

> **TIP:** Chances are that if you do enough prewriting and thinking on paper, you will eventually discover the point and support of your paragraph.

Create a scratch outline that could serve as a guide if you were to write a paragraph on your best or worst job experience.

Activity

5

Writing a First Draft

To write your first draft, begin by reading the prewriting you completed for the assignment. Then review your working topic sentence and your scratch outline. Make sure that each item in your outline supports and develops the main point in your working topic sentence. If it doesn't, cross it out. For example, let's say Gene's scratch outline had these items: (1) hard work, (2) poor pay, (3) poor working conditions, and (4) friendly coworkers. Gene would want to eliminate item 4 because it does not support his working topic sentence—"The apple plant was my worst job."

Once you have reviewed your outline, you're ready to write your first draft. Start by writing down or typing your working topic sentence. Then put down the first item from your scratch outline in sentence form. Now write, one sentence at a time, all the specific details for that item that you gathered during prewriting. For example, look at Gene's first draft on page 26. After explaining that the work was hard, Gene included the following supporting detail: "For ten hours a night, I stacked cartons that rolled down a metal track. . . ." This information is from the list Gene made during prewriting (see page 20).

When you are finished with the first outline item, go on to the next one. Following your scratch outline like a blueprint, continue to put down information gathered in your prewriting under the remaining items in your outline. Don't worry yet about grammar, punctuation, or spelling. You don't want to take time to correct sentences that you might decide to remove later.

New details and ideas may pop into your mind as you write. That's only natural. Just add the new information to your draft. Remember that writing is a process: You discover more and more about what you want to say as you work. Developing new information helps make your paragraph more convincing. More important, it shows that you are thinking critically as you work.

Writing a First Draft: A Student Model

Here is Gene's first draft, done in longhand.

~~The apple plant job was my worst.~~ Working in an apple plant was the worst job I ever had. The work was physicaly hard. For ~~a long time~~ ten hours a night, I stacked cartons that rolled down a metal track in a tracter trailer. Each carton had cans or bottles of apple juice, and they were heavy. At the same time, I had to keep a mental count of all the cartons I had loaded. The pay for the job was a bad feature. I was getting the minamum wage at that time plus a quarter extra for night shift. I had to work a lot to get a decent take-home pay. Working conditions were poor at the apple plant, we were limited to ~~short breaks~~ two ten-minute breaks. The truck-loading dock where I was most of the time was a cold and lonely place. Then by myself cleaning up. DETAILS!

> **TIP:** After Gene finished the first draft, he was able to put it aside until the next day. You will benefit as well if you can allow some time between finishing a draft and starting to revise.

Activity

6

See if you can fill in the missing words in the following explanation of Gene's first draft.

1. Gene presents his _____ in the first sentence and then crosses it out and revises it right away to make it read smoothly and clearly.

2. Notice that he continues to accumulate specific supporting details as he writes the draft. For example, he crosses out and replaces "a long time"

   with the more specific _____; he crosses out and

   replaces "short breaks" with the more specific _____.

3. There are various misspellings—for example, _____.
    Gene doesn't worry about spelling at this point. He just wants to get down
    as much of the substance of his paragraph as possible.

4. There are various punctuation errors, especially the run-on and the
    fragment near the (*beginning, middle, end*) _____ of
    the paragraph.

5. Near the close of his paragraph, Gene can't think of added details to
    insert, so he simply prints "_____" as a reminder to
    himself for the next draft.

Revising

www.mhhe.com/langan

Revising is as much a stage in the writing process as prewriting, outlining, and
doing the first draft. *Revising* means that you rewrite a paragraph, building upon
what has already been done, in order to make it stronger. One writer said about
revision, "It's like cleaning house—getting rid of all the junk and putting things
in the right order." It is not just "straightening up"; instead, you must be ready
to roll up your sleeves and do whatever is needed to create an effective paragraph.
Too many students think that a first draft *is* the paragraph. They start to become
writers when they realize that revising a rough draft three or four times is often
at the heart of the writing process.

   Here are some quick tips that can help make revision easier. First, set your
first draft aside for a while. You can then come back to it with a fresher, more
objective point of view. Second, work from typed or printed text, preferably
double-spaced so you'll have room to handwrite changes later. You'll be able to
see the paragraph more impartially if it is typed than if you were just looking at
your own familiar handwriting. Next, read your draft aloud. Hearing how your
writing sounds will help you pick up problems with meaning as well as with
style. Finally, as you do all these things, write additional thoughts and changes
above the lines or in the margins of your paragraph. Your written comments can
serve as a guide when you work on the next draft.

   There are two stages to the revision process:

- Revising content
- Revising sentences

Revising Content

To revise the content of your paragraph, ask the questions at the top of the
next page.

1. **Is my paragraph unified?**
    *   Do I have a main idea that is clearly stated at the beginning of my paragraph?
    *   Do all my supporting points truly support and back up my main idea?
2. **Is my paragraph supported?**
    *   Are there separate supporting points for the main idea?
    *   Do I have specific evidence for each supporting point?
    *   Is there plenty of specific evidence for the supporting points?
3. **Is my paragraph organized?**
    *   Do I have a clear method of organizing my paper?
    *   Do I use transitions and other connecting words?

The next two chapters (Chapters 3 and 4) give you practice in achieving *unity, support,* and *organization* in your writing.

Revising Sentences

To revise individual sentences in your paragraph, ask the following questions:

1. Do I use *parallelism* to balance my words and ideas?
2. Do I have a *consistent point of view?*
3. Do I use *specific* words?
4. Do I use *active* verbs?
5. Do I use words effectively by *avoiding slang, clichés, pretentious language,* and *wordiness?*
6. Do I *vary my sentences* in length and structure?

Chapter 5 will give you practice in revising sentences.

Revising: A Student Model

For his second draft, Gene used a word-processing program on a computer. He then printed out a double-spaced version of his paragraph, leaving himself plenty of room for handwritten revisions. Here is Gene's second draft plus the handwritten changes and additions that became his third draft.

Gene made his changes in longhand as he worked on the second draft. As you will see when you complete the activity below, his revision serves to make the paragraph more unified, supported, and organized.

Fill in the missing words.

1. To clarify the organization, Gene adds at the beginning of the first supporting point the transitional phrase "_____," and he sets off the third supporting point with the word "_____."

2. In the interest of (*unity, support, organization*) _____, he crosses out the sentence "_____." He realizes that this sentence is not a relevant detail to support the idea that the work was physically hard.

Activity

7

3. To add more (*unity, support, organization*) _____, he changes "a lot of hours" to "_____"; he changes "on the dock" to "_____"; he changes "cold temperatures" to "_____."

4. In the interest of eliminating wordiness, he removes the words "_____" from the sixth sentence.

5. To achieve parallelism, Gene changes "the half hour for lunch was not paid" to "_____."

6. For greater sentence variety, Gene combines two short sentences, beginning the second part of the sentence with the subordinating word "_____."

7. To create a consistent point of view, Gene changes "You felt this isolation" to "_____."

8. Finally, Gene replaces the somewhat vague "bad" in "The vats were a bad place to be on a cold morning, and the job was a bad one to have" with two more precise words: "_____" and "_____."

Editing

The last major stage in the writing process is editing—checking a paragraph for mistakes in grammar, punctuation, usage, and spelling. Editing as well as proof-reading (checking a paragraph for typos and other careless errors) is explained in detail on pages 125–127.

Editing: A Student Model

After typing into his word-processing file all the revisions in his paragraph, Gene printed out another clean draft of the paragraph. He now turned his attention to editing changes, as shown on the next page.

My Job in an Apple Plant

Working in an apple plant was the worst job I ever had. First of all, the
work was ~~physicaly~~ *physically* hard. For ten hours a night, I took cartons that rolled
down a metal track and stacked them onto wooden skids in a ~~tracter~~ *tractor*
trailer. Each carton contained ~~25~~ *twenty-five* pounds of bottled apple juice, and they
came down the track almost nonstop. The second bad feature of the job
was the pay. I was getting the ~~minamum~~ *minimum* wage at that time, $3.65 an
hour, *,P* Plus just a quarter extra for working the night shift. I had to work
over sixty hours a week to get a decent take-home pay. Finally, I hated the
working conditions. We were limited to two ten-minute breaks and an
unpaid half hour for lunch. Most of my time was spent outside on the
loading dock in near-zero-degree temperatures. And I was very lonely on
the job because I had no interests in common with the other workers. I
felt this isolation especially when the production line shut down for the
night, and I ~~had to clean~~ *spent two hours by myself cleaning* the apple vats. The vats were an ugly place to be
on a cold morning, and the job was a bitter one to have.

Once again, Gene made his changes in longhand right on the printout of his
paragraph. To note these changes, complete the activity below.

Fill in the missing words.

1. As part of his editing, Gene checked and corrected the _____
   of three words, *physically, tractor,* and *minimum.*

2. He added _____ to set off an introductory phrase ("First of
   all") and an introductory word ("Finally") and also to connect the two
   complete thoughts in the final sentence.

3. He corrected a fragment ("_____") by using a comma
   to attach it to the preceding sentence.

4. He realized that a number like "25" should be _____ as
   "twenty-five."

Activity

8

5. And since revision can occur at any stage of the writing process, including editing, Gene makes one of his details more vivid by adding the descriptive words "_____."

All that remained for Gene to do was to enter his corrections, print out the final draft of the paragraph, and proofread it for any typos or other careless errors. He was then ready to hand it in to his instructor.

Review Activities

www.mhhe.com/langan

You now have a good overview of the writing process, from prewriting to first draft to revising to editing. The remaining chapters in Part One will deepen your sense of the four goals of effective writing: unity, support, organization or coherence, and sentence skills.

To reinforce much of the information about the writing process that you have learned in this chapter, you can now work through the following activities:

1. Taking a writing inventory
2. Considering purpose and audience
3. Prewriting
4. Outlining
5. Revising

1 Taking a Writing Inventory

Activity

9

To evaluate your approach to the writing process, answer the questions below. This activity is not a test, so try to be as honest as possible. Becoming aware of your writing habits can help you make helpful changes in your writing.

1. When you start work on a paper, do you typically do any prewriting?

    _____ Yes   _____ Sometimes   _____ No

2. Which of the following techniques do you use?

    _____ Freewriting   _____ Clustering

    _____ Questioning   _____ Topic sentence and scratch outline

    _____ List making   _____ Other (please describe)

    _____ Summarizing

3. Which prewriting technique or techniques work best for you or do you think will work best for you?

4. Many students have said they find it helpful to handwrite a first draft and then type that draft on a computer. They then print the draft out and revise it by hand. Describe your own way of drafting and revising a paper.

5. After you write the first draft of a paper, do you have time to set it aside for a while so that you can come back to it with a fresh eye?

6. How many drafts do you typically write when doing a paper?

7. When you revise, are you aware that you should be working toward a paper that is unified, solidly supported, and clearly organized? Has this chapter given you a better sense that unity, support, and organization are goals to aim for?

8. Do you revise a paper for the effectiveness of its sentences as well as for its content?

9. What (if any) information has this chapter given you about prewriting that you will try to apply in your writing?

10. What (if any) information has this chapter given you about revising that you will try to apply in your writing?

2 Considering Purpose and Audience

Purpose

Of course, the *purpose* of completing any college writing assignment is to fulfill a course requirement and to get a grade. But all writing—whether done for a class, a job, or any other reason—is aimed at accomplishing something far more specific. In most cases, you will be given an assignment that explains or at least hints at that purpose. You will be able to spot clues about purpose by looking for key words in the assignment such as *define, contrast, argue, illustrate,* or *explain causes and eff*ects.

For example, an assignment for a history paper might ask you to *explain* the causes of World War I. An essay question on a biology midterm might call for the *definition* of photosynthesis. A political science assignment might ask you to *contrast* the parliamentary system of government used in several European nations with the federal system used in the United States. If you are enrolled in a technical writing course, you might be asked to *describe* a machine or *analyze* a natural or mechanical *process*. Each of these tasks asks you to accomplish a specific aim, a specific purpose.

Having a clear idea of your purpose is just as important for writing you do outside of college (what some call "real-world writing"). For example, say your employer asks you to write a report that recommends the purchase of a particular model of photocopier from a choice of three. You first might have to *contrast* each on the basis of cost, ease of use, features, and reliability. Then you might have to *argue* that even though copier A is more expensive than copiers B and C, it is preferable because it can work well with your company's computers. Note that unlike a college writing assignment, the job you have been given by your employer does not specify the approaches (*contrasting* and *arguing*) you will have to take to complete the project. You will have to figure that out for yourself by considering the writing's purpose before you begin.

As you begin gathering information for your paragraph or essay, keep your purpose in mind. You might want to read your assignment several times, looking for key words such as those mentioned above, and then summarize your purpose in a short sentence of your own on a piece of scrap paper. Keep this sentence in front of you throughout the prewriting stage.

Audience

The *audience* for a piece of writing is its reader or readers, and like purpose, audience should be considered early in the writing process. Many college students believe that the only person who will read their writing is the professor. In some cases, this is correct. However, college professors often share a student's work with others in the class as a way to illustrate good writing techniques. Also, students often write letters or other pieces for their school newspaper. In addition, they are sometimes required to write documents when applying for scholarships, transferring to other colleges, or applying to graduate schools.

When you are writing for the world outside of college, determining your audience becomes even more important. In most cases, more than one reader will be involved. Let's say you graduate with a degree in criminal justice and become a police officer. You will have to write up incident and arrest reports that might be read by other police officers, lawyers, judges, and members of city government, as well as by ordinary citizens whose knowledge of the law and police procedures might be limited.

You will read more about audience and purpose as you continue to learn about the writing process and about various methods to develop paragraphs in Part Two.

3 Prewriting and Scratch Outline

Below are examples of how the different techniques could be used to develop the topic "Inconsiderate Drivers." Identify each technique by writing F (for free-writing), Q (for questioning), L (for listing), C (for clustering), or SO (for scratch outline) in the answer space.

Activity

10

_____   High beams on
              Weave in and out at high speeds
              Treat street like a trash can
              Open car door onto street without looking
              Stop on street looking for an address
              Don't use turn signals
              High speeds in low-speed zones
              Don't take turns merging
              Use horn when they don't need to
              Don't give walkers the right of way
              More attention to cell phone than the road

_____

What is one example of an inconsiderate driver?	A person who turns suddenly without signaling.
Where does this happen?	At city intersections or on smaller country roads.
Why is this dangerous?	You have to be alert and slow down yourself to avoid rear-ending the car in front.
What is another example of inconsideration on the road?	Drivers who come toward you at night with their high beams on.

_____ Some people are inconsiderate drivers.
1. In city:
   a. Stop in middle of street
   b. Turn without signaling
2. On highway:
   a. Leave high beams on
   b. Stay in passing lane
   c. Cheat during a merge
3. Both in city and on highway:
   a. Throw trash out of window
   b. Pay more attention to cell phone than to road

_____

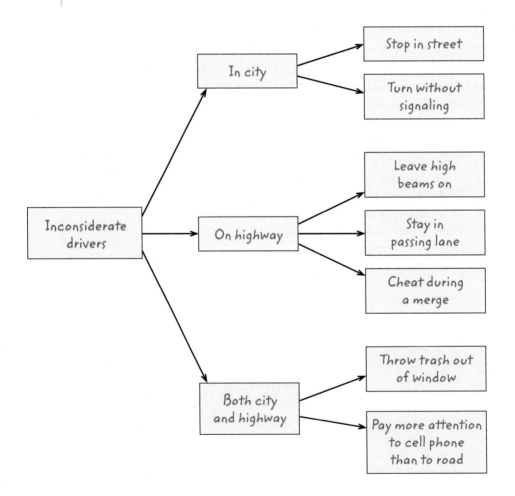

———   I was driving home last night after class and had three people try to blind me by coming at me with their high beams on. I had to zap them all with my high beams. Rude drivers make me crazy. The worst are the ones that use the road as a trash can. People who throw butts and cups and hamburger wrappings and other stuff out the car windows should be tossed into a trash dumpster. If word got around that this was the punishment maybe they would wise up. Other drivers do dumb things as well. I hate the person who will just stop in the middle of the street and try to figure out directions or look for a house address. Why don't they pull over to the side of the street? That hardly seems like too much to ask. Instead, they stop all traffic while doing their own thing. Then there are the people who keep what they want to do a secret. They're not going to tell you they plan to make a right- or left-hand turn. You've got to figure it out yourself when they suddenly slow down in front of you. Then there are all the people on their cell phones yakking away and not paying attention to their driving.

4 Outlining

As already mentioned (see page 24), outlining is central to writing a good paragraph. An outline lets you see, and work on, the bare bones of a paragraph, without the distraction of cluttered words and sentences. It develops your ability to think clearly and logically. Outlining provides a quick check on whether your paragraph will be *unified*. It also suggests right at the start whether your paragraph will be adequately *supported*. And it shows you how to plan a paragraph that is *well organized*.

www.mhhe.com/langan

The following series of exercises will help you develop the outlining skills so important to planning and writing a solid paragraph.

One key to effective outlining is the ability to distinguish between general ideas and specific details that fit under those ideas. Read each group of specific ideas below. Then circle the letter of the general idea that tells what the specific ideas have in common. Note that the general idea should not be too broad or too narrow. Begin by trying the example item, and then read the explanation that follows.

Activity

11

EXAMPLE

Specific ideas: runny nose, coughing, sneezing, sore throat

The general idea is:

a. cold symptoms.

b. symptoms.

c. throat problems.

EXPLANATION   It is true that the specific ideas are all symptoms, but they have in common something even more specific—they are all symptoms of the common cold. Therefore, answer *b* is too broad; the correct answer is *a*. Answer *c* is too narrow because it doesn't cover all the specific ideas; it covers only the final item in the list ("sore throat").

---

1. *Specific ideas:* leaking toilet, no hot water, broken window, roaches

   The general idea is:

   a. problems.

   b. kitchen problems.

   c. apartment problems.

2. *Specific ideas:* count to ten, take a deep breath, go for a walk

   The general idea is:

   a. actions.

   b. ways to calm down.

   c. ways to calm down just before a test.

3. *Specific ideas:* putting sticky tape on someone's chair, putting a "kick me" sign on someone's back, putting hot pepper in someone's cereal

   The general idea is:

   a. jokes.

   b. practical jokes.

   c. practical jokes played on teachers.

4. *Specific ideas:* going to bed earlier, eating healthier foods, reading for half an hour each day, trying to be kinder

   The general idea is:

   a. resolutions.

   b. problems.

   c. solutions.

5. *Specific ideas:* money problems, family problems, relationship problems, health problems

   The general idea is:

   a. poor grades.

   b. causes of poor grades.

   c. effects of poor grades.

In the following items, the specific ideas are given but the general ideas are unstated. Fill in each blank with a general heading that accurately describes the list provided.

Activity

12

EXAMPLE

> *General idea:* Household Chores
>
> *Specific ideas:* washing dishes
> preparing meals
> taking out trash
> dusting

1. *General idea:* _____
   Specific ideas: convenient work hours
   short travel time to job
   good pay
   considerate boss

2. *General idea:* _____
   Specific ideas: greed
   cowardice
   selfishness
   dishonesty

3. *General idea:* _____
   Specific ideas: order the invitations
   get the bride's gown
   rent the tuxedos
   hire a photographer

4. *General idea:* _____
   Specific ideas: "Your mother stinks."
   "Your father's a bum."

"You look like an ape."

"Your car is a real piece of junk."

5. *General idea:* _____

   Specific ideas: "I like your dress."

   "You look great in red."

   "Your new haircut looks terrific."

   "You did very well on the exam."

Activity

13

Major and minor ideas are mixed together in the two paragraphs outlined below. Put the ideas in logical order by filling in the outlines.

1. *Topic sentence:* People can be classified by how they treat their cars.

   Seldom wax or vacuum car
   Keep every mechanical item in top shape
   Protective owners
   Deliberately ignore needed maintenance
   Indifferent owners
   Wash and polish car every week
   Never wash, wax, or vacuum car
   Abusive owners
   Inspect and service car only when required by state law

   a. _____

      (1) _____

      (2) _____

   b. _____

      (1) _____

      (2) _____

   c. _____

      (1) _____

      (2) _____

2. *Topic sentence:* Living with an elderly parent has many benefits.

   Advantages for elderly person
   Live-in baby-sitter
   Learn about the past
   Advantages for adult children

Serve useful role in family
Help with household tasks
Advantages for grandchildren
Stay active and interested in young people
More attention from adults

a. _____

    (1) _____

    (2) _____

b. _____

    (1) _____

    (2) _____

c. _____

    (1) _____

    (2) _____

Again, major and minor ideas are mixed together. In addition, in each outline one of the three major ideas is missing and must be added. Put the ideas in logical order by filling in the outlines that follow (summarizing as needed) and adding a third major idea.

Activity 14

1. *Topic sentence:* Extending the school day would have several advantages.

   Help children academically
   Parents know children are safe at the school
   More time to spend on basics
   Less pressure to cover subjects quickly
   More time for extras like art, music, and sports
   Help working parents
   More convenient to pick up children at 4 or 5 P.M.
   Teachers' salaries would be raised

a. _____

    (1) _____

    (2) _____

b. _____

    (1) _____

    (2) _____

c. _____

    1. _____

    2. _____

2. *Topic sentence:* By following certain hints about food, exercise, and smoking, you can increase your chances of dying young.

Don't ever walk if you can ride instead.
Choose foods such as bacon and lunch meats that are laced with nitrites and other preservatives.
Be very selective about what you eat.
If you begin to cough or feel short of breath, keep smoking.
If a friend invites you to play an outdoor sport, open a beer instead and head for your La-Z-Boy recliner.
Resist the urge to exercise.
Choose foods from one of four essential groups: fat, starch, sugar, and grease.
Smoke on a regular basis.

    a. _____

        (1) _____

        (2) _____

    b. _____

        (1) _____

        (2) _____

    c. _____

        (1) _____

        (2) _____

Activity 15

Read the following two paragraphs. Then outline each one in the space provided. Write out the topic sentence in each case and summarize in a few words the primary and secondary supporting material that fits under the topic sentence.

1.

Why I'm a Stay-at-Home Baseball Fan

I'd much rather stay at home and watch ball games on television than go to the ballpark. First, it's cheaper to watch a game at home. I don't have to spend fifteen dollars for a ticket and another ten dollars for a parking space. If I want some refreshments, I can have what's already in the refrigerator instead of shelling out another six dollars for a limp, lukewarm hot dog and a watery Coke. Also, it's more comfortable at home. I avoid a bumper-to-bumper drive to the ballpark and pushy crowds who want to go through the same gate I do. I can lie quietly on my living-room sofa instead of sitting on a hard stadium seat with noisy people all around me. Most of all, watching a game on television is more informative. Not only do I see all the plays that I might miss from my fifteen-dollar seat, but I see some of them two and three times in instant replay. In addition, I get each play explained to me in glorious detail. If I were at the ballpark, I wouldn't know that the pitch our third baseman hit was a high and inside slider or that his grand-slam home run was a record-setting seventh in his career. The other fans can spend their money; put up with traffic, crowds, and hard seats; and guess at the plays. I'll take my baseball lying down—at home.

Topic sentence: _____

_____

a. _____

    (1) _____

    (2) _____

b. _____

    (1) _____

    (2) _____

c. _____

    (1) _____

    (2) _____

2.

Slow Down to Slim Down

It might sound strange, but one reason people gain weight is lack of time. Most of us live such busy lives that exercising and following a sensible diet—the two most important ways to stay slim—are difficult. Walking, running, or working out at least three times a week demands sacrifice. To fit it into our schedules, we need to wake up extra early or make time after long hours at school or work, when all we want to do is lie on the couch. Moreover, physical exercise may not be part of our daily routine.

To save twenty precious minutes, we drive to the post office or drugstore rather than walk, or we take the elevator to the fifth floor rather than the stairs, just to squeeze out another ten minutes. However, our need for more time also affects our diet. Too often we skip breakfast, which causes us to overeat later in the day, or we head for the drive-through and pick up some cholesterol-loaded monstrosity containing nearly 1,000 calories. Then, at lunch, we grab a burger and french fries, which we devour—in five minutes or less—while at work, while we're studying, or even while we're driving our cars. And instead of spending time cooking sensible, healthful dinners at home, we opt for fat-soaked, calorie-filled fried chicken takeout so we can get to our second jobs on time, start a ton of homework, or run off to fulfill a family obligation. In short then, we need to make time—as hard as that is—to do what's right for our bodies and ourselves. Weight gain is a major health threat because it can lead to a number of serious illnesses such as arthritis, diabetes, and heart disease. It can also affect our self-esteem and even cause depression. The lesson is clear: We need to slow down to slim down.

Topic sentence: _____

a. _____

   (1) _____

   (2) _____

b. _____

   (1) _____

   (2) _____

   (3) _____

      _____

c. _____

   (1) _____

   (2) _____

Activity | 5 Revising

16   Listed in the box below are five stages in the process of composing a paragraph titled "Dangerous Places."

> 1. **Prewriting (list)**
> 2. **Prewriting (freewriting and questioning) and scratch outline**
> 3. **First draft**
> 4. **Revising (second draft)**
> 5. **Revising (final draft)**

The five stages appear in scrambled order below and on the next page. Write the number 1 in the blank space in front of the first stage of development and number the remaining stages in sequence.

_____   There are some places where I never feel safe. For example, public restrooms. The ~~dirt and graffiti~~ dirt on the floors and the graffiti scrawled on the walls ~~make the room seem dangerous~~ create a sense of danger. I'm also afraid in parking lots. ~~Late at night, I don't like walking in the lot After class, I don't like the parking lot.~~ When I leave my night class or the shopping mall late the walk to the car is scary. ~~Most parking lots have large lights which make me feel at least a little better.~~ I feel least safe in our laundry room. . . . It is a depressing place . . . Bars on the windows, . . . pipes making noises, . . . cement steps the only way out. . . .

_____   Dangerous Places
Highways
Cars—especially parking lots
Feel frightened in our laundry room
Big crowds—concerts, movies
Closed-in places
Bus and train stations
Airplane
Elevators and escalators

_____   **Dangerous Places**

There are some places where I never feel completely safe. For example, I seldom feel safe in public restrooms. I worry that I'll suddenly be alone there and that someone will come in to mug me. The ugly graffiti often scrawled on the walls, along with the grime and dirt in the room and crumpled tissues and paper towels on the floor, add to my sense of unease and danger. I also feel unsafe in large, dark, parking lots. When I leave my night class a little late, or I am one of the few leaving the mall at 10 P.M., I dread the walk to my car. I am afraid that someone may be lurking behind another car, ready to mug me. And I fear that my car will not start, leaving me stuck in the dark parking lot. The place where I feel least safe is the basement laundry room in our apartment building. No matter what time I do my laundry, I seem to be the only person there. The windows are barred, and the only exit is a steep flight of cement steps. While I'm folding the clothes, I feel trapped. If anyone unfriendly came down those steps, I would have nowhere to go. The pipes in the room make sudden gurgles, clanks, and hisses, adding to my unsettledness. Places like public restrooms, dark parking lots, and the basement laundry room give me the shivers.

_____   There are some places where I never feel completely safe. For example, I never feel safe in public restrooms. If I'm alone there, I worry that someone will come in to rob and mug me. The dirt on the floors and the graffiti scrawled on the walls create a sense of danger. I feel unsafe in large, dark parking lots. When I leave my night class a little late or I leave the mall at 10 P.M., the walk to the car is scary. I'm afraid that someone may be behind a car. Also that my car won't start. Another place I don't feel safe is the basement laundry room in our apartment building. No matter when I do the laundry, I'm the only person there. The windows are barred and there are steep steps. I feel trapped when I fold the clothes. The pipes in the room make frightening noises such as hisses and clanks. Our laundry room and other places give me the shivers.

_____   Some places seem dangerous and unsafe to me. For example, last night I stayed till 10:15 after night class and walked out to parking lot alone. Very scary. Also, other places I go to every day, such as places in my apartment building. Also frightened by big crowds and public restrooms.

Why was the parking lot scary?	What places in my building scare me?
Dark	Laundry room (especially)
Only a few cars	Elevators
No one else in lot	Lobby at night sometimes
Could be someone behind a car	Outside walkway at night
Cold	

2   Parking lots
3   Laundry room
1   Public restrooms

The author of "Dangerous Places" in Activity 16 made a number of editing changes between the second draft and the final draft. Compare the two drafts and, in the spaces provided below, identify five of the changes.

1. _____

2. _____

3. _____

4. _____

5. _____

3

The First and Second Steps in Writing

This chapter will show you how to

- begin a paragraph by making a point of some kind
- provide specific evidence to support that point
- write a simple paragraph

There are many different reasons for going to college. Perhaps you are studying hospitality management like the students pictured here. This chapter contains two student paragraphs detailing each of the writer's reasons for being in college. Think about your own reasons for attending college. You may want to make a list of these reasons. At the end of this chapter you will be asked to write your own paragraph on why you are in college.

Chapter 2 emphasized how prewriting and revising can help you become an effective writer. This chapter focuses on the first two steps in writing an effective paragraph:

1. Begin with a point.
2. Support the point with specific evidence.

Chapters 4 and 5 then look at the third and fourth steps in writing:

3. Organize and connect the specific evidence (pages 86–107).
4. Write clear, error-free sentences (pages 103–138).

www.mhhe.com/langan

Step 1: Begin with a Point

Your first step in writing is to decide what point you want to make and to write that point in a single sentence. The point is commonly known as a *topic sentence*. As a guide to yourself and to the reader, put that point in the first sentence of your paragraph. Everything else in the paragraph should then develop and support in specific ways the single point given in the first sentence. (For information about using a working topic sentence to develop a scratch outline, see pages 23–25 in Chapter 2.)

Read the two student paragraphs below about families today. Which paragraph clearly supports a single point? Which paragraph rambles on in many directions, introducing a number of ideas but developing none of them?

Activity

1

Paragraph A

> ### Changes in the Family
>
> Changes in our society in recent years have weakened family life. First of all, today's mothers spend much less time with their children. A generation or two ago, most households got by on Dad's paycheck and Mom stayed home. Now many mothers work, and their children attend an after-school program, stay with a neighbor, or go home to an empty house. Another change is that families no longer eat together. In the past, Mom would be home to fix a full dinner—salad, pot roast, potatoes, and vegetables, with homemade cake or pie to top it off. Dinner today is more likely to be takeout food or frozen dinners eaten at home, or fast food eaten out, with different members of the family eating at different times. Finally, television has taken the place of family conversation and togetherness. Back when there were traditional meals, family members would have a chance to eat together, talk with each other, and share events of the day in a leisurely manner. But now families are more likely to be looking at the TV set than talking to one another. Most homes even have several TV sets, which people watch in separate rooms. Clearly, modern life is a challenge to family life.

Paragraph B

The Family

Family togetherness is very important. However, today's mothers spend much less time at home than their mothers did, for several reasons. Most fathers are also home much less than they used to be. In previous times, families had to work together running a farm. Now children are left at other places or are home alone much of the time. Some families do find ways to spend more time together despite the demands of work. Another problem is that with parents gone so much of the day, nobody is at home to prepare wholesome meals for the family to eat together. The meals Grandma used to make would include pot roast and fried chicken, mashed potatoes, salad, vegetables, and delicious homemade desserts. Today's takeout foods and frozen meals can provide good nutrition. Some menu choices offer nothing but high-fat and high-sodium choices. People can supplement prepared foods by eating sufficient vegetables and fruit. Finally, television is also a big obstacle to togetherness. It sometimes seems that people are constantly watching TV and never talking to each other. Even when parents have friends over, it is often to watch something on TV. TV must be used wisely to achieve family togetherness.

Complete the following statement: Paragraph _____ is effective because it makes a clear, single point in the first sentence and goes on in the remaining sentences to support that single point.

Paragraph A starts with a point—that changes in our society in recent years have weakened family life—and then supports that idea with examples about mothers' working, families' eating habits, and television.

Paragraph B, on the other hand, does not make and support a single point. At first we think the point of the paragraph may be that "family togetherness is very important." But there is no supporting evidence showing how important family togetherness is. Instead, the line of thought in paragraph B swerves about like a car without a steering wheel. In the second sentence, we read that "today's mothers spend much less time at home than their mothers did, for several reasons." Now we think for a moment that this may be the main point and that the author will list and explain some of those reasons. But the paragraph then goes on to comment on fathers, families in previous times, and families who find ways to spend time together. Any one of those ideas could be the focus of the paragraph, but none is. By now we are not really surprised at what happens in the rest of the paragraph. We are told about the absence of anyone "to prepare wholesome meals for the family," about what "the meals Grandma used to make" would be like, and about nutrition. The author then goes on to make a couple of points about how much people watch TV. The paragraph ends with yet another idea that does not support any previous point and that itself could be the point of a paragraph: "TV must be used wisely to achieve family togetherness." No single idea in this paragraph is developed, and the result for the reader is confusion.

In summary, while paragraph A is unified, paragraph B shows a complete lack of unity.

Step 2: Support the Point with Specific Evidence

The first essential step in writing effectively is to start with a clearly stated point. The second basic step is to support that point with specific evidence. Consider the supported point that you just read:

Point

Changes in our society in recent years have weakened family life.

Support

1. Mothers
   a. Most stayed home a generation ago
   b. Most work now, leaving children at an after-school program, or with a neighbor, or in an empty house
2. Eating habits
   a. Formerly full homemade meals, eaten together
   b. Now prepared foods at home or fast food out, eaten separately
3. Television
   a. Watching TV instead of conversing
   b. Watching in separate rooms instead of being together

The supporting evidence is needed so that we can *see and understand for ourselves* that the writer's point is sound. The author of "Changes in the Family" has supplied specific supporting examples of how changes in our society have weakened family life. The paragraph has provided the evidence that is needed for us to understand and agree with the writer's point.

Now consider the following paragraph.

Good-Bye, Tony

I have decided not to go out with Tony anymore. First of all, he was late for our first date. He said that he would be at my house by 8:30, but he did not arrive until 9:30. Second, he was bossy. He told me that it would be too late to go to the new Chris Rock comedy that I wanted to see and that we would go instead to a new action film with the Rock. I told him that I didn't like violent movies, but he said that I could shut my eyes during the bloody parts. Only because it was a first date did I let him have his way. Finally, he was abrupt. After the movie, rather than sug- gesting a hamburger or a drink, he drove right out to a back road near Oakcrest High School and started making out with me. What he did a half hour later angered me most of all. He cut his finger on my earring and immediately said we had to go right home. He was afraid the scratch would get infected if he didn't put Bactine and a Band-Aid on it. When he dropped me off, I said, "Good-bye, Tony," in a friendly enough way, but in my head I thought, "Good-bye forever, Tony."

The author's point is that she has decided not to go out with Tony anymore. See if you can summarize in the spaces below the three reasons she gives to support her decision:

Reason 1: _____

Reason 2: _____

Reason 3: _____

Notice what the supporting details in this paragraph do. They provide you, the reader, with a basis for understanding why the writer made the decision she did. Through specific evidence, the writer has explained and communicated her point successfully. The evidence that supports the point in a paragraph often consists of a series of reasons introduced by signal words (the author here uses *First of all, Second,* and *Finally*) and followed by examples and details that sup- port the reasons. That is true of the sample paragraph above: Three reasons are provided, followed by examples and details that back up those reasons.

The Point as an "Umbrella" Idea

You may find it helpful to think of the point as an "umbrella" idea. Under the writer's point fits all of the other material of the paragraph. That other material is made up of specific supporting details—evidence such as examples, reasons, or facts. The diagram to the right shows the relationship for the paragraph "Good-Bye, Tony."

Both of the paragraphs that follow resulted from the assignment to "Write a paragraph that details your reasons for being in college." Both writers make the point that they have various reasons for attending college. Which paragraph then goes on to provide plenty of specific evidence to back up its point? Which paragraph is vague and repetitive and lacks the concrete details needed to show us exactly why the author decided to attend college?

Activity

2

> **HINT:** Imagine that you've been asked to make a short film based on each paragraph. Which one suggests specific pictures, locations, words, and scenes you could shoot? That is the one that uses concrete details.

Paragraph A

Reasons for Going to College

I decided to attend college for various reasons. One reason is self-respect. For a long time now, I have had little self-respect. I spent a lot of time doing nothing, just hanging around or getting into trouble, and eventually I began to feel bad about it. Going to college is a way to start feeling better about myself. By accomplishing things, I will improve my self-image. Another reason for going to college is that things happened in my life that made me think about a change. For one thing, I lost the part-time job I had. When I lost the job, I realized I would have to do something in life, so I thought about school. I was in a rut and needed to get out of it but did not know how. But when something happens that is out of your control, then you have to make some kind of decision. The most important reason for college, though, is to fulfill my dream. I know I need an education, and I want to take the courses I need to reach the position that I think I can handle. Only by qualifying yourself can you get what you want. Going to college will help me fulfill this goal. These are the main reasons why I am attending college.

Paragraph B

Why I'm in School

There are several reasons I'm in school. First of all, my father's attitude made me want to succeed in school. One night last year, after I had come in at 3 A.M., my father said, "Mickey, you're a bum. When I look at my son, all I see is a good-for-nothing bum." I was angry, but I knew my father was right in a way. I had spent the last two years working at odd jobs at a pizza parlor and luncheonette, trying all kinds of drugs with my friends. That night, though, I decided I would prove my father wrong. I would go to college and be a success. Another reason I'm in college is my girlfriend's encouragement. Marie has already been in school for a year, and she is doing well in her computer courses. Marie helped me fill out my application and register for courses. She even lent me sixty-five dollars for textbooks. On her day off, she lets me use her car so I don't have to take the college bus. The main reason I am in college is to fulfill a personal goal: for the first time in my life, I want to finish something. For example, I quit high school in the eleventh grade. Then I enrolled in a government job-training program, but I dropped out after six months. I tried to get a high school equivalency diploma, but I started missing classes and eventually gave up. Now I am in a special program where I will earn my high school degree by completing a series of five courses. I am determined to accomplish this goal and to then go on and work for a degree in hotel management.

Complete the following statement: Paragraph _____ provides clear, vividly detailed reasons why the writer decided to attend college.

Paragraph B is the one that solidly backs up its point. The writer gives us specific reasons he is in school. On the basis of such evidence, we can clearly understand his opening point. The writer of paragraph A offers only vague, general reasons for being in school. We do not get specific examples of how the writer was "getting into trouble," what events occurred that forced the decision, or even what kind of job he or she wants to qualify for. We sense that the feeling expressed is sincere, but without particular examples we cannot really see why the writer decided to attend college.

Reinforcing Point and Support

You have learned the two most important steps in writing effectively: making a point and supporting that point. Take a few minutes now to do the following activity. It will strengthen your ability to recognize a *point* and the *support* for that point.

In the following groups, one statement is the general point and the other statements are specific support for the point. Identify each point with a P and each statement of support with an S.

Activity

3

EXAMPLE

_S_ My college is only three miles from my house.

_S_ It's on a bus line that passes a block from my house.

_S_ When the weather is good, I can walk to school in about forty-five minutes.

_P_ For me, the college I attend is easy to get to.

> **EXPLANATION**   The point—that the writer's college is easy for the writer to get to—is strongly supported by the three specific details stated.

1. _____ This has been a wonderful week.

   _____ I won $100 in the state lottery.

   _____ I scored a 96 on my chemistry exam.

   _____ My boss just gave me a raise.

2. _____ Some people skip breakfast.

   _____ Some people have poor eating habits.

   _____ Some people always order supersize portions.

   _____ Some people eat almost no fruits or vegetables.

3. _____ My blood pressure has dropped.

   _____ This new exercise program must be working.

   _____ I have lost ten pounds in three weeks.

   _____ I don't tire as easily as I used to.

4. _____ Cats are clean and do not require much attention.

   _____ Cats like living indoors and are safe to have around children.

   _____ Cats are inexpensive to feed and easy to keep healthy.

   _____ There are definite advantages to having a cat as a pet.

5. _____   She is eating less red meat, fewer fatty foods, and more vegetables.

_____   Jane is taking better care of herself.

_____   She exercises at least four times a week.

_____   Jane made sure to get a flu shot this year.

6. _____   My work hours are flexible.

_____   I love my job at the day care center.

_____   The children are easy to work with.

_____   The center is bright and cheerful.

7. _____   The bread the waiter brought us is stale.

_____   We've been waiting for our main course for more than an hour.

_____   It is time to speak to the restaurant manager.

_____   The people next to us are awfully loud.

8. _____   Carla asks you questions about yourself.

_____   Carla is a pleasure to be around.

_____   Carla has a great smile.

_____   Carla really listens when you talk.

9. _____   The library subscribes to more than five hundred magazines and newspapers.

_____   Students have online access to thirty-five academic databases to which the college subscribes.

_____   Several expert librarians are always present to help students locate resources.

_____   Our college library has excellent resources.

_____   The library's DVD collection has recently been expanded.

_____   There are more than 150,000 books in our library.

10. _____   My older brother is a computer nerd.

_____   My sister wants to go to dental school.

_____   My younger brother wants to become a history teacher.

_____   The children in my family have different academic and career goals.

_____   I have a flair for foreign languages and want to become a diplomat.

11. _____ Though a mosquito is small, it has power.

_____ A mosquito can find you in the dark.

_____ A mosquito can keep you awake all night.

_____ A mosquito can make you scratch yourself until you bleed.

12. _____ Because sending e-mail is so simple, family and friends may use e-mail messages to stay in close touch.

_____ When people are upset, they may send off an angry e-mail before they consider the consequences.

_____ The jokes, petitions, and other e-mails that friends so easily forward can become a real nuisance.

_____ The ease of using e-mail can be both a blessing and a curse.

13. _____ When some people answer the phone, their first words are "Who's this?"

_____ Some people never bother to identify themselves when calling someone.

_____ Some people have terrible telephone manners.

_____ Some people hang up without even saying good-bye.

14. _____ One mother created what she called the homework zone—the kitchen table after dinner—where she and her young children did their assignments.

_____ Some adult students have taken classes at a nearby community college during their lunch hour.

_____ Adult students often find creative ways to balance school, employment, and family responsibilities.

_____ By listening to recorded lectures in the car, working students turn travel time into learning time.

15. _____ Moviegoers can take several simple steps to save money at the movie theater.

_____ Bringing homemade popcorn to the movies is cheaper than buying expensive theater popcorn.

_____ Buying candy at a grocery store, not a theater, cuts candy costs in half.

_____ Going to movies early in the day reduces ticket prices by as much as $3 each.

The Importance of *Specific* Details

The point that opens a paragraph is a general statement. The evidence that supports a point is made up of specific details, reasons, examples, and facts.

Specific details have two key functions. First of all, details *excite the reader's interest.* They make writing a pleasure to read, for we all enjoy learning particulars about other people—what they do and think and feel. Second, details *support and explain a writer's point;* they give the evidence needed for us to see and understand a general idea. For example, the writer of "Good-Bye, Tony" provides details that make vividly clear her decision not to see Tony anymore. She specifies the exact time Tony was supposed to arrive (8:30) and when he actually arrived (9:30). She mentions the kind of film she wanted to see (a new Chris Rock movie) and the one that Tony took her to instead (a violent movie). She tells us what she may have wanted to do after the movie (have a hamburger or a drink) and what they did instead (making out); she even specifies the exact location of the place Tony took her (a back road near Oakcrest High School). She explains precisely what happened next (Tony "cut his finger on my earring") and even mentions by name (Bactine and a Band-Aid) the treatments he planned to use.

The writer of "Why I'm in School" provides equally vivid details. He gives clear reasons for being in school (his father's attitude, his girlfriend's encouragement, and his wish to fulfill a personal goal) and backs up each reason with specific details. His details give us many sharp pictures. For instance, we hear the exact words his father spoke: "Mickey, you're a bum." He tells us exactly how he was spending his time ("working at odd jobs at a pizza parlor and luncheonette, trying all kinds of drugs with my friends"). He describes how his girlfriend helped him (filling out the college application, lending money and her car). Finally, instead of stating generally that "you have to make some kind of decision," as the writer of "Reasons for Going to College" does, he specifies that he has a strong desire to finish college because he dropped out of many schools and programs in the past: high school, a job-training program, and a high school equivalency course.

In both "Good-Bye, Tony" and "Why I'm in School," then, the vivid, exact details capture our interest and enable us to share in the writer's experience. We see people's actions and hear their words; the details provide pictures that make each of us feel "I am there." The particulars also allow us to understand each writer's point clearly. We are shown exactly why the first writer has decided not to see Tony anymore and exactly why the second writer is attending college.

Each of the five points below is followed by two attempts at support (*a* and *b*). Write S (for *specific*) in the space next to the one that succeeds in providing specific support for the point. Write X in the space next to the one that lacks supporting details.

1. My brother-in-law is a workaholic.

    _____ a. He works twelve hours a day at the accounting firm he started. Then he comes home, gulps down some dinner, opens his briefcase, turns on his computer, and puts in another three hours.

    _____ b. He's at it all the time. He spends a lot of time at the office even though he's the boss. Then he comes home and does more work. Sometimes he's working late into the night.

2. The prices in the amusement park were outrageously high.

    _____ a. The food seemed to cost twice as much as it would in a supermarket and was sometimes of poor quality. The rides also cost a lot, and so I had to tell the children that they were limited to a certain number of them.

    _____ b. The cost of the log flume, a ride that lasts roughly three minutes, was ten dollars a person. Then I had to pay four dollars for an eight-ounce cup of Coke and six dollars for a hot dog.

3. My cat is extremely bright.

    _____ a. He knows how to solve problems. He also recognizes people he knows.

    _____ b. When he gets locked in the basement, he simply grasps the door latch, pulls down on it, and opens the door. He also distinguishes between family members and strangers. When a classmate of mine came by last week, my cat jumped on my lap and rubbed himself against my face, but he refused to go near our guest.

4. The so-called "bargains" at the yard sale were junk.

    _____ a. The tables were filled with useless stuff no one could possibly want. They were the kinds of things that should be thrown away, not sold.

    _____ b. The "bargains" included two headless dolls, blankets filled with holes, scorched potholders, and a plastic Christmas tree with several branches missing.

Activity 4

5. The key to success in college is organization.

_____ a. Knowing what you're doing, when you have to do it, and so on, is a big help for a student. A system is crucial in achieving an ordered approach to study. Otherwise, things become very disorganized, and it is not long before grades will begin to drop.

_____ b. Organized students never forget paper or exam dates, which are marked on a calendar above their desks. And instead of having to cram for exams, they study their clear, neat classroom and textbook notes on a daily basis.

EXPLANATION   The specific support for point 1 is _a_. The sentence goes beyond telling us that the brother-in-law is a workaholic; it also gives examples of his day and evening work habits. For point 2, answer _b_ gives specific prices (ten dollars for a ride, four dollars for a Coke, and six dollars for a hot dog) to support the idea that the amusement park was expensive. For point 3, answer _b_ vividly describes the cat's behavior to prove that he is bright. Point 4 is supported by answer _b_, which lists specific examples of useless items that were offered for sale—from headless dolls to a broken plastic Christmas tree. We cannot help but agree with the writer's point that the items were not bargains but junk. Point 5 is backed up by answer _b,_ which identifies two specific strategies of organized students: They mark important dates on calendars above their desks, and they take careful notes and study them on a daily basis.

In each case the specific evidence enables us _to see for ourselves_ that the writer's point is valid.

Activity

5

Follow the directions for Activity 4.

1. Professor DeMarco is an excellent math teacher.

_____ a. He keeps extra office hours for students who are having trouble understanding the homework or the material presented in class. He questions students individually in class to make sure that everyone understands what is being discussed. If not, he explains the subject again in a different way to make it clearer.

_____ b. He cares about students, makes his classes interesting, and has taught me a great deal.

2. Students have practical uses for computers.

   _____ a. Students stay in touch with friends by e-mail. They often shop over the Internet. They do all their research online.

   _____ b. Students have an easier way now to communicate with their friends. They can also save time now: They have no need to go out to buy things but can shop from home. Also, getting information they need for papers no longer requires spending time in the library.

3. Rico knew very little about cooking when he got his first apartment.

   _____ a. He had to live on whatever he had in the freezer for a while. He was not any good in the kitchen and had to learn very slowly. More often than not, he would learn how to cook something only by making mistakes first.

   _____ b. He lived on macaroni and cheese TV dinners for three weeks. His idea of cooking an egg was to put a whole egg in the microwave, where it exploded. Then he tried to make a grilled cheese sandwich by putting slices of cheese and bread in a toaster.

4. Speaking before a group is a problem for many people.

   _____ a. They become uncomfortable even at the thought of speaking in public. They will go to almost any length to avoid speaking to a group. If they are forced to do it, they can feel so anxious that they actually develop physical symptoms.

   _____ b. Stage fright, stammering, and blushing are frequent reactions. Some people will pretend to be ill to avoid speaking publicly. When asked to rank their worst fears, people often list public speaking as even worse than death.

5. Small children can have as much fun with ordinary household items as with costly toys.

   _____ a. A large sheet thrown over a card table makes a great hideout or playhouse. Banging pot covers together makes a tremendous crash that kids love. Also, kids like to make long, winding fences out of wooden clothespins.

   _____ b. Kids can make musical instruments out of practically anything. The result is a lot of noise and fun. They can easily create their own play areas as well by using a little imagination. There is simply no need to have to spend a lot of money on playthings.

The Importance of *Adequate* Details

One of the most common and most serious problems in students' writing is inadequate development. You must provide *enough* specific details to support fully the point you are making. You could not, for example, submit a paragraph about your brother-in-law being rude and provide only a single short example. You would have to add several other examples or provide an extended example of your brother-in-law's rudeness. Without such additional support, your paragraph would be underdeveloped.

At times, students try to disguise an undersupported point by using repetition and wordy generalities. You saw this, for example, in paragraph A ("Reasons for Going to College") on page 53. Be prepared to do the plain hard work needed to ensure that each of your paragraphs has full, solid support.

Activity

6

The following paragraphs were written on the same topic, and each has a clear opening point. Which one is adequately developed? Which one has few particulars and uses mostly vague, general, wordy sentences to conceal the fact that it is starved for specific details?

Paragraph A

Florida

Florida, the Sunshine State, is known as a place where many senior citizens spend their retirement because of the fabulous weather. However, this state offers something for people of all ages. Recreational opportunities are abundant. First, Florida is a peninsula—that is, two-thirds of it is surrounded by water—so there are plenty of places to go swimming, boating, fishing, wind surfing, and water skiing. In the interior, Florida offers many gorgeous lakes for similar activities or simply for observing animals such as alligators, snakes, panthers, tortoises, herons, ibis, egrets, cranes, and flamingos in their native habitats. Florida is also an entertainment mecca. Besides the most famous attractions—Disney World, Universal Studios, and Busch Gardens—there are theme parks such as SeaWorld, Legoland, and Discovery Cove. In addition, every major city has theaters, museums, and concert halls of all kinds. One of the most fascinating is the Salvador Dalí Museum in St. Petersburg, which features the works of the famous Spanish artist. Floridians are also proud of their great professional athletic teams, such as the Miami Dolphins, the Tampa Bay Buccaneers, the Florida Marlins, the Tampa Bay Rays, and the Miami Heat.

continued

Daytona Beach, right off Route 95 on Florida's eastern coast, is home to what some people call the World Series of stock car racing. Finally, Florida has many fine colleges and universities, from local community colleges, such as Miami-Dade Community College, to Florida State University and the University of Florida. Perhaps all of this is why this state has had the greatest rate of population growth in the country.

Paragraph B

Florida

Lots of older people retire to Florida because of the weather. After all, it's not called the Sunshine State for nothing. However, that is not the only reason that more and more people are moving to Florida from other parts of the country. There's simply a lot to do there, which makes the state very attractive to potential newcomers. First, there's water sports. One can swim or just relax at one of Florida's many beaches. Then there are many lakes where the state's exotic wildlife can be seen in their natural habitats. Also, Florida is an entertainment mecca. Theme parks attract millions of visitors from all over the world the year round. Seniors, adults, and children really love these places. They are certainly family friendly. In addition, every major city has theaters, museums, and concert halls of all kinds. Floridians also love their professional sports teams, and almost every professional sport is represented, including stock car racing. Finally, there are many excellent colleges and universities in the state. Perhaps all of this is why this state has had the greatest rate of population growth in the country.

Complete the following statement: Paragraph _____ provides an adequate number of specific details to support its point.

Paragraph A offers detailed examples of Florida's many attractions. Paragraph B, on the other hand, is underdeveloped. Paragraph B speaks only of "water sports" such as swimming, but paragraph A mentions boating, fishing, surfing, and water skiing, as well. Paragraph B talks in a general way about Florida as an entertainment mecca, but paragraph A mentions specific attractions such as Disney World and Universal Studios. When discussing Florida's sports, paragraph B claims that the state has many professional teams, but paragraph A names several teams, such as the Dolphins and the Marlins. In short, paragraph A has the detail that paragraph B lacks.

To check your understanding of the chapter so far, see if you can answer the following questions.

1. It has been observed: "To write well, the first thing that you must do is decide what nail you want to drive home." What is meant by *nail*?

   _____

2. How do you drive home the nail in the paragraph?

   _____

   _____

3. What are the two reasons for using specific details in your writing?

   a. _____

   b. _____

Practice in Making and Supporting a Point

You now know the two most important steps in competent writing: (1) making a point and (2) supporting that point with specific evidence. The purpose of this section is to expand and strengthen your understanding of these two basic steps.

You will first work through a series of activities on *making* a point:

1. Identifying Common Errors in Topic Sentences
2. Understanding the Two Parts of a Topic Sentence
3. Selecting a Topic Sentence
4. Writing a Topic Sentence: I
5. Writing a Topic Sentence: II

You will then sharpen your understanding of specific details by working through a series of activities on *supporting* a point:

6. Recognizing Specific Details: I
7. Recognizing Specific Details: II
8. Providing Supporting Evidence
9. Identifying Adequate Supporting Evidence
10. Adding Details to Complete a Paragraph
11. Writing a Simple Paragraph

1 Identifying Common Errors in Topic Sentences

When writing a point, or topic sentence, people sometimes make mistakes that undermine their chances of producing an effective paper. One mistake is to substitute an announcement of the topic for a true topic sentence. Other mistakes include writing statements that are too broad or too narrow. Following are examples of all three errors, along with contrasting examples of effective topic sentences.

Announcement

My car is the concern of this paragraph.

The statement above is a simple announcement of a subject, rather than a topic sentence expressing an idea about the subject.

Statement That Is Too Broad

Many people have problems with their cars.

The statement is too broad to be supported adequately with specific details in a single paragraph.

Statement That Is Too Narrow

My car is a Ford Focus.

The statement above is too narrow to be expanded into a paragraph. Such a narrow statement is sometimes called a *dead-end statement* because there is no place to go with it. It is a simple fact that does not need or call for any support.

Effective Topic Sentence

I hate my car.

The statement above expresses an opinion that could be supported in a paragraph. The writer could offer a series of specific supporting reasons, examples, and details to make it clear why he or she hates the car.

Here are additional examples:

Announcements

The subject of this paper will be my apartment.

I want to talk about increases in the divorce rate.

Statements That Are Too Broad

The places where people live have definite effects on their lives.

Many people have trouble getting along with others.

Statements That Are Too Narrow

I have no hot water in my apartment at night.

Almost one of every two marriages ends in divorce.

Effective Topic Sentences

My apartment is a terrible place to live.

The divorce rate is increasing for several reasons.

Activity 7

For each pair of sentences below, write A beside the sentence that only *announces* a topic. Write OK beside the sentence that *advances an idea* about the topic.

1. _____ a. This paper is about what not to do on a first date.

   _____ b. There are three things to avoid if you don't want to make your first date with someone your last.

2. _____ a. I am going to write about my job as a gas station attendant.

   _____ b. Working as a gas station attendant was the worst job I ever had.

3. _____ a. Keeping to a strict budget is this paragraph's focus.

   _____ b. College students can save money by giving up cigarettes and beer.

4. _____ a. In several ways, my college library is inconvenient to use.

   _____ b. This paragraph will deal with the college library.

5. _____ a. My paper will discuss the topic of procrastinating.

   _____ b. The following steps will help you stop procrastinating.

Activity 8

For each pair of sentences below, write TN beside the statement that is *too narrow* to be developed into a paragraph. Write OK beside the statement in each pair that could be developed into a paragraph.

1. _____ a. I do push-ups and sit-ups each morning.

   _____ b. Exercising every morning has had positive effects on my health.

2. _____ a. José works nine hours a day and then goes to school three hours a night.

   _____ b. José is an ambitious man.

3. _____ a. I started college after being away from school for seven years.

   _____ b. Several of my fears about returning to school have proved to be groundless.

4. _____ a. I watched a show on the Discovery Channel.

_____ b. The Discovery Channel show on chimpanzees that I watched provided information on language acquisition that I can use when writing my psychology paper.

5. _____ a. My brother was depressed yesterday for several reasons.

_____ b. Yesterday my brother had to pay fifty-two dollars for a motor tune-up.

For each pair of sentences below, write TB beside the statement that is *too broad* to be supported adequately in a short paper. Write OK beside the statement that makes a limited point.

Activity

9

1. _____ a. Angela is very intelligent.

_____ b. Angela has the qualifications to be a great lawyer.

2. _____ a. Married life is the best way of living.

_____ b. Teenage marriages often end in divorce for several reasons.

3. _____ a. Aspirin can have several harmful side effects.

_____ b. Drugs are dangerous.

4. _____ a. I've always done poorly in school.

_____ b. I flunked math last semester for several reasons.

5. _____ a. Computers are changing our society.

_____ b. Using computers to teach schoolchildren is a mistake.

2 Understanding the Two Parts of a Topic Sentence

As stated earlier, the point that opens a paragraph is often called a *topic sentence.* When you look closely at a point, or topic sentence, you can see that it is made up of two parts:

1. The *limited topic*
2. The writer's *attitude* toward, or idea about, the limited topic

The writer's attitude, point of view, or idea is usually expressed in one or more *key words.* All the details in a paragraph should support the idea expressed in the key words. In each of the topic sentences below, a single line appears under the topic and a double line under the idea about the topic (expressed in a key word or key words):

My dog is extremely stubborn.

Texting while driving is against the law in many states.

The kitchen is the most widely used room in my house.

Voting should be required by law in the United States.

My pickup truck is the most reliable vehicle I have ever owned.

In the first sentence, the topic is *dog,* and the key words that express the writer's idea about his topic are that his dog is *extremely stubborn.* In the second sentence, the topic is *texting while driving,* and the key words that determine the focus of the paragraph are *against the law.* Notice each topic and key word or key words in the other three sentences as well.

Activity

10

For each point below, draw a single line under the topic and a double line under the idea about the topic.

1. Billboards should be abolished.

2. My boss is an ambitious man.

3. Politicians are often self-serving.

4. The house provided every comfort a young person would want.

5. Television commercials are often insulting.

6. Spaniards eat dinner very late.

7. The middle child is often a neglected member of the family.

8. The language in many movies today is offensive.

9. Nurses at our local hospital are well trained.

10. Homeowners today are more energy-conscious than ever before.

11. My car is a tempermental machine.

12. The capital of Hungary, which is Budapest, was once two separate cities.

13. Finding information for research papers has become easier because of the Internet.

14. The zoo contains many exotic animals.

15. Regulations in the school cafeteria should be strictly enforced.

16. The national speed limit should be raised.

17. The legislature voted to reduce tuition at all state colleges.

18. The city's traffic-light system has both values and drawbacks.

19. Insects serve many useful purposes.

20. Serious depression often has several warning signs.

3 Selecting a Topic Sentence

Remember that a paragraph is made up of a topic sentence and a group of related sentences developing the topic sentence. It is also helpful to remember that the topic sentence is a *general* statement. The other sentences provide specific support for the general statement.

Each group of sentences below could be written as a short paragraph. Circle the letter of the topic sentence in each case. To find the topic sentence, ask yourself, "Which is a general statement supported by the specific details in the other three statements?"

    Begin by trying the example item below. First circle the letter of the sentence you think expresses the main idea. Then read the explanation.

Activity

11

EXAMPLE

    a. If you stop carrying matches or a lighter, you can cut down on impulse smoking.

    b. If you sit in no-smoking areas, you will smoke less.

    (c.) You can behave in ways that will help you smoke less.

    d. By keeping a record of when and where you smoke, you can identify the most tempting situations and then avoid them.

EXPLANATION   Sentence *a* explains one way to smoke less. Sentences *b* and *d* also provide specific ways to smoke less. In sentence *c,* however, no one specific way is explained. The words *ways that will help you smoke less* refer only generally to such methods. Therefore, sentence *c* is the topic sentence; it expresses the author's main idea. The other sentences support that idea by providing examples.

---

1.   a.   The kitchen and the baths had been remodeled.
        b.   The house was well maintained.
        c.   The roof, furnace, and air conditioner were new.
        d.   The yard had just been landscaped.
2.   a.   This car costs less than comparable models.
        b.   My car is economical.
        c.   It gets forty-one miles per gallon.
        d.   After 75,000 miles, I have replaced only the tires and brakes.

3. a. The last time I ate at the diner, I got food poisoning and was sick for two days.
   b. The city inspector found roaches and mice in the diner's kitchen.
   c. Our town diner is a health hazard and ought to be closed down.
   d. The toilets in the diner often back up, and the sinks have only a trickle of water.

4. a. The History Channel and the Discovery Channel are informative.
   b. Viewers of shows like *This Old House* can learn a lot about home maintenance.
   c. Television can be a tool for education.
   d. Several cable networks offer shows discussing important health issues.

5. a. In early colleges, students were mostly white males.
   b. Colleges of two centuries ago were quite different from today's schools.
   c. All students in early colleges had to take the same courses.
   d. The entire student body at early schools would be only a few dozen people.

4 Writing a Topic Sentence: I

Activity

12

The following activity will give you practice in writing an accurate point, or topic sentence—one that is neither too broad nor too narrow for the supporting material in a paragraph. Sometimes you will construct your topic sentence after you have decided which details you want to discuss. An added value of this activity is that it shows you how to write a topic sentence that will exactly match the details you have developed.

1. *Topic sentence:* _____

   _____

   a. Thomas Jefferson read Latin, Greek, French, Italian, and other foreign languages.
   b. His library contained more than 6,400 books.
   c. He designed his magnificent mansion at Monticello after teaching himself architecture.
   d. He was an excellent writer, an accomplished musician, and a political genius.

2. *Topic sentence:* _____

   _____

   a. Only about thirty people came to the dance, instead of the expected two hundred.
   b. The band arrived late and spent an hour setting up.
   c. There were at least three males at the dance to every female.
   d. An hour after the dance started, it ended because of a power failure.

3. *Topic sentence:* _____

_____

    a. We had to wait half an hour even though we had reserved a table.
    b. Our appetizer and main course arrived at the same time.
    c. The busboy ignored our requests for more water.
    d. The wrong desserts were served to us.

4. *Topic sentence:* _____

_____

    a. People who settled the American frontier had to clear dense forests.
    b. They had to fight off deadly diseases that threatened them and their animals.
    c. The weather, which was unpredictable, sometimes destroyed their crops.
    d. Because knowledge of farming methods was limited, they sometimes failed to grow enough food to sustain themselves.

5. *Topic sentence:* _____

_____

    a. The crowd scenes were crudely spliced from another film.
    b. Mountains and other background scenery were just painted cardboard cutouts.
    c. The "sync" was off, so that you heard voices even when the actors' lips were not moving.
    d. The so-called monster was just a spider that had been filmed through a magnifying lens.

5 Writing a Topic Sentence: II

Often you will start with a general topic or a general idea of what you want to write about. You may, for example, want to write a paragraph about some aspect of school life. To come up with a point about school life, begin by limiting your topic. One way to do this is to make a list of all the limited topics you can think of that fit under the general topic.

Following are five general topics and a series of limited topics that fit under them. Make a point out of *one* of the limited topics in each group.

Activity

13

> **HINT:** To create a topic sentence, ask yourself, "What point do I want to make about _____ (*my limited topic*)?"

EXAMPLE

Recreation

- Movies
- Dancing
- TV shows
- Reading
- Sports parks

Your point: *Sports parks today have some truly exciting games.*

1. Your school
   - Instructor
   - Cafeteria
   - Specific course
   - Particular room or building
   - Particular policy (attendance, grading, etc.)
   - Classmate

   Your point: _____

   _____

2. Job
   - Pay
   - Boss
   - Working conditions
   - Duties
   - Coworkers
   - Customers or clients

   Your point: _____

   _____

3. Money
   - Budgets
   - Credit cards
   - Dealing with a bank
   - School expenses
   - Ways to get it
   - Ways to save it

Your point: _____

_____

4. Living dangerously
   - Sky diving
   - Drag racing
   - Unprotected sex
   - Drinking and driving
   - Snowbarding and skiing accidents

   Your point: _____

   _____

5. Sports
   - A team's chances
   - At your school
   - Women's team
   - Recreational versus spectator
   - Favorite team
   - Outstanding athlete

   Your point: _____

   _____

6 Recognizing Specific Details: I

Specific details are examples, reasons, particulars, and facts. Such details are needed to support and explain a topic sentence effectively. They provide the evidence needed for readers to understand, as well as to feel and experience, a writer's point.

Here is a topic sentence followed by two sets of supporting sentences. Which set provides sharp, specific details?

Topic Sentence

Some poor people must struggle to make meals for themselves.

Set A

They gather up whatever free food they can find in fast-food restaurants and take it home to use however they can. Instead of planning well-balanced meals, they base their diet on anything they can buy that is cheap and filling.

Set B

Some make tomato soup by adding hot water to the free packets of ketchup they get at McDonald's. Others buy cans of cheap dog food and fry it like hamburger.

Set B provides specific details: Instead of a general statement about "free food they find in fast-food restaurants and take . . . home to use however they can," we get a vivid detail we can see and picture clearly: "make tomato soup [from] free packets of ketchup." Instead of a general statement about how the poor will "base their diet on anything they can buy that is cheap and filling," we get exact and vivid details: "Others buy cans of cheap dog food and fry it like hamburger."

Specific details are often like the information we might find in a movie script. They provide us with such clear pictures that we could make a film of them if we wanted to. You would know just how to film the information given in set B. You would show a poor person breaking open a packet of ketchup from McDonald's and mixing it with water to make a kind of tomato soup. You would show some-one opening a can of dog food and frying its contents like hamburger.

In contrast, the writer of set A fails to provide the specific information needed. If you were asked to make a film based on set A, you would have to figure out for yourself what particulars you were going to show.

When you are working to provide specific supporting information in a paper, it might help to ask yourself, "Could someone easily film this information?" If the answer is "yes," you probably have good details.

| Activity 14 | Each topic sentence below is followed by two sets of supporting details (*a* and *b*). Write S (for *specific*) in the space next to the set that provides specific support for the point. Write G (for *general*) next to the set that offers only vague, general support. |

1. *Topic sentence*: Attila the Hun was a fierce and bloody ruler.

    _____ a. After he became king of the Huns (A.D. 434), a people who lived in an area of eastern Europe that approximates the site of modern Hungary, Attila murdered his brother and coruler, Bleda. Then he wreaked havoc on eastern and central Europe, conquering many peoples who lived in that area, which now includes Poland, the Czech Republic, Austria, Slovakia, and Romania. In 450, he invaded Gaul (now France), which was a Roman province, and later Italy, where he killed thousands of people, wiped out several villages and small cities, and burned farmland.

    _____ b. Attila became king of the Huns in the fifth century. The Huns lived in central Europe. Shortly after taking the throne, he killed his brother. Then he attacked his neighbors, conquering many of the people around him. He also invaded France and Italy, where he killed thousands of others and caused much destruction.

2. *Topic sentence:* Roberta is very aggressive.

   _____ a. Her aggressiveness is apparent in both her personal and her professional life. She is never shy about extending social invitations. And while some people are turned off by her aggressive attitude, others are impressed by it and enjoy doing business with her.

   _____ b. When she meets a man she likes, she is quick to say, "Let's go out sometime. What's your phone number?" In her job as a furniture salesperson, she will follow potential customers out onto the sidewalk as she tries to persuade them to buy.

3. *Topic sentence:* Our new kitten causes us lots of trouble.

   _____ a. He has shredded the curtains in my bedroom with his claws. He nearly drowned when he crawled into the washing machine. And my hands look like raw hamburger from his playful bites and scratches.

   _____ b. He seems to destroy everything he touches. He's always getting into places where he doesn't belong. Sometimes he plays too roughly, and that can be painful.

4. *Topic sentence:* My landlord is softhearted.

   _____ a. Even though he wrote them himself, he sometimes ignores the official apartment rules in order to make his tenants happy.

   _____ b. Although the lease states "No pets," he brought my daughter a puppy after she told him how much she missed having one.

5. *Topic sentence:* The library is a distracting place to try to study.

   _____ a. It's hard to concentrate when a noisy eight-person poker game is going on on the floor beside you. It's also distracting to overhear remarks like, "Hey, Baby, what's your mother's address? I want to send her a thank-you card for having such a beautiful daughter."

   _____ b. Many students meet in the library to do group activities and socialize with one another. Others go there to flirt. It's easy to get more interested in all that activity than in paying attention to your studies.

7 Recognizing Specific Details: II

Activity

15

At several points in the following paragraphs, you are given a choice of two sets of supporting details. Write S (for *specific*) in the space next to the set that provides specific support for the point. Write G (for *general*) next to the set that offers only vague, general support.

Paragraph 1

My daughter's boyfriend is a good-for-nothing young man. After knowing him for just three months, everyone in our family is opposed to the relationship. For one thing, Russell is lazy.

_____ a. He is always finding an excuse to avoid putting in an honest day's work. He never pitches in and helps with chores around our house, even when he's asked directly to do so. And his attitude about his job isn't any better. To hear him tell it, he deserves special treatment in the workplace. He thinks he's gone out of his way if he just shows up on time.

_____ b. After starting a new job last week, he announced this Monday that he wasn't going to work because it was his *birthday*—as if he were somebody special. And when my husband asked Russell to help put storm windows on the house next Saturday, Russell answered that he uses his weekends to catch up on sleep.

Another quality of Russell's which no one likes is that he is cheap.

_____ c. When my daughter's birthday came around, Russell said he would take her out to Baldoni's, a fancy Italian restaurant. Then he changed his mind. Instead of spending a lot of money on a meal, he said, he wanted to buy her a really nice pair of earrings. So my daughter cooked dinner for him at her apartment. But there was no present, not even a little one. He claims he's waiting for a jewelry sale at Macy's. I don't think my daughter will ever see that "really nice" gift.

_____ d. He makes big promises about all the nice things he's going to do for my daughter, but he never comes through. His words are cheap, and so is he. He's all talk and no action. My daughter isn't greedy, but it hurts her when Russell says he's going to take her someplace nice or give her something special and then nothing happens.

Worst of all, Russell is mean.

_____ e. Russell seems to get special pleasure from hurting people when he feels they have a weak point. I have heard him make remarks that to him were funny but were really very insensitive. You've got to wonder about someone who needs to be ugly to other people just for the sake of being powerful. Sometimes I want to let him know how I feel.

_____ f. When my husband was out of work, Russell said to him, "Well, you've got it made now, living off your wife." After my husband glared at him, he said, "Why're you getting sore? I'm just kidding." Sometimes he snaps at my daughter, saying things like "Don't make me wait—there are plenty of other babes who would like to take your place." At such times I want to toss him out to the curb.

Everyone in the family is waiting anxiously for the day when my daughter will see Russell the way the rest of us see him.

Paragraph 2

Many adult children move back in with their parents for some period of time. Although living with Mom and Dad again has some advantages, there are certain problems that are likely to arise. One common problem is that children may expect their parents to do all the household chores.

_____ a. They never think that they should take on their share of work around the house. Not only do they not help with their parents' chores; they don't even take responsibility for the extra work that their presence creates. Like babies, they go through the house making a mess that the parents are supposed to clean up. It's as if they think their parents are their servants.

_____ b. They expect meals to appear on the table as if by magic. After they've eaten, they go off to work or play, never thinking about who's going to do the dishes. They drop their dirty laundry beside the washing machine, assuming that Mom or Dad will attend to it and return clean, folded clothes to their bedroom door. And speaking of their bedrooms: Every day they await the arrival of Mom's Maid Service to make the bed, pick up the floor, and dust the furniture.

Another frequent problem is that parents forget their adult children are no longer adolescents.

_____ c. Parents like this want to know everything about their adult children's lives. They don't think their kids, even though they are adults, should have any privacy. Whenever they see their children doing anything, they want to know all the details. It's as though their children are still teenagers who are expected to report all their activities. Naturally, adult children get irritated when they are treated as if they were little kids.

_____ d. They may insist upon knowing far more about their children's comings and goings than the children want to share. For example, if such parents see their adult son heading out the door, they demand, "Where are you going? Who will you be with? What will you be doing? What time will you be back?" In addition, they may not let their adult child have any privacy. If their daughter and a date are sitting in the living room, for instance, they may join them there and start peppering the young man with questions about his family and his job, as if they were interviewing him for the position of son-in-law.

Finally, there may be financial problems when an adult child returns to live at home.

_____ e. Having an extra adult in the household creates extra expenses. But many adult children don't offer to help deal with those extra costs. Adult children often eat at home, causing the grocery bill to climb. They may stay in a formerly unused room, which now needs to be heated and lit. They produce extra laundry to be washed. They run up the family's cell-phone bills. For all these reasons, adult children should expect to pay a reasonable fee to their parents for room and board.

_____ f. It's expensive to have another adult living in the household. Adult children would be paying a lot of bills on their own if they weren't staying with their parents. It's only fair that they share the expenses at their parents' house. They should consider all the ways that their living at home is increasing their parents' expenses. Then they should insist on covering their share of the costs.

8 Providing Supporting Evidence

Activity

16

Provide three details that logically support each of the following points, or topic sentences. Your details can be drawn from your own experience, or they can be invented. In each case, the details should show in a specific way what the point expresses in only a general way. You may state your details briefly in phrases, or as complete sentences.

EXAMPLE

The student had several ways of passing time during the dull lecture.

_____

_____

_____

1. I could tell I was coming down with the flu.

   _____

   _____

   _____

2. There are several ways to save gas.

   _____

   _____

   _____

3. I had car problems recently.

   _____

   _____

   _____

4. When your money gets tight, there are several ways to economize.

   _____

   _____

   _____

5. Some people have dangerous driving habits.

   _____

   _____

   _____

9 Identifying Adequate Supporting Evidence

Two of the following paragraphs provide sufficient details to support their topic sentences convincingly. Write AD, for *adequate development,* beside those paragraphs. There are also three paragraphs that, for the most part, use vague, general, or wordy sentences as a substitute for concrete details. Write U, for *underdeveloped,* beside those paragraphs.

Activity

17

_____ 1.   **My Husband's Stubbornness**

My husband's worst problem is his stubbornness. He simply will not let any kind of weakness show. If he isn't feeling well, he refuses to admit it. He will keep on doing whatever he is doing and will wait until the symptoms get almost unbearable before he will even hint that anything is the matter with him. Then things are so far along that he has to spend more time recovering than he would if he had a different attitude. He also hates to be wrong. If he is wrong, he will be the last to admit it. This happened once when we went shopping, and he spent an endless amount of time going from one place to the next. He insisted that one of them had a fantastic sale on things he wanted. We never found a sale, but the fact that this situation happened will not change his attitude. Finally, he never listens to anyone else's suggestions on a car trip. He always knows he's on the right road, and the results have led to a lot of time wasted getting back in the right direction. Every time one of these incidents happens, that only means that it is going to happen again in the future.

_____ 2.   **The Aztecs**

Before the Spaniards came to Mexico, the native inhabitants had developed advanced civilizations. For example, when the Europeans arrived, the Aztecs controlled much of the southwestern portion of present-day Mexico. They had built cities that were as large as, or larger than, many European cities of the sixteenth century. In fact, their capital, Tenochtitlán, had 200,000 to 300,000 inhabitants, more than any European capital. The Aztecs built immense temples and government buildings, and they developed a vibrant economy. In the central market of Tenochtitlán, 60,000 people conducted business each day. They also developed a writing system based on pictographs (small pictures), wrote poetry, recorded their history, and composed music. Their government and armies were highly organized. They created a system to collect taxes, they practiced a sophisticated system of religion, and they even took a census.

_____ 3.   **Attitudes toward Food**

As children, we form attitudes toward food that are not easily changed. In some families, food is love. Not all families are like this, but some children grow up with this attitude. Some families think of food as something precious and not to be wasted. The attitudes children pick up about food are hard to change in adulthood. Some families celebrate with food. If a child learns an attitude, it is hard to break this later. Someone once said: "As the twig is bent, so grows the tree." Children are very impressionable, and they can't really think for themselves when they are small. Children learn from the parent figures in their lives, and later from their peers. Some families have healthy attitudes about food. It is important for adults to teach their children these healthy attitudes. Otherwise, the children may have weight problems when they are adults.

_____ 4. **Qualities in a Friend**

There are several qualities I look for in a friend. A friend should give support and security. A friend should also be fun to be around. Friends can have faults, like anyone else, and sometimes it is hard to overlook them. But a friend can't be dropped because he or she has faults. A friend should stick to you, even in bad times. There is a saying that "a friend in need is a friend indeed." I believe this means that there are good friends and fair-weather friends. The second type is not a true friend. He or she is the kind of person who runs when there's trouble. Friends don't always last a lifetime. Someone you believed to be your best friend may lose contact with you if you move to a different area or go around with a different group of people. A friend should be generous and understanding. A friend does not have to be exactly like you. Sometimes friends are opposites, but they still like each other and get along. Since I am a very quiet person, I can't say that I have many friends. But these are the qualities I believe a friend should have.

_____ 5. **An Unsafe Place**

We play touch football on an unsafe field. First of all, the grass on the field is seldom mowed. The result is that we have to run through tangled weeds that wrap around our ankles like trip wires. The tall grass also hides some gaping holes lurking beneath. The best players know the exact positions of all the holes and manage to detour around them like soldiers zig-zagging across a minefield. Most of us, though, endure at least one sprained ankle per game. Another danger is the old baseball infield that we use as the last twenty yards of our gridiron. This area is covered with stones and broken glass. No matter how often we clean it up, we can never keep pace with the broken bottles hurled on the field by the teenagers we call the "night shift." These people apparently hold drinking parties every night in the abandoned dugout and enjoy throwing the empties out on the field. During every game, we try to avoid falling on especially big chunks of Budweiser bottles. Finally, encircling the entire field is an old, rusty chain-link fence full of tears and holes. Being slammed into the fence during the play can mean a painful stabbing by the jagged wires. All these dangers have made us less afraid of opposing teams than of the field where we play.

10 Adding Details to Complete a Paragraph

Each of the following paragraphs needs specific details to back up its supporting points. In the spaces provided, add a sentence or two of realistic details for each supporting point. The more specific you are, the more convincing your details are likely to be.

Activity

18

1.

A Pushover Instructor

We knew after the first few classes that the instructor was a pushover. First of all, he didn't seem able to control the class.

_____

_____

_____

In addition, he made some course requirements easier when a few students complained.

_____

_____

_____

Finally, he gave the easiest quiz we had ever taken.

_____

_____

_____

2.

Helping a Parent in College

There are several ways a family can help a parent who is attending college. First, family members can take over some of the household chores that the parent usually does.

_____

_____

_____

Also, family members can make sure that the student has some quiet study time.

_____

_____

_____

Last, families can take an interest in the student's problems and accomplishments.

_____

_____

_____

11 Writing a Simple Paragraph

You know now that an effective paragraph does two essential things: (1) It makes a point. (2) It provides specific details to support that point. You have considered a number of paragraphs that are effective because they follow these two basic steps or ineffective because they fail to follow them.

You are ready, then, to write a simple paragraph of your own. Choose one of the three assignments below, and follow carefully the guidelines provided.

Writing Assignment

1

Turn back to the activity on page 78, and select the point for which you have the best supporting details. Develop that point into a paragraph by following these steps.

a. If necessary, rewrite the point so that the first sentence is more specific or suits your purpose more exactly. For example, you might write the second point as follows: "Saving gas will help you economize and protect the environment."

b. Provide several sentences of information to develop each of your three supporting details fully. Make sure that all the information in your paragraph truly supports your point.

c. Use the words *First of all, Second,* and *Finally* to introduce your three supporting details.

d. Conclude your paragraph with a sentence that refers to your opening point. This last sentence "rounds off" the paragraph and lets the reader know that your discussion is complete. For example, the paragraph "Changes in the Family" on page 49 begins with "Changes in our society in recent years have weakened family life." It closes with a statement that refers to, and echoes, the opening point: "Clearly, modern life is a challenge to family life."

e. Supply a title based on your point. For instance, point 4 on page 79 might have the title "Ways to Economize."

Use the following list to check your paragraph for each of the above items:

YES	NO	
____	____	Do you begin with a point?
____	____	Do you provide relevant, specific details that support the point?
____	____	Do you use the words *First of all, Second,* and *Finally* to introduce your three supporting details?
____	____	Do you have a closing sentence?

YES   NO

_____ _____ Do you have a title based on your point?

_____ _____ Are your sentences clear and free of obvious errors?

Writing Assignment

2 In this chapter you have read two paragraphs (pages 53–54) on reasons for being in college. For this assignment, write a paragraph describing your own reasons for being in college. You might want to look first at the following list of common reasons students give for going to school. Write a check mark next to each reason that applies to you. If you have reasons for being in college that are not listed here, add them to the list. Then select your three most important reasons for being in school, and generate specific supporting details for each reason.

Before starting, reread paragraph A on page 53. *You must provide comparable specific details of your own.* Make your paragraph truly personal; do not fall back on vague generalities like those in paragraph B on page 54. As you work on your paragraph, use the checklist for Writing Assignment 1 as a guide.

**APPLY IN
MY CASE**   ## Reasons Students Go to College

_____   To have some fun before getting a job

_____   To prepare for a specific career

_____   To please their families

_____   To educate and enrich themselves

_____   To be with friends who are going to college

_____   To take advantage of an opportunity they didn't have before

_____   To find a husband or wife

_____   To see if college has anything to offer them

_____   To do more with their lives than they've done so far

_____   To take advantage of Veterans Administration benefits or other special funding

_____   To earn the status that they feel comes with a college degree

_____   To get a new start in life

_____   Other: _____

Writing Assignment

3

Write three paragraphs about an activity that you find positive or self-fulfilling. It could take place at school, at home, at work, at your place of worship, or anywhere at all. Each topic sentence should state a different reason you find this activity so positive. Topic sentences for such paragraphs might resemble these:

1. I enjoy volunteering at the animal shelter because I know how much the organization needs a helping hand.
2. Volunteering at the animal shelter helps me forget my everyday troubles.
3. Working at the shelter has taught me much about caring for animals.

In each case, develop the paragraph with as many specific details as you can. Use the checklist for Writing Assignment 1 as a guide while you are working on the paragraphs.

4

The Third Step in Writing

This chapter will show you how to

- organize specific evidence in a paper by using a clear method of organization
- connect the specific evidence by using transitions and other connecting words

Look at this photograph, and write a paragraph in which you tell a new college student how to study for an important exam. Once you have read through Chapter 4, read your paragraph again. Did you use time order, emphatic order, *or a combination of both to organize your paragraph?*

You know from Chapter 3 that the first two steps in writing an effective paragraph are making a point and supporting the point with specific evidence. This chapter deals with the third step. You'll learn the chief ways to organize and connect the supporting information in a paper.

Step 3: Organize and Connect the Specific Evidence

www.mhhe.com/langan

At the same time that you are generating the specific details needed to support a point, you should be thinking about ways to organize and connect those details. All the details in your paper must *cohere,* or stick together; when they do, your reader will be able to move smoothly from one bit of supporting information to the next. This chapter discusses the following ways to organize and connect supporting details: (1) common methods of organization, (2) transition words, and (3) other connecting words.

Common Methods of Organization: Time Order and Emphatic Order

Time order and emphatic order are common methods used to organize the supporting material in a paper. (You will learn more specialized methods of development in Part Two of the book.)

Time order simply means that details are listed as they occur in time. *First* this is done; *next* this; *then* this; *after* that, this; and so on. Here is a paragraph that organizes its details through time order.

How I Relax

    The way I relax when I get home from school on Thursday night is, first of all, to put my three children to bed. Next, I run hot water in the tub and put in lots of scented bubble bath. As the bubbles rise, I undress and get into the tub. The water is relaxing to my tired muscles, and the bubbles are tingly on my skin. I lie back and put my feet on the water spigots, with everything but my head under the water. I like to stick my big toe up the spigot and spray water over the tub. After about ten minutes of soaking, I wash myself with scented soap, get out and dry myself off, and put on my nightgown. Then I go downstairs and make myself a ham, lettuce, and tomato sandwich on rye bread and pour myself a tall glass of iced tea with plenty of sugar and ice cubes. I carry these into the

---

continued

living room and turn on the television. To get comfortable, I sit on the couch with a pillow behind me and my legs under me. I enjoy watching *The Daily Show* or a late movie. The time is very peaceful after a long, hard day of housecleaning, cooking, washing, and attending night class.

Fill in the missing words: "How I relax" uses the following words to help show time order: _____, _____, _____, _____, and _____.

Emphatic order is sometimes described as "save-the-best-'til-last" order. It means that the most interesting or important detail is placed in the last part of a paper. (In cases where all details seem equal in importance, the writer should impose a personal order that seems logical or appropriate to the details.) The last position in a paper is the most emphatic position because the reader is most likely to remember the last thing read. *Finally, last of all,* and *most important* are typical words and phrases showing emphasis. The following paragraph organizes its details through emphatic order.

The *National Enquirer*

There are several reasons why the *National Enquirer* is so popular. First of all, the paper is advertised on television. In the ads, attractive-looking people say, with a smile, "I want to know!" as they scan the pages of the *Enquirer.* The ads reassure people that it's all right to want to read stories such as "Heartbreak for Jennifer Lopez" or "Prince's Fiancée in New Royal Topless Scandal." In addition, the paper is easily available. In supermarkets, convenience stores, and drugstores, the *Enquirer* is always displayed in racks close to the cash register. As customers wait in line, they can't help being attracted to the paper's glaring headlines. Then, on impulse, customers will add the paper to their other purchases. Most of all, people read the *Enquirer* because they love gossip. We find other people's lives fascinating, especially if those people are rich and famous. We want to see and read about their homes, their clothes, and their friends, lovers, and families. We also take a kind of mean delight in their unflattering photos and problems and mistakes, perhaps because we envy them. Even though we may be ashamed of our interest, it's hard to resist buying a paper that promises "The Forbidden Love of Paris Hilton" or "Film Star Who Now Looks Like a Cadaver," or even "Hollywood Star Wars: Who Hates Whom and Why." The *Enquirer* knows how to get us interested and make us buy.

Fill in the missing words: The paragraph lists a total of _____ different reasons people read the *National Enquirer.* The writer of the paragraph feels that the most important reason is _____. He or she signals this reason by using the emphasis words _____.

Some paragraphs use a *combination of time order and emphatic order.* For example, "Good-Bye, Tony" on page 52 includes time order: It moves from the time Tony arrived to the end of the evening. In addition, the writer uses emphatic order, ending with her most important reason (signaled by the words *most of all*) for not wanting to date Tony anymore.

Transition Words

Look at the following items. Then check (✓) the one that is easier to read and understand.

_____ Our landlord repainted our apartment. He replaced the dishwasher.

_____ Our landlord repainted our apartment. Also, he replaced the dishwasher.

You probably found the second item easier to understand. The word *also* makes it clear that the writer is adding a second way the landlord has been of help. *Transitions,* or *transition words,* are signal words that help readers follow the direction of the writer's thoughts. They show the relationship between ideas, connecting thoughts. They are "bridge" words, carrying the reader across from one idea to the next.

Paperback books cost less than hardbacks. ___ALSO___ , they are easier to carry.

Two major types of transitions are of particular help when you write: words that show *addition* and words that show *time.*

Words That Show Addition

Check (✓) the item that is easier to read and understand.

1. _____ a. A drinking problem can destroy a person's life. It can tear a family apart.

_____ b. A drinking problem can destroy a person's life. In addition, it can tear a family apart.

www.mhhe.com/langan

2. _____ a. One way to lose friends is always to talk and never to listen. A way to end friendships is to borrow money and never pay it back.

_____ b. One way to lose friends is always to talk and never to listen. Another way to end friendships is to borrow money and never pay it back.

In the pair of sentences about a drinking problem, the words *In addition* help make the relationship between the two sentences clear. The author is describing two effects of a drinking problem: it can destroy a life and a family. *In addition, another,* and words like these are known as *addition words.* In the pair of sentences about losing friends, you probably found the second item easier to understand. The word *Another* makes it clear that the writer is describing a second way to lose friends.

Addition words signal added ideas. They help writers organize information and present it clearly to readers. Some common words that show addition are listed in the following box.

Addition Words

one	to begin with	in addition
first	another	next
first of all	second	last (of all)
for one thing	also	finally

Words That Show Time

Check (✓) the item that is easier to read and understand.

1. _____ a. I had blood work done. I went to the doctor.

_____ b. I had blood work done. Then I went to the doctor.

The word *Then* in the second item makes clear the relationship between the sentences. After having blood work done, the writer goes to the doctor. *Then* and words like it are *time words,* which carry the reader from one idea to the next.

I had blood work done. ————— I went to the doctor.

Here are some more pairs of sentences. Check (✓) the item in each pair that contains a time word and so is easier to read and understand.

2. _____ a. Every week my uncle studies the food ads to see which stores have the best specials. He clips all the coupons.

_____ b. Every week my uncle studies the food ads to see which stores have the best specials. Next, he clips all the coupons.

3. _____ a. Carmen took a very long shower. There was no hot water left for anyone else in the house.

_____ b. Carmen took a very long shower. After that, there was no hot water left for anyone else in the house.

In the pair of sentences about the uncle, the word *Next* helps make the relationship between the two sentences clear. The uncle studies ads, and then he clips coupons. In the second pair of sentences, the word *after* makes the relationship clear. After Carmen's long shower, there was no hot water left for anyone else.

Time words tell us *when* something happened in relation to when something else happened. They help writers organize and make clear the order of events, stages, and steps in a process. Below are some common words that show time.

Time Words

before	**next**	**later**
first	**as**	**after**
second	**when**	**finally**
third	**while**	**then**

1. Fill in each blank with the appropriate addition transition from the list that follows. Use each transition once.

another finally one

Activity

1

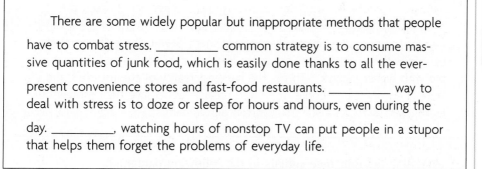

There are some widely popular but inappropriate methods that people have to combat stress. _____ common strategy is to consume massive quantities of junk food, which is easily done thanks to all the ever-present convenience stores and fast-food restaurants. _____ way to deal with stress is to doze or sleep for hours and hours, even during the day. _____, watching hours of nonstop TV can put people in a stupor that helps them forget the problems of everyday life.

www.mhhe.com/langan

2. Fill in each blank with the appropriate time transition from the list that follows. Use each transition once.

    then   next   before   first   after

    I do not like to write. In fact, I dislike writing so much that I have developed a series of steps for postponing the agony of doing writing assignments. _____ I tell myself that to proceed without the proper equipment would be unwise. So I go out to buy a new pen, and this kills at least an hour. _____, I begin to stare at the blank page. _____ long, however, I realize that writing may also require thought, so I begin to think deeply about my subject. Soon I feel drowsy. This naturally leads to the conclusion that I need a nap because I can't throw myself into my writing until I am at my very best. _____ a refreshing nap, I again face the blank page. It is usually at this stage that I actually write a sentence or two—disappointing ones. I _____ wisely decide that I need inspiration, perhaps from an interesting magazine or my new XBox game. If I feel a bit guilty, I comfort myself with the knowledge that, as any artist knows, you can't rush these things.

---

3. Underline the three *addition* signals in the following paragraph.

    I am opposed to state-supported lotteries for a number of reasons. First of all, by supporting lotteries, states are supporting gambling. I don't see anything morally wrong with gambling, but it is a known cause of suffering for many people who do it to excess. The state should be concerned with relieving suffering, not causing it. Another objection I have to state lotteries is the kind of advertising they do on television. The commercials promote the lotteries as an easy way to get rich. In fact, the odds against getting rich are astronomical. Last, the lotteries take advantage of the people who can least afford them. Studies have shown that people with lower incomes are more likely to play the lottery than people with higher incomes. This is the harshest reality of the lotteries: the state is encouraging people of limited means not to save their money but to throw it away on a state-supported pipe dream.

---

4. Underline the four *time* signals in the following paragraph.

> It is often easy to spot bad drivers on the road because they usually make more than one mistake: They make their mistakes in series. First, for example, you may notice that a man is tailgating you. Then, almost as soon as you notice, he has passed you in a no-passing zone. That's two mistakes already in a matter of seconds. Next, almost invariably, you see him speed down the road and pass someone else. Finally, as you watch in disbelief, glad that he's out of your way, he speeds through a red light or cuts across oncoming traffic in a wild left turn.

Other Kinds of Transitions

In the following box are other common transitional words, grouped according to the kind of signal they give readers. In the paragraphs you write, you will most often use addition words (like *first, also, another,* and *finally*), but all of the following signals are helpful to know as well.

Other Common Transitional Words

Space signals: **next to, across, on the opposite side, to the left, to the right, in front, in back, above, below, behind, nearby**

Change-of-direction signals: **but, however, yet, in contrast, otherwise, still, on the contrary, on the other hand**

Illustration signals: **for example, for instance, specifically, as an illustration, once, such as**

Conclusion signals: **therefore, consequently, thus, then, as a result, in summary, to conclude, last of all, finally**

---

1. Underline the four space signals in the following paragraph:

Activity

2

> The Lincoln Memorial is located in Washington, D.C. Its cornerstone was laid in 1915. Around the Memorial's exterior are thirty-six columns representing the thirty-six states of the nation at the time of President Abraham Lincoln's death in 1865. In front of the building is a large and imposing staircase leading to three large rooms. In the middle room is a statue of the President sitting in a large chair. To the left and right of this room are the north and south chambers, on the walls of which are inscribed quotations from Lincoln's Gettysburg Address and Second Inaugural Address.

2. Underline the four *change-of-direction signals* in the following paragraph.

In some ways, train travel is superior to air travel. People always marvel at the speed with which airplanes can zip from one end of the country to another. Trains, on the other hand, definitely take longer. But sometimes longer can be better. Traveling across the country by train allows you to experience the trip more completely. You get to see the cities and towns, mountains and prairies that too often pass by unnoticed when you fly. Another advantage of train travel is comfort. Traveling by plane means wedging yourself into a narrow seat with your knees bumping the back of the seat in front of you and, if you're lucky, being handed a "snack" consisting of a bag of pretzels. In contrast, the seats on most trains are spacious and comfortable, permitting even the longest-legged traveler to stretch out and watch the scenery just outside the window. And when train travelers grow hungry, they can get up and stroll to the dining car, where they can order anything from a simple snack to a full meal. There's no question that train travel is definitely slow and old-fashioned compared with air travel. However, in many ways it is much more civilized.

3. Underline the three *illustration signals* in the following selection.

Status symbols are all around us. The cars we drive, for instance, say something about who we are and how successful we have been. The auto makers depend on this perception of automobiles, designing their commercials to show older, well-established people driving luxury sedans and young, fun-loving people driving to the beach in sports cars. Clothing, too, has always been a status symbol. Specifically, schoolchildren are often rated by their classmates according to the brand names of their clothing. Another example of a status symbol is the cell phone. This device, not so long ago considered a novelty, is now used by almost everyone. Being without a cell phone in the twenty-first century is like being without a regular phone in the 1990s.

4. Underline the *conclusion signal* in the following paragraph.

A hundred years ago, miners used to bring caged canaries down into the mines with them to act as warning signals. If the bird died, the miners knew that the oxygen was running out. The smaller animal would be affected much more quickly than the miners. In the same way, animals are acting as warning signals to us today. Baby birds die before they can hatch because pesticides in the environment cause the adults to lay eggs with paper-thin shells. Fish die when lakes are contaminated with acid rain or poisonous mercury. The dangers in our environment will eventually affect all life on earth, including humans. Therefore, we must pay attention to these early warning signals. If we don't, we will be as foolish as a miner who ignored a dead canary—and we will die.

Other Connecting Words

In addition to transitions, there are three other kinds of connecting words that help tie together the specific evidence in a paper: *repeated words, pronouns,* and *synonyms.*

www.mhhe.com/langan

Repeated Words

Many of us have been taught by English instructors—correctly so—not to repeat ourselves in writing. However, repeating key words can help tie ideas together. In the paragraph that follows, the word *business* is repeated to remind readers of the key idea on which the discussion is centered. Underline the word the six times it appears.

Everyone remembers Thomas Alva Edison (1847–1931) as a great inventor; after all, he was issued more than one thousand patents by the United States government, more than any other person to date. However, he also had a head for business. When he was ten years old, he started a fresh produce business, growing vegetables on his family farm and selling them locally. Later, he began selling sandwiches, newspapers, and other goods to train commuters, a business that grew to such an extent that he had to hire other boys to help him. In 1870, Edison established a business in New Jersey manufacturing stock tickers and telegraph equipment. By 1872, sponsored by the Western Union Company, he opened a laboratory in Menlo Park, New Jersey. This new business yielded such extraordinary inventions as the phonograph, a new telephone transmitting device, and of course the incandescent lightbulb. By the time the United States entered World War I (1917), Edison had become a very wealthy man, having patented, manufactured, and marketed inventions affecting every sector of American business, from the film industry to cement manufacturing.

Pronouns

Pronouns (*he, she, it, you, they, this, that,* and others) are another way to connect ideas as you develop a paper. Using pronouns to take the place of other words or ideas can help you avoid needless repetition. (Be sure, though, to use pronouns with care in order to avoid the unclear or inconsistent pronoun references described in Chapters 28 and 29 of this book.) Underline the eight pronouns in the passage that follows, noting at the same time the words that the pronouns refer to.

> A professor of nutrition at a major university recently advised his students that they could do better on their examinations by eating lots of sweets. He told them that the sugar in cakes and candy would stimulate their brains to work more efficiently, and that if the sugar was eaten for only a month or two, it would not do them any harm.

Synonyms

Using *synonyms*—words that are alike in meaning—can also help move the reader from one thought to the next. In addition, the use of synonyms increases variety and interest by avoiding needless repetition of the same words. Underline the three words used as synonyms for *false ideas* in the following passage.

> There are many false ideas about suicide. One wrong idea is that a person who talks about suicide never follows through. The truth is that about three out of every four people who commit suicide notify one or more other persons ahead of time. Another misconception is that a person who commits suicide is poor or downtrodden. Actually, poverty appears to be a deterrent to suicide rather than a predisposing factor. A third myth about suicide is that people bent on suicide will eventually take their lives one way or another, whether or not the most obvious means of suicide is removed from their reach. In fact, since an attempt at suicide is often a kind of cry for help, removing a convenient means of taking one's life, such as a gun, shows people bent on suicide that someone cares enough about them to try to prevent it.

Activity

3

Read the selection below, and then answer the questions about it that follow.

My Worst Experience of the Week

¹The registration process at State College was a nightmare. ²The night before registration officially began, I went to bed anxious about the whole matter, and nothing that happened the next day served to ease

---

continued

my tension. [3]First, even though I had paid my registration fee early last spring, the people at the bursar's office had no record of my payment. [4]And for some bizarre reason, they wouldn't accept the receipt I had. [5]Consequently, I had to stand in line for two hours, waiting for someone to give me a slip of paper, which stated that I had, in fact, paid my registration fee. [6]The need for this new receipt seemed ludicrous to me, since all along I had proof that I had paid. [7]I was next told that I had to see my adviser in the Law and Justice Department and that the department was in Corridor C of the Triad Building. [8]I had no idea what or where the Triad was. [9]But, finally, I found my way to the ugly gray-white building. [10]Then I began looking for Corridor C. [11]When I found it, everyone there was a member of the Communications Department. [12]No one seemed to know where Law and Justice had gone. [13]Finally, one instructor said she thought Law and Justice was in Corridor A. [14]"And where is Corridor A?" I asked. [15]"I don't know," the teacher answered. [16]"I'm new here." [17]She saw the bewildered look on my face and said sympathetically, "You're not the only one who's confused." [18]I nodded and walked numbly away. [19]I felt as if I were fated to spend the rest of the semester trying to complete the registration process, and I wondered if I would ever become an official college student.

Questions

1. How many times is the key word *registration* used? _____

2. Write here the pronoun that is used for *people at the bursar's office* (sentence 4): _____; *Corridor C* (sentence 11): _____; *instructor* (sentence 17): _____.

3. Write here the words that are used as a synonym for *receipt* (sentence 5):

    _____

    the words that are used as a synonym for *Triad* (sentence 9):

    _____

    the word that is used as a synonym for *instructor* (sentence 15):

    _____

Complete the following statements.

1. *Time order* means _____

    _____

2. *Emphatic order* means _____

    _____

3. _____ are signal words that help readers follow the
    direction of a writer's thought.

4. In addition to transitions, three other kinds of connecting words
    that help link sentences and ideas are repeated words, _____,
    and _____.

Practice in Organizing and Connecting Specific Evidence

You now know the third step in effective writing: organizing and connecting the specific evidence used to support the main point of a paper. This closing section will expand and strengthen your understanding of the third step in writing.

You will work through the following series of activities:

*   Organizing through Time Order
*   Organizing through Emphatic Order
*   Organizing through a Combination of Time Order and Emphatic Order
*   Identifying Transitions
*   Identifying Transitions and Other Connecting Words

Organizing through Time Order

Activity

4

Use time order to organize the scrambled list of sentences below. Write the number 1 beside the point that all the other sentences support. Then number each supporting sentence as it occurs in time.

_____ Once you have settled on a working thesis, continue researching by taking notes.

_____ Writing a research paper should be done as a process.

_____ Narrow your subject to a limited research topic that the instructor approves.

_____ Use index cards to record your research notes—not loose-leaf paper. Cards make it much easier to organize information when the time comes to write an outline.

_____ Edit the final, revised version of your paper. Write a "Works Cited" list, "References" list, or bibliography (depending upon which citation style you are using).

_____ After you've completed taking notes, start outlining. Your instructor may require a long, formal outline, but a scratch outline will do at this stage just to get you started.

_____ First, choose a broad subject to write about that interests you—unless, of course, your instructor has already assigned you one.

_____ Next, do some preliminary research. Make sure your topic can be easily researched in the library or electronically. Then limit or refine your topic even more.

_____ Revise your rough draft as many times as needed. You may find that you have to add information at this point to further develop some of your ideas. If so, don't panic. This is not unusual. Simply take some time to go back to the researching stage.

_____ After completing your preliminary research, ask yourself what exactly you want to prove or say about your topic. Use this idea to write a working thesis, which should state the point your paper will make.

_____ Finally, proofread your edited copy as carefully as you can.

_____ Using the outline as a blueprint, draft the paper, remembering to cite or identify the sources of material you've taken from researched sources. Use a documentation style required by your instructor.

Organizing through Emphatic Order

Use emphatic order (order of importance) to arrange the following scrambled list of sentences. Write the number 1 beside the point that all the other sentences support. Then number each supporting sentence, starting with what seems to be the least important detail and ending with the most important detail.

_____ The people here are all around my age and seem to be genuinely friendly and interested in me.

_____ The place where I live has several important advantages.

_____ The schools in this neighborhood have a good reputation, so I feel that my daughter is getting a good education.

Activity

5

_____ The best thing of all about this area, though, is the school system.

_____ Therefore, I don't have to put up with public transportation or worry about how much it's going to cost to park each day.

_____ The school also has an extended after-school program, so I know my daughter is in good hands until I come home from work.

_____ First of all, I like the people who live in the other apartments near mine.

_____ Another positive aspect of this area is that it's close to where I work.

_____ That's more than I can say for the last place I lived, where people stayed behind locked doors.

_____ The office where I'm a receptionist is only a six-block walk from my house.

_____ In addition, I save a lot of wear and tear on my car.

Organizing through a Combination of Time Order and Emphatic Order

Activity

6

Use a combination of time and emphatic order to arrange the scrambled list of sentences below. Write the number 1 beside the point that all the other sentences support. Then number each supporting sentence. Paying close attention to transitional words and phrases will help you organize and connect the supporting sentences.

_____ I did not see the spider but visited my friend in the hospital, where he suffered through a week of nausea and dizziness because of the poison.

_____ We were listening to the radio when we discovered that nature was calling.

_____ As I got back into the car, I sensed, rather than felt or saw, a presence on my left hand.

_____ After these two experiences, I suspect that my fear of spiders will be with me until I die.

_____ The first experience was the time when my best friend received a bite from a black widow spider.

_____ I looked down at my hand, but I could not see anything because it was so dark.

_____ I had two experiences when I was sixteen that are the cause of my *arachnophobia,* a terrible and uncontrollable fear of spiders.

_____ We stopped the car at the side of the road, walked into the woods a few feet, and watered the leaves.

_____ My friend then entered the car, putting on the dashboard light, and I almost passed out with horror.

_____ I saw the bandage on his hand and the puffy swelling when the bandage was removed.

_____ Then it flew off my hand and into the dark bushes nearby.

_____ I sat in the car for an hour afterward, shaking and sweating and constantly rubbing the fingers of my hand to reassure myself that the spider was no longer there.

_____ But my more dramatic experience with spiders happened one evening when another friend and I were driving around in his car.

_____ Almost completely covering my fingers was a monstrous brown spider, with white stripes running down each of a seemingly endless number of long, furry legs.

_____ Most of all, I saw the ugly red scab on his hand and the yellow pus that continued oozing from under the scab for several weeks.

_____ I imagined my entire hand soon disappearing as the behemoth relentlessly devoured it.

_____ At the same time, I cried out "Arghh!" and flicked my hand violently back and forth to shake off the spider.

_____ For a long, horrible second it clung stickily, as if intertwined for good among the fingers of my hand.

Identifying Transitions

Fill in each blank with the appropriate addition transition from the following list. Use each transition once.

Activity

7

| also | second | for one thing | last of all |

Why School May Frighten a Young Child

School may be frightening to young children for a number of reasons.

_____, the regimented environment may be a new and disturbing experience. At home, children may have been able to do what they wanted when they wanted to do it. In school, however, they are given set times for talking, working, playing, eating, and even using the restroom.

continued

A _____ source of anxiety may be the public method of discipline that some teachers use. Whereas at home children are scolded in private, in school they may be held up to embarrassment and ridicule in front of their peers. "Bonnie," the teacher may say, "why are you the only one in class who didn't do your homework?" Or, "David, why are you the only one who can't work quietly at your seat?" Children may _____ be frightened by the loss of personal attention. Their little discomforts or mishaps, such as tripping on the stairs, may bring instant sympathy from a parent; in school, there is often no one to notice, or the teacher is frequently too busy to care and just says, "Go do your work. You'll be all right."

_____, a child may be scared by the competitive environment of the school. At home, one hopes, such competition for attention is minimal. But in school, children may vie for the teacher's approving glance or tone, or for stars on a paper, or for favored seats in the front row. For these and other reasons, it is not surprising that children may have difficulty adjusting to school.

Activity 8

Fill in each blank with the appropriate time transition from the list that follows. Use each transition once.

then   first   after   as   later

A Victory for Big Brother

In one of the most terrifying scenes in all of literature, George Orwell in his classic novel *1984* describes how a government known as Big Brother destroys a couple's love. The couple, Winston and Julia, fall in love and meet secretly, knowing the government would not approve. _____ informers turn them in, a government agent named O'Brien takes steps to end their love. _____ he straps Winston down and explains that he has discovered Winston's worst fear. _____ he sets a cage with two giant, starving sewer rats on the table next to Winston. He says that when he presses a lever, the door of the cage will slide up, and the rats will shoot out like bullets and bore straight into Winston's face. _____ Winston's eyes dart back and forth, revealing his terror, O'Brien places his hand on the lever. Winston knows that the only way out is for Julia to take his place. Suddenly, he hears his own voice screaming, "Do it to Julia!

continued

Not me! Julia!" Orwell does not describe Julia's interrogation, but when Julia and Winston see each other _____, they realize that each has betrayed the other. Their love is gone. Big Brother has won.

Fill in each blank with the appropriate addition or change-of-direction transition from the list that follows. Use each transition once.

Activity

9

however   also   next   finally   but   first

Watching TV Football

Watching a football game on television may seem like the easiest thing in the world. _____, like the game of football itself, watching a game correctly is far more complicated than it appears. _____ is the matter of what company you invite. The ideal number of people depends on the size of your living room. You should _____ invite at least one person who will be rooting for the opposite team. There's nothing like a little rivalry to increase the enjoyment of a football game. _____, you must attend to the refreshments. Make sure to have on hand plenty of everyone's favorite drinks, along with the essential chips, dips, and pretzels. You may even want something more substantial on hand, like sandwiches or pizza. If you do, make everyone wait until the moment of kickoff before eating. Waiting will make everything taste much better.

_____, there is one bit of sports equipment you should have on hand: a football. In the spirit of the occasion, it is good to have a football to toss around outside during halftime. _____ if your team happens to be getting trounced, you may decide not to wait until halftime.

Fill in each blank with the appropriate addition or change-of-direction transitions from the list that follows. Use each transition once.

Activity

10

fourth	but	yet	another
for one thing	second	however	last

Avoidance Tactics

Getting down to studying for an exam or writing a paper is hard, and so it is tempting for students to use one of the following five avoidance tactics in order to put the work aside. _____, students may say to themselves, "I can't do it." They adopt a defeatist attitude at the start and give up without a struggle. They could get help with their work by using such college services as tutoring programs and skill labs, _____ they refuse even to try. A _____ avoidance technique is to say, "I'm too busy." Students may take on an extra job, become heavily involved in social activities, or allow family problems to become so time-consuming that they cannot concentrate on their studies. _____ if college really matters to a student, he or she will make sure that there is enough time to do the required work. _____ avoidance technique is expressed by the phrase "I'm too tired." Typically, sleepiness occurs when it is time to study or go to class and then vanishes when the pressure of school is off. This sleepiness is a sign of work avoidance. A _____ excuse is to say, "I'll do it later." Putting things off until the last minute is practically a guarantee of poor grades on tests and papers. When everything else—watching TV, calling a friend, or even cleaning the oven—seems more urgent than studying, a student may simply be escaping academic work. _____, some students avoid work by saying to themselves, "I'm here and that's what counts." Some students live under the dangerous delusion that, since they possess a college ID, a parking sticker, and textbooks, the course work will somehow take care of itself. _____ once a student has a college ID, he or she has only just begun. Doing the necessary studying, writing, and reading will bring real results: good grades, genuine learning, and a sense of accomplishment.

Activity

11

Fill in each blank with the appropriate transition from the following list. Use each transition once.

Addition transitions: first of all, second, finally

Time transition: when

Illustration transition: once

Change-of-direction transition: however

Conclusion transition: as a result

Joining a Multicultural Club

One of the best things I've done in college is joining a multicultural club.

_____, the club has helped me become friendly with a diverse group of people. At any time in my apartment, I can have someone from Pakistan or Sweden chatting about music, or someone from Russia or

Uganda talking about politics. _____, I watched a Spanish student serve *chocolate con churros* to three students from China. They had

never tasted such a thing before, but they liked it. A _____ benefit of the club is that it's helped me realize how similar people are.

_____ the whole club first assembled, we wound up having a conversation about dating and sex that included the perspectives of people from fifteen countries and six continents! It was clear we all shared the feeling that sex was fascinating. The talk lasted for hours, with many different people describing the wildest or funniest dating experience they had had. Only a few students, particularly those from the United States

and Japan, seemed bashful. _____, the club has reminded me about the dangers of stereotyping. Before I joined the club, my only direct experience with people from China was ordering meals in the local

Chinese restaurant. _____, I believed that most Chinese people

ate lots of rice and worked in restaurants. In the club, _____ I met Chinese people who were soccer players, English majors, and math tutors. I've also seen Jewish and Muslim students—people who I thought would never get along—drop their preconceived notions and become friends. Even more than my classes, the club has been an educational experience for me.

Identifying Transitions and Other Connecting Words

This activity will give you practice in identifying transitions and other connecting words that are used to help tie ideas together.

Activity

12

Section A—Transitions

Locate the transitional word in each sentence, and write it in the space provided.

1. I decided to pick up a drop-add form from the registrar's office. However, I changed my mind when I saw the long line of students waiting there.

_____

2. In England, drivers use the left-hand side of the road. Consequently, in a car the steering wheel is on the right side.

_____

3. Crawling babies will often investigate new objects by putting them in their mouths. Therefore, parents should be alert for any pins, tacks, or other dangerous items on floors and carpets.

_____

4. One technique that advertisers use is to have a celebrity endorse a product. The consumer then associates that product with the star qualities of the celebrity.

_____

Section B—Repeated Words

In the space provided, write the repeated words.

5. The tall ships moved majestically into the harbor. Along the docks were thousands of people who had come to witness the harbor spectacle.

_____

6. Many researchers believe that people have weight set-points their bodies try to maintain. This may explain why many dieters return to their original weight.

_____

7. At the end of the concert, thousands of fans held up lighters in the darkened stadium. The sea of lighters signaled that the fans wanted an encore.

_____

8. Establishing credit is important for everyone. A good credit history is often necessary when you are applying for a loan or credit card.

_____

Section C—Synonyms

In the space provided, write the synonym for the underlined word.

9. Entering the five-thousand-year-old tomb, the archaeologists found that it had been ransacked by thieves hundreds of years before. However, several of the fine earthen jars had been left intact by the robbers.

_____

10. Women's <u>clothes</u>, in general, use less material than men's clothes. Yet women's garments usually cost more than men's.

_____

11. The temperance movement in this country sought to ban <u>alcohol</u>. Drinking liquor, movement leaders said, led to violence, poverty, prostitution, and insanity.

_____

12. For me, <u>apathy</u> quickly sets in when the weather becomes hot and sticky. This listlessness disappears when the humidity decreases.

_____

Section D—Pronouns

In the space provided, write the word referred to by the underlined pronoun.

13. At the beginning of the twentieth century, bananas were still an oddity in the United States. Some people even attempted to eat <u>them</u> with the skin on.

_____

14. Canning vegetables is easy and economical. <u>It</u> can also be very dangerous.

_____

15. Members of the United States Congress seem always to be campaigning. After all, <u>they</u> have to stand for reelection every two years.

_____

The Fourth Step in Writing

Write a paragraph about your initial reaction to this photograph. The U.S. Constitution places very few restrictions on freedom of speech. What limits do you think should be placed on free expression? Why?

Step 4: Write Clear, Error-Free Sentences

So far, this book has emphasized the first three steps in writing an effective paragraph: making a point (Chapter 3), supporting the point (Chapter 3), and organizing and connecting the evidence (Chapter 4). This chapter focuses on the fourth step: writing clear, error-free sentences. You'll learn how to revise a paragraph so that your sentences flow smoothly and clearly. Then you'll review how to edit a paragraph for mistakes in grammar, punctuation, and spelling.

Revising Sentences

The following strategies will help you to revise your sentences effectively.

- Use parallelism.
- Use a consistent point of view.
- Use specific words.
- Use concise wording.
- Vary your sentences.

Use Parallelism

Words in a pair or a series should have a parallel structure. By balancing the items in a pair or a series so that they have the same kind of structure, you will make a sentence clearer and easier to read. Notice how the parallel sentences that follow read more smoothly than the nonparallel ones.

www.mhhe.com/langan

Nonparallel (Not Balanced)	**Parallel (Balanced)**
I resolved to lose weight, to study more, and *watching* less TV.	I resolved to lose weight, to study more, and to watch less TV. (A balanced series of to verbs: *to lose, to study, to watch*)
A consumer group rates my car as noisy, expensive, and *not having much safety*.	A consumer group rates my car as noisy, expensive, and unsafe. (A balanced series of descriptive words: *noisy, expensive, unsafe*)
Lola likes wearing soft sweaters, eating exotic foods, and *to bathe* in scented bath oil.	Lola likes wearing soft sweaters, eating exotic foods, and bathing in scented bath oil. (A balanced series of *-ing* words: *wearing, eating, bathing*)

Nonparallel (Not Balanced)	Parallel (Balanced)
Single life offers more freedom of choice; *more security is offered by marriage.*	Single life offers more freedom of choice; marriage offers more security. (Balanced verbs and word order: *single life offers . . . ; marriage offers . . .*)

> **TIP:** You need not worry about balanced sentences when writing first drafts. But when you rewrite, try to put matching words and ideas into matching structures. Such parallelism will improve your writing style.

Activity 1

Cross out and revise the unbalanced part of each of the following sentences.

EXAMPLE

When Gail doesn't have class, she uses her time to clean house, ~~getting~~ *to get* her laundry done, and to buy groceries.

1. Lola plans to become a model, a lawyer, or to go into nursing.

2. Filling out an income tax form is worse than wrestling a bear or to walk on hot coals.

3. The study-skills course taught me how to take more effective notes, to read a textbook chapter, and preparing for exams.

4. Home Depot has huge sections devoted to plumbing equipment, electrical supplies, and ₍tools needed for carpentry.

5. When visiting Chicago, make sure to visit its wonderful art museum, eat some deep-dish pizza, and taking a stroll along the Lake Michigan shoreline.

6. Filled with talent and ambitious, Eduardo worked hard at his sales job.

7. Viewing the Grand Canyon for the first time, we felt exeitement, peaceful, and awed at the same time.

8. Cindy's cat likes sleeping in the dryer, lying in the bathtub, and to chase squirrels.

9. The weather was hot, there were crowds in the city, and the buses were on strike.

10. People in the lobby munched popcorn, sipped sodas, and were shuffling their feet impatiently.

Use a Consistent Point of View

Consistency with Verbs

Do not shift verb tenses unnecessarily. If you begin writing a paper in the present tense, don't shift suddenly to the past. If you begin in the past, don't shift without reason to the present. Notice the inconsistent verb tenses in the following example:

Incorrect   The shoplifter *walked* quickly toward the front of the store. When a clerk *shouts* at him, he *started* to run.

The verbs must be consistently in the present tense:

Correct   The shoplifter *walks* quickly toward the front of the store. When a clerk *shouts* at him, he *starts* to run.

Or the verbs must be consistently in the past tense:

Correct   The shoplifter *walked* quickly toward the front of the store. When a clerk *shouted* at him, he *started* to run.

In each passage, one verb must be changed so that it agrees in tense with the other verbs. Cross out the incorrect verb, and write the correct form above each crossed-out verb.

Activity

2

EXAMPLE

Kareem wanted to be someplace else when the dentist ~~carries~~ *carried* in a long needle.

1. I listened to music and surfed the Internet before I decide to do some homework.

2. The hitchhiker stopped me as I walks from the turnpike rest station and said, "Are you on your way to San Jose?"

3. During both World War I and World War II, Switzerland was neutral. Therefore, some refugees from Nazi Germany escape to that country.

4. Molly's grandfather was a college English professor. Only after he retires did he learn to read Italian.

5. In the movie, artillery shells exploded on the hide of the reptile monster. The creature just grinned, tosses off the shells, and kept eating people.

6. Several months a year, monarch butterflies come to live in a spot along the California coast. Thousands and thousands of them hang from the trees and fluttered through the air in large groups.

7. After waking up each morning, Harry stays in bed for a while. First he stretches and yawned loudly, and then he plans his day.

8. The salespeople at Biggs's Department Store are very helpful. When people asked for a product the store doesn't carry or is out of, the salesperson recommends another store.

9. The American Revolution began in 1775, when the British fire upon Americans at Lexington and Concord, Massachusetts. However, trouble had been brewing since Britain imposed new taxes on the colonies in 1766.

10. Smashed cars, ambulances, and police cars blocked traffic on one side of the highway. On the other side, traffic slows down as drivers looked to see what had happened.

Consistency with Pronouns

Pronouns should not shift point of view unnecessarily. When writing a paper, be consistent in your use of first-, second-, or third-person pronouns.

Type of Pronoun	Singular	Plural
First-person pronouns	I (my, mine, me)	we (our, us)
Second-person pronouns	you (your)	you (your)
Third-person pronouns	he (his, him)	they (their, them)
	she (her)	
	it (its)	

TIP: Any person, place, or thing, as well as any indefinite pronoun like *one, anyone, someone,* and so on, is a third-person word.

If you start writing in the third person *she,* don't jump suddenly to the second person *you.* Or if you are writing in the first person *I,* don't shift unexpectedly to *one.* Look at the examples that follow.

Inconsistent	Consistent
I enjoy movies like *The Return of the Vampire* that frighten *you*. (A very common mistake people make is to let *you* slip into their writing after they start with another pronoun.)	I enjoy movies like *The Return of the Vampire* that frighten me.
As soon as a tourist enters Arlington National Cemetery, where many of America's military heroes are buried, *you* begin to realize how costly the price of liberty is.	As soon as a tourist enters Arlington National Cemetery, where many of America's military heroes are buried, *he or she* begins to realize how costly the price of liberty is.
(Again, *you* is a shift in point of view.)	(See also the coverage of *his or her* references on pages 484–485.)

Cross out inconsistent pronouns in the following sentences, and write the correct form of the pronoun above each crossed-out word. You may have to change the form of the verb as well.

Activity

3

EXAMPLE

My dreams are always the kind that haunt ~~you~~ *me* the next day.

1. Whenever we take our children on a trip, you have to remember to bring snacks, tissues, and toys.

2. In our society, we often need a diploma before you can be hired for a job.

3. This summer, I worked for the city sanitation department, a job in which you learn a lot about people's consumption habits.

4. If a student organizes time carefully, you can accomplish a great deal of work.

5. Although I know you should watch your cholesterol intake, I can never resist an ear of corn dripping with melted butter.

6. Good conversationalists have the ability to make the person they were talking to feel as if they are the only other person in the room.

7. We never go to the Salad Bowl anymore, because you wait so long to be seated and the waiters usually make mistakes with the order.

8. I read over my notes before class because one can never tell when there will be a quiz.

9. Our time was limited, so we decided not to go to the Gettysburg National Military Park because you would need to spend an entire day for a worthwhile visit.

10. In my job as store manager, I'm supposed to be nice to the customer even if they are being totally unreasonable.

Use Specific Words

To be an effective writer, you must use specific words rather than general words. Specific words create pictures in the reader's mind. They help capture interest and make your meaning clear. Compare the following general and specific sentences:

General	Specific
The boy came down the street.	Theo ran down Woodlawn Avenue.
A bird appeared on the grass.	A blue jay swooped down onto the frost-covered lawn.
She stopped the car.	Jackie slammed on the brakes of her Hummer.

The specific sentences create clear pictures in our minds. The details *show* us exactly what has happened.

Here are four ways to make your sentences specific.

1. Use exact names.
   She loves her *car*.
   Renée loves her *Honda*.

2. Use lively verbs.
   The garbage truck *went* down Front Street.
   The garbage truck *rumbled* down Front Street.

3. Use descriptive words (modifiers) before nouns.
   A girl peeked out the window.
   A *chubby six-year-old* girl peeked out the *dirty kitchen* window.

4. Use words that relate to the five senses: sight, sound, taste, smell, and touch.
   That woman is a karate expert.
   That *tiny, silver-haired* woman is a karate expert. (*sight*)

   When the dryer stopped, a signal sounded.
   When the dryer stopped, a *loud buzzer* sounded. (*sound*)

Lola offered me an orange slice.

Lola offered me a *sweet, juicy* orange slice. (*taste*)

The real estate agent opened the door of the closet.

The real estate agent opened the door of the *cedar-scented* closet. (*smell*)

I pulled the blanket around me to fight off the wind.

I pulled the *fluffy* blanket around me to fight off the *chilling* wind. (*touch*)

This activity will give you practice in replacing vague, indefinite words with sharp, specific words. Add three or more specific words to replace the general word or words underlined in each sentence. Make changes in the wording of a sentence as necessary.

Activity

4

EXAMPLE

My bathroom cabinet contains <u>many drugs</u>.

My bathroom cabinet contains aspirin, antibiotics, tranquilizers, and

codeine cough medicine.

1. At the shopping center, we visited <u>several stores</u>.

   _____

   _____

2. Sunday is my day to take care of <u>chores</u>.

   _____

   _____

3. Lola enjoys <u>various activities</u> in her spare time.

   _____

   _____

4. I spent most of my afternoon <u>doing homework</u>.

   _____

   _____

5. Recently we rented <u>several</u> films about vampires.

   _____

   _____

Activity

5

Again, you will practice changing vague, indefinite writing into lively, image-filled writing that helps capture the reader's interest and makes your meaning clear. With the help of the methods described on pages 49–62 and 71–82, add specific details to the sentences that follow. Note the examples.

EXAMPLE

The person got out of the car.
The elderly man painfully lifted himself out of the white Buick station wagon.

The fans enjoyed the victory.
Many of the fifty thousand fans stood, waved banners, and cheered wildly when Barnes scored the winning touchdown.

1. The college offers a variety of intramural sports.

    _____

    _____

2. The animal ran away.

    _____

    _____

3. An accident occurred.

    _____

    _____

4. The instructor came into the room.

    _____

    _____

5. Luis is interested in electronic gadgets.

    _____

    _____

    _____

    _____

Use Concise Wording

Wordiness—using more words than necessary to express a meaning—is often a sign of lazy or careless writing. Your readers may resent the extra time and energy they must spend when you have not done the work needed to make your writing direct and concise.

Here are examples of wordy sentences:

> Anne is of the opinion that the death penalty should be allowed.

> The country of Colombia has as its capital the city known as Bogotá.

Omitting needless words improves the sentences:

> Anne supports the death penalty.

> The capital of Colombia is Bogotá.

The following box lists some wordy expressions that could be reduced to single words.

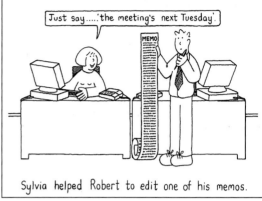

Just say.....'the meeting's next Tuesday'.

Sylvia helped Robert to edit one of his memos.

www.CartoonStock.com

Wordy Form	Short Form
a large number of	many
a period of a week	a week
arrive at an agreement	agree
at an earlier point in time	before
at the present time	now
big in size	big
owing to the fact that	because
during the time that	while
five in number	five
for the reason that	because
good benefit	benefit
in every instance	always
in my own opinion	I think
in the event that	if
in the near future	soon
in this day and age	today
is able to	can
large in size	large
plan ahead for the future	plan
postponed until later	postponed
red in color	red
return back	return

Rewrite the following sentences, omitting needless words.

1. After a lot of careful thinking, I have arrived at the conclusion that drunken drivers should receive jail terms.

    _____

    _____

2. The movie that I went to last night, which was fairly interesting, I must say, was enjoyed by me and my girlfriend.

    _____

    _____

3. Ben finally made up his mind after a lot of indecisions and decided to look for a new job.

    _____

    _____

4. The headquarters of the U.S. Central Intelligence Agency, which collects information important to maintaining the security and safety of the entire nation, is located in Langley, Virginia, a suburb just outside of the nation's capital, which is Washington, D.C.

    _____

    _____

    _____

5. The agency that is known as the U.S. Central Intelligence Agency grew out of what was called the Office of Strategic Services, an organization founded in the year 1942 to gather strategic information important and useful in fighting the Second World War.

    _____

    _____

    _____

Vary Your Sentences

One aspect of effective writing is to vary your sentences. If every sentence follows the same pattern, writing may become monotonous. This chapter explains four ways you can create variety and interest in your writing style. The first two ways involve coordination and subordination—important techniques for achieving different kinds of emphasis.

The following are four methods you can use to make your sentences more varied and more sophisticated:

- Add a second complete thought (coordination).
- Add a dependent thought (subordination).
- Begin with a special opening word or phrase.
- Place adjectives or verbs in a series.

Revise by Adding a Second Complete Thought (Coordination)

When you add a second complete thought to a simple sentence, the result is a *compound* (or double) sentence. The two complete statements in a compound sentence are usually connected by a comma plus a joining, or *coordinating,* word (*and, but, for, or, nor, so, yet*).

Use a compound sentence when you want to give equal weight to two closely related ideas. The technique of showing that ideas have equal importance is called *coordination.* Following are some compound sentences. Each contains two ideas that the writer regards as equal in importance.

> The Roman Colosseum was where gladiatorial contests once took place, but it is now a major tourist attraction.
>
> I repeatedly failed the math quizzes, so I decided to drop the course.
>
> Darrell turned all the lights off, and then he locked the office door.

Combine the following pairs of simple sentences into compound sentences. Use a comma and a logical joining word (*and, but, for, so, yet*) to connect each pair.

Activity 7

HINT: If you are not sure what *and, but, for,* and *so* mean, see pages 448–449.

EXAMPLE

- The cars crept along slowly.
- Visibility was poor in the heavy fog.

  The cars crept along slowly, for visibility was poor in the heavy fog.

---

1. • The Vikings sailed as far west as North America.
    • They built cities as far east as Russia.

    _____

    _____

2. • George Washington did not have an extensive military education.
    • When he became general of the Continental Army, he got some on-the-job training.

    _____

    _____

3. • The Wailing Wall in Jerusalem is an important religious site for Jews.
    • It is visited by people of all faiths.

    _____

    _____

4. • Mold grew on my leather boots.
    • The closet was warm and humid.

    _____

    _____

5. • My father has a high cholesterol count.
    • He continues to eat red meat almost every day.

    _____

    _____

Revise by Adding a Dependent Thought (Subordination)

When you add a dependent thought to a simple sentence, the result is a complex sentence.* A dependent thought begins with a word or phrase such as one of the following.

Dependent Words		
after	if, even if	when, whenever
although, though	in order that	where, wherever
as	since	whether
because	that, so that	which, whichever
before	unless	while
even though	until	who, whoever
how	what, whatever	whose

---

*The two parts of a complex sentence are sometimes called an *independent clause* and a *dependent clause*. A *clause* is simply a word group that contains a subject and a verb. An independent clause expresses a complete thought and can stand alone. A dependent clause does not express a complete thought in itself and "depends on" the independent clause to complete its meaning. Dependent clauses always begin with a dependent, or subordinating, word.

A *complex* sentence is used to emphasize one idea over another. Look at the following complex sentence:

Although I lowered the thermostat, my heating bill remained high.

The idea that the writer wants to emphasize here—*my heating bill remained high*—is expressed as a complete thought. The less important idea—*Although I lowered my thermostat*—is subordinated to this complete thought. The technique of giving one idea less emphasis than another is called *subordination.*

Following are other examples of complex sentences. In each case, the part starting with the dependent word is the less emphasized part of the sentence.

Even though I was tired, I stayed up to watch the horror movie.

Before I take a bath, I check for spiders in the tub.

When Vera feels nervous, she pulls on her earlobe.

Use logical subordinating words to combine the following pairs of simple sentences into sentences that contain a dependent thought. Place a comma after a dependent statement when it starts the sentence.

Activity

8

EXAMPLE

- Our team lost.
- We were not invited to the tournament.
  Because our team lost, we were not invited to the tournament.
  _____

1. • I receive my degree in June.
   • I will begin applying for jobs.
   _____

   _____

2. • Sona doesn't enjoy cooking.
   • She often eats at restaurants.
   _____

   _____

3. • Ronald Reagan started his career as a radio announcer.
   • He ended it by holding the highest office in the land.
   _____

   _____

4. • My bank pays little compound interest on savings accounts.

   • My money doesn't grow very fast.

   _____

   _____

5. • The final exam covered sixteen chapters.

   • The students complained.

   _____

   _____

Revise by Beginning with a Special Opening Word or Phrase

Among the special openers that can be used to start sentences are (1) -*ed* words, (2) -*ing* words, (3) -*ly* words, (4) *to* word groups, and (5) prepositional phrases. Here are examples of all five kinds of openers:

-*ed* word

Tired from a long day of work, Sharon fell asleep on the sofa.

-*ing* word

Using a thick towel, Mel dried his hair quickly.

-*ly* word

Reluctantly, I agreed to rewrite the paper.

***to* word group**

To get to the church on time, you must leave now.

prepositional phrase

With Fred's help, Martha planted the evergreen shrubs.

Activity 9

Combine each pair of simple sentences into one sentence by using the opener shown at the left and omitting repeated words. Use a comma to set off the opener from the rest of the sentence.

EXAMPLE

-*ing* word   • The toaster refused to pop up.

   • It buzzed like an angry hornet.

   Buzzing like an angry hornet, the toaster refused to pop up.

   _____

1. • In 1980, the U.S. Olympic hockey team was determined to take the
     gold medal.
   • It beat the Soviet team, which was rated the world's finest.

   _____

   _____

   -ed word

2. • The star player glided down the court.
   • He dribbled the basketball like a pro.

   _____

   _____

   -ing word

3. • No pedestrians were hurt when a large chunk of ice fell from the roof
     of the building.
   • That was lucky.

   _____

   _____

   -ly word

4. • The little boy likes to annoy his parents.
   • He pretends not to hear them.

   _____

   _____

   **to word
   group**

5. • People must wear rubber-soled shoes.
   • They must do this in the gym.

   _____

   _____

   **prepositional
   phrase**

Revise by Placing Adjectives or Verbs in a Series

Various parts of a sentence may be placed in a series. Among these parts are
adjectives (descriptive words) and verbs. Here are examples of both in a series.

Adjectives

The *black, smeary* newsprint rubbed off on my *new butcher-block* table.

Verbs

The quarterback *fumbled* the ball, *recovered* it, and *sighed* with relief.

Activity

10

In each group, combine the simple sentences into one sentence by using adjectives or verbs in a series and by omitting repeated words. In most cases, use a comma between the adjectives or verbs in a series.

EXAMPLE

- Before Christmas, I made fruitcakes.
- I decorated the house.
- I wrapped dozens of toys.

Before Christmas, I made fruitcakes, decorated the house, and wrapped dozens of toys.

1. • Alexander Hamilton was the first secretary of the Treasury of the United States.
   • He signed the Constitution.
   • He wrote most of the *Federalist Papers*.

   _____

   _____

2. • Lights appeared in the fog.
   • The lights were flashing.
   • The lights were red.
   • The fog was soupy.
   • The fog was gray.

   _____

   _____

3. • George Washington Carver found about three hundred uses for peanuts.
   • He also discovered additional uses for sweet potatoes and soybeans.
   • He invented ways to improve the production of paint, plastics, and gasoline.

   _____

   _____

   _____

4. • Lola picked sweater hairs off her coat.
   • The hairs were fuzzy.
   • The hairs were white.
   • The coat was brown.

- The coat was suede.

_____

_____

5.　•　The contact lens fell onto the floor.
- The contact lens was thin.
- The contact lens was slippery.
- The floor was dirty.
- The floor was tiled.

_____

_____

Editing Sentences

www.mhhe.com/langan

After revising sentences in a paragraph so that they flow smoothly and clearly, you need to edit the paragraph for mistakes in grammar, punctuation, mechanics, usage, and spelling. Even if a paragraph is otherwise well written, it will make an unfavorable impression on readers if it contains such mistakes. To edit a paragraph, check it against the agreed-upon rules or conventions of written English—simply called *sentence skills* in this book. Here are the most common of these conventions:

- Write complete sentences rather than fragments.
- Do not write run-ons.
- Use verb forms correctly.
- Make sure that subject, verbs, and pronouns agree.
- Eliminate faulty modifiers.
- Use pronoun forms correctly.
- Use capital letters where needed.
- Use the following marks of punctuation correctly: apostrophe, quotation marks, comma, semicolon, colon, hyphen, dash, parentheses.
- Use correct manuscript form.
- Eliminate slang, clichés, and pretentious words.
- Check for possible spelling errors.
- Eliminate careless errors.

These sentence skills are treated in detail in Part Five of this book, and they can be referred to easily as needed. Both the list of sentence skills on the inside back cover and the correction symbols on page 633 include page references so that you can turn quickly to any skill you want to check.

Tips for Editing

Here are four tips that can help you edit the next-to-final draft of a paragraph for sentence-skills mistakes:

1. Have at hand two essential tools: a good dictionary (see page 559) and a grammar handbook (you can use the one in this book on pages 411–633).

2. Use a sheet of paper to cover your paragraph so that you will expose only one sentence at a time. Look for errors in grammar, spelling, and typing. It may help to read each sentence out loud. If a sentence does not read clearly and smoothly, chances are something is wrong.

3. Pay special attention to the kinds of errors you tend to make. For example, if you tend to write run-ons or fragments, be on the lookout for those errors.

4. Try to work on a printed draft, where you'll be able to see your writing more objectively than you can on a handwritten page or computer screen; use a pen with colored ink so that your corrections will stand out.

A Note on Proofreading

Proofreading means checking the final, edited draft of your paragraph closely for typos and other careless errors. An effective strategy is to read your paper backward, from the last sentence to the first. This helps keep you from getting caught up in the flow of the paper and missing small mistakes. Here are six useful proofing symbols.

Proofing Symbol	Meaning	Example
∧	insert missing letter or word	bel∧eve
ℐ	omit	in the ~~the~~ meantime
∽	reverse order of words or letters	once a upon time
#	add space	all#together
⌒	close up space	foot ball
cap, lc	Add a capital (or a lowercase) letter	My persian Cat

If you have to make a lot of corrections, type in the corrections and reprint the page.

In the spaces below this paragraph, write the numbers of the ten word groups that contain fragments or run-ons. Then, in the spaces between the lines, edit by making the necessary corrections. One is done for you as an example.

> ¹Two groups of researchers have concluded that "getting cold" has little to do with "catching a cold." ²When the experiment was done for the first time, ³Researchers exposed more than four hundred people to the cold virus, ⁴Then divided those people into three groups. ⁵One group, wearing winter coats, sat around in ten-degree temperature. the second group was placed in sixty-degree temperature, ⁶With the third group staying in a room, ⁷Where it was eighty degrees. ⁸The number of people who actually caught colds was the same, ⁹In each group. ¹⁰Other researchers repeated this experiment ten years later. ¹¹This time they kept some subjects cozy and warm they submerged others in a tank filled with water, ¹²Whose temperature had been lowered to seventy-five degrees. ¹³They made others sit around in their underwear in forty-degree temperature. ¹⁴The results were the same, the subjects got sick at the same rate. ¹⁵Proving that people who get cold do not always get colds.

1. _____ 2. _____ 3. _____ 4. _____ 5. _____

6. _____ 7. _____ 8. _____ 9. _____ 10. _____

HINT: A series of editing tests appears on pages 615–633. You will probably find it most helpful to take these tests after reviewing the sentence-skills handbook in Part Five.

Practice in Revising Sentences

You now know the fourth step in effective writing: revising and editing sentences. You also know that practice in *editing* sentences is best undertaken after you have worked through the sentence skills in Part Five. The focus in this closing section, then, will be on *revising* your work—using a variety of methods to ensure that your sentences flow smoothly and are clear and interesting. You will work through review tests that cover the following topics:

- Using parallelism
- Using a consistent point of view
- Using specific words
- Using concise wording
- Varying your sentences

Using Parallelism

Review Test 1

Cross out the unbalanced part of each sentence. In the space provided, revise the unbalanced part so that it matches the other item or items in the sentence. The first one is done for you as an example.

1. Our professor warned us that he would give surprise tests, ~~the assignment of term papers~~, and allow no makeup exams.

   assign term papers _____

2. Making a big dinner is a lot more fun than to clean up after it.

   _____

3. The street-corner preacher stopped people walking by, was asking them questions, and handed them pamphlets.

   _____

4. My teenage daughter enjoys shopping for new clothes, to try different cosmetics, and reading fashion magazines.

   _____

5. Many of today's action movies have attractive actors, fantastic special effects, and dialogue that is silly.

   _____

6. While you're downtown, please pick up the dry cleaning, return the library books, and the car needs washing, too.

   _____

7. I want a job that pays high wages, provides a complete benefits package, and offering opportunities for promotion.

   _____

8. As the elderly woman climbed the long staircase, she breathed hard and was grabbing the railing tightly.

_____

9. I fell into bed at the end of the hard day, grateful for the sheets that were clean, soft pillow, and cozy blanket.

_____

10. Ray's wide smile, clear blue eyes, and expressing himself earnestly all make him seem honest, even though he is not.

_____

Review Test 2

Cross out the unbalanced part of each sentence. In the space provided, revise the unbalanced part so that it matches the other item or items in the sentence.

1. The neighborhood group asked the town council to repair the potholes and that a traffic light be installed.

_____

2. Pesky mosquitoes, humidity that is high, and sweltering heat make summer an unpleasant time for me.

_____

3. The afternoon mail brought advertisements that were unwanted, bills I couldn't pay, and magazines I didn't like.

_____

4. Our house has a broken garage door, shutters that are peeling, and a crumbling chimney.

_____

5. My car needed the brakes replaced, the front wheels aligned, and recharging of the battery.

_____

6. I had to correct my paper for fragments, misplaced modifiers, and there were apostrophe mistakes.

_____

7. We do not want to stay home during our vacation, but a trip is not something we can afford.

_____

8. Penicillin, the first wonder drug, has many uses: to treat syphilis, to fight bacterial infections in wounds, and even curing eye and ear infections.

   _____

9. Having a headache, my stomach being upset, and a bad case of sunburn did not put me in a good mood for the evening.

   _____

10. The state of Georgia offers a varied landscape with the Blue Ridge Mountains in the north and the Okefenokee Swamp is found in the south.

    _____

Using a Consistent Point of View

Review Test 3

In the following passage, change verbs as needed so that they are consistently in the past tense. Cross out each incorrect verb and write the correct form above it, as shown in the example. You will need to make nine corrections.

Late one rainy night, Mei Ling woke to the sound of steady dripping. When she got out of bed to investigate, a drop of cold water ~~splashes~~ *splashed* onto her arm. She ~~looks~~ *looked* up just in time to see another drop form on the ceiling, hang suspended for a moment, and fall to the carpet. Stumbling to the kitchen, Mei Ling ~~reaches~~ *reached* deep into one of the cabinets and ~~lifts~~ *lifted* out a large roasting pan. As she did so, pot lids and baking tins clattered out and ~~crash~~ *crashed* onto the counter. Mei Ling ignored them, stumbled back to the bedroom, and ~~places~~ *placed* the pan on the floor under the drip. But a minute after sliding her icy feet under the covers, Mei Ling realized she ~~is~~ *was* in trouble. The sound of each drop hitting the metal pan echoed like a gunshot in the quiet room. Mei Ling ~~feels~~ *felt* like crying, but she finally thought of a solution. She got out of bed and ~~returns~~ *returned* a minute later with a thick bath towel. She lined the pan with the towel and ~~crawls~~ *crawled* back into bed.

Review Test 4

Cross out the inconsistent pronouns in the following sentences and revise by writing the correct form of the pronoun above each crossed-out word.

EXAMPLE

>   *I*
> I dislike waitressing, for ~~you~~ can never count on a fair tip.

1. Joseph lives in a place where you can ski year round.

2. While traveling through England, Melissa asked her tour guide if you would be able to see the Tower of London from her hotel room.

3. I drink coffee at work because you need a regular jolt of energy.

4. As we entered the house, you could hear someone giggling in the hallway.

5. Tourists should visit the Louvre Museum in Paris because you can get an education in art just by looking at the paintings.

6. In this company, a worker can take a break only after a relief person comes to take your place.

7. Sometimes the Bradleys take the turnpike route, but it costs you five dollars in tolls.

8. As we sat in class waiting for the test results, you could feel the tension.

9. My brother was told that you must get a B in Advanced Algebra to take Calculus I.

10. My favorite subject is abnormal psychology because the case studies make one seem so normal by comparison.

Using Specific Words

Review Test 5

Revise the following sentences, replacing vague, indefinite words with sharp, specific ones.

1. The refrigerator was well stocked with *food.*

    _____

    _____

    _____

2. Lin brought *lots of reading materials* to keep her busy in the hospital waiting room.

_____

_____

3. To do well in school, a student needs *certain qualities.*

_____

_____

4. The table at the wedding reception was full of *a variety of appetizers.*

_____

_____

5. As I grew older and less stupid, I realized that money cannot buy *certain things.*

_____

_____

Review Test 6

With the help of the methods described on pages 114–115 and summarized below, add specific details to the sentences that follow.

1. Use exact names.
2. Use lively verbs.
3. Use descriptive words (modifiers) before nouns.
4. Use words that relate to the senses—sight, hearing, taste, smell, touch.

1. The audience loved her performance.

_____

_____

2. I relaxed.

_____

_____

3. The room was cluttered.

_____

_____

4. The child threw the object.

_____

_____

5. The valley looked beautiful.

_____

_____

Using Concise Wording

Review Test   7

Rewrite the following sentences, omitting needless words.

1. There was this one girl in my class who rarely, if ever, did her homework.

_____

_____

2. Judging by the looks of things, it seems to me that it will probably rain very soon.

_____

_____

3. Seeing as how the refrigerator is empty of food, I will go to the supermarket in the very near future.

_____

_____

4. In this day and age it is almost a certainty that someone you know will be an innocent victim of criminal activity.

_____

_____

5. In my personal opinion it is correct to say that the spring season is the most beautiful period of time in the year.

_____

_____

Review Test 8

Rewrite the following sentences, omitting needless words.

1. Workers who are employed on a part-time basis are attractive to a business because they do not have to be paid as much as full-time workers for a business.

   _____

   _____

2. During the time that I was sick and out of school, I missed a total of three math tests.

   _____

   _____

3. The game, which was scheduled for later today, has been canceled by the officials because of the rainy weather.

   _____

   _____

4. At this point in time, I am quite undecided and unsure about just which classes I will take during this coming semester.

   _____

   _____

5. An inconsiderate person located in the apartment next to mine keeps her radio on too loud a good deal of the time, with the result being that it is disturbing to everyone in the neighboring apartments.

   _____

   _____

Varying Your Sentences

Review Test 9

Using coordination, subordination, or both, combine each of the following groups of simple sentences into one longer sentence. Omit repeated words. Various combinations are possible, so for each group, try to find the combination that flows most smoothly and clearly.

1. • My grandmother is eighty-six.
   • She drives to Florida alone every year.

    • She believes in being self-reliant.

_____

_____

2. • Dr. Martin Luther King Jr. was a Baptist minister.
    • He led the Southern Christian Leadership Conference.
    • He helped create this organization in 1957.

_____

_____

3. • The United States Constitution was adopted in 1787.
    • The Declaration of Independence was written in 1776.
    • Both documents were approved at meetings in Philadelphia.

_____

_____

4. • A volcano erupts.
    • It sends tons of ash into the air.
    • This creates flaming orange sunsets.

_____

_____

5. • A telephone rings late at night.
    • We answer it fearfully.
    • It could bring tragic news.

_____

_____

Review Test 10

Using coordination, subordination, or both, combine each of the following groups of simple sentences into two longer sentences. Omit repeated words. Various combinations are possible, so for each group, try to find the combination that flows most smoothly and clearly.

1. • Wendy pretended not to overhear her coworkers.
    • She couldn't stop listening.
    • She felt deeply embarrassed.

- They were criticizing her work.

_____

_____

_____

2. • Tony got home from the shopping mall.
   • He discovered that his rented tuxedo did not fit.
   • The jacket sleeves covered his hands.
   • The pants cuffs hung over his shoes.

_____

_____

_____

3. • The boys waited for the bus.
   • The wind shook the flimsy shelter.
   • They shivered with cold.
   • They were wearing thin jackets.

_____

_____

_____

4. • The First Amendment to the United States Constitution guarantees freedom of religion.
   • It also guarantees freedom of assembly.
   • Other rights it guarantees are freedom of speech and freedom of the press.

_____

_____

_____

5. • Gary was leaving the store.
   • The shoplifting alarm went off.
   • He had not stolen anything.
   • The clerk had forgotten to remove the magnetic tag.
   • The tag was on a shirt Gary had bought.

_____

_____

_____

Review Test 11

Part A

Combine the simple sentences into one sentence by using the opener shown in the margin and omitting repeated words. Use a comma to set off the opener from the rest of the sentence.

1. • We were exhausted from four hours of hiking.   *-ed* word

   • We decided to stop for the day.

   _____

   _____

2. • Gus was staring out the window.   *-ing* word

   • He didn't hear the instructor call on him.

   _____

   _____

3. • The surgeon closed the incision of the patient on whom she had just   *-ly* word
     operated.

   • She was careful when she did this.

   _____

   _____

4. • Steve traveled to Cairo, Egypt.   **to word group**

   • He wanted to see the Great Pyramid.

   _____

   _____

5. • Joanne goes online to e-mail her friends.   **prepositional phrase**

   • She does this during her lunch breaks.

   _____

   _____

Part B

Combine the simple sentences in each group into one sentence by using adjectives or verbs in a series and by omitting repeated words. In most cases, use a comma between the adjectives or verbs in a series.

6. The photographer waved a teddy bear at the baby.
   He made a funny face.

He quacked like a duck.

_____

_____

7. The bucket held a bunch of daisies.
   The bucket was shiny.
   The bucket was aluminum.
   The daisies were fresh.
   The daisies were white.

_____

_____

8. Amy poured herself a cup of coffee.
   She pulled her hair back into a ponytail.
   She opened her textbook.
   She sat down at her desk.
   She fell asleep.

_____

_____

9. The box in the dresser drawer was stuffed with letters.
   The box was cardboard.
   The dresser drawer was locked.
   The letters were faded.
   The letters were about love.

_____

_____

10. The speaker was eloquent.
    The speaker was learned.
    He moved to the podium.
    The podium was on the stage of the auditorium.
    The auditorium was crowded.

_____

_____

Four Bases for Revising Writing

Very often, our own interests and goals are different from those our parents want for us. Look at this illustration and write a paragraph about a time you "did your own thing" instead of following a loved one's wishes. Why did you make the decision you did? How did the other person react? Looking back, do you still feel you made the right decision?

In the preceding chapters, you learned four essential steps in writing an effective paragraph. The box below shows how these steps lead to four standards, or bases, you can use in revising your writing.

Four Steps ⟶	Four Bases
1. **If you make one point and stick to that point,**	your writing will have *unity*.
2. **If you back up the point with specific evidence,**	your writing will have *support*.
3. **If you organize and connect the specific evidence,**	your writing will have *coherence*.
4. **If you write clear, error-free sentences,**	your writing will demonstrate effective *sentence skills*.

This chapter discusses the four bases—unity, support, coherence, and sentence skills—and shows how these four bases can be used to evaluate and revise a paragraph.

Base 1: Unity

Understanding Unity

The following two paragraphs were written by students on the topic "Why Students Drop Out of College." Read them and decide which one makes its point more clearly and effectively, and why.

Paragraph A

Why Students Drop Out

Students drop out of college for many reasons. First of all, some students are bored in school. These students may enter college expecting nonstop fun or a series of fascinating courses. When they find out that college is often routine, they quickly lose interest. They do not want to take dull required courses or spend their nights studying, so they drop out. Students also drop out of college because the work is harder than they

continued

thought it would be. These students may have made decent grades in high school simply by showing up for class. In college, however, they may have to prepare for two-hour exams, write fifteen-page term papers, or make detailed presentations to a class. The hard work comes as a shock, and students give up. Perhaps the most common reason students drop out is that they are having personal or emotional problems. Younger students, especially, may be attending college at an age when they are also feeling confused, lonely, or depressed. These students may have problems with roommates, family, boyfriends, or girlfriends. They become too unhappy to deal with both hard academic work and emotional troubles. For many types of students, dropping out seems to be the only solution they can imagine.

Paragraph B

Student Dropouts

There are three main reasons students drop out of college. Some students, for one thing, are not really sure they want to be in school and lack the desire to do the work. When exams come up, or when a course requires a difficult project or term paper, these students will not do the required studying or research. Eventually, they may drop out because their grades are so poor they are about to flunk out anyway. Such students sometimes come back to school later with a completely different attitude about school. Other students drop out for financial reasons. The pressures of paying tuition, buying textbooks, and possibly having to support themselves can be overwhelming. These students can often be helped by the school because financial aid is available, and some schools offer work-study programs. Finally, students drop out because they have personal problems. They cannot concentrate on their courses because they are unhappy at home, they are lonely, or they are having trouble with boyfriends or girlfriends. Instructors should suggest that such troubled students see counselors or join support groups. If instructors would take a more personal interest in their students, more students would make it through troubled times.

Fill in the blanks: Paragraph _____ makes its point more clearly and effectively because _____

_____

_____

Activity

1

Paragraph A is more effective because it is *unified.* All the details in paragraph A are *on target;* they support and develop the single point expressed in the first sentence—that students drop out of college for many reasons.

On the other hand, paragraph B contains some details irrelevant to the opening point—that there are three main reasons students drop out. These details should be omitted in the interest of paragraph unity. Go back to paragraph B and cross out the sections that are off target—the sections that do not support the opening idea.

You should have crossed out the following sections: "Such students sometimes . . . attitude about school"; "These students can often . . . work-study programs"; and "Instructors should suggest . . . through troubled times."

The difference between these two paragraphs leads us to the first base, or standard, of effective writing: *unity.* To achieve unity is to have all the details in your paragraph related to the single point expressed in the topic sentence, the first sentence. Each time you think of something to put in, ask yourself whether it relates to your main point. If it does not, leave it out. For example, if you were writing about a certain job as the worst job you ever had and then spent a couple of sentences talking about the interesting people you met there on that job, you would be missing the first and most essential base of good writing.

www.mhhe.com/langan

Checking for Unity

To check a paragraph for unity, ask yourself these questions:

1. Is there a clear opening statement of the point of the paragraph?
2. Is all the material on target in support of the opening point?

Base 2: Support

Understanding Support

The following student paragraphs were written on the topic "A Quality of Some Person You Know." Both are unified, but one communicates more clearly and effectively. Which one, and why?

Paragraph A

My Generous Grandfather

My grandfather is the most generous person I know. He worked two jobs—one as a barber, the other as a part-time tailor—thirteen hours per day, six days a week for forty years. He sent three children through college and even paid my aunt's law school tuition. My father and my two aunts weren't spoiled, but Grandpa gave them all they needed to live a comfortable and fulfilling life. Now at age seventy, he's still working (only thirty hours per week) so he can help his six grandchildren, some of whom are beginning college this year. Finally, my grandfather serves his community. He is a member of the local council of the Knights of Columbus, a fraternal organization that has raised hundreds of thousand of dollars for homeless shelters, child care facilities, and our community hospital. A hero, for me, is someone who dedicates his life to others; that's my grandfather!

Paragraph B

My Generous Grandfather

My grandfather is the most generous person I know. He gave up a life of his own in order to give his children everything they wanted. Not only did he give up many years of his life to raise his children properly, but he is now sacrificing many more years to his grandchildren. His generosity is also evident in his relationship with his neighbors, his friends, and the members of his church. He has been responsible for many good deeds and has always been there to help all the people around him in times of trouble. Everyone knows that he will gladly lend a helping hand. He is so generous that you almost have to feel sorry for him. If one day he suddenly became selfish, it would be earthshaking. That's my grandfather.

Fill in the blanks: Paragraph _____ makes its point more clearly and effectively because _____

_____

_____

Activity

2

Paragraph A is more effective, for it offers specific examples that show us the grandfather in action. We see for ourselves why the writer describes the grandfather as generous.

Paragraph B, on the other hand, gives no specific evidence. The writer tells us repeatedly that the grandfather is generous but never provides examples of his generosity. Exactly how did the grandfather sacrifice for his children and grandchildren? Did he hold two jobs so his children could attend college? Did he pay for his daughter's law school tuition? Is he still working to help his grandchildren with their college tuition? What does he do for the community? Does he work for organizations that help the less fortunate? We want to see and judge for ourselves whether the writer is making a valid point about the grandfather, but without specific details, we cannot do so.

Consideration of these two paragraphs leads us to the second base of effective writing: *support.* After realizing the importance of specific supporting details, one student writer revised a paragraph she had done on a restaurant job as the worst job she ever had. In the revised paragraph, instead of talking about "unsanitary conditions in the kitchen," she referred to such specifics as "green mold on the bacon" and "ants in the potato salad." All your paragraphs should include many vivid details!

www.mhhe.com/langan

Checking for Support

To check a paragraph for support, ask yourself these questions:

1. Is there *specific* evidence to support the opening point?
2. Is there *enough* specific evidence?

Base 3: Coherence

Understanding Coherence

The following two paragraphs were written on the topic "The Best or Worst Job You Ever Had." Both are unified and both are supported. However, one communicates more clearly and effectively. Which one, and why?

Paragraph A

Pantry Helper

My worst job was as a pantry helper in one of San Diego's well-known restaurants. I had an assistant from three to six in the afternoon who did little but stand around and eat the whole time she was there. She would listen for the sound of the back door opening, which was a sure sign the boss was coming in. The boss would testily say to me, "You've got a lot of things to do here, Alice. Try to get a move on." I would come in at two o'clock to relieve the woman on the morning shift. If her day was busy, that meant I would have to prepare salads, slice meat and cheese, and so on. Orders for sandwiches and cold platters would come in and have to be prepared. The worst thing about the job was that the heat in the kitchen, combined with my nerves, would give me an upset stomach by seven o'clock almost every night. I might be going to the storeroom to get some supplies, and one of the waitresses would tell me she wanted a bacon, lettuce, and tomato sandwich on white toast. I would put the toast in and head for the supply room, and a waitress would holler out that her customer was in a hurry. Green flies would come in through the torn screen in the kitchen window and sting me. I was getting paid only $7.05 an hour. At five o'clock, when the dinner rush began, I would be dead tired. Roaches scurried in all directions whenever I moved a box or picked up a head of lettuce to cut.

Paragraph B

My Worst Job

The worst job I ever had was as a waiter at the Westside Inn. First of all, many of the people I waited on were rude. When a baked potato was hard inside or a salad was flat or their steak wasn't just the way they wanted it, they blamed me, rather than the kitchen. Or they would ask me to light their cigarettes, or chase flies from their tables, or even take their children to the bathroom. Also, I had to contend not only with the customers but with the kitchen staff as well. The cooks and busboys were often undependable and surly. If I didn't treat them just right, I would wind up having to apologize to customers because their meals came late or their water glasses weren't filled. Another reason I didn't like the job was that I was always moving. Because of the constant line at the door, as

---

continued

soon as one group left, another would take its place. I usually had only a twenty-minute lunch break and a ten-minute break in almost nine hours of work. I think I could have put up with the job if I had been able to pause and rest more often. The last and most important reason I hated the job was my boss. She played favorites, giving some of the waiters and waitresses the best-tipping repeat customers and preferences on holidays. She would hover around during my break to make sure I didn't take a second more than the allotted time. And even when I helped out by working through a break, she never had an appreciative word but would just tell me not to be late for work the next day.

<table>
<tr><td>

Activity

3

</td><td>

Fill in the blanks: Paragraph _____ makes its point more clearly and effectively because _____

_____

_____

</td></tr>
</table>

Paragraph B is more effective because the material is organized clearly and logically. Using emphatic order, the writer gives us a list of four reasons why the job was so bad: rude customers, an unreliable kitchen staff, constant motion, and—most of all—an unfair boss. Further, the writer includes transitional words that act as signposts, making movement from one idea to the next easy to follow. The major transitions are *First of all, Also, Another reason,* and *The last and most important reason.*

While paragraph A is unified and supported, the writer does not have any clear and consistent way of organizing the material. Partly, emphatic order is used, but this is not made clear by transitions or by saving the most important reason for last. Partly, time order is used, but it moves inconsistently from two to seven to five o'clock.

These two paragraphs lead us to the third base of effective writing: *coherence.* The supporting ideas and sentences in a composition must be organized so that they cohere, or "stick together." As has already been mentioned, key techniques for tying material together are a clear method of organization (such as time order or emphatic order), transitions, and other connecting words.

Checking for Coherence

To check a paragraph for coherence, ask yourself these questions:
1. Does the paragraph have a clear method of organization?
2. Are transitions and other connecting words used to tie the material together?

Base 4: Sentence Skills

Understanding Sentence Skills

Two versions of a paragraph are given below. Both are unified, supported, and organized, but one version communicates more clearly and effectively. Which one, and why?

Paragraph A

Falling Asleep Anywhere

[1]There are times when people are so tired that they fall asleep almost anywhere. [2]For example, there is a lot of sleeping on the bus or train on the way home from work in the evenings. [3]A man will be reading the newspaper, and seconds later it appears as if he is trying to eat it. [4]Or he will fall asleep on the shoulder of the stranger sitting next to him. [5]Another place where unplanned naps go on is the lecture hall. [6]In some classes, a student will start snoring so loudly that the professor has to ask another student to shake the sleeper awake. [7]A more embarrassing situation occurs when a student leans on one elbow and starts drifting off to sleep. [8]The weight of the head pushes the elbow off the desk, and this momentum carries the rest of the body along. [9]The student wakes up on the floor with no memory of getting there. [10]The worst place to fall asleep is at the wheel of a car. [11]Police reports are full of accidents that occur when people lose consciousness and go off the road. [12]If the drivers are lucky, they are not seriously hurt. [13]One woman's car, for instance, went into a river. [14]She woke up in four feet of water and thought it was raining. [15]When people are really tired, nothing will stop them from falling asleep—no matter where they are.

Paragraph B

"Falling Asleep Anywhere"

[1]There are times when people are so tired that they fall asleep almost anywhere. [2]For example, on the bus or train on the way home from work. [3]A man will be reading the newspaper, seconds later it appears as if he is trying to eat it. [4]Or he will fall asleep on the shoulder of the stranger sitting next to him. [5]Another place where unplanned naps go on are in the lecture hall. [6]In

continued

some classes, a student will start snoring so loudly that the professor has to ask another student to shake the sleeper awake. [7]A more embarrassing situation occurs when a student leans on one elbow and starting to drift off to sleep. [8]The weight of the head push the elbow off the desk, and this momentum carries the rest of the body along. [9]The student wakes up on the floor with no memory of getting there. [10]The worst time to fall asleep is when driving a car. [11]Police reports are full of accidents that occur when people conk out and go off the road. [12]If the drivers are lucky they are not seriously hurt. [13]One womans car, for instance, went into a river. [14]She woke up in four feet of water. [15]And thought it was raining. [16]When people are really tired, nothing will stop them from falling asleep—no matter where they are.

Activity

4

Fill in the blanks: Paragraph _____ makes its point more clearly and effectively

because _____

_____

_____

Paragraph A is more effective because it incorporates *sentence skills,* the fourth base of competent writing.

Activity

5

See if you can identify the ten sentence-skills mistakes in paragraph B. Do this, first of all, by going back and underlining the ten spots in paragraph B that differ in wording or punctuation from paragraph A. Then try to identify the ten sentence-skills mistakes by circling what you feel is the correct answer in each of the ten statements below.

> **HINT:** Comparing paragraph B with the correct version may help you guess correct answers even if you are not familiar with the names of certain skills.

1. The title should not be set off with
   a. capital letters.
   b. quotation marks.

2. In word group 2, there is a
   a. missing comma.
   b. missing apostrophe.
   c. sentence fragment.
   d. dangling modifier.

3. In word group 3, there is a
   a. run-on.
   b. sentence fragment.
   c. mistake in subject-verb agreement.
   d. mistake involving an irregular verb.

4. In word group 5, there is a
   a. sentence fragment.
   b. spelling error.
   c. run-on.
   d. mistake in subject-verb agreement.

5. In word group 7, there is a
   a. misplaced modifier.
   b. dangling modifier.
   c. mistake in parallelism.
   d. run-on.

6. In word group 8, there is a
   a. nonstandard English verb.
   b. run-on.
   c. comma mistake.
   d. missing capital letter.

7. In word group 11, there is a
   a. mistake involving an irregular verb.
   b. sentence fragment.
   c. slang phrase.
   d. mistake in subject-verb agreement.

8. In word group 12, there is a
   a. missing apostrophe.
   b. missing comma.
   c. mistake involving an irregular verb.
   d. sentence fragment.

9. In word group 13, there is a
   a. missing quotation mark.
   b. mistake involving an irregular verb.
   c. missing apostrophe.
   d. missing capital letter.

10. In word group 15, there is a
   a. mistake in parallelism.
   b. mistake involving an irregular verb.
   c. sentence fragment.
   d. mistake in pronoun point of view.

You should have chosen the following answers:

1. b   2. c   3. a   4. d   5. c
6. a   7. c   8. b   9. c   10. c

Part Five of this book explains these and other sentence skills. You should review all the skills carefully. Doing so will ensure that you know the most important rules of grammar, punctuation, and usage—rules needed to write clear, error-free sentences.

Checking for Sentence Skills

Sentence skills and the other bases of effective writing are summarized in the following chart and on the inside back cover of the book.

www.mhhe.com/langan

A Summary of the Four Bases of Effective Writing

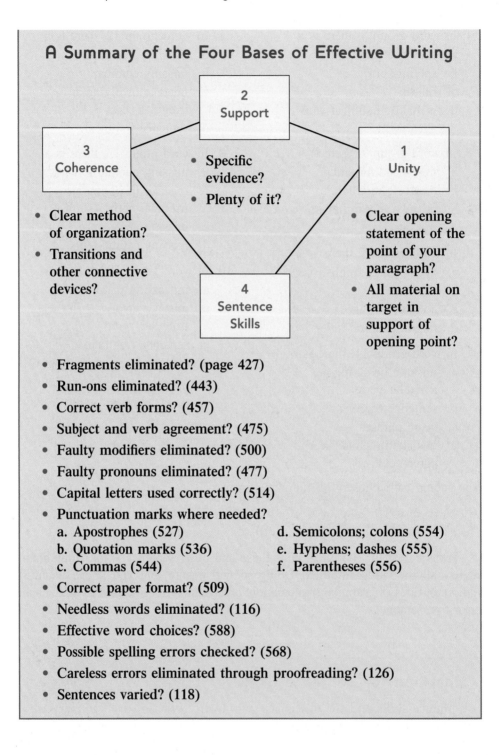

2 Support
- Specific evidence?
- Plenty of it?

3 Coherence
- Clear method of organization?
- Transitions and other connective devices?

1 Unity
- Clear opening statement of the point of your paragraph?
- All material on target in support of opening point?

4 Sentence Skills

- Fragments eliminated? (page 427)
- Run-ons eliminated? (443)
- Correct verb forms? (457)
- Subject and verb agreement? (475)
- Faulty modifiers eliminated? (500)
- Faulty pronouns eliminated? (477)
- Capital letters used correctly? (514)
- Punctuation marks where needed?
  a. Apostrophes (527)   d. Semicolons; colons (554)
  b. Quotation marks (536)   e. Hyphens; dashes (555)
  c. Commas (544)   f. Parentheses (556)
- Correct paper format? (509)
- Needless words eliminated? (116)
- Effective word choices? (588)
- Possible spelling errors checked? (568)
- Careless errors eliminated through proofreading? (126)
- Sentences varied? (118)

Practice in Using the Four Bases

You are now familiar with four bases, or standards, of effective writing: unity, support, coherence, and sentence skills. In this closing section, you will expand and strengthen your understanding of the four bases as you work through the following activities:

1. Evaluating Scratch Outlines for Unity
2. Evaluating Paragraphs for Unity
3. Evaluating Paragraphs for Support
4. Evaluating Paragraphs for Coherence
5. Revising Paragraphs for Coherence
6. Evaluating Paragraphs for All Four Bases: Unity, Support, Coherence, and Sentence Skills

1 Evaluating Scratch Outlines for Unity

The best time to check a paragraph for unity is at the outline stage. A scratch outline, as explained on page 23, is one of the best techniques for getting started with a paragraph.

Look at the following scratch outline that one student prepared and then corrected for unity.

I had a depressing weekend.
1. Hay fever bothered me
2. Had to pay seventy-seven-dollar car bill
3. ~~Felt bad~~
4. Boyfriend and I had a fight
5. ~~Did poorly in my math test today as a result~~
6. My mother yelled at me unfairly

Four reasons support the opening statement that the writer was depressed over the weekend. The writer crossed out "Felt bad" because it was not a reason for her depression. (Saying that she felt bad is only another way of saying that she was depressed.) She also crossed out the item about the math test because the point she is supporting is that she was depressed over the weekend.

In each outline, cross out the items that do not support the opening point. These items must be omitted in order to achieve paragraph unity.

1. In 1699, the Pennsylvania Religious Society of Friends argued against the evil of slavery.
    a. Pennsylvania is named after William Penn.
    b. They argued that taking someone's freedom is the same as taking his or her life.
    c. The wealth that comes from slavery is the product of violence.
    d. The Civil War ended slavery in the United States.
    e. The Society of Friends denied the claim that the Bible allowed slavery.

2. The twentieth century achieved much toward the control of infectious diseases.
    a. Penicillin and other antibacterial medicines were discovered.
    b. Sanitary sewer systems were built in many cities.
    c. School lunch programs offered low-cost meals to students.
    d. Many communities developed water purification systems.
    e. More was learned about psychological diseases.

3. There are several ways to get better mileage in your car.
    a. Check air pressure in tires regularly.
    b. Drive at no more than fifty-five miles per hour.
    c. Orange and yellow cars are the most visible.
    d. Avoid jackrabbit starts at stop signs and traffic lights.
    e. Always have duplicate ignition and trunk keys.

4. My swimming instructor helped me overcome my terror of the water.
    a. He talked with me about my fears.
    b. I was never good at sports.
    c. He showed me how to hold my head under water and not panic.
    d. I held on to a floating board until I was confident enough to give it up.
    e. My instructor was on the swimming team at his college.

5. Fred Wilkes is the best candidate for state governor.
    a. He has fifteen years' experience in the state senate.
    b. His son is a professional football player.
    c. He has helped stop air and water pollution in the state.
    d. His opponent has been divorced.
    e. He has brought new industries and jobs to the state.

2 Evaluating Paragraphs for Unity

Each of the following five paragraphs contains sentences that are off target— sentences that do not support the opening point—and so the paragraphs are not unified. In the interest of paragraph unity, such sentences must be omitted.

Cross out the irrelevant sentences and write the numbers of those sentences in the spaces provided. The number of spaces will tell you the number of irrelevant sentences in each paragraph.

1.   **A Kindergarten Failure**

¹In kindergarten I experienced the fear of failure that haunts many schoolchildren. ²My moment of panic occurred on my last day in kindergarten at Charles Foos Public School in Riverside, California. ³My family lived in California for three years before we moved to Omaha, Nebraska, where my father was a personnel manager for Mutual of Omaha. ⁴Our teacher began reading a list of names of all those students who were to line up at the door in order to visit the first-grade classroom. ⁵Our teacher was a pleasant-faced woman who had resumed her career after raising her own children. ⁶She called off every name but mine, and I was left sitting alone in the class while everyone else left, the teacher included. ⁷I sat there in absolute horror. ⁸I imagined that I was the first kid in human history who had flunked things like crayons, sandbox, and sliding board. ⁹Without getting the teacher's permission, I got up and walked to the bathroom and threw up into a sink. ¹⁰Only when I ran home in tears to my mother did I get an explanation of what had happened. ¹¹Since I was to go to a parochial school in the fall, I had not been taken with the other children to meet the first-grade teacher at the public school. ¹²My moment of terror and shame had been only a misunderstanding.

The numbers of the irrelevant sentences: _____ _____

2.   **How to Prevent Cheating**

¹Instructors should take steps to prevent students from cheating on exams. ²To begin with, instructors should stop reusing old tests. ³A test that has been used even once is soon known on the student grapevine. ⁴Students will check with their friends to find out, for example, what was on Dr. Thompson's biology final last term. ⁵They may even manage to find a copy of the test itself, "accidentally" not turned in by a former student of Dr. Thompson's. ⁶Instructors should also take some commonsense precautions at test time. ⁷They should make students separate themselves—by at least one seat—during an exam, and they should watch the class closely. ⁸The best place for the instructor to sit is in the rear of the room, so that a student is never sure if the instructor is looking at him or her. ⁹Last of all, instructors must make it clear to students that there will be stiff penalties for cheating. ¹⁰One of the problems with our school systems is a lack of discipline. ¹¹Instructors never used to give in to students' demands or put up with bad behavior, as they do today. ¹²Anyone caught cheating should

immediately receive a zero for the exam. [13]A person even suspected of cheating should be forced to take an alternative exam in the instructor's office. [14]Because cheating is unfair to honest students, it should not be tolerated.

The numbers of the irrelevant sentences: _____ _____

3.   **Other Uses for Cars**

[1]Many people who own a car manage to turn the vehicle into a trash can, a clothes closet, or a storage room. [2]People who use their cars as trash cans are easily recognized. [3]Empty snack bags, hamburger wrappers, pizza cartons, soda cans, and doughnut boxes litter the floor. [4]On the seats are old scratched CDs, blackened fruit skins, crumpled receipts, crushed cigarette packs, and used tissues. [5]At least the trash stays in the car, instead of adding to the litter on our highways. [6]Other people use a car as a clothes closet. [7]The car contains several pairs of shoes, pants, or shorts, along with a suit or dress that's been hanging on the car's clothes hanger for over a year. [8]Sweaty, smelly gym clothes will also find a place in the car, a fact passengers quickly discover. [9]The world would be better off if people showed more consideration of others. [10]Finally, some people use a car as a spare garage or basement. [11]In the backseats or trunks of these cars are bags of fertilizer, beach chairs, old textbooks, chainsaws, or window screens that have been there for months. [12]The trunk may also contain an extra spare tire, a dented hubcap, a gallon container of window washer fluid, and old stereo equipment. [13]If apartments offered more storage space, probably fewer people would resort to using their cars for such storage purposes. [14]All in all, people get a lot more use out of their cars than simply the miles they travel on the road.

The numbers of the irrelevant sentences: _____ _____ _____

4.   **Why Adults Visit Amusement Parks**

[1]Adults visit amusement parks for several reasons. [2]For one thing, an amusement park is a place where it is acceptable to "pig out" on junk food. [3]At the park, everyone is drinking soda and eating popcorn, ice cream, or hot dogs. [4]No one seems to be on a diet, and so buying all the junk food you can eat is a guilt-free experience. [5]Parks should provide stands where healthier food, such as salads or cold chicken, would be sold. [6]Another reason people visit amusement parks is to prove themselves. [7]They want to visit the park that has the newest, scariest ride in order to say that they went on the Parachute Drop, the seven-story Elevator, the Water Chute, or the Death Slide. [8]Going on a scary ride is a way to feel courageous and adventurous without taking much of a risk. [9]Some

rides, however, can be dangerous. [10]Rides that are not properly inspected or maintained have killed people all over the country. [11]A final reason people visit amusement parks is to escape from everyday pressures. [12]When people are poised at the top of a gigantic roller coaster, they are not thinking of bills, work, or personal problems. [13]A scary ride empties the mind of all worries—except making it to the bottom alive. [14]Adults at an amusement park may claim they have come for their children, but they are there for themselves as well.

The numbers of the irrelevant sentences: _____ _____ _____

5. **American Technology**

[1]America has provided the world with a flood of technology that has improved human life. [2]This is especially true for the twentieth century. [3]For example, the American industrialist Henry Ford set up an automobile assembly line, which made it possible to mass-produce automobiles that used interchangeable parts. [4]As a result, Ford was able to manufacture cars that everyday Americans could afford. [5]The Ford Motor Company is still in existence, selling cars all over the world. [6]The first successful flying machine was built by the Wright brothers who, in 1903, were able to keep their experimental plane flying for twelve seconds at Kitty Hawk, North Carolina. [7]Today, the Boeing Company of Seattle, Washington, is one of two leading builders of jetliners in the world. [8]The transistor, which replaced vacuum tubes in radios and televisions and which led to the development of the personal computer, was developed by two American companies: Bell Labs and Texas Instruments. [9]A transistor is a device used to increase the power of electronic signals or for switching signals. [10]In 1942, Enrico Fermi, who had immigrated to America, and Leo Szilard worked on the Manhattan Project, which built the first atomic reactor. [11]Eventually, this led to the development of the atomic bomb, which was dropped on the Japanese cities of Hiroshima and Nagasaki in 1945. [12]With the dawning of the atomic age, it was possible to make use of nuclear power for many peaceful purposes, such as the generation of electricity and the development of devices and treatments used in nuclear medicine. [13]In the 1930s, a German, Konrad Zuse, invented the first programmable computer. [14]The computer we know today was largely the product of the work of scientists at several American companies and universities, including IBM, Remington Rand, and Harvard University.

The numbers of the irrelevant sentences: _____ _____ _____

_____ _____

3 Evaluating Paragraphs for Support

Activity

8

The five paragraphs that follow lack sufficient supporting details. In each paragraph, identify the spot or spots where more specific details are needed.

1.

Chicken: Our Best Friend

¹Chicken is the best-selling meat today for a number of good reasons. ²First of all, its reasonable cost puts it within everyone's reach. ³Chicken is popular, too, because it can be prepared in so many different ways. ⁴It can, for example, be cooked by itself, in spaghetti sauce, or with noodles and gravy. ⁵It can be baked, boiled, broiled, or fried. ⁶Chicken is also convenient. ⁷Last and most important, chicken has a high nutritional value. ⁸Four ounces of chicken contain twenty-eight grams of protein, which is almost half the recommended daily dietary allowance.

Fill in the blanks: The first spot where supporting details are needed occurs after sentence number _____. The second spot occurs after sentence number _____.

2.

A Car Accident

¹I was on my way home from work when my terrible car accident took place. ²As I drove my car around the curve of the expressway exit, I saw a number of cars ahead of me. ³They were backed up because of a red light at the main road. ⁴I slowly came to a stop behind a dozen or more cars. ⁵In my rearview mirror, I then noticed a car coming up behind me that did not slow down or stop. ⁶I had a horrible, helpless feeling as I realized the car would hit me. ⁷I knew there was nothing I could do to signal the driver in time, nor was there any way I could get away from the car. ⁸Minutes after the collision, I picked up my glasses, which were on the seat beside me. ⁹My lip was bleeding, and I got out a tissue to wipe it. ¹⁰The police arrived quickly, along with an ambulance for the driver of the car that hit me. ¹¹My car was so damaged that it had to be towed away. ¹²Today, eight years after the accident, I still relive the details of the experience whenever a car gets too close behind me.

Fill in the blank: The point where details are needed occurs after sentence number _____.

3.

Tips on Bringing Up Children

¹In some ways, children should be treated as mature people. ²For one thing, adults should not use baby talk with children. ³Using real words with children helps them develop language skills more quickly. ⁴Baby talk makes children feel patronized, frustrated, and confused, for they want to understand and communicate with adults by learning their speech. ⁵So animals should be called cows and dogs, not "moo-moos" and "bow-wows."

⁶Second, parents should be consistent when disciplining children. ⁷For example, if a parent tells a child, "You cannot have dessert unless you put away your toys," it is important that the parent follow through on the warning. ⁸By being consistent, parents will teach children responsibility and give them a stable center around which to grow. ⁹Finally, and most important, children should be allowed and encouraged to make simple decisions. ¹⁰Parents will thus be helping their children prepare for the complex decisions that they will have to deal with in later life.

Fill in the blank: The spot where supporting details are needed occurs after sentence number _____.

4.   **Being on TV**

¹People act a little strangely when a television camera comes their way. ²Some people behave as if a crazy puppeteer were pulling their strings. ³Their arms jerk wildly about, and they begin jumping up and down for no apparent reason. ⁴Often they accompany their body movements with loud screams, squeals, and yelps. ⁵Another group of people engage in an activity known as the cover-up. ⁶They will be calmly watching a sports game or other televised event when they realize the camera is focused on them. ⁷The camera operator can't resist zooming in for a close-up of these people. ⁸Then there are those who practice their funny faces on the unsuspecting public. ⁹They take advantage of the television time to show off their talents, hoping to get that big break that will carry them to stardom. ¹⁰Finally, there are those who pretend they are above reacting for the camera. ¹¹They wipe an expression from their faces and appear to be interested in something else. ¹²Yet if the camera stays on them long enough, they will slyly check to see if they are still being watched. ¹³Everybody's behavior seems to be slightly strange in front of a TV camera.

Fill in the blanks: The first spot where supporting details are needed occurs after sentence number _____. The second spot occurs after sentence number _____.

5.   **Culture Conflict**

¹I am in a constant tug-of-war with my parents over conflicts between their Vietnamese culture and American culture. ²To begin with, my parents do not like me to have American friends. ³They think that I should spend all my time with other Vietnamese people and speak English only when necessary. ⁴I get into an argument whenever I want to go to a fast-food restaurant or a movie at night with my American friends. ⁵The conflict with my parents is even worse when it comes to plans for a career. ⁶My parents want me to get a degree in science and then go on to medical school. ⁷On the other hand, I think I want to become a teacher. ⁸So far I

have been taking both science and education courses, but soon I will have to concentrate on one or the other. [9]The other night my father made his attitude about what I should do very clear. [10]The most difficult aspect of our cultural differences is the way our family is structured. [11]My father is the center of our family, and he expects that I will always listen to him. [12]Although I am twenty-one years old, I still have a nightly curfew at an hour which I consider insulting. [13]Also, I am expected to help my mother perform certain household chores that I've really come to hate. [14]My father expects me to live at home until I am married to a Vietnamese man. [15]When that happens, he assumes I will obey my husband just as I obey him. [16]I do not want to be a bad daughter, but I want to live like my American female friends.

Fill in the blanks: The first spot where supporting details are needed occurs after sentence number _____. The second spot occurs after sentence number _____. The third spot occurs after sentence number _____.

4 Evaluating Paragraphs for Coherence

Activity

9

Answer the questions about coherence that follow each of the two paragraphs below.

1.
Why I Bought a Handgun

[1]I bought a handgun to keep in my house for several reasons. [2]Most important, I have had a frightening experience with an obscene phone caller. [3]For several weeks, a man has called me once or twice a day, sometimes as late as three in the morning. [4]As soon as I pick up the phone, he whispers something obscene or threatens me by saying, "I'll get you." [5]I decided to buy a gun because crime is increasing in my neighborhood. [6]One neighbor's house was burglarized while she was at work; the thieves not only stole her appliances but also threw paint around her living room and slashed her furniture. [7]Not long after this incident, an elderly woman from the apartment house on the corner was mugged on her way to the supermarket. [8]The man grabbed her purse and threw her to the ground, breaking her hip. [9]Buying a gun was my response to listening to the nightly news. [10]It seemed that every news story involved violence of some kind—rapes, murders, muggings, and robberies. [11]I wondered if some of the victims in the stories would still be alive if they had been able to frighten the criminal off with a gun. [12]As time passed, I became more convinced that I should keep a gun in the house.

a. The paragraph should use emphatic order. Write 1 before the reason that seems slightly less important than the other two reasons, 2 before the second-most-important reason, and 3 before the most important reason.

_____ Obscene phone caller

_____ Crime increase in neighborhood

_____ News stories about crime

b. Before which of the three reasons should the transitional words *First of all* be added? _____

c. Before which of the three reasons could the transition *In addition* be added? _____

d. Which words show emphasis in sentence 2? _____

e. In sentence 8, to whom does the pronoun *her* refer? _____

f. How often does the key word *gun* appear in the paragraph?

_____

g. What is a synonym for *burglarized* in sentence 6? _____

2.

Apartment Hunting

[1]Apartment hunting is a several-step process. [2]Visit and carefully inspect the most promising apartments. [3]Check each place for signs of unwanted guests such as roaches or mice. [4]Make sure that light switches and appliances work and that there are enough electrical outlets. [5]Turn faucets on and off and flush the toilet to be sure that the plumbing works smoothly. [6]Talk to the landlord for a bit to get a sense of him or her as a person. [7]If a problem develops after you move in, you want to know that a decent and capable person will be there to handle the matter. [8]Find out what's available that matches your interests. [9]Your town newspaper and local real estate offices can provide you with a list of apartments for rent. [10]Family and friends may be able to give you leads. [11]And your school may have a housing office that keeps a list of approved apartments for rent. [12]Decide just what you need. [13]If you can afford no more than $400 a month, you need to find a place that will cost no more than that. [14]If you want a location that's close to work or school, you must take that factor into account. [15]If you plan to cook, you want a place with a workable kitchen. [16]By taking these steps, you should be ready to select the apartment that is best for you.

a. The paragraph should use time order. Write 1 before the step that should come first, 2 before the intermediate step, and 3 before the final step.

_____ Visit and carefully inspect the most promising apartments.

_____ Decide just what you need.

_____ Find out what's available that matches your interests.

   b. Before which of three steps could the transitional words *The first step is to* be added? _____

   c. Before which step could the transitional words *After you have decided what you are looking for, the next step is to* be added? _____

   d. Before which step could the transitional words *The final step* be added? _____

   e. To whom does the pronoun *him or her* in sentence 6 refer?

   _____

   f. What is a synonym for *landlord* in sentence 7? _____

   g. What is a synonym for *apartment* in sentence 13? _____

5 Revising Paragraphs for Coherence

The two paragraphs in this section begin with a clear point, but in each case the supporting material that follows the point is not coherent. Read each paragraph and the comments that follow it on how to organize and connect the supporting material. Then do the activity for the paragraph.

Paragraph 1

A Difficult Period

Since I arrived in the Bay Area in midsummer, I have had the most difficult period of my life. I had to look for an apartment. I found only one
place that I could afford, but the landlord said I could not move in until it
was painted. When I first arrived in San Francisco, my thoughts were to
stay with my father and stepmother. I had to set out looking for a job so
that I could afford my own place, for I soon realized that my stepmother
was not at all happy having me live with them. A three-week search led to
a job shampooing rugs for a housecleaning company. I painted the apartment myself, and at least that problem was ended. I was in a hurry to get
settled because I was starting school at the University of San Francisco in
September. A transportation problem developed because my stepmother
insisted that I return my father's bike, which I was using at first to get to
school. I had to rely on a bus that often arrived late, with the result that I
missed some classes and was late for others. I had already had a problem
with registration in early September. My counselor had made a mistake

---

continued

with my classes, and I had to register all over again. This meant that I was one week late for class. Now I'm riding to school with a classmate and no longer have to depend on the bus. My life is starting to order itself, but I must admit that at first I thought it was hopeless to stay here.

EXPLANATION   The writer of this paragraph has provided a good deal of specific evidence to support the opening point. The evidence, however, needs to be organized. Before starting the paragraph, the writer should have decided to arrange the details by using time order. He or she could then have listed in a scratch outline the exact sequence of events that made for such a difficult period.

Activity

10

Here is a list of the various events described by the writer of paragraph 1. Number the events in the correct time sequence by writing 1 in front of the first event that occurred, 2 in front of the second event, and so on.

Since I arrived in the Bay Area in midsummer, I have had the most difficult period of my life.

_____ I had to search for an apartment I could afford.

_____ I had to find a job so that I could afford my own place.

_____ My stepmother objected to my living with her and my father.

_____ I had to paint the apartment before I could move in.

_____ I had to find an alternative to unreliable bus transportation.

_____ I had to register again for my college courses because of a counselor's mistake.

Your instructor may now have you rewrite the paragraph on separate paper. If so, be sure to use time signals such as *first, next, then, during, when, after,* and *now* to help guide your reader from one event to the next.

Paragraph 2

Childhood Cruelty

When I was in grade school, my classmates and I found a number of excuses for being cruel to a boy named Andy Poppovian. Sometimes Andy gave off a strong body odor, and we knew that several days had passed since he had taken a bath. Andy was very slow in speaking, as well as very careless

---

continued

in personal hygiene. The teacher would call on him during a math or grammar drill. He would sit there silently for so long before answering that she sometimes said, "Are you awake, Andy?" Andy had long fingernails that he never seemed to cut, with black dirt caked under them. We called him "Poppy," or we accented the first syllable in his name and mispronounced the rest of it and said to him, "How are you today, POP-o-van?" His name was funny. Other times we called him "Popeye," and we would shout at him. "Where's your spinach today, Popeye?" Andy always had sand in the corners of his eyes. When we played tag at recess, Andy was always "it" or the first one who was caught. He was so physically slow that five guys could dance around him and he wouldn't be able to touch any of them. Even when we tried to hold a regular conversation with him about sports or a teacher, he was so slow in responding to a question that we got bored talking with him. Andy's hair was always uncombed, and it was often full of white flakes of dandruff. Only when Andy died suddenly of spinal meningitis in seventh grade did some of us begin to realize and regret our cruelty toward him.

EXPLANATION   The writer of this paragraph provides a number of specifics that support the opening point. However, the supporting material has not been organized clearly. Before writing this paragraph, the author should have (1) decided to arrange the supporting evidence by using emphatic order and (2) listed in a scratch outline the reasons for the cruelty to Andy Poppovian and the supporting details for each reason. The writer could also have determined which reason to use in the emphatic final position of the paper.

Activity
11

Create a clear outline for paragraph 2 by filling in the scheme below. The outline is partially completed.

When I was in grade school, my classmates and I found a number of excuses for being cruel to a boy named Andy Poppovian.

Reason   1. *Funny name* _____

Details   a. _____

           b. _____

           c. _____

Reason   2. *Physically slow* _____

Details   a. _____

           b. *Five guys could dance around him* _____

3. _____   Reason

   a. _____   Details

   b. *In regular conversation* _____

4. _____   Reason

   a. _____   Details

   b. *Sand in eyes* _____

   c. _____

   d. _____

Your instructor may have you rewrite the paragraph on separate paper. If so, be sure to introduce each of the four reasons with transitions such as *First, Second, Another reason,* and *Finally.* You may also want to use repeated words, pronouns, and synonyms to help tie your sentences together.

www.mhhe.com/langan

6 Evaluating Paragraphs for All Four Bases: Unity, Support, Coherence, and Sentence Skills

In this activity, you will evaluate paragraphs in terms of all four bases: unity, support, coherence, and sentence skills. Evaluative comments follow each paragraph below. Circle the letter of the statement that best applies in each case.

Activity

12

1.   **Drunk Drivers**

     People caught driving while drunk—even first offenders—should be jailed. Drunk driving, first of all, is more dangerous than carrying around a loaded gun. In addition, a jail term would show drivers that society will no longer tolerate such careless and dangerous behavior. Finally, severe penalties might encourage solutions to the problem of drinking and driving. People who go out for a good time and intend to have several drinks would always designate one person, who would stay completely sober, as the driver.

   a. The paragraph is not unified.

   b. The paragraph is not adequately supported.

   c. The paragraph is not well organized.

   d. The paragraph does not show a command of sentence skills.

   e. The paragraph is well written in terms of the four bases.

2.   **Bullying**

     In recent years, the frequency of bullying in schools has increased. The National Education Association estimates that 160,000 children stay home from school regularly. Because they fear being bullied. In fact, fifteen percent of absenteeism is caused by the fear of being bullied, and at least one out of every six children is a victim of bullying. Believed to have low esteem, psychologists once thought that bullies were children who had been bullied themselves, either at school or at home. And that they intimidated others to bolster their egos. However, new research shows that many bullies have high self-esteem, they engage in such behavior because they take pleasure in threatening and even harming others. Bullying can be stopped. The *Stop Bulling* Web site advisees victims of bullying to report it to teachers or counselors. Also to join groups in which others will lend support against bullies. Finally, to confront the bully if it's safe to do so.

a. The paragraph is not unified.

b. The paragraph is not adequately supported.

c. The paragraph is not well organized.

d. The paragraph does not show a command of sentence skills.

e. The paragraph is well written in terms of the four bases.

3.

Asking Girls Out

There are several reasons I have trouble asking girls to go out with me. I have asked some girls out and have been turned down. This is one reason that I can't talk to them. At one time I was very shy and quiet, and people sometimes didn't even know I was present. I can talk to girls now as friends, but as soon as I want to ask them out, I usually start to become quiet, and a little bit of shyness comes out. When I finally get the nerve up, the girl will turn me down, and I swear that I will never ask another one out again. I feel sure I will get a refusal, and I have no confidence in myself. Also, my friends mock me, though they aren't any better than I am. It can become discouraging when your friends get on you. Sometimes I just stand there and wait to hear what line the girl will use. The one they use a lot is "We like you as a friend, Ted, and it's better that way." All my past experiences with girls have been just as bad. One girl used me to make her old boyfriend jealous. Then when she succeeded, she started going out with him again. I had a bad experience when I took a girl to the prom. I spent a lot of money on her. Two days later, she told me that she was getting serious with another guy. I feel that when I meet a girl I have to be sure I can trust her. I don't want her to turn on me.

a. The paragraph is not unified.

b. The paragraph is not adequately supported.

c. The paragraph is not well organized.

d. The paragraph does not show a command of sentence skills.

e. The paragraph is well written in terms of the four bases.

4.

A Change in My Writing

A technique of my present English instructor has corrected a writing problem that I've always had. In past English courses, I had major problems with commas in the wrong places, bad spelling, capitalizing the wrong words, sentence fragments, and run-on sentences. I never had any big problems with unity, support, or coherence, but the sentence skills were another matter. They were like little bugs that always appeared to infest my writing. My present instructor asked me to rewrite papers, just concentrating on sentence skills. I thought that the instructor was crazy because I didn't feel that rewriting would do any good. I soon became certain that my instructor was out of his mind, for he made me rewrite my first paper four times. It was very frustrating, for I became tired of doing the same paper over and over. I wanted to belt my instructor against the wall when I'd show him each new draft and he'd find skills mistakes and say, "Rewrite." Finally, my papers began to improve and the sentence skills began to fall into place. I was able to see them and correct them before turning in a paper, whereas I couldn't before. Why or how this happened I don't know, but I think that rewriting helped a lot. It took me most of the semester, but I stuck it out and the work paid off.

a. The paragraph is not unified.
b. The paragraph is not adequately supported.
c. The paragraph is not well organized.
d. The paragraph does not show a command of sentence skills.
e. The paragraph is well written in terms of the four bases.

5.

Luck and Me

I am a very lucky man, though the rest of my family has not always been lucky. Sometimes when I get depressed, which is too frequently, it's hard to see just how lucky I am. I'm lucky that I'm living in a country that is free. I'm allowed to worship the way I want to, and that is very important to me. Without a belief in God a person cannot live with any real certainty in life. My relationship with my wife is a source of good fortune for me. She gives me security, and that's something I need a lot. Even with these positive realities in my life, I still seem to find time for insecurity, worry, and, worst of all, depression. At times in my life I have had bouts of terrible luck. But overall, I'm a very lucky guy. I plan to further develop the positive aspects of my life and try to eliminate the negative ones.

a. The paragraph is not unified.
b. The paragraph is not adequately supported.
c. The paragraph is not well organized.
d. The paragraph does not show a command of sentence skills.
e. The paragraph is well written in terms of the four bases.

Paragraph Development

This photograph is clearly making a statement. Write a paragraph about what you think that statement is and why you came to that conclusion. You may want to use personal experience to strengthen the support in your paragraph.

PREVIEW

7 Introduction to Paragraph Development

The photograph above pictures an activity that is part of the yearly celebration of Kwanzaa. Can you think of a special tradition that you share with family, friends, or other members of your culture? Write a paragraph about this special tradition.

Important Considerations in Paragraph Development

Before you begin work on particular types of paragraphs, there are several general considerations about writing to keep in mind: knowing your subject, knowing your purpose, and knowing your audience.

Knowing Your Subject

Whenever possible, write on a subject that interests you. If you do, you will find it easier to put more time into your work. Even more important, try to write on a subject that you already know something about. If you do not have direct experience with the subject, you should at least have indirect experience—knowledge gained through thinking, prewriting, reading, or talking about the subject.

If you are asked to write on a topic about which you have no experience or knowledge, you should do whatever research is required to gain the information you need. Chapters 19 and 20 show you how to look up relevant information at the library and online, and how to write a research paper. Without direct or indirect experience, or the information you gain through research, you may not be able to provide the specific evidence needed to develop whatever point you are trying to make. Your writing will be starved for specifics.

Knowing Your Purpose and Audience

The three most common purposes of writing are *to inform, to persuade,* and *to entertain.* Each is described briefly below.

- To **inform**—to give information about a subject. Authors who are writing to inform want to provide facts that will explain or teach something to readers. For example, an informative paragraph about sandwiches might begin, "Eating food between two slices of bread—a sandwich—is a practice that has its origins in eighteenth-century England."

- To **persuade**—to convince the reader to agree with the author's point of view on a subject. Authors who are writing to persuade may give facts, but their main goal is to argue or prove a point to readers. A persuasive paragraph about sandwiches might begin, "There are good reasons why every sandwich should be made with whole grain bread."

- To **entertain**—to amuse and delight; to appeal to the reader's senses and imagination. Authors write to entertain in various ways, through fiction and nonfiction. An entertaining paragraph about sandwiches might begin, "What I wanted was a midnight snack, but what I got was better—the biggest, most magical sandwich in the entire world."

Much of the writing assigned in this book will involve some form of argumentation or persuasion. You will advance a point or thesis and then support it in a variety of ways. To some extent, also, you will write papers to inform—to provide readers with information about a particular subject. And since, in practice, writing often combines purposes, you might also find yourself providing vivid or humorous details in order to entertain your readers.

In Chapter 2, you learned that the audience of a piece of writing is its readers and that, like purpose, audience should be considered early in the writing process. In college, your primary audience will be your instructor. Your instructor, though, is really representative of the larger audience you should see yourself as writing for—an audience of educated adults who expect you to present your ideas in a clear, direct, organized way.

Some instructors will also require you to share your work with other students, either in small groups or with the class as a whole. In some cases, your writing will be judged on how well it informs or persuades your classmates. Therefore, you must keep them in mind as you write. In addition, you may have occasion to write a letter to your local or college newspaper to express a complaint or an opinion that others will read. Other situations in which you will want to keep your audience in mind include applying for transfer to another college, for graduate school, or for a scholarship.

After you graduate, you will have ample opportunity to write to a wide range of audiences. This is when you will have to pay even more attention to evaluating your audience. For example, careers in science and the technologies require employees to write to other experts, who may know a great deal about the subject. On the other hand, scientists and technologists are often required to write to laypersons, whose knowledge of a subject might vary from adequate to nonexistent. The same is true of those who pursue careers in business, law enforcement, the legal and medical professions, the military, education, or government work.

Let's say you get a job in a town's public works department as a road engineer and the town decides to install new storm sewers on a stretch of road on a steep hill. You may be asked to write a letter to residents who live on that road explaining why the job is necessary, what will be done, how long it will take, and why they will have to take a long detour to and from home during construction. Explaining such a project to another road engineer might not be difficult, since he or she will know about the technicalities of road grading, sewer installation, and paving. Your explanation will be fairly straightforward and will use technical terminology that this reader is sure to understand. In addition, you won't have to convince your engineering colleague that the inconvenience to residents will be worthwhile; it will be obvious to him or her that the improvements will make the road much safer. However, if you are writing to the residents— people who may not have any knowledge about road construction and repair— you would avoid using technical terminology, which they might not understand.

In addition, you might have to make a real effort to convince these readers that the inconvenience they will experience during construction is worth the outcome—a much safer road.

Here are a few questions you should ask yourself when evaluating any audience. The answers to these questions will help determine your approach to any writing project.

1. *How much does the audience already know about the subject?* On the one hand, if you incorrectly assume that your readers know very little, you might bore them with too much basic information. On the other hand, if you incorrectly assume that they know more than they do, you might confuse them by using unfamiliar technical terminology or neglecting to provide enough informative detail.

2. *Why might the reader need or want to read this material?* In college, your English professor will use your papers to evaluate your writing skills and determine how you can strengthen them. He or she will probably also use them to establish your course grade. If, however, you are writing to a group of residents whose road is going to be closed for repaving, you will have to meet different expectations. They will want to know why the road is being paved, how long the work will take, and what benefits they will reap from it. As taxpayers, they may also want to know how much the repaving will cost.

3. *Is your purpose simply to inform the audience? Or is it to convince readers of something as well?* If your purpose is to convince or persuade, you may want to use some of the techniques for writing arguments in Chapter 16. For example, if you are writing a letter to the editor of your local newspaper in support of the new school budget, you may have to persuade voters to approve the budget even though it is sure to raise their property taxes.

4. *What type of language should be used?* Are you writing to peers, other college students? Or are you communicating with professors, business and community leaders, or government officials? With peers, you might want to use language that is relaxed, friendly, and informal, language that will win their confidence. If you're writing to a professor or to a government official or an employer, you will have to be more formal. (You can read more about effective word choice in Chapter 43.)

A Note on Tone

It will be helpful for you to write some papers for a more specific audience. By so doing, you will develop an ability to choose words and adopt a tone of voice that is just right for a given purpose and a given group of people. *Tone* reveals the attitude that a writer has toward a subject. It is expressed through the words and details the writer selects. Just as a speaker's voice can project a range of feelings, a writer's voice can project one or more tones, or feelings: anger, sympathy, hopefulness, sadness, respect, dislike, and so on.

Activity

1

To appreciate differences in tone, look at the six statements below, which express different attitudes about a shabby apartment. Six different tones are used. Label each statement with the tone you think is present.

a. bitter	c. matter-of-fact	e. tolerant and accepting
b. sentimental	d. humorous	f. optimistic and hopeful

_____ 1. This place may be shabby, but since both of my children were born while we lived here, it has a special place in my heart.

_____ 2. The apartment is not fancy, but it meets my needs.

_____ 3. If only there were some decent jobs out there, I wouldn't be reduced to living in this miserable dump.

_____ 4. This place does need some repairs, but I'm sure the landlord will be making improvements sometime soon.

_____ 5. When we move away, we're planning to release three hundred cockroaches and two mice so we can leave the place exactly as we found it.

_____ 6. It's a small two-bedroom apartment that needs to be repainted and have the kitchen plumbing repaired.

EXPLANATION   The tone of item 1 is sentimental. "It has a special place in my heart" expresses tender emotions. In item 2, the words "meets my needs" show that the writer is tolerant, accepting the situation while recognizing that it could be better. We could describe the tone of item 3 as bitter. The writer resents a situation that forces him or her to live in a "miserable dump." Item 4 is optimistic and hopeful, since the writer is expecting the apartment to be improved soon. The tone of item 5 is humorous. Its writer claims to be planning a comic revenge on the landlord. The tone of item 6 is matter-of-fact and objective, simply describing what needs to be done.

The "Purpose and Audience" Assignment in Each Chapter

In this part of the book, an assignment at the end of each chapter asks you to write with a very specific purpose in mind and for a very specific audience. You will be asked, for example, to imagine yourself as an aide at a day care center preparing instructions for children, as a high school graduate explaining to the school's principal why the school deserves a high or low rating, as an apartment tenant complaining to a landlord about neighbors, as a reporter for your college newspaper describing a potential vacation spot, and as an employee describing a new job opening at your workplace. Through these and other assignments, you will learn how to adjust your style and tone of voice to a given writing situation.

Tips on Using a Computer

- If you are using your school's computer center, allow yourself enough time. You may have to wait for a computer or printer to be free. In addition, you may need several sessions at the computer and printer to complete your paper.

- Every word-processing program allows you to save your writing by hitting one or more keys. Save your work file frequently as you write your draft. A saved file is stored safely on the computer or network. Work that is not saved may be lost if the computer crashes or if the power is turned off.

- Keep your work in two places—the hard drive or network you are working on and, if you have one, a backup USB drive. At the end of each session with the computer, copy your work onto the USB drive or e-mail a copy to yourself. Then if the hard drive or network becomes damaged, you'll have the backup copy.

- Print out your work at least at the end of every session. Then not only will you have your most recent draft to work on away from the computer, you'll also have a copy in case something should happen to your electronic file.

- Work in single spacing so that you can see as much of your writing on the screen at one time as possible. Just before you print out your work, change to double spacing.

- Before making major changes in a paper, create a copy of your file. For example, if your file is titled "Worst Job," create a file called "Worst Job 2." Then make all your changes in that file. If the changes don't work out, you can always go back to the original file.

Using a Computer at Each Stage of the Writing Process

Following are some ways to make word processing a part of your writing. Note that the sections that follow correspond to the stages of the writing process described in Chapter 2, pages 16–32.

Prewriting

If you're a fast typist, many kinds of prewriting will work well on the computer. With freewriting in particular, you can get ideas onto the screen almost as quickly as they occur to you. A passing thought that could be productive is not likely to get lost. You may even find it helpful, when freewriting, to dim the screen of your monitor so that you can't see what you're typing. If you temporarily can't see the screen, you won't have to worry about grammar or spelling or typing errors (all of which do not matter in prewriting); instead, you can concentrate on getting down as many ideas and details as possible about your subject.

After any initial freewriting, questioning, and list making on a computer, it's often very helpful to print out a hard copy of what you've done. With a clean printout in front of you, you'll be able to see everything at once and revise and expand your work with handwritten comments in the margins of the paper.

Word processing also makes it easy for you to experiment with the wording of the point of your paper. You can try a number of versions in a short time. After you have decided on the version that works best, you can easily delete the other versions—or simply move them to a temporary "leftover" section at the end of the paper.

If you have prepared a list of items, you may be able to turn that list into an outline right on the screen. Delete the ideas you feel should not be in your paper (saving them at the end of the file in case you change your mind), and add any new ideas that occur to you. Then use the cut and paste functions to shuffle the supporting ideas around until you find the best order for your paper.

Writing Your First Draft

Like many writers, you may want to write out a first draft by hand and then type it into the computer for revision. Even as you type your handwritten draft, you may find yourself making some changes and improvements. And once you have a draft on the screen, or printed out, you will find it much easier to revise than a handwritten one.

If you feel comfortable composing directly on the screen, you can benefit from the computer's special features. For example, if you have written an anecdote in your freewriting that you plan to use in your paper, simply copy the story from your freewriting file and insert it where it fits in your paper. You can refine it then or later. Or if you discover while typing that a sentence is out of place, cut it out from where it is and paste it wherever you wish. And if while writing you realize that an earlier sentence can be expanded, just move your cursor back to that point and type in the added material.

Revising

It is during revision that the virtues of word processing really shine. All substituting, adding, deleting, and rearranging can be done easily within an existing file. All changes instantly take their proper places within the paper, not scribbled above the line or squeezed into the margin. You can concentrate on each change you want to make, because you never have to type from scratch or work on a messy draft. You can carefully go through your paper to check that all your supporting evidence is relevant and to add new support as needed here and there. Anything you decide to eliminate can be deleted with a keystroke. Anything you add can be inserted precisely where you choose. If you change your mind, all you have to do is delete or cut and paste. Then you can sweep through the paper focusing on other changes: improving word choice, increasing sentence variety, eliminating wordiness, and so on.

> **TIP:** If you are like some students, you will find it convenient to print out a hard copy of your file at various points throughout the revision. You can then revise in longhand—adding, crossing out, and indicating changes—and later quickly make those changes in the document.

Editing and Proofreading

Editing and proofreading also benefit richly from word processing. Instead of crossing or whiting out mistakes, or rewriting an entire paper to correct numerous errors, you can make all necessary changes within the most recent draft. If you find editing or proofreading on the screen hard on your eyes, print out a copy. Mark any corrections on that copy, and then transfer them to the final draft.

If the word-processing program you're using includes spelling and grammar checks, by all means use them. The spell-check function tells you when a word is not in the computer's dictionary. Keep in mind, however, that the spell-check cannot tell you how to spell a name correctly or when you have mistakenly used, for example, *their* instead of *there*. To a spell-check, *Thank ewe four the compliment* is as correct as *Thank you for the compliment*. Also use the grammar check with caution. Any errors it doesn't uncover are still your responsibility, and it sometimes points out mistakes where there are none.

A word-processed paper, with its clean appearance and attractive formatting, looks so good that you may think it is in better shape than it really is. Do not be fooled by your paper's appearance. Take sufficient time to review your grammar, punctuation, and spelling carefully.

> **TIP:** Even after you hand in your paper, save the computer file. Your teacher may ask you to do some revising, and then the file will save you from having to type the paper from scratch.

Using Peer Review

Often, it is a good idea to have another student respond to your writing before you hand it in to the instructor. On the day a composition is due, or on a day when you are writing paragraphs or essays in class, your instructor may ask you to pair up with another student. That student will read your composition, and you will read his or hers.

Ideally, read the other paragraph or essay aloud while your partner listens. If that is not practical, read it in a whisper while he or she looks on. As you read, both you and your partner should look and listen for spots where the composition does not read smoothly and clearly. Check or circle the trouble spots where your reading snags.

Your partner should then read your work, marking possible trouble spots while doing so. Then each of you should do the following three things.

1 Identification

On a separate sheet of paper, write at the top the title and author of the composition you have read. Under it, put your name as the reader of the paragraph or essay.

2 Scratch Outline

"X-ray" the paper for its inner logic by making up a scratch outline. The scratch outline need be no more than twenty words or so, but it should show clearly the logical foundation on which the paragraph or essay is built. It should identify and summarize the overall point of the paper and the three areas of support for the point.

Your outline should be organized like this:

Point: _____

Support:

   1. _____

   2. _____

   3. _____

For example here is a scratch outline of the paper on page 213 about the benefits of exercise:

Point: Effects of exercise can change one's life.

Support:

1. Burns calories for weight loss

2. Helps heart and circulatory system

3. Helps improve emotional health

3 Comments

Under the outline, write the heading "Comments." Here is what you should comment on.

- Look at the spots where your reading of the composition snagged: Are words missing or misspelled? Is there a lack of parallel structure? Are there mistakes with punctuation? Is the meaning of a sentence confusing? Try to figure out what the problems are and suggest ways of fixing them.

- Are there spots in the paragraph or essay where you see problems with *unity, support,* or *organization*? (You'll find it helpful to refer to the checklist on the inside back cover of this book.) If so, offer comments. For example, for an essay, you might say, "More details are needed in the first supporting paragraph," or "Some of the details in the last supporting paragraph don't really back up your point."

- Finally, make note of something you really liked about the composition, such as good use of transitions or an especially realistic or vivid specific detail.

After you have completed your evaluation of the paragraph or essay, give it to your partner.

Your instructor may provide you with the option of rewriting your composition in light of this feedback. Whether or not you rewrite, be sure to hand in the peer evaluation form with your paragraph or essay.

Doing a Personal Review

1. While you're writing and revising a paragraph or essay, you should be constantly evaluating it in terms of *unity, support,* and *organization*. Use as a guide the detailed checklist on the inside back cover of this book.

2. After you've finished the next-to-final draft of a composition, check it for the *sentence skills* listed on the inside back cover. It may also help to read your work out loud. If a given sentence does not sound right—that is, if it does not read clearly and smoothly—chances are something is wrong. In that case, revise or edit as necessary until your composition is complete.

Patterns of Paragraph Development

Traditionally, writing has been divided into the following patterns of development.

• **Exposition**	• **Description**
Examples	• **Narration**
Process	• **Argumentation**
Cause and effect	
Comparison and contrast	
Definition	
Division and classification	

In *exposition,* the writer provides information about and explains a particular subject. Patterns of development within exposition include giving *examples,* detailing a *process* of doing or making something, analyzing *causes and effects, comparing* and *contrasting, defining* a term or concept, and *dividing* something into parts or *classifying* it into categories.

In addition to the six exposition patterns of development, three other patterns are common: *description, narration,* and *argumentation.* A *description* is a verbal picture of a person, place, or thing. In *narration,* a writer tells the story of something that happened. Finally, in *argumentation,* a writer attempts to support a controversial point or defend a position on which there is a difference of opinion.

The pages ahead present individual chapters on each pattern. You will have a chance, then, to learn nine different patterns or methods for organizing material in your papers. Each pattern has its own internal logic and provides its own special strategies for imposing order on your ideas.

As you practice each pattern, you should remember the Tip on the next page.

TIP: While each paragraph that you write will involve one predominant pattern, very often one or more additional patterns may be involved as well. For instance, the paragraph "Good-Bye, Tony" (page 52) presents a series of causes leading to an effect—that the writer will not go out with Tony again. But the writer also presents examples to explain each of the causes (Tony was late; he was bossy; he was abrupt). And there is an element of narration, as the writer presents examples that occur from the beginning to the end of the date.

No matter which pattern or patterns you use, each paragraph will probably involve some form of argumentation. You will advance a point and then go on to support your point. To convince the reader that your point is valid, you may use exemplification, narration, description, or some other pattern of organization. Among the paragraphs you will read in Part Two, one writer supports the point that a favorite outdoor spot is like "heaven" by providing a number of descriptive details. Another labels a certain experience in his life as heartbreaking and then uses a narrative to demonstrate the truth of his statement. A third writer advances the opinion that good horror movies can be easily distinguished from bad horror movies and then supplies comparative information about both to support her claim. Much of your writing, in short, will have the purpose of persuading your reader that the idea you have advanced is valid.

The Progression in Each Chapter

After each type of paragraph development is explained, student papers illustrating that type are presented. These are followed by questions about the paragraphs. The questions relate to unity, support, and coherence—three of the four bases of effective writing. You are then asked to write your own paragraph. In most cases, the first assignment is fairly structured and provides a good deal of guidance for the writing process. The other assignments offer a wide choice of writing topics. The fourth assignment always requires some simple research, and the fifth assignment requires writing with a specific purpose and for a specific audience.

8

Exemplification

This chapter will explain and illustrate how to

- develop an exemplification paragraph
- write an exemplification paragraph
- revise an exemplification paragraph

In addition, you will read and consider

- three student paragraphs

Is the United States a health-conscious nation? Look at this photograph and write a paragraph in which you answer that question. Use examples found in the media, in the photograph, or in your own daily observations to support your point.

www.mhhe.com/langan

In our daily conversations, we often provide *examples*—that is, details, particulars, specific instances—to explain statements that we make. Consider the several statements and supporting examples in the box below.

Statement	Examples
Wal-Mart was crowded today.	There were at least four carts waiting at each of the checkout counters, and it took me forty-five minutes to get through a line.
The corduroy shirt I bought is poorly made.	When I washed it, the colors began to fade, one button cracked and another fell off, a shoulder seam opened, and the sleeves shrank almost two inches.
Success in college requires students to practice commonsense habits.	Regular attendance is necessary for mastering the complex ideas taught in college. Keeping up with the assigned reading prepares students for class and increases their grasp of the material. Careful note taking is essential to studying for and passing examinations.

In each case, the examples help us *see for ourselves* the truth of the statement that has been made. In paragraphs, too, explanatory examples help the audience fully understand a point. Lively, specific examples also add interest to a paragraph.

In this chapter, you will be asked to provide a series of examples to support a topic sentence. Providing examples to support a point is one of the simplest and most common methods of paragraph development. First read the paragraphs ahead; they all use examples to develop their points. Then answer the questions that follow.

Paragraphs to Consider

Inconsiderate Drivers

¹Some people are inconsiderate drivers. ²In the city, they will at times stop right in the middle of the street while looking for a certain home or landmark. ³If they had any consideration for the cars behind them, they would pull over to the curb first. ⁴Other drivers will be chatting on their

continued

cell phones and then slow down unexpectedly at a city intersection to make a right or left turn. [5]The least they could do is use their turn signals to let those behind them know in advance of their intention. [6]On the highway, a common example of inconsiderateness is night drivers who fail to turn off their high beams, creating glare for cars approaching in the other direction. [7]Other rude highway drivers move to the second or passing lane and then stay there, making it impossible for cars behind to go around them. [8]Yet other drivers who act as if they have special privileges are those who do not wait their turn in bottleneck situations where the cars in two lanes must merge alternately into one lane. [9]Perhaps the most inconsiderate drivers are those who throw trash out their windows, creating litter that takes away some of the pleasure of driving and that must be paid for with everyone's tax dollars.

Office Politics

[1]Office politics is a destructive game played by several types of people. [2]For instance, two supervisors may get into a conflict over how to do a certain job. [3]Instead of working out an agreement like adults, they carry on a power struggle that turns the poor employees under them into human Ping-Pong balls being swatted between two angry players. [4]Another common example of office politics is the ambitious worker who takes credit for other people's ideas. [5]He or she will chat in a "friendly" fashion with inexperienced employees, getting their ideas about how to run the office more smoothly. [6]Next thing you know, Mr. or Ms. Idea-Stealer is having a closed-door session with the boss and getting promotion points for his or her "wonderful creativity." [7]Yet another illustration of office politics is the spy. [8]This employee acts very buddy-buddy with other workers, often dropping little comments about things he or she doesn't like in the workplace. [9]The spy encourages people to talk about their problems at work, that they don't like their boss, the pay, and the working conditions. [10]Then the spy goes straight back and repeats all he or she has heard to the boss, and the employees get blamed for their "poor attitude." [11]A final example of office politics is people who gossip. [12]Too often, office politics can turn a perfectly fine work situation into a stressful one.

A Visit to Utah's National Parks

¹Some of the most interesting national parks in the United States are found in Utah. ²For example, Zion National Park contains a canyon that is almost one-half mile deep. ³It also features massive cliffs of deep red and brown that overlook rivers and green, wooded trails. ⁴Visitors to Bryce Canyon National Park are treated to interesting rock formations shaped by wind erosion. ⁵Included are several large solid rock horseshoes, which are topped with delicate stone columns in fantastic shapes. ⁶South Dakota's Badlands National Park is another place one can see landforms created by erosion. ⁷In most cases, it's the wind that has cut the stone, but in others water from rivers—long dried up—has done the sculpting. ⁸Utah's Arches National Park is well named because of its stone arches. ⁹Tourists are often seen photographing the park's beautiful red-rock formations, whose shading varies with changes in sunlight as the day goes on. ¹⁰Petroglyphs, or engravings in the surface of rocks, can be found in Canyonlands National Park in the southeastern part of Utah. ¹¹Many of these carvings are more than one thousand years old. ¹²Finally, Capitol Reef National Park is interesting because of its large white rock that looks a lot like the United States Capitol in Washington, D.C.

About Unity

1. Which two sentences in "A Visit to Utah's National Parks" are irrelevant to the point that "interesting national parks . . . are found in Utah"?

    _____   _____

About Support

2. In "Inconsiderate Drivers," how many examples are given of inconsiderate drivers?

    _____ two _____ four _____ six _____ seven

3. After which sentence in "Office Politics" are specific details needed?

    _____

About Coherence

4. What are the four transition words or phrases that are used to introduce each new example in "Office Politics"?

    _____   _____   _____   _____

Questions

5. Identify at least three transitional words or phrases used to introduce examples in "A Visit to Utah's National Parks."

    _____   _____   _____

6. Which paragraph clearly uses emphatic order to organize its details, saving for last what the writer regards as the most important example?

    _____

Developing an Exemplification Paragraph

Development through Prewriting

Backing up your statements with clear, specific illustrations is the key to a successful examples paragraph. When Charlene, the writer of "Office Politics," was assigned an examples paragraph, she at first did not know what to write about.

Then her instructor made a suggestion. "Imagine yourself having lunch with some friends," the instructor said. "You're telling them *how* you feel about something and *why*. Maybe you're saying, 'I am so mad at my boyfriend!' or 'My new apartment is really great.' You wouldn't stop there—you'd continue by saying what your boyfriend does that is annoying, or in what way your apartment is nice. In other words, you'd be making a general point and backing it up with examples. That's what you need to do in this paragraph."

That night, Charlene was on the telephone with her brother. She was complaining about the office where she worked. "Suddenly I realized what I was doing," Charlene said. "I was making a statement—I hate the politics in my office—and giving examples of those politics. I knew what I could write about!"

Charlene began preparing to write her paragraph by freewriting. She gave herself ten minutes to write down everything she could think of on the subject of politics in her office. This is what she wrote:

Of all the places I've ever worked this one is the worst that way. Can't trust anybody there—everybody's playing some sort of game. Worst one of all is Bradley and the way he pretends to be friendly with people. Gets them to complain about Ms. Bennett and

continued

Mr. Hankins and then runs back to them and reports everything. He should realize that people are catching on to his game and figuring out what a jerk he is. Melissa steals people's ideas and then takes credit for them. Anything to get brownie points. She's always out for herself first, you can tell. Then there's all the gossip that goes on. You think you're in a soap opera or something, and it's kind of fun in a way but it also is very distracting people always talking about each other and worrying about what they say about you. And people talk about our bosses a lot. Nobody knows why Ms. Bennett and Mr. Hankins hate each other so much but they each want the workers on their side. You do something one boss's way, but then the other boss appears and is angry that you're not doing it another way. You don't know what to do at times to keep people happy.

Charlene read over her freewriting and then spent some time asking questions about her paragraph. "Exactly what do I want my point to be?" she asked. "And exactly how am I going to support that point?" Keeping those points in mind, she worked on several scratch outlines and wound up with the following:

Office politics are ruining the office.
1. Bradley reports people's complaints.
2. Melissa steals ideas.
3. People gossip.
4. Ms. Bennett and Mr. Hankins make workers choose sides.

Working from this outline, she then wrote the following first draft:

My office is being ruined by office politics. It seems like everybody is trying to play some sort of game to get ahead and don't care what it does to anybody else. One example is Bradley. Although he pretends to be friendly with people he isn't sincere. What he is trying to do is get them to complain about their bosses. Once they do, he goes back to the bosses and tells them what's been said and gets the worker in trouble. I've seen the same kind of thing happen at two other offices where I've worked. Melissa is another example of someone who plays office politics games. She steals other people's ideas and takes the credit for them. I had a good idea once on how to reduce office memos. I told her we ought to use e-mail to send office memos instead of typing them on paper. She went to Ms. Bennett and pretended the idea was hers. I guess I was partly to blame for not acting on the idea myself. And Ms. Bennett and Mr. Hankins hate each other and try to get us to take sides in their conflict. Then there is all the gossip that goes on. People do a lot of backbiting, and you have to be very careful about your behavior or people will start talking about you. All in all, office politics is really a problem where I work.

Development through Revising

After completing her first draft, Charlene put it aside until the next day. When she reread it, this was her response:

"I think the paragraph would be stronger if I made it about office politics in general instead of just politics in my office. The things I was writing about happen in many offices, not just in mine. And our instructor wants us to try some third-person writing. Also, I need to make better use of transitions to help the reader follow as I move from one example to another."

With these thoughts in mind, Charlene began revising her paragraph, and after several drafts she produced the paragraph that appears on page 182.

Writing an Exemplification Paragraph

Writing Assignment

1

The assignment here is to complete an unfinished paragraph (in the box), which has as its topic sentence, "People use MP3 players for more than just listening to music." Provide the supporting details needed to develop the examples. The first example is done for you.

Uses for MP3 Players

    People use MP3 players for more than just listening to music. Many people wear earpieces connected to iPods or other MP3 players just so they can drown out annoying noises.

In a large city, being exposed to the roar of buses and trains for more than a few minutes can be nerve-wracking. Then there are the cars and taxis that blow their horns at each other and at pedestrians as they bully their way through traffic.

Being plugged into an electronic device can also come in handy on a crowded bus, train, or other type of public transportation.

_____

_____

_____

Listening to background music on an MP3 player can help one concentrate on important tasks even when in busy places where others are coming and going and talking among themselves.

_____

_____

_____

Finally, listening to these devices helps drown out unwanted noise at home.

_____

_____

_____

Prewriting

a. On a separate piece of paper, jot down a couple of answers for each of the following questions.

*   How can being plugged into an MP3 player help people avoid noise pollution on a bus, train, or other type of public transportation? What kinds of noise distractions have you experienced when using public transportation?

*   What tasks do you find easier to concentrate on when listening to music that comes through an earpiece? Why does the music make it easier to concentrate on these tasks even when you are in a place that is crowded and noisy? Name specific places that you often find crowded and noisy.

*   What kinds of unwanted noises annoy or disturb you at home? Does such noise break your concentration when you are trying to do something important? What are some of these tasks or projects?

Your instructor may ask you to work with one or two other students in generating the details needed to develop the three examples in the paragraph. The

groups may then be asked to read their details aloud, with the class deciding which details are the most effective for each example.

Here and in general in your writing, try to generate *more* supporting material than you need. You are then in a position to choose the most convincing details for your paragraph.

b. Read over the details you have generated and decide which sound most effective. Jot down additional details as they occur to you.

c. Take your best details, reshape them as needed, and use them to complete the paragraph explaining why people plug into electronic devices.

Revising

Read over the paragraph you have written. Ask yourself these questions.

FOUR BASES Checklist for Exemplification

About *Unity*

✓ Do all of the examples I provide support the central idea that people use MP3 players for several reasons?

About *Support*

✓ Are there enough examples to make my point about MP3 players and convince others to agree with me?

✓ Do I appeal to my readers' senses with vivid, specific examples?

About *Coherence*

✓ Have I presented the examples in my paragraph in the most effective order?

About *Sentence Skills*

✓ Have I used specific rather than general words?

✓ Are my sentences varied in length and structure?

✓ Have I checked for spelling and other sentence skills, as listed on the inside back cover of the book?

Continue revising your work until you can answer "yes" to all these questions.

Writing Assignment

2   Write an examples paragraph about one quality of a person you know well. The person might be a member of your family, a friend, a roommate, a boss or supervisor, a neighbor, an instructor, or someone else. Here is a list of descriptions that you might consider choosing from. Feel free to choose another description that does not appear here.

Honest	Hardworking	Jealous
Bad-tempered	Supportive	Materialistic
Ambitious	Suspicious	Sarcastic
Prejudiced	Open-minded	Self-centered
Considerate	Lazy	Spineless
Argumentative	Independent	Good-humored
Softhearted	Stubborn	Cooperative
Energetic	Flirtatious	Self-disciplined
Patient	Irresponsible	Sentimental
Reliable	Stingy	Defensive
Generous	Trustworthy	Dishonest

Persistent	Aggressive	Insensitive
Shy	Courageous	Unpretentious
Sloppy	Compulsive	Tidy

Prewriting

a. Select the individual you will write about and the quality of this person that you will focus on. For example, you might choose a self-disciplined cousin. Her quality of self-discipline will then be the point of your paper.

b. Make a list of examples that will support your point. A list for the self-disciplined cousin might look like this:
Exercises every day for forty-five minutes
Never lets herself watch TV until homework is done
Keeps herself on a strict budget
Organizes her school papers in color-coordinated notebooks
Eats no more than one dessert every week
Balances her checkbook the day her statement arrives

c. Read over your list and see how you might group the items into categories. The list above, for example, could be broken into three categories: schoolwork, fitness, and money.
Exercises every day for forty-five minutes (fitness)
Never lets herself watch TV until homework is done (schoolwork)
Keeps herself on a strict budget (money)
Organizes her school papers in color-coordinated notebooks (schoolwork)
Eats no more than one dessert every week (fitness)
Balances her checkbook the day her bank statement arrives (money)

d. Prepare a scratch outline made up of the details you've generated, with those details grouped into appropriate categories.

1. Self-disciplined about fitness
   A. Exercises every day for forty-five minutes
   B. Eats no more than one dessert every week
2. Self-disciplined about schoolwork
   A. Never lets herself watch TV until homework is done
   B. Organizes her school papers in color-coordinated notebooks
3. Self-disciplined about money
   A. Keeps herself on a strict budget
   B. Balances her checkbook the day her bank statement arrives

e. Write the topic sentence of your paragraph. You should include the name of the person you're writing about, your relationship to that person, and the specific quality you are focusing on. For example, you might write, "Keisha, a schoolmate of mine, is very flirtatious," or "Stubbornness is Uncle Carl's outstanding characteristic." And a topic sentence for the paragraph about the self-disciplined cousin might be "My cousin Mari is extremely self-disciplined."

Remember to focus on only *one* characteristic. Also remember to focus on a *specific* quality, not a vague, general quality. For instance, "My English instructor is a nice person" is too general.

f. Now you have a topic sentence and an outline and are ready to write the first draft of your paragraph. Remember, as you flesh out the examples, that your goal is not just to *tell* us about the person but to *show* us the person by detailing his or her words, actions, or both.

Revising

It's hard to criticize your own work honestly, especially right after you've finished writing. If at all possible, put your paragraph away for a day or so and then return to it. Better yet, wait a day and then read it aloud to a friend whose judgment you trust.

Read the paragraph with these questions in mind.

FOUR BASES Checklist for Exemplification

About *Unity*

☑ Does my topic sentence clearly state whom I am writing about, what that person's relationship is to me, and what quality of that person I am going to focus on?

☑ Do the examples I provide truly show that my subject has the quality I am writing about?

About *Support*

☑ Have I provided enough specific details to solidly support my point that my subject has a certain quality?

About *Coherence*

☑ Have I organized the details in my paragraph into several clearly defined categories?

☑ Have I used transitional words such as *also, in addition, for example,* and *for instance* to help the reader follow my train of thought?

About *Sentence Skills*

- ☑ Have I used a consistent point of view throughout my paragraph?
- ☑ Have I used specific rather than general words?
- ☑ Have I used concise wording?
- ☑ Are my sentences varied?
- ☑ Have I checked for spelling and other sentence skills, as listed on the inside back cover of the book?

Continue revising your work until you and your reader can answer "yes" to all these questions.

Writing Assignment 3

Write a paragraph that uses examples to develop one of the following statements or a related statement of your own.

1. The computer is an invaluable tool for students.

2. _____ is a place where it's easy to spend a lot of money.

3. Abundant evidence exists that the United States has become a health-conscious nation.

4. Despite modern appliances, many household chores are still drudgery.

5. One of my instructors, _____, has some good (*or* unusual) teaching techniques.

6. Wasted electricity is all around us.

7. Temptations to eat fattening foods are all around us.

8. _____ (name a relative or good friend) is the most generous person I know.

9. Today, some people are wearing ridiculous fashions.

10. It's easy to find opportunities to exercise in your normal, daily routine even without going to a gym or jogging.

Be sure to choose examples that truly support your topic sentence. They should be relevant facts, statistics, personal experiences, or incidents you have heard or read about. Organize your paragraph by listing several examples that support your point. Save the most vivid, most convincing, or most important example for last.

Writing Assignment

4 As this cartoon suggests, the diet of many Americans is not healthy. We eat too much junk food and far too much cholesterol. Write a paragraph with a topic sentence like one of those below:

www.CartoonStock.com

The diet of the average American is unhealthy.

The diet of many American families is unhealthy.

Many schoolchildren in America do not have a healthy diet.

Using strategies described in Chapter 19 (pages 370–385), you might research the topic with keywords such as "unhealthy American diets." Combine information you find with your own observations to provide a series of examples that support your point.

Writing Assignment

5 **Writing for a Specific Purpose and Audience**

In this examples paragraph, you will write with a specific purpose and for a specific audience. Imagine that you are writing a television review for a college newspaper read by students just like you and your classmates. Your purpose will be to *recommend* the television programs you think are most worth watching.

Notice that the topic for this assignment is very broad. How can you discuss the many television shows you think are worth watching in a single paragraph? You decide to do some prewriting to narrow your topic.

Here's where paying attention to the specific needs or interests of your intended audience—students like you—can help. Through prewriting, you realize that reality shows, game shows, and crime dramas are among this group's favorite types of television programs. You decide to limit your paragraph to shows from one of these categories.

The next step is to express the point you want to make in a topic sentence. For example, you might start with "The most entertaining (reality shows, game shows, crime dramas) this season are _____, _____, and _____."

You see that you will have to do some more prewriting—in this case, research—to develop specific details for your paragraph. Begin by watching various episodes of the type of show you have chosen. Take detailed notes on what qualities make a specific show particularly entertaining. Is it suspenseful, clever, humorous, realistic? Write down examples that illustrate each of these qualities. Now, pick three shows you would recommend to readers.

When you write your outline, list the titles of the shows as your major headings. Then under each heading list two or three specific details that make that show particularly entertaining. For example, you might describe how a character's outrageous actions in a particular episode made you laugh.

After you have written the first draft of your paragraph, read it to make sure that your topic sentence is limited and clear, that you have included enough detail, and that your paragraph is both unified and coherent. Then revise and edit.

9

Process

Reproduced with permission of Yahoo! Inc. © 2010 Yahoo! Inc. Yahoo! And the Yahoo! Logo are registered trademarks of Yahoo! Inc.

Write a paragraph that informs a particular reader how to "surf the Web." For instance, you might tell film buffs how to find out about their favorite directors, or budding astronomers where to find help online, or students where to find help in one or more of their courses. Be sure to imagine a specific audience with specific interests and take readers through the process of surfing the Web step by step.

Every day we perform many activities that are *processes*—that is, series of steps carried out in a definite order. Many of these processes are familiar and automatic: for example, tying shoelaces, changing sheets, using a vending machine, and starting a car. We are thus seldom aware of the sequence of steps making up each activity. In other cases, such as when we are asked for directions to a particular place, or when we try to read and follow the directions for a new game, we may be painfully conscious of the whole series of steps involved in the process.

In this section, you will be asked to write a process paragraph—one that explains clearly how to do or make something. To prepare for this assignment, you should first read the student process papers below and then respond to the questions that follow.

www.mhhe.com/langan

TIP: In process writing, you are often giving instructions to the reader, so the pronoun *you* can appropriately be used. Two of the following model paragraphs use *you*—as indeed does much of this book, which gives instruction on how to write effectively. As a general rule, though, do not use *you* in your writing.

Paragraphs to Consider

www.mhhe.com/langan

Sneaking into the House at Night

¹The first step I take is bringing my key along with me. ²Obviously, I don't want to have to knock on the door at 1:30 in the morning and rouse my parents out of bed. ³Second, I make it a point to stay out past midnight. ⁴If I come in before then, my father is still up, and I'll have to face his disapproving look. ⁵All I need in my life is for him to make me feel guilty. ⁶Trying to make it as a college student is as much as I'm ready to handle. ⁷Next, I am careful to be very quiet upon entering the house. ⁸This involves lifting the front door up slightly as I open it, so that it does not creak. ⁹It also means treating the floor and steps to the second floor like a minefield, stepping carefully over the spots that squeak. ¹⁰When I'm upstairs, I stop briefly in the bathroom without turning on the light. ¹¹Finally, I tiptoe to my room, put my clothes in a pile on a chair, and slip quietly into bed. ¹²With my careful method of sneaking into the house at night, I have avoided some major hassles with my parents.

Protecting Your Skin

[1]Being exposed to the sun or ultraviolet light regularly or for long periods can harm your skin. [2]It can even cause skin cancer. [3]You can do several things to prevent this. [4]First, stay away from tanning booths. [5]They are simply not safe. [6]They use ultraviolet rays, which over time can cause severe damage. [7]Second, and for the same reason, don't use sun lamps or sit in the sun with a shiny reflector under your chin. [8]Many young people use artificial tanning devices or sit under sun reflectors to clear up their complexions. [9]However, there are many safer methods to solve acne problems. [10]Next, even if you don't have fair skin, avoid exposure to the sun especially during the hours of 11 A.M. to 3 P.M., when its rays are strongest. [11]Finally and most important, wear a hat and cover your arms and legs when you have to be out in the sun for any length of time. [12]Use a sunscreen that has a sun protection factor (SPF) of 30 as well. [13]However, remember that many sun protectors wash off when you go swimming, so they must be reapplied. [14]Also, realize that even the best sunscreen can't protect you from prolonged exposure.

Dealing with Verbal Abuse

[1]If you are living with someone who abuses you verbally with criticism, complaints, and insults, you should take steps to change your situation. [2]First, realize that you are not to blame for his or her abusive behavior. [3]This may be difficult for you to believe. [4]Years of verbal abuse have probably convinced you that you're responsible for everything that's wrong with your relationship. [5]But that is a lie. [6]If your partner is verbally abusive, it is that person's responsibility to learn why he or she chooses to deal with problems by saying nasty things. [7]Perhaps he observed his father treating his mother that same way. [8]Maybe she never learned any more positive ways to deal with negative emotions, like anger, fear, or disappointment. [9]Steps two and three need to be done one right after the other. [10]Step two is for you to announce that you will no longer tolerate being verbally abused. [11]State that you are a person who deserves respect and civil behavior, and that you will accept no less. [12]Next, offer to go with him or her to talk to a counselor who will help both of you learn new ways to communicate. [13]While your partner learns to express his or

continued

her feelings without attacking you, you can learn to stand up for yourself and express your feelings clearly. [14]If he or she refuses to take responsibility for changing abusive behavior, then you must consider step four: to leave that person. [15]You were not put here on earth to have your self-concept demolished by serving as someone else's verbal punching bag.

About Unity

1. Which paragraph lacks an opening topic sentence?

   _____

2. Which two sentences in "Sneaking into the House at Night" should be eliminated in the interest of paragraph unity? (*Write the sentence numbers here.*)

   _____   _____

About Support

3. After which sentence in "Protecting Your Skin" are supportive details or examples needed?

   _____

4. Summarize the four steps in the process of dealing with verbal abuse.

   a. _____

   b. _____

   c. _____

   d. _____

About Coherence

5. Which of these paragraphs use or uses time order?

   _____

   Which use or uses emphatic order?

   _____

6. Which transition words introduce the first, second, and third steps in "Sneaking into the House at Night"?

   _____   _____   _____

Questions

Developing a Process Paragraph

Development through Prewriting

To be successful, a process essay must explain clearly each step of an activity. The key to preparing to write such an essay is thinking through the activity as though you're doing it for the first time. Selma is the author of "Dealing with Verbal Abuse." As she considered possible topics for her paper, she soon focused on a situation in her own life: living with an abusive man. Selma had not known how to change her situation. But with the help of a counselor, she realized there were steps she could take—a process she could follow. She carried out that process and finally left her abusive partner. Remembering this, Selma decided to write about how to deal with abuse.

She began by making a list of the steps she followed in coping with her own abusive relationship. This is what she wrote:

Tell him you won't accept any more abuse.

Open your own checking account.

Apply for credit cards in your own name.

Offer to go with him to counseling.

Realize you're not to blame.

Learn to stand up for yourself.

Go into counseling yourself if he won't do it.

Call the police if he ever becomes violent.

Leave him if he refuses to change.

Next, she numbered the steps in the order in which she had performed them. She crossed out some items she realized weren't really part of the process of dealing with verbal abuse.

2   Tell him you won't accept any more abuse.

~~Open your own checking account.~~

~~Apply for credit cards in your own name.~~

3   Offer to go with him to counseling.

1   Realize you're not to blame.

5   Learn to stand up for yourself.

4   Go into counseling yourself if he won't do it.

~~Call the police if he ever becomes violent.~~

6   Leave him if he refuses to change.

Then Selma grouped her items into four steps. Those steps were (1) realize you're not to blame; (2) tell the abuser you won't accept more abuse; (3) get into counseling, preferably with him; and (4) if necessary, leave him.

Selma was ready to write her first draft. Here it is.

Some people think that "abuse" has to mean getting punched and kicked, but that's not so. Verbal abuse can be as painful inside as physical abuse is on the outside. It can make you feel worthless and sad. I know because I lived with a verbally abusive man for years. Finally I found the courage to deal with the situation. Here is what I did. With the help of friends, I finally figured out that I wasn't to blame. I thought it was my fault because that's what he always told me—that if I wasn't so stupid, he wouldn't criticize and insult me. When I told him I wanted him to stop insulting and criticizing me, he just laughed at me and told me I was a crybaby. One of my friends suggested a counselor, and I asked Harry to go talk to him with me. We went together once but Harry wouldn't go back. He said he didn't need

continued

anyone to tell him how to treat his woman. I wasn't that surprised because Harry grew up with a father who treated his mother like dirt and his mom just accepts it to this day. Even after Harry refused to go see the counselor, though, I kept going. The counselor helped me see that I couldn't make Harry change, but I was still free to make my own choices. If I didn't want to live my life being Harry's verbal punching bag, and if he didn't want to change, then I would have to. I told Harry that I wasn't going to live that way anymore. I told him if he wanted to work together on better ways to communicate, I'd work with him. But otherwise, I would leave. He gave me his usual talk about "Oh, you know I don't really mean half the stuff I say when I'm mad." I said that wasn't a good enough excuse, and that I did mean what I was saying. He got mad all over again and called me every name in the book. I stuck around for a little while after that but then realized "This is it. I can stay here and take this or I can do what I know is right for me." So I left. It was a really hard decision but it was the right one. Harry may be angry at me forever but I know now that his anger and his verbal abuse are his problem, not mine.

Development through Revising

After Selma had written her first draft, she showed it to a classmate for her comments. Here is what the classmate wrote in response:

In order for this to be a good process essay, I think you need to do a couple of things.

First, although the essay is based on what you went through, I think it's too much about your own experience. I'd suggest you take

continued

yourself out of it and just write about how any person could deal with any verbally abusive situation. Otherwise this paper is about you and Harry, not the process.

Second, you need a clear topic sentence that tells the reader what process you're going to explain.

Third, I'd use transitions like "first" and "next" to make the steps in the process clearer. I think the steps are all there, but they get lost in all the details about you and Harry.

When Selma reread her first draft, she agreed with her classmate's suggestions. She then wrote the version of "Dealing with Verbal Abuse" that appears on page 198.

Writing a Process Paragraph

Choose one of the topics below to write about in a process paragraph.

How to feed a family on a budget

How to break up with a boyfriend or girlfriend

How to balance a checkbook

How to change a car or bike tire

How to get rid of house or garden pests, such as mice, roaches, or wasps

How to play a simple game like checkers, tic-tac-toe, or an easy card game

How to shorten a skirt or pants

How to meet new people, for either dating or friendship

How to plant a garden

How to deal with a nosy person

How to fix a leaky faucet, a clogged drain, or the like

How to build a campfire or start a fire in a fireplace

How to study for an important exam

How to conduct a yard or garage sale

How to wash dishes efficiently, clean a bathroom, or do laundry

Prewriting

a. Begin by freewriting on your topic for ten minutes. Do not worry about spelling, grammar, organization, or other matters of form. Just write whatever comes into your head regarding the topic. Keep writing for more than ten minutes if ideas keep coming to you. This freewriting will give you a base of raw material to draw from during the next phase of your work on the paragraph. After freewriting, you should have a sense of whether there is enough material available

for you to write a process paragraph about the topic. If so, continue as explained below. If there is not enough material, choose another topic and freewrite about *it* for ten minutes.

b. Write a clear, direct topic sentence stating the process you are going to describe. For instance, if you are going to describe a way to study for major exams, your topic sentence might be "My study-skills instructor has suggested a good way to study for major exams." Or you can state in your topic sentence the process and the number of steps involved: "My technique for building a campfire involves four main steps."

c. List all the steps you can think of that may be included in the process. Don't worry, at this point, about how each step fits or whether two steps overlap. Here, for example, is the list prepared by the author of "Sneaking into the House at Night":

Quiet on stairs

Come in after Dad's asleep

House is freezing at night

Bring key

Know which steps to avoid

continued

Lift up front door

Late dances on Saturday night

Don't turn on bathroom light

Avoid squeaky spots on floor

Get into bed quietly

d. Number your items in the order in which they occur; strike out items that do not fit in the list; add others that come to mind. The author of "Sneaking into the House at Night" did this step as follows:

~~Quiet on stairs~~

2   Come in after Dad's asleep

~~House is freezing at night~~

1   Bring key

5   Know which steps to avoid

3   Lift up front door

~~Late dances on Saturday night~~

6   Don't turn on bathroom light

4   Avoid squeaky spots on floor

8   Get into bed quietly

7   Undress quietly

e. Use your list as a guide to write the first draft of your paragraph. As you write, try to think of additional details that will support your opening sentence. Do not expect to finish your composition in one draft. After you complete your first rough draft, in fact, you should be ready to write a series of drafts as you work toward the goals of unity, support, and coherence.

Revising

After you have written the first draft of your paragraph, set it aside for a while if you can. Then read it out loud, either to yourself or (better yet) to a friend or classmate who will be honest with you about how it sounds. You (or you and your friend) should keep these points in mind.

FOUR BASES Checklist for Process

About *Unity*

✓ An effective process composition describes a series of events in a way that is clear and easy to follow. Are the steps in your paragraph described in a clear, logical way?

About *Support*

✓ Does your paragraph explain every necessary step so that a reader could perform the task described?

About *Coherence*

✓ Have you used transitions such as *first, next, also, then, after, now, during,* and *finally* to make the paper move smoothly from one step to another?

About *Sentence Skills*

✓ Is the point of view consistent? For example, if you begin by writing "This is how I got rid of mice" (first person), do not switch to "You must buy the right traps" (second person). Write this paragraph either from the first-person point of view (using *I* and *we*) or from the second-person point of view (*you*)—do not jump back and forth from one to the other.

✓ Have you corrected any sentence-skills mistakes that you noticed while reading the paragraph out loud? Have you checked the composition for sentence skills, including spelling, as listed on the inside back cover of this book?

Continue revising your work until you and your reader can answer "yes" to all these questions.

Writing Assignment

2

Write a paragraph about one of the following processes. For this assignment, you will be working with more general topics than those in Writing Assignment 1. In fact, many of the topics are so broad that entire books have been written about them. A big part of your task, then, will be to narrow the topic down enough so that it can be covered in one paragraph. Then you'll have to invent your own steps for the process. In addition, you'll need to make decisions about how many steps to include and the order in which to present them.

> How to break a bad habit such as smoking, overeating, or excess drinking
>
> How to improve a course you have taken
>
> How to make someone you know happy
>
> How to be less concerned about yourself and more concerned about others
>
> How to improve the place where you work
>
> How to show appreciation to others
>
> How to make someone forgive you
>
> How to be more "green"
>
> How to make your life less hectic
>
> How to conserve energy
>
> How to fail at something (the paragraph written on this topic is intended to be funny)
>
> How to flirt

Prewriting

a. Choose a topic that appeals to you. Then ask yourself, "How can I make this broad, general topic narrow enough to be covered in a paragraph?" A logical way to proceed would be to think of a particular time you have gone through this process. For instance, if the general topic is "How to decorate economically," you might think about a time you decorated your own apartment.

b. Write a topic sentence about the process you are going to describe. Your topic sentence should clearly reflect the narrowed-down topic you have chosen. If you chose the topic described in step *a,* for example, your topic sentence could be "I made my first apartment look nice without spending a fortune."

c. Make a list of as many different items as you can think of that concern your topic. Don't worry about repeating yourself, about putting the items in order, or about whether details are major or minor, or about spelling. Simply make a list of everything about your topic that occurs to you. Here, for instance, is a list of items generated by the student writing about decorating her apartment on a budget:

Bought pretty towels and used them as wall hangings

Trimmed overgrown shrubs in front yard

Used old mayonnaise jars for vases to hold flowers picked in the
   yard

Found an old oriental rug at a yard sale

Painted mismatched kitchen chairs in bright colors

Kept dishes washed and put away

Bought a slipcover for a battered couch

Used pink lightbulbs

Hung pretty colored sheets over the windows

d. Next, decide what order you will present your items in and number them. (As in the example of "decorating an apartment," there may not be an order that the steps *must* be done in. If that is the case, you'll need to make a decision about a sequence that makes sense, or that you followed yourself.) As you number your items, strike out items that do not fit in the list and add others that you think of, like this:

6 Bought pretty towels and used them as wall hangings

~~Trimmed overgrown shrubs in front yard~~

7 Used old mayonnaise jars for vases to hold flowers picked in the
   yard

4 Found an old oriental rug at a yard sale

continued

2 Painted mismatched kitchen chairs in bright colors

~~Kept dishes washed and put away~~

1 Bought a slipcover for a battered couch

8 Used pink lightbulbs

5 Hung pretty colored sheets over the windows

3 Built bookshelves out of cinder blocks and boards

e. Referring to your list of steps, write the first draft of your paper. Add additional steps as they occur to you.

Revising

If you can, put your first draft away for a day or so and then return to it. Read it out loud to yourself or, better yet, to a friend who will give you honest feedback.

Here are questions to ask yourself as you read over your first draft and the drafts to follow.

FOUR BASES Checklist for Process

About *Unity*

☑ Have I included a clear topic sentence that tells what process I will be describing?

☑ Is the rest of my paragraph on target in support of my topic sentence?

About *Support*

☑ Have I included all the essential information so that anyone reading my paper could follow the same process?

About *Coherence*

☑ Have I made the sequence of steps easy to follow by using transitions like *first, second, then, next, during,* and *finally*?

continued

About *Sentence Skills*

   ☑ Have I used a consistent point of view throughout my paragraph?

   ☑ Have I used specific rather than general words?

   ☑ Have I used concise wording?

   ☑ Are my sentences varied?

   ☑ Have I checked for spelling and other sentence skills, as listed on the inside back cover of the book?

Continue revising your work until you can answer "yes" to all these questions.

Writing Assignment

3 Reading regularly can improve a person's life. What steps can somebody take to make him- or herself a better reader? Alternatively, what can a person do to encourage a child to read? Write a paragraph that discusses a series of steps by which an adult might become a more avid reader or by which a child might be encouraged to read more.

Writing Assignment

4 Write a paragraph for a younger brother, sister, or other relative on how to succeed at a job interview. You can find information on the Internet, so do some research on the topic first. Read at least three different Web sites for information. Your reading will help you think about how to proceed. Remember, however, that any information you take from another source, such as a Web site, must be expressed completely in your own words.

Condense the information you find into four or five basic steps. Choose the steps that seem most important to you and that are repeated most often or that are stressed in the various Web sites you researched. Remember that you can use only the *information* found in these sources, not the *actual words*. Once again, make sure to rephrase that information into your own words. Otherwise you may commit plagiarism. See pages 393–394 for important information about plagiarism.

Writing | Assignment

Writing for a Specific Purpose and Audience

5

In this process paragraph, you will write with a specific purpose and for a specific audience. You have two options.

Option 1

Imagine that you have a part-time job helping out in a day care center. The director, who is pleased with your work and wants to give you more responsibility, has put you in charge of a group activity (for example, an exercise session, an alphabet lesson, or a valentine-making project). But before you actually begin the activity, the director wants to see a summary of how you would go about it. What advance preparation would be needed, and what exactly would you be doing throughout the time of the project? Write a paragraph explaining the steps you would follow in conducting the activity.

Option 2

Pretend you have been asked to write a letter or e-mail message to members of your college's next incoming class. Explain one thing that these future college students can do to improve their chances of succeeding. For example, explain how to take notes, how to study for an exam, or how to make use of the college's tutoring services.

10

Cause and Effect

This chapter will explain and illustrate how to

- develop a cause-and-effect paragraph
- write a cause-and-effect paragraph
- revise a cause-and-effect paragraph

In addition, you will read and consider

- three student cause-and-effect paragraphs

Write a paragraph in which you explain the effects of a massive natural disaster, like the one pictured here, on your town or city. Think about how such an event might affect public and private transportation, schools and colleges, businesses and industries. How might it affect you personally?

What caused Will to drop out of school? Why are reality TV shows so popular? Why does our football team do so poorly each year? How has retirement affected Mom? What effects does divorce have on children? Every day we ask such questions and look for answers. We realize that situations have causes and also effects—good or bad. By examining causes and effects, we seek to understand and explain things.

In this section, you will be asked to do some detective work by examining the causes or the effects of something. First read the three paragraphs that follow and answer the questions about them. All three paragraphs support their opening points by explaining a series of causes or a series of effects.

www.mhhe.com/langan

Paragraphs to Consider

The Benefits of Exercise

[1]The effects of regular exercise can change a person's life. [2]First, walking or running three miles a day can burn about 250 calories. [3]That adds up to a weight loss of about half a pound a week even without dieting! [4]Over a year, about twenty-six pounds can be shed. [5]Second, exercise helps the heart and circulatory system, thereby increasing the flow of oxygen and, in the long run, lessening the chances of contracting heart disease. [6]Perhaps most significantly, however, exercise releases endorphins, compounds produced by glands in the body, which help fight depression and improve one's emotional health!

Senior Savers

[1]Many college students are amazed over how frugal their grandparents are, never wasting food, cutting grocery coupons out of the newspaper, and using tools and appliances until they literally fall apart. [2]There are several reasons that so many seniors are frugal. [3]The first is that many of them grew up during or just after the Great Depression. [4]They were taught by their parents, many of whom experienced the sting of being unemployed for lengthy periods, that every penny counted. [5]The Depression ended during the early 1940s, when the United States entered World War II. [6]Second, many seniors today are on fixed incomes. [7]Because of inflation, they fear that they will not have enough money to support themselves for the rest of their lives. [8]Those who have investments in stocks, bonds,

continued

and real estate have seen their net worth decrease greatly during economic downturns. [9]Third, many of these people are afraid that they won't be able to afford medical insurance in the future unless they keep enough money in reserve now. [10]Medical insurance costs are a concern even for young people. [11]Fourth and most important, seniors are very generous people, who want to leave as much as they can to their grandchildren—people like you—when they leave this world!

Why I Stopped Smoking

[1]For one thing, I realized that my cigarette smoke bothered others, irritating people's eyes and causing them to cough and sneeze. [2]They also had to put up with my stinking smoker's breath. [3]Also, cigarettes are a messy habit. [4]Our house was littered with ashtrays piled high with butts, matchsticks, and ashes, and the children were always knocking them over. [5]Cigarettes are expensive, and I estimated that the carton a week that I was smoking cost me about $2,000 a year. [6]Another reason I stopped was that the message about cigarettes being harmful to health finally got through to me. [7]I'd known they could hurt the smoker—in fact, a heavy smoker I know from work is in Eagleville Hospital now with lung cancer. [8]But when I realized what secondhand smoke could do to my wife and children, causing them bronchial problems and even increasing their risk of cancer, it really bothered me. [9]Cigarettes were also inconvenient. [10]Whenever I smoked, I would have to drink something to wet my dry throat, and that meant I had to keep going to the bathroom all the time. [11]I sometimes seemed to spend whole weekends doing nothing but smoking, drinking, and going to the bathroom. [12]Most of all, I resolved to stop smoking because I felt exploited. [13]I hated the thought of wealthy, greedy corporations making money off my sweat and blood. [14]The rich may keep getting richer, but—at least as regards cigarettes—with no thanks to me.

Questions

About Unity

1. What two sentences in "Senior Savers" do not support the opening idea and should be omitted?

   _____   _____

2. Which of the above paragraphs lacks a topic sentence?

   _____

About Support

3. How many separate causes are given in "Why I Stopped Smoking"?

    _____ four   _____ six   _____ seven   _____ eight

4. How many effects of regular exercise are discussed in "The Benefits of Exercise"?

    _____ one   _____ two   _____ three   _____ four

About Coherence

5. What transition words or phrases are used to introduce the four reasons listed in "Senior Savers"?

    _____   _____   _____   _____

6. In "The Benefits of Exercise," what words signal the effect the author thinks is most important?

    _____

Developing a Cause-and-Effect Paragraph

Development through Prewriting

In order to write a good cause-and-effect paragraph, you must clearly define an effect (*what* happened) and the contributing causes (*why* it happened). In addition, you will need to provide details that support the causes and effects you're writing about.

Jerome is the student author of "Why I Stopped Smoking." As soon as the topic occurred to him, he knew he had his *effect* (he had stopped smoking). His next task was to come up with a list of *causes* (reasons he had stopped). He decided to make a list of all the reasons for his quitting smoking that he could think of. This is what he came up with:

Annoyed others
Messy
Bad for health
Expensive

Taking his list, Jerome then jotted down details that supported each of those reasons:

Annoyed others
Bad breath
Irritates eyes
Makes other people cough
People hate the smell

Messy
Ashtrays, ashes, butts everywhere
Messes up my car interior

Bad for health
Marco in hospital with lung cancer
Secondhand smoke dangerous to family
My morning cough

Expensive
Carton a week costs more than $2,000 a year
Tobacco companies getting rich off me

Jerome then had an effect and four causes with details to support them. On the basis of this list, he wrote a first draft.

My smoking annoyed other people, making them cough and burning their eyes. I bothered them with my smoker's breath. Nonsmokers usually hate the smell of cigarettes and I got embarrassed when nonsmokers visited my house. I saw them wrinkle their noses in disgust at the smell. It is a messy habit. My house was full of loaded ashtrays that the kids were always knocking over.

continued

My car was messy too. A guy from work, Marco, who has smoked for years, is in the hospital now with lung cancer. It doesn't look as though he's going to make it. Secondhand smoke is bad for people too and I worried it would hurt my wife and kids. Also I realized I was coughing once in a while. The price of cigarettes keeps going up and I was spending too much on smokes. When I see things in the paper about tobacco companies and their huge profits it made me mad.

Development through Revising

The next day, Jerome traded first drafts with his classmate Roger. This is what Roger had to say about Jerome's work.

The biggest criticism I have is that you haven't used many transitions to tie your sentences together. Without them, the paragraph sounds like a list, not a unified piece of writing.

Is one of your reasons more important than the others? If so, it would be good if you indicated that.

You could add a little more detail in several places. For instance, how could secondhand smoke hurt your family? And how much were you spending on cigarettes?

As Jerome read his own paper, he realized he wanted to add one more reason to his paragraph: the inconvenience to himself. "Maybe it sounds silly to write about always getting drinks and going to the bathroom, but that's one of the ways that smoking takes over your life that you never think about when you start," he said. Using Roger's comments and his own new idea, he produced the paragraph that appears on page 214.

Writing a Cause-and-Effect Paragraph

1 Choose one of the three topic sentences and brief outlines below. Each is made up of three supporting points (causes or effects). Your task is to turn the topic sentence and outline into a cause or effect paragraph.

Option 1

Topic sentence: There are several reasons why some high school graduates are unable to read.

(1) Failure of parents (*cause*)
(2) Failure of schools (*cause*)
(3) Failure of students themselves (*cause*)

Option 2

Topic sentence: Living with roommates (or family) makes attending college difficult.

(1) Late-night hours (*cause*)
(2) More temptations to cut class (*cause*)
(3) More distractions from studying (*cause*)

Option 3

Topic sentence: Attending college has changed my personality in positive ways.

(1) More confident (*effect*)
(2) More knowledgeable (*effect*)
(3) More adventurous (*effect*)

Prewriting

a. After you've chosen the option that appeals to you most, jot down all the details you can think of that might go under each of the supporting points. Use a separate piece of paper for your lists. Don't worry yet about whether you can use all the items—your goal is to generate more material than you need. Here, for example, are some of the details generated by the author of "The Benefits of Exercise" to back up her supporting points:

Topic sentence: The effects of regular exercise can change a person's life.

1. *Helps lose weight*

   a. *Running/walking three miles can burn about 250 calories*

   b. *This adds up to half a pound a week*

   c. *Can lose about twenty-six pounds a year*

   d. *Swimming or lifting weights for an hour equally effective*

2. *Helps circulatory system, lungs*

   a. *Lowers heart rate*

   b. *Increases oxygen flow*

   c. *Lessens chances of developing heart disease*

   d. *Increases lung capacity*

3. *Helps improve emotional health*

   a. *Makes for better sleep*

   b. *Relieves tension*

   c. *Releases endorphins, which help fight depression*

   d. *Improves emotional outlook*

   b. Now go through the details you have generated and decide which are most effective. Strike out the ones you decide are not worth using. Do other details occur to you? If so, jot them down as well.

   c. Now you are ready to write your paragraph. Begin the paragraph with the topic sentence you chose. Make sure to develop each of the supporting points from the outline into a complete sentence, and then back it up with the best of the details you have generated.

Revising

Review your paragraph with these questions in mind.

FOUR BASES Checklist for Cause and Effect

About *Unity*

  ☑ Have I begun the paragraph with the topic sentence provided?

  ☑ Are any sentences in my paragraph not directly relevant to this topic sentence?

About *Support*

  ☑ Is each supporting point stated in a complete sentence?

  ☑ Have I provided effective details to back up each supporting point?

About *Coherence*

  ☑ Have I used transitions such as *in addition, another thing,* and *also* to make relationships between the sentences clear?

About *Sentence Skills*

  ☑ Have I avoided wordiness?

  ☑ Have I proofread the paragraph for sentence-skills errors, including spelling, as listed on the inside back cover of the book?

Revise your paragraph until you are sure the answer to each question is "yes."

Writing Assignment

2

Most of us find it easy to criticize other people, but we may find it harder to give compliments. In this assignment, you will be asked to write a one-paragraph letter praising someone. The letter may be to a person you know (for instance, a parent, relative, or friend); to a public figure (an actor, politician, religious leader, sports star, and so on); or to a company or an organization (for example, a newspaper, a government agency, a store where you shop, or the manufacturer of a product you own).

Prewriting

a. The fact that you are writing this letter indicates that its recipient has had an *effect* on you: You like, admire, or appreciate the person or organization. Your job will be to put into words the *causes,* or reasons, for this good feeling. Begin by making a list of reasons for your admiration. Here, for example, are a few reasons a person might praise an automobile manufacturer:

> My car is dependable.
>
> The price was reasonable.
>
> I received prompt action on a complaint.
>
> The car is well-designed.
>
> The car dealer was honest and friendly.
>
> The car has needed little maintenance.

Reasons for admiring a parent might include these:

> You are patient with me.
>
> You are fair.
>
> You have a great sense of humor.
>
> You encourage me in several ways.
>
> I know you have made sacrifices for me.

Develop your own list of reasons for admiring the person or organization you've chosen.

b. Now that you have a list of reasons, you need details to back up each reason. Jot down as many supporting details as you can for each reason. Here is what the writer of a letter to the car manufacturer might do:

My car is dependable.

Started during last winter's coldest days when neighbors' cars wouldn't start

Has never stranded me anywhere

The price was reasonable.

Costs less than other cars in its class

Came standard with more options than other cars of the same price

I received prompt action on a complaint.

When I complained about rattle in door, manufacturer arranged for a part to be replaced at no charge

The car is well-designed.

Controls are easy to reach

Dashboard gauges are easy to read

The car dealer was honest and friendly.

No pressure, no fake "special deal only today"

The car has needed little maintenance.

Haven't done anything but regular tune-ups and oil changes

---

c. Next, select from your list the three or four reasons that you can best support with effective details. These will make up the body of your letter.

d. For your topic sentence, make the positive statement you wish to support. For example, the writer of the letter to the car manufacturer might begin like this: "I am a very satisfied owner of a 2010 Accord."

e. Now combine your topic sentence, reasons, and supporting details, and write a draft of your letter.

Revising

If possible, put your letter aside for a day. Then read it aloud to a friend. As you and he or she listen to your words, you should both keep these questions in mind.

FOUR BASES Checklist for Cause and Effect

About *Unity*

☑ Is the topic sentence a positive statement that is supported by the details?

☑ Is the rest of my letter on target in support of my topic sentence?

About *Support*

☑ Does the letter clearly state several different reasons for liking and admiring the person or organization?

☑ Is each of those reasons supported with specific evidence?

About *Coherence*

☑ Are the sentences linked with transitional words and phrases?

About *Sentence Skills*

☑ Have I avoided wordiness?

☑ Are my sentences varied?

☑ Have I checked for spelling and other sentence skills, as listed on the inside back cover of the book?

Continue revising your work until you and your reader can answer "yes" to all these questions.

Writing Assignment

3 Look at the poster pictured here. What does it seem to suggest? How do the woman's expression and clenched fists help you better understand the meaning of the poster?

Write a paragraph about a particular addiction. You might write about someone you know who is addicted to smoking, drinking, shopping, playing video games, or surfing the Internet. In your paragraph, discuss several possible reasons for this addiction, or several effects on the person's life.

Here are some sample topic sentences for such a paragraph:

My cousin is addicted to overeating, and her addiction is harming her in a number of ways.

There were at least three reasons why I became addicted to cigarettes.

Although shopping can be a pleasant activity, addictive shopping can be destructive for several reasons.

Writing Assignment

4 Discover the reasons behind an event making news in your town or state, on your campus, or in the nation or world. For example, you might want to focus on the causes of

A change in parking regulations or fees

A tax increase

An increase in tuition

The election of a particular politician

The announcement that a particular business is hiring or laying off workers

An increase or decrease in the number of police patrols

The opening or closing of a firehouse

The construction or closing of a public school

Research the causes behind this development in current print and online newspapers or newsmagazines or on radio and television news shows. Decide on the major cause or causes of this development and their specific effects. Below is a sample topic sentence for this assignment.

> The fifth accident in two months caused by drag racing along Oak Boulevard has created serious concern among residents, who are demanding that police patrol that road more frequently.

Notice that the sentence contains general words such as *concern, demanding,* and *frequently,* which can summarize specific supporting details. Support for *frequently,* for example, might include details about how often the police now patrol and how often people would like them to do so.

Writing Assignment

Writing for a Specific Purpose and Audience

5

In this paragraph, you will write with a specific purpose and for a specific audience. Choose one of the following options.

Option 1

Assume that most of the students who graduated from your high school gave the school a positive (or negative) rating when they completed a school evaluation during the week before graduation. What could be the causes for their responses?

Recall your own high school experience, and freewrite about possible causes for why you might have given your school either a positive or a negative evaluation if you had had the chance to do so. Then write a letter to the principal of the school in which you explain the reasons you believe it deserves the rating you would have given it.

Option 2

Your roommate has been complaining that it's impossible to succeed in Mr. X's class because the class is too stressful. You volunteer to attend the class and see for yourself. Afterward, you decide to write a letter to the instructor calling attention to the stressful conditions and suggesting concrete ways to deal with them. Write this letter, explaining in detail the causes and effects of stress in the class.

11 Comparison or Contrast

This chapter will explain and illustrate how to

- develop a comparison or contrast paragraph
- write a comparison or contrast paragraph
- revise a comparison or contrast paragraph

In addition, you will read and consider

- three student comparison or contrast paragraphs
- two common methods of development in a comparison or contrast paragraph

Look at the this photograph and write a paragraph in which you compare or contrast attending a sporting event in person or viewing one on television. Be sure to note how spectators in the photo are acting. Use one or more examples from this photo to support your point.

Comparison and contrast are two everyday thought processes. When we *compare* two things, we show how they are similar; when we *contrast* two things, we show how they are different. We might compare or contrast two brand-name products (for example, Nike versus New Balance running shoes), two television shows, two instructors, two jobs, two friends, or two courses of action we could take in a given situation. The purpose of comparing or contrasting is to understand both of the two things more clearly and, at times, to make judgments about them.

There are two common methods of developing a comparison or contrast paragraph. Read the two paragraphs that follow and try to explain the difference in the two methods of development.

Paragraphs to Consider

> ### Landenburg: Then and Now
>
> [1]Landenburg has changed for the better over the last ten years. [2]Twenty years ago, the town experienced an economic downturn. [3]The electrical supply factory, which employed more than five hundred people, had just closed down. [4]The hundred-year-old high school needed repair: Its roof leaked, the masonry was cracked, the heating system was undependable, and its outside walls were covered with graffiti. [5]The science labs contained only outdated or broken equipment. [6]Students were using books that were very old, and pages were missing in some of them. [7]Barker Avenue, the town's main shopping area, contained several boarded-up storefronts, and most of the other stores advertised going-out-of-business sales. [8]There were always plenty of parking spaces because fewer and fewer customers shopped there. [9]It was as if an economic disease had attacked the heart of Landenburg. [10]About ten years ago, however, things changed. [11]The local economy got better. [12]A manufacturer of automobile brake pads relocated in Landenburg, building a huge factory just outside of town. [13]Then a restaurant supply factory moved in, and last year the state university broke ground for an extension campus two miles away. [14]As a result, many new jobs have been created, and with increased tax revenues, the town was able to replace the old high school with one that has modern laboratories and offers students brand-new books. [15]The new jobs have also boosted consumer confidence. [16]The downtown shopping area has several new stores and restaurants. [17]A ten-screen movie complex just opened, and not one of the town's commercial buildings is for rent. [18]And because of the increased activity, downtown parking spaces are sometimes impossible to find. [19]The entire town seems to have gotten a lot healthier.

Day versus Evening Students

[1]As a part-time college student who has taken both day and evening courses, I have observed notable differences between day and evening students. [2]First of all, day and evening students differ greatly in age, styles, and interests. [3]The students in my daytime classes are all about the same age, with similar clothing styles and similar interests. [4]Most are in their late teens to early twenties, and whether male or female, they pretty much dress alike. [5]Their uniform consists of jeans, a T-shirt, running shoes, a baseball cap, and maybe a gold earring or two. [6]They use the same popular slang, talk about the same movies and TV shows, and know the same musical artists. [7]But students in my evening courses are much more diverse. [8]Some are in their late teens, but most range from young married people in their twenties and thirties to people my grandparents' age. [9]Generally, their clothing is more formal than the day students'. [10]They are dressed for the workplace, not for a typical college classroom. [11]Many of the women wear skirts or dresses; the men often wear dress shirts or sweaters. [12]And they are more comfortable talking about mortgages or work schedules or child care than about what was on TV last night. [13]Day and evening students also have very different responsibilities. [14]For day students, college and a part-time job are generally the only major responsibilities. [15]They have plenty of time to study and get assignments done. [16]However, evening students lead much more complicated lives than most day students. [17]They may come to campus after putting in a nine-to-five day at work. [18]Most have children to raise or grandchildren to baby-sit for. [19]When they miss a class or hand in an assignment late, it's usually because of a real problem, such as a sick child or an important deadline at work. [20]Finally, day and evening students definitely have different attitudes toward school. [21]Day students often seem more interested in the view out the window or the cute classmate in the next row than in what the instructor is saying. [22]They doze, draw cartoons, whisper, and write notes instead of paying attention. [23]In contrast, evening students sit up straight, listen hard, and ask the instructor lots of questions. [24]They obviously are there to learn, and they don't want their time wasted. [25]In short, day students and night students are as different as . . . day and night.

The student writer of "Day versus Evening Students" uses the different appearances of day and evening students to support his or her argument. Looking at the woman pictured here, would you say she is a day or an evening student, or not a student at all? What generalizations do we often make about people based on their appearance? Are these generalizations fair? Write a paragraph in which you explore this topic.

Complete this comment: The difference in the methods of contrast in the two paragraphs is that

_____

_____

_____

Compare your answer with the following explanation of the two methods of development used in comparison or contrast paragraphs.

Methods of Development

There are two common methods, or formats, of development in a comparison or contrast paper. One format presents the details *one side at a time*. The other presents the details *point by point*. Each format is explained below.

One Side at a Time

Look at the outline of "Landenburg: Then and Now":

Topic sentence: Landenburg has changed for the better over the last ten years.

A. Landenburg 20 years ago (first half of paragraph)

   1. Economic downturn

   2. Electrical supply factory closes

   3. More than 500 jobs lost

   4. High school in disrepair, poorly equipped

   5. Many downtown shops closed or closing

B. Landenburg today (second half of paragraph)

   1. Things change; local economy better

   2. New companies more in; state university building extension campus

   3. New jobs created

   4. New high school built—modern labs, new books

   5. Revival of downtown shopping district

When you use the one-side-at-a-time method, follow the same order of points of contrast or comparison for each side, as in the outline above. For example, both the first half of the paper and the second half begin with the same idea: the state of the economy. Then both sides go on to companies, jobs, the high school, and so on.

Point by Point

Now look at the outline of "Day versus Evening Students":

Topic sentence: There are notable differences between day and night students.

A. Age and related interests and tastes in clothing
   1. Youthful nature of day students
   2. Older nature of evening students
B. Amount of responsibilities
   1. Lighter responsibilities of day students
   2. Heavier responsibilities of evening students
C. Attitude toward school
   1. Casual attitude of day students
   2. Serious attitude of evening students

The outline shows how the two kinds of students are contrasted point by point. First, the writer contrasts the ages, clothing styles, and interests of daytime students and evening students. Next, the writer contrasts the limited responsibilities of the daytime students with the heavier responsibilities of the evening students. Finally, the writer contrasts the casual attitude toward school of the daytime students and the serious attitude of the evening students.

When you begin a comparison or contrast paper, you should decide right away which format you are going to use: one side at a time or point by point. An outline is an essential step in helping you decide which format will be more workable for your topic. Keep in mind, however, that an outline is just a guide, not a permanent commitment. If you later feel that you've chosen the wrong format, you can reshape your outline to the other format.

Complete the partial outlines provided for the two paragraphs that follow.

---

1.   **The United States Congress: Two Branches**

      The United States Congress, the federal government's law-making branch, is made up of two different bodies: the Senate and the House of Representatives. The Senate consists of one hundred members, two from each state. Until 1913, senators were elected by state legislatures, but the Seventeenth Amendment to the Constitution, approved in that year, now requires the direct election of senators by each state's citizens. Senators serve six-year terms, and about one-third of the members are eligible for reelection every two years. The presiding officer of the Senate is the vice president of the United States. The House of Representatives has 435 members representing congressional districts across the United States. The boundaries of a congressional district are determined, theoretically at least, by the number of people residing in the district. Therefore, while New Jersey has eleven congressional districts, Wyoming, with a much smaller population, has only one. Members of the House serve for two-year terms, at the end of which all members must be reelected if they wish to continue. The presiding officer of this body is the Speaker of the House, who is elected by members of the majority party. Whenever the two branches pass different versions of a bill, a committee consisting of both representatives and senators meets to resolve the differences.

Topic sentence: The United States Congress, the federal government's law-making branch, is made up of two different bodies: the Senate and the House of Representatives.

    a. The Senate
        (1) Consists of 100 members
        (2) Before 1913 was elected by state legislature; today is elected by citizens
        (3) Senators serve six-year terms, one-third up for reelection every two years
        (4) VP is presiding officer

    b. House of Representatives
        (1) Consists of 435 members; each congressional district contains about same number of people
        (2) Members directly elected by citizens of district
        (3) Members serve two-year terms, then must be reelected to continue
        (4) Speaker of the House is presiding officer—elected by members of House's majority party.

    c. Joint committee of House and Senate resolves differences in bills

Complete the following statement: Paragraph 1 uses the _____ method of development.

---

2.   **Good and Bad Horror Movies**

A good horror movie is easily distinguishable from a bad one. A good horror movie, first of all, has both male and female victims. Both sexes suffer terrible fates at the hands of monsters and maniacs. Therefore, everyone in the audience has a chance to identify with the victim. Bad horror movies, on the other hand, tend to concentrate on women, especially half-dressed ones. These movies are obviously prejudiced against half the human race. Second, a good horror movie inspires compassion for its characters. For example, the audience will feel sympathy for the victims in the horror classics about the Wolfman, played by Lon Chaney Jr., and also for the Wolfman himself, who is shown to be a sad victim of fate. In contrast, a bad horror movie encourages feelings of aggression and violence in viewers. For instance, in the *Halloween* films, the murders are seen from the murderer's point of view. The effect is that the audience stalks the victims along with the killer and feels the same thrill he does. Finally, every good horror movie has a sense of humor. In *Alien*, as a crew member is coughing and choking just before the horrible thing bursts out of his chest, a colleague chides him, "The food ain't *that* bad, man." Humor provides relief from the horror and makes the characters more human. A bad horror movie, though, is humorless and boring. One murder is piled on top of another, and the characters are just cardboard figures. Bad horror movies may provide cheap thrills, but the good ones touch our emotions and live forever.

Topic sentence: A good horror movie is easily distinguished from a bad one.

   a. Kinds of victims

      (1) _____

      (2) _____

   b. Effect on audience

      (1) _____

      (2) _____

c. Tone

(1) _____

(2) _____

Complete the following statement: Paragraph 2 uses the _____ method of development.

Additional Paragraphs to Consider

Read these additional paragraphs of comparison or contrast, and then answer the questions that follow.

My Broken Dream

[1]When I became a police officer in my town, the job was not as I had dreamed it would be. [2]I began to dream about being a police officer at about age ten. [3]I could picture myself wearing a handsome blue uniform with an impressive-looking badge on my chest. [4]I could also picture myself driving a powerful patrol car through town and seeing everyone stare at me with envy. [5]But most of all, I dreamed of wearing a gun and using all the equipment that "TV cops" use. [6]I knew everyone would be proud of me. [7]I could almost hear the guys on the block saying, "Boy, Steve made it big. [8]Did you hear he's a cop?" [9]I dreamed of leading an exciting life, solving big crimes, and meeting lots of people. [10]I knew that if I became a cop, everyone in town would look up to me. [11]However, when I actually did become a police officer, I soon found out that the reality was different. [12]My first disappointment came when I was sworn in and handed a well-used, baggy uniform. [13]My disappointment continued when I was given a badge that looked like something pulled out of a cereal box. [14]I was assigned a beat-up old junker and told that it would be my patrol car. [15]It had a striking resemblance to a car that had lost in a demolition derby at a stock-car raceway. [16]Disappointment seemed to continue. [17]I soon found out that I was not the envy of all my friends. [18]When I drove through town, they acted as if they had not seen me, despite the gun and nightstick at my side. [19]I was told I was crazy doing this kind of job by people I thought would look up to me. [20]My job was not as exciting as I had dreamed it would be, either. [21]Instead of solving robberies and murders every day, I found that I spent a great deal of time comforting a local resident because a neighborhood dog had watered his favorite bush.

Two Views on Toys

[1]Children and adults have very different preferences. [2]First, there is the matter of taste. [3]Adults pride themselves on taste, while children ignore the matter of taste in favor of things that are fun. [4]Adults, especially grandparents, pick out tasteful toys that go unused, while children love the cheap playthings advertised on television. [5]Second, of course, there is the matter of money. [6]The new games on the market today are a case in point. [7]Have you ever tried to lure a child away from some expensive game in order to get him or her to play with an old-fashioned game or toy? [8]Finally, there is a difference between an adult's and a child's idea of what is educational. [9]Adults, filled with memories of their own childhood, tend to be fond of the written word. [10]Today's children, on the other hand, concentrate on anything electronic. [11]These things mean much more to them than to adults. [12]Next holiday season, examine the toys that adults choose for children. [13]Then look at the toys the children prefer. [14]You will see the difference.

Ice Hockey and Soccer

[1]Like ice hockey, soccer is a game whose aim is scoring goals against the opposing team. [2]Both are team sports in which the most important position is that of goaltender or goalie. [3]This is the player who defends the team's goal or net. [4]Unlike ice hockey, which is played on an indoor ice rink or a frozen pond or lake, soccer is played outside on a grassy field. [5]In an ice hockey match, only six players from each team can be on the ice at one time. [6]Ice hockey players wear a lot of protective equipment such as helmets, shin guards, and padded gloves. In a soccer match, each team fields eleven players. [7]Both sports require a great deal of energy. [8]Ice hockey players seem to be constantly in motion, and soccer players race up and down the field almost nonstop. [9]However, they wear little protective gear. [10]Their uniforms consist of soccer shoes, socks, shorts, and jerseys.

About Unity

1. Which paragraph lacks a topic sentence?

   _____

2. Which paragraph has a topic sentence that is too broad?

   _____

About Support

3. Which paragraph contains almost no specific details?

   _____

4. Which paragraph provides the most complete support?

   _____

About Coherence

5. What method of development (one side at a time or point by point) is used in "My Broken Dream"?

   _____

   In "Two Views in Toys"?

   _____

6. Which paragraph offers specific details but lacks a clear, consistent method of development?

   _____

Developing a Comparison or Contrast Paragraph

Development through Prewriting

Molly, the author of "Landenburg: Then and Now," had little trouble thinking of a topic for her comparison or contrast paper.

"My instructor said, 'You might compare or contrast two individuals, two places, two situations, or the same place at different times.' I immediately thought about the town in which I was born—the difference that ten years has made is amazing."

Because she is a person who likes to think visually, Molly started preparing for her paragraph by clustering. She found this a helpful way to "see" the differences between her hometown as it is now and as it was.

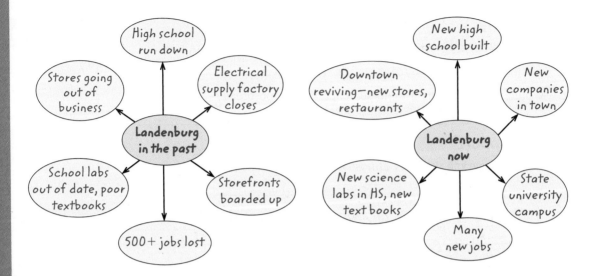

Taking a detail first from the "Landenburg in the past" part of the diagram, then one from the "Landenburg now" part, then another from the "Landenburg in the past" section, and so on, Molly began to write her paragraph using the point-by-point method:

Landenburg has changed for the better over the last 10 years. Twenty years ago, the town experienced an economic downturn. The electrical supply factory closed down about 10 years ago. However, things changed when a maker of automobile brake pads built a factory just outside of town. When the electrical supply factory closed, more than 500 people lost their jobs. The new company brought back many of those jobs. In addition, there's another new factory that manufactures restaurant equipment, and it employs about 150 additional people. Last year, the state university broke ground for a new extension campus. When the economy was bad, there was little money to spend on education, and the old high school was in disrepair. The science labs were outdated, and the textbooks were old and falling apart.

Molly stopped here because she wasn't satisfied with the way the paragraph was developing. "I wanted the reader to picture the way Landenburg had been years ago without interrupting that picture with a description of what it's like today. So I decided to try the one-side-at-a time approach, instead." Here is Molly's next draft:

Landenburg: Then and Now

Landenburg has changed for the better over the last ten years. Twenty years ago, the town experienced an economic downturn. The electrical supply factory had just closed down. The old high school needed repair. I remember my grandmother telling me that she had graduated from Landenburg High School and that she had met my grandfather there in an algebra class. The high school's outside walls were covered with graffiti. Students used books that were very old. Barker Avenue, the town's main shopping area, looked like a ghost town. It was as if an economic disease had attacked Landenburg. About ten years ago, however, things changed. A manufacturer of automobile brake pads decided to relocate in Landenburg, and it built a huge factory just outside of town. I worked there one summer and made enough to pay for half of my college tuition that year. It was hard, dirty work, and there was no air conditioning. So on really hot days, I was miserable. As a result of this new factory, however, many new jobs have replaced those lost when the electrical supply factory closed, and with increased tax revenues, the town was able to replace the old high school. The entire town seems to have gotten a lot healthier. The new jobs have also boosted consumer confidence. The downtown shopping area is busier than ever. A ten-screen movie complex just opened. A restaurant supply factory decided to move in, and last year the state university broke ground for an extension campus two miles away. These events have also helped build confidence.

Development through Revising

Molly's instructor reviewed her first draft. Here are his comments:

> All of this is very interesting, but some of your details are out of order—for example, you mention the opening of the restaurant-equipment plant and the work on the state university's extension campus after discussing the creation of new jobs and the boost in consumer confidence. Shouldn't the order be reversed? After all, the new plant and the new college campus are among the reasons that the local economy is getting better.
>
> More descriptive details are needed! For instance, you say that the downtown area once "looked like a ghost town." Exactly what does a ghost town look like? Describe what you saw there. Also, what do you mean by "the old high school needed repair"? How old was it, and what kind of repairs did it need?
>
> You include some unnecessary information; for example, the details about your grandmother and grandfather meeting in a high school algebra class and those that have to do with your work at the brake-pad factory. Everything in your paragraph should support your topic sentence.

Following her instructor's suggestions (and remembering a few more details she wanted to include), Molly wrote the version of her paragraph that appears on page 227.

Writing a Comparison or Contrast Paragraph

Writing Assignment

1

Write a comparison or contrast paragraph on one of the topics below:

Two holidays
A holiday celebrated in different
   ways by different cultures
Two instructors
Two types of diets
Two coworkers
Two members of a team
   (or two teams)
Two times in your life
Two singers or groups
Two drivers
Two dogs, cats, or other pets
Two ways to solve a problem

Two characters in the same movie
   or TV show
Two homes
Two neighborhoods
Teachers in two high schools
   or colleges
Two members of a family
Two cartoon strips
Two cars
Two bosses or supervisors
Two jobs you have held
Two types of computers
Two magazines

Prewriting

a. Choose your topic, the two subjects you will write about.

b. Decide whether your paragraph will *compare* the two subjects (discuss their similarities) or *contrast* them (discuss their differences). Students most often choose to write about differences. For example, you might write about how a musical group you enjoy differs from a musical group you dislike. You might discuss important differences between two employers you have had or between two neighborhoods you've lived in. You might contrast a job you've had in a car factory with a job you've had as a receptionist.

c. Write a direct topic sentence for your paragraph. Here's an example: "My job in a car-parts factory was very different from my job as a receptionist."

d. Come up with at least three strong points to support your topic sentence. If you are contrasting two jobs, for example, your points might be that they differed greatly (1) in their physical setting, (2) in the skills they required, and (3) in the people they brought you into contact with.

e. Use your topic sentence and supporting points to create a scratch outline for your paragraph. For the paragraph about jobs, the outline would look like this:

> _Topic sentence:_ My job in a car-parts factory was very different from my job as a receptionist.
> 1. The jobs differed in physical setting.
> 2. The jobs differed in the skills they required.
> 3. The jobs differed in the people they brought me into contact with.

f. Under each of your supporting points, jot down as many details as occur to you. Don't worry yet about whether the details all fit perfectly or whether you will be able to use them all. Your goal is to generate a wealth of material to draw on. An example:

> _Topic sentence:_ My job in a car-parts factory was very different from my job as a receptionist.
> 1. _The jobs differed in physical setting._
>   Factory loud and dirty
>   Office clean and quiet
>   Factory full of machines, hunks of metal, tools
>   Office full of desks, files, computers
>   Factory smelled of motor oil
>   Office smelled of new carpet

continued

> Windows in factory too high and grimy to look out of
>
> Office had clean windows onto street
>
> 2. The jobs differed in the skills and behavior they required.
>
> Factory required physical strength
>
> Office required mental activity
>
> Didn't need to be polite in factory
>
> Had to be polite in office
>
> Didn't need to think much for self in factory
>
> Constantly had to make decisions in office
>
> 3. The jobs differed in the people they brought me into contact with.
>
> In factory, worked with same crew every day
>
> In office, saw constant stream of new customers
>
> Most coworkers in factory had high-school education or less
>
> Many coworkers and clients in office well educated
>
> Coworkers in factory spoke variety of languages
>
> Rarely heard anything but English in office

g. Decide which format you will use to develop your paragraph: one side at a time or point by point. Either is acceptable; it is up to you to decide which you prefer. The important thing is to be consistent: whichever format you choose, be sure to use it throughout the entire paragraph.

h. Write the first draft of your paragraph.

Revising

Put your writing away for a day or so. You will return to it with a fresh perspective and a better ability to critique what you have done.

Reread your work with these questions in mind.

FOUR BASES Checklist for Comparison or Contrast

About *Unity*

☑ Does my topic sentence make it clear what two things I am comparing or contrasting?

☑ Do all sentences in the paragraph stay on-topic?

About *Support*

☑ Have I compared or contrasted the subjects in at least three important ways?

☑ Have I provided specific details that effectively back up my supporting points?

About *Coherence*

☑ If I have chosen the point-by-point format, have I consistently discussed a point about one subject, then immediately discussed the same point about the other subject before moving on to the next point?

☑ If I have chosen the one-side-at-a-time format, have I discussed every point about one of my subjects, then discussed the same points *in the same order* about the second subject?

☑ Have I used appropriate transitions, such as *first, in addition, also,* and *another way,* to help readers follow my train of thought?

About *Sentence Skills*

☑ Have I carefully proofread my paragraph, using the list on the inside back cover of the book, and corrected all sentence-skills mistakes, including spelling?

Continue revising your work until you can answer "yes" to all these questions.

Writing Assignment

2

Write a paragraph in which you compare or contrast your life in the real world with your life in an imagined "perfect world." Your paragraph may be humorous or serious.

Prewriting

a. As your "real life" and "ideal life" are too broad for a paragraph, choose three specific areas to focus on. You might select any of the areas below, or think of a specific area yourself.

work   friends
money   possessions
romance   housing
physical location   talents
personal appearance

b. Write the name of one of your three areas (for example, "work") across the top of a page. Divide the page into two columns. Label one column "real world" and the other "perfect world." Under "real world," write down as many details as you can think of describing your real-life work situation. Under "perfect world," write down details describing what your perfect work life would be like. Repeat the process on separate pages for your other two major areas.

c. Write a topic sentence for your paragraph. Here's an example: "In my perfect world, my life would be quite different in the areas of work, money, and housing."

d. Decide which approach you will take: one side at a time or point by point.

e. Write a scratch outline that reflects the format you have selected. The outline for a point-by-point format would look like this:

Topic sentence: In my perfect world, my life would be quite different in the areas of work, money, and housing.

1. Work

   a. Real-life work

   b. Perfect-world work

continued

2. Money
   a. Real-life money
   b. Perfect-world money
3. Housing
   a. Real-life housing
   b. Perfect-world housing

The outline for a one-side-at-a-time format would look like this:

Topic sentence: In my perfect world, my life would be quite different in the areas of work, money, and housing.
1. Real life
   a. Work
   b. Money
   c. Housing
2. Perfect world
   a. Work
   b. Money
   c. Housing

    f. Drawing from the three pages of details you generated in step *b*, complete your outline by jotting down your strongest supporting details for each point.

    g. Write the first draft of your paragraph.

Revising

Reread your paragraph, and then show it to a friend who will give you honest feedback. You should both review it with these questions in mind.

FOUR BASES Checklist for Comparison or Contrast

About *Unity*

☑ Does the topic sentence make it clear what three areas of life are being compared or contrasted?

☑ Is the rest of my paragraph on target in support of my topic sentence?

About *Support*

☑ Does the paragraph provide specific details that describe both the "real-life" situation and the "perfect-world" situation?

About *Coherence*

☑ Does the paragraph follow a consistent format: point by point or one side at a time?

About *Sentence Skills*

☑ Have I used a consistent point of view throughout my paragraph?

☑ Have I used specific rather than general words?

☑ Have I avoided wordiness?

☑ Are my sentences varied?

☑ Have I checked for spelling and other sentence skills, as listed on the inside back cover of the book?

Continue revising your work until you and your reader can answer "yes" to all these questions.

Writing Assignment

3

Write a contrast paragraph on one of the topics below.

Neighborhood stores versus a shopping mall

Driving on an expressway versus driving on country roads

People versus *Us Weekly* (or any other two popular magazines)

Camping in a tent versus camping in a recreational vehicle

Working parents versus stay-at-home parents

Shopping at a department store versus shopping online

A used car versus a new one

Recorded music versus live music

PG-rated movies versus R-rated movies

News in a newspaper versus news on television or the Internet

Yesterday's toys versus today's toys

Fresh food versus canned or frozen food

An ad on television or online versus an ad for the same product in a magazine

Amateur sports teams versus professional teams

Follow the directions for prewriting and rewriting given in Writing Assignment 2.

Writing Assignment

4 Write a paragraph in which you contrast two types of students at your college. Pick two types you know well. For example, contrast a student who is highly motivated with one who is not, or contrast one who has to work at a job with one who can afford not to work. You might also contrast the needs, the duties, or the daily schedules of a student who is a parent with those of a student who is not.

Writing Assignment

5 ## Writing for a Specific Purpose and Audience

In this comparison and contrast paragraph, you will write with a specific purpose and for a specific audience. Imagine that you are living in an apartment building in which new tenants are making life unpleasant for you. Write a letter of complaint to your landlord comparing *and* contrasting life before and after the tenants arrived.

Your purpose is to get your landlord to do something about the problem or problems created by the new tenants. To achieve this purpose, use as many specific and convincing details as you can. For example, don't just write that your neighbors have lots of parties. Instead, say that guests come and go until 2 or 3 A.M. or that the music is so loud it shakes the walls and keeps you up all night.

Your audience—the landlord—has an interest in keeping *all* tenants happy. So you might also explain that many of the other tenants have been complaining about the newcomers or that the police have been called during their parties.

You might want to focus on one or more of the following:

Noise   Parking situation

Trash   Damage to the building

Safety hazards

Definition

This chapter will explain and illustrate how to

- develop a definition paragraph
- write a definition paragraph
- revise a definition paragraph

In addition, you will read and consider

- three student definition paragraphs

What are some words that come to mind as you look at this photograph? Write a paragraph in which you define one of these terms. For example, you may look at the photograph and think "challenge," "frustration," "obstacle," or "courage."

In talking with other people, we sometimes offer informal definitions to explain just what we mean by a particular term. Suppose, for example, we say to a friend, "Karen can be so clingy." We might then expand on our idea of "clingy" by saying, "You know, a clingy person needs to be with someone every single minute. If Karen's best friend makes plans that don't include her, she becomes hurt. And when she dates someone, she calls him several times a day and gets upset if he even goes to the grocery store without her. She hangs on to people too tightly." In a written definition, we make clear in a more complete and formal way our own personal understanding of a term. Such a definition typically starts with one meaning of a term. The meaning is then illustrated with a series of examples or a story.

The simplest way to state the meaning of a word is to follow the lead of scientists, who first classify an animal or plant by general category or class (*genus*) and then by the specific characteristics of the animal or plant (*species*). Thus you could say that a dog is a mammal (general category) that has four legs, a tail, and an ability to bark (specific characteristics). In one of the paragraphs that follow, the writer begins by defining *hypnotherapy* as a "medical treatment" (general category). The definition then explains that this treatment is used "while the patient is hypnotized" (specific characteristic).

After discussing the meaning of a term, provide as many examples and details as you can to clarify your point. In the paragraph entitled "The Liberal Arts," which follows, the writer gives several examples of the types of subjects included in the liberal arts. In "Hypnotherapy" the writer supplies a few examples of the uses of this medical practice.

To continue developing your definition, you might consider defining by contrast. That means telling your reader what the term does *not* mean or distinguishing it from other terms with which it is sometimes confused. For example, the writer of "Hynotherapy" contrasts that term with *mesmerism*. The author of "The Liberal Arts" contrasts the liberal arts course of study with vocational, professional, and technical courses of study.

In this section, you will be asked to write a paragraph that begins with a one-sentence definition; that sentence will be the topic sentence. The three student papers below are all examples of definition paragraphs. Read them and then answer the questions that follow.

Paragraphs to Consider

Hypnotherapy

[1]Hypnotherapy is a medical treatment that is used while the patient is hypnotized. [2]The word *hypnosis* comes from the Greek word *hypnos*, which means "sleep." [3]Under hypnosis, the patient is very susceptible to suggestions from the doctor, who uses these suggestions to aid in the treatment. [4]The British surgeon James Braid used this method during minor operations to lessen the patient's discomfort. [5]Today, it is used to treat insomnia, depression, and emotional problems. [6]Hypnotherapy has been used to ease a pregnant woman's anxiety, even during childbirth. [7]Mesmerism, founded by Franz Anton Mesmer, is often confused with hypnotism and therefore with hypnotherapy. [8]Mesmer studied medicine at the University of Vienna, but he was also an astrologer. [9]However, mesmerism has been discredited as a therapy by the medical profession. [10]Mesmer's claim that he could use a force called "animal magnetism" to probe a subject's unconscious was proven false by Braid and those who followed him.

Disillusionment

[1]Disillusionment is the feeling we have when one of our most cherished beliefs is stolen from us. [2]I learned about disillusionment firsthand the day Mr. Keller, our eighth-grade teacher, handed out the grades for our class biology projects. [3]I had worked hard to assemble what I thought was the best insect collection any school had ever seen. [4]For weeks, I had set up homemade traps around our house, in the woods, and in vacant lots. [5]At night, I would stretch a white sheet between two trees, shine a lantern on it, and collect the night-flying insects that gathered there. [6]With my own money, I had bought killing jars, insect pins, gummed labels, and display boxes. [7]I carefully arranged related insects together, with labels listing each scientific name and the place and date of capture. [8]Slowly and painfully, I wrote and typed the report that accompanied my project at the school science fair. [9]In contrast, my friend Eddie did almost nothing for his project. [10]He had his father, a psychologist, build an impressive maze complete with live rats and a sign that read, "You are the trainer." [11]A person could lift a little plastic door, send a rat running through the maze, and then hit a button to release a pellet of rat food as a reward. [12]This

continued

exhibit turned out to be the most popular one at the fair. [13]I felt sure that our teacher would know that Eddie could not have built it, and I was certain that my hard work would be recognized and rewarded. [14]Then the grades were finally handed out, and I was crushed. [15]Eddie had gotten an A plus, but my grade was a B. [16]I suddenly realized that honesty and hard work don't always pay off in the end. [17]The idea that life is not fair, that sometimes it pays to cheat, hit me with such force that I felt sick. [18]I will never forget that moment.

The Liberal Arts

[1]Most colleges offer at least some liberal arts classes. [2]The vast majority, in fact, offer liberal arts courses of study. [3]These are unlike professional, vocational, or technical courses of study, which focus on specific skills or on areas that prepare students for certain specific occupations. [4]Instead, the liberal arts tend to be wider in scope and to provide all students—not just those majoring in a liberal arts subject—with the general knowledge they will need to be well-rounded members of the community. [5]The liberal arts, which are often grouped with the natural sciences, include communication, literature, history, language, the social sciences, philosophy, and mathematics. [6]In addition to teaching an accepted body of knowledge, liberal arts classes also teach students the kinds of skills they will need to continue learning on their own after they graduate. [7]For example, many courses in literature, history, and philosophy require critical reading, research, and writing. [8]The term *liberal* comes from the Latin word *liber*, meaning "free," for when the liberal arts were taught in antiquity they were intended for free men. [9]Training in specific skills, on the other hand, was reserved for slaves. [10]The liberal arts are also called the humanities, because they aim at helping people become more civilized, that is, more human.

Questions

About Unity

1. Which paragraph places its topic sentence within the paragraph rather than, more appropriately, at the beginning?

_____

2. Which sentence in "Hypnotherapy" should be omitted in the interest of paragraph unity? (*Write the sentence number here.*) _____

About Support

3. Which paragraph develops its definition through examples?

_____

4. Which paragraph develops its definition through a single extended example?

_____

About Coherence

5. Which paragraph uses emphatic order, saving the best detail for last?

_____

6. Which paragraph uses time order to organize its details?

_____

Developing a Definition Paragraph

Development through Prewriting

When Harry, the author of "Disillusionment," started working on his assignment, he did not know what he wanted to write about. He looked around the house for inspiration. His two-year-old twins racing around the room made him think about defining "energy." The fat cat asleep on a sunny windowsill suggested that he might write about "laziness" or "relaxation." Still not sure of a topic, he looked over his notes from that day's class. His instructor had jotted a list of terms on the blackboard, saying, "Maybe you could focus on what one of these words has meant in your own life." Harry looked over the words he had copied down: _honesty, willpower, faith, betrayal, disillusionment._ "When I got to the word 'disillusionment,' the eighth-grade science fair flashed into my mind," Harry said. "That was a bitter experience that definitely taught me what disillusionment was all about."

Because the science fair had occurred many years before, Harry had to work to remember it well. He decided to try the technique of questioning himself to come up with the details of what had happened. Here are the questions Harry asked himself and the answers he wrote:

When did I learn about disillusionment?
When I was in eighth grade

Where did it happen?
At the school science fair

continued

Who was involved?

Me, Eddie Loomis and his father, and Mr. Keller

What happened?

I had worked very hard on my insect collection. Eddie had done almost nothing but he had a rat maze that his father had built. I got a B on my project while Eddie got an A+.

Why was the experience so disillusioning?

I thought my hard work would be rewarded. I was sure Mr. Keller would recognize that I had put far more effort into my project than Eddie had. When Eddie won, I learned that cheating can pay off and that honest work isn't always rewarded.

How did I react?

I felt sick to my stomach. I wanted to confront Mr. Keller and Eddie and make them see how unfair the grades were. But I knew I'd just look like a poor loser, so I didn't do anything.

On the basis of this experience, how would I define disillusionment?

It's finding out that something you really believed in isn't true.

Drawing from the ideas generated by his self-questioning, Harry wrote the following draft of his paragraph:

Disillusionment is finding out that one of your most important beliefs isn't true. I learned about disillusionment at my eighth-grade science fair. I had worked very hard on my project, an insect collection. I was sure it would get an A. I had worked so hard on it, even spending nights outside making sure it was very good. My friend Eddie also did a project, but he barely worked on his at all.

continued

Instead, he had his father build a maze for a rat to run through. The trainer lifted a little plastic door to let the rat into the maze, and if it completed the maze, the trainer could release a pellet of food for it to eat. It was a nice project, but the point is that Eddie hadn't made it. He just made things like the banner that hung over it. Mr. Keller was our science teacher. He gave Eddie an A+ and me just a B. So that really taught me about disillusionment.

Development through Revising

The next day, Harry's instructor divided the class into groups of three. The groups reviewed each member's paragraph. Harry was grouped with Curtis and Jocelyn. After reading through Harry's paper several times, the group had the following discussion:

"My first reaction is that I want to know more about your project," said Jocelyn. "You give details about Eddie's, but not many about your own. What was so good about it? You need to show us, not just tell us. Also, you said that you worked very hard, but you didn't show us how hard."

"Yeah," said Harry. "I remember my project clearly, but I guess the reader has to know what it was like and how much effort went into it."

Curtis said, "I like your topic sentence, but when I finished the paragraph I wasn't sure what 'important belief' you'd learned wasn't true. What would you say that belief was?"

Harry thought a minute. "I'd believed that honest hard work would always be rewarded. I found out that it doesn't always happen that way, and that cheating can actually win."

Curtis nodded. "I think you need to include that in your paper."

Jocelyn added, "I'd like to read how you felt or reacted after you saw your grade, too. If you don't explain that, the paragraph ends sort of abruptly."

Harry agreed with his classmates' suggestions. After he had gone through several revisions, he produced the version that appears on page 249.

Writing a Definition Paragraph

Writing Assignment

1 Write a paragraph that defines the term *TV addict*. Base your paragraph on the topic sentence and three supporting points provided below.

Topic sentence: Television addicts are people who will watch all the programs they can, for as long as they can, without doing anything else.

(1) TV addicts, first of all, will watch anything on the tube, no matter how bad it is. . . .

(2) In addition, addicts watch more hours of TV than normal people do. . . .

(3) Finally, addicts feel that TV is more important than other people or any other activities that might be going on. . . .

Prewriting

a. Generate as many examples as you can for each of the three qualities of a TV addict. You can do this by asking yourself the following questions:

- What are some truly awful shows that I (or TV addicts I know) watch just because the television is turned on?

- What are some examples of the large amounts of time that I (or TV addicts I know) watch television?

- What are some examples of ways that I (or TV addicts I know) neglect people or give up activities in order to watch TV?

Write down every answer you can think of for each question. At this point, don't worry about writing full sentences or even about grammar or spelling. Just get your thoughts down on paper.

b. Look over the list of examples you have generated. Select the strongest examples you have thought of. You should have at least two or three for each quality. If not, ask yourself the questions in step *a* again.

c. Write out the examples you will use, this time expressing them in full, grammatically correct sentences.

d. Start with the topic sentence and three points provided in the assignment. Fill in the examples you've generated to support each point and write a first draft of your paragraph.

Revising

Put your first draft away for a day or so. When you come back to it, reread it critically, asking yourself these questions.

FOUR BASES Checklist for Definition

About *Unity*

☑ Have I used the topic sentence and the three supporting points that were provided?

☑ Does every sentence in my paragraph help define the term *TV addict*?

About *Support*

☑ Have I backed up each supporting point with at least two examples?

☑ Does each of my examples truly illustrate the point that it backs up?

About *Coherence*

☑ Have I used appropriate transitional language (*another, in addition, for example*) to tie my thoughts together?

☑ Are all the transitional words correctly used?

About *Sentence Skills*

☑ Have I carefully proofread my paragraph, using the list on the inside back cover of the book, and corrected all sentence-skills mistakes, including spelling?

☑ Have I used a consistent point of view throughout my paragraph?

Keep revising your paragraph until you can answer "yes" to each question.

Writing Assignment

2 Write a paragraph that defines one of the following terms. Each term refers to a certain kind of person.

Charmer	Fool	Nerd	Slob
Clown	Good neighbor	Optimist	Snob
Con artist	Good sport	Pessimist	Spaz
Control freak	Know-it-all	Player	Traitor
Fair-weather friend	Leader	Princess	Workaholic
Flake	Loser	Showoff	

Prewriting

a. Write a topic sentence for your definition paragraph. This is a two-part process:

- *First,* place the term in a class, or category. For example, if you are writing about a certain kind of person, the general category is *person.* If you are describing a type of friend, the general category is *friend.*

- *Second,* describe what you consider the special feature or features that set your term apart from other members of its class. For instance, say what *kind* of person you are writing about or what *type* of friend.

In the following topic sentence, try to identify three things: the term being defined, the class it belongs to, and the special feature that sets the term apart from other members of the class.

A chocoholic is a person who craves chocolate.

The term being defined is *chocoholic.* The category it belongs to is *person.* The words that set *chocoholic* apart from any other person are *craves chocolate.*

Below is another example of a topic sentence for this assignment. It is a definition of *whiner.* The class, or category, is underlined: A whiner is a type of person. The words that set the term *whiner* apart from other members of the class are double-underlined.

A whiner is a <u>person</u> who <u><u>feels wronged by life.</u></u>

In the following sample topic sentences, underline the class and double-underline the special features.

A shopaholic is a person who needs new clothes to be happy.

The class clown is a student who gets attention through silly behavior.

A worrywart is a person who sees danger everywhere.

b. Develop your definition by using one of the following methods:

Examples. Give several examples that support your topic sentence.

Extended example. Use one longer example to support your topic sentence.

Contrast. Support your topic sentence by contrasting what your term *is* with what it is *not.* For instance, you may want to define a *fair-weather friend* by contrasting his or her actions with those of a true friend.

c. Once you have created a topic sentence and decided how to develop your paragraph, make a scratch outline. If you are using a contrast method of development, remember to present the details one side at a time or point by point (see pages 229–230).

d. Write a first draft of your paragraph.

Revising

As you revise your paragraph, keep these questions in mind.

FOUR BASES Checklist for Definition

About *Unity*

☑ Does my topic sentence (1) place my term in a class and (2) name some special features that set it apart from its class?

☑ Is the rest of my paragraph on target in support of my topic sentence?

About *Support*

☑ Have I made a clear choice to develop my topic sentence through several examples, or one extended example, or contrast?

About *Coherence*

☑ If I have chosen to illustrate my topic through contrast, have I consistently followed either a point-by-point or a one-side-at-a-time format?

☑ Have I used appropriate transitions (*another, in addition, in contrast, for example*) to tie my thoughts together?

About *Sentence Skills*

☑ Have I used a consistent point of view throughout my paragraph?

☑ Have I used specific rather than general words?

☑ Have I avoided wordiness?

☑ Are my sentences varied?

☑ Have I checked for spelling and other sentence skills, as listed on the inside back cover of the book?

Continue revising your work until you can answer "yes" to all these questions.

Writing Assignment

3 Write a paragraph that defines one of the abstract terms below.

Arrogance	Family	Persistence
Assertiveness	Fear	Practicality
Class	Freedom	Rebellion
Common sense	Gentleness	Responsibility
Conscience	Innocence	Self-control
Curiosity	Insecurity	Sense of humor
Danger	Jealousy	Shyness
Depression	Nostalgia	Violence
Escape	Obsession	

As a guide in writing your paper, use the suggestions for prewriting and rewriting in Writing Assignment 2. Remember to place your term in a class or category and to describe what *you* feel are the distinguishing features of that term.

After writing your topic sentence, check that it is complete and correct by doing the following:

- Single-underline the category of the term you're defining.
- Double-underline the term's distinguishing characteristic or characteristics.

Here are three sample topic sentences:

Laziness is the trait of resisting all worthwhile work as much as possible.

Jealousy is the feeling of wanting a possession or quality that someone else has.

A family is a group whose members are related to one another in some way.

Writing Assignment

4 Since stress affects all of us to some degree—in the workplace, in school (as shown in the photograph on the next page), in our families, and in our everyday lives—it is a useful term to explore. Write a paragraph defining *stress*. Organize your paragraph in one of these ways:

- Use a series of examples (see pages 181–184) of stress.
- Use narration (see pages 293–306) to provide one longer example of stress: Create a hypothetical person (or use a real person) and show how this person's typical day illustrates your definition of *stress*.

Using strategies described in Chapter 19 (pages 369–385), do some research on stress. Your reading will help you think about how to proceed with the paper.

> **HINT** Do not simply write a series of general, abstract sentences that repeat and reword your definition. If you concentrate on providing specific support, you will avoid the common trap of getting lost in a maze of generalities.
>
> Make sure your paper is set firmly on the four bases: unity, support, coherence, and sentence skills. Edit the next-to-final draft of the paragraph carefully for sentence-skills errors, including spelling.

Writing Assignment

Writing for a Specific Purpose and Audience

5

In this definition paragraph, you will write with a specific purpose and for a specific audience. Choose one of the following options.

Option 1

Imagine that at the place where you work, one employee has just quit, creating a new job opening. Since you have been working there for a while, your boss has asked you to write a description of the position. That description, a detailed definition of the job, will be sent to employment agencies. These agencies will be responsible for interviewing candidates. Choose any position you know about, and write a paragraph defining it. First state the purpose of the job, and then list its duties and responsibilities. Finally, describe the qualifications for the position. Below is a sample topic sentence for this assignment.

> Purchasing-department secretary is a <u>position</u> in which someone <u>provides a variety of services</u> to the purchasing-department managers.

In a paragraph with that topic sentence, the writer would go on to list and explain the various services the secretary must provide.

Option 2

Alternatively, imagine that a new worker has been hired, and your boss has asked you to explain "team spirit" to him or her. The purpose of your explanation will be to give the newcomer an idea of the kind of teamwork that is expected in this workplace. Write a paragraph that defines in detail what your boss means by *team spirit*. Use examples or one extended example to illustrate each of your general points about team spirit.

Option 3

Earlier you read a paragraph defining *hypnotherapy*. Write a paragraph in which you define another scientific term. If you need to, complete some background research on the Internet, but make sure that the information you put into your paragraph is in your own words and reflects your own phrasing. Here are a few terms you might choose from:

Absolute zero	Inertia
Doppler effect	Isotope
Electromagnetism	Magnetic resonance imaging
Global warming	Photosynthesis
Greenhouse effect	Tsunami
Hypertension	Vulcanism

If these terms don't interest you, try defining a term that comes from our use of computers or other electronic equipment. Here are a few examples:

Blog	HTML	Spam
Computer virus	Network	Spyware
Facebook	PDF	Texting
Home page	Search engine	YouTube

Division-Classification

13

This chapter will explain and illustrate how to

- develop a division-classification paragraph
- write a division-classification paragraph
- revise a division-classification paragraph

In addition, you will read and consider

- three student division-classification paragraphs

Music comes in many forms. Write a paragraph in which you discuss three different styles of music and what makes each one unique and different.

If you were doing the laundry, you might begin by separating the clothing into piles. You would then put all the whites in one pile and all the colors in another. Or you might classify the laundry not according to color but according to fabric—putting all cottons in one pile, polyesters in another, and so on. *Classifying* is the process of taking many things and separating them into categories. We generally classify to better manage or understand many things. Librarians classify books into groups (fiction, travel, health, etc.) to make them easier to find. A scientist sheds light on the world by classifying all living things into two main groups: animals and plants.

Dividing, in contrast, is taking one thing and breaking it down into parts. We often divide, or analyze, to better understand, teach, or evaluate something. For instance, a tinkerer might take apart a clock to see how it works; a science text might divide a tree into its parts to explain their functions. A music reviewer may analyze the elements of a band's performance—for example, the skill of the various players, rapport with the audience, selections, and so on.

In short, if you are classifying, you are sorting *numbers of things* into categories. If you are dividing, you are breaking *one thing* into parts. It all depends on your purpose—you might classify flowers into various types or divide a single flower into its parts.

In this section, you will be asked to write a paragraph in which you classify a group of things into categories according to a single principle. To prepare for this assignment, first read the paragraphs below, and then work through the questions and the activity that follow.

Paragraphs to Consider

Types of E-Mail

[1]As more and more people take advantage of e-mailing, three categories of e-mail have emerged. [2]One category of e-mail is junk mail, or spam. [3]When most people sign on to their computers, they are greeted with a flood of get-rich-quick schemes, invitations to pornographic Web sites, and ads for a variety of unwanted products. [4]E-mail users quickly become good at hitting the "delete" button to get rid of this garbage. [5]The second category that clogs most people's electronic mailbox is forwarded mail, most of which also gets deleted without being read. [6]The third and best category of e-mail is genuine personal e-mail from genuine personal friends or colleagues. [7]Getting such real, thoughtful e-mail can almost make up for the irritation of the other two categories.

The Diversity of Africa

[1]We often think of Africa as a place covered with jungles and inhabited by people who practice the same culture. [2]The northern part of Africa is mainly desert, except for the very edge, which borders the Mediterranean Sea. [3]The Sahara, the world's largest desert, is located in this part of the continent. [4]So are countries such as Morocco, Algeria, Libya, Mauritania, and Egypt. In these countries the vast majority of the population speaks Arabic and practices Islam. [5]In the middle of the continent, one finds the Sudan, Africa's largest country, which offers a wide variety of landscapes: desert, grassland, and mountain. [6]Other countries found in the middle part of Africa are Ethiopia, the Congo, Nigeria, Ghana, Uganda, and Kenya. [7]The best-known countries in the southern part of the continent are Angola, Zimbabwe, Zambia, and South Africa. [8]The landscape in the first three of these southern countries consists mostly of grasslands with some mountains. [9]The languages of these countries include English as well as native tongues. [10]Many southern African countries have Christian majorities. [11]In Mauritius, however, there are more Hindus than Christians or Muslims. [12]Finally, the nation of South Africa seems to mirror the rest of the continent in its diversity. [13]Here there are mountains, grasslands, and seashore. [14]Eleven official languages are spoken in this country: Afrikaans, English, isiNdebele, isiXhosa, isiZulu, Sepedi, Sesotho, Setswana, siSwati, Tshivenda, and Xitsonga. [15]What's more, several very different faiths are represented in South Africa, including Hinduism, Judaism, Islam, many sects of Christianity, and a wide variety of native religions.

Three Kinds of Dogs

[1]A city walker will notice that most dogs fall into one of three categories. [2]First there are the big dogs, which are generally harmless and often downright friendly. [3]They walk along peacefully with their masters, their tongues hanging out and big goofy grins on their faces. [4]Apparently they know they're too big to have anything to worry about, so why not be nice? [5]Second are the spunky medium-sized dogs. [6]When they see a stranger approaching, they go on alert. [7]They prick up their ears, they raise their hackles, and they may growl a little deep in their throats. [8]"I could tear you up," they seem to be saying, "but I won't if you behave yourself." [9]Unless the walker leaps for their master's throat, these dogs usually won't do anything more than threaten. [10]The third category is made up of the shivering neurotic

continued

little yappers whose shrill barks could shatter glass and whose needle-like little teeth are eager to sink into a friendly outstretched hand. [11]Walkers always
wonder about these dogs—don't they know that people who really wanted
to could squash them under their feet like bugs? [12]Apparently not, because
of all the dogs a walker meets, these provide the most irritation. [13]Such dogs
are only one of the potential hazards that the city walker encounters.

Questions

About Unity

1. Which paragraph lacks a topic sentence?

_____

2. Which sentence in "Three Kinds of Dogs" should be eliminated in the
   interest of paragraph unity? (*Write the sentence number here.*) _____

About Support

3. Of the three parts of Africa discussed in "The Diversity of Africa," which
   one needs more specific detail?

_____

4. After which sentence in "Types of E-Mail" are supporting details needed?
   (*Write the sentence number here.*) _____

About Coherence

5. Which paragraph uses emphatic order to organize its details?

_____

6. Which words in the emphatic-order paragraph signal the most important detail?

_____

Activity 1

This activity will sharpen your sense of the classifying process. In each of the
ten groups, cross out the one item that has not been classified on the same basis
as the other three. Also, indicate in the space provided the single principle of
classification used for the remaining three items. Note the examples.

EXAMPLE

Water
a. Cold
b. ~~Lake~~
c. Hot
d. Lukewarm
Unifying principle:
Temperature

Household pests
a. ~~Mice~~
b. Ants
c. Roaches
d. Flies
Unifying principle:
Insects

1. Eyes
   a. Blue
   b. Nearsighted
   c. Brown
   d. Hazel
   Unifying principle:

   _____

2. Mattresses
   a. Double
   b. Twin
   c. Queen
   d. Firm
   Unifying principle:

   _____

3. Zoo animals
   a. Flamingo
   b. Peacock
   c. Polar bear
   d. Ostrich
   Unifying principle:

   _____

4. Vacation
   a. Summer
   b. Holiday
   c. Seashore
   d. Weekend
   Unifying principle:

   _____

5. Books
   a. Novels
   b. Biographies
   c. Boring
   d. Short stories
   Unifying principle:

   _____

6. Wallets
   a. Leather
   b. Plastic
   c. Stolen
   d. Fabric
   Unifying principle:

   _____

7. Newspaper
   a. Wrapping garbage
   b. Editorials
   c. Making paper planes
   d. Covering floor while painting
   Unifying principle:

   _____

8. Students
   a. First-year
   b. Transfer
   c. Junior
   d. Sophomore
   Unifying principle:

   _____

9. Exercise
   a. Running
   b. Swimming
   c. Gymnastics
   d. Fatigue
   Unifying principle:

   _____

10. Leftovers
    a. Cold chicken
    b. Feed to dog
    c. Reheat
    d. Use in a stew
    Unifying principle:

    _____

Developing a Division-Classification Paragraph

Development through Prewriting

Marcus walked home from campus to his apartment, thinking about the assignment to write a division-classification paragraph. As he strolled along his familiar route, his observations made him think of several possibilities. "First I thought of writing about the businesses in my neighborhood, dividing them into the ones run by Hispanics, Asians, and African Americans," he said. "When I stopped in at my favorite coffee shop, I thought about dividing the people who hang out there. There is a group of old men who meet to drink coffee and play cards, and there are students like me, but there didn't seem to be a third category and I wasn't sure two was enough. As I continued walking home, though, I saw Mr. Enriquez and his big golden retriever, and a woman with two nervous little dogs that acted as if they wanted to eat me, and the newsstand guy with his mutt that's always guarding the place, and I thought 'Dogs! I can classify types of dogs.'"

But how would he classify them? Thinking further, Marcus realized that he thought of dogs as having certain personalities depending on their size. "I know there are exceptions, of course, but since this was going to be a lighthearted, even comical paragraph, I thought it would be OK if I exaggerated a bit." He wrote down his three categories:

> Big dogs
> Medium-sized dogs
> Small dogs

Under each division, then, he wrote down as many characteristics as he could think of:

Big dogs	Medium-sized dogs	Small dogs
calm	spunky	nervous
friendly	energetic	trembling
good-natured	ready to fight	noisy
dumb	protective	yappy
lazy	friendly if they know you	snappy
		annoying

Marcus then wrote a topic sentence: "Dogs seem to fall into three categories." Using that topic sentence and a scratch outline he produced from his prewriting, he wrote the following paragraph:

Most dogs seem to fall into one of three categories. First there are the big dumb friendly dogs. They give the impression of being sweet but not real bright. One example of this kind of dog is Lucy. She's a golden retriever belonging to a man in my neighborhood. Lucy goes everywhere with Mr. Enriquez. She doesn't even need a leash but just follows him. Dogs like Lucy never bother anybody. She just lies at Mr. Enriquez's feet when he stops to talk to anyone. The guy who runs the corner newsstand I pass every day has a spunky medium-sized dog. Once the dog knows you he's friendly and even playful. But he's always on the lookout for a stranger who might mean trouble. For a dog who's not very big he can make himself look pretty fierce if he wants to. Then there are my least favorite kind of dogs. Little nervous yappy ones. My aunt used to have a Chihuahua like that. It knew me for nine years and still went crazy shaking and yipping at me every time we met. She loved that dog but I can't imagine why. If I had a dog it would definitely come from category 1 or 2.

Development through Revising

Marcus traded his first draft with a fellow student, Rachel, and asked her to give him feedback. Here are the comments Rachel wrote on his paper:

Most dogs seem to fall into three categories. First there are the big dumb friendly dogs. They give the impression of being sweet but not real bright. One example of this kind of dog is Lucy, a golden retriever belonging to a man in my neighborhood. Lucy goes everywhere with Mr. Enriquez. She doesn't even need a leash but just follows him everywhere. Lucy never bothers you. She just lies at Mr. Enriquez's feet when he stops to talk to anyone. The guy who runs the corner newsstand I pass every day has a spunky medium-sized dog. Once the dog knows you he's friendly and even playful. But he's always on the lookout for a stranger who might mean trouble. For a dog who's not very big he can make himself look pretty fierce if he wants to scare you. Then there are my least favorite kind of dogs. Little nervous yappy ones. My aunt used to have a Chihuahua like that. It knew me for nine years and still went crazy shaking and yipping at me every time we met. She loved that dog but I can't imagine why. If I had a dog it would definitely come from category 1 or 2.

This is a change in point of view—you haven't been using "you" before.

Is this the beginning of a second category? That's not clear.

Not a complete sentence.

Another change in point of view—you've gone from writing in the third person to "you" to "me."

Marcus—I think you need to make your three categories clearer. Your first one is OK—"big dogs," which you say are friendly—but categories 2 and 3 aren't stated as clearly. It's distracting to have your point of view change from third person to "you" to "me."

Since you're trying to divide and classify all dogs, I'm not sure it's a good idea to talk only about three individual dogs. This way it sounds as if you're just describing those three dogs instead of putting them into three groups.

When Marcus considered Rachel's comments and reread his paragraph, he agreed with what she had written. "I realized it was too much about three particular dogs and not enough about the categories of dogs," he said. "I decided to revise it and focus on the three classes of dogs."

Marcus then wrote the version that appears on page 263.

Writing a Division-Classification Paragraph

Writing Assignment

1

Below are four options to develop into a classification paragraph. Each one presents a topic to classify into three categories. Choose one option to develop into a paragraph.

OPTION **1**

Supermarket shoppers

(1) Slow, careful shoppers

(2) Average shoppers

(3) Hurried shoppers

OPTION **2**

Eaters

(1) Very conservative eaters

(2) Typical eaters

(3) Adventurous eaters

OPTION **3**

Students

(1) Those who work hard to achieve a goal

(2) Those who don't know why they're in college

(3) Those who just want to get by

OPTION **4**

Types of attitudes toward sex

(1) Overly strict and puritanical

(2) Healthy

(3) Promiscuous

Prewriting

a. Begin by freewriting on your topic. For five or ten minutes, simply write down everything that comes into your head when you think about "students," "types of eaters," or whichever topic you chose. Don't worry about grammar, spelling, or organization—just write.

b. Now that you've "loosened up your brain" a little, try asking yourself questions about the topic and writing down your answers. If you are writing about supermarket shoppers, for instance, you might ask questions like these:

How do the three kinds of shoppers prepare for their shopping trip?

How many aisles will each kind of shopper visit?

What do the different kinds of shoppers bring along with them—lists, calculators, coupons, etc.?

How long does each type of shopper spend in the store?

Write down whatever answers occur to you for these and other questions. Again, do not worry at this stage about writing correctly. Instead, concentrate on getting down all the information you can think of that supports your three points.

c. Reread the material you have accumulated. If some of the details you have written make you think of even better ones, add them. Select the details that best support your three points. Number them in the order you will present them.

  d. Restate your topic as a grammatically complete topic sentence. For example, if you're writing about eaters, your topic sentence might be "Eaters can be divided into three categories." Turn each of your three supporting points into a full sentence as well.

  e. Using your topic sentence and three supporting sentences and adding the details you have generated, write the first draft of your paragraph.

Revising

Put away your work for a day or so. Then reread it with a critical eye, asking yourself or a peer reviewer these questions.

FOUR BASES Checklist for Division-Classification

About *Unity*

☑ Does my paragraph include a complete topic sentence and three supporting points?

☑ While classifying the various types of my chosen topic, have I also kept that subject unified?

About *Support*

☑ Have I backed up each supporting point with strong, specific details?

☑ Have I given examples of each type of shopper, eater, student, or attitude toward sex?

About *Coherence*

☑ Does the paragraph successfully classify types of shoppers, eaters, students, or attitudes toward sex?

About *Sentence Skills*

☑ Have I carefully proofread my paragraph, using the list on the inside back cover of the book, and corrected all sentence-skills mistakes, including spelling?

☑ Have I used specific rather than general words?

Continue revising your work until you can answer "yes" to all these questions.

Writing Assignment

2

Write a classification paragraph on one of the following topics:

First dates

Drivers

Mothers or fathers

Kinds of clothes students wear

Baseball, basketball, football,
   or hockey players

Instructors

Sports fans

Celebrities

Attitudes toward life

Commercials

Employers

Internet users   Retail customers

Moviegoers   Presents

Restaurant servers   Neighbors

Rock, pop, rap, or country singers   Houseguests

Prewriting

a. Classify members of the group you are considering writing about into three categories. Remember: *You must use a single principle of division when you create your three categories.* For example, if your topic is "school courses" and you classify them into easy, moderate, and challenging, your basis for classification is "degree of difficulty." It would not make sense to have as a fourth type "foreign language" (the basis of such a categorization would be "subject matter") or "early morning" (the basis of that classification would be "time of day the classes meet"). You *could* categorize school courses on the basis of subject matter or time of day they meet, for almost any subject can be classified in more than one way. In a single paper, however, you must choose *one* basis for classification and stick to it.

b. Once you have a satisfactory three-part division, spend at least five minutes freewriting about each of your three points. Don't be concerned yet with grammar, spelling, or organization. Just write whatever comes into your mind about each of the three points.

    c. Expand your topic into a fully stated topic sentence.

    d. At this point, you have all three elements of your paragraph: the topic sentence, the three main points, and the details needed to support each point. Now weave them all together in one paragraph.

Revising

Do not attempt to revise your paragraph right away. Put it away for a while, if possible until the next day. When you reread it, try to be as critical of it as you would be if someone else had written it. As you go over the work, ask yourself these questions.

FOUR BASES Checklist for Division-Classification

About *Unity*

☑ Have I divided my topic into three distinct parts?

☑ Is each of those parts based on the same principle of division?

About *Support*

☑ Have I provided effective details to back up each of my three points?

☑ Have I given each of the three parts approximately equal weight, devoting the same amount of time to each part?

About *Coherence*

☑ Have I used appropriate transitions and other connective devices to weave my paragraph together?

About *Sentence Skills*

☑ Have I used a consistent point of view throughout my paragraph?

☑ Have I used specific rather than general words?

☑ Have I avoided wordiness and used concise wording?

☑ Are my sentences varied?

☑ Have I checked for spelling and other sentence skills, as listed on the inside back cover of the book?

Continue revising until you are sure the answer to each question is "yes."

Writing Assignment 3

There are many ways you could classify your fellow students. Pick out one of your courses and write a paragraph in which you classify the students in that class according to one underlying principle. You may wish to choose one of the classification principles below.

Attitude toward the class   Punctuality

Participation in the class   Attendance

Method of taking notes in class   Level of confidence

Performance during oral reports,
speeches, presentations, lab sessions

If you decide, for instance, to classify students according to their attitude toward class, you might come up with these three categories:

Students actually interested in learning the material

Students who know they need to learn the material, but don't want to overdo it

Students who find the class a good opportunity to catch up with lost sleep

Of course, you may use any other principle of classification that seems appropriate. Follow the steps listed under "Prewriting" and "Revising" for Writing Assignment 2.

Writing Assignment 4

When we go to a restaurant, we probably hope that the service will be helpful, the atmosphere will be pleasant, and the food will be tasty. But as the cartoon shown on the following page suggests, restaurants that are good in all three respects may be hard to find. Write a review of a restaurant, analyzing its (1) service, (2) atmosphere, and (3) food. Visit a restaurant for this assignment, or draw on an experience you have had recently. Freewrite or make a list of observations about such elements as

Quantity of food you receive   Attitude of the servers

Taste of the food   Efficiency of the servers

Temperature of the food   Decor (consider if it's a chain restaurant)

Freshness of the ingredients   Level of cleanliness

How the food is presented   Noise level and music, if any
(garnishes, dishes, and so on)

Feel free to write about details other than those listed above. Just be sure each detail fits into one of your three categories: food, service, or atmosphere.

"The little sad faces next to some items mean they don't taste very good."

For your topic sentence, rate the restaurant by giving it from one to five stars, on the basis of your overall impression. Include the restaurant's name and location in your topic sentence. Here are some examples:

Guido's, an Italian restaurant downtown, deserves three stars.

The McDonald's on Route 70 merits a four-star rating.

The Circle Diner in Westfield barely earns a one-star rating.

Writing Assignment

5 | Writing for a Specific Purpose and Audience

In this division-classification paragraph, you will write with a specific purpose and for a specific audience. Pretend you are working at a car wash, a beauty salon, a restaurant, an automobile service center, or some other establishment that offers three different versions of a service: economy, full-service, and high-end. For each service, explain what is covered, what is done, and what is charged. Another option is to describe three versions of a product sold where you work. For example, let's say you're employed by a fast-food hamburger restaurant. You might describe three different versions of the same meal by discussing what they cost, what they include, and what size each part of the meals comes in.

Description

This chapter will explain and illustrate how to

- develop a descriptive paragraph
- write a descriptive paragraph
- revise a descriptive paragraph

In addition, you will read and consider

- three student descriptive paragraphs

Just as an artist uses paint to create a picture for viewers, writers use words to paint a picture in their readers' minds. Try to recreate this painting with words by writing a paragraph in which you describe the painting to someone who has never seen it.

When you describe something or someone, you give your readers a picture in words. To make this "word picture" as vivid and real as possible, you must observe and record specific details that appeal to your readers' senses (sight, hearing, taste, smell, and touch). More than any other type of writing, a descriptive paragraph needs sharp, colorful details.

Here is a description in which only the sense of sight is used:

A rug covers the living-room floor.

In contrast, here is a description rich in sense impressions:

A thick, reddish-brown shag rug is laid wall to wall across the living-room floor. The long, curled fibers of the shag seem to whisper as you walk through them in your bare feet, and when you squeeze your toes into the deep covering, the soft fibers push back at you with a spongy resilience.

Sense impressions include sight (*thick, reddish-brown shag rug; laid wall to wall; walk through them in your bare feet; squeeze your toes into the deep covering; push back*), hearing (*whisper*), and touch (*bare feet, soft fibers, spongy resilience*). The sharp, vivid images provided by the sensory details give us a clear picture of the rug and enable us to share the writer's experience.

In addition to sensory detail, you can include details about how a person behaves, how a thing operates, or what happens in a place. In other words, you can relate actions to help convey your *dominant impression* of your subject. This is called *narration,* a writing technique discussed in Chapter 15. For example, in "Paradise Pond," a paragraph that follows, the writer includes certain actions such as the golfers warning him about certain "critters" that live in the pond. He also tells us about his fishing bobber plunging into the water as a bass tugs at the end of his line. In "My Teenage Son's Room," the writer mentions the gerbil that scratches "against the cage wall." In addition we get a picture of the writer's son, Greg, tossing balls of papers into a "'basket'—the trash can."

In this chapter, you will be asked to describe a person, place, or thing for your readers by using words rich in sensory details. To prepare for the assignment, first read the three paragraphs ahead and then answer the questions that follow.

Paragraphs to Consider

My Teenage Son's Room

[1]I push open the door with difficulty. [2]The doorknob is loose and has to be jiggled just right before the catch releases from the doorjamb. [3]Furthermore, as I push at the door, it runs into a basketball shoe lying on the floor. [4]I manage to squeeze in through the narrow opening. [5]I am

continued

immediately aware of a pungent odor in the room, most of which is coming from the closet, to my right. [6]That's the location of a white wicker clothes hamper, heaped with grass-stained jeans, sweat-stained T-shirts, and smelly socks. [7]But the half-eaten burrito, lying dried and unappetizing on the bedside table across the room, contributes a bit of aroma, as does the glass of curdled sour milk sitting on the sunny windowsill. [8]To my left, the small wire cage on Greg's desk is also fragrant, but pleasantly. [9]From its nest of sweet-smelling cedar chips, the gerbil peers out at me with its bright eyes, its tiny claws scratching against the cage wall. [10]The floor around the wastebasket that is next to the desk is surrounded by what appears to be a sprinkling of snowballs. [11]They're actually old wadded-up school papers, and I can picture Greg sitting on his bed, crushing them into balls and aiming them at the "basket"—the trash can. [12]I glance at the bed across from the desk and chuckle because pillows stuffed under the tangled nest of blankets make it look as if someone is still sleeping there, though I know Greg is in history class right now. [13]I step carefully through the room, trying to walk through the obstacle course of science-fiction paperbacks, a wristwatch, sports magazines, and a dust-covered computer on which my son stacks empty soda cans. [14]I leave everything as I find it, but tape a note to Greg's door saying, "Isn't it about time to clean up?"

Paradise Pond

[1]It wasn't a pond at all, just a large water hole on a golf course. [2]But it was my little piece of heaven. [3]Long shards of sweet grass rose on every shore, completely encircling the water except for a small clearing where I could fish. [4]Sometimes a musty, half-sweet odor rose from the brown muck that collected around the green and yellow grass, but usually the air was clear, cool, and refreshing. [5]I was after blue gills and bass, which had somehow found their way into the pond and which I could sometimes see swimming in the sandy shallows. [6]On the other side of the pond, the golfers, playing hole 10, scowled at me, and they called out warnings about "critters" that lived there. [7]The only other sound was the crack of a steel seven iron that struck a ball and sent it flying toward the flag, which waved in the cool, silent breeze. [8]I only chuckled, my eyes fixed on the bobber that I was certain would soon plunge deep into the water as a large-mouth bass tugged on the line.

Karla

¹Karla, my brother's new girlfriend, is a catlike creature. ²Framing her face is a layer of sleek black hair that always looks just-combed. ³Her face, with its wide forehead, sharp cheekbones, and narrow, pointed chin, resembles a triangle. ⁴Karla's skin is a soft, velvety brown. ⁵Her large brown eyes slant upward at the corners, and she emphasizes their angle with a sweep of maroon eye shadow. ⁶Karla's habit of looking sidelong out of the tail of her eye makes her appear cautious, as if she were expecting something to sneak up on her. ⁷Her nose is small and flat. ⁸The sharply outlined depression under it leads the observer's eye to a pair of red-tinted lips. ⁹With their slight upward tilt at the corners, Karla's lips make her seem self-satisfied and secretly pleased. ¹⁰One reason Karla may be happy is that she recently was asked to be in a local beauty contest. ¹¹Her long neck and slim body are perfectly in proportion with her face. ¹²Karla manages to look elegant and sleek no matter how she is standing or sitting, for her body seems to be made up of graceful angles. ¹³Her slender hands are tipped with long, polished nails. ¹⁴Her narrow feet are long, too, but they appear delicate even in flat-soled running shoes. ¹⁵Somehow, Karla would look perfect in a cat's jeweled collar.

Questions

About Unity

1. Which paragraph lacks a topic sentence?

   _____

2. Which sentence in the paragraph about Karla should be omitted in the interest of paragraph unity? (*Write the sentence number here.*) _____

About Support

3. Label as *sight, touch, hearing,* or *smell* all the sensory details in the following sentences taken from the three paragraphs. The first sentence is done for you as an example.

   a. Sometimes a musty, half-sweet *smell* odor rose from the brown *sight* muck that collected around the green *sight* and yellow grass, but usually the air was *sight* clear, cool, and *touch* refreshing.

   b. I only chuckled, my eyes fixed on the bobber that I was certain would soon plunge deep into the water as a large-mouth bass tugged on the line.

   c. Her slender hands are tipped with long, polished nails.

   d. That's the location of a white wicker clothes hamper, heaped with grass-stained jeans, sweat-stained T-shirts, and smelly socks.

4. After which sentence in "Paradise Pond" are specific details needed?

_____

About Coherence

5. Spatial signals (*above, next to, to the right,* and so on) are often used to help organize details in a descriptive paragraph. List four space signals that appear in "My Teenage Son's Room":

_____   _____   _____   _____   ____   _____

6. The writer of "Karla" organizes the details by observing Karla in an orderly way. Which of Karla's features is described first? _____ Which is described last? _____ Check the method of spatial organization that best describes the paragraph:

_____ Interior to exterior

_____ Near to far

_____ Top to bottom

Developing a Descriptive Paragraph

Development through Prewriting

When Victor was assigned a descriptive paragraph, he thought at first of describing his own office at work. He began by making a list of details he noticed while looking around the office.

adjustable black chair	*computer*
beige desk	*pictures of Marie and kids on desk*
piles of papers	*desk calendar*

But Victor quickly became bored. Here is how he describes what happened next:

   "As I wrote down what I saw in my office, I was thinking, 'What a drag.' I gave up and worked on something else. Later that evening I told my wife that I was going to write a boring paragraph about my boring office. She started laughing at me. I said, 'What's so funny?' and she said, 'You're so certain that a writing assignment has to be boring that you deliberately chose a subject that bores you. How about writing about something you care about?' At first I was annoyed, but then I realized she was right. When I hear 'assignment' I automatically think 'pain in the neck' and just want to get it over with."

Victor's attitude is not uncommon. Many students who are not experienced writers don't take the time to find a topic that interests them. They grab the one closest at hand and force themselves to write about it just for the sake of completing the assignment. Like Victor, they ensure that they (and probably their instructors as well) will be bored with the task.

That evening, Victor remembered the days when, as a boy, he used to fish "the pond," really a water hole on a local public golf course in Florida. "As I remembered the 'pond,' I recalled a lot of descriptive details—sounds, smells, sights," said Victor. "I realized not only that it would be more fun to describe a place like that than my bland, boring office, but also that I would actually find it an interesting challenge to make my reader see the pond through my words."

Victor now began to make a list of details about the pond:

Brown muck surrounding the pond

Tall sweet grass

Golfers on the 10th hole

Steel clubs cracking against hard golf balls

A clear spot in the weeds—a place to fish

Blue gills, large-mouth bass

Musty smell, sweet

"Watch out for snakes, kid"

Bobber plunges into the water—a strike

Great feeling at the end of the line, bass tugs away

As he looked over his list of details, the word that came to mind was "paradise." Victor remembered this place fondly, as a beautiful and peaceful haven. He decided his topic sentence would be "It was my little piece of heaven." He then wrote this first draft:

It was my little piece of heaven, beautiful and peaceful. Grass completely surrounded the pond except for one small clearing where I could fish. All I cared about was catching fish, and I kept my eye on that bobber, waiting for it to disappear into the water. The golfers warn me to watch for snakes. I didn't care about the golfers' warnings. The only other sound is a club hitting the ball. An odor rose from the muck that collects around the grass, but it's not bad. Usually the air is refreshing. Watch out for the "critters."

Development through Revising

The next day, Victor's instructor asked to see the students' first drafts. This is what she wrote in response to Victor's:

This is a very good beginning. You have provided some strong details that appeal to the reader's sense of smell, hearing, and sight.

In your next draft, organize your paragraph better. Try spatial order. For example, you might describe the grass that surrounds the pond, then mention the fact that you found an open spot to fish from, and then tell us about the golfers' warnings. You can then end logically by explaining how you reacted to their warnings.

I encourage you to become even more specific in your details. For instance, what kind of fish were you after? As you work on each sentence, ask yourself if you can add more descriptive details to paint a more vivid picture in words.

In response to his instructor's suggestions, Victor rewrote the paragraph, beginning with the sweet grass on the shore. Then he mentioned the fish in the water. Next he focused on the golfers on the other side of the pond. He ended the paragraph with a sentence that brought the reader back to his fishing on the shoreline. He then added some more vivid details throughout and produced the paragraph that appears on page 277.

Writing a Descriptive Paragraph

Writing Assignment

1   Write a paragraph describing a certain person's room. Use as your topic sentence "I could tell by looking at the room that a _____ lived there." There are many kinds of people who could be the focus for such a paragraph. You can select any one of the following, or think of another type of person.

Photographer	Cheerleader
Cook	Football player
Student	Actor
Musician	Dancer
Hunter	Carpenter
Slob	Baby
Outdoors person	Cat or dog lover
Doctor	World traveler
Music lover	Drug addict
TV addict	Little boy or girl
Camper	Alcoholic
Computer expert	In-line skater

Prewriting

a. After choosing a topic, spend a few minutes making sure it will work. Prepare a list of all the details you can think of that support the topic. For example, a student who planned to describe a soccer player's room made this list:

soccer balls

shin guards

posters of professional soccer teams

soccer trophies

shirt printed with team name and number

autographed soccer ball

medals and ribbons

photos of player's own team

sports clippings

radio that looks like soccer ball

soccer socks

soccer shorts

HINT: If you don't have enough details, choose another type of person. Check your new choice by listing details before committing yourself to the topic.

---

b. You may want to use other prewriting techniques, such as freewriting or questioning, to develop more details for your topic. As you continue prewriting, keep the following in mind:

- Everything in the paragraph should support your point. For example, if you are writing about a soccer player's room, every detail should serve to show that the person who lives in that room plays and loves soccer. Other details—for example, the person's computer, tropical fish tank, or daily "to-do" list—should be omitted.

- Description depends on the use of specific rather than general descriptive words. For example:

General	Specific
Mess on the floor	The obstacle course of science-fiction paper-backs, a wristwatch, sports magazines, and a dust-covered computer on which my son stacks empty soda cans.
Ugly turtle tub	Large plastic tub of dirty, stagnant-looking water containing a few motionless turtles
Bad smell	Unpleasant mixture of strong chemical deodorizers, urine-soaked newspapers, and musty sawdust
Nice skin	Soft, velvety brown skin

Remember that you want your readers to experience the room vividly. Your words should be as detailed as a clear photograph, giving readers a real feel for the room. Appeal to as many senses as possible. Most of your description will involve the sense of sight, but you may be able to include details about touch, hearing, and smell as well.

- Spatial order is a good way to organize a descriptive paragraph. Move as a visitor's eye might move around the room, from right to left or from larger items to smaller ones. Here are a few transition words that show spatial relationships:

to the left	across from	on the opposite side
to the right	above	nearby
next to	below	

Such transitions will help prevent you—and your reader—from getting lost as the description proceeds.

c. Before you write, see if you can make a scratch outline based on your list. Here is one possible outline of the paragraph about the soccer player's room. Note that the details are organized according to spatial order—from the edges of the room in toward the center.

Topic sentence: I could tell by looking at the room that a soccer player lived there.

1. Walls

2. Bookcase

3. Desk

4. Chair

5. Floor

    d. Then proceed to write a first draft of your paragraph.

Revising

Read your descriptive paragraph slowly out loud to a friend. Ask the friend to close his or her eyes and try to picture the room as you read. Read it aloud a second time. Ask your friend to answer these questions.

FOUR BASES Checklist for Description

About *Unity*

  ☑ Does every detail in the paragraph support the topic sentence? Here's one way to find out: Ask your friend to imagine omitting the key word or words (in the case of our example, "soccer player") in your topic sentence. Would readers know what word should fit in that empty space?

About *Support*

  ☑ Are the details specific and vivid rather than general?

  ☑ Has the writer included details that appeal to as many senses as possible?

continued

About *Coherence*

✔ Does the paragraph follow a logical spatial order?

✔ Has the writer used transitions (such as *on top of, beside, to the left of*) to help the reader follow that order?

About *Sentence Skills*

✔ Has the writer carefully proofread his or her paragraph, using the list on the inside back cover of the book, and corrected all sentence-skills mistakes, including spelling?

Continue revising your work until you and your reader can answer "yes" to all these questions.

Writing Assignment

2   Write a paragraph describing a specific person. Select a dominant impression of the person, and use only details that will convey that impression. You might want to write about someone who falls into one of these categories:

www.mhhe.com/langan

TV or movie personality	Coworker
Brother or sister	Clergyman or clergywoman
Employer	Police officer
Child	Store owner or manager
Older person	Bartender
Close friend	Joker
Enemy or rival	Doctor or nurse

Prewriting

a. Reread the paragraph about Karla that appears earlier in this chapter. Note the dominant impression that the writer wanted to convey: that Karla is a catlike person. Having decided to focus on that impression, the writer included only details that contributed to her point. Similarly, you should focus on one dominant aspect of your subject's appearance, personality, or behavior.

   Once you have chosen the person you will write about and the impression you plan to portray, put that information into a topic sentence. Here are some examples of topic sentences that mention a particular person and the dominant impression of that person:

> Kate gives the impression of being permanently nervous.
>
> The candidate for the Senate looked like a movie star.
>
> The child was an angelic little figure.
>
> The dental receptionist was extremely reassuring.
>
> The TV newscaster seems as synthetic as a piece of Styrofoam.
>
> Our neighbor is a fussy person.
>
> The rock singer seemed to be plugged into some special kind of energy source.
>
> The police office inspired confidence.
>
> My friend Jeffrey is a slow, deliberate person.
>
> The owner of that grocery store seems burdened with troubles.

b. Make a list of the person's qualities that support your topic sentence. Write quickly; don't worry if you find yourself writing down something that doesn't quite fit. You can always edit the list later. For now, just write down all the details that occur to you that support the dominant impression you want to convey. Include details that involve as many senses as possible (sight, sound, hearing, touch, smell). For instance, here's a list one writer jotted down to support the sentence "The child was an angelic little figure":

> soft brown ringlets of hair
>
> pink cheeks
>
> wide shining eyes
>
> shrieking laugh
>
> joyful smile
>
> starched white dress
>
> white flowers in hair

c. Edit your list, striking out details that don't support your topic sentence and adding others that do. The author of the paragraph on an angelic figure crossed out one detail from the original list and added a new one:

soft brown ringlets of hair

pink cheeks

wide shining eyes

~~shrieking laugh~~

joyful smile

starched white dress

white flowers in hair

sweet singing voice

d. Decide on a spatial order of organization. In the example above, the writer ultimately decided to describe the child from head to toe.

e. Make a scratch outline for your paragraph, based on the organization you have chosen.

f. Then proceed to write a first draft of your paragraph.

Revising

Put your paragraph away for a day or so if at all possible. Then ask yourself and a peer editor these questions.

FOUR BASES Checklist for Description

About *Unity*

✓   Does my topic sentence make a general point about the person?

About *Support*

✓   Do descriptions of the appearance, tone of voice, and expressions of the people involved paint a clear picture of the person?

continued

About *Coherence*

☑ Have I used transitional words, such as *first, later,* and *then*?

About *Sentence Skills*

☑ Have I used a consistent point of view throughout my paragraph?

☑ Have I used specific rather than general words?

☑ Have I avoided wordiness?

☑ Are my sentences varied?

☑ Have I checked for spelling and other sentence skills, as listed on the inside back cover of the book?

Continue revising your work until you can answer "yes" to all these questions.

Writing Assignment

3

www.CartoonStock.com

Write a paragraph describing the cartoon shown here so that a person who has never seen it will be able to visualize it and fully understand it.

In order to write such a complete description, you must notice and report *every detail* in the cartoon. The details include such things as the way the room is arranged; the objects present in the room; what the characters are doing with those objects; the expressions on the characters' faces; and any motions that are occurring. Remember as you are describing the cartoon to give special attention to the same elements that the cartoonist gives special attention to. Your goal should be this: Someone who reads your description of the cartoon will understand it as fully as someone who saw the cartoon itself.

Writing Assignment

4 Write a paragraph describing an animal you have spent some time with—a pet, a friend's pet, an animal you've seen in a park or zoo or even on television. Write a paragraph about how the animal looks and behaves. Select details that support a dominant impression of your subject. Once you decide on the impression you wish to convey, compose a topic sentence, like either of those below, that summarizes the details you will use.

The appearance of a gorilla named Koko gives no hint of the animal's intelligence and gentleness.

A cute squirrel who has taken up residence in my backyard exhibits surprising agility and energy.

Remember to provide colorful, detailed descriptions to help your readers picture the features and behavior you are writing about. Note the contrast in the two items below.

Lacks rich descriptive details: The squirrel was gray and enjoyed our deck.

Includes rich descriptive details: On our deck, the young gray squirrel dug a hole in the dirt in a planter full of marigolds and then deposited an acorn in the hole, his fluffy tail bobbing enthusiastically all the while.

Writing Assignment

5 Pretend you are a reporter for your college newspaper. You have been given an assignment to visit a place that other students might be thinking about visiting during a day off or when they are on vacation. Your assignment is to describe your overall impression of this place and to recommend—or not—that your fellow students make an effort to visit it as well.

A museum

A town, county, state, or national park or any other place where nature can be observed

A place of worship

A shopping mall

A particularly interesting area of town

A public monument or an interesting office building

An old record shop or an antique shop

A roller skating rink

A bowling alley

A shooting range

A restaurant

A library

A hospital

A sports stadium or arena

Another college campus

A hardware store, toy store, sports shop, or clothing store

Remember that a place is often characterized by what happens there. Thus, if you are describing a place of worship, you might want to visit during a service. As you take notes about the appearance of the place, also record what goes on during the service, what the congregation does, what duties the clergy or other officials perform. You might also describe the sound of the music or the chanting, if there is any, and even quote important words or phrases used in the service.

Again, decide on a dominant impression you want to convey of the place, and use only those details that will support that impression. Follow the notes on prewriting, writing, and revising for Writing Assignment 2.

Writing Assignment

6

Writing for a Specific Purpose and Audience

In this description paragraph, you will write with a specific purpose and for a specific audience. Choose one of the following options.

Option 1

Imagine that you are an interior designer. A new dormitory is going to be built on campus, and you have been asked to create a sample dormitory room for two students. Write a paragraph describing your design of the room, telling what it would include and how it would be arranged. In your prewriting for this assignment, you might list all the relevant student needs you can think of, such as a good study space, storage space, and appropriate lighting and colors. Then put all the parts together so that they work well as a whole. Use a spatial order in your paragraph to help readers "see" your room. Begin with the following topic sentence or something like it. In each case, pretend that you are writing to some-one who might use such a room. For example, think about the needs of students and teachers if designing a classroom.

> My design for a dormitory room offers both efficiency and comfort for two students.

Feel free to use a less-than-serious tone.

Option 2

Alternatively, write a paragraph describing your design of another type of room, including any of the following:

Child's bedroom	Kitchen
Schoolroom	Porch
Restaurant	Bakery

Narration

This chapter will explain and illustrate how to

- develop a narrative paragraph
- write a narrative paragraph
- revise a narrative paragraph

In addition, you will read and consider

- three student narrative paragraphs

Adults sentimentally think of childhood as a time of happy, carefree innocence, as depicted in this photograph. Yet during childhood most of us witnessed events that began to make us aware that life was not always happy or fair. What such events do you remember? Select one and write a paragraph about it. What impression did it make on you?

At times we make a statement clear by relating in detail something that has happened. In the story we tell, we present the details in the order in which they happened. A person might say, for example, "I was embarrassed yesterday," and then go on to illustrate the statement with the following narrative:

> I was hurrying across campus to get to a class. It had rained heavily all morning, so I was hopscotching my way around puddles in the pathway. I called to two friends ahead to wait for me, and right before I caught up to them, I came to a large puddle that covered the entire path. I had to make a quick choice of either stepping into the puddle or trying to jump over it. I jumped, wanting to seem cool, since my friends were watching, but didn't clear the puddle. Water splashed everywhere, drenching my shoe, sock, and pants cuff, and spraying the pants of my friends as well. "Well done, Dave!" they said. My embarrassment was all the greater because I had tried to look so casual.

The speaker's details have made his moment of embarrassment vivid and real for us, and we can see and understand just why he felt as he did.

In addition to vivid details that convey action, you might want to include both characters and *dialogue* (what people say) in your narrative. For example, in "Heartbreak" we meet Bonnie, the writer's former girlfriend. When he asks her about her new love interest ("Who is Blake?"), Bonnie asks him, "What do you want to hear about—my classes or Blake?" An even greater use of character and dialogue is made in "Losing My Father." In fact, Laura, the writer, reports a fairly long conversation with her father, quoting him and herself frequently.

In this section, you will be asked to tell a story that illustrates or explains some point. The paragraphs below all present narrative experiences that support a point. Read them and then answer the questions that follow.

Paragraphs to Consider

Heartbreak

^{1}Bonnie and I had gotten engaged in August, just before she left for college at Penn State. ^{2}A week before Thanksgiving, I drove up to see her as a surprise. ^{3}When I knocked on the door of her dorm room, she was indeed surprised, but not in a pleasant way. ^{4}She introduced me to her roommate, who looked uncomfortable and quickly left. ^{5}I asked Bonnie

continued

how classes were going, and at the same time I tugged on the sleeve of my heavy sweater in order to pull it off. [6]As I was slipping it over my head, I noticed a large photo on the wall—of Bonnie and a tall guy laughing together. [7]It was decorated with paper flowers and a yellow ribbon, and on the ribbon was written "Bonnie and Blake." [8]"What's going on?" I said. [9]I stood there stunned and then felt anger that grew rapidly. [10]"Who is Blake?" I asked. [11]Bonnie laughed nervously and said, "What do you want to hear about—my classes or Blake?" [12]I don't really remember what she then told me, except that Blake was a sophomore math major. [13]I felt a terrible pain in the pit of my stomach, and I wanted to rest my head on someone's shoulder and cry. [14]I wanted to tear down the sign and run out, but I did nothing. [15]Clumsily I pulled on my sweater again. [16]My knees felt weak, and I barely had control of my body. [17]I opened the room door, and suddenly more than anything I wanted to slam the door shut so hard that the dorm walls would collapse. [18]Instead, I managed to close the door quietly. [19]I walked away understanding what was meant by a broken heart.

Losing My Father

[1]Although my father died ten years ago, I felt that he'd been lost to me four years earlier. [2]Dad had been diagnosed with Alzheimer's disease, an illness that destroys the memory. [3]He couldn't work any longer, but in his own home he got along pretty well. [4]I lived hundreds of miles away and wasn't able to see my parents often. [5]So when my first child was a few weeks old, I flew home with the baby to visit them. [6]After Mom met us at the airport, we picked up Dad and went to their favorite local restaurant. [7]Dad was quiet, but kind and gentle as always, and he seemed glad to see me and his new little grandson. [8]Everyone went to bed early. [9]In the morning, Mom left for work. [10]I puttered happily around in my old bedroom. [11]I heard Dad shuffling around in the kitchen, making coffee. [12]Eventually I realized that he was pacing back and forth at the foot of the stairs as if he were uneasy. [13]I called down to him, "Everything all right there? [14]I'll be down in a minute." [15]"Fine!" he called back, with forced-sounding cheerfulness. [16]Then he stopped pacing and called up to me, "I must be getting old and forgetful. [17]When did you get here?" [18]I was surprised, but made myself answer calmly. [19]"Yesterday afternoon. [20]Remember, Mom met us at the airport, and then we went to The Skillet for dinner." [21]"Oh, yes," he said. [22]"I had roast beef." [23]I began to relax. [24]But then he continued, hesitantly, "And . . . who are you?" [25]My breath stopped

continued

as if I'd been punched in the stomach. [26]When I could steady my voice, I answered, "I'm Laura; I'm your daughter. [27]I'm here with my baby son, Max." [28]"Oh" was all he said. [29]"Oh." [30]And he wandered into the living room and sat down. [31]In a few minutes I joined him and found him staring blankly out the window. [32]He was a polite host, asking if I wanted anything to eat, and if the room was too cold. [33]I answered with an aching heart, mourning for his loss and for mine.

The End of Smallpox

[1]The deadly infectious disease known as smallpox killed millions over the centuries. [2]Today, however, the disease has been completely eliminated. [3]Smallpox began in Africa, some scientists believe, and then moved to Asia thousands of years ago. [4]The first signs that smallpox could be eradicated came about one thousand years ago in Asia. [5]About the year 1040, it was discovered that pulverizing the scabs of smallpox victims and blowing the dust into the nose of a healthy person would make that person immune. [6]Then, at the end of the eighteenth century, a British doctor, Edward Jenner, found that farmworkers who got cowpox, a disease that attacks cows and oxen, became immune to smallpox. [7]Cowpox also affects rodents such as mice and voles. [8]Soon thereafter, Jenner developed a vaccine by using the pus in a farmworker's cowpox boil to make a serum that he injected into a healthy young boy. [9]Several weeks later, the boy was exposed to smallpox, but he never developed the disease. [10]In the late 1960s, an attempt to eradicate smallpox was launched by the World Health Organization, and since 1980, no additional cases of smallpox have been reported.

Questions

About Unity

1. Which paragraph lacks a topic sentence?

_____

Write a topic sentence for the paragraph.

_____

_____

2. Which sentence in "The End of Smallpox" should be omitted in the interest of paragraph unity? (Write the sentence number here.) _____

About Support

3. What is for you the best (most real and vivid) detail or image in the paragraph "Heartbreak"?

_____

_____

What is the best detail or image in "Losing My Father"?

_____

_____

What is the best detail or image in "The End of Smallpox"?

_____

_____

4. Which two paragraphs include the actual words spoken by the participants?

_____

_____

About Coherence

5. Do the three paragraphs use time order or emphatic order to organize details?

_____

6. What are the five transition words used in "The End of Smallpox"?

_____

_____

Developing a Narrative Paragraph

Development through Prewriting

Gary's instructor was helping her students think of topics for their narrative paragraphs. "A narrative is simply a story that illustrates a point," she said. "That point is often about an emotion you felt. Looking at a list of emotions may help you think of a topic. Ask yourself what incident in your life has made you feel any of these emotions."

The instructor then jotted these feelings on the board:

Anger	Thankfulness
Embarrassment	Loneliness
Jealousy	Sadness
Amusement	Terror
Confusion	Relief

As Gary looked over the list, he thought of several experiences in his life. "The word 'angry' made me think about a time when I was a kid. My brother took my skateboard without permission and left it in the park, where it got stolen. 'Amused' made me think of when I watched my roommate, who claimed he spoke Spanish, try to bargain with a street vendor in Mexico. He got so flustered that he ended up paying even more than the vendor had originally asked for. When I got to 'sad', though, I thought about when I visited Bonnie and found out she was dating someone else. 'Sad' wasn't a strong enough word, though— I was heartbroken. So I decided to write about heartbreak."

Gary's first step was to do some freewriting. Without worrying about spelling or grammar, he simply wrote down everything that came into his mind concerning his visit to Bonnie. Here is what he came up with:

> I hadn't expected to see Bonnie until Christmas. We'd got engaged just before she went off to college. The drive to Penn State took ten hours each way and that seemed like to much driving for just a weekend visit. But I realized I had a long weekend over Thanksgiving I decided to surprise her. I think down deep I knew something was wrong. She had sounded sort of cool on the phone and she hadn't been writing as often. I guess I wanted to convince myself that everything was OK. We'd been dating since we were 16 and I couldn't imagine not being with her. When I knocked at her dorm door I remember how she was smiling when she opened the door. Her expression changed to one of surprise. Not happy surprise. I hugged her and she sort of hugged me back but like you'd hug your brother. Another girl was in the room. Bonnie said, "This is

continued

Pam," and Pam shot out of the room like I had a disease. Everything seemed wrong and confused. I started taking off my sweater and then I saw it. On a bulletin board was this photo of Bonnie with Blake, the guy she had been messing around with. They broke up about a year later, but by then I never wanted to see Bonnie again. I couldn't believe Bonnie would start seeing somebody else when we were planning to get married. It had even been her idea to get engaged. Before she left for college. Later on I realized that wasn't the first dishonest thing she'd done. I got out of there as quick as I could.

Development through Revising

Gary knew that the first, freewritten version of his paragraph needed work. Here are the comments he made after he reread it the following day.

"Although my point is supposed to be that my visit to Bonnie was heartbreaking, I didn't really get that across. I need to say more about how the experience felt.

"I've included some information that doesn't really support my point. For instance, what happened to Bonnie and Blake later isn't important here. Also, I think I spend too much time explaining the circumstances of the visit. I need to get more quickly to the point where I arrived at Bonnie's dorm.

"I think I should include more dialogue, too. That would make the reader feel more like a witness to what really happened."

With this self-critique in mind, Gary revised his paragraph until he had produced the version that appears on page 294.

Writing a Narrative Paragraph

Writing | Assignment

1 Write a paragraph about an experience in which a certain emotion was predominant. The emotion might be fear, pride, satisfaction, embarrassment, or any of these:

Frustration	Sympathy	Shyness
Love	Bitterness	Disappointment
Sadness	Violence	Happiness
Terror	Surprise	Jealousy
Shock	Nostalgia	Anger
Relief	Loss	Hate
Envy	Silliness	Nervousness

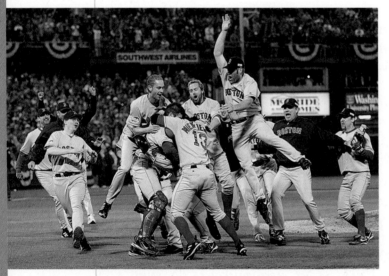

The experience you write about should be limited in time, like the experiences in two of the paragraphs in this chapter ("Heartbreak" and "Losing My Father"), which occurred within relatively short periods.

A good way to bring your event to life is to include some dialogue. Words that you or someone else said can help make a situation come alive. First, though, be sure to check the section on quotation marks on pages 536–543.

Prewriting

a. Begin by freewriting. Think of an experience or event that caused you to feel a certain emotion strongly. Then spend ten minutes writing freely about the experience. Do not worry at this point about such matters as spelling or grammar or putting things in the right order. Instead, just try to get down all the details you can think of that seem related to the experience.

b. This preliminary writing will help you decide whether your topic is promising enough to develop further. If it is not, choose another emotion and repeat step *a*. If it does seem promising, do two things:

- First, write your topic sentence, underlining the emotion you will focus on. For example, "My first day in kindergarten was one of the <u>scariest</u> days of my life."
- Second, make up a list of all the details involved in the experience. Then number these details according to the order in which they occurred.

c. Referring to your list of details, write a rough draft of your paragraph. Use time signals such as *first, then, after, next, while, during,* and *finally* to help connect details as you move from the beginning to the middle to the end of your narrative. Be sure to include not only what happened but also how you felt about what was going on.

Revising

Put your first draft away for a day or so. When you return to it, read it over, asking yourself these questions.

FOUR BASES Checklist for Narration

About *Unity*

☑ Does my topic sentence clearly state what emotion the experience made me feel?

☑ Are there any off-topic sentences I should eliminate for the sake of paragraph unity?

About *Support*

☑ Have I included some dialogue to make the experience come alive?

☑ Have I explained how I felt as the experience occurred?

About *Coherence*

☑ Have I used time order to narrate the experience from beginning to end?

☑ Have I used time signals to connect one detail to the next?

continued

About *Sentence Skills*

☑ Have I carefully proofread my paragraph, using the list on the inside back cover of the book, and corrected all sentence-skills mistakes, including spelling?

☑ Is the first-person point of view in my paragraph consistent?

☑ Did I use verb tenses consistently and correctly? (This is especially important when relaying a story.)

Continue revising your work until you can answer "yes" to all these questions.

Writing Assignment

2 Narrate a real-life event you have witnessed. Listed below are some places where interesting personal interactions often happen. Think of an event that you saw happen at one of these places, or visit one of them and take notes on an incident to write about.

The traffic court or small-claims court in your area

The dinner table at your or someone else's home

A waiting line at a supermarket, unemployment office, ticket counter, movie theater, or cafeteria

A doctor's office

An audience at a movie, concert, or sports event

A classroom

A restaurant

A student lounge

Prewriting

a. Decide what point you will make about the incident. What one word or phrase characterizes the scene you witnessed? Your narration of the incident will emphasize that characteristic.

b. Write your topic sentence. The topic sentence should state where the incident happened as well as your point about it. Here are some possibilities:

> I witnessed a *heartwarming* incident at Taco Bell yesterday.
>
> Two fans at last week's baseball game got into a *hilarious* argument.

The scene at our family dinner table Monday was one of complete *confusion*.

A *painful* dispute went on in Atlantic County small-claims court yesterday.

c. Use the questioning technique to remind yourself of details that will make your narrative come alive. Ask yourself questions like these and write down your answers:

Whom was I observing?

How were they dressed?

What were their facial expressions like?

What tones of voice did they use?

What did I hear them say?

d. Drawing details from the notes you have written, write the first draft of your paragraph. Remember to use time signals such as *then, after that, during, meanwhile,* and *finally* to connect one sentence to another.

Revising

After you have put your paragraph away for a day, read it to a friend who will give you honest feedback. You and your friend should consider these questions.

FOUR BASES Checklist for Narration

About *Unity*

☑   Does my topic sentence make a general point about the incident?

About *Support*

☑   Do descriptions of the appearance, tone of voice, and expressions of the people involved paint a clear picture of the incident?

About *Coherence*

☑   Is the sequence of events made clear by transitional words such as *first, later,* and *then*?

continued

About *Sentence Skills*

✓   Have I used a consistent point of view throughout my paragraph?

✓   Have I used specific rather than general words?

✓   Have I avoided wordiness?

✓   Are my sentences varied?

✓   Have I checked for spelling and other sentence skills, as listed on the inside back cover of the book?

Continue revising your work until you and your reader can answer "yes" to all these questions.

Writing Assignment

3   In a story, something happens. The *Peanuts* cartoon on the following page is a little story about the would-be writer, Snoopy, who gets a rejection letter and loses his temper. For this assignment, tell a story about something that happened to you.

Make sure that your story has a point, expressed in the first sentence of the paragraph. If necessary, tailor your narrative to fit your purpose. Use time order to organize your details (*first* this happened; *then* this; *after* that, this; *next,* this; and so on). Concentrate on providing as many specific details as possible so that the reader can really share your experience. Try to make it as vivid for the reader as it was for you when you first experienced it.

Use one of the topics below or a topic of your own choosing. Whatever topic you choose, remember that your story must illustrate or support a point stated in the first sentence of your paper.

A time you lost your temper

A moment of great happiness or sadness

Your best or worst date

A time you took a foolish risk

An incident that changed your life

A time when you did or did not do the right thing

Your best or worst holiday or birthday, or some other day

A time you learned a lesson or taught a lesson to someone else

An occasion of triumph in sports or some other area

© United Feature Syndicate, Inc.

You may wish to refer to the suggestions for prewriting and revising in Writing Assignments 1 and 2.

Writing Assignment

4

Write a paragraph that shows, through a personal experience, the truth or falsity of a popular belief such as one from the list below.

Haste makes waste.

Don't count your chickens before they hatch.

A bird in the hand is worth two in the bush.

It isn't what you know; it's who you know.

You really never know people until you see them in an emergency.

If you don't help yourself, no one else will.

An ounce of prevention is worth a pound of cure.

You get what you pay for.

A fool and his money are soon parted.

Nice guys finish last.

Begin with a topic sentence that expresses your agreement or disagreement with the saying or belief—for example:

"Never give advice to a friend" is not always good advice, as I learned after helping a friend reunite with her boyfriend.

Remember that the purpose of your story is to support your topic sentence. Omit details that don't support it. Also feel free to make up details that will.

Writing Assignment

5 Writing for a Specific Purpose and Audience

In this narrative paragraph, you will write with a specific purpose and for a specific audience. Imagine that a younger brother, sister, or friend must make an important decision. Perhaps he or she must decide whether to drop a difficult class or what to do about a coworker who is stealing from the cash register. Narrate a story from your experience (or from the experience of someone you know) that relates to the decision this younger person must make. Also, state the lesson that the story teaches. Here are more suggestions for decisions to write about:

Should he or she live at home, in the dorm, or in an apartment with friends?

How should he or she deal with friends who are involved with drugs, stealing or some other dangerous behavior?

Refer to the suggestions for prewriting and revising in Writing Assignments 1 and 2.

Argument

This chapter will explain and illustrate how to

- develop an argument paragraph
- write an argument paragraph
- revise an argument paragraph

In addition, you will read and consider

- three student argument paragraphs

Do paparazzi have a right to follow a celebrity's every move, snapping photographs all along the way? Write a paragraph in which you argue for or against the outrageous tactics of the paparazzi.

Most of us know someone who enjoys a good argument. Such a person usually challenges any sweeping statement we might make. "Why do you say that?" he or she will ask. "Give your reasons." Our questioner then listens carefully as we cite our reasons, waiting to see if we really do have solid evidence to support our point of view. In an argument such as the one going on in the cartoon, the two parties each present their supporting evidence. The goal is to determine who has the more solid evidence to support his or her point of view. A questioner may make us feel a bit nervous, but we may also appreciate the way he or she makes us think through our opinions.

The ability to advance sound, compelling arguments is an important skill in everyday life. We can use argument to get an extension on a term paper, obtain a favor from a friend, or convince an employer that we are the right person for a job. Understanding persuasion based on clear, logical reasoning can also help us see through the sometimes faulty arguments advanced by advertisers, editors, politicians, and others who try to bring us over to their side.

REAL LIFE ADVENTURES © 2002 GarLanCo Productions. Reprinted with permission of Universal Press Syndicate

Provide Logical Support

The best way to prove a point or to persuade someone to do something is simply to provide enough evidence or support for your position. Thus, if you are trying to persuade the president of your college to hire more librarians, you might explain that you had to wait for more than an hour to get the help you needed when recently researching a paper topic.

But you wouldn't stop there. You might get a hundred other students to attest to the same problem by signing a petition. You might also find out the student-librarian ratios at other colleges and compare them with the ratio at your school. Finally, you might conduct a survey to estimate the number of students who use the library each semester or the number of research papers that are assigned at your school each term. All of this would provide hard evidence to help you make your case. Of course, you would want to present your position logically and fairly. In this case, it seems only logical and fair that if students are being requested to do library research, enough librarians should be on hand to assist them.

Anticipate Opposing Arguments

Another way to strengthen your argument is to anticipate and address opposing arguments. Let's say the college's budget is stretched to the limit. If so, the college president might respond to your argument simply by stating that the lack of funds prevents the hiring of more librarians. If you believe this to be true, the first thing to do is to admit that it is. The next is to offer a solution to the problem, perhaps by suggesting that money from a less important aspect of college operations be shifted to the library's budget. Of course, if you don't believe that the opposing argument is true, you will have to disprove it convincingly before you move on.

Establish Your Credibility

Yet another important requirement for arguing persuasively is to establish your credibility. In other words, you will need to convince your readers that you know what you are talking about and that your opinion is sound. For example, in "Living Alone," a student paragraph that follows, the writer establishes his credibility by telling us that he "lived alone for ten years before [he] got married."

Appeal to Your Audience

Finally, remember that tone and audience are even more important to argument than to other types of writing. While you may want to appeal to your readers' self-interest and emotions, try to remain as clear and logical as you can. For example, at the end of "Bashing Men," another paragraph that follows, the author recounts a common joke whose point is that no "decent man" exists, in order to help convince us that there is simply too much man-bashing in society. Doing so clearly appeals to readers' sense of fair play. At the same time, the writer never uses language that is inflammatory or inappropriate. The tone in this paragraph is, at times, emphatic, but it is always fair and controlled.

In this chapter, you will be asked to argue a position and defend it with a series of solid reasons. In a general way, you are doing the same thing with all the paragraph assignments in the book: making a point and then supporting it. The difference here is that, in a more direct and formal manner, you will advance a point about which you feel strongly and seek to persuade others to agree with you.

Paragraphs to Consider

Let's Ban Proms

[1]While many students regard proms as peak events in high school life, I believe that high school proms should be banned. [2]One reason is that even before the prom takes place, it causes problems. [3]Teenagers are separated into "the ones who were asked" and "the ones who weren't." [4]Being one of those who weren't asked can be heartbreaking to a sensitive young person. [5]Another pre-prom problem is money. [6]The price of the various

continued

items needed can add up quickly to a lot of money. [7]The prom itself can be unpleasant and frustrating, too. [8]At the beginning of the evening, the girls enviously compare dresses while the boys sweat nervously inside their rented suits. [9]During the dance, the couples who have gotten together only to go to the prom have split up into miserable singles. [10]When the prom draws to a close, the popular teenagers drive off happily to other parties while the less popular ones head home, as usual. [11]Perhaps the main reason proms should be banned, however, is the drinking and driving that go on after the prom is over. [12]Teenagers pile into their cars on their way to "after-proms" and pull out the bottles and cans stashed under the seat. [13]By the time the big night is finally over, at 4 or 5 A.M., students are trying to weave home without encountering the police or a roadside tree. [14]Some of them do not make it, and prom night turns into tragedy. [15]For all these reasons, proms have no place in our schools.

Bashing Men

[1]Our culture now puts down men in ways that would be considered very offensive if the targets were women. [2]For instance, men are frequently portrayed in popular culture as bumbling fools. [3]The popular TV show *The Simpsons*, for instance, shows the father, Homer, as a total idiot, dishonest and childish. [4]His son, Bart, is equally foolish; but the mother, Marge, and the sister, Lisa, are levelheaded and responsible. [5]Little children love the "Berenstain Bears" books, which are supposed to teach lessons about subjects including honesty, bad habits, and going to the doctor. [6]In every book, while the mother bear gives her cubs good advice, the father bear acts stupidly and has to be taught a lesson along with the kids. [7]In addition, society teaches us to think of men as having no value in a family other than to contribute money. [8]Popular stars go on national TV and proclaim that because they are financially independent women, their babies don't need a father. [9]Families on welfare are denied benefits if the children's father stays in the home—apparently if he isn't bringing in money, the family is better-off without him. [10]The welfare system is deeply flawed in other ways as well. [11]And women tell each other men-bashing jokes that would be considered sexist and offensive if they were directed at women. [12]Here's one: "Question: A woman has a flat tire. [13]Santa Claus, Oprah Winfrey, and a decent man all stop to help her. [14]Who actually changes the tire?" [15]The answer: "Oprah, of course. [16]The other two are fictional characters." [17]Women deserve to be treated with respect, but that doesn't mean men should be put down.

Living Alone

[1]Living alone is quite an experience. [2]I know because I lived alone for ten years before I got married. [3]People who live alone, for one thing, have to learn to do all kinds of tasks by themselves. [4]They must learn—even if they have had no experience—to change fuses, put up curtains and shades, temporarily dam an overflowing toilet, cook a meal, and defrost a refrigerator. [5]When there is no father, husband, mother, or wife to depend on, a person can't fall back on the excuse, "I don't know how to do that." [6]Those who live alone also need the strength to deal with people. [7]Alone, singles must face noisy neighbors, unresponsive landlords, dishonest repair people, and aggressive bill collectors. [8]Because there are no buffers between themselves and the outside world, people living alone have to handle every visitor—friendly or unfriendly—alone. [9]Finally, singles need a large dose of courage to cope with occasional panic and unavoidable loneliness. [10]That weird thump in the night is even more terrifying when there is no one in the next bed or the next room. [11]Frightening weather or unexpected bad news is doubly bad when the worry can't be shared. [12]Even when life is going well, little moments of sudden loneliness can send shivers through the heart. [13]Struggling through such bad times taps into reserves of courage that people may not have known they possessed. [14]Facing everyday tasks, confronting all types of people, and handling panic and loneliness can shape singles into brave, resourceful, and more independent people.

About Unity

1. The topic sentence in "Living Alone" is too broad. Circle the topic sentence below that states accurately what the paragraph is about.

   a. Living alone can make one a better person.

   b. Living alone can create feelings of loneliness.

   c. Living alone should be avoided.

2. Which sentence in "Bashing Men" should be eliminated in the interest of paragraph unity? (*Write the sentence number here.*) _____

3. How many reasons are given to support the topic sentence in each paragraph?

   a. In "Let's Ban Proms" _____ one _____ two _____ three _____ four

   b. In "Bashing Men" _____ one _____ two _____ three _____ four

   c. In "Living Alone" _____ one _____ two _____ three _____ four

4. After which sentence in "Let's Ban Proms" are more specific details needed? _____

About Coherence

5. Which paragraph uses a combination of time and emphatic order to organize its details? _____

6. What are the three main transition words in "Living Alone"?

_____   _____   _____

Complete the outline below of "Bashing Men." Summarize in a few words the supporting material that fits under the topic sentence: After *1, 2,* and *3,* write in the three main points of support for the topic sentence. In the spaces after the numbers, write in the examples used to support those three main points. Two items have been done for you as examples.

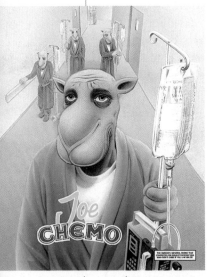

Images can make visual arguments as well. What visual argument does this spoof-ad make? Is it effective? Why or why not?

Topic sentence: Our culture now puts down men in ways that would be considered very offensive if the targets were women.

1. _____

_____

a. _____

_____

b. Berenstain Bears

2. _____

_____

a. _____

_____

b. Welfare benefits cut off if father in home

3. _____

_____

a. _____

_____

Developing an Argument Paragraph

Development through Prewriting

Yolanda is the student author of "Let's Ban Proms." She decided on her topic after visiting her parents' home one weekend and observing her younger brother's concern about his upcoming prom.

"I really felt bad for Martin as I saw what he was going through," Yolanda said. "He's usually a happy kid who enjoys school. But this weekend he wasn't talking about his track meets or term papers or any of the things he's usually chatting about. Instead he was all tied up in knots about his prom. The girl he'd really wanted to go with had already been asked, and so friends had fixed him up with a girl he barely knew who didn't have a date either. Neither of them was excited about being together, but they felt that they just 'had' to go. And now he's worried about how to afford renting a tux, and how will he get a cool car to go in, and all that stuff. It's shaping up to be a really stressful, expensive evening. When I was in high school, I saw a lot of bad things associated with the prom, too. I hate to see young kids feeling pressured to attend an event that is fun for only a few."

Yolanda began prewriting by making a list of all the negative aspects of proms. This is what she came up with:

Drinking after prom

Car accidents (most important!)

Competition for dates

Preparation for prom cuts into school hours

Rejection of not being asked

Waste of school money

Going with someone you don't like

Separates popular from unpopular

Expensive

Bad-tempered chaperones

Next, Yolanda numbered the details in the order she was going to present them. She also struck out details she decided not to use:

6   Drinking after prom

7   Car accidents (most important!)

3   Competition for dates

~~Preparation for prom cuts into school hours~~

1   Rejection of not being asked

~~Waste of school money~~

4   Going with someone you don't like

5   Separates popular from unpopular

2   Expensive

~~Bad-tempered chaperones~~

Drawing from these notes, Yolanda wrote the following first draft of her paragraph:

In my opinion, high school proms should be banned. First, they cause unhappiness by separating students into "the ones who were asked" and "the ones who weren't." Proms are also expensive, as anyone who has attended one knows. The competition for dates can damage previously strong friendships. Many couples get together only in order to have a date for the prom and do not enjoy each other's company. After the prom, too, the kids are separated into "more popular" and "less popular" groups, with the popular ones going to after-prom parties. The biggest reason to ban proms, though, is the prom-night drinking that commonly occurs. Teenagers hide liquor in their cars and then try to drive home drunk. Some of them do not make it. For all these reasons, proms should be banned.

Development through Revising

Yolanda's instructor reviewed her first draft and made these comments:

The order of your paragraph could be made stronger. Although you make good use of emphatic order (by ending with "the biggest reason to ban proms"), it's less clear that the paragraph is also organized according to time—in other words, you move from before the prom starts to during the prom to after it. Better use of transitional language will make the organization more clear.

Also, you could make the paragraph more alive by including concrete details and illustrations. Your main points would be stronger with such support.

With these comments in mind, Yolanda revised her paragraph until she produced the version that appears on pages 309–310.

Writing an Argument Paragraph

Writing Assignment

1

Develop an argument paragraph based on one of the following statements:

Condoms should (*or* should not) be made available in high schools.

_____ (*name a specific athlete*) is the athlete most worthy of admiration in his *or* her sport.

Television is one of the best (*or* worst) inventions of this century.

_____ make the best (*or* worst) pets.

Cigarette and alcohol advertising should (*or* should not) be banned.

Teenagers make poor parents.

_____ is one public figure today who can be considered a hero.

This college needs a better _____ (cafeteria *or* library *or* student center *or* grading policy *or* attendance policy).

Prewriting

a. Make up brief outlines for any three of the statements above. Make sure you have three separate and distinct reasons for each statement. Below is an example of a brief outline for a paragraph making another point.

> *Large cities should outlaw passenger cars.*
>
> 1. *Cut down on smog and pollution*
>
> 2. *Cut down on noise*
>
> 3. *Make more room for pedestrians*

b. Decide, perhaps through discussion with your instructor or classmates, which of your outlines is the most promising for development into a paragraph. Make sure your supporting points are logical by asking yourself in each case, "Does this item truly support my topic sentence?"

c. Do some prewriting. Prepare a list of all the details you can think of that might actually support your point. Don't limit yourself; include more details than you can actually use. Here, for example, are details generated by the writer of "Living Alone":

Deal with power failures	*Noisy neighbors*
Nasty landlords	*Develop courage*
Scary noises at night	*Do all the cooking*
Spiders	*Home repairs*
Bill collectors	*Obscene phone calls*
Frightening storms	*Loneliness*

d. Decide which details you will use to develop your paragraph. Number the details in the order in which you will present them. Because presenting the strongest reason last (emphatic order) is the most effective way to organize an argument paragraph, be sure to save your most powerful reason for last. Here is how the author of "Living Alone" made decisions about details:

1	Deal with power failures
4	Nasty landlords
7	Scary noises at night
	~~Spiders~~
6	Bill collectors
8	Frightening storms
5	Noisy neighbors
10	Develop courage
2	Do all the cooking
3	Home repairs
	~~Obscene phone calls~~
9	Loneliness

e. Write the first draft of your paragraph. As you write, develop each reason with specific details. For example, in "Living Alone," notice how the writer makes the experience of living alone come alive with phrases like "That weird thump in the night" or "little moments of sudden loneliness can send shivers through the heart."

Revising

Put your paragraph away for a day or so. Then look over the checklist that follows.

FOUR BASES Checklist for Argument

About *Unity*

☑ Imagine that your audience is a jury who will ultimately render a verdict on your argument. Have you presented a convincing case? If you were on the jury, would you both understand and be favorably impressed by this argument?

☑ Does every one of your supporting points help prove the argument stated in your topic sentence?

About *Support*

☑ Have you backed up your points of support with specific details?

☑ Have you appealed to your readers' senses with these details?

About *Coherence*

☑ Have you used emphatic order in your paragraph, saving the most important, strongest detail for last?

About *Sentence Skills*

☑ Have you used strong verbs (rather than *is* and *to be*) throughout?

☑ Have you used active verbs in your writing?

☑ Have you checked your paper for sentence-skills mistakes, including spelling? Use the checklist on the inside back cover of this book.

Continue revising your work until you can answer "yes" to all these questions.

Writing Assignment

2   Write a paragraph in which you take a stand on one of the controversial points below. Support the point with three reasons.

Students should not be required to attend high school.

All handguns should be banned.

The death penalty should exist for certain crimes.

Abortion should remain legal.

Federal prisons should be coed, and prisoners should be allowed to marry.

The government should set up centers where sick or aged persons can go voluntarily to commit suicide.

Parents should never hit their children.

Prostitution should be legalized.

Prewriting

a. As a useful exercise to help you begin developing your argument, your instructor might give class members a chance to "stand up" for what they believe in. One side of the front of the room should be designated *strong agreement* and the other side *strong disagreement,* with an imaginary line representing varying degrees of agreement or disagreement in between. The instructor will read one value statement at a time from the list above, and students will move to the appropriate spot, depending on their degree of agreement or disagreement. Some time will be allowed for students, first, to discuss with those near them the reasons they are standing where they are; and, second, to state to those at the other end of the scale the reasons for their position.

b. Begin your paragraph by writing a sentence that expresses your attitude toward one of the value statements above—for example, "I feel that prostitution should be legalized."

c. Outline the reason or reasons you hold the opinion that you do. Your support may be based on your own experience, the experience of someone you know, or logic. For example, an outline of a paragraph based on one student's logic looked like this:

I feel that prostitution should be legalized for the following reasons:

1. Prostitutes would then have to pay their fair share of income tax.

2. Government health centers would administer regular checkups. This would help prevent the spread of AIDS and venereal disease.

3. Prostitutes would be able to work openly and independently and would not be controlled by pimps and gangsters.

4. Most of all, prostitutes would be less looked down on—an attitude that is psychologically damaging to those who may already have emotional problems.

d. Write a first draft of your paragraph, providing specific details to back up each point in your outline.

Revising

Put your paragraph away for at least a day. Ask a friend whose judgment you trust to read and critique it. Your friend should consider each of these questions.

FOUR BASES Checklist for Argument

About *Unity*

☑ Does the topic sentence clearly state the writer's opinion on a controversial subject?

About *Support*

☑ Does the paragraph include at least three separate and distinct reasons that support the author's argument?

☑ Is each of the three reasons backed up by specific, relevant evidence?

About *Coherence*

☑ Has the author saved the most powerful reason for last?

About *Sentence Skills*

☑ Has the author used a consistent point of view throughout the paragraph?

☑ Has the author used specific rather than general words?

☑ Has the author avoided wordiness?

☑ Has the author checked for spelling and other sentence skills, as listed on the inside back cover of the book?

Continue revising your work until you and your reader can answer "yes" to all these questions.

Writing Assignment 3

Where do you think it is best to bring up children—in the country, the suburbs, or the city? Write a paragraph in which you argue that one of those three environments is best for families with young children. Your argument should cover two types of reasons: (1) the advantages of living in the environment you've chosen and (2) the disadvantages of living in the other places. Use the following, or something much like it, for your topic sentence:

For families with young children, (*the country, a suburb,* or *the city*)

_____ is the best place to live.

For each reason you advance, include at least one persuasive example. For instance, if you argue that the cultural life in the city is one important reason to live there, you should explain in detail how going to a science museum is interesting and helpful to children. After deciding on your points of support, arrange them in a brief outline, saving your strongest point for last. In your paragraph, introduce each of your reasons with an addition transition, such as *first of all, another, also,* and *finally.*

Writing Assignment 4

Write a paper in which you use research findings to help support one of the following points:

Cigarettes should be illegal.

Any person convicted of drunken driving should be required to spend time in jail.

Drivers should not be permitted to use cellphones.

Everyone should own a pet.

High schools should (*or* should not) pass out birth-control devices and information to students.

Homosexuals should (*or* should not) be allowed in the armed forces.

Schools should be open all year round.

Advertising should not be permitted on young children's TV shows.

Same-sex marriage should be legal.

Chapter 19, "Using the Library and the Internet" (pages 370–385), will show you how to use keywords and search engines to think about your topic and do research. See if you can organize your paper in the form of three separate and distinct reasons that support the topic. Put these reasons into a scratch outline and use it as a guide in writing your paragraph.

Writing Assignment

5 | Writing for a Specific Purpose and Audience

In this argument paragraph, you will write with a specific purpose and for a specific audience. Imagine that you have finally met Mr. or Ms. Right—but your parents don't approve of him or her. Specifically, they are against your doing one of the following:

Continuing to see this person

Seriously dating this person and no one else

Moving in together

Getting married at the end of the school year

Write a letter to your parents explaining in detail why you have made your choice. Do your best to convince them that it is a good choice.

If this assignment doesn't appeal to you, write a paragraph to your parents, your siblings, or other loved ones explaining why you have decided to take some action they might disagree with. Here are some examples:

Changing your religion

Changing your academic major

Leaving school for a semester to work or to travel

Joining a particular organization

Getting a piercing or a tattoo

Leaving home or moving out of the dorm to live in an apartment

Joining the military

Renting an apartment with a member of the opposite sex

Dating someone of a different race or religion

Additional Paragraph Assignments

17

Permission from Chemistry.com, a company of Match.com.

Imagine that you have subscribed to an online dating service. Write a paragraph in which you describe yourself. Your goal is to give interested members of the dating service a good idea of what you are like.

This chapter will provide

- additional writing assignments especially suited for practice at the beginning of the course
- additional writing assignments for measuring progress at the end of the course
- fifteen additional writing assignments in all

This chapter contains a variety of paragraph writing assignments. The earlier assignments are especially suited for writing practice at the beginning of a course; the later ones can be used to measure progress at the end of the course. In general, more detailed instructions are provided with the earlier assignments; fewer guidelines appear for the later ones, so that writers must make more individual decisions about exactly how to proceed. In short, the section provides a wide range of writing assignments. Many choices are possible, depending on the needs and interests of students and the purposes of the instructor.

Writing Assignment

1

Your instructor may pass out slips of paper and ask you to write, in the middle of the slip, your name; in the top left-hand corner, the best or worst job (or chore) you have ever had; in the top right-hand corner, the best or worst instructor you have ever had; in the lower left-hand corner, the best or worst place you have ever eaten in; in the lower right-hand corner, the best or worst thing that has happened to you in the past week. The instructor may also participate by writing on the board. Here is one student's paper.

Baby-sitting for my sister   *B. O. Sullivan*
                                   (tenth-grade history teacher)

               Gail Battaglia

Fourth Street Diner   *Trying to register*

You should then get together with any person in the room whom you do not know, exchange papers, and talk for a bit about what you wrote. Then the two of you should join another pair, with members of the resulting group of four doing two things:

- Mastering the first names of all the members of the group, so that, if asked, you could introduce the instructor to everyone in the group.
- Giving a "mini" speech to the group in which you talk with *as much specific detail as possible* about any one of the four responses on your slip of paper. During or after this speech, other members of the group should ask questions to get as full a sense as possible of why the experience described was "best" or "worst."

Finally, you should write a paragraph about any one of the best or worst experiences. The main purpose in writing this paragraph is to provide plenty of specific details that *show clearly* why your choice was "best" or "worst." The paragraph on page 6 is an example of one student's response to this assignment.

Writing Assignment 2

Interview someone in the class. Take notes as you ask the person a series of questions.

How to Proceed

a. Begin by asking a series of factual questions about the person. You might ask such questions as

> Where is the person from? Where does he or she live now?
>
> Does the person have brothers or sisters? Does the person live with other people, or alone?
>
> What kinds of jobs (if any) has the person had? Where does he or she work now?
>
> What are the person's school or career plans? What courses is he or she taking?
>
> What are the person's favorite leisure activities?

Work at getting specific details rather than general ones. You do not want your introduction to include lines such as "Regina graduated from high school and worked for a year." You want to state specific places and dates: "Regina graduated from DeWitt Clinton High School in the Bronx in 2008. Within a week of graduation, she had gotten a job as a secretary for a branch of the Allstate Insurance Company located in Queens." Or if you are writing about a person's favorite activities, you do not want to simply say, "Regina enjoys watching TV in her few spare hours." Instead, go on and add details such as "Her favorite shows are *60 Minutes, The Colbert Report,* and *CSI: NY.*"

b. Then ask a series of questions about the person's attitudes and thoughts on various matters. You might ask the person's feeling about his or her

> Writing ability
>
> Parents
>
> Boss (if any)

Courses

Past schooling

Strengths and talents

Areas for self-improvement

You might also ask what things make the person angry or sad or happy, and why.

c. After collecting all this information, use it in two paragraphs. Begin your introduction to the person with a line like "This is a short introduction to _____. Here is some factual information about him (her)." Then begin your second paragraph with the line "Now let's take a brief look at some of _____'s attitudes and beliefs."

Writing Assignment

3   Keep a journal for one week, or for whatever time period your instructor indicates. At some point during each day—perhaps right before going to bed—write for fifteen minutes or more about some of the specific happenings, thoughts, and feelings of your day. You do not have to prepare what to write or be in the mood or worry about making mistakes; just write down whatever words come out. As a minimum, you should complete at least one page in each writing session.

Keeping a journal will help you develop the habits of thinking on paper and writing in terms of specific details. Also, the journal can serve as a sourcebook of ideas for possible papers.

A sample journal entry was given on pages 12–13 in Chapter 1. It includes general ideas that the writer might develop into paragraphs—for example:

Working at a department store means that you have to deal with some irritating customers.

Certain preparations are advisable before you quit a job.

See if you can construct another general point from this journal entry that might be the basis for a detailed and interesting paragraph. Write the point in the space below.

_____

Writing Assignment

4

Make up and write a *realistic* dialogue between two or more people. Don't have your characters talk like cardboard figures; have them talk the way people would in real life. Also, make sure their voices are consistent. (Do not have them suddenly talk out of character.)

The dialogue should deal with a lifelike situation. It may, for example, be a discussion or argument of some kind between two friends or acquaintances, a husband and wife, a parent and child, a brother and sister, two people who are dating, a clerk and customer, or other people. The conversation may or may not lead to a decision or action of some kind.

When writing dialogue, enclose your characters' exact words within quotation marks. (You should first review the material on quotation marks on pages 536–543.) Begin a new paragraph to mark each change in speaker. Also, include brief descriptions of whether your characters smile, sit down or stand up, or make other facial gestures or movements during the conversation. And be sure to include a title for your dialogue. The example that follows can serve as a guide.

A Supermarket Conversation

The supermarket checker rang up the total and said to the young woman in line, "That'll be $43.61."

The young woman fumbled with her pocketbook and then said in an embarrassed voice, "I don't think I have more than $40. How much did you say it was again?"

"It's $43.61," the checker said in a sharp, impatient tone.

As the young woman searched her pocketbook for the dollars she needed, the checker said loudly, "If you don't have enough money, you'll have to put something back."

A middle-aged man behind the young woman spoke up. "Look, ma'am, I'll lend you a couple of dollars."

"No, I couldn't do that," said the young woman. "If . . . I don't think I need those sodas," she said hesitantly.

"Look, lady, make up your mind. You're holding up the line," the checker snapped.

The man turned to the checker and said coldly, "Why don't you try being a little more courteous to people? If we weren't here buying things, you'd be out of a job."

Writing | Assignment

5   Write three paragraphs, each of which explains a different reason for choosing the college you are now attending. Topic sentences for each of these paragraphs may resemble one of the following.

> I chose Auburn Community College because it is very affordable.
>
> Salem University has an excellent accounting program.
>
> I chose Rutherford Technical Institute because its instructors have professional experience in the latest technologies.
>
> The sports management program at Caro College provides excellent preparation in both physical education and business management.

Make sure to develop each paragraph with detail that will prove the point your topic sentence is making. For example, if you claim that Salem University has an excellent accounting program, you might back up your claim by mentioning that all of the professors are certified public accountants, that graduates of the program are often hired by large accounting firms at high salaries, and that *U.S. News & World Report* magazine ranked Salem's accounting program among the country's top five.

Writing | Assignment

6   Getting comfortable is a quiet pleasure in life that we all share. Write a paper about the special way you make yourself comfortable, providing plenty of specific details so that the reader can really see and understand your method. Use transition words such as *first, next, then, in addition, also, finally,* and so on, to guide readers through your paper. Transitions act like signposts on an unfamiliar route—they prevent your readers from getting lost.

A student paragraph on getting comfortable ("How I Relax") is on pages 87–88.

Writing Assignment 7

Write in detail about a person who provided help at an important time in your life. State in the first sentence who the person is and the person's relationship to you (friend, father, cousin, etc.). For example, "My grandmother gave me a lot of direction during the difficult time when my parents were getting divorced." Then show through specific examples (the person's words and actions) why he or she was so special for you.

For example, you could say that your grandfather made sure to call you every day or that he attended all of your basketball games, soccer matches, or drama performances. You might add that in particularly trying moments your grandfather used to take you for long walks in the park, along the lake, or in other peaceful places, to encourage you and cheer you up with words of comfort and wisdom.

Writing Assignment 8

Describe a favorite childhood place that made you feel secure, safe, private, or in a world of your own. Here are some possibilities:

A closet

Under a piece of furniture

A grandparent's room

A basement or attic

The woods

A shed or barn

A tree

A bunk bed

Begin with a topic sentence something like this:

"_____ was a place that made me feel

_____ when I was a child." Keep the point of your topic sentence in mind as you describe this place. Include only details that will support the idea that your place was one of security, safety, privacy, or the like.

Writing Assignment

9 Write a paragraph providing examples of one quality or habit that helps make you unique. One student's response to this assignment follows.

Floor-Cleaning Freak

The one habit that makes me unique is that I am a floor-cleaning freak. I use my DustBuster to snap up crumbs seconds after they fall. When a rubber heel mark appears on my vinyl floor, I run for the steel wool. As I work in my kitchen preparing meals, I constantly scan the tiles, looking for spots where some liquid has been spilled or for a crumb that has somehow miraculously escaped my vision. After I scrub and wax my floors, I stand to one side of the room and try to catch the light in such a way as to reveal spots that have gone unwaxed. As I travel from one room to the other, my experienced eye is faithfully searching for lint that may have invaded my domain since my last passing. If I discover an offender, I discreetly tuck it into my pocket. The amount of lint I have gathered in the course of the day is the ultimate test of how diligently I am performing my task. I give my vacuum cleaner quite a workout, and I spend an excessive amount on replacement bags. My expenses for floor-cleaners and wax are alarmingly high, but somehow this does not stop me. Where my floors are concerned, money is not a consideration!

Writing Assignment

10 Write about techniques you use to make it through a day of school or work. These may include

Caffeine

A system of rewards

Humor

Food

Fantasizing

Speaking with friends

Praying or meditating

Just keeping busy

www.CartoonStock.com

You might organize the paragraph by using time order. Show how you turn to your supports at various times during the day in order to cope with fatigue or boredom. For example, in the morning you might use coffee (with its dose of caffeine) to get started. Later in the day, you might go on to use other supports, such as drinking a Red Bull.

Writing Assignment 11

Imagine that all the televisions in the United States go blank, starting tonight. What would you and your family or friends do on a typical night without television? You may want to write about

What each individual would be doing

What you could do together

Problems the lack of TV would cause

Benefits of quality time without TV

Choose any of these approaches, or some other single approach, in writing about your life without TV.

Writing Assignment 12

Write a paper on one of the following topics. Begin with a clear, direct sentence that states exactly what your paper will be about. For example, if you choose the first topic, your opening sentence might be "There were several delightful childhood games I played that occupied many of my summer days." An opening sentence for the second topic might be "The work I had to do to secure my high school diploma is one of the special accomplishments of my life." Be sure to follow your opening sentence with plenty of specific supporting details that develop your topic.

A way you had fun as a child

A special accomplishment

A favorite holiday and why it is your favorite

Some problems a family member or friend is having

A superstition or fear

A disagreement you have had with someone

A debt you have repaid or have yet to repay

The sickest you've ever been

How your parents (or you and a special person in your life) met

Your father's or mother's attitude toward you

Writing Assignment

13 Write a paper on one of the following topics. Follow the instructions given for Assignment 12.

A wish or dream you have or had

Everyday pleasures

Ways you were punished by your parents as a child

Ways you were rewarded by your parents as a child

A difficult moment in your life

An experience you or someone you know has had with drugs

Your weaknesses as a student

Your strengths as a student

A time a prayer or wish was answered

Something you would like to change

Writing Assignment

14 Write a paper on one of the following topics:

Crime	Music	Books
Lies	Exercise	Transportation
Television	Debt	Exhaustion
Plants	Parking meters	Cellphones
Comic books	Hunger	Video games

Suggestions on How to Proceed

a. You might begin by writing several statements about your general topic. For example, suppose that you choose to do a paper on the subject "Neighborhood." Here are some statements you might write:

My neighborhood is fairly rural.

The neighborhood where I grew up was unique.

Many city neighborhoods have problems with crime.

My new neighborhood has no playgrounds for children.

Everyone in my neighborhood seems to mow the lawn almost daily.

My neighborhood became a community when it was faced with a hurricane last summer.

My neighborhood is a noisy place.

b. Choose (or revise) one of the statements that you could go on to develop in a paragraph. You should not select a narrow statement like "My new neighborhood has no playgrounds for children," for it is a simple factual sentence needing no support. Nor should you begin with a point such as "Many city neighborhoods have problems with crime," which is too broad for you to develop adequately in a single paragraph. (See also the information on topic sentences on pages 65–75.)

c. After you have chosen a promising sentence, make a scratch outline of supporting details that will develop the point of that sentence. For example, one student provided the following outline:

My neighborhood is a noisy place.

1. *Businesses*

   a. *Bar with loud music*

   b. *Twenty-four-hour drive-in burger restaurant*

2. *Children*

   a. *Skating and biking while carrying loud radios*

   b. *Street games*

3. *Traffic*

   a. *Truck route nearby*

   b. *Horn-blowing during frequent delays at intersection*

---

d. While writing your paper, use the checklist on the inside back cover to make sure you can answer "yes" to the questions about unity, support, and coherence. Also, refer to the checklist when you edit the next-to-final draft of your paper for sentence-skills mistakes, including spelling.

Writing Assignment

15 Write a paper on one of the topics below. Follow the instructions given for Assignment 14.

YouTube	Tryouts	Illness
Babies	Facebook	Success
Vacation	Hospital	Failure
Red tape	Parties	Wisdom teeth
Dependability	Criticism	Home

Essay Development

Write two to three paragraphs about your plans after graduating college.

18

Writing the Essay

Technology continues to change the way people communicate in their personal, college, and business lives. Write two or more paragraphs about a technology you use frequently that has changed the way you communicate with others.

What Is an Essay?

Differences between an Essay and a Paragraph

An *essay* is simply a paper of several paragraphs, rather than one paragraph, that supports a single point. In an essay, subjects can and should be treated more fully than they would be in a single-paragraph paper.

The main idea or point developed in an essay is called the *thesis statement* or *thesis sentence* (rather than, as in a paragraph, the *topic sentence*). The thesis statement appears in the introductory paragraph, and it is then developed in the supporting paragraphs that follow. A short concluding paragraph closes the essay.

The Form of an Essay

The diagram on page 339 shows the form of an essay. You can refer to this as a guide while writing your own essays.

In some situations, you may need to include additional supporting paragraphs, but for this chapter's purposes, we will be focusing on papers with three supporting paragraphs.

A Model Essay

Gene, the writer of the paragraph on working in an apple plant (page 8), later decided to develop his subject more fully. Here is the essay that resulted.

www.mhhe.com/langan

My Job in an Apple Plant

[1]In the course of working my way through school, I have taken many jobs I would rather forget. [2]I have spent nine hours a day lifting heavy automobile and truck batteries off the end of an assembly belt. [3]I have risked the loss of eyes and fingers working a punch press in a textile factory. [4]I have served as a ward aide in a mental hospital, helping care for brain-damaged men who would break into violent fits at unexpected moments. [5]But none of these jobs was as dreadful as my job in an apple plant. [6]The work was physically hard; the pay was poor; and, most of all, the working conditions were dismal.

Introductory paragraph

continued

First
supporting
paragraph

[7]First, the job made enormous demands on my strength and energy. [8]For ten hours a night, I took cartons that rolled down a metal track and stacked them onto wooden skids in a tractor trailer. [9]Each carton contained twelve heavy bottles of apple juice. [10]A carton shot down the track about every fifteen seconds. [11]I once figured out that I was lifting an average of twelve tons of apple juice every night. [12]When a truck was almost filled, I or my partner had to drag fourteen bulky wooden skids into the empty trailer nearby and then set up added sections of the heavy metal track so that we could start routing cartons to the back of the empty van. [13]While one of us did that, the other performed the stacking work of two men.

Second
supporting
paragraph

[14]I would not have minded the difficulty of the work so much if the pay had not been so poor. [15]I was paid the minimum wage at that time, $3.65 an hour, plus just a quarter extra for working the night shift. [16]Because of the low salary, I felt compelled to get as much overtime pay as possible. [17]Everything over eight hours a night was time-and-a-half, so I typically worked twelve hours a night. [18]On Friday I would sometimes work straight through until Saturday at noon—eighteen hours. [19]I averaged over sixty hours a week but did not take home much more than $220.

Third
supporting
paragraph

[20]But even more than the low pay, what upset me about my apple plant job was the working conditions. [21]Our humorless supervisor cared only about his production record for each night and tried to keep the assembly line moving at breakneck pace. [22]During work I was limited to two ten-minute breaks and an unpaid half hour for lunch. [23]Most of my time was spent outside on the truck loading dock in near-zero-degree temperatures. [24]The steel floors of the trucks were like ice; the quickly penetrating cold made my feet feel like stone. [25]I had no shared interests with the man I loaded cartons with, and so I had to work without companionship on the job. [26]And after the production line shut down and most people left, I had to spend two hours alone scrubbing clean the apple vats, which were coated with a sticky residue.

Concluding
paragraph

[27]I stayed on the job for five months, all the while hating the difficulty of the work, the poor money, and the conditions under which I worked. [28]By the time I quit, I was determined never to do such degrading work again.

Introductory Paragraph

> Introduction
> Thesis statement
> Plan of development:
> Points 1, 2, 3

The *introduction* attracts the reader's interest.

The *thesis statement* (or *thesis sentence*) states the main idea advanced in the essay.

The *plan of development* is a list of points that support the thesis. The points are presented in the order in which they will be developed in the essay.

First Supporting Paragraph

> Topic sentence (point 1)
> Specific evidence

The *topic sentence* advances the first supporting point for the thesis, and the *specific evidence* in the rest of the paragraph develops that first point.

Second Supporting Paragraph

> Topic sentence (point 2)
> Specific evidence

The *topic sentence* advances the second supporting point for the thesis, and the *specific evidence* in the rest of the paragraph develops that second point.

Third Supporting Paragraph

> Topic sentence (point 3)
> Specific evidence

The *topic sentence* advances the third supporting point for the thesis, and the *specific evidence* in the rest of the paragraph develops that third point.

Concluding Paragraph

> Summary, conclusion, or both

A *summary* is a brief restatement of the thesis and its main points. A *conclusion* is a final thought or two stemming from the subject of the essay.

Important Points about the Essay

Introductory Paragraph

An introductory paragraph has certain purposes or functions and can be constructed using various methods.

Purposes of the Introduction

An introductory paragraph should do three things:

1. Attract the reader's *interest*. Using one of the suggested methods of introduction described below can help draw the reader into your essay.

2. Present a *thesis sentence*—a clear, direct statement of the central idea that you will develop in your essay. The thesis statement, like a topic sentence, should have a key word or key words reflecting your attitude about the subject. For example, in the essay on the apple plant job, the key word is *dreadful.*

3. Indicate a *plan of development*—a preview of the major points that will support your thesis statement, listed in the order in which they will be presented. In some cases, the thesis statement and plan of development may appear in the same sentence. In some cases, also, the plan of development may be omitted.

Activity

1

1. In "My Job in an Apple Plant," which sentences are used to attract the reader's interest?

   _____ sentences 1 to 3 _____ 1 to 4 _____ 1 to 5

2. The thesis in "My Job in an Apple Plant" is presented in

   _____ sentence 4 _____ sentence 5 _____ sentence 6

3. Is the thesis followed by a plan of development?

   _____ Yes _____ No

4. Which words in the plan of development announce the three major supporting points in the essay? Write them below.

   a. _____

   b. _____

   c. _____

Common Methods of Introduction

Here are some common methods of introduction. Use any one method, or a combination of methods, to introduce your subject in an interesting way.

1. **Broad statement.** Begin with a broad, general statement of your topic and narrow it down to your thesis statement. Broad, general statements ease the reader into your thesis statement by providing a background for it. In "My Job in an Apple Plant," Gene writes generally on the topic of his worst jobs and then narrows down to a specific worst job.

2. **Contrast.** Start with an idea or situation that is the opposite of the one you will develop. This approach works because your readers will be surprised, and then intrigued, by the contrast between the opening idea and the thesis that follows it. Here is an example of a "contrast" introduction by a student writer:

   When I was a girl, I never argued with my parents about differences between their attitudes and mine. My father would deliver his judgment on an issue, and that was usually the end of the matter. Discussion seldom changed his mind, and disagreement was not tolerated. But the situation is different with today's parents and children. My husband and I have to contend with radical differences between what our children think about a given situation and what we think about it. We have had disagreements with all three of our daughters, Stephanie, Diana, and Giselle.

3. **Relevance.** Explain the importance of your topic. If you can convince your readers that the subject applies to them in some way, or is something they should know more about, they will want to continue reading. The introductory paragraph of "Sports-Crazy America" (page 346) provides an example of a "relevance" introduction.

4. **Anecdote.** Use an incident or brief story. Stories are naturally interesting. They appeal to a reader's curiosity. In your introduction, an anecdote will grab the reader's attention right away. The story should be brief and should be related to your central idea. The incident in the story can be something that happened to you, something that you may have heard about, or something that you

have read about in a newspaper or magazine. Here is an example of a paragraph that begins with a story:

> The husky man pushes open the door of the bedroom and grins as he pulls out a .38 revolver. An elderly man wearing thin pajamas looks at him and whimpers. In a feeble effort at escape, the old man slides out of his bed and moves to the door of the room. The husky man, still grinning, blocks his way. With the face of a small, frightened animal, the old man looks up and whispers, "Oh, God, please don't hurt me." The grinning man then fires four times. The television movie cuts now to a soap commercial, but the little boy who has been watching the set has begun to cry. Such scenes of direct violence on television must surely be harmful to children for a number of psychological reasons.

5. **Questions.** Ask your readers one or more questions. These questions catch the readers' interest and make them want to read on. Here is an example of a paragraph that begins with questions:

> What would happen if we were totally honest with ourselves? Would we be able to stand the pain of giving up self-deception? Would the complete truth be too much for us to bear? Such questions will probably never be answered, for in everyday life we protect ourselves from the onslaught of too much reality. All of us cultivate defense mechanisms that prevent us from seeing, hearing, or feeling too much. Included among such defense mechanisms are rationalization, reaction formation, and substitution.

Note, however, that the thesis itself must not be a question.

6. **Quotation.** A quotation can be something you have read in a book or an article. It can also be something that you have heard: a popular saying or proverb ("Never give advice to a friend"); a current or recent advertising slogan ("Just do it"); a favorite expression used by your friends or family ("My father always says . . ."). Using a quotation in your introductory paragraph lets you add someone else's voice to your own. Here is an example of a paragraph that begins with a quotation:

> "Evil," wrote the philosopher Martin Buber, "is lack of direction." In my school days as a fatherless boy, with a mother too confused by her own life to really care for me, I strayed down a number of dangerous paths. Before my eighteenth birthday, I had been a car thief, a burglar, and a drug dealer.

7. **Startling statement or statistic.** Some essays start with statements or statistics (numbers) that may shock readers and get them so interested that they want to read more. Read the following paragraph, which uses both statistics and a startling statement:

> The Spanish influenza (flu) was a pandemic that, between 1918 and 1920, reached every corner of the earth, including the Arctic and the most remote Pacific islands. Unlike most other flus, this one attacked healthy young men and women primarily, not the very old or the very young. Scientists estimate that the disease killed between 50 million and 100 million people worldwide. Even more significantly, the Spanish influenza was caused by a strain of the H1N1 virus that threatens the world today.

Supporting Paragraphs

Most essays have three supporting points, developed in three separate paragraphs. (Some essays will have two supporting points; others, four or more.) Each of the supporting paragraphs should begin with a topic sentence that states the point to be detailed in that paragraph. Just as the thesis provides a focus for the entire essay, the topic sentence provides a focus for each supporting paragraph.

1. What is the topic sentence for the first supporting paragraph of "My Job in an Apple Plant"? (*Write the sentence number here.*) _____

2. What is the topic sentence for the second supporting paragraph? _____

3. What is the topic sentence for the third supporting paragraph? _____

Activity

2

Transitional Sentences

In paragraphs, transitions and other connective devices (pages 89–98) are used to help link sentences. Similarly, in an essay *transitional sentences* are used to help tie the supporting paragraphs together. Such transitional sentences usually occur near the end of one paragraph or the beginning of the next.

In "My Job in an Apple Plant," the first transitional sentence is this:

> I would not have minded the difficulty of the work so much if the pay had not been so poor.

In this sentence, the key word *difficulty* reminds us of the point of the first supporting paragraph, while *pay* tells us the point to be developed in the second supporting paragraph.

Activity

3

Here is the other transitional sentence in "My Job in an Apple Plant":

> But even more than the low pay, what upset me about my apple plant job was the working conditions.

Complete the following statement: In the sentence above, the key words _____ echo the point of the second supporting paragraph, and the key words _____ announce the topic of the third supporting paragraph.

Concluding Paragraph

The concluding paragraph often summarizes the essay by briefly restating the thesis and, at times, the main supporting points. Also, the conclusion brings the paper to a natural and graceful end, sometimes leaving the reader with a final thought on the subject.

Activity

4

1. Which sentence in the concluding paragraph of "My Job in an Apple Plant" restates the thesis and supporting points of the essay? _____

2. Which sentence contains the concluding thought of the essay? _____

Essays to Consider

Read the three student essays below and then answer the questions that follow.

Get Rid of the Dog

[1]What is this mania Americans have for dogs? [2]Why do so many American homes contain dogs? [3]Why do so many television programs, commercials, and even movies glorify canines? [4]And why is it that an entire aisle in the supermarket is devoted to food and supplies for dogs and other household pets? [5]It's a mystery. [6]At best, a dog is an expensive nuisance; at worst, it can destroy a house and even cause chaos within a family.

[7]First, dogs are an expensive nuisance because they need a great deal of attention. [8]If the owner does not live in a house with a large backyard, he or she will have to walk the animal at least twice a day (or pay someone else to do this). [9]And before leaving town on a vacation or business trip, he or she will have to hire a house sitter or arrange for the animal to be boarded at an expensive kennel. [10]Regular veterinarian visits are required too, and these are usually costly.

[11]Another reason not to own one of these beasts is that dogs can destroy a house. [12]Puppies are in the habit of chewing up rugs, shoes, furniture, and molding. [13]Large dogs have been known to eat their way out of rooms by chewing through a door or wall. [14]Dogs that enjoy playing in the rain or digging holes in the backyard usually wind up covered with mud, which they quickly transfer to the carpets and upholstery upon reentering the house.

[15]Worst of all, dogs can even disrupt family harmony. [16]Picture a father, mother, and two children sitting down to dinner. [17]Enter the family dog, which begins to beg even before the first bite is taken. [18]It knows that little Jeremy is a sucker who will sneak whatever food he doesn't like to the dog when his parents aren't looking. [19]When Dad catches his son in the act, however, he reprimands him, reminding Jeremy that he has forbidden feeding Fido from the table on numerous occasions. [20]As he grabs the animal by the collar and attempts to toss him outside, the children react by whining and even crying. [21]In the end a simple family meal has been transformed into a circus.

[22]How do I know all of this? [23]I myself am the owner of a ten-pound cairn terrier, and I am the sucker who always breaks down and feeds him from the table. [24]The truth is that I simply can't resist that sweet, sad face when he puts his paws on my knee and begs for more.

Sports-Crazy America

[1]Almost all Americans are involved with sports in some way. [2]They may play basketball or volleyball or go swimming or skiing. [3]They may watch football or basketball games on the high school, college, or professional level. [4]Sports may seem like an innocent pleasure, but it is important to look under the surface. [5]In reality, sports have reached a point where they play too large a part in daily life. [6]They take up too much media time, play too large a role in the raising of children, and give too much power and prestige to athletes.

[7]The overemphasis on sports can be seen most obviously in the vast media coverage of athletic events. [8]It seems as if every bowl game play-off, tournament, trial, bout, race, meet, or match is shown on one television channel or another. [9]On Saturday and Sunday, a check of *TV Guide* will show countless sports programs on network television alone, and countless more on cable stations. [10]In addition, sports make up about 30 percent of local news at six and eleven o'clock, and network world news shows often devote several minutes to major American sports events. [11]Radio offers a full roster of games and a wide assortment of sports talk shows. [12]Furthermore, many daily newspapers such as *USA Today* are devoting more and more space to sports coverage, often in an attempt to improve circulation. [13]The newspaper with the biggest sports section is the one people will buy.

Maria Sharapova
and her Aquaracer Diamonds

WHAT ARE YOU MADE OF?

TAGHeuer
SWISS AVANT-GARDE SINCE 1860

Available at TAG Heuer Westfield, London and selected
fine jewellers nationwide. For further information
please call 0800 037 9656 or visit www.tagheuer.com

[14]The way we raise and educate our children also illustrates our sports mania. [15]As early as age six or seven, kids are placed in little leagues, often to play under screaming coaches and pressuring parents. [16]Later, in high school, students who are singled out by the school and by the community are not those who are best academically but those who are best athletically. [17]And college sometimes seems to be more about sports than about learning. [18]The United States may be the only country in the world where people often think of their colleges as teams first and schools second. [19]The names Ohio State, Notre Dame, and Southern Cal mean "sports" to the public.

continued

[20]Our sports craziness is especially evident in the prestige given to athletes in the United States. [21]For one thing, we reward them with enormous salaries. [22]In 2006, for example, baseball players averaged over $2.8 million a year; the average annual salary in the United States was $44,389. [23]Besides their huge salaries, athletes receive the awe, the admiration, and sometimes the votes of the public. [24]Kids look up to someone like LeBron James or Tom Brady as a true hero; adults wear the jerseys and jackets of their favorite teams. [25]Former players become senators and congressmen. [26]And a famous athlete like Serena Williams needs to make only one commercial for advertisers to see the sales of a product boom.

[27]Americans are truly mad about sports. [28]Perhaps we like to see the competitiveness we experience in our daily lives acted out on playing fields. [29]Perhaps we need heroes who can achieve clear-cut victories in a short time, of only an hour or two. [30]Whatever the reason, the sports scene in this country is more popular than ever.

An Interpretation of *Lord of the Flies*

[1]Modern history has shown us the evil that exists in human beings. [2]Assassinations are common, governments use torture to discourage dissent, and six million Jews were exterminated during World War II. [3]In *Lord of the Flies*, William Golding describes a group of schoolboys shipwrecked on an island with no authority figures to control their behavior. [4]One of the boys soon yields to dark forces within himself, and his corruption symbolizes the evil in all of us. [5]First, Jack Merridew kills a living creature; then, he rebels against the group leader; and finally, he seizes power and sets up his own murderous society.

[6]The first stage in Jack's downfall is his killing of a living creature. [7]In Chapter 1, Jack aims at a pig but is unable to kill. [8]His upraised arm pauses "because of the enormity of the knife descending and cutting into living flesh, because of the unbearable blood," and the pig escapes. [9]Three chapters later, however, Jack leads some boys on a successful hunt. [10]He returns triumphantly with a freshly killed pig and reports excitedly to the others, "I cut the pig's throat." [11]Yet Jack twitches as he says this, and he wipes his bloody hands on his shorts as if eager to remove the stains. [12]There is still some civilization left in him.

[13]After the initial act of killing the pig, Jack's refusal to cooperate with Ralph shows us that this civilized part is rapidly disappearing. [14]With no adults around, Ralph has made some rules. [15]One is that a signal fire must

continued

be kept burning. [16]But Jack tempts the boys watching the fire to go hunting, and the fire goes out. [17]Another rule is that at a meeting, only the person holding a special seashell has the right to speak. [18]In Chapter 5, another boy is speaking when Jack rudely tells him to shut up. [19]Ralph accuses Jack of breaking the rules. [20]Jack shouts: "Bollocks to the rules! We're strong—we hunt! If there's a beast, we'll hunt it down! We'll close in and beat and beat and beat—!" [21]He gives a "wild whoop" and leaps off the platform, throwing the meeting into chaos. [22]Jack is now much more savage than civilized.

[23]The most obvious proof of Jack's corruption comes in Chapter 8, when he establishes his own murderous society. [24]Insisting that Ralph is not a "proper chief" because he does not hunt, Jack asks for a new election. [25]After he again loses, Jack announces, "I'm going off by myself . . . . Anyone who wants to hunt when I do can come too." [26]Eventually, nearly all the boys join Jack's "tribe." [27]Following his example, they paint their faces like savages, sacrifice to "the beast," brutally murder two of their schoolmates, and nearly succeed in killing Ralph as well. [28]Jack has now become completely savage— and so have the others.

[29]Through Jack Merridew, then, Golding shows how easily moral laws can be forgotten. [30]Freed from grown-ups and their rules, Jack learns to kill living things, defy authority, and lead a tribe of murdering savages. [31]Jack's example is a frightening reminder of humanity's potential for evil. [32]The "beast" the boys try to hunt and kill is actually within every human being.

Questions

1. In which essay does the thesis statement appear in the last sentence of the introductory paragraph? _____

2. In the essay on *Lord of the Flies,* which sentence of the introductory paragraph contains the plan of development? _____

3. Which method of introduction is used in "Get Rid of the Dog"?

   a. General to narrow   c. Incident or story
   b. Stating importance of topic   d. Questions

4. Write a brief outline of the three points developed in "Get Rid of the Dog":

   a. _____

   b. _____

   c. _____

5. Which *two* essays use a transitional sentence between the first and second supporting paragraphs?

   _____

6. *Complete the following statement:* Emphatic order is shown in the last supporting paragraph of "Get Rid of the Dog" with the words _____;

   in the last supporting paragraph of "Sports-Crazy America" with the words

   _____ ; and in the last supporting paragraph of "An

   Interpretation of *Lord of the Flies*" with the words _____ .

7. Which essay uses time order as well as emphatic order to organize its

   three supporting paragraphs? _____

8. List four major transitions used in the supporting paragraphs of "An

   Interpretation of *Lord of the Flies*." _____

   a. _____   c. _____

   b. _____   d. _____

9. Which essay includes a sentence in the concluding paragraph that summarizes three supporting points?

   _____

10. Which essay includes two final thoughts in its concluding paragraph?

   _____

Planning the Essay

Determining Audience and Purpose

When you are writing an essay, planning is crucial for success. Start by thinking about your purpose (what you want your essay to accomplish) and intended audience (the person or persons who will read the essay).

In Chapter 2, you learned that, often, an assignment clearly states or at least hints at what the essay is supposed to accomplish—its intended purpose. Key words such as *define, contrast, argue, illustrate,* or *explain causes and effects,* can reveal the assignment's purpose. The box on pages 359–360 explains such terms, and Chapters 8–16 discuss how to develop specific types of paragraphs for these purposes. So before you begin collecting information for your essay through prewriting (Chapter 2), spend a few minutes thinking about the purpose your paper is intended to fulfill.

Now determine who your reader is. Sometimes this will simply be your instructor. At other times you may be writing for a wider and more diverse audience, such as the other students in your class, the student body of your college, or the employees of a company you work for.

To clearly define your audience, ask yourself these questions:

1. Why does this person want to read my essay? What does he or she want to gain or learn from it?

2. Does the reader need to make a decision based upon what I have written? Is the reader leaning one way or the other? Does the reader hold an opinion that is opposite to the one I am defending?

3. Is the reader simply seeking new information, or does he or she need to answer a specific question or to solve a specific problem?

4. Is the reader looking for a recommendation on a course of action. (For example, a movie reviewer makes recommendations aimed at people choosing a movie to see.)

5. How much does my reader know about my subject? Is he new to the subject, or does she know a lot about it already? Will I have to define basic terms, or can I use these terms without explaining what they mean? (For example, you might define the word *tweeting* to a senior citizen who does not own a computer. But would you have to explain this term to one of your peers?)

6. Am I writing to readers who have strong political, religious, or other beliefs? If you are stating an opposite opinion, you might have to be extra careful to word your ideas so as not to offend the audience.

Once you have answered these questions in your head, on a piece of paper, or on a computer, you will have a much clearer idea of your audience's background, needs, and purpose for reading. More important, you will be able to tailor your essay so that it contains ideas, information, and techniques that will appeal to your intended audience and, thus, improve your chances of writing an effective essay.

Outlining the Essay

Another important step in planning the essay is by outlining. You can make a plan of your essay by outlining in two ways.

1. Prepare a scratch outline. This should consist of a short statement of the thesis followed by the main supporting points for the thesis. Here is Gene's scratch outline for his essay on the apple plant:

   Working at an apple plant was my worst job.
   1. *Hard work*
   2. *Poor pay*
   3. *Bad working conditions*

   Do not underestimate the value of this initial outline—or the work involved in achieving it. Be prepared to do a good deal of plain hard thinking at this first and most important stage of your essay.

2. Prepare a more detailed outline. The outline form that follows will serve as a guide. Your instructor may ask you to submit a copy of this form either before you actually write an essay or along with your finished essay.

Form for Planning an Essay

To write an effective essay, use a form like the one that follows.

Opening remarks

Thesis statement _____   Introduction

_____

Plan of development

Body

| *Topic sentence 1* _____ |
| _____ |
| Specific supporting evidence |

| *Topic sentence 2* _____ |
| _____ |
| Specific supporting evidence |

| *Topic sentence 3* _____ |
| _____ |
| Specific supporting evidence |

Conclusion

| Summary, closing remarks, or both |

Practice in Writing the Essay

In this section, you will expand and strengthen your understanding of the essay form as you work through the following activities.

1 Understanding the Two Parts of a Thesis Statement

In this chapter, you have learned that effective essays center on a thesis, or main point, that a writer wishes to express. This central idea is usually presented as a *thesis statement* in an essay's introductory paragraph.

A good thesis statement does two things. First, it tells readers an essay's *topic*. Second, it presents the *writer's attitude, opinion, idea,* or *point* about that topic. For example, look at the following thesis statement:

| Celebrities are often poor role models. |

In this thesis statement, the topic is *celebrities;* the writer's main point is celebrities are *often poor role models.*

For each thesis statement below, <u>single-underline</u> the topic and <u><u>double-underline</u></u> the main point that the writer wishes to express about the topic.

1. Several teachers have played important roles in my life.

2. A period of loneliness in life can actually have certain benefits.

3. Owning an old car has its own special rewards.

4. Learning to write takes work, patience, and a sense of humor.

5. Advertisers use several clever sales techniques to promote their message.

6. The police in large cities often have to do more than fight crime.

7. Working part time and going to college full time requires self-sacrifice, energy, and an ability to manage one's time.

8. My study habits in college benefited greatly from a course on note taking, textbook study, and test-taking skills.

9. The best teachers encourage their students, provide them with extra help, and present the material in a clear and interesting manner.

10. Parents should take certain steps to encourage their children to enjoy reading.

2 Supporting the Thesis with Specific Evidence

The first essential step in writing a successful essay is to form a clearly stated thesis. The second basic step is to support the thesis with specific reasons or details.

To ensure that your essay will have adequate support, you may find an informal outline very helpful. Write down a brief version of your thesis idea, and then work out and jot down the three points that will support your thesis.

Here is the scratch outline that was prepared for one essay:

The college cafeteria is poorly managed.

The checkout lines are always long.

The floor and tables are often dirty.

Food choices are often limited.

A scratch outline like the one above looks simple, but developing it often requires a good deal of careful thinking. The time spent on developing a logical outline is invaluable, though. Once you have planned the steps that logically support your thesis, you will be in an excellent position to go on to write an effective essay.

Activity

6

Following are five informal outlines in which two points (*a* and *b*) are already provided. Complete each outline by adding a third logical supporting point (*c*).

1. Poor grades in school can have various causes.
    a. Family problems
    b. Study problems

    c. _____

2. My landlord adds to the stress in my life.
    a. Keeps raising the rent
    b. Expects me to help maintain the apartment

    c. _____

3. My mother (*or some other adult*) has three qualities I admire.
    a. Sense of humor
    b. Patience

    c. _____

4. The first day in college was nerve-racking.
    a. Meeting new people
    b. Dealing with the bookstore

    c. _____

5. Staying healthy while carrying a full course load in college takes planning.
    a. Set aside at least seven hours a day for sleep
    b. Choose foods that are nutritious; avoid those loaded with sugar and fat

    c. _____

3 Identifying Introductions

The box lists seven common methods for introducing an essay; each is discussed in this chapter.

1. Broad statement	5. Question
2. Contrast	6. Quotation
3. Relevance	7. Startling statement or statistic
4. Incident or story	

After reviewing the seven methods of introduction on pages 341–343, refer to the box above and read the following seven introductory paragraphs. Then, in the space provided, write the number of the kind of introduction used in each paragraph. Each kind of introduction is used once.

Paragraph A

_____ Is bullying a natural, unavoidable part of growing up? Is it something that everyone has to endure as a victim, or practice as a bully, or tolerate as a bystander? Does bullying leave deep scars on its victims, or is it fairly harmless? Does being a bully indicate some deep-rooted problems, or is it not a big deal? These and other questions need to be looked at as we consider the three forms of bullying: physical, verbal, and social.

Paragraph B

_____ In a perfect school, students would treat each other with affection and respect. Differences would be tolerated, and even welcomed. Kids would become more popular by being kind and supportive. Students would go out of their way to make sure one another felt happy and comfortable. But most schools are not perfect. Instead of being places of respect and tolerance, they are places where the hateful act of bullying is widespread.

Paragraph C

_____ Students have to deal with all kinds of problems in schools. There are the problems created by difficult classes, by too much homework, or by personality conflicts with teachers. There are problems with scheduling the classes you need and still getting some of the ones you want. There are problems with bad cafeteria food, grouchy principals, or overcrowded classrooms. But one of the most difficult problems of all has to do with a terrible situation that exists in most schools: bullying.

Paragraph D

_____ Eric, a new boy at school, was shy and physically small. He quickly became a victim of bullies. Kids would wait after school, pull out his shirt, and punch and shove him around. He was called such names as "Mouse Boy" and "Jerk Boy." When he sat down during lunch hour, others would leave his table. In gym games he was never thrown the ball, as if he didn't exist. Then one day he came to school with a gun. When the police were called, he told them he just couldn't take it anymore. Bullying had hurt him badly, just as it hurts many other students. Every member of a school community should be aware of bullying and the three hateful forms that it takes: physical, verbal, and social bullying.

Paragraph E

_____ A British prime minister once said, "Courage is fire, and bullying is smoke." If that is true, there is a lot of "smoke" present in most schools today. Bullying in schools is a huge problem that hurts both its victims and the people who practice it. Physical, verbal, and social bullying are all harmful in their own ways.

Paragraph F

_____ A pair of students bring guns and homemade bombs to school, killing a number of their fellow students and teachers before taking their own lives. A young man hangs himself on Sunday evening rather than attend school the following morning. A junior high school girl is admitted to the emergency room after cutting her wrists. What do all these horrible reports have to do with each other? All were reportedly caused by a terrible practice that is common in schools: bullying.

Paragraph G

_____ It is estimated that 23 percent of all students in American middle schools have experienced bullying. More than 20 percent have admitted to engaging in bullying themselves. Moreover, 8 percent complain of being bullied at least once each week. At times, victims of bullying become depressed, suffer from chronic health problems, and even contemplate suicide!

4 Revising an Essay for All Four Bases: Unity, Support, Coherence, and Sentence Skills

You know from your work on paragraphs that there are four "bases" a paper must cover to be effective. In the following activity, you will evaluate and revise an essay in terms of all four bases: *unity, support, coherence,* and *sentence skills.*

Activity 8

Comments follow each supporting paragraph and the concluding paragraph. Circle the letter of the *one* statement that applies in each case.

A Hateful Activity: Bullying

Paragraph 1: Introduction

Eric, a new boy at school, was shy and physically small. He quickly became a victim of bullies. Kids would wait after school, pull out his shirt, and punch and shove him around. He was called such names as "Mouse Boy" and "Jerk Boy." When he sat down during lunch hour, others would leave his table. In gym games he was never thrown the ball, as if he didn't exist. Then one day he came to school with a gun. When the police were called, he told them he just couldn't take it anymore. Bullying had hurt him badly, just as it hurts many other students. Every member of a school community should be aware of bullying and the three hateful forms that it takes: physical, verbal, and social bullying.

Paragraph 2: First Supporting Paragraph

Bigger or meaner kids try to hurt kids who are smaller or unsure of themselves. They'll push kids into their lockers, knock books out of their hands, or shoulder them out of the cafeteria line. In gym class, a bully often likes to kick kids' legs out from under them while they are running. In the classroom, bullies might kick the back of the chair or step on the foot of the kids they want to intimidate. Bullies will corner a kid in a bathroom. There the victim will be slapped around, will have his or her clothes half pulled off, and might even be shoved into a trash can. Bullies will wait for kids after school and bump or wrestle them around, often while others are looking on. The goal is to frighten kids as much as possible and try to make them cry. Physical bullying is more common among boys, but it is not unknown for girls to be physical bullies as well. The victims are left bruised and hurting, but often in even more pain emotionally than bodily.

a. Paragraph 2 contains an irrelevant sentence.
b. Paragraph 2 lacks transition words.
c. Paragraph 2 lacks supporting details at one key spot.
d. Paragraph 2 contains a fragment and a run-on.

Paragraph 3: Second Supporting Paragraph

Perhaps even worse than physical attack is verbal bullying, which uses words, rather than hands or fists, as weapons. We may be told that "sticks and stones may break my bones, but words can never harm me," but few of us are immune to the pain of a verbal attack. Like physical bullies, verbal bullies tend to single out certain targets. From that moment on, the victim is subject to a hail of insults and put-downs. These are usually delivered in public, so the victim's humiliation will be greatest: "Oh, no; here comes the nerd!" "Why don't you lose some weight, blubber boy?" "You smell as bad as you look!" "Weirdo." "Fairy." "Creep." "Dork." "Slut." "Loser." Verbal bullying is an equal-opportunity activity, with girls as likely to be verbal bullies as boys. If parents don't want their children to be bullies like this, they shouldn't be abusive themselves. Meanwhile, the victim retreats farther and farther into his or her shell, hoping to escape further notice.

a. Paragraph 3 contains an irrelevant sentence.
b. Paragraph 3 lacks transition words.
c. Paragraph 3 lacks supporting details at one key spot.
d. Paragraph 3 contains a fragment and a run-on.

Paragraph 4: Third Supporting Paragraph

As bad as verbal bullying is, many would agree that the most painful type of bullying of all is social bullying. Many students have a strong need for the comfort of being part of a group. For social bullies, the pleasure of belonging to a group is increased by the sight of someone who is refused entry into that group. So, like wolves targeting the weakest sheep in a herd, the bullies lead the pack in isolating people who they decide are different. Bullies do everything they can to make those people feel sad and lonely. In class and out of it, the bullies make it clear that the victims are ignored and unwanted. As the victims sink farther into isolation and depression, the social bullies—who seem to be female more often than male—feel all the more puffed up by their own popularity.

a. Paragraph 4 contains an irrelevant sentence.
b. Paragraph 4 lacks transition words.
c. Paragraph 4 lacks supporting details at one key spot.
d. Paragraph 4 contains a fragment and a run-on.

Paragraph 5: Concluding Paragraph

Whether bullying is physical, verbal, or social, it can leave deep and lasting scars. If parents, teachers, and other adults were more aware of the types of bullying, they might help by stepping in. Before the situation becomes too extreme. If students were more aware of the terrible pain that bullying causes, they might think twice about being bullies themselves, their awareness could make the world a kinder place.

a. Paragraph 5 contains an irrelevant sentence.
b. Paragraph 5 lacks transition words.
c. Paragraph 5 lacks supporting details at one key spot.
d. Paragraph 5 contains a fragment and a run-on.

Essay Exams

In many classes, instructors administer examinations with questions to be answered in short but fully developed essays. Here are a few suggestions for taking such exams and completing such essays.

1. Keep to a schedule. Reserve enough time to complete the essay, depending on how much the essay contributes to the overall test grade. For example, if the essay question is worth 50 points of the test's 100 points, plan to spend at least half the test period writing the essay.

2. Make sure you understand the test question well. Read through it a few times if you have to. Then follow the directions carefully.

3. Look for key words to determine exactly what the question is asking you to do. This is perhaps the most important part of the process. If the question asks you to *analyze* the long-term effects of the Civil War, you will need to do more than just say that the South lost and some of its major cities were greatly damaged. If you are asked to *compare* and *contrast* the economies of the South and North before the Civil War, you will have to do more than simply explain how they were different (contrast). If you are asked to explain what *causes* a tsunami, don't describe the devastation when the 2004 tsunami struck southern Asia.

Here is a list of key terms you might encounter on essay exams.

Term	Meaning	Example
Analyze	Divide into component parts or aspects, and then explain how each part relates to the whole.	*Analyze* the imagery in William Shakespeare's Sonnet 116.
Compare	Draw similarities between items.	*Compare* the composition of the ancient Roman senate to that of the modern United States Senate.
Contrast	Explain differences between items.	How are the jobs of a local police officer and an FBI agent *different*?
Describe	Create a verbal picture. However, sometimes *describe* means "discuss" or even "narrate" in any essay exam.	*Describe* the symptoms seen in people who suffered from bubonic plague. *Describe* (discuss) the economic effects of recent income tax rate reductions.
Discuss	Explain, analyze, and/or evaluate.	*Discuss* the advantages of regular aerobic exercise.
Enumerate	List items	*Enumerate* the rights guaranteed in the Bill of Rights.
Evaluate	Weigh, assess, or appraise.	*Evaluate* the effectiveness of using electronic calculators to teach college algebra.

continued

Explain	List causes or effects or tell how something is done, for example, depending on the rest of the question.	*Explain* the *effects* of America's entry into World War II on its economy. *Explain* the *process* that immigrants must go through to become citizens.
Illustrate	Provide examples.	*Illustrate* the following statement: "The computer is an invaluable academic tool."
Interpret	Analyze and explain the meaning or significance of something.	*Interpret* the significance of the religious imagery used in two of Hawthorne's short stories.
Prove	Provide a logical argument supported by facts.	*Prove* the claim that the Greek gods displayed human qualities.
Trace	Track the progress of something.	*Trace* the major developments that ended apartheid in South Africa.

4. Jot down a rough outline of what you want to say in your essay.
5. Leave enough time to edit and proofread your essay for glaring errors before you submit your test paper to the instructor.

Essay Assignments

HINTS: Keep the points below in mind when writing an essay on any of the topics that follow.

1. Plan your essay: Determine your purpose and audience. Prepare both a scratch outline and a more detailed outline.

2. While writing your essay, use the checklist below to make sure that your essay touches all four bases of effective writing.

FOUR BASES Checklist for Essays

Base 1: *Unity*

☑ Clearly stated thesis in the introductory paragraph of your essay

☑ All the supporting paragraphs on target in backing up your thesis

Base 2: *Support*

☑ Three separate supporting points for your thesis

☑ *Specific* evidence for each of the three supporting points

☑ *Plenty* of specific evidence for each supporting point

Base 3: *Coherence*

☑ Clear method of organization

☑ Transitions and other connecting words

☑ Effective introduction and conclusion

Base 4: *Sentence Skills*

☑ Clear, error-free sentences (use the checklist on the inside back cover of this book)

Writing Assignment

1

Your House or Apartment

Write an essay on the advantages or disadvantages (not both) of the house or apartment where you live. In your introductory paragraph, describe briefly the place you plan to write about. End the paragraph with your thesis statement and a plan of development. Remember that a plan of development lists the major points that support your thesis in the order in which they will be presented. Here are some suggested thesis statements:

The best features of my apartment are its large windows, roomy closets, and great location.

The drawbacks of my house are its unreliable oil burner, tiny kitchen, and old-fashioned bathroom.

An inquisitive landlord, sloppy neighbors, and platoons of cockroaches came along with our rented house.

My apartment has several advantages, including friendly neighbors, lots of storage space, and a good security system.

Writing Assignment

2 | A Big Decision

Write an essay about the worst or the best decision you have made within the past year. Explain the decision and show how its effects have convinced you that it was the worst or best thing to do. For example, if you write about limiting your hours at work so you could spend more time studying, explain what effects this decision had on your grades, on your self-confidence, or on your lifestyle.

To get started, make a list of all the major decisions you made last year that have resulted in failure or success. Then pick the one that has had the most important consequences for you. Make a brief outline as in the following examples.

Thesis: Buying a used car to commute to school was the worst
decision I made last year.
1. Unreliable—late for class or missed class
2. Expenses of insurance, repairs
3. Led to an accident

> _Thesis:_ Deciding to join a gym was the best decision I made last year.
>
> 1. Lost a lot of weight
> 2. Built stamina, self-esteem
> 3. Made new friends

Writing Assignment 3

What If?

Write an essay in which you explain the effects on your community caused by one of the following problems:

1. A massive hurricane hits the state, knocking out all cell phone towers and destroying thousands of telephone poles.
2. Oil imports to the United States from foreign countries suddenly stop.
3. A large percentage of the doctors in your area decide to move out of state.
4. Public school teachers go on strike.
5. The town's water supply gets contaminated.
6. The town government goes broke, and there is no money to pay firefighters and police.
7. A giant storm drops 48 inches of snow on the area in five hours.

Writing Assignment 4

Single Life

Write an essay on the advantages or drawbacks of single life. To get started, make a list of all the advantages and drawbacks you can think of. Advantages might include

Fewer expenses	More personal freedom
Fewer responsibilities	More opportunities to move or travel

Drawbacks might include

Parental disapproval

Being alone at social events

No companion for shopping, movies, and so on

Sadness at holiday time

After you make up two lists, select the thesis for which you feel you have more supporting material. Then organize your material into a scratch outline. Be sure to include an introduction, a clear topic sentence for each supporting paragraph, and a conclusion.

Alternatively, write an essay on the advantages or drawbacks of married life. Follow the directions given above.

Writing Assignment

5 | Influences on Your Writing

Are you as good a writer as you want to be? Write an essay analyzing the reasons you have become a good writer or explaining why you are not as good as you'd like to be. Begin by considering some factors that may have influenced your writing ability.

Your family background: Did you see people writing at home? Did your parents respect and value the ability to write?

Your school experience: Did you have good writing teachers? Did you have a history of failure or success with writing? Was writing fun, or was it a chore? Did your school emphasize writing?

Social influences: How did your school friends do at writing? What were your friends' attitudes toward writing? What feelings about writing did you pick up from TV or the movies?

You might want to organize your essay by describing the three greatest influences on your skill (or your lack of skill) as a writer. Show how each of these has contributed to the present state of your writing.

Writing Assignment

6 | Abolishing Unjust, Unnecessary Rules

Write an essay in which you discuss three rules, requirements, laws, policies, or regulations that you think should be abolished because they are unjust or are unnecessary or because of any other reason you believe is appropriate. Among the examples you might wish to discuss are the following:

A code enforced by a club, sorority, or house of worship to which you belong

A policy your employer wants you to follow

A graduation requirement at your high school or college

A law enforced by your state or community

A rule or practice your family observes

If you want, pick three unrelated rules or policies enforced by different organizations or people. In your thesis statement, however, explain why you oppose these laws or rules. For example, let's say that your employer wants you to wear conservative clothes to work even though you work in the stockroom; that your college wants you to complete a course covering computer programs that you've already mastered; and that the volunteer fire company you belong to requires your attendance at a Halloween dance. Your thesis might read as follows: "Certain rules and regulations, like those enforced by my employer, my college, and my fire company, are simply unnecessary." Note that such a thesis includes a plan of development. In other words, you will discuss your employer first, your college second, and your fire company last.

Writing Assignment

7

Reviewing a TV Show or Movie

Write an essay about a television show or movie you have seen very recently. The thesis of your essay will be that the show (or movie) has both good and bad features. (If you are writing about a TV series, be sure that you evaluate only one episode.)

In your first supporting paragraph, briefly summarize the show or movie. Don't get bogged down in small details here; just describe the major characters briefly and give the highlights of the action.

In your second supporting paragraph, explain what you feel are the best features of the show or movie. Listed below are some examples of good features you might write about:

Suspenseful, ingenious, or realistic plot

Good acting

Good scenery or special effects

Surprise ending

Good music

Believable characters

In your third supporting paragraph, explain what you feel are the worst features of the show or movie. Here are some possibilities:

Far-fetched, confusing, or dull plot

Poor special effects

Bad acting

Cardboard characters

Unrealistic dialogue

Remember to cover only a few features in each paragraph; do not try to include everything.

Writing Assignment

8 Your High School

Imagine that you are an outside consultant called in as a neutral observer to examine the high school you attended. After your visit, you must send the school board a five-paragraph letter in which you describe the most striking features (good, bad, or both) of the school and the evidence for each of these features.

In order to write the letter, you may want to think about the following features of your high school:

Attitude of the teachers, student body, or administration

Condition of the buildings, classrooms, recreational areas, and so on

Curriculum

How classes are conducted

Extracurricular activities

Crowded or uncrowded conditions

Be sure to include an introduction, a clear topic sentence for each supporting paragraph, and a conclusion.

Writing Assignment

9 Parents and Children

The older we get, the more we see our parents in ourselves.

Write a paragraph in which you describe three characteristics you have "inherited" from a parent. Ask yourself a series of questions: "How am I like my mother (or father)?" "When and where am I like her (or him)?" "Why am I like her (or him)?"

One student used the following thesis statement: "Although I hate to admit it, I know that in several ways I'm just like my mom." She then went on to describe how she works too hard, worries too much, and judges other people too harshly. Be sure to include examples for each characteristic you mention.

Writing Assignment

Influential People   10

Who are the three people who have been the most important influences in your life? Write an essay describing each of these people and explaining how each of them has helped you. For example:

It was my aunt who first impressed upon me the importance of a college education.

If it weren't for my father, I wouldn't be in college today.

My best friend has helped me with my college education in several ways.

To develop support for this essay, make a list of all the ways each person helped you get your bearings and focus on a college path. Alternatively, you could do some freewriting about each person you're writing about. These prewriting techniques—listing and freewriting—are both helpful ways of getting started with an essay and thinking about it on paper.

Writing Assignment

Heroes for the Human Race   11

Many people would agree that three men who died in recent years were a credit to the human race. Christopher Reeve played Superman in the movies but became one in real life by fighting a spinal-cord injury. Charles Schultz was the creator

of the world-famous comic strip *Peanuts,* whose characters dealt with anxieties we could all understand. Fred Rogers starred in the well-known television show *Mr. Rogers' Neighborhood,* which children and adults still watch today. Write an essay in which three separate supporting paragraphs explain in detail why each of these men can be regarded as a hero for humanity. Chapter 20, "Writing a Research Paper" (pages 386–410), will show you how to do the necessary research.

Writing Assignment

12   Writing for a Specific Purpose and Audience

Perhaps you've heard the old saying "Some people are their own worst enemies." We all know people who, unfortunately, find ways to hurt themselves or contribute to their own lack of success. Write two short essays in the form of letters to two different people you know who engage in behavior that is harmful or that may someday prove harmful to them. Your purpose here is to convince both of them to change that behavior before they hurt themselves any further.

Your audience for each letter is the letter's recipient. Pretend that the first person to whom you are writing is the sensitive type. He or she is easily moved and emotional and does not take criticism well. With this reader, you will have to be gently persuasive and, while stroking his or her ego, suggest reasonable ways to change. Pretend that your second correspondent is tougher, more hardheaded, and self-assured. In this case, your tone will have to be stronger and more direct. You might have to paint a grisly picture of the way your reader might end up if this behavior doesn't change.

Both letters can be structured in the same way.

1. In the beginning remind your reader that you value your friendship (or other type of relationship) and that you wish him or her only the best. Make this point part of your explanation for writing the letter in the first place.

2. Describe your reader's destructive behavior in two or more supporting paragraphs. Recall events in which this behavior was very apparent, or discuss the obvious effects it is having on your reader's personality, lifestyle, or relationships with others.

3. In the concluding paragraph suggest changes he or she should make. If necessary, suggest that he or she seek professional counseling or join a support group.

Research Skills

Choose a hobby or interest you might like to find out more about. Using the search engine of your choice, visit several Web sites that are related to your interest. Choose a site that you like and write a paragraph describing both the activity and the Web site to someone unfamiliar with both. What appeals to you about the activity? What makes the Web site fun, informative, and/or amusing to people who share your interest?

19 Using the Library and the Internet

This chapter will explain and illustrate how to use the library and the Internet to

- find books on your topic
- find articles on your topic

This chapter will also show you how to

- evaluate Internet sources

Write an essay about using the Internet as a tool for research. To support your main point, provide examples of specific sites that you have found useful. What kinds of information has the Internet made available? Remember to be specific.

This chapter provides the basic information you need to use your college library and the Internet with confidence. You will learn that for most research topics there are two basic steps you should take:

1. Find books on your topic.
2. Find articles on your topic.

You will learn, too, that while using the library is the traditional way of doing such research, a home computer with Internet access now enables you to investigate any topic.

Using the Library

Most students know that libraries provide study space, computer workstations, and copying machines. They are also aware of a library's reading area, which contains recent copies of magazines and newspapers. But the true heart of a library is the following: a *main desk,* the library's *catalog or catalogs of holdings, book stacks,* and the *periodicals storage area.* Each of these is discussed in the pages that follow.

Main Desk

The main desk is usually located in a central spot. Check at the main desk to see whether a brochure describes the layout and services of the library. You might also ask whether the library staff provides tours of the library. If not, explore your library to find each of the areas described below.

Make up a floor plan of your college library. Label the main desk, catalogs (in print or computerized), book stacks, and periodicals area.

Activity

1

Library Catalog

For almost any research project, the *library catalog* is the starting point. It is a list of all the holdings of the library. In most cases, library catalogs are computerized and can be accessed on terminals located in the library. Increasingly, catalogs can be accessed online, so you may be able to check a library's book holdings on your home computer.

Finding a Book—Author, Title, and Subject

There are three ways to search for a book: by author, by title, and by subject. For example, suppose you want to see if the library has the book *Amazing Grace*, by Jonathan Kozol. You can check for the book in any of three ways:

1. You can do an *author* search and look it up under "Kozol, Jonathan." An author is always listed under his or her last name.

2. You can do a *title* search and look it up under "Amazing Grace." Note that you always look up a book under the first word in the title, excluding the words *A, An,* or *The.*

3. If you know the subject that the book deals with—in this case, poor children—you can do a *subject* search and look it up under "Poor children."

Here is the author entry in a computerized catalog for Kozol's book *Amazing Grace:*

Author:	Kozol, Jonathan
Title:	Amazing Grace
Publisher:	New York: Crown, 1995
LC Subjects:	1. Poor children—New York (N.Y.) 2. Racism and racial segregation—New York (N.Y.) 3. Children of minorities—New York (N.Y.) 4. AIDS, asthma, illnesses of children.
Call Number:	362.709 Koz
Material:	Book
Location:	Cherry Hill
Status:	Available

Note that in addition to giving you the publisher (Crown) and year of publication (1995), the entry also tells you the *call number*—where to find the book in the library. If the computerized catalog is part of a network of libraries, you may also learn at what branch or location the book is available. If the book is not at your library, you can probably arrange for an interlibrary loan.

Using Subject Headings to Research a Topic

Generally, if you are looking for a particular book, it is easier to search by *author* or by *title*. On the other hand, if you are researching a topic, then you should search by *subject.*

The subject section performs three valuable functions:

- It will give you a list of books on a given topic.
- It will often provide related topics that might have information on your subject.
- It will suggest to you more limited topics, helping you narrow your general topic.

Chances are you will be asked to do a research paper of about five to fifteen pages. You do not want to choose a topic so broad that it could be covered only by an entire book or more. Instead, you want to come up with a limited topic that can be adequately supported in a relatively short paper. As you search the subject section, take advantage of ideas that it might offer on how you can narrow your topic.

Part A   Answer the following questions about your library's catalog.

1. Explain how to look up a book by its title and then by its author, using the catalog found at your college library.

   _____

2. Which type of catalog search will help you research and limit a topic?

   _____

Part B   Use your library's catalog to answer the following questions.

1. What is the title of one book by Alice Walker?

   _____

2. What is the title of one book by George Will?

   _____

3. Who is the author of *The Making of the President*? (Remember to look up the title under *Making,* not *The.*)

   _____

4. Who is the author of *Angela's Ashes*? _____

5. List two books and their authors dealing with the subject of adoption:

a. _____

_____

b. _____

_____

6. Look up a book titled *The Road Less Traveled* or *Passages* or *The American Way of Death* and give the following information:

a. Author _____

b. Publisher _____

c. Date of publication _____

d. Call number _____

e. Subject headings _____

7. Look up a book written by Barbara Tuchman or Russell Baker or Bruce Catton and give the following information:

a. Title _____

b. Publisher _____

c. Date of publication _____

d. Call number _____

e. Subject headings _____

Book Stacks

The *book stacks* are the area of the library in which books are shelved according to call numbers. The *call number,* as distinctive as a Social Security number, always appears on the catalog entry for any book. It is also printed on the spine of every book in the library.

If your library has *open stacks* (an area that you are permitted to enter), here is how to find a book. Suppose you are looking for *Amazing Grace,* which has the call number HV[875] / N48 / K69 in the Library of Congress system. (Libraries using the Dewey decimal system have call letters made up entirely of numbers rather than letters and numbers. However, you use the same basic method to locate a book.) First, you go to the section of the stacks that holds the H's. After you locate the H's, you look for the HV's. After that, you look for HV875. Finally, you look for HV875 / N48 /K69, and you have the book.

If your library has *closed stacks* (stacks that you are not permitted to enter), you will have to write down the title, author, and call number on a request form. (Such forms will be available near the card catalog or computer terminals.) You'll then give the form to a library staff person, who will locate the book and bring it to you.

Use the book stacks to answer one of the following sets of questions. Choose the questions that relate to the system of classifying books used by your library.

Library of Congress system (letters and numbers)

1. Books in the BF21 to BF833 area deal with

   a. philosophy.

   b. sociology.

   c. psychology.

   d. history.

2. Books in the HV580 to HV5840 area deal with which type of social problem?

   a. Drugs

   b. Suicide

   c. White-collar crime

   d. Domestic violence

3. Books in the PR4740 to PR4757 area deal with

   a. James Joyce.

   b. Jane Austen.

   c. George Eliot.

   d. Thomas Hardy.

Dewey decimal system (numbers)

1. Books in the 320 area deal with

   a. self-help.

   b. divorce.

   c. science.

   d. politics.

2. Books in the 636 area deal with

   a. animals.

   b. computers.

   c. marketing.

   d. senior citizens.

3. Books in the 709 area deal with

   a. camping.

   b. science fiction.

   c. art.

   d. poetry.

Periodicals

The first step in researching a topic is to check for relevant books; the second step is to locate relevant periodicals. *Periodicals* (from the word *periodic,* which means "at regular periods") are magazines, journals, and newspapers. Periodicals often contain recent information about a given subject, or very specialized information about a subject, which may not be available in a book.

The library's catalog lists its periodicals, just as it lists the library's books. To find articles in these periodicals, however, you need to consult a periodicals index. One widely used index, *Readers' Guide to Periodical Literature,* comes in print and electronic versions. Many other indexes can be accessed through *online databases.*

Readers' Guide to Periodical Literature

The familiar green volumes of the *Readers' Guide* can be found in nearly every library. They list articles published in more than two hundred popular magazines, such as *Newsweek, Health, People, Ebony, Redbook,* and *Popular Science.* Articles are listed alphabetically under both subject and author. For example, if you wanted to learn the names of articles published on the subject of child abuse within a certain time span, you would look under the heading "Child abuse."

Here is a typical entry from the *Readers' Guide:*

Subject heading   Title of article   Author of article   "Illustrated"

Psychology
Getting Inside a Teen Brain S. Begley il *Newsweek*
    p. 58–59 F 28 '00

Page   Date   Name of magazine
numbers

Note the sequence in which information about the article is given:

1. Subject heading.

2. Title of the article. In some cases, bracketed words ([ ]) after the title help make clear what the article is about.

3. Author (if it is a signed article). The author's first name is always abbreviated.

4. Whether the article has a bibliography (*bibl*) or is illustrated with pictures (*il*). Other abbreviations sometimes used are shown in the front of the *Readers' Guide.*

5. Name of the magazine. Before 1988, the *Readers' Guide* used abbreviations for most of the magazines indexed. For example, the magazine *Popular Science* is abbreviated *Pop Sci.* If necessary, refer to the list of magazines in the front of the index to identify abbreviations.

6. Page numbers on which the article appears.

7. Date when the article appeared. Dates are abbreviated. For example, *Mr* stands for March, *Ag* for August, *O* for October. Other abbreviations are shown in the front of the *Guide.*

The *Readers' Guide* is published in monthly supplements. At the end of a year, a volume is published covering the entire year. You will see in your library large green volumes that say, for instance, *Readers' Guide 2000* or *Readers' Guide 2008.* You will also see the small monthly supplements for the current year.

The drawback of *Readers' Guide* is that it gives you only a list of articles; you must then go to your library's catalog to see if the library actually has copies of the magazines that contain those articles. If you're lucky and it does, you must take the time to locate the relevant issue and then to read and take notes on the articles or make copies of them.

The *Readers' Guide* may also be available at your library in an electronic version. If so, you can quickly search for articles on a given subject simply by typing in a keyword or key phrase.

Online Databases

Most college and public libraries provide online computer-search services known as *online databases* or *library subscription services*. Using any of these services, you can type in keywords and quickly search many periodicals for articles on your subject. Some databases, such as General Science Index, cover a specific discipline, but others, such as Academic Search Premier, are more general.

Often, articles you find will appear as "full text." This means that you can print the entire article from your computer. In other cases, only an *abstract* (summary) of the article will be available. However, abstracts are valuable too, because they allow you to determine whether the article is relevant to your research and whether you should continue searching for the full text.

Finally, database articles appear in *HTML* or *PDF* format or in both. Articles in HTML (*hypertext markup language*) have been reformatted for publication on the Internet. Those in PDF (*portable document format*) are exact reproductions of a print document.

Your library may use a service that provides access to many online databases. EBSCOhost, Infotrac, and ProQuest are such services. Here are a few online databases that have proven useful for new student researchers.

Academic Search Premier covers a variety of disciplines and includes full-text articles and abstracts of articles from more than 4,400 periodicals.

CGP (Catalog of U.S. Government Publications) contains documents published by the U.S. government.

Cumulative Index to Nursing and Allied Health Literature (CINAHL) provides access to articles found in more than 1,800 professional journals in the health professions.

ERIC (Education Resources Information Center) makes available articles from professional journals, reports, and speeches having to do with education.

General Science Index lists articles on biology, chemistry, physics, and the other physical sciences.

JSTOR (Journal Storage) provides full-text articles found in back issues of journals in the humanities, social sciences, and natural sciences.

New York Times **Index** lists articles published in this newspaper since 1913.

PsychInfo is published by the American Psychological Association. It includes abstracts of books, articles, and doctoral dissertations in psychology. It also provides access to full-text articles through PsycARTICLES.

Wilson Humanities Index covers more than 500 English-language periodicals in disciplines such as archaeology, the classics, art, history, theater, music, literature, philosophy, and religion.

Activity

4

At this point in the chapter, you now know the two basic steps in researching a topic in the library. What are the steps?

1. _____

2. _____

Activity

5

1. Look up a recent article on Internet shopping using one of your library's periodicals indexes and fill in the following information:
   a. Name of the index you used _____
   b. Article title _____
   c. Author (if given) _____
   d. Name of magazine _____
   e. Pages _____   f. Date _____

2. Look up a recent article on violence in schools using one of your library's periodicals indexes and fill in the following information:
   a. Name of the index you used _____
   b. Article title _____
   c. Author (if given) _____
   d. Name of magazine _____
   e. Pages _____   f. Date _____

3. Using one of the online databases to which your college subscribes, find an article on organic gardening.
   a. Name of the database you used _____
   b. Article title _____
   c. Author (if given) _____
   d. Name of magazine, journal, or newspaper _____
   e. Pages (if given) _____   f. Date _____

Using the Internet

www.mhhe.com/langan

Find Books on Your Topic

To find current books, go to your college's catalog, which you may be able to access from home, and look for books published recently. Another approach is to go online and search the Web site of a commercial bookseller such as Amazon.com (www.amazon.com) or Barnes and Noble Books (www.barnesandnoble.com). You can search for books on these sites for free, and you are under no obligation to buy a book.

Use the "Browse" Tab

On the Web site of a commercial bookseller, click on "Books" and then "Browse." You'll get a list of general categories to search. Suppose you are reporting on the development of the modern telescope. When you click "Browse subjects" on Amazon.com, you get a list of categories that includes "Science." Clicking on that category displays a list of subcategories, one of which is "Astronomy and space science." Clicking on this subcategory brings up more subcategories, including "Telescopes." Finally, clicking on "Telescopes" gives you a list of recent books on the topic. You can click on each title for information about each book. All this browsing can be done very easily and will help you research your topic quickly.

Use the "Search" Box

If you are preparing a paper on some aspect of photography, type the word "photography" in the search box. You'll then get a list of books on that subject. Just looking at the list may help you narrow your subject and decide on a specific topic to develop. For instance, one student typed "photography" in the search box on Barnes and Noble's site and got a list of 13,000 books on the subject. Considering only part of that list helped her realize that she wanted to write on some aspect of photography during the U.S. Civil War. She typed "Civil War photography" and got a list of 200 titles. After looking at information about twenty of those books, she was able to decide on a limited topic for her paper.

A Note on the Library of Congress

The commercial bookstore sites described are especially quick and easy to use. But you should know that to find additional books on your topic, you can also visit the Library of Congress Web site (www.loc.gov). The Library of Congress, in Washington, D.C., has copies of all books published in the United States. Its online catalog contains about twelve million entries. You can browse this catalog by subject or search by keywords. The search form permits you to check only those books that interest you. Click on the "Full Record" option to view publication information about a book, as well as its call numbers. You can then try to obtain the book from your college library or through an interlibrary loan.

Other Points to Note

Remember that at any time you can use your printer to quickly print information presented on the screen. (For example, the student planning a paper on photography in the Civil War could print a list of the twenty books, along with sheets of information about individual books.) You could then go to your library knowing exactly what books you want to borrow. If your own local or school library is accessible online, you can visit in advance to find out whether it has the books you want. Also, if you have time and money, you may want to purchase them from a local bookshop or an online bookstore, such as Amazon. Used books are often available at greatly reduced cost, and they often ship out in only a few days.

Find Articles on Your Topic

There are many online sources that will help you find articles on your subject. Following are descriptions of some of them.

Online Magazine, Newspaper, and Journal Articles

As already mentioned, your library may subscribe to online databases (see the sample list on pages 377–378) that you can use to access articles on your subject. Another online research service, one that you can subscribe to individually on a home computer, is *Question.* You may be able to get a free one-day trial subscription or pay for a monthly subscription at limited cost. This service provides millions of newspaper articles as well as thousands of book chapters and television and radio transcripts.

Search Engines

An Internet search engine will help you quickly go through a vast amount of information on the Web to find articles about almost any topic. One extremely helpful search engine is Google; you can access it by typing "www.google.com." A screen will then appear with a box in which you can type one or more keywords. For example, if you are thinking of doing a paper on Habitat for Humanity, you simply enter the words "Habitat for Humanity." Within a second or so you will get a list of nearly three million articles and sites on the Web about Habitat for Humanity.

You should then try to narrow your topic by adding other keywords. For instance, if you typed "Habitat for Humanity's hurricane relief efforts," you would get a list of about 390,000 articles and sites. If you narrowed your potential topic further by typing "Habitat for Humanity's hurricane relief effort in New Orleans," you would get a list of 78,600 items. Google does a superior job of returning hits that are genuinely relevant to your search, so just scanning only the early part of a list may be enough to provide you with the information you need.

Very often your challenge with searches will be getting too much information rather than too little. Try making

Google, Inc.

Results from a keyword search on Google using "Habitat for Humanity's hurricane relief effort in New Orleans."

your keywords more specific, or use different combinations of keywords. You might also try another search engine, such as www.yahoo.com. In addition, consult the search engine's built-in "Advanced Search" feature for tips on successful searching.

Finally, remember while you search to save the addresses of relevant Web sites that you may want to visit again. The browser that you are using (for example, Internet Explorer or Safari) will probably have a "Bookmark" or "Favorite Places" option. With the click of a mouse, you can bookmark a site. You will then be able to return to it simply by clicking on its name in a list, rather than having to remember and type its address.

Evaluating Internet Sources

Keep in mind that the quality and reliability of information you find on the Internet may vary widely. Anyone with a bit of computer know-how can create a Web site and post information there. That person may be a Nobel Prize winner, a leading authority in a specialized field, a high school student, or a crackpot. Be careful, then, to look closely at your source in the following ways.

Evaluating Online Sources

1. **Internet address:** In a Web address, the three letters after the "dot" identify the domain. The most common domains are .com, .edu, .gov, .net, and .org. You can't always determine a Web site's reliability by the domain type. Almost anyone can get a Web address ending in *.com* or *.org*. So you must examine every Web site carefully. Consider these three points: author, internal evidence, and date.

2. **Author:** What credentials does the author have? What academic degrees does he or she hold? Does the author work for a college, university, well-respected think tank, or research group? Has he or she published other material on the topic?

3. **Internal evidence:** Does the author seem to proceed objectively— presenting all sides of the issue fairly before stating his or her own views?

   Does the sponsor of the Web site seem to be an objective source? For example, it would be fair to assume that a Web article from the American Medical Association discussing irradiated food treats the subject objectively. Can you say the same for an article appearing on the Web site of an irradiated-food distributor?

   Does the author provide adequate support for his or her views? Or does he or she make unsupported generalizations—claims that are simply not backed up with studies or the opinions of other experts?

   Was the article first published in a print version? Is the publisher of this print version reliable? If the article was not first published in print, could it have been, or is it so outlandish that no publisher would take the financial risk of backing it?

4. **Date:** Is the information up to date? Check at the top or bottom of the document for copyright, publication, or revision dates. Knowing such data will help you decide whether the material is current enough for your purposes. For example, would a ten-year-old article on computer viruses yield useful information for a paper that discusses ways to protect today's computers? Probably not.

Part A Go to www.google.com and search for the word "democracy." Then complete the items below.

1. How many items did your search yield? _____

2. In the early listings, you will probably find each of the following domains: edu, gov, org, and com. Pick one site with each domain and write its full address.

   a. Address of one .com site you found: _____

   b. Address of one .gov site: _____

   c. Address of one .org site: _____

   d. Address of one .edu site: _____

Part B Circle *one* of the sites you identified above and use it to complete the following evaluation.

3. Name of site's author or authoring institution: _____

4. Is site's information current (within two years)? _____

5. Does the site serve obvious business purposes (with advertising or attempts to sell products)? _____

6. Does the site have an obvious connection to a governmental, commercial, business, or religious organization? If so, which one?

   _____

7. Does the site's information seem fair and objective?

   _____

   _____

8. Based on the information above, would you say the site appears reliable?

   _____

Practice in Using the Library and the Internet

Use your library or the Internet to research a subject that interests you. Select one of the following areas or (with your instructor's permission) an area of your own choice:

Assisted suicide	Same-sex marriage
Interracial adoption	Global warming
Ritalin and children	Nursing home costs
Sexual harassment	Pro-choice movement today

Pro-life movement today

Health insurance reform

Pollution of drinking water

Problems of retirement

Cremation

Capital punishment

Prenatal care

Acid rain

New aid for people with disabilities

New remedies for allergies

Censorship on the Internet

Prison reform

Drug treatment programs

Sudden infant death syndrome

New treatments for insomnia

Organ donation

Child abuse

Voucher system in schools

Food poisoning (salmonella)

Alzheimer's disease

Holistic healing

Best job prospects today

Heroes for today

Computer use and carpal tunnel syndrome

Noise control

Animals nearing extinction

Animal rights movement

Anti-gay violence

Drug treatment programs for adolescents

Fertility drugs

Witchcraft today

New treatments for AIDS

Mind-body medicine

Origins of Kwanzaa

Hazardous substances in the home

Airbags

Gambling and youth

Nongraded schools

Forecasting earthquakes

Ethical aspects of hunting

Ethics of cloning

Recent consumer frauds

Stress reduction in the workplace

Sex on television

Everyday addictions

Toxic waste disposal

Self-help groups

Telephone crimes

Date rape

Steroids

Surrogate mothers

Vegetarianism

HPV immunizations

Steroids and professional athletes

The Aztecs

The Maya

All-electric cars

Magna Carta

Charter schools

Cyberbullying

The next ice age

Timbuktu

Violence on television

Declaration of Independence

Bill of Rights

Research the topic first through a subject search in your library's catalog or that of an online bookstore. Then research the topic through a periodicals index (print or online). On a separate sheet of paper, provide the following information:

1. Topic

2. Three books that either cover the topic directly or at least touch on the topic in some way. Include

   Author

   Title

   Place of publication

   Publisher

   Date of publication

3. Three articles on the topic published in 2005 or later. Include

   Title of article

   Author (if given)

   Title of magazine

   Date

   Pages (if given)

4. Finally, write a paragraph describing exactly how you went about researching your topic. In addition, include a photocopy or printout of one of the three articles.

20

Writing a Research Paper

This chapter will explain and illustrate

- the six steps in writing a research paper:

  STEP 1: Select a topic that you can readily research

  STEP 2: Limit your topic, make the purpose of your paper clear, and assess your audience

  STEP 3: Gather information on your limited topic

  STEP 4: Plan your paper and take notes on your limited topic

  STEP 5: Write the paper

  STEP 6: Use an acceptable format and method of documentation

This chapter also provides

- a model research paper

If you were to write a research paper on college, what would you focus on? "College" itself is too broad a topic to cover in one paper. You would need to select a more limited topic. For example, you could focus on the first-class treatment received by many college star athletes or the benefits of attending smaller colleges over larger universities. Looking at these photos, can you think of other college-themed topics you might cover in a research paper?

Step 1: Select a Topic That You Can Readily Research

Researching at a Local or College Library

Start with a *subject* search of your library's catalog (as described on pages 371–374), and see whether there are several books on your general topic. For example, if you choose the broad topic "divorce," try to find at least three books on that topic. Make sure the books are available on the library shelves.

Next, go to a *periodicals index* in your library (see pages 375–377) to see if there are a fair number of magazine, newspaper, or journal articles on your topic. You can use the *Readers' Guide to Periodical Literature* (described on page 376) to find articles in back issues of periodicals that your library may keep. Also, your library may subscribe to electronic databases such as Academic Search Premier, JSTOR, and Wilson Humanities Index (described on pages 377–378), which will allow you to find articles published in a far greater range of publications. For instance, when Sara Hughes, author of the model research paper "Divorce Mediation," visited her local library, she typed the search term "divorce" into a computer that connected her to Academic Search Premier. In searching this database, she found hundreds of titles, with publication information and the complete text of articles about divorce.

Researching on the Internet

The first step is to go to the *subjects* section of the Web site of a large bookseller—such as Barnes and Noble or Amazon.com—or library catalog to find books. (You don't have to buy the books; you're just browsing for information.)

Sara Hughes checked out both Barnes and Noble and Amazon. "At Barnes and Noble, the category I clicked on first was 'Parenting and Families.' Under that were many subcategories, including 'Divorce.' I clicked on it, and got back 733 books! Scrolling through these titles, I noticed that there were several different themes: mostly 'how to survive a divorce' books, but also books on other topics, like 'how to stay involved in your children's lives when you're not living with them.' Others were about all kinds of emotional, legal, and financial aspects of divorce." There were so many books that Sara felt frustrated and decided to return to Barnes and Noble later, after searching online for newspaper and magazine articles.

She started with the Internet search engine Google (see page 381). "First I typed the word 'divorce' in the keyword box," says Sara. "But I got more than a hundred million hits! Then I narrowed my topic to 'the process of divorce,' but that was still too general, so I kept narrowing to things like 'divorce costs' and 'divorce alternatives.' I was still getting too many hits, but I saw that some of the first ones seemed really promising.

"In order to look just for newspaper or magazine articles, I went directly to the sites of some popular publications such as *Time* (time.com), *Newsweek* (newsweek.com), and *USA Today* (usatoday.com). I was able to search each one for recent articles on divorce; however, I would have had to pay about two dollars to read each article online. So I wrote down the title, date, and page number of the articles I was interested in and looked up the ones that were available in the back-issue section of the library and on the electronic databases my library subscribes to. I found plenty of recent material on my subject. In *USA Today,* I found an article entitled 'A Kindler, Gentler Divorce?', which really grabbed my attention. In it was a term I had never heard before: 'divorce mediation.' I learned that divorce mediation helps people divorce without becoming bitter enemies in the process. It definitely sounded like a topic worth exploring. So I went back to Google and typed in 'divorce mediation.' I began to read these articles and realized that this was a far more limited topic than the one I had before. Now I was beginning to have a focus."

Encouraged, Sarah returned to the Barnes and Noble site and typed in "divorce mediation." That brought up a far more manageable list of forty-one books. As she clicked on their titles, she noticed that for some of them she could access reviews, a summary and a table of contents. That helped her narrow her focus even more; she decided to write about the advantages of divorce mediation over traditional divorce. With that in mind, she picked out ten books that looked promising. When she went to her college library, she found that it had six of the ten; she then bought one more book in paperback at a local bookstore. (Remember that if you can't find a book in your local or college library, you can always ask the librarians to obtain it from another library through interlibrary loan. However, be aware that interlibrary loans take days or even weeks.)

Sarah's search was successful. However, for your own research, if not enough books and articles are available to you, try changing your topic. After all, you can't write a research paper for which research materials are not readily available.

Step 2: Limit Your Topic, Make the Purpose of Your Paper Clear, and Assess Your Audience

A research paper should *thoroughly* develop a *limited* topic. It should be narrow and deep, rather than broad and shallow. Therefore, as you read through books and articles on your general topic, look for ways to limit the topic.

For instance, as Sarah read through materials on the general topic "divorce," she chose to limit her paper to divorce mediation. Furthermore, she decided to limit it even more by focusing on the advantages of mediated divorce over more traditional adversarial divorce. The general topic "violence in the media" might be narrowed to instances of copycat crimes inspired by movies or TV. After doing some reading on protests against the death penalty, you might decide to limit your paper to cases in which executed people were later proved innocent. The broad subject "learning disabilities" could be reduced to the widespread use of the drug Ritalin or possible causes of dyslexia. "AIDS" might be limited to federal funding to fight the disease; "personal debt" could be narrowed to the process an individual goes through in declaring bankruptcy.

The subject headings in your library's catalog and periodicals index will give you helpful ideas about how to limit your subject. For example, under the subject heading "Divorce" in the book file at Sarah's library were titles suggesting many limited directions for research: helping children cope with divorce, cooperative parenting after a divorce, the financial toll of divorce, fathers and custody rights. Under the subject heading "Divorce" in the library's periodicals index were subheadings and titles of many articles that suggested additional limited topics that a research paper might explore: how women can learn more about family finances in the event of a divorce, how parents can move past their own pain to focus on children's welfare, becoming a divorce mediator, divorce rates in second marriages. The point is that *subject headings and related headings, as well as book and article titles, may be of great help to you in narrowing your topic.* Take advantage of them.

Do not expect to limit your topic and make your purpose clear all at once. You may have to do quite a bit of reading as you work out the limited focus of your paper. Note that many research papers have one of two general purposes. Your purpose might be to make and defend a point of some kind. (For example, your purpose in a paper might be to provide evidence that gambling should be legalized.) Or, depending on the course and the instructor, your purpose might simply be to present information about a particular subject. (For instance, you might be asked to write a paper describing the most recent scientific findings about what happens when we dream.)

In Chapters 2 and 18, you learned that assessing the needs of an audience is an important step in the writing process. Chances are that your research paper will probably be read only by your instructor, although he or she might want to share it with the rest of the class. Even if your instructor is your only reader, you will need to keep his or her needs in mind as you research your paper. For example, pretend you are writing a paper on the medical breakthroughs resulting from adult-stem-cell research. Your composition instructor's training is probably in English, not biology or medicine, so he or she might not be familiar with certain technical terms like *undifferentiated cells* (cells that have not yet developed into specific cell types) or *somatic stem cells* (another term for the stem cells of an adult body). Of course, you will have become familiar with such terms through your research; nonetheless, you will have to define them for your reader to make sure that he or she can follow your paper easily.

To introduce a reader to a process with which he or she is unfamiliar, you might want to determine the most frequently asked questions (called "FAQs" online) about the subject. As such, you might be able to anticipate the reader's needs even better. For example, Sarah Hughes, the student writing a paper on "divorce mediation," came upon a Web site that listed several frequently asked questions about her topic. Some of these seemed so important to her (*What is the cost? How long does mediation take?* for example) that she made a point of discussing them in her paper because there was a good chance her reader might ask such questions.

Step 3: Gather Information on Your Limited Topic

After you have a good sense of your limited topic, you can begin gathering information. A helpful way to proceed is to sign out the books that you need from your library. In addition, make copies of all relevant articles from magazines, newspapers, or journals. If your library has an online periodicals database, you may be able to print copies of those articles.

In other words, take the steps needed to get all your important source materials together in one place. You can then sit and work on these materials in a quiet, unhurried way in your home or some other place of study.

Step 4: Plan Your Paper and Take Notes on Your Limited Topic

Preparing a Scratch Outline

As you carefully read through the material you have gathered, think constantly about the specific content and organization of your paper. Begin making decisions about exactly what information you will present and how you will arrange it. Prepare a scratch outline for your paper that shows both its thesis and the areas of support for the thesis. It may help to try to plan at least three areas of support.

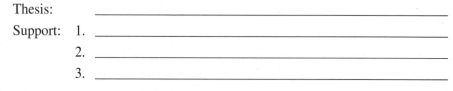

Here, for example, is the brief outline that Sarah Hughes prepared for her paper on divorce mediation:

Thesis: Divorce mediation is an alternative to the painful, expensive
            process of a traditional divorce.

Support: 1. Saves time and money
            2. Produces less hostility
            3. Produces more acceptable agreement between ex-spouses

---

Taking Notes

With a tentative outline in mind, you can begin taking notes on the information that you expect to include in your paper. Write your notes on four- by six-inch or five- by eight-inch cards or on computer files. The notes you take can be in the form of *direct quotations, paraphrases, summaries,* or all three.

A *direct quotation* must be written *exactly* as it appears in the original work. But as long as you don't change the meaning, you may omit words from a quotation if they are not relevant to your point. Show such an omission with three spaced periods (known as an *ellipsis*) in place of the deleted words.

www.mhhe.com/langan

Original Passage

If you choose to follow the traditional path through this adversarial system, you will each hire lawyers who will fight on your behalf like ancient knights, charging each other with lances. Each knight, highly skilled in the intricacies of jousting but untrained in other ways to resolve conflict, will try to win by seizing for his client as much booty (children and property) as possible.

Direct Quotation with Ellipsis

"[Y]ou will each hire lawyers who will fight on your behalf like ancient knights, charging each other with lances. Each knight . . . will try to win by seizing for his client as much booty (children and property) as possible."

(Note that the capital letter in brackets shows that the word was capitalized by the student and did not begin the sentence in the original source.)

A *paraphrase* uses about the same number of words as the original. However, you express the information in your own words, structuring the ideas in your own way. A paraphrase accurately reports the original information, but it does so in a completely new way.

Reread the original statement on Sarah's direct-quotation note card on page 391. Then compare it to a paraphrase of that statement.

Paraphrase

People who decide to hire highly skilled and experienced divorce attorneys usually end up in a bitter fight (the only strategies the attorneys know how to use) in which one side tries to deprive the other of as much as it can, including the house, the cars, the furniture, and even the kids.

In a *summary,* you condense the original material by expressing it in your own words. Summaries may be written as lists, as brief paragraphs, or both. Following is one of Sarah Hughes's summary note cards.

Abusive spouse

If there has been a recent history of physical abuse, mediation should not be attempted. If the abuse has been mental/verbal, mediation may not be successful if abused partner is very intimidated.

Butler/Walker, 46–47

Keep in mind the following points about your research notes:

- Write on only one side of each card or sheet of paper.
- Write only one kind of information, from one source, on any one card or sheet. For example, the sample card above has information on only one idea (abusive spouse) from one source (Butler/Walker).
- At the top of each card or sheet, write a heading that summarizes its content. This will help you organize the different kinds of information that you gather.
- Identify the source and page number at the bottom.

Whether you quote, paraphrase, or summarize, be sure to record the exact source and page from which you take each piece of information. In a research paper, you must document all information that is not common knowledge or a matter of historical record. For example, the birth and death dates of Dr. Martin Luther King Jr. are established facts and do not need documenting. On the other hand, the number of adoptions granted to single people in 2008 is a specialized fact that should be documented. As you read several sources on a subject, you will develop a sense of what authors regard as generally shared or common information and what is more specialized information that must be documented.

A Note on Plagiarism

If you do not document information that is not your own, you will be stealing. The formal term is *plagiarizing*—using someone else's work as if it were your own, whether you borrow a single idea, a sentence, or an entire essay. Plagiarism is a direct violation of academic ethics; if you pass someone else's work off as your own, you risk being failed or even expelled. Equally, plagiarism deprives you of what can be a most helpful and organizational experience—researching and writing about a selected topic in detail.

www.mhhe.com/langan

There are two types of plagiarism: intended and unintended. The first is worse than the second, but both must be avoided.

One example of *intended plagiarism* is submitting someone else's paper as if it were your own. Another is copying an article from a magazine, newspaper, the Internet, or any other source and turning it in as your own. Keep in mind that teachers can easily discover whether a student has taken material from an Internet source by typing a sentence or two from the student's paper into a search engine such as Google; the source is often quickly identified.

Intended plagiarism, described above, is rather obvious and easy to avoid. Unintended plagiarism, the other type, is trickier. *Unintended plagiarism* occurs when the note taker writes a paraphrase or summary that too closely resembles the original because it uses some of the same structure or some of the same words as the original.

On page 392, you can see an acceptable paraphrase based on an original passage about "divorce mediation." Here is an example of an unacceptable paraphrase of that original passage. Compare it to the acceptable paraphrase on page 392.

Unacceptable Paraphrase

People who decide to use the <u>traditional path</u> and pursue an <u>adversarial</u> divorce will each hire attorneys <u>who will fight</u> each other for their clients. Each lawyer will probably be very good at what he or she does but will probably be <u>untrained in other ways to resolve</u> the problem. And each side will try <u>to seize as much</u> from the other (houses, <u>children</u>, etc.) <u>as possible.</u>

As you can see, similar or identical phrases are underlined. In addition, the structure of the unacceptable paraphrase is identical to that of the original source.

With the possibility of plagiarism in mind, then, be sure to take careful, documented notes during your research. Remember that if you use another person's material—whether you quote directly, paraphrase, or summarize—*you must acknowledge your source.* Moreover, when you cite a source properly, you give credit where it is due, you provide your readers with a way to locate the original material on their own, and you demonstrate that your work has been carefully researched.

www.mhhe.com/langan

Step 5: Write the Paper

After you have finished reading and note taking, you should have a fairly clear idea of the plan of your paper. Make a *final outline* and use it as a guide to write your first full draft. If your instructor requires an outline as part of your paper, you should prepare either a *topic outline,* which contains your thesis plus supporting words and phrases, or a *sentence outline,* which contains all complete sentences. In the model paper shown on pages 401–410, a topic outline appears on page 402. You will note that Roman numerals are used for first-level headings, capital letters for second-level headings, and Arabic numerals for third-level headings.

In your *introduction,* include a thesis statement expressing the purpose of your paper and indicate the plan of development that you will follow. The section on writing an introductory paragraph for an essay (pages 341–343) is also appropriate for the introductory section of a research paper.

As you move from *introduction* to *main body* to *conclusion,* strive for unity, support, and coherence so that your paper will be clear and effective. Repeatedly ask yourself, "Does each of my supporting paragraphs develop the thesis of my paper?" Use the checklist on the inside back cover of this book to make sure that your paper touches all four bases of effective writing.

Step 6: Use an Acceptable Format and Method of Documentation

Format

The model paper on pages 401–410 shows acceptable formats for a research paper, including the style recommended by the Modern Language Association (MLA). Be sure to note carefully the comments and directions set in small print in the margins of each page.

Documentation of Sources

You must tell the reader the sources (books, articles, and so on) of the borrowed material in your paper. Whether you quote directly, paraphrase, or summarize ideas in your own words, you must acknowledge your sources. In the past, you may have used footnotes and a bibliography to cite your sources. Here you will learn a simplifed and widely accepted documentation style used by the Modern Language Association.

Citations within a Paper

When citing a source, you must mention the author's name and the relevant page number. The author's name may be given either in the sentence you are writing or in parentheses following the sentence. Here are two examples:

> Paula James, the author of *The Divorce Mediation Handbook*, has witnessed the divorce process from both sides—actually, *three* sides. First, she went through a traditional divorce herself. In her words, "we simply turned our destinies over to our two attorneys. . . . Many thousands of dollars later we were divorced, but with resentment and distrust and no idea of how we would jointly raise our child" (xvi).
>
> By contrast, mediation costs are far more reasonable. Most mediators charge between $100 and $350 an hour (Friedman 19).

There are several points to note about citations within the paper:

- When an author's name is provided within the parentheses, only the last name is given.

- There is no punctuation between the author's name and the page number.

- The parenthetical citation is placed after the borrowed material but before the period at the end of the sentence.

- If you are using more than one work by the same author, include a shortened version of the title within the parenthetical citation. For example, suppose you were using two books by Paula James and you included a second quotation from her book *The Divorce Mediation Handbook*. Your citation within the text would be

(James, *Handbook* 39).

Note that a comma separates the author's last name from the abbreviated title and page number.

- Use the abbreviation *qtd. in* when citing a quotation from another source. For example, a quotation from Lynn Jacob on the third page of Sarah Hughes's paper (see page 405) is from a work written not by Jacob but by Ann Field. The citation is therefore handled as follows:

As pointed out by Lynn Jacob, president of the Academy of Family Mediators, "the legal system is designed so that the more the couples fight, the more money the lawyers earn" (qtd. in Field 136).

Citations at the End of a Paper

End your paper with a list of works cited that includes all the sources actually used in the paper. (Don't list other sources, no matter how many you have read.) Look at the "Works Cited" list in the research paper on page 410, and note the following:

- Begin the "Works Cited" list on a new page, not on the last page of the paper's text.
- Organize entries alphabetically according to the authors' last names. Do not number the entries.
- Double-space the entries, and insert no extra space between entries.
- After the first line of an entry, indent each additional line in that entry half an inch.
- Italicize (do not underline) titles of books, periodicals, and other independently published works.
- Do not include URLs in Web entries.
- Include the publication medium, such as "Print," "Web," "DVD," or "Television."
- If no publisher's name appears in a Web source, write *N.p.* When no date appears on a Web site, write *n.d.*

Model Entries for a "Works Cited" List

Model entries for a "Works Cited" list are given below. Use these entries as a guide when you prepare your own list.

Book by One Author

Maggio, Theresa. *The Stone Boudoir: Travels through the Hidden Villages of Sicily.* Cambridge, MA: Perseus, 2003. Print.

Note that the author's last name is written first. In addition, when citing a book, always provide the full title, which you should copy from the inside title page.

Include a subtitle by placing a colon after the main title and then copying the subtitle word for word.

Two or More Entries by the Same Author

Nuland, Sherman B. *How We Die: Reflections on Life's Final Chapter.* New York:

   Vintage, 1995. Print.

—. *The Mysteries Within: A Surgeon Reflects on Medical Myths.* New York:

   Simon & Schuster, 2000. Print.

If you cite two or more entries by the same author (in the example above, the second book is also by Nuland), do not repeat the author's name. Instead, substitute for it three hyphens followed by a period. Then give the remaining information as usual. Arrange works by the same author alphabetically by title. Ignore the words *A, An*, and *The* when alphabetizing by title.

Book by Two or More Authors

Baxandall, Rosalyn, and Elizabeth Ewen. *Picture Windows: How the Suburbs*

   Happened. New York: Basic Books, 2000. Print.

For a book with two or more authors give all the authors' names but reverse only the first name.

Magazine Article

Bowden, Charles. "Unseen Sahara." *National Geographic* Oct. 2009: 100–11.

   Print.

Newspaper Article

Zoroya, Gregg. "A Hunger for Heroes." *USA Today* 28 Feb. 2000: D1–2. Print.

The final letter and numbers refer to pages 1 and 2 of section D. If the article is not printed on consecutive pages, list the first page, followed by a plus sign "+" (in that case, the example above would read "D1+"). Also, when citing newspaper titles, omit the introductory *The* (for example *Boston Globe*, not *The Boston Globe*).

Article in Professional Journal

Andrews, Elmer. "The Gift and the Craft: An Approach to the Poetry of Seamus

   Heaney." *Twentieth Century Literature* 31.4 (1985): 368–69. Print.

Editorial or Letter

"Drugs and Preschoolers." Editorial. *Philadelphia Inquirer* 28 Feb. 2000: A10. Print.

Selection in an Edited Collection

Feist, Raymond E. "The Wood Boy." *Legends: Short Novels by the Masters of Modern Fantasy.* Ed. Robert Silverberg. New York: Tor Books, 1998. 176–211. Print.

Revised or Later Edition

Davis, Mark H. *Social Psychology.* 4th ed. New York: McGraw-Hill, 2000. Print.

Note that the abbreviations *Rev. ed., 2nd ed., 3rd ed.,* and so on, are placed right after the title.

Chapter or Section in a Book by One Author

Secunda, Victoria. "A New Sense of Family." *Losing Your Parents, Finding Yourself: The Defining Turning Point of Adult Life.* New York: Hyperion, 2000. 242–59. Print.

Pamphlet

Health Scams: Don't Take the Risk. Washington, D.C.: U.S. Food and Drug Administration, 2009. Print.

Television Program

"Not As Private As You Think." *60 Minutes.* Narr. Lesley Stahl. Prod. Rome Hartman. CBS. 13 Aug. 2000. Television.

Film

The Departed. Dir. Martin Scorsese. Warner Bros., 2006. Film.

Sound Recording

Mayer, John. "Gravity." *Continuum.* Aware Records, 2006. LP.

DVD or Videocassette

"To the Moon." *Nova.* Narr. Liev Schrieber. PBS Video, 1999. Videocassette.

Personal Interview

Cornell, Matthew R. Personal interview. 17 Sept. 2009.

Article in a Reference Database

De Sousa, Avinash. "The Role of Music Therapy in Psychiatry." *Alternative Ther-*
    apies in Health & Medicine 11.6 (2005): 52–53. *Academic Search Premier.*
    Web. 8 Jan. 2010.

The first date (2005) refers to the publication date; the second (8 Jan. 2010) refers to the exact day the student researcher accessed the information.

Article in an Online Magazine

Begley, Sharon. "It's in Our Genes. So What?" *Newsweek Online* 25 Nov. 2009.
    Web. 18 Feb. 2010.

Article on a Web Site

"Galileo's Telescope." *The Galileo Project*. Rice University. 1995. Web. 9 Mar.
    2009.

No author is given, so the article is cited first, followed by the title of the Web site (*The Galileo Project*), followed by the sponsor of the Web site (Rice University). The first date (1995) refers to when the material was electronically published, updated, or posted; the second date (9 Mar. 2009) refers to when the student researcher accessed the source.

Electronic Mail (E-mail) Posting

Capuana, Louis. "Re: Once upon a Time." Message to John Verga. 10 Apr. 2008.
    E-mail.

Activity 1

On a separate sheet of paper, convert the information in each of the following references into the correct form for a "Works Cited" list. Use the appropriate model above as a guide.

1. An article by Alex Yannis titled "In New League, Women Get Payoff and Payday" on page D5 of the April 13, 2001, issue of the *New York Times*.

2. An article by Nancy Franklin titled "Nonsense and Sensibility" on pages 96–97 of the March 6, 2000, issue of the *New Yorker*.

3. A book by Francis McInerney and Sean White called *Futurewealth: Investing in the Second Great Wave of Technology* and published in New York by St. Martin's in 2000.

4. A book by Ellen N. Junn and Chris Boyatzis titled *Child Growth and Development* and published in a seventh edition by McGraw-Hill in New York in 2000.

5. An article by Melinda Liu and Leila Abboud titled "Generation Superpower" dated April 11, 2001, and found on April 12, 2007, in the online version of *Newsweek*.

Model Paper

While the *MLA Handbook* does not require a title page or an outline for a paper, your instructor may ask you to include one or both. Here is a model title page.

Divorce Mediation: A Better Alternative

by

Sarah Hughes

English 101

Professor Martinez

8 March 2010

Option 1: Model Title Page

The title should begin about one-third of the way down the page. Center the title. Double-space between lines of the title and your name. Also center and double-space the instructor's name and the date.

Papers written in MLA style use the simple format shown below. There is no title page or outline.

½ inch

Hughes 1

1 inch

Sarah Hughes

Professor Martinez

English 101

8 March 2010

Divorce Mediation: A Better Alternative

Divorce is never easy. Even if two people both want to part, ending a marriage is a painful experience. In order to become divorced, most people go through a process that increases this pain. Starting with the lawsuit that one partner has to file against the other, the two take on the roles of enemies. . . .

Option 2: Model First Page with Top Heading

Double-space between lines. Leave a one-inch margin on all sides.

Model Outline Page

Use this format if your instructor asks you to submit an outline of your paper.

After the title page, number all pages in upper-right corner—one-half inch from the top. Place your name before the page number. Use lowercase Roman numerals on outline pages. Use Arabic numbers on pages following the outline.

The word *Outline* **(without underlining or quotation marks) is centered one inch from the top. Double-space between lines. Leave a one-inch margin on all sides.**

Hughes i

Outline

Thesis: Divorce mediation offers several advantages over the traditional process of divorce.

I. Introduction

   A. Traditional divorce

      1. Casts divorcing couple in the role of enemies

      2. Expensive and painful

   B. Mediation

      1. Description of mediation process

      2. Growing popularity of mediation

II. Advantages of mediation in terms of money and time

   A. Traditional divorce

      1. Lawyers' fees charged for every step

      2. Lawyers' and courts' involvement slows process down

   B. Mediation

      1. Mediators' fees lower than lawyers'

      2. Couple controls costs of case

      3. Mediated divorces completed more quickly

III. Emotional benefits of mediation

   A. Traditional divorce

      1. Pits clients against one another

      2. Produces hostility and distrust

   B. Mediation encourages clients to work cooperatively

IV. Advantages of mediation in terms of divorce agreement

   A. Traditional divorce leaves clients with attorney-negotiated agreement that may not work well for them

   B. Mediation creates agreement that both clients can live with

V. Who shouldn't use mediation

VI. Conclusion

Here is a full model paper. It assumes that the writer has included a title page.

Hughes 1

Divorce Mediation: A Better Alternative

Divorce is never easy. Even if two people both want to break up, ending a marriage is a painful experience. In order to become divorced, most people go through a process that increases this pain. Starting with the lawsuit that one partner files against the other, the two take on the roles of enemies. As author Paula James describes it,

> You will each hire lawyers who will fight on your behalf like ancient knights, charging each other with lances. Each knight . . . will try to win by seizing for his client as much booty (children and property) as possible. You will stand on the sidelines wringing your hands while you watch the battle—and, of course, pay your knight a high hourly fee. One peculiarity of this battle is that the wounds inflicted don't appear on the other warrior; they appear on you, your spouse, and your children. (3)

But there is an alternative to this traditional, ugly divorce process. It is called divorce mediation. Couples who use divorce mediation find that it saves them time and money, it produces less hostility, and it leaves them with an agreement they can respect.

What is divorce mediation? According to a 2009 article entitled "Divorce Litigation Alternatives," it is a process in which "the parties engage the services of a specially trained impartial third party to facilitate a mutually satisfactory resolution of the divorce" (Schonfeld and Kessler). The mediator, who is usually a lawyer or a therapist, helps the couple hammer out a divorce agreement they both find acceptable. This is done in as few or as many meetings as necessary. Each spouse will probably hire a personal lawyer to review the agreement before it is made final. But the spouses, not "hired gun" lawyers, are responsible

---

Marginal annotations:

Double-space between lines of the text. Leave a one-inch margin all the way around the page. Your name and the page number should be typed one-half inch from the top of the page.

Source is identified by name.

Direct quotations of five typed lines or more are indented ten spaces from the left margin. Quotation marks are not used.

The spaced periods (ellipsis) show that material from the original source has been omitted.

Only the page number is needed, as the author has already been named in the text.

Thesis, followed by plan of development.

Both authors' names are given since both appear in the "Works Cited" entry.

for creating it. In fact, as Cathy Gale, an Australian divorce law specialist, indicates, if lawyers are involved at all, their job is "to coach and support their clients to do the negotiating themselves" (qtd. in Towers 29).

During the process, the mediator doesn't favor one partner over the other. Instead, the mediator maintains, in the words of the lawyer and mediator Gary Friedman, an attitude of "positive neutrality." Friedman explains the term by saying, "While I am largely neutral as to the outcome, . . . I am not neutral as to process. On the contrary, I am actively engaged in trying to ensure that each party takes responsibility for him- or herself, and making sure that all decisions are sound for both of them" (26).

Source is identified by name and area of expertise.

Once the couple is satisfied with the agreement, it is filed in court and approved by a judge in a brief hearing. In many states, the couple does not even need to attend that hearing. Couples can thus complete a divorce without ever seeing the inside of a courtroom.

There are no official statistics to tell how many divorcing couples use mediation, but it is definitely becoming a popular option. According to the Academy of Family Mediators in Boston, the number of mediators has increased exponentially (Valente B7). And courts in twenty-five states now *require* couples involved in child-custody disputes to work with a mediator (Field 136).

This typical citation is made up of the author's last name and the relevant page number. "Works Cited" then provides full information about the source.

One practical advantage of mediation is that it is less expensive and less time-consuming. In a traditional divorce, after each partner retains a lawyer and sets the divorce machine in motion, costs mount up quickly. A lawyer's fee "may exceed $500 per hour . . . for each spouse" ("Avoiding the War"). The lawyers bill their clients for every phone call made, every letter written, every hearing attended, every

Citation for an online source. No page number is given because the online document does not provide one.

Hughes 3

meeting held to iron out another wrinkle in the process. In addition, when people divorce, they must make decisions about countless details. Even if the spouses are not far apart in their thinking, those decisions take time. If the husband and wife are deeply divided, the bills can become staggering. According to Field, "An uncontested, amiable divorce may cost $5,000 per partner and drag on for more than a year. . . . A warring duo . . . could wind up spending $30,000 apiece, and the case might span an entire Presidential administration" (136). The couple's financial welfare is not the top concern of courts and attorneys. As pointed out by Lynn Jacob, president of the Academy of Family Mediators, "the legal system is designed so that the more the couples fight, the more money the lawyers earn" (qtd. in Field 136).

The abbreviation qtd. means quoted. The quoted material is not capitalized because the student has blended it into a sentence with an introductory phrase.

By contrast, mediation costs are far more reasonable. Most mediators charge between $100 and $350 an hour (Friedman 19). Because both spouses are present for all mediating sessions, they are in control of how high the costs mount. Although there is no "typical" divorce, it is clear that mediated divorces tend to be much less expensive than others. In Friedman's experience, a mediated divorce in which there is "substantial disagreement" costs between $2,000 and $5,000 (19). Ken Waldron, a mediator with the Madison (Wisconsin) Center for Divorce Mediation, estimates that most mediated divorces end up costing one-half to one-third less than an attorney-negotiated divorce (Schuetz 10). Mediator Paula James describes mediated divorces as costing "a fraction" of attorney-negotiated ones (60).

Quotation marks acknowledge that the phrase is copied from the previous citation.

Second, mediated divorces are finalized much more quickly than divorces fought out in the courts. Couples divorcing in the traditional way spend a long time going through the following cycle: meet with attorney, wait for attorney to talk with spouse's attorney, wait for spouse's attorney to talk with spouse, wait for spouse's attorney to return with response. Mediating couples don't have to do any of that. They also don't have the ordeal of endless hearings, court delays, and their attorneys' own schedule problems. Mediating couples can do a large part of the work of their divorce agreement outside their meetings with the mediator. Most mediating couples really want to get their agreement finished, for both financial and emotional reasons. Because they have the guidance of a professional to help them work through difficult points, they tend to work efficiently. According to an article by Meg Lundstrom in *BusinessWeek*, most mediated divorces are completed in four to eight sessions, or six to twenty-four hours (228). Gary Friedman's estimate is about the same: four to six meetings spaced over a period of two to three months (18). A typical mediation center advertising online, Divorce Solutions of New York, N.Y., says, "The entire divorce process takes approximately 2–3 months, as opposed to 2–3 years in the adversarial process" ("Mediation: How It Works").

Citation for an online source with no author.

A third important point is that mediated divorces leave less hostility behind them. It's true that a divorce produces feelings of grief, anger, and frustration for almost everyone. But mediation can help people deal with these feelings. By contrast, an attorney-fought divorce seems designed to make the splitting partners hate each other as much as possible. Before she wrote *The Divorce Mediation Handbook,* Paula James had witnessed the divorce process from both sides—actually, *three* sides. First, she went through a traditional divorce herself. In her words, "we simply turned our destinies over to our two attorneys. . . . Many thousands of dollars later we were divorced, but with resentment and distrust and no idea of how we would jointly raise our child" (xvi).

Hughes 5

Later, James became an attorney herself and represented clients in traditional divorces. She describes how she and her colleagues routinely dug for dirt about possible affairs, alcohol abuse, shady business dealings, child neglect, and any other personal weaknesses they could use as ammunition in court. By the end of such an ordeal, she writes, couples were "deeply in debt, very angry, and distrustful of one another" (10).

Finally, James began working as a divorce mediator. As a mediator she works with many clients who may no longer be the best of friends but who want to remain on decent terms with their ex-spouses, for their own sake as well as for the sake of any children. One such client, Terri, expressed the feelings of many people who want a mediated divorce. She called James after having talked with an attorney. Terri was horrified by the attorney's fee ($5,000 to start) and what he told her. " 'He said that Eli and I are now adversaries, that I must do everything I can to protect myself from him and to get as much money as possible. . . . ,' Terri said. 'That's not what I want. I'm sorry that our marriage hasn't worked out, but I'm not trying to take Eli to the cleaners' " (10). Terri and Eli then started working with James. By listening carefully to them both, and stepping in occasionally to help them explain their fears and priorities rather than attack one another, James helped Terri and Eli work out an agreement in a short time and for a reasonable fee. "They left my office looking more relaxed than when they had entered," she reported (15). According to the Divorce Law Information Service Center's home page, "In family law disputes, mediation is often preferred over litigation because it facilitates future communication between the parties which is necessary when the future of the children is at stake."

In the long run, the biggest advantage of mediated divorce is that it helps couples develop an agreement they will be willing to live with.

Single quotation marks are used for a quotation within a quotation.

The authors of "Divorce Litigation Alternatives" assert, "[A]s mediated agreements represent a genuine compromise between the interests of the parties, the likelihood of future disputes is reduced. Most importantly, where the welfare of the children is a concern, mediation promotes their best interest, by discouraging the escalation of parental conflict" (Schonfeld and Kessler). Attorney-negotiated agreements tend to fall into rigid, traditional patterns: She gets the house; he gets the car; the kids spend every other weekend and six weeks in the summer with him. But mediated agreements are generally more creative and in tune with the divorcing couple's lives. One couple described by Field, in a *Cosmopolitan* article, Vivian and Bill, had been fighting bitterly over the mail-order business they had built together. Each insisted that he or she should take over the business entirely.

> Without lawyers, judges, or formal courtroom rules to get in the way, the mediator got Vivian and Bill to agree on a general plan whereby one spouse would keep the business, buy out the other, and lend him or her enough money to start a new venture. Then he instructed them to calculate their company's net worth. Finally, the material helped them realize on their own that Vivian, who'd had more contact with overseas suppliers, should keep the business; Bill, who was more aggressive, would do better taking the loan and launching a new product line. (Field 137)

Once they are used to the idea, most couples like the idea of creating an agreement that really works for them. In the words of Paula James, "[The divorcing couple] aren't ignorant children who must be silenced while their lawyers do the talking" (xvii).

Although mediation has clear advantages, it is not right for everyone. Most mediation experts agree with Butler and Walker, who

Brackets indicate that the words inside them were supplied by the student and did not appear in the original source.

Hughes 7

say that mediation "would not be an appropriate way to negotiate a fair settlement" if one of the divorcing partners feels unable or too frightened to stand up to the other. Examples are situations characterized by "intimidation or fear of violence," "a recent history of domestic violence or child abuse," or "severe intellectual or emotional limitations" (6). In such cases, it is probably best for the weaker partner if an attorney does his or her negotiating.

In conclusion, while divorce is never a pleasant experience, divorce mediation can save a couple time and money, help them keep a civil relationship, and produce an agreement that they both feel is reasonable. According to the Academy of Family Mediators, 70 to 90 percent of couples are satisfied with the terms of their mediated divorces (Lundstrom 228). This high figure shows that mediation is a more civilized and respectful way to achieve a divorce than the traditional courtroom method.

The conclusion provides a summary and restates the thesis.

A mediating couple, Sam and Jane, said it best:

[Sam said,] "I really do appreciate your help. This was a lot easier than I thought it would be."

Jane smiled. "We both thought we were going to end up in a huge fight. Doing it this way was so much better." (Qtd. in James xi)

Hughes 8

Works Cited

"Avoiding the War." *Divorce without War*. Divorce without War. 2008. Web. 18 Feb. 2010.

Butler, Carol A., and Dolores D. Walker. *The Divorce Mediation Answer Book*. New York: Kodansha America, 1999.

Divorce Law Information Service Center. "Mediation." *Divorcelawinfo .com*. Epoq US. 2010. Web. 19 Feb. 2010.

Field, Ann. "Divorce Mediation and Other (Cheap) Ways to Split." *Cosmopolitan* Aug. 1995: 136–37. Print.

Friedman, Gary J. *A Guide to Divorce Mediation*. New York: Workman, 1993. Print.

James, Paula. *The Divorce Mediation Handbook*. San Francisco: Jossey-Bass, 1997. Print.

Lundstrom, Meg. "A Way to 'Take the War Out' of Divorce." *BusinessWeek* 16 Nov. 1998: 228. Print.

"Mediation: How It Works." *Divorce Solutions*. Divorce Solutions. 2010. Web. 18 Feb. 2010.

Schonfeld, Esther, and Deena Kessler. "Divorce Litigation Alternatives." *5 Towns Jewish Times*. 5 Towns Jewish Times. 27 Nov. 2009. Web. 18 Feb. 2010.

Schuetz, Lisa. "Mediation Offers an Alternative When Dealing with Divorce." *Wisconsin State Journal* 31 May 1998: 10. Print.

Towers, Katherine. "Parting with Dignity." *Herald Sun* [Melbourne, Austral.] 27 Apr. 2009: 29–30. *Newspaper Source*. Web. 21 Feb. 2010.

Valente, Judith. "A Kinder, Gentler Divorce?" *USA Today* 25 Aug. 1997: B7. Print.

"Works Cited" should be centered at the top of a new page.

The list should be double-spaced.

Titles of books, magazines, newspapers, Web sites, and database services should be italicized.

The date an online source is accessed—in this case, February 18, 2010—should be added after the word "Web."

Handbook of Sentence Skills

*What is confusing about these signs? How could
you change their wording or appearance to keep
each one's message consistent and coherent?*

Sentence-Skills Diagnostic Test

Part 1

This test will help you check your knowledge of important sentence skills. Certain parts of the following word groups are underlined. Write *X* in the answer space if you think a mistake appears at the underlined part. Write *C* in the answer space if you think the underlined part is correct.

A series of headings ("Fragments," "Run-Ons," and so on) will give you clues to the mistakes to look for. However, you do not have to understand the label to find a mistake. What you are checking is your own sense of effective written English.

Fragments

_____ 1. Until his mother called him twice. Barry did not get out of bed. He had stayed up too late the night before.

_____ 2. After I slid my aching bones into the hot water of the tub, I realized there was no soap. I didn't want to get out again.

_____ 3. Mother elephants devote much of their time to child care. Nursing their babies up to eight years.

_____ 4. A country in Central American bordered by Mexico to the north. Guatemala is famous for its coffee.

_____ 5. I love to eat and cook Italian food, especially lasagna and ravioli. I make everything from scratch.

_____ 6. One of my greatest joys in life is eating desserts. Such as blueberry cheesecake and vanilla cream puffs. Almond fudge cake makes me want to dance.

Run-Ons

_____ 7. We couldn't view the Picasso exhibit because the museum is closed on Mondays.

_____ 8. The window shade snapped up like a gunshot her cat leaped four feet off the floor.

_____ 9. Billy is the meanest little kid on his block, he eats only the heads of animal crackers.

_____ 10. The Allies landed in Normandy in June 1944, the war in Europe was over in less than a year.

_____ 11. My first boyfriend was five years old. We met every day in the playground sandbox.

_____ 12. The store owner watched the shopper carefully, she suspected him of stealing from her before.

Standard English Verbs

_____ 13. Jed tows cars away for a living and is ashamed of his job.

_____ 14. You snored like a chain saw last night.

_____ 15. After Massachusetts exiled Roger Williams in 1635, he settle in what is now Providence, Rhode Island.

_____ 16. Charlotte react badly whenever she gets caught in a traffic jam.

Irregular Verbs

_____ 17. Henry Folger gived the money to establish the Folger Shakespeare Library in Washington, D.C.

_____ 18. She had written four poems and a short story before she was twelve.

_____ 19. When the mud slide started, the whole neighborhood began going downhill.

_____ 20. Juan has rode the bus to school for two years while saving for a car.

Subject-Verb Agreement

_____ 21. There is long lines at the checkout counter.

_____ 22. The little girl have a painful ear infection.

_____ 23. One of the crooked politicians was jailed for a month.

_____ 24. The Allegheny and Monongahela Rivers joins in Pittsburgh to form the Ohio River.

Consistent Verb Tense

_____ 25. The South had a rural economy before the Civil War begins in 1861.

_____ 26. The first thing Jerry does every day is weigh himself. The scale informs him what kind of meals he can eat that day.

_____ 27. Sandy eats a nutritional breakfast, skips lunch, and then enjoys a big dinner.

_____ 28. His parents stayed together for his sake; only after he graduates from college were they divorced.

Pronoun Agreement, Reference, and Point of View

_____ 29. Every smoker endangers their lungs.

_____ 30. I enjoy movies, like *The Return of the Vampire,* that frighten me.

_____ 31. Every guest at the party dressed like their favorite cartoon character.

_____ 32. People who visit foreign countries must carry their passports.

_____ 33. As the cats fought, they knocked the lamp against the glass, breaking it.

_____ 34. I love hot peppers, but they do not always agree with me.

Pronoun Types

_____ 35. Him and Antoine joined the soccer team.

_____ 36. No one is a better cook than she.

Adjectives and Adverbs

_____ 37. Bonnie ran quick up the steps, taking them two at a time.

_____ 38. Parts of Holland are more lower than sea level.

Misplaced Modifiers

_____ 39. He swatted the wasp that stung him with a newspaper.

_____ 40. Charlotte returned the hamburger that was spoiled to the supermarket.

_____ 41. Jamal test-drove a car at the dealership with power windows and a sunroof.

_____ 42. Smiling, the house was entered by Mildred's prom date.

Dangling Modifiers

_____ 43. Tapping a pencil on the table, Ms. Garcia asked for the students' attention.

_____ 44. Walking across the field, a river came into view.

_____ 45. While I was waiting for the bus, rain began to fall.

_____ 46. Falling to the ground, the rising sun was greeted by the tan beachcombers.

Faulty Parallelism

_____ 47. The sky got dark, lightning flashed, the wind howled, and a massive storm <u>approaching</u> the city.

_____ 48. The recipe instructed me to chop onions, to peel carrots, and <u>to boil a pot</u> of water.

_____ 49. In London, we ate fish and chips, visited the British Museum, and <u>traveling</u> around the city in a double-decker bus.

_____ 50. Jackie enjoys shopping for new clothes, <u>surfing the Internet</u>, and walking her dog.

Capital Letters

_____ 51. After being out in a cold drizzling rain, I looked forward to a bowl of <u>campbell's</u> soup for lunch.

_____ 52. Julio is taking a vacation in <u>august</u> this year.

_____ 53. A woman screamed, "<u>He's</u> stolen my purse!"

_____ 54. During the <u>Winter</u> months, my grandfather burns wood in his Franklin stove.

Apostrophe

_____ 55. The <u>Wolfman's</u> bite is worse than his bark.

_____ 56. <u>Clydes</u> quick hands reached out to break his son's fall.

_____ 57. We <u>can't</u> go to Paris without visiting the Eiffel Tower.

_____ 58. They <u>didn't</u> study as hard as they should have for the test.

Quotation Marks

_____ 59. Mark Twain once said, "<u>The</u> more I know about human beings, the more I like my dog."

_____ 60. Say something tender to me, "<u>whispered Tony to Lola.</u>"

_____ 61. "Ask not what your country can do for <u>you, said</u> President Kennedy."

_____ 62. "To err is human," Alexander Pope wrote, "<u>to forgive divine.</u>"

Comma

_____ 63. Some major European capitals include London Paris Rome Madrid and Berlin.

_____ 64. Although he had little formal education Thomas Alva Edison became a great inventor.

_____ 65. Sandra didn't have to study much for her algebra final, for she was a mathematical genius.

_____ 66. The large clock which was in the library's foyer told us that the place was closing.

_____ 67. Dogs, according to most cat lovers, are inferior pets.

_____ 68. His father shouted "Why don't you go out and get a job?"

Commonly Confused Words

_____ 69. We were grateful to hear that the storm would not effect us.

_____ 70. Your never too old to learn a foreign language.

_____ 71. They're planning to trade in their old car.

_____ 72. Its important to get this job done properly.

_____ 73. Will you except this job if it's offered to you, or keep looking for something better?

_____ 74. Who's the culprit who left the paint can on the table?

Effective Word Choice

_____ 75. The effects of the drought are still persisting.

_____ 76. The movie was a real bomb, so we left early.

_____ 77. Arthur never goes to fast-food restaurants; he avoids them like the plague.

_____ 78. Jason's face turned red in color after he swallowed the hot peppers.

Part 2 (Optional)

Do Part 2 at your instructor's request. This second part of the test will provide more detailed information about skills you need to know. On a separate piece of paper, number and correct all the items in Part One that you marked with an X. For example, suppose you had marked the following word groups with an X. (Note that these examples are not taken from the test.)

  4. If football games disappeared entirely from television. I would not even miss them. Other people in my family would perish.

  7. The kitten suddenly saw her reflection in the mirror, she jumped back in surprise.

 15. Nashville Tennessee is the capital of country music.

 29. The first woman to obtain a medical license in Italy Maria Montessori was a pioneer in education for children.

Here is how you should write your corrections on a separate sheet of paper.

  4. television, I

  7. mirror, and

 15. Nashville, Tennessee

 29. in Italy, Maria

There are more than forty corrections to make in all.

REPAIRS IN PROGRESS

STAIRWELL CLOSE
TO ALL TRAFFIC

To ensure your safety, these stairs
are undergoing extensive repairs

We apologize for the inconvenience.

To access Columbus please use the
stairwell at the east end (back toward
the lake) of the Sheraton Hotel.

*How could you change this sign's wording to make it
grammatically correct? What specific errors do you see?*

Subjects and Verbs

21

The basic building blocks of English sentences are subjects and verbs. Understanding them is an important first step toward mastering a number of sentence skills.

Every sentence has a subject and a verb. Who or what the sentence speaks about is called the <u>subject</u>; what the sentence says about the subject is called the <u>verb</u>.

> The <u>children</u> <u>laughed</u>.
>
> Several <u>branches</u> <u>fell</u>.
>
> Most <u>students</u> <u>passed</u> the test.
>
> That <u>man</u> <u>is</u> a hero.

www.mhhe.com/langan

A Simple Way to Find a Subject

To find a subject, ask *who* or *what* the sentence is about. As shown below, your answer is the subject.

> *Who* is the first sentence about? <u>Children</u>
>
> *What* is the second sentence about? Several <u>branches</u>
>
> *Who* is the third sentence about? Most <u>students</u>
>
> *Who* is the fourth sentence about? That <u>man</u>

A Simple Way to Find a Verb

To find a verb, ask what the sentence *says about* the subject. As shown below, your answer is the verb.

> What does the first sentence *say about* the children? They <u>laughed</u>.
>
> What does the second sentence *say about* the branches? They <u>fell</u>.
>
> What does the third sentence *say about* the students? They <u>passed</u>.
>
> What does the fourth sentence *say about* that man? He <u>is</u> (a hero).

A second way to find the verb is to put *I, you, we, he, she, it,* or *they* (whichever form is appropriate) in front of the word you think is a verb. If the result makes sense, you have a verb. For example, you could put *they* in front of *laughed* in the first sentence above, with the result, *they laughed,* making sense. Therefore you know that *laughed* is a verb. You could use *they* or *he,* for instance, to test the other verbs as well.

Finally, it helps to remember that most verbs show action. In the sentences already considered, the three action verbs are *laughed, fell,* and *passed.* Certain other verbs, known as *linking verbs,* do not show action. They do, however, give information about the subject. In "That man is a hero," the linking verb *is* tells us that the man is a hero. Other common linking verbs include *am, are, was, were, feel, appear, look, become,* and *seem.*

Activity	In each of the following sentences, draw one line under the subject and two lines under the verb.
1	

1. Blood flows from the heart to the lungs via the pulmonary arteries.
2. The curious child stared silently at the shopping mall Santa.
3. The city-states of ancient Greece were ruled by various kinds of governments.
4. Cotton shirts feel softer than polyester ones.
5. The fog rolled into the cemetery.
6. Yoko invited her friends to dinner.
7. A green fly stung her on the ankle.
8. Every year, the Nile River flooded the land it bordered, depositing fertile soil on its banks.
9. The elderly man sat for a few minutes on the park bench.
10. With their fingers, the children drew pictures on the steamed window.

More about Subjects and Verbs

1. A pronoun (a word such as *he, she, it, we, you,* or *they* used in place of a noun) can serve as the subject of a sentence. For example:

   He seems like a lonely person.
   They both like to gamble.

   Without a surrounding context (so that we know who *He* or *They* refers to), such sentences may not seem clear, but they *are* complete.

2. A sentence may have more than one verb, more than one subject, or several subjects and verbs:

> My heart skipped and pounded.
>
> The money and credit cards were stolen from the wallet.
>
> Dave and Ellen prepared the report together and presented it to the class.

3. The subject of a sentence never appears within a prepositional phrase. A *prepositional phrase* is simply a group of words that begins with a preposition. Following is a list of common prepositions.

Prepositions

about	before	by	inside	over
above	behind	during	into	through
across	below	except	of	to
among	beneath	for	off	toward
around	beside	from	on	under
at	between	in	onto	with

Cross out prepositional phrases when you are looking for the subject of a sentence.

> ~~Under my pillow~~ I found a quarter left ~~by the tooth fairy~~.
>
> One ~~of the yellow lights at the school crossing~~ began flashing.
>
> The comics pages ~~of the newspaper~~ have disappeared.
>
> ~~In spite of my efforts~~, Bob dropped out ~~of school~~.
>
> ~~During a rainstorm~~, I sat ~~in my car~~ reading magazines.

4. Many verbs consist of more than one word. Here, for example, are some of the many forms of the verb *smile.*

Forms of *smile*

smile	smiled	should smile
smiles	were smiling	will be smiling
does smile	have smiled	can smile
is smiling	had smiled	could be smiling
are smiling	had been smiling	must have smiled

5. Words like *not, just, never, only,* and *always* are not part of the verb, although they may appear within the verb.

> Larry did not finish the paper before class.
>
> The road was just completed last week.

6. No verb preceded by *to* is ever the verb of a sentence.

> My car suddenly began to sputter on the freeway.
>
> I swerved to avoid a squirrel on the road.

7. No *ing* word by itself is ever the verb of a sentence. (It may be part of the verb, but it must have a helping verb in front of it.)

> They leaving early for the game. (not a sentence, because the verb is not complete)
>
> They are leaving early for the game. (a sentence)

Activity

2

Draw a single line under the subjects and a double line under the verbs in the following sentences. Be sure to include all parts of the verb.

1. A large meteor heading for Earth raced across the galaxy.
2. Parts of my car were manufactured in Canada.
3. Vampires and werewolves are repelled by garlic.
4. Three people in the long bank line looked impatiently at their watches.
5. The pelting rain had pasted wet leaves all over the car.
6. She has decided to find a new apartment.
7. The trees in the mall were glittering with tiny white lights.
8. The puppies slipped and tumbled on the vinyl kitchen floor.
9. Spain and Portugal occupy the Iberian Peninsula and share a border.
10. We have not met our new neighbors in the apartment building.

Review Test

Draw a single line under subjects and a double line under verbs. Crossing out prepositional phrases may help you to find the subjects.

1. A cloud of fruit flies hovered over the bananas.

2. Candle wax dripped onto the table and hardened into pools.

3. Professors Medina and Guggen both knew how to read Sanskrit.

4. The receptionists in my doctor's office always seem willing to help.

5. The children slept soundly in their beds.

6. They have just decided to go on a diet together.

7. Psychology and graphic design are my favorite subjects.

8. The sofa in the living room has not been cleaned for over a year.

9. The water stains on her suede shoes did not disappear with brushing.

10. Fred was fond of Mexican food; he often brought home takeout from Anita's Latin Bistro.

Sentence Sense

What Is Sentence Sense?

As a speaker of English, you already possess the most important of all sentence skills. You have *sentence sense*—an instinctive feel for where a sentence begins, where it ends, and how it can be developed. You learned sentence sense automatically and naturally, as part of learning the English language, and you have practiced it through all the years that you have been speaking English. It is as much a part of you as your ability to speak and understand English is a part of you.

Sentence sense can help you recognize and avoid fragments and run-ons, two of the most common and most serious sentence-skills mistakes in written English. Sentence sense will also help you to place commas, spot awkward and unclear phrasing, and add variety to your sentences.

You may ask, "If I already have this 'sentence sense,' why do I still make mistakes in punctuating sentences?" One answer could be that your past school experiences in writing were unrewarding or unpleasant. English courses may have been a series of dry writing topics and heavy doses of "correct" grammar and usage, or they may have given no attention at all to sentence skills. For any of these reasons, or perhaps for other reasons, the instinctive sentence skills you practice while *speaking* may turn off when you start *writing*. The very act of picking up a pen or sitting down to type may shut down your natural system of language abilities and skills.

Turning On Your Sentence Sense

Chances are that you don't *read a paper aloud* after you write it, and that you don't do the next best thing: read it "aloud" in your head. But reading aloud is essential to turn on the natural language system within you. By reading aloud, you will be able to hear the points where your sentences begin and end. In addition, you will be able to pick up any trouble spots where your thoughts are not communicated clearly and well.

The activities that follow will help you turn on and rediscover the enormous language power within you. You will be able to see how your built-in sentence sense can guide your writing just as it guides your speaking.

Each item that follows lacks basic punctuation. There is no period to mark the end of one sentence and no capital letter to mark the start of the next. Read each item aloud (or in your head) so that you "hear" where each sentence begins and ends. Your voice will tend to drop and pause at the point of each sentence break. Draw a light slash mark (/) at every point where you hear a break. Then go back and read the item a second time. If you are now sure of each place where a split occurs, insert a period and change the first small letter after it to a capital. Minor pauses are often marked in English by commas; these are already inserted. Part of item 1 is done for you as an example.

1. I take my dog for a walk on Saturdays in the big park by the lake. I do this very early in the morning before children come to the park that way I can let my dog run freely. *H*he jumps out the minute I open the car door and soon sees the first innocent squirrel. *T*then he is off like a shot and doesn't stop running for at least half an hour.

2. Lola hates huge tractor trailers that sometimes tailgate her Honda Civic the enormous smoke-belching machines seem ready to swallow her small car she shakes her fist at the drivers, and she screams out many angry words recently she had a very satisfying dream she broke into an army supply depot and stole a bazooka she then became the first person in history to murder a truck.

3. When I sit down to write, my mind is blank all I can think of is my name, which seems to me the most boring name in the world often I get sleepy and tell myself I should take a short nap other times I start daydreaming about things I want to buy sometimes I decide I should make a telephone call to someone I know the piece of paper in front of me is usually still blank when I leave to watch my favorite television show.

4. One of the biggest regrets of my life is that I never told my father I loved him I resented the fact that he had never been able to say the words "I love you" to his children even during the long period of my father's illness, I remained silent and unforgiving then one morning he was dead, with my words left unspoken a guilt I shall never forget tore a hole in my heart I determined not to hold in my feelings with my daughters they know they are loved, because I both show and tell them this all people, no matter who they are, want to be told that they are loved.

5. the Federalists, a faction that arose during the administration of President George Washington (1789–97), favored a strong central government it was led by Alexander Hamilton, Washington's secretary of the Treasury. Hamilton and his followers also believed in supporting the rights of landowners and business people they were opposed by the Democratic-Republican Party the Federalists were against the war of 1812 with Great Britain however, President James Madison, a member of the opposing party, was reelected therefore, the war continued by 1824, the Federalists had lost much of their power, and soon the party went out of existence.

Summary: Using Sentence Sense

You probably did well in locating the end stops in these selections—proving to yourself that you *do* have sentence sense. This instinctive sense will help you deal with fragments and run-ons, perhaps the two most common sentence-skills mistakes.

Remember the importance of *reading your paper aloud.* By reading aloud, you turn on the natural language skills that come from all your experience of speaking English. The same sentence sense that helps you communicate effectively in speaking will help you communicate effectively in writing.

Fragments

23

Introductory Activity

Every sentence must have a subject and a verb and must express a complete thought. A word group that lacks a subject or a verb and that does not express a complete thought is a <u>fragment</u>. Underline the statement in each numbered item that you think is *not* a complete sentence.

1. Because I could not sleep. I turned on my light and read.

2. Calling his dog's name. Todd walked up and down the street.

3. My little sister will eat anything. Except meat, vegetables, and fruit.

4. The reporter turned on her laptop. Then began to type quickly.

Understanding the answers: Read and complete each explanation.

1. *Because I could not sleep* is not a complete sentence. The writer does not complete the _____ by telling us what happened because he could not sleep. Correct the fragment by joining it to the sentence that follows it:
   Because I could not sleep, I turned on my light and read.

2. *Call his dog's name* is not a complete sentence. This word group has no _____ and no verb, and it does not express a complete thought. Correct the fragment by adding it to the sentence that follows it:
   Calling his dog's name, Todd walked up and down the street.

3. *Except meat, vegetables, and fruit* is not a complete sentence. Again, the word group has no subject and no

   _____, and it does not express a complete thought. Correct the fragment by adding it to the sentence that comes before it:
   My little sister will eat anything except meat, vegetables, and fruit.

(continued)

> 4. *Then began to type quickly* is not a complete sentence.
>
> This word group has no _____. One way to correct the fragment is to add the subject *she:*
> Then she began to type quickly.
>
> See Appendix A for answers.

What Are Fragments?

Every sentence must have a subject and a verb and must express a complete thought. A word group that lacks a subject or a verb and does not express a complete thought is a *fragment.* The most common types of fragments are

1. Dependent-word fragments
2. *-ing* and *to* fragments
3. Added-detail fragments
4. Missing-subject fragments

Once you understand what specific kinds of fragments you write, you should be able to eliminate them from your writing. The following pages explain all four types of fragments.

Dependent-Word Fragments

Some word groups that begin with a dependent word are fragments. Here is a list of common dependent words.

Dependent Words		
after	if, even if	when, whenever
although, though	in order that	where, wherever
as	since	whether
because	that, so that	which, whichever
before	unless	while
even though	until	who, whoever
how	what, whatever	whose

Whenever you start a sentence with one of these words, you must be careful that a fragment does not result.

The word group beginning with the dependent word *After* in the example below is a fragment.

> After I learned the price of new cars. I decided to keep my old pickup.

A *dependent statement*—one starting with a dependent word such as *After*—cannot stand alone. It depends on another statement to complete the thought. "After I learned the price of new cars" is a dependent statement. It leaves us hanging. We expect to find out—in the same sentence—*what happened after* the writer learned the price of new cars. When a writer does not follow through and complete a thought, a fragment results.

To correct the fragment, simply follow through and complete the thought:

> After I learned the price of new cars, I decided to keep my old pickup.

Remember, then, that *dependent statements by themselves are fragments.* They must be attached to a statement that makes sense standing alone.

Here are two other examples of dependent-word fragments:

> My daughter refused to stop smoking. Unless I quit also.

> He made an early appointment. Which he did not intend to keep.

"Unless I quit also" is a fragment; it does not make sense standing by itself. We want to know—in the same statement—*what would not happen unless* the writer quit also. The writer must complete the thought. Likewise, "Which he did not intend to keep" is not in itself a complete thought. We want to know in the same statement what *which* refers to.

Correcting a Dependent-Word Fragment

In most cases you can correct a dependent-word fragment by attaching it to the sentence that comes after it or to the sentence that comes before it:

> After I learned the price of new cars, I decided to keep my old pickup.
> (*The fragment has been attached to the sentence that comes after it.*)

> My daughter refused to quit smoking unless I quit also.
> (*The fragment has been attached to the sentence that comes before it.*)

> He made an early appointment, which he did not intend to keep.
> (*The fragment has been attached to the sentence that comes before it.*)

Another way of connecting a dependent-word fragment is simply to eliminate the dependent word by rewriting the sentence:

I learned the price of new cars and decided to keep my old pickup.

She wanted me to quit also.

He did not intend to keep it.

Do not use this method of correction too frequently, however, for it may cut down on interest and variety in your writing style.

TIPS:

1. Use a comma if a dependent-word group comes at the beginning of a sentence (see also page 429):

    After I learned the price of new cars, I decided to keep my old pickup.

    However, do not generally use a comma if the dependent-word group comes at the end of a sentence:

    My daughter refused to stop smoking unless I quit also.

    He made an early appointment, which he did not intend to keep.

2. Sometimes the dependent words *who, that, which,* or *where* appear not at the very start, but near the start, of a word group. A fragment often results:

    The town council decided to put more lights on South Street.
    A place where several people have been mugged.

    "A place where several people have been mugged" is not in itself a complete thought. We want to know in the same statement *where the place was* that several people were mugged. The fragment can be corrected by attaching it to the sentence that comes before it:

    The town council decided to put more lights on South Street, a place where several people have been mugged.

Activity

1

Turn each of the following dependent-word groups into a sentence by adding a complete thought. Put a comma after the dependent-word group if a dependent word starts the sentence.

EXAMPLES

Although I arrived in class late
Although I arrived in class late, I still did well on the test.

_____

The little boy who plays with our daughter
The little boy who plays with our daughter just came down with

German measles.

1. After we stopped for gas

_____

_____

2. If I lend you twenty dollars

_____

_____

3. The car that we bought

_____

_____

4. When I made the Dean's List

_____

_____

5. Before my father got married

_____

_____

Working with a partner, underline the dependent-word fragment or fragments in each item. Then correct each fragment by attaching it to the sentence that comes before or the sentence that comes after it—whichever sounds more natural. Put a comma after the dependent-word group if it starts the sentence.

Activity

2

1. When a flock of birds is resting in the trees. One always acts as a lookout. It will warn the others of possible danger.

_____

_____

_____

2. Bill always turns on the radio in the morning to hear the news. He wants to get an update on world events. Before he gets on with his day.

_____

_____

_____

3. Although Mr. Simon is over eighty years old. He walks briskly to work every day. He seems like a much younger man. Since he is so active and involved in life.

_____

_____

_____

4. Canadian football is similar to football played in the United States. Although in Canada the field is 110 yards long. While in the United States, it is 100 yards long.

_____

_____

_____

5. Last week, I missed work twice. Because of a snowstorm. Which made it hard to pay all my bills this week.

_____

_____

_____

-ing and *to* Fragments

When an *-ing* word appears at or near the start of a word group, a fragment may result. Such fragments often lack a subject and part of the verb. Underline the word groups in the examples below that contain *-ing* words. Each is a fragment.

Example 1

I spent almost two hours on the phone yesterday. Trying to find a garage to repair my car. Eventually I had to have it towed to a garage in another town.

Example 2

Maggie was at first happy with the used SUV she bought from a neighbor. <u>Not realizing until a week later that the vehicle averaged just nine miles per gallon of gas.</u>

Example 3

He looked forward to the study period at school. <u>It being the only time he could sit unbothered and dream about his future.</u> He imagined himself as a lawyer with lots of money and women to spend it on.

People sometimes write *-ing* fragments because they think the subject in one sentence will work for the next word group as well. Thus, in the first example, the writer thinks that the subject *I* in the opening sentence will also serve as the subject for "Trying to find a garage to repair my car." But the subject must actually be *in* the sentence.

Correcting *-ing* Fragments

1. Attach the *-ing* fragment to the sentence that comes before it or the sentence that comes after it, whichever makes sense. Example 1 could read: "I spent almost two hours on the phone yesterday, trying to find a garage to repair my car."

2. Add a subject and change the *-ing* verb part to the correct form of the verb. Example 2 could read: "She did not realize until a week later that the vehicle averaged just nine miles per gallon of gas."

3. Change *being* to the correct form of the verb *be* (*am, are, is, was, were*). Example 3 could read: "It was the only time he could sit unbothered and dream about his future."

Correcting *to* Fragments

When *to* appears at or near the start of a word group, a fragment sometimes results:

I plan on working overtime. To get this job finished. Otherwise, my boss may get angry at me.

The second word group is a fragment and can be corrected by adding it to the preceding sentence:

I plan on working overtime to get this job finished.

Activity	Underline the *-ing* fragment in each of the items that follow. Then make it a sentence by rewriting it, using the method described in parentheses.

3   EXAMPLE

A thunderstorm was brewing. A sudden breeze shot through the windows.
<u>Driving the stuffiness out of the room.</u>
(Add the fragment to the preceding sentence.)

A sudden breeze shot through the windows, driving the stuffiness out

of the room.

(In the example, a comma is used to set off "driving the stuffiness out of the room," which is extra material placed at the end of the sentence.)

1. Establishing a research laboratory in Menlo Park, New Jersey (1876). Edison set the standard for modern industrial research.
   (Add the fragment to the sentence that comes after it.)

   _____

   _____

2. He works 10 hours a day. Then going to class for 2½ hours. It is no wonder he writes fragments.
   (Connect the fragment by adding the subject *he* and changing *going* to the proper form of the verb, *goes*.)

   _____

   _____

3. Charlotte loved the classic movie *Gone with the Wind,* but Clyde hated it. His chief objection being that it lasted four hours.
   (Correct the fragment by changing *being* to the proper verb form, *was*.)

   _____

   _____

Activity	Underline the *-ing* or *to* fragment or fragments in each item. Then rewrite each item, using one of the methods of correction described on page 433.

4   1. A mysterious package arrived on my porch yesterday. Bearing no return address. I half expected to find a bomb inside.

   _____

   _____

2. Jack bundled up and went outside on the bitterly cold day. To saw wood for his fireplace. He returned half frozen with only two logs.

   _____

   _____

3. Tariq read an entire novel on his seventeen-hour flight. Traveling to South Africa. He also wrote three letters.

   _____

   _____

4. Being an excellent math student. Nadia had no difficulty impressing her algebra professor.

   _____

   _____

5. Typing furiously. Luis attempted to finish his paper before class. However, he didn't leave time for proofreading. The result being a paper riddled with errors.

   _____

   _____

Added-Detail Fragments

Added-detail fragments lack a subject and a verb. They often begin with one of the following words.

also	**except**	**including**
especially	**for example**	**such as**

See if you can locate and underline the one added-detail fragment in each of the examples that follow:

Example 1

I love to cook and eat Italian food. Especially spaghetti and lasagna. I make everything from scratch.

Example 2

The class often starts late. For example, yesterday at a quarter after nine instead of at nine sharp. Today the class started at five after nine.

Example 3

He failed a number of courses before he earned his degree. Among them, English I, Economics, and General Biology.

People often write added-detail fragments for much the same reason they write *-ing* fragments. They think the subject and verb in one sentence will serve for the next word group as well. But the subject and verb must be in *each* word group.

Correcting Added-Detail Fragments

1. Attach the fragment to the complete thought that precedes it. Example 1 could read: "I love to cook and eat Italian food, especially spaghetti and lasagna."

2. Add a subject and a verb to the fragment to make it a complete sentence. Example 2 could read: "The class often starts late. For example, yesterday it began at a quarter after nine instead of at nine sharp."

3. Change words as necessary to make the fragment part of the preceding sentence. Example 3 could read: "Among the courses he failed before he earned his degree were English I, Economics, and General Biology."

Activity

5

Underline the fragment in each of the items below. Then make it a sentence by rewriting it, using the method described in parentheses.

EXAMPLE

I am always short of pocket money. <u>Especially for everyday items like magazines and sodas.</u> Luckily my friends often have change.
(Add the fragment to the preceding sentence.)

I am always short of pocket money, especially for everyday items like

magazines and sodas.

1. There are many little things wrong with this apartment. For example, defective lights and leaking faucets. The landlord is not good about making repairs. (Correct the fragment by adding the subject and verb *it has*.)

_____

_____

2. I could feel Bill's anger building. Like a land mine ready to explode. I was silent because I didn't want to be the one to set it off. (Add the fragment to the preceding sentence.)

   _____

   _____

3. We took several unnecessary supplies on our two-day camping trip. Among other things, three bottles of shampoo and a portable television. (Correct the fragment by adding the subject and verb *we brought*.)

   _____

   _____

Underline the added-detail fragment in each item. Then rewrite that part of the item needed to correct the fragment. Use one of the three methods of correction described above.

Activity

6

1. It's always hard for me to get up for work. Especially on Monday after a holiday weekend. However, I always wake up early on free days.

   _____

   _____

2. Tony has enormous endurance. For example, the ability to run five miles in the morning and then play basketball all afternoon.

   _____

   _____

3. Montgomery is the capital of Alabama. As well as being a major furniture-manufacturing center.

   _____

   _____

4. I love visiting Arizona. Especially Sedona. However, I always bring a lot of sun protection.

   _____

   _____

5. One of my greatest joys in life is eating desserts. Such as cherry cheesecake and vanilla cream puffs. Almond fudge cake makes me want to dance.

   _____

   _____

Missing-Subject Fragments

In each example below, underline the word group in which the subject is missing.

Example 1

The truck skidded on the rain-slick highway. But missed a telephone pole on the side of the road.

Example 2

Michelle tried each of the appetizers on the table. And then found that, when the dinner arrived, her appetite was gone.

People write missing-subject fragments because they think the subject in one sentence will apply to the next word group as well. But the subject, as well as the verb, must be in *each* word group to make it a sentence.

Correcting Missing-Subject Fragments

1. Attach the fragment to the preceding sentence. Example 1 could read: "The truck skidded on the rain-slick highway but missed a telephone pole on the side of the road."

2. Add a subject (which can often be a pronoun standing for the subject in the preceding sentence). Example 2 could read: "She then found that, when the dinner arrived, her appetite was gone."

Activity

7

Work with a partner to underline the missing-subject fragment in each item. Together, rewrite that part of the item needed to correct the fragment. Use one of the two methods of correction described above.

1. I tried on an old suit hanging in our basement closet. And discovered, to my surprise, that it was too tight to button.

   _____

   _____

2. When Mary had a sore throat, friends told her to gargle with salt water. Or suck on an ice cube. The worst advice she got was to avoid swallowing.

   _____

   _____

3. Montana is bordered by North Dakota and South Dakota to the east. Also by Wyoming to the south. To the north of the state lies Canada.

   _____

   _____

TIP: Check for Fragments

1. Read your paper aloud from the *last* sentence to the *first.* You will be better able to see and hear whether each word group you read is a complete thought.

2. If you think a word group is a fragment, ask yourself: Does this contain a subject and a verb and express a complete thought?

3. More specifically, be on the lookout for the most common fragments:
    *   Dependent-word fragments (starting with words such as *after, because, since, when,* and *before*)
    *   *-ing* and *to* fragments (*-ing* or *to* at or near the start of a word group)
    *   Added-detail fragments (starting with words such as *for example, such as, also,* and *especially*)
    *   Missing-subject fragments (a verb is present but not the subject)

Review Test   1

Turn each of the following word groups into a complete sentence. Use the spaces provided.

EXAMPLES

With sweaty palms

With sweaty palms, I walked in for the job interview.

Even when it rains

The football teams practice even when it rains.

1. When the alarm sounded

_____

_____

2. Mariana, who is now an excellent student

_____

_____

3. Were having a party

_____

_____

4. To pass the course

_____

_____

5. Geraldo, who is very impatient

_____

_____

6. During the holiday season

_____

_____

7. Over the next hill

_____

_____

8. Before the movie started

_____

_____

9. Known as the "City of Brotherly Love," Philadelphia

_____

_____

10. Feeling very confident

_____

_____

Review Test 2

Each word group in the student paragraph following is numbered. In the space provided, write C if a word group is a *complete sentence;* write F if it is a *fragment.* You will find seven fragments in the paragraph.

A Disastrous First Date

¹My first date with Donna was a disaster. ²I decided to take her to a small Italian restaurant. ³That my friends told me had reasonable prices. ⁴I looked over the menu and realized I could not pronounce the names of the dishes. ⁵Such as "veal piccata" and "fettucini alfredo." ⁶Then I noticed a burning smell. ⁷The candle on the table was starting to blacken. ⁸And scorch the back of my menu. ⁹Trying to be casual, I quickly poured half my glass of water onto the menu. ¹⁰When the waiter returned to our table. ¹¹He asked me if I wanted to order some wine. ¹²I ordered a bottle of Blue Nun. ¹³The only wine that I had heard of and could pronounce. ¹⁴The waiter brought the wine, poured a small amount into my glass, and waited. ¹⁵I said, "You don't have to stand there. We can pour the wine ourselves." ¹⁶After the waiter put down the wine bottle and left. ¹⁷Donna told me I was supposed to taste the wine. ¹⁸Feeling like a complete fool. ¹⁹I managed to get through the dinner. ²⁰However, for weeks afterward, I felt like jumping out of a tenth-story window.

1. _____
2. _____
3. _____
4. _____
5. _____
6. _____
7. _____
8. _____
9. _____
10. _____
11. _____
12. _____
13. _____
14. _____
15. _____
16. _____
17. _____
18. _____
19. _____
20. _____

On a separate piece of paper, correct the fragments you have found. Attach each fragment to the sentence that comes before or after it, or make whatever other change is needed to turn the fragment into a sentence.

Review Test 3

Underline the two fragments in each item. Then rewrite the item in the space provided, making the changes needed to correct the fragments.

EXAMPLE

The people at the sandwich shop save money. <u>By watering down the coffee.</u> Also, <u>using the cheapest grade of hamburger.</u> Few people go there anymore.

The people at the sandwich shop save money by watering down the coffee. Also, they use the cheapest grade of hamburger. . . .

1. Gathering speed with enormous force. The plane was suddenly in the air. Then it began to climb sharply. And several minutes later leveled off.

_____

_____

_____

2. After visiting Montevideo, the capital of Uruguay. We flew to Buenos Aires, Argentina. And then to Santiago, Chile.

   _____

   _____

   _____

3. Running untouched into the end zone. The halfback raised his arms in triumph. Then he slammed the football to the ground. And did a little victory dance.

   _____

   _____

   _____

4. The Greek scientist Archimedes (287–212 B.C.) invented many interesting devices. Such as huge mirrors that, reflecting the sun's rays, set the invading Roman ships on fire. However, his efforts at repelling the enemy were unsuccessful.

   _____

   _____

   _____

5. While we waited in a line to see the Claude Monet paintings at the museum. A famous actor entered the building. And caused an enormous commotion.

   _____

   _____

   _____

Review Test   4

Write quickly for five minutes about what you like to do in your leisure time. Don't worry about spelling, punctuation, finding exact words, or organizing your thoughts. Just focus on writing as many words as you can without stopping.

After you have finished, go back and make whatever changes are needed to correct any fragments in your writing.

Run-Ons

24

Introductory Activity

A run-on occurs when two sentences are run together with no adequate sign given to mark the break between them. Shown below are four run-ons and four correctly marked sentences. See if you can complete the statement that explains how each run-on is corrected.

1. He is the meanest little kid on his block he eats only the heads of animal crackers. *Run-on*

   He is the meanest little kid on his block. He eats only the heads of animal crackers. *Correct*

   The run-on has been corrected by using a _____ and a capital letter to separate the two complete thoughts.

2. Fred Grencher likes to gossip about other people, he doesn't like them to gossip about him. *Run-on*

   Fred Grencher likes to gossip about other people, but he doesn't like them to gossip about him. *Correct*

   The run-on has been corrected by using a joining word,

   _____, to connect the two complete thoughts.

3. The chain on my bike likes to chew up my pants, it leaves grease marks on my ankle as well. *Run-on*

   The chain on my bike likes to chew up my pants; it leaves grease marks on my ankles as well. *Correct*

   The run-on has been corrected by using a _____ to connect the two closely related thoughts.

4. The window shade snapped up like a gunshot, her cat leaped four feet off the floor. *Run-on*

   When the window shade snapped up like a gunshot, her cat leaped four feet off the floor. *Correct*

   The run-on has been corrected by using the subordinating word _____ to connect the two closely related thoughts.

See Appendix A for answers.

What Are Run-Ons?

As previously mentioned, a *run-on* is two complete thoughts run together with no adequate sign given to mark the break between them.* Some run-ons have no punctuation at all to mark the break between the thoughts. Such run-ons are known as *fused sentences:* They are fused, or joined together, as if they were only one thought.

Fused Sentences

My grades are very good this semester my social life rates only a C.

Our father was a madman in his youth he would do anything on a dare.

In other run-ons, known as *comma splices,* a comma is used to connect, or "splice" together, the two complete thoughts. However, a comma alone is *not enough* to connect two complete thoughts. Some connection stronger than a comma alone is needed.

Comma Splices

My grades are very good this semester, my social life rates only a C.

Our father was a madman in his youth, he would do anything on a dare.

Comma splices are the most common kind of run-on. Students sense that some kind of connection is needed between two thoughts and so put a comma at the dividing point. But the comma alone is not sufficient: A stronger, clearer mark is needed between the two thoughts.

A Warning about Words That Can Lead to Run-Ons People often write run-ons when the second complete thought begins with one of the following words.

I	we	there	now
you	they	this	then
he, she, it		that	next

Remember to be on the alert for run-ons whenever you use one of those words in writing a paper.

---

*Notes:

1 Some instructors feel that the term *run-ons* should be applied only to fused sentences, not to comma splices. But for many other instructors, and for our purposes in this book, the term *run-on* applies equally to fused sentences and comma splices. The point is that you do not want either fused sentences or comma splices in your writing.

2 Some instructors refer to each complete thought in a run-on as an *independent clause*. A *clause* is simply a group of words having a subject and a verb. A clause may be *independent* (expressing a complete thought and able to stand alone) or *dependent* (not expressing a complete thought and not able to stand alone). A run-on is two independent clauses that are run together with no adequate sign given to mark the break between them.

Correcting Run-Ons

Here are four common methods of correcting a run-on:

1. Use a period and a capital letter to break the two complete thoughts into separate sentences.

> My grades are very good this semester. My social life rates only a C.
> Our father was a madman in his youth. He would do anything on a dare.

2. Use a comma plus a joining word (*and, but, for, or, nor, so, yet*) to connect the two complete thoughts.

> My grades are very good this semester, but my social life rates only a C.
> Our father was a madman in his youth, for he would do anything on a dare.

3. Use a semicolon to connect the two complete thoughts.

> My grades are very good this semester; my social life rates only a C.
> Our father was a madman in his youth; he would do anything on a dare.

4. Use subordination.

> Although my grades are very good this semester, my social life rates only a C.
> Because my father was a madman in his youth, he would do anything on a dare.

The following pages will give you practice in all four methods of correcting a run-on. The use of subordination is explained on page 452.

Method 1: Period and a Capital Letter

One way of correcting a run-on is to use a period and a capital letter at the break between the two complete thoughts. Use this method especially if the thoughts are not closely related or if another method would make the sentence too long.

Locate the split in each of the following run-ons. Each is a *fused sentence*—that is, each consists of two sentences that are fused, or joined together, with no punctuation between them. Reading each fused sentence aloud will help you "hear" where a major break or split in the thought occurs. At such a point, your voice will probably drop and pause.

Correct the run-on by putting a period at the end of the first thought and a capital letter at the start of the next thought.

Activity

1

EXAMPLE

Martha Grencher shuffled around the apartment in her slippers. Her husband couldn't stand their slapping sound on the floor.

1. A felt-tip pen is easy to ruin just leave it lying around without its cap.

2. Astigmatism is an eye defect it can be the result of disease or of an injury.

3. Last summer no one swam in the lake a little boy had dropped his pet piranhas into the water.

4. A horse's teeth never stop growing they will eventually grow outside the horse's mouth.

5. Cuba is only 80 miles south of the United States it is one of the few Communist countries left in the world.

6. Ice water is the best remedy for a burn using butter is like adding fat to a flame.

7. Cryptography is the science of creating and breaking codes it was first practiced in ancient Egypt.

8. The Purple Heart is awarded to a member of the military wounded in battle my grandfather has two Purple Hearts.

9. Lobsters are cannibalistic this is one reason they are hard to raise in captivity.

10. Last week a student brought a gun to school the principal has now decided to install metal detectors at the school's entrance.

Activity 2

Working in pairs, locate the split in each of the following run-ons. Some of the run-ons are fused sentences, and some are *comma splices*—run-ons spliced, or joined together, with only a comma. Correct each run-on by putting a period at the end of the first thought and a capital letter at the start of the next thought.

1. A bird got into the house through the chimney we had to catch it before our cat did.

2. Some so-called health foods are not so healthy many are made with oils that raise cholesterol levels.

3. We sat only ten feet from the magician we still couldn't see where all the birds came from.

4. Jerome needs only five hours of sleep each night his wife needs at least seven.

5. Our image of dentistry will soon change dentists will use lasers instead of drills.

6. Gail got to school early to study for a math test when she got there, she found school had closed because of a water-main break.

7. There were several unusual hairstyles at the party one woman had bright green braids.

8. Todd saves all his magazines once a month, he takes them to a nearby nursing home.

9. The mountain ranges of Europe include the Pyrenees and the Alps the Himalayas are in Asia.

10. In the nineteenth century, showboats had stages on which actors and musicians performed they sailed up and down major rivers such as the Mississippi.

Write a second sentence to go with each of the sentences that follow. Start the second sentence with the word given at the right. Your sentences can be serious or playful.

Activity

3

EXAMPLE

Jackie works for the phone company. _She climbs telephone poles in all_   She
kinds of weather.

1. The new Asian restaurant on Main Street looks interesting. _____   It

_____

2. My uncle has a peculiar habit. _____   He

_____

3. Lola studied for the math test for two hours. _____   Then

_____

4. I could not understand why the car would not start. _____   It

_____

5. Last year's class trip took us to an amazing zoo, where we saw a number   Our
of interesting animals. _____

_____

Method 2: Comma and a Joining Word

A second way of correcting a run-on is to use a comma plus a joining word to connect the two complete thoughts. Joining words (also called *conjunctions*) include *and, but, for, or, nor, so,* and *yet*. Here is what the four most common joining words mean:

and   in addition to, along with

> His feet hurt from the long hike, and his stomach was growling.

(*And* means "in addition": His feet hurt from the long hike; *in addition,* his stomach was growling.)

but   however, except, on the other hand, just the opposite

> I remembered to get the cocoa, but I forgot the marshmallows.

(*But* means "however": I remembered to get the cocoa; *however,* I forgot the marshmallows.)

for   because, the reason that, the cause of something

> She was afraid of not doing well in the course, for she had always had bad luck with English before.

(*For* means "because" or "the reason that": She was afraid of not doing well in the course; *the reason* was that she had always had bad luck with English before.)

> **HINT:** If you are not comfortable using *for,* use *because* instead in the activities that follow. If you do use *because,* omit the comma before it.

so   as a result, therefore

> The windshield wiper was broken, so she was in trouble when the rain started.

(*So* means "as a result": The windshield wiper was broken; *as a result,* she was in trouble when the rain started.)

Activity

4

Insert the joining word (*and, but, for, so*) that logically connects the two thoughts in each sentence.

1. The Vikings were the first Europeans to land in the Americas, _____ Columbus is usually given credit for the discovery.

2. The Law of the Sea treaty agreed to in 1982 prohibits ocean pollution, _____ it also limits a nation's territorial waters to 12 miles.

3. Clyde asked his wife if she had any bandages, _____ he had just sliced his finger with a paring knife.

4. A group of teens talked and giggled loudly during the movie, _____ the ushers asked them to leave.

5. The restaurant was beautiful, _____ the food was overpriced.

Add a complete, closely related thought to go with each of the following statements. Use a comma plus the joining word at the right when you write the second thought.

Activity 5

EXAMPLE

Lola spent the day walking barefoot *, for the heel of one of her shoes had come off.* — for

1. She wanted to go to the party _____ — but

2. Tony washed his car in the morning _____ — and

3. The day was dark and rainy _____ — so

4. We missed the bus this morning _____ — for

5. I wish I could spend more time with my family _____ — but

Method 3: Semicolon

A third method of correcting a run-on is to use a semicolon to mark the break between two thoughts. A *semicolon* (;) is made up of a period above a comma and is sometimes called a *strong comma*. The semicolon signals more of a pause than a comma alone but not quite the full pause of a period.

Semicolon Alone Here are some earlier sentences that were connected with a comma plus a joining word. Notice that a semicolon alone, unlike a comma alone, can be used to connect the two complete thoughts in each sentence:

> The Law of the Sea treaty agreed to in 1982 prohibits ocean pollution; it also limits a nation's territorial waters to 12 miles.

> She was afraid of not doing well in the course; she had always had bad luck with English before.

> The restaurant was beautiful; the food was overpriced.

The semicolon can add to sentence variety. For some people, however, the semicolon is a confusing mark of punctuation. Keep in mind that if you are not comfortable using it, you can and should use one of the first two methods of correcting a run-on.

Activity

6

Insert a semicolon where the break occurs between the two complete thoughts in each of the following run-ons.

EXAMPLE

> I missed the bus by seconds;there would not be another for half an hour.

1. Some people have trouble with standardized tests the very idea of taking one makes them panic.

2. Pat retired at age forty she had won $6 million in the state lottery.

3. The current was too strong Byron decided not to risk crossing the river.

4. Tony never goes to a certain gas station anymore he found out that the service manager overcharged him for a valve job.

5. The washer shook and banged with its unbalanced load then it began to walk across the floor.

Semicolon with a Transitional Word A semicolon is sometimes used with a transitional word and a comma to join two complete thoughts.

> We were short of money; therefore, we decided not to eat out that weekend.

> The roots of a geranium have to be crowded into a small pot; otherwise, the plants may not flower.

> I had a paper to write; however, my brain had stopped working for the night.

Following is a list of common transitional words (also known as *adverbial conjunctions*). Brief meanings are given for the words.

Transitional Word	Meaning
however	but
nevertheless	but
on the other hand	but
instead	as a substitute
meanwhile	in the intervening time
otherwise	under other conditions
indeed	in fact
in addition	and
also	and
moreover	and
futhermore	and
as a result	in consequence
thus	as a result
consequently	as a result
therefore	as a result

Choose a logical transitional word from the list in the box and write it in the space provided. Put a semicolon *before* the connector and a comma *after* it.

EXAMPLE

Activity

7

Exams are over _____ *; however,* _____ I still feel tense and nervous.

1. I did not understand her point _____ I asked her to repeat it.

2. John wasn't willing to pay $200 for a fancy dinner _____ he had no problem investing this amount in stocks.

3. Post offices are closed for today's holiday _____ no mail will be delivered.

4. Mac and Alana didn't have a fancy wedding _____ they used their money for a nice honeymoon.

5. We're sure he didn't get the invitation _____ he would have come to the party.

Punctuate each sentence by using a semicolon and a comma.

EXAMPLE

My brother's asthma was worsening;as a result, he quit the soccer team.

1. We observed a blue heron standing by the side of the lake in addition we saw an ibis that had built a nest nearby.

2. Arnie tried to straighten his tie however he almost strangled himself.

3. Our instructor was absent therefore the test was postponed.

4. I had no time to shop for a gift instead I gave my friend a gift certificate to her favorite store.

5. Lola loves the velvety texture of cherry Jell-O moreover she loves to squish it between her teeth.

Method 4: Subordination

A fourth method of joining related thoughts is to use subordination. *Subordination* is a way of showing that one thought in a sentence is not as important as another thought.

Here are three earlier sentences that have been recast so that one idea is subordinated to (made less important than) the other idea:

When the window shade snapped up like a gunshot, her cat leaped four feet off the floor.

Because my father was a madman in his youth, he would do anything on a dare.

Although my grades are very good this year, my social life rates only a C.

Notice that when we subordinate, we use dependent words such as *when, because,* and *although.* Here is a brief list of common dependent words.

Common Dependent Words		
after	before	unless
although	even though	until
as	if	when
because	since	while

Choose a logical dependent word from the box on page 452 and write it in the space provided. Then team up with a partner and compare your answers.

EXAMPLE

_____*Because*_____ I had so much to do, I never even turned on the TV last night.

1. _____ the roads became snow covered, we decided to stay home.

2. _____ "All Natural" was printed in large letters on the yogurt carton, the fine print listing the ingredients told a different story.

3. _____ Phil had eaten a second helping of lasagna, he had no room left for dessert.

4. _____ the vampire movie was over, my children were afraid to go to bed.

5. _____ you have a driver's license and two major credit cards, that store will not accept your check.

TIP: Check for Run-Ons

1. To see if a sentence is a run-on, read it aloud and listen for a break marking two complete thoughts. Your voice will probably drop and pause at the break.

2. To check an entire paper, read each sentence aloud from the *last* one to the *first*. Doing so will help you hear and see each complete thought.

3. Be on the lookout for words that can lead to run-on sentences:

I	he, she, it	they	this	next
you	we	there	that	then

4. Correct run-on sentences by using one of the following methods:

   • Period and capital letter
   • Comma and joining word (*and, but, for, or, nor, so, yet*)
   • Semicolon
   • Subordination

Review Test 1

Some of the run-ons that follow are fused sentences, having no punctuation between the two complete thoughts; others are comma splices, having only a comma between the two complete thoughts. Correct the run-ons by using one of the following three methods:

- Period and capital letter
- Comma and joining word
- Semicolon

Do not use the same method of correction for every sentence.

EXAMPLE

Three people did the job, *but* I could have done it alone.

1. Seven vampire movies were released this month we saw every one of them.

2. The course on the history of UFOs sounded interesting, it turned out to be very dull.

3. That clothing store is a strange place to visit you keep walking up to dummies that look like real people.

4. Everything on the menu of the Pancake House sounded delicious they wanted to order the entire menu.

5. Chung has a photographic memory after reading a page of text, he can recite it word for word.

6. Marc used to be a fast-food junkie now he eats only vegetables and sunflower seeds.

7. The college has been able to operate within its budget it won't need to raise tuition.

8. The boy smiled joyously, his silver braces flashed in the sun.

9. My boss does not know what he is doing half the time then he tries to tell me what to do.

10. In the next minute, 100 people will die, over 240 babies will be born.

Review Test 2

Correct each run-on by using subordination. Choose from among the following dependent words.

after	before	unless
although	even though	until
as	if	when
because	since	while

EXAMPLE

My eyes have been watering all day, I can tell the pollen count is high.

Because my eyes have been watering all day, I can tell the pollen count is high.

1. There are a number of suits and jackets on sale, they all have very noticeable flaws.

   _____

   _____

2. Many computer systems come with printers, I had to pay extra for mine.

   _____

   _____

3. Marilyn took Professor Stewart's Introduction to Literature class, she had a greater appreciation for poetry.

   _____

   _____

4. The power went off for an hour during the night, all the clocks in the house must be reset.

   _____

   _____

5. Gas-saving hybrid vehicles are now available, they make up only a fraction of the new-car market.

   _____

   _____

Review Test 3

There are two run-ons in each passage. Correct them by using the following methods:

- Period and capital letter
- Comma and one of these joining words: *and, but,* or *so*
- One of these dependent words: *although, because,* or *when*

1. The medical researcher was honored by her colleagues who could have dreamed that a cure for such a deadly disease could ever be found? Her research had taken years she was persistent. She never gave up.

_____

_____

_____

2. Small feet were admired in ancient China, some female infants had their feet tightly bound. The feet then grew into a tiny, deformed shape. The women could barely walk their feet were crippled for life.

_____

_____

_____

3. Kanye insisted on dressing himself for nursery school. It was a cold winter day, he put on shorts and a tank top. He also put on cowboy boots over his bare feet. He liked his image in the mirror his mother made him change.

_____

_____

_____

4. A stimulating scent such as peppermint can help people concentrate better. The idea has practical applications, studies have shown that students do better on tests when peppermint is in the air. Maybe scented air could improve students' performance, it might help office workers be more alert, too.

_____

_____

_____

Standard English Verbs

Introductory Activity

Underline what you think is the correct form of the verb in each of the sentences below:

As a boy, he (enjoy, enjoyed) watching nature shows on television.

He still (enjoy, enjoys) watching such shows today as an adult.

When my car was new, it always (start, started) in the morning.

Now it (start, starts) only sometimes.

A couple of years ago, when Maya (cook, cooked) dinner, you needed an antacid tablet.

Now, when she (cook, cooks), neighbors invite themselves over to eat with us.

On the basis of those examples, see if you can complete the following statements:

1. The first example in each pair refers to a (past, present) action, and the regular verb ends in _____.

2. The second example in each pair refers to a (past, present) action, and the regular verb ends in _____.

See Appendix A for answers.

Many people have grown up in communities where nonstandard verb forms are used in everyday life. Such forms include *I thinks, he talk, it done, we has, you was,* and *she don't.* Community dialects have richness and power but are a drawback in college and the world at large, where standard English verb forms must be used. Standard English helps ensure clear communication among English-speaking people everywhere, and it is especially important in the world of work.

This chapter compares community dialect and standard English forms of one regular verb and three common irregular verbs.

www.mhhe.com/langan

Regular Verbs: Dialect and Standard Forms

The chart below compares community dialect (nonstandard) and standard English forms of the regular verb *smile.*

Smile			
Community Dialect (Do not use in your writing)		**Standard English** (Use for clear communication)	
Present tense			
I~~ smiles~~	we ~~smiles~~	I smile	we smile
you smiles	you smiles	you smile	you smile
~~he, she~~, it smile	they ~~smiles~~	he, she, it smiles	they smile
Past tense			
I~~ smile~~	we ~~smile~~	I smiled	we smiled
you smile	you smile	you smiled	you smiled
~~he, she~~, it smile	they ~~smile~~	he, she, it smiled	they smiled

One of the most common nonstandard forms results from dropping the endings of regular verbs. For example, people might say "David never *smile* anymore" instead of "David never *smiles* anymore." Or they will say "Before he lost his job, David *smile* a lot" instead of "Before he lost his job, David *smiled* a lot." To avoid such nonstandard usage, memorize the forms shown above for the regular verb *smile.* Then use the activities that follow to help you develop a habit of including verb endings when you write.

Present-Tense Endings

The verb ending -*s* or -*es* is needed with a regular verb in the present tense when the subject is *he, she, it,* or any *one person* or *thing*. Consider the following examples of present-tense endings.

He	He yell*s*.
She	She throw*s* things.
It	It really anger*s* me.
One person	Their son storm*s* out of the house.
One person	Their frightened daughter crouch*es* behind the bed.
One thing	At night the house shake*s*.

All but one of the ten sentences that follow need *s* or *es* verb endings. Cross out the nonstandard verb forms, and write the standard forms in the spaces provided. Mark the one sentence that needs no change with a *C* for *correct*.

Activity 1

EXAMPLE

_____wants_____ Dana always ~~want~~ the teacher's attention.

_____ 1. Recently, I bought a computer that operate very fast.

_____ 2. Don't eat a fish that smell funny.

_____ 3. Claire plan to enter the contest.

_____ 4. Whole-wheat bread taste better to me than rye bread.

_____ 5. Bob work as a security guard at the mall.

_____ 6. The city seem to glow in the early morning sun.

_____ 7. You make me angry sometimes.

_____ 8. Troy run faster than anybody else on the track team.

_____ 9. She live in a rough section of town.

_____ 10. Martha like mystery novels better than romances.

Activity	Work with a partner to rewrite the short passage below, adding present *-s* or *-es*
2	verb endings wherever needed.

Terri work in a big office downtown. Her cubicle sit right next to another worker's. This worker drive Terri crazy. He make more noise than you can imagine. Every day he bring a bag of raw carrots to work. The crunching noise fill the air. After he eat the carrots, he chew gum. He pop it so loud it sound like gunfire.

_____

_____

_____

_____

_____

Past-Tense Endings

The verb ending *-d* or *-ed* is needed with a regular verb in the past tense.

A midwife deliver*ed* my baby.

The visitor puzzl*ed* over the campus map.

The children watch*ed* cartoons all morning.

Activity	All but one of the ten sentences that follow need *-d* or *-ed* verb endings. Cross
3	out the nonstandard verb forms, and write the standard forms in the spaces provided. Mark the one sentence that needs no change with a *C*.

EXAMPLE

____*failed*____   Yesterday I ~~fail~~ a chemistry quiz.

_____   1. Lily want to go to the concert on Saturday.

_____   2. The Vietnamese student struggle with the new language.

_____   3. In the past, the requirement for a bachelor of arts degree include two years' study of a foreign language.

_____   4. The tired mother turned on the TV for him.

_____   5. Many newcomers to the community attend the recent town hall meeting.

_____   6. The weather forecaster promise blue skies, but rain began early this morning.

_____ 7. Sam attempt to put out the candle flame with his finger.

_____ 8. However, he end up burning himself.

_____ 9. On the bus, Yolanda listen to music on her iPod.

_____ 10. As the photographer was about to take a picture of the smiling baby, a sudden noise frighten the child and made her cry.

Rewrite the following short passage, adding past-tense -*d* or -*ed* verb endings wherever needed.

Activity

4

    I smoke for two years and during that time suffer no real side effects. Then my body attack me. I start to have trouble falling asleep, and I awaken early every morning. My stomach digest food very slowly, so that at lunchtime I seem to be still full with breakfast. My lips and mouth turn dry, and I swallow water constantly. Also, mucus fill my lungs and I cough a lot. I decide to stop smoking when my wife insist I take out more life insurance for our family.

_____

_____

_____

_____

_____

_____

Three Common Irregular Verbs: Dialect and Standard Forms

The following charts compare community dialect and standard English forms of the common irregular verbs *be, have,* and *do.* (For more on irregular verbs, see pages 466–474.)

Be

Community Dialect		Standard English	
(Do not use in your writing)		**(Use for clear communication)**	

Present tense

~~I be~~ (or is)	~~we be~~	I am	we are
you be	~~you be~~	you are	you are
~~he, she~~, it be	~~they be~~	he, she, it is	they are

Past tense

~~I were~~	~~we was~~	I was	we were
you was	~~you was~~	you were	you were
~~he, she~~, it were	~~they was~~	he, she, it was	they were

Have

Community Dialect		Standard English	
(Do not use in your writing)		**(Use for clear communication)**	

Present tense

~~I has~~	~~we has~~	I have	we have
you has	~~you has~~	you have	you have
~~he, she~~, it have	~~they has~~	he, she, it has	they have

Past tense

~~I has~~	~~we has~~	I had	we had
you has	~~you has~~	you had	you had
~~he, she~~, it have	~~they has~~	he, she, it had	they had

Do

Community Dialect		Standard English	
(Do not use in your writing)		(Use for clear communication)	
Present tense			
I does	we does	I do	we do
you does	you does	you do	you do
he, she, it do	they does	he, she, it does	they do
Past tense			
I done	we done	I did	we did
you done	you done	you did	you did
he, she, it done	they done	he, she, it did	they did

TIP: Many people have trouble with the negative form of *do.* They will say, for example, "He don't agree" instead of "He doesn't agree," or they will say "The door don't work" instead of "The door doesn't work." Be careful to avoid the common mistake of using *don't* instead of *doesn't.*

Underline the standard form of *be, have,* or *do.*

Activity

5

1. Crystal (have, has) such a nice singing voice that she often sings solos at our choir concerts.
2. The women at the factory (is, are) demanding to be paid the same wages as men.
3. The island of Corsica (has, have) belonged to France since the eighteenth century.
4. Rod and Arlene (was, were) ready to leave for the movies when the baby began to wail.
5. Our art class (done, did) the mural on the wall of the cafeteria.
6. If I (have, has) the time later, I will help you set up your new laser printer.
7. Jesse (be, is) the best basketball player at our school.
8. The Finnish government (has, have) installed stop signals in road pavements because pedestrians who are texting sometimes get hurt when they cross the street.

9. Vanessa wears the same perfume that Anya (do, does), but their clothing styles are very different.

10. The science instructor said that the state of California (be, is) likely to have a major earthquake any day.

Activity

6

Fill in each blank with the standard form of *be*, *have*, or *do*.

1. My 2008 Wizbang SUV _____ a real personality.

2. I think it _____ almost human.

3. When it rains hard, my car just _____ not want to start, as if it _____ worried about getting wet.

4. Like me, the car _____ a problem dealing with freezing weather.

5. On cold days, I just want to stay in bed; my Wizbang _____ a hard time getting started as well.

6. Also, we _____ the same feeling about rainstorms.

7. I hate driving to school in a downpour, and so _____ the car.

8. When the car _____ stopped at a light, it stalls.

9. The habits my car _____ may be annoying.

10. But they _____ understandable.

Review Test   1

Underline the standard verb form.

1. Johanna (love, loves) to walk in the rain.

2. Manuel and Yvonne (do, does) their grocery shopping first thing in the morning when the store is nearly empty.

3. In 1976, Manila (became, become) the capital of the independent Republic of the Philippines.

4. Dan (climb, climbed) up on the roof to see where the water was coming in.

5. Both of the ships (was, were) built in Brooklyn, New York.

6. As soon as she gets home from work, Missy (boil, boils) some water to make tea.

7. My daughter often (watch, watches) TV after the rest of the family is in bed.

8. The old lawnmower usually (start, starts) the first time I pull the cord.

9. Jeannie (has, have) just one contact lens; she lost the other one in the bathroom sink.

10. I remember how my wet mittens (use, used) to steam on the hot school radiator.

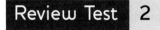

Cross out the two nonstandard verb forms in each sentence below. Then write the standard English verbs in the spaces provided.

EXAMPLE

_____*is*_____ When our teacher ~~be~~ angry, his eyelid ~~begin~~ to twitch.

_____*begins*_____

_____ 1. My mother work for the local newspaper; she take classified
_____   ads over the phone.

_____ 2. Caesar conquer Gaul in 58 B.C.; he then invade Britain.
_____

_____ 3. Peter and his sister owns a fast-food restaurant that offer
_____   gourmet takeout.

_____ 4. Henry love to go camping until two thieves in the campground
_____   remove his cooler, stove, and sleeping bag from his tent.

_____ 5. Last week the supermarket have a special on orange juice,
_____   just when I needs some.

_____ 6. Although my little girls knows they shouldn't tease the cat,
_____   they often dresses up the animal in doll clothes.

_____ 7. Whenever my brothers watches *Monday Night Football,* they
_____   screams at the TV as if they are actually at the game.

_____ 8. The large red fire engines gleams in the afternoon sun as
_____   they rushes through traffic on the busy boulevard.

_____ 9. I show the receipt to the manager to prove that the clerk
_____   had accidentally overcharge me.

_____ 10. As far as our son be concerned, oatmeal taste like soggy
_____   cardboard.

26

Irregular Verbs

A Brief Review of Regular Verbs

Every verb has four principal parts: present, past, past participle, and present participle. These parts can be used to build all the verb *tenses* (the times shown by a verb).

The past and past participle of a regular verb are formed by adding *-d* or *-ed* to the present. The *past participle* is the form of the verb used with the helping verbs *have, has,* or *had* (or some form of *be* with passive verbs). The *present participle* is formed by adding *-ing* to the present. Here are the principal forms of some regular verbs. Most verbs in English are regular.

Present	Past	Past Participle	Present Participle
crash	crashed	crashed	crashing
shiver	shivered	shivered	shivering
kiss	kissed	kissed	kissing
apologize	apologized	apologized	apologizing
tease	teased	teased	teasing

List of Irregular Verbs

Irregular verbs have irregular forms in the past tense and past participle. For example, the past tense of the irregular verb *know* is *knew,* and the past participle is *known.*

Almost everyone has some degree of trouble with irregular verbs. When you are unsure about the form of a verb, you can check the following list of irregular verbs. (The present participle is not shown on this list because it is formed simply by adding *-ing* to the base form of the verb.) Or you can check a dictionary, which gives the principal parts of irregular verbs.

Present	Past	Past Participle
arise	arose	arisen
awake	awoke *or* awaked	awoken *or* awaked
be (am, are, is)	was (were)	been
become	became	become
begin	began	begun
bend	bent	bent
bite	bit	bitten
blow	blew	blown

Present	Past	Past Participle
break	broke	broken
bring	brought	brought
build	built	built
burst	burst	burst
buy	bought	bought
catch	caught	caught
choose	chose	chosen
come	came	come
cost	cost	cost
cut	cut	cut
do (does)	did	done
draw	drew	drawn
drink	drank	drunk
drive	drove	driven
eat	ate	eaten
fall	fell	fallen
feed	fed	fed
feel	felt	felt
fight	fought	fought
find	found	found
fly	flew	flown
forget	forgot	forgotten
freeze	froze	frozen
get	got	got *or* gotten
give	gave	given
go (goes)	went	gone
grow	grew	grown
have (has)	had	had
hear	heard	heard
hide	hid	hidden
hold	held	held
hurt	hurt	hurt
keep	kept	kept

Present	Past	Past Participle
know	knew	known
lay	laid	laid
lead	led	led
leave	left	left
lend	lent	lent
let	let	let
lie	lay	lain
lose	lost	lost
make	made	made
meet	met	met
pay	paid	paid
ride	rode	ridden
ring	rang	rung
rise	rose	risen
run	ran	run
say	said	said
see	saw	seen
sell	sold	sold
send	sent	sent
shake	shook	shaken
shrink	shrank	shrunk
shut	shut	shut
sing	sang	sung
sit	sat	sat
sleep	slept	slept
speak	spoke	spoken
spend	spent	spent
stand	stood	stood
steal	stole	stolen
stick	stuck	stuck
sting	stung	stung
swear	swore	sworn
swim	swam	swum

Present	Past	Past Participle
take	took	taken
teach	taught	taught
tear	tore	torn
tell	told	told
think	thought	thought
throw	threw	thrown
wake	woke *or* waked	woken *or* waked
wear	wore	worn
win	won	won
write	wrote	written

Activity 1

Cross out the incorrect verb form in each of the following sentences. Then write the correct form of the verb in the space provided.

EXAMPLE

_____*drew*_____ The little boy ~~drawed~~ on the marble table with permanent ink.

_____ 1. Tomatoes were once thought to be poisonous, and they were growed only as ornamental shrubs.

_____ 2. On the last day of swim class, every student swimmed the whole length of the pool.

_____ 3. When we felled asleep last night, no one believed we would have six inches of snow in the morning.

_____ 4. The snow freezed in clumps on our gloves as we went down the ice-covered hill.

_____ 5. Every time the church bells ringed, we knew an hour had passed.

_____ 6. Only seven people have ever knowed the formula for Coca-Cola.

_____ 7. Amy blowed up animal-shaped balloons for her son's birthday party.

_____ 8. I shaked the bottle of medicine before I took a teaspoonful of it.

_____ 9. While waiting for the doctor to arrive, I sitted in a plastic chair for over two hours.

_____ 10. The pile of bones on the plate showed how much chicken the family had ate.

For each of the italicized verbs, fill in the three missing forms in the following order:

(*a*) **Present tense, which takes an -*s* ending when the subject is *he, she, it,* or any *one person* or *thing* (see pages 459–460)**

(*b*) **Past tense**

(*c*) **Past participle—the form that goes with the helping verb *have, has,* or *had***

After completing the activity, compare answers with a partner.

EXAMPLE

My uncle likes to give away certain things. He *(a)* _____*gives*_____ old, threadbare clothes to the Salvation Army. Last year he *(b)* _____*gave*_____ me a worthless television set whose picture tube was burned out. He has *(c)* _____*given*_____ away stuff that a junk dealer would reject.

1. I like to *freeze* Hershey bars. A Hershey bar *(a)* _____ in half an hour. Once I *(b)* _____ a bottle of Pepsi. I put it in the freezer to chill and then forgot about it. Later I opened the freezer and discovered that it had *(c)* _____ and exploded.

2. Natalie *speaks* French. She *(a)* _____ German, too. Her grandmother *(b)* _____ both languages and taught them to her. Since she was a baby, Natalie has *(c)* _____ them both as well as she speaks English.

3. My cousin has always liked to *write*. He usually *(a)* _____ short stories. However, he just *(b)* _____ a book of poetry, which he is getting published. He has even *(c)* _____ a play.

4. I *go* to parties a lot. Often Camille *(a)* _____ with me. She *(b)* _____ with me just last week. I have *(c)* _____ to parties every Friday for the past month.

5. My brother likes to *throw* things. Sometimes he *(a)* _____ socks into his bureau drawer. In high school he *(b)* _____ footballs while quarterbacking the team. And he has *(c)* _____ Frisbees in our backyard for as long as I can remember.

6. I would like to *see* a UFO. I spend hours looking at the night sky, hoping to *(a)* _____ one. A neighbor of ours claims he *(b)* _____ one last month. But he says he has *(c)* _____ the Abominable Snowman, too.

7. I often *lie* down for a few minutes after a hard day's work. Sometimes my cat *(a)* _____ down near me. Yesterday was Saturday, so I *(b)* _____ in bed all morning. I probably would have *(c)* _____ in bed all afternoon, but I wanted to get some planting done in my vegetable garden.

8. To *teach* in college has been Claire's life-long dream. Currently, she *(a)* _____ English at the YWCA to newly arrived immigrants. Last year, she *(b)* _____ at a private high school, and before that she *(c)* _____ at the local community college part time.

9. The government plans to *give* citizens more tax credits in order to encourage energy savings. It already *(a)* _____ a $3,000 credit to those who buy hybrid vehicles. Last year, it *(b)* _____ my uncle a tax credit for installing solar panels on his house, and it *(c)* _____ him money the year before to help pay for the cost of replacement windows.

10. Martha likes to *eat*. She *(a)* _____ as continuously as some people smoke. Once she *(b)* _____ a large pack of cookies in half an hour. Even if she has *(c)* _____ a heavy meal, she often starts munching snacks right afterward.

Review Test | 1

Underline the correct verb in the parentheses.

1. As I began my speech, my hands (shaked, shook) so badly I nearly dropped my notes.

2. Oscar came into the gym and (began, begun) to practice on the parallel bars.

3. The food she donated (feed, fed) three families during the holidays.

4. Even though my father (teached, taught) me how to play baseball, I never enjoyed any part of the game.

5. When I (lent, lend) him the money yesterday, I knew he would pay me back.

6. The bank had (growed, grown) from a small savings and loan to a large regional mortgage company.

7. Lola (brang, brought) a sweatshirt with her, for she knew the mountains got cold at night.

8. The red maple that had (stood, standed) in the yard for one hundred years was blown over by a strong wind.

9. The audience (burst, bursted) into laughter when the comedian told his favorite joke.

10. Anthony (sweared, swore) that he had locked the front door.

11. Someone (leaved, left) his or her books in the classroom.

12. Fran's muscle was (tore, torn) when she slipped on the wet pavement.

13. If I hadn't (threw, thrown) away the receipt, I could have gotten my money back.

14. I would have (become, became) very angry if you had not intervened.

15. As the flowerpot (fell, falled) from the windowsill, the little boy yelled, "Bombs away!"

Review Test 2

Write short sentences that use the form indicated for the following irregular verbs.

EXAMPLE

Past of *grow* *I grew eight inches in one year.*

1. Past of *know* _____

   _____

2. Past participle of *build* _____

   _____

3. Past of *fall* _____

   _____

4. Past of *stand* _____

   _____

5. Past of *bring* _____

   _____

6. Past participle of *speak* _____

   _____

7. Past of *swim* _____

   _____

8. Past participle of *fly* _____

   _____

9. Past participle of *see* _____

   _____

10. Past of *drive* _____

    _____

Subject-Verb Agreement

27

Introductory Activity

As you read each pair of sentences below, write a check mark beside the sentence that you think uses the underlined word correctly.

There <u>was</u> too many people talking at once. _____

There <u>were</u> too many people talking at once. ____✓____

The onions in that spaghetti sauce <u>gives</u> me heartburn.

_____

The onions in that spaghetti sauce <u>give</u> me heartburn.

_____

The mayor and her husband <u>attends</u> our church. _____

The mayor and her husband <u>attend</u> our church. _____

Everything <u>seem</u> to slow me down when I'm in a hurry.

_____

Everything <u>seems</u> to slow me down when I'm in a hurry.

_____

See Appendix A for answers.

A verb must agree with its subject in number. A *singular subject* (one person or one thing) takes a singular verb. A *plural subject* (more than one person or thing) takes a plural verb. Mistakes in subject-verb agreement are sometimes made in the situations listed below (each situation is explained on the following pages):

1. When words come between the subject and the verb
2. When a verb comes before the subject
3. With compound subjects
4. With indefinite pronouns

Words between Subject and Verb

Words that come between the subject and the verb do not change subject-verb agreement. In the sentence

> The tomatoes in this salad are brown and mushy.

the subject (tomatoes) is plural, and so the verb (are) is plural. The words *in this salad* that come between the subject and the verb do not affect subject-verb agreement.

To help find the subject of certain sentences, you should cross out prepositional phrases (see page 421):

> Nell, ~~with her three dogs close behind~~, runs around the park every day.
> The seams ~~in my new coat~~ have split after only two wearings.

Activity

1

Underline the correct verb form in the parentheses.

1. The decisions of the judge (seem, seems) questionable.
2. The flakes in this cereal (taste, tastes) like sawdust.
3. The list of books for my American literature course (are, is) posted on the class Web site.
4. Many people in Europe (speak, speaks) several languages.
5. An ability to read a compass and a map (are, is) essential to surviving in the wild.
6. That silk flower by the candles (look, looks) real.
7. Opinions about the latest renovations to the Student Center (was, were) discussed at the meeting.
8. The rust spots on the back of Emily's car (need, needs) to be cleaned with a special polish.

9. The collection of medicine bottles in my parents' bathroom (overflow, overflows) the cabinet shelves.

10. A schedule of all the intramural tennis matches (appear, appears) on the coach's office door.

Verb before Subject

A verb agrees with its subject even when the verb comes *before* the subject. Words that may precede the subject include *there, here,* and, in questions, *who, which, what,* and *where.*

On Glen's doorstep were two police officers.

There are many pizza places in our town.

Here is your receipt.

Where are they going to sleep?

If you are unsure about the subject, look at the verb and ask *who* or *what.* With the first example above, you might ask, "*Who* were on the doorstep?" The answer, *police officers,* is the subject.

Working with a partner, write the correct form of the verb in each space provided.

Activity 2

is, are	1. What _____ your middle name?
was, were	2. Among the guests _____ a private detective.
do, does	3. Where _____ you go when you want to be alone?
is, are	4. There _____ many interesting things to see in Mexico.
rest, rests	5. In that grave _____ the bones of my great-grandfather.
was, were	6. There _____ so many important problems to be solved that we got to work immediately.
is, are	7. Why _____ the lights turned off?
stand, stands	8. Across the street _____ the post office.
is, are	9. Here _____ the tickets for tonight's game.
has, have	10. When _____ the people of this city ever not been able to trust the police?

Compound Subjects

Subjects joined by *and* generally take a plural verb.

Maple syrup and sweet butter taste delicious on pancakes.

Fear and ignorance have a lot to do with hatred.

When subjects are joined by *either . . . or, neither . . . nor, not only . . . but also,* the verb agrees with the subject closer to the verb.

Neither TV shows nor the Internet is as enjoyable to me as spending time with my friends.

The nearer subject, *Internet,* is singular, and so the verb is singular.

Activity

3

Write the correct form of the verb in the space provided.

stays, stay

1. Our cats and dog _____ at a neighbor's house when we go on vacation.

Is, Are

2. _____ the birthday cake and ice cream ready to be served?

holds, hold

3. Staples and Scotch tape _____ all our old photo albums together.

was, were

4. Tom and Pam _____ able to pay for their new car in cash.

support, supports

5. Neither the mayor nor the members of the city council _____ the new state mandate.

are, is

6. Tokyo and Beijing _____ capitals of Asian countries.

was, were

7. Owning a car and having money in my pocket _____ the chief ambitions of my adolescence.

visits, visit

8. My aunt and uncle from Ireland _____ us every other summer.

was, were

9. Before they saw a marriage therapist, Peter and Jenny _____ planning to get divorced.

favor, favors

10. Not only the dean but also the faculty members _____ adopting changes to the curriculum.

Indefinite Pronouns

The following words, known as *indefinite pronouns,* always take singular verbs.

(-*one* words)	(-*body* words)	(-*thing* words)	
one, no one	nobody	nothing	each
anyone	anybody	anything	either
everyone	everybody	everything	neither
someone	somebody	something	

TIP: *Both* always takes a plural verb.

Write the correct form of the verb in the space provided.

Activity

4

is, are   1. Everybody at my new school _____ friendly.

has,   2. Neither of them _____ made it to the wrestling finals.
have

knows,   3. Nobody in my family _____ how to swim.
know

believe,   4. Each of three candidates _____ he or she won the debate.
believes

tell, tells 5. Something _____ me that she will succeed.

pitches,   6. If each of us _____ in, we can finish this job in an hour.
pitch

was,   7. Everyone we invited _____ asked to bring a story to share.
were

provides, 8. Neither of the restaurants _____ facilities for the
provide   handicapped.

likes,   9. No one in our family _____ housecleaning, but we all
like   take a turn at it.

steals,   10. Someone in our neighborhood _____ vegetables from
steal   people's gardens.

Review Test 1

Underline the correct verb in parentheses.

1. The damage caused by the recent snowstorms (amount, amounts) to less than we expected.

2. No one who attended last night's lecture (fail, fails) to realize the seriousness of the problem.

3. The packages in the shopping bag (was, were) a wonderful mystery to the children.

4. My exercise class of five students (meets, meet) every Thursday afternoon.

5. The living room, which is much larger than ours, (contain, contains) fewer pieces of furniture.

6. Business contacts and financial backing (is, are) all that I need to establish my career as an interior designer.

7. Each of those breakfast cereals (contains, contain) a high proportion of sugar.

8. Those large paintings on the gallery's far wall (fascinate, fascinates) me.

9. All the cars on my block (has, have) to be moved one day a month for street cleaning.

10. Some people (know, knows) more about their favorite TV characters than they do about the members of their own family.

Review Test 2

Each of the following passages contains *two* mistakes in subject-verb agreement. Find these two mistakes and cross them out. Then write the correct form of each verb in the space provided.

1. Some people who visit Spain stays in hotels that were once convents and monasteries. Two of my professors, who spent their junior years studying abroad, recalls staying in one.

   a. _____

   b. _____

2. Everyone who comes to the product demonstration receive a coupon for a 20 percent discount. Customers will need it. Not one of the products are bargain-priced.

   a. _____

   b. _____

3. All the neighbors meets once a year for a block party. Everyone talks and dances far into the night. Huge bowls of delicious food sits on picnic tables. Afterward, everyone goes home and sleeps all day.

   a. _____

   b. _____

4. The members of the swimming team paces nervously beside the pool. Finally, an official blows a whistle. Into the pool dive a swimmer with thick, tan arms. He paddles quickly through the water.

   a. _____

   b. _____

5. When Lin Soo comes home from school each day, her work is just beginning. The members of her family all works in their small restaurant. Nobody rest until the last customer is served. Only then do Lin Soo and her brother start their homework.

   a. _____

   b. _____

28

Pronoun Agreement and Reference

Introductory Activity

Read each pair of sentences below. Then write a check mark beside the sentence that you think uses the underlined word or words correctly.

Someone in my neighborhood lets their dog run loose.

_____

Someone in my neighborhood lets his or her dog run loose.

_____

After Tony reviewed his notes with Bob, he passed the exam with ease. _____

After reviewing his notes with Bob, Tony passed the exam with ease. _____

See Appendix A for answers.

Pronouns are words that take the place of nouns (persons, places, or things). In fact, the word *pronoun* means "for a noun." Pronouns are shortcuts that keep you from unnecessarily repeating words in writing. Here are some examples of pronouns:

> Shirley has not finished the paper *she* was assigned. (*She* is a pronoun that replaces *Shirley.*)
>
> Tony swung so heavily on the tree branch that *it* snapped. (*It* replaces *branch.*)
>
> When the three little pigs saw the wolf, *they* pulled out cans of Mace. (*They* is a pronoun that takes the place of *pigs.*)

This chapter presents rules that will help you avoid two common mistakes people make with pronouns. The rules are as follows:

1. A pronoun must agree in number with the word or words it replaces.
2. A pronoun must refer clearly to the word it replaces.

Pronoun Agreement

www.mhhe.com/langan

A pronoun must agree in number with the word or words it replaces. If the word a pronoun refers to is singular, the pronoun must be singular; if that word is plural, the pronoun must be plural. (Note that the word a pronoun refers to is also known as the *antecedent.*)

> Barbara agreed to lend me her Ray Charles CDs.

> People walking the trail must watch their step because of snakes.

In the first example, the pronoun *her* refers to the singular word *Barbara;* in the second example, the pronoun *their* refers to the plural word *People.*

Write the appropriate pronoun (*their, they, them, it*) in the blank space in each of the following sentences.

Activity

1

EXAMPLE

I lifted the pot of hot potatoes carefully, but ____*it*____ slipped out of my hand.

1. People should try to go into a new situation with _____ minds open, not with opinions already firmly formed.

2. Fred never misses his daily workout; he believes _____ keeps him healthy.

3. Citizens of New Orleans are proud of _____ city's heritage.

4. For some students, college is often their first experience with an unsupervised learning situation, and _____ are not always ready to accept the responsibility.

5. Our new neighbors moved in three months ago, but I have yet to meet _____

Indefinite Pronouns

The following words, known as *indefinite pronouns,* are always singular.

(*-one* words)	(*-body* words)	
one, no one	nobody	each
anyone	anybody	either
everyone	everybody	neither
someone	somebody	

If a pronoun in a sentence refers to one of those singular words, the pronoun should be singular.

Each father felt that his child should have won the contest.

One of the women could not find her purse.

Everyone must be in his seat before the instructor takes attendance.

In each example, the circled pronoun is singular because it refers to one of the special singular words.

The last example is correct if everyone in the class is a man. If everyone in the class is a woman, the pronoun would be *her.* If the class has both women and men, the pronoun form would be *his or her:*

Everyone must be in his or her seat before the instructor takes attendance.

Some writers follow the traditional practice of using *his* to refer to both women and men. Many now use *his or her* to avoid an implied sexual bias. To avoid using *his* or the somewhat awkward *his or her,* a sentence can often be rewritten in the plural:

Students must be in their seats before the instructor takes attendance.

Underline the correct pronoun. Check your answers against a partner's.

1. Some young man has blocked the parking lot exit with (his, their) sports car.
2. An elderly, stylishly dressed gentleman sporting a top hat and tails made (his, their) way into the fashionable restaurant.
3. Neither of the men arrested as terrorists would reveal (his, their) real name.
4. Anyone who joins the Women's Civic Club can add (her, their) voice to the discussions held at monthly meetings.
5. Each of the president's female advisers offered (her, their) opinion about the abortion bill.

Activity

2

www.mhhe.com/langan

Pronoun Reference

A sentence may be confusing and unclear if a pronoun appears to refer to more than one word, or if the pronoun does not refer to any specific word. Look at this sentence:

> Joe almost dropped out of high school, for he felt *they* emphasized discipline too much.

Who emphasized discipline too much? There is no specific word that *they* refers to. Be clear:

> Joe almost dropped out of high school, for he felt *the teachers* emphasized discipline too much.

Below are sentences with other kinds of faulty pronoun reference. Read the explanations of why they are faulty and look carefully at how they are corrected.

Faulty	Clear
June told Margie that *she* lacked self-confidence. (*Who* lacked self-confidence: June or Margie? Be clear.)	June told Margie, "You lack self-confidence." (Quotation marks, which can sometimes be used to correct an unclear reference, are explained on pages 536–543.)
Nancy's mother is a hairdresser, but Nancy is not interested in *it*. (There is no specific word that *it* refers to. It would not make sense to say, "Nancy is not interested in hairdresser.")	Nancy's mother is a hairdresser, but Nancy is not interested in becoming one.

Ron blamed the police officer for the ticket, *which* was foolish. (Does *which* mean that the ticket was foolish or that Ron's blaming the officer was foolish? Be clear.)

Foolishly, Ron blamed the police officer for the ticket.

Activity 3

Rewrite each of the following sentences to make the vague pronoun reference clear. Add, change, or omit words as necessary.

EXAMPLE

Our cat was friends with our hamster until he bit him.

Until the cat bit the hamster, the two were friends.

1. They found him not guilty, and she set him free immediately.

   _____

2. They claim that if the American colonists had lost the Revolutionary War, we would still be governed by Britain.

   _____

   _____

3. Telephone operators provide assistance when they're not working correctly.

   _____

   _____

4. Jeanne told Maria she had been promoted.

   _____

5. I love Parmesan cheese on veal, but it does not always digest well.

   _____

Review Test 1

Cross out the pronoun error in each sentence, and write the correction in the space provided at the left. Then circle the letter that correctly describes the type of error that was made.

EXAMPLES

his (or her)   Each player took ~~their~~ position on the court.

Mistake in: (a.) pronoun agreement.   b. pronoun reference.

the store   I was angry that ~~they~~ wouldn't give me cash back when I returned the sweater I had bought.

Mistake in: a. pronoun agreement.   (b.) pronoun reference.

_____ 1. Dan asked Mr. Sanchez if he could stay an extra hour at work today.

Mistake in: a. pronoun agreement. b. pronoun reference.

_____ 2. Both the front door and the back door of the abandoned house had fallen off its hinges.

Mistake in: a. pronoun agreement. b. pronoun reference.

_____ 3. I've been taking cold medicine, and now it is better.

Mistake in: a. pronoun agreement. b. pronoun reference.

_____ 4. Arthur was angry when they said he was getting a ticket for speeding.

Mistake in: a. pronoun agreement b. pronoun reference

_____ 5. Each one of the Boy Scouts was required to bring their sleeping bags.

Mistake in: a. pronoun agreement b. pronoun reference

_____ 6. An annual flu shot is a good idea; they will help children and older people stay healthy.

Mistake in: a. pronoun agreement. b. pronoun reference.

_____ 7. Everyone who wishes to run for office must submit their petition by April 1.

Mistake in: a. pronoun agreement b. pronoun reference

_____ 8. Indira could not believe that they had changed the immigration laws again.

Mistake in: a. pronoun agreement. b. pronoun reference.

_____ 9. At the dental office, I asked him if it was really necessary to take X-rays of my mouth again.

Mistake in: a. pronoun agreement. b. pronoun reference.

_____ 10. At the restaurant, he recited a long list of specials that weren't on the menu.

Mistake in: a. pronoun agreement b. pronoun reference

Review Test 2

Underline the correct word in parentheses.

1. Philip is the kind of father who likes to keep in close contact with (his, their) children.

2. Hoping to be first in line when (they, the ushers) opened the doors, we arrived two hours early for the concert.

3. If a person really wants to appreciate good coffee, (he or she, they) should drink it black.

4. I have been interested in gardening ever since my grandmother kept (a garden, one) in her backyard.

5. Lois often visits the reading center in school, for she finds that (they, the tutors) give her helpful instruction.

6. Nobody in our house can express (his or her, their) opinion without starting an argument.

7. As the room got colder, everybody wished for (his or her, their) coat.

8. Each of my brothers has had (his, their) apartment broken into.

9. If someone is going to write a composition, (he or she, they) should prepare at least one rough draft.

10. My uncle gets into the movies for half price; (that discount, it) is one of the advantages of being a senior citizen.

This chapter describes some common types of pronouns: subject and object pronouns, possessive pronouns, and demonstrative pronouns.

www.mhhe.com/langan

Subject and Object Pronouns

Pronouns change their form depending on the purpose they serve in a sentence. In the box that follows is a list of subject and object pronouns.

Subject Pronouns	Object Pronouns
I	me
you	you (*no change*)
he	him
she	her
it	it (*no change*)
we	us
they	them

Subject Pronouns

Subject pronouns are subjects of verbs.

> *She* is wearing blue nail polish on her toes. (*She* is the subject of the verb *is wearing.*)
>
> *They* ran up three flights of stairs. (*They* is the subject of the verb *ran.*)
>
> *We* children should have some privacy too. (*We* is the subject of the verb *should have.*)

Rules for using subject pronouns, and several kinds of mistakes people sometimes make with subject pronouns, are explained in the pages that follow.

Rule 1 Use a subject pronoun in spots where you have a compound (more than one) subject.

Incorrect	Correct
Sally and *me* are exactly the same size.	Sally and *I* are exactly the same size.
Her and *me* share our wardrobes with each other.	*She* and *I* share our wardrobes with each other.

> **TIP:** If you are not sure what pronoun to use, try each pronoun by itself in the sentence. The correct pronoun will be the one that sounds right. For example, "Her shares her wardrobe" does not sound right. "She shares her wardrobe" does.

Rule 2 Use a subject pronoun after forms of the verb *be*. Forms of *be* include *am, are, is, was, were, has been,* and *have been.*

It was *I* who called you a minute ago and then hung up.

It may be *they* entering the diner.

It was *he* who put the white tablecloth into the washing machine with a red sock.

The sentences above may sound strange and stilted to you because they are seldom used in conversation. When we speak with one another, forms such as "It was me," "It may be them," and "It is him" are widely accepted. In formal writing, however, the grammatically correct forms are still preferred.

> **TIP:** To avoid having to use the subject pronoun form after *be,* you can simply reword a sentence. Here is how the preceding examples could be reworded:
>
> I was the one who called you a minute ago and then hung up.
>
> They may be the ones entering the diner.
>
> He put the white tablecloth into the washing machine with a red sock.

Rule 3 Use subject pronouns after *than* or *as*. The subject pronoun is used because a verb is understood after the pronoun.

Mark can hold his breath longer than *I* (can). (The verb *can* is understood after *I*.)

Her thirteen-year-old daughter is as tall as *she* (is). (The verb *is* is understood after *she*.)

You drive much better than *he* (drives). (The verb *drives* is understood after *he*.)

> **TIP:** Avoid mistakes by mentally adding the "missing" verb at the end of the sentence.

Object Pronouns

Object pronouns (for example, *me, him, her, us, them*) are the objects of verbs or prepositions. (*Prepositions* are connecting words like *for, at, about, to, before, by, with,* and *of.* See also page 421.)

Lee pushed *me.* (*Me* is the object of the verb *pushed.*)

We dragged *them* all the way home. (*Them* is the object of the verb *dragged.*)

She wrote all about *us* in her diary. (*Us* is the object of the preposition *about.*)

Vera passed a note to *him* as she walked to the pencil sharpener. (*Him* is the object of the preposition *to.*)

People are sometimes uncertain about which pronoun to use when two objects follow the verb.

Incorrect	Correct
I argued with his sister and *he.*	I argued with his sister and *him.*
The cashier cheated Rick and *I.*	The cashier cheated Rick and *me.*

> **TIP:** If you are not sure which pronoun to use, try each pronoun by itself in the sentence. The correct pronoun will be the one that sounds right. For example, "I argued with he" does not sound right; "I argued with him" does.

Underline the correct subject or object pronoun in each of the following sentences. Then show whether your answer is a subject or an object pronoun by circling S or O in the margin. The first one is done for you as an example.

Activity

1

(S) O   1. Darcy and (she, her) kept dancing even after the band stopped playing.

S   O   2. Both Sam and (I, me) submitted proposals for the project.

S   O   3. Dawn is good at bowling, but her little sister is even better than (she, her).

S   O   4. Their track team won because they practiced more than (we, us).

S   O   5. (We, Us) choir members get to perform for the governor.

S   O   6. The rest of (they, them) came to the wedding by train.

S   O   7. (Her, She) and Albert have teamed up to study for the chemistry exam.

S   O   8. Between you and (I, me), I don't believe in flying saucers.

S   O   9. Tony and (he, him) look a lot alike, but they're not even related.

S   O   10. Gordon asked Steve and (her, she) to join his study group.

Possessive Pronouns

Possessive pronouns show ownership or possession.

> Using a small branch, Stu wrote *his* initials in the wet cement.
>
> The furniture is *mine,* but the car is *hers.*

Here is a list of possessive pronouns:

my, mine	our, ours
your, yours	your, yours
his	their, theirs
her, hers	
its	

TIP: A possessive pronoun *never* uses an apostrophe. (See also page 531.)

Incorrect	Correct
That earring is *her's.*	That earring is *hers.*
The orange cat is *theirs'.*	The orange cat is *theirs.*

Cross out the incorrect pronoun form in each of the sentences below. Write the correct form in the space at the left.

EXAMPLE

_____ours_____   The house with the maroon shutters is ~~ours~~'.

_____ 1. A porcupine has no quills on it's belly.

_____ 2. The desk chair we just bought is less comfortable than her's

_____ 3. You can easily tell which team is ours' by when we cheer.

_____ 4. It's banks swollen, the river nearly overflowed into the middle of town.

_____ 5. Grandma's silverware and dishes will be yours' when you get married.

Demonstrative Pronouns

Demonstrative pronouns point to or single out a person or thing. There are four demonstrative pronouns:

this	**these**
that	**those**

Generally speaking, *this* and *these* refer to things close at hand; *that* and *those* refer to things farther away. These four pronouns are commonly used in the role of demonstrative adjectives as well.

This milk has gone sour.

My wife insists on saving all *these* cooking magazines.

I almost tripped on *that* roller blade at the bottom of the steps.

Those plants in the corner don't get enough light.

> **TIP:** Do not use *them, this here, that there, these here,* or *those there* to point out. Use only *this, that, these,* or *those.*

Activity	Cross out the incorrect form of the demonstrative pronoun and write the correct form in the space provided.

3

EXAMPLE

_____Those_____   ~~Those there~~ tires look worn.

_____   1.   This here child has a high fever.

_____   2.   Them birds you see on the lawn are crows.

_____   3.   These here mistakes in your paper need correcting.

_____   4.   That there umpire won't stand for any temper tantrums.

_____   5.   I am saving them old baby clothes for my daughter's dolls.

Review Test

Underline the correct word in the parentheses.

1. Professor Santelli reviewed my paper. His comments about (its, it's) structure were quite helpful.

2. The vase on my dresser belonged to my grandmother, and the candlesticks on the windowsill were (hers', hers) as well.

3. My boyfriend offered to drive his mother and (I, me) to the mall to shop for his birthday present.

4. (Them, Those) little marks on the floor are scratches, not crumbs.

5. Dad bought my brother and (I, me) snow shovels for Christmas, as a subtle reminder of what awaited us.

6. When Lin and (she, her) drove back from the airport, they talked so much that they missed their exit.

7. (That there, That) man wearing the tweed hat is my Uncle Mort.

8. Antonia's pet-sitting service has earned her so much money that (she, her) and her sister Diana are opening up a grooming business as well.

9. The waitress brought our food to the people at the next table and gave (theirs, theirs') to us.

10. Since it was so hot out, Lana and (he, him) felt they had a good excuse to study at the beach.

Adjectives and Adverbs

Adjectives

What Are Adjectives?

Adjectives describe nouns (the names of persons, places, or things) or pronouns.

> Ernie is a *rich* man. (The adjective *rich* describes the noun *man.*)
>
> He is also *generous*. (The adjective *generous* describes the pronoun *he.*)
>
> Our *gray* cat sleeps a lot. (The adjective *gray* describes the noun *cat.*)
>
> She is *old*. (The adjective *old* describes the pronoun *she.*)

Adjectives usually come before the word they describe (as in *rich man* and *gray cat*). But they come after forms of the verb *be* (*is, are, was, were,* and so on). They also follow verbs such as *look, appear, seem, become, sound, taste,* and *smell.*

> That speaker was *boring*. (The adjective *boring* describes the speaker.)
>
> The Petersons are *homeless*. (The adjective *homeless* describes the Petersons.)
>
> The soup looked *good*. (The adjective *good* describes the soup.)
>
> But it tasted *salty*. (The adjective *salty* describes the pronoun *it.*)

Using Adjectives to Compare

For nearly all one-syllable adjectives and some two-syllable adjectives, add *-er* when comparing two things and *-est* when comparing three or more things.

> My sister's handwriting is *neater* than mine, but Mother's is the *neatest.*
>
> Charles is *wealthier* than Thomas, but James is the *wealthiest* of the brothers.
>
> Note: The *y* in *wealthy* has been changed to an *i*.

For some two-syllable adjectives and all longer adjectives, add *more* when comparing two things and *most* when comparing three or more things.

In general, scorpion venom is *more poisonous* than bee venom, but the *most poisonous* venom comes from snakes.

Basketball is *more exciting* than baseball, but football is the *most exciting* sport of all.

You can usually tell when to use *more* and *most* by the sound of a word. For example, you can probably tell by its sound that "carefuller" would be too awkward to say and that *more careful* is thus correct.

There are many words for which both *-er* or *-est* and *more* or *most* are equally correct. For instance, either "a more fair rule" or "a fairer rule" is correct.

To form negative comparisons, use *less* and *least.*

When kids called me "Dum-dum," I tried to look *less* hurt than I felt.

Arthur spent *less* time on the project than anyone else, yet he won first prize.

Suzanne is the most self-centered, *least* thoughtful person I know.

Points to Remember about Comparing

Point 1 Use only one form of comparison at a time. In other words, do not use both an *-er* ending and *more* or both an *-est* ending and *most.*

Incorrect	Correct
My southern accent is always *more stronger* after I visit my family in Georgia.	My southern accent is always *stronger* after I visit my family in Georgia.
My *most luckiest* day was the day I met my wife.	My *luckiest* day was the day I met my wife.

Point 2 Learn the irregular forms of the following words.

	Comparative (for Comparing Two Things)	Superlative (for Comparing Three or More Things)
bad	worse	worst
good, well	better	best
little (in amount)	less	least
much, many	more	most

Do not use both *more* and an irregular comparative or *most* and an irregular superlative.

Incorrect	Correct
It is *more better* to stay healthy than to have to get healthy.	It is *better* to stay healthy than to have to get healthy.
Yesterday I went on the *most best* date of my life—and all we did was go on a picnic.	Yesterday I went on the *best* date of my life—and all we did was go on a picnic.

Add to each sentence the correct form of the word in the margin.

Activity

1

EXAMPLES

bad

The _____*worst*_____ meal I have ever had was at Bert's Bacteria Bonanza and Barbecue.

wonderful

The day I sold my boat was even ___*more wonderful*___ than the day I bought it.

good

1. The Grammy awards are given to the _____ recording artists of each year.

intelligent

2. Sandra is even _____ than her sister, who holds a doctorate in physics.

angry

3. Among all of the protesters, he seemed to be the _____.

light

4. A pound of feathers is no _____ than a pound of stones.

little

5. The _____ expensive way to accumulate a wardrobe is to buy used clothing whenever possible.

Adverbs

What Are Adverbs?

Adverbs—most end in *-ly*—describe verbs, adjectives, or other adverbs.

The referee *suddenly* stopped the fight. (The adverb *suddenly* describes the verb *stopped*.)

Her yellow rosebushes are *absolutely* beautiful. (The adverb *absolutely* describes the adjective *beautiful*.)

The auctioneer spoke so *terribly* fast that I couldn't understand him. (The adverb *terribly* describes the adverb *fast*.)

www.mhhe.com/langan

A Common Mistake with Adverbs and Adjectives

People often mistakenly use an adjective instead of an adverb after a verb.

Incorrect	Correct
I jog *slow*.	I jog *slowly*.
The nervous witness spoke *quiet*.	The nervous witness spoke *quietly*.
The first night I quit smoking, I wanted a cigarette *bad*.	The first night I quit smoking, I wanted a cigarette *badly*.

Activity

2

Underline the adjective or adverb needed. (Remember: Adjectives describe nouns or pronouns. Adverbs describe verbs, adjectives, or other adverbs.)

1. During a quiet moment in class, my stomach rumbled (loud, loudly).

2. I'm a (slow, slowly) reader, so I have to put aside more time to study than some of my friends.

3. Thinking no one was looking, my daughter (quick, quickly) peeked into the bag to see what we had bought for her.

4. The train raced (swift, swiftly) across the frozen prairie.

5. Mr. Mendoza is (slight, slightly) younger than his wife, but he looks much older than she.

Well and *Good*

Two words that are often confused are *well* and *good*. *Good* is an adjective; it describes nouns. *Well* is usually an adverb, and when it is, it describes verbs. *Well* (rather than *good*) is also used to refer to a person's health.

Activity

3

Write *well* or *good* in each of the sentences that follow. Compare your answers with a partner's.

1. I could tell by the broad grin on Della's face that the news was _____.

2. They say my grandfather sang so _____ that even the wind stopped to listen.

3. After she got a flu shot, Kathy did not feel _____.

4. The artist who painted the mural at our school did a _____ job.

5. People who eat _____ usually know something about nutrition.

Review Test

Underline the correct word in the parentheses.

1. In Egypt, silver was once (more valued, most valued) than gold.
2. The doctor predicted that Ben would soon be (good, well) enough to go home.
3. The (little, less) time I spend worrying about a problem, the easier it is to solve.
4. Light walls make a room look (more large, larger) than dark walls do.
5. One of the (brightest, most brightest) women I have ever met never had the opportunity to go to college.
6. The moth (continuous, continuously) thumped against the screen.
7. The Amish manage (good, well) without radios, telephones, or television.
8. When the prisoners of war were taken into the military compound, the guards were warned not to treat them (bad, badly).
9. It is (good, better) to teach people to fish than to give them fish.
10. Our new senator is (more honest, honester) than the last.

31 Misplaced and Dangling Modifiers

Because of misplaced or dangling words, each of the sentences below has more than one possible meaning. In each case, see if you can explain the *intended* meaning and the *unintended* meaning.

1. Clyde and Charlotte decided to have two children on their wedding day.

    Intended meaning: _____

    _____

    Unintended meaning: _____

    _____

2. The students no longer like the math instructor who failed the test.

    Intended meaning: _____

    _____

    Unintended meaning: _____

    _____

3. While smoking a pipe, my dog sat with me by the crackling fire.

    Intended meaning: _____

    _____

    Unintended meaning: _____

    _____

4. Busy talking on a cell phone, his car went through a red light.

    Intended meaning: _____

    _____

    Unintended meaning: _____

    _____

See Appendix A for answers.

What Misplaced Modifiers Are and How to Correct Them

Modifiers are descriptive words. *Misplaced modifiers* are words that, because of awkward placement, do not describe the words the writer intended them to describe. Misplaced modifiers often obscure the meaning of a sentence. To avoid them, place words as close as possible to what they describe.

Misplaced Words	Correctly Placed Words
Tony bought an old car from a crooked dealer *with a faulty transmission.* (The *dealer* had a faulty transmission?)	Tony bought an old car with a faulty transmission from a crooked dealer. (The words describing the old car are now placed next to "car.")
I *nearly* earned two hundred dollars last week. (You just missed earning two hundred dollars, but in fact earned nothing?)	I earned nearly two hundred dollars last week. (The meaning—that you earned a little under two hundred dollars—is now clear.)
Bill yelled at the howling dog *in his underwear.* (The *dog* wore underwear?)	Bill, in his underwear, yelled at the howling dog. (The words describing Bill are placed next to "Bill.")

Underline the misplaced word or words in each sentence. Then rewrite the sentence, placing related words together and thereby making the meaning clear.

Activity

1

EXAMPLES

The suburbs <u>nearly</u> had five inches of rain.

The suburbs had nearly five inches of rain.

We could see the football stadium <u>driving across the bridge.</u>

Driving across the bridge, we could see the football stadium.

1. I saw mountains of uncollected trash walking along the city streets.

_____

2. Samantha could only hear the music blaring in her ear, nothing else.

_____

3. Angel walked through his girlfriend's front door wearing a smirk.

_____

4. The hikers saw a large stand of stately pines walking up the mountain.

_____

5. The driver could not read the detour sign along the Mexican highway written in Spanish.

_____

_____

6. Roger visited the old house still weak with the flu.

_____

7. The phone almost rang fifteen times last night.

_____

8. Yesterday, Maud spotted a family of squirrels drinking coffee on her deck.

_____

9. We decided to send our daughter to college on the day she was born.

_____

10. Fred always opens the bills that arrive in the mailbox with a sigh.

_____

www.mhhe.com/langan

What Dangling Modifiers Are and How to Correct Them

A modifier that opens a sentence must be followed immediately by the word it is meant to describe. Otherwise, the modifier is said to be *dangling,* and the sentence takes on an unintended meaning. For example, in the sentence

> While smoking a pipe, my dog sat with me by the crackling fire.

the unintended meaning is that the *dog* was smoking the pipe. What the writer meant, of course, was that *he,* the writer, was smoking the pipe. The dangling modifier could be corrected by placing *I,* the word being described, directly after the opening modifier and revising as necessary:

> While smoking a pipe, *I sat with* my dog by the crackling fire.

The dangling modifier could also be corrected by placing the subject within the opening word group:

> While *I was* smoking my pipe, my dog sat with me by the crackling fire.

Here are other sentences with dangling modifiers. Read the explanations of why they are dangling and look carefully at how they are corrected.

Dangling	Correct
Swimming at the lake, a rock cut Sue's foot.	Swimming at the lake, Sue cut her foot on a rock.
(*Who* was swimming at the lake? The answer is not *rock* but *Sue*. The subject *Sue* must be added.)	*Or:* When Sue was swimming at the lake, she cut her foot on a rock.
While eating my sandwich, five mosquitoes bit me.	While *I* was eating my sandwich, five mosquitoes bit me.
(*Who* is eating the sandwich? The answer is not *five mosquitoes,* as it unintentionally seems to be, but *I*. The subject *I* must be added.)	*Or:* While eating my sandwich, *I* was bitten by five mosquitoes.
Getting out of bed, the tile floor was so cold that Yoko shivered all over.	Getting out of bed, *Yoko* found the tile floor so cold that she shivered all over.
(*Who* got out of bed? The answer is not *tile floor* but *Yoko*. The subject *Yoko* must be added.)	*Or:* When *Yoko* got out of bed, the tile floor was so cold that she shivered all over.
To join the team, a C average or better is necessary.	To join the team, *you* must have a C average or better.
(*Who* is to join the team? The answer is not *C average* but *you*. The subject *you* must be added.)	*Or:* For *you* to join the team, a C average or better is necessary.

The preceding examples make clear the two ways of correcting a dangling modifier. Decide on a logical subject and do one of the following:

1. Place the subject *within* the opening word group.

    When Sue was swimming at the lake, she cut her foot on a rock.

TIP: In some cases an appropriate subordinating word such as *when* must be added, and the verb may have to be changed slightly as well.

---

2. Place the subject right *after* the opening word group.

    Swimming at the lake, Sue cut her foot on a rock.

Ask *Who?* as you look at the opening words in each sentence. The subject that answers the question should be nearby in the sentence. If it is not, provide the logical subject by using either method of correction described above.

EXAMPLE

While setting up camp, a bear was spotted.

While we were setting up camp, we spotted a bear.

_____

or *While setting up camp, we spotted a bear.*

_____

1. Watching the horror movie, goose bumps covered my spine.

_____

_____

2. After putting on a wool sweater, the room didn't seem as cold.

_____

_____

3. Walking down the stairs, loud music could be heard.

_____

_____

4. To assess the effects of a possible tuition hike, several students were interviewed.

_____

_____

5. Joining several college clubs, Antonio's social life became more active.

_____

_____

6. While visiting the Jungle Park Safari, a baboon scrambled onto the hood of their car.

_____

_____

7. When only a boy, that wild horse was trained.

_____

_____

8. Standing at the ocean's edge, the wind coated my glasses with a salty film.

_____

_____

9. After laughing for two hours straight, Rita's stomach started to ache.

_____

_____

10. Using binoculars, the hawk was clearly seen following its prey.

_____

_____

Review Test   1

Underline the misplaced word or words in each sentence. Write *M* for *misplaced modifier* or *C* for *correct* in front of each sentence.

_____ 1. Having been held up, the police were called by the store owner.

_____ 2. Having been held up, the store owner called the police.

_____ 3. I noticed a crack in the window walking into the delicatessen.

_____ 4. Walking into the delicatessen, I noticed a crack in the window.

_____ 5. Though he thought the job was long-term, Sam worked in Phoenix only one day.

_____ 6. Though he thought the job was long-term, Sam only worked in Phoenix one day.

_____ 7. With great delight, the children were ready to devour the luscious dessert.

_____ 8. The children were ready to devour the luscious dessert with great delight.

_____ 9. In a secondhand store, Willie found a television set that had been stolen from me last month.

_____ 10. Willie found a television set in a secondhand store that had been stolen from me last month.

_____ 11. Willie found, in a secondhand store, a television set that had been stolen from me last month.

_____ 12. After working a double shift she just was interested in a night's sleep.

_____ 13. After working a double shift she was interested just in a night's sleep.

_____ 14. The corn soaked up the rain newly planted in the parched soil.

_____ 15. The corn, newly planted in the parched soil, soaked up the rain.

Review Test   2

Write _D_ for _dangling_ or _C_ for _correct_ in the blank next to each sentence. Remember that the opening words are a dangling modifier if they have no nearby logical subject to modify.

_____ 1. Advertising on _Craigslist,_ Ian's car was quickly sold.

_____ 2. By advertising on _Craigslist,_ Ian quickly sold his car.

_____ 3. After painting the downstairs, the house needed airing to clear out the fumes.

_____ 4. After we painted the downstairs, the house needed airing to clear out the fumes.

_____ 5. Believing Venice to be the most romantic city in Europe, a visit there was planned for our honeymoon.

_____ 6. Believing Venice to be the most romantic city in Europe, we planned a visit there for our honeymoon.

_____ 7. After picking out a suit, a tie and a shirt were added to my list.

_____ 8. After picking out a suit, I added a tie and a shirt to my list.

_____ 9. Casting his fishing line into the lake, a largemouth bass could be felt grabbing his bait.

_____ 10. Casting his fishing line into the lake, Matthew could feel a largemouth bass grabbing his bait.

_____ 11. Looking through the telescope, I saw a brightly lit object come into view.

_____ 12. As I was looking through the telescope, a brightly lit object came into view.

_____ 13. Looking through the telescope, a brightly lit object came into my view.

_____ 14. While we were having a picnic lunch of hamburgers and hot dogs, two deer passed through the campsite.

_____ 15. While having a picnic lunch of hamburgers and hot dogs, two deer passed through the campsite.

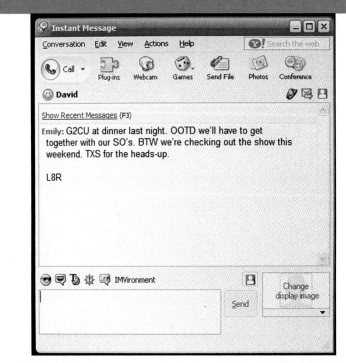

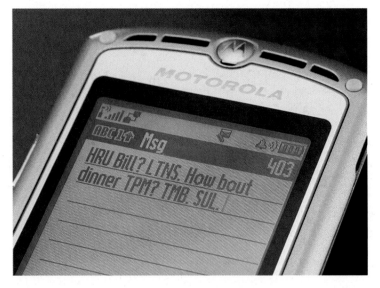

Abbreviations are the norm in instant messages and text messages, as shown here. But are these abbreviations appropriate in your college papers? Why or why not?

Paper Format

32

When you hand in a paper for any of your courses, probably the first thing you will be judged on is its format. It is important, then, that you do certain things to make your papers look attractive, neat, and easy to read.

www.mhhe.com/langan

Here are guidelines to follow in preparing a paper for an instructor:

1. Use full-size theme or printer paper, 8½ by 11 inches.

2. Leave wide margins (1 to 1½ inches) on all four sides of each page. In particular, do not crowd the right-hand or bottom margin. The white space makes your paper more readable; also, the instructor has room for comments.

3. If you write by hand:

   a. Use a pen with blue or black ink (*not* a pencil).

   b. Do not overlap letters. Do not make decorative loops on letters. On narrow-ruled paper, write only on every other line.

   c. Make all your letters distinct. Pay special attention to *a, e, i, o,* and *u*—five letters that people sometimes write illegibly.

   d. Keep your capital letters clearly distinct from small letters. You may even want to print all the capital letters.

   e. Make commas, periods, and other punctuation marks firm and clear. Leave a slight space after each period.

4. Center the title of your paper on the first line of page 1. Do *not* put quotation marks around the title, do not underline it, and do not put a period after it. Capitalize all the major words in a title, including the first word. Short connecting words within a title such as *of, for, the, in,* and *to* are not capitalized. Skip a line between the title and the first line of your text.

5. Indent the first line of each paragraph about five spaces (half an inch) from the left-hand margin.

6. When you type, use double-spacing between lines. Also double-space after a period.

7. Whenever possible, avoid breaking (hyphenating) words at the end of lines. If you must break a word, break only between syllables (see page 556). Do not break words of one syllable.

8. Write your name, the date, and the course number where your instructor asks for them.

Also keep in mind these important points about the *title* and *first sentence* of your paper:

9. The title should simply be several words that tell what the paper is about. It should usually *not* be a complete sentence. For example, if you are writing a paper about one of the most frustrating jobs you have ever had, the title could be just "A Frustrating Job."

10. Do not rely on the title to help explain the first sentence of your paper. The first sentence must be independent of the title. For instance, if the title of your paper is "A Frustrating Job," the first sentence should *not* be "It was working as a babysitter." Rather, the first sentence might be "Working as a babysitter was the most frustrating job I ever had."

Activity

1

Identify the mistakes in format in the following lines from a student paper. Explain the corrections in the spaces provided. One correction is provided as an example.

		"Charles Darwin: his voyage on the ship beagle"
		He was a man who put forth the theories of evolution and natu-
		ral selection. Darwin was the naturalist aboard the English ship Beagle
		(1831-36), which made a nearly five-year journey all over the globe.
		Its official mission was to chart the coastline of South America.
		However, on that journey, Darwin started collecting information that
		would form the basis of his scientific career.

1. _Hyphenate only between syllables._

2. _____

3. _____

4. _____

5. _____

6. _____

Often a title can be based on the topic sentence—the sentence that expresses the main idea of the paper. Following are five topic sentences from student papers. Working with a partner, write a suitable and specific title for each paper, basing the title on the topic sentence. (Note the example.)

Activity

2

EXAMPLE

  Compromise in a Relationship
  _____

  Learning how to compromise is essential to a good relationship.

1. *Title:* _____

   Some houseplants are dangerous to children and pets.

2. *Title:* _____

   Some herbicides can be as dangerous to human beings as to weeds.

3. *Title:* _____

   You don't have to be a professional to take good photographs if you keep a few guidelines in mind.

4. *Title:* _____

   My husband is compulsively neat.

5. *Title:* _____

   Insulating a home well can save the owner a great deal of money on heating and cooling.

As has already been stated, you must *not* rely on the title to help explain your first sentence. In four of the five sentences that follow, the writer has, inappropriately, used the title to help explain the first sentence.

Rewrite these four sentences so that they stand independent of the title. Write *Correct* under the one sentence that is independent of the title.

Activity

3

EXAMPLE

  Title: My Career Plans

  First sentence: They have changed in the last six months.

  Rewritten: My career plans have changed in the last six months.

1. *Title:* Contending with Dogs

   First sentence: This is the main problem in my work as a mail carrier.

   Rewritten: _____

2. *Title:* Study Skills

    First sentence: Good study skills are necessary if a person is to do well in college.

    Rewritten: _____

    _____

3. *Title*: Black Bears

    First Sentence: We saw several of them as we drove across the Blue Ridge Mountains.

    Rewritten: _____

    _____

4. *Title:* The Renaissance

    First Sentence: It was the period that followed the Middle Ages in Europe.

    Rewritten: _____

    _____

5. *Title:* Cell Phones

    First sentence: Many motorists have learned the hard way just how dangerous these handy tools can be.

    Rewritten: _____

    _____

Review Test

In the space provided, rewrite the following sentences from a student paper. Correct the mistakes in format.

	"beijing: china's capital then and now"
	This city is the capital of the People's Republic of China. It is the
	second largest city city in China; Shanghai is the largest. For more
	than seven hundred years, on and off, Beijing has been the seat of
	the Chinese government. For a time, its name was Peking. However,
	when the Communists took over the country in 1949, they gave the
	city back its ancient name. Important tourist sites in and near
	Beijing include the Forbidden City, the Summer Palace, the Beijing
	Zoo, and the Great Wall.

33

Capital Letters

Introductory Activity

Items 1–13 You probably know a good deal about the uses of capital letters. Answering the questions below will help you check your knowledge.

1. Write the full name of a person you know: _____

2. In what country were you born? _____

3. What is your present street address? _____

4. Name a country where you would like to travel: _____

5. Name a school that you attended: _____

6. Give the name of a store where you buy food: _____

7. Name a company where someone you know works: _____

8. What day of the week gives you the best chance to relax? _____

9. What holiday is your favorite? _____

10. What brand of car do you drive, or what brand of television or computer do you own? _____

11. What is the title of this textbook? _____

12. What is the title of your favorite movie? _____

13. Write the name of a river or a mountain range: _____

Items 14–16 Three capital letters are needed in the lines below. Underline the words that you think should be capitalized. Then write them, capitalized, in the spaces provided.

the masked man reared his silvery-white horse, waved good-bye, and rode out of town. My heart thrilled when i heard someone say, "that was the Lone Ranger. You don't see his kind much, anymore."

14. _____   15. _____   16. _____

See Appendix A for answers.

Main Uses of Capital Letters

Capital letters are used with

1. The first word in a sentence or a direct quotation
2. Names of persons and the word *I*
3. Names of particular places
4. Names of days of the week, months, and holidays
5. Names of commercial products (brand names)
6. Names of organizations such as religious and political groups, associations, companies, unions, and clubs
7. Titles of books, magazines, newspapers, articles, stories, poems, films, podcasts, television shows, songs, papers that you write, and the like

Each use is illustrated on the pages that follow.

First Word in a Sentence or Direct Quotation

The panhandler touched me and asked, "Do you have any change?"

(Capitalize the first word in the sentence.)

(Capitalize the first word in the direct quotation.)

"If you want a ride," said Tawana, "get ready now. Otherwise, I'm going alone."

(*If* and *Otherwise* are capitalized because they are the first words of sentences within a direct quotation. But *get* is not capitalized, because it is part of the first sentence within the quotation.)

Names of Persons and the Word *I*

Last night I ran into Tony Curry and Lola Morrison.

Names of Particular Places

Charlotte graduated from Fargone High School in Orlando, Florida. She then moved with her parents to Bakersfield, California, and worked for a time there at Alexander's Gift House. Eventually she married and moved with her husband to the Naval Reserve Center in Atlantic County, New Jersey. She takes courses two nights a week at Stockton State College. On weekends she and her family often visit the nearby Wharton State Park and go canoeing on the Mullica River. She does volunteer work at Atlantic City Hospital in connection with the First Christian Church. In addition, she works during the summer as a hostess at Convention Hall and the Holiday Inn.

But   Use small letters if the specific name of a place is not given.

Charlotte sometimes remembers her unhappy days in high school and at the gift shop where she worked after graduation. She did not imagine then that she would one day be going to college and doing volunteer work for a church and a hospital in the community where she and her husband live.

Names of Days of the Week, Months, and Holidays

I was angry at myself for forgetting that Sunday was Mother's Day.

During July and August, Fred works a four-day week, and he has Mondays off.

Bill still has a scar on his ankle from a cherry bomb that exploded near him one Fourth of July and a scar on his arm where he stabbed himself with a fishhook on a Labor Day weekend.

But   Use small letters for the seasons—summer, fall, winter, spring.

Names of Commercial Products

After brushing with Colgate toothpaste in the morning, Clyde typically has a glass of Tropicana orange juice and Total cereal with milk, followed by a Marlboro cigarette.

My sister likes to play Monopoly and Cranium; I like chess and poker; my brother likes Scrabble, baseball, and table tennis.

But   Use small letters for the *type* of product (toothpaste, orange juice, cereal, cigarette, and so on).

Names of Organizations Such as Religious and Political Groups, Associations, Companies, Unions, and Clubs

Fred Grencher was a Lutheran for many years but converted to Catholicism when he married. Both he and his wife, Martha, are members of the Democratic Party. Both belong to the American Automobile Association. Martha works part-time as a refrigerator salesperson at Sears. Fred is a mail carrier and belongs to the Postal Clerks' Union.

Tony met Lola when he was a Boy Scout and she was a Campfire Girl; she asked him to light her fire.

Titles of Books, Magazines, Newspapers, Articles, Stories, Poems, Films, Television Shows, Songs, Papers That You Write, and the Like

On Sunday Lola read the first chapter of *I Know Why the Caged Bird Sings,* a book required for her writing course. She looked through her parents' copy of the *New York Times.* She then read an article titled "Thinking about a Change in Your Career" and a poem titled "Some Moments Alone" in *Cosmopolitan* magazine. At the same time, she listened to an old Beatles album, *Abbey Road.* In the evening she watched *60 Minutes* on television and an old movie, *High Noon,* starring Gary Cooper. Then from 11 P.M. to midnight she worked on a paper titled "Uses of Leisure Time in Today's Culture" for her sociology class.

Cross out the words that need capitals in the following sentences. Then write the capitalized forms of the words in the spaces provided. The number of spaces tells you how many corrections to make in each case.

Copyright © 2012 The McGraw-Hill Companies, Inc. All rights reserved.

Activity

1

EXAMPLE

I brush with ~~crest~~ toothpaste but get cavities all the time. _____*Crest*_____

1. A spokesperson for general motors announced that the prices of all chevrolets will rise next year.

   _____   _____   _____

2. In may 2008 mario's family moved here from brownsville, Texas.

   _____   _____   _____

3. Nathaniel hawthrone wrote a novel entitled the scarlet letter and a short story called "young goodman brown."

   _____   _____   _____

4. Andy went to the local ford dealership, where he asked about the prices of cars. For now, however, he'll continue to ride his schwinn bicycle to school, or perhaps borrow his brother's harley davidson motorcycle.

   _____   _____   _____

5. A greyhound bus almost ran over Tony as he was riding his yamaha to a friend's home in florida.

   _____   _____   _____

6. Before I lent my nikon camera to Janet, I warned her, "be sure to return it by friday."

   _____   _____   _____

7. Before christmas George took his entire paycheck, went to sears, and bought a twenty-two-inch zenith flat-screen television.

_____   _____   _____

8. On their first trip to New York City, Fred and Martha visited the empire State Building and Times square. They also saw the New York mets play at the old Shea Stadium.

_____   _____   _____

9. Clyde was listening to Ray Charles's recording of "America the beautiful," Charlotte was reading an article in *Reader's digest* titled "let's Stop Peddling Sex," and their son was watching *sesame Street*.

_____   _____   _____   _____

10. When a sign for a burger king rest stop appeared on the highway, anita said, "let's stop here. I'm exhausted."

_____   _____   _____   _____

Other Uses of Capital Letters

Capital letters are also used with

1. Names that show family relationships
2. Titles of persons when used with their names
3. Specific school courses
4. Languages
5. Geographic locations
6. Historical periods and events
7. Races, nations, and nationalities
8. Opening and closing of a letter

Each use is illustrated on the pages that follow.

Names That Show Family Relationships

I got Mother to babysit for me.

I went with Grandfather to the church service.

Uncle Carl and Aunt Lucy always enclose twenty dollars with birthday cards.

But   Do not capitalize words like *mother, father, grandmother, aunt,* and so on, when they are preceded by a possessive word (*my, your, his, her, our, their*).

I got my mother to babysit for me.

I went with my grandfather to the church service.

My uncle and aunt always enclose twenty dollars with birthday cards.

Titles of Persons When Used with Their Names

I wrote to Senator Grabble and Congresswoman Punchie.

Professor Snorrel sent me to Chairperson Ruck, who sent me to Dean Rappers.

He drove to Dr. Helen Thompson's office after the cat bit him.

But   Use small letters when titles appear by themselves, without specific names.

I wrote to my senator and my congresswoman.

The professor sent me to the chairperson, who sent me to the dean.

He drove to the doctor's office after the cat bit him.

Specific School Courses

I got an A in both Accounting and Small Business Management, but I got a C in Human Behavior.

But   Use small letters for general subject areas.

I enjoyed my business courses but not my psychology or language courses.

Languages

She knows German and Spanish, but she speaks mostly American slang.

Geographic Locations

I grew up in the Midwest. I worked in the East for a number of years and then moved to the West Coast.

But   Use small letters for directions.

A new high school is being built at the south end of town.

Because I have a compass in my car, I know that I won't be going east or west when I want to go north.

Historical Periods and Events

Hector did well answering an essay question about the Second World War, but he lost points on a question about the Great Depression.

Races, Nations, and Nationalities

The research study centered on African Americans and Hispanics.

They have German knives and Danish glassware in the kitchen, an Indian wood carving in the bedroom, Mexican sculptures in the study, and a Turkish rug in the living room.

Opening and Closing of a Letter

Dear Sir:

Dear Madam:

Sincerely yours,

Truly yours,

> TIP: Capitalize only the first word in a closing.

Activity

2

Working with a partner, cross out the words that need capitals in the following sentences. Then write the capitalized forms of the words in the spaces provided. The number of spaces tells you how many corrections to make in each case.

1. The first european city I ever visited was london; the last was rome.

   _____   _____   _____

2. The e-mail letter began, "dear friend—You must send twenty copies of this message if you want good luck."

   _____   _____

3. A retired army officer, captain Evert Johnson, is teaching a course called military history. He once served in the middle east.

   _____   _____   _____

4. aunt Sarah and uncle Hal, who are mormons, took us to their church services when we visited them in the midwest.

   _____   _____   _____   _____

5. While visiting san francisco, Liza stopped in at a buddhist temple and talked to a chinese lawyer there.

   _____   _____   _____   _____

Unnecessary Use of Capitals

Many errors in capitalization are caused by using capitals where they are not needed.

Cross out the incorrectly capitalized words in the following sentences. Then write the correct forms of the words in the spaces provided. The number of spaces tells you how many corrections to make in each sentence.

1. My cousin is taking a course in Russian History at a College in Moscow.

   _____   _____

2. I love the television Commercials of some Insurance companies; they make Me break out laughing.

   _____   _____   _____

3. A front-page Newspaper story about the crash of a commercial Jet has made me nervous about my Overseas trip.

   _____   _____   _____

4. During a Terrible Blizzard in 1888, People froze to Death on the streets of New York.

   _____   _____   _____   _____

5. I asked the Bank Officer at Citibank, "How do I get a Card to use the automatic teller machines?"

   _____   _____   _____

Review Test 1

Cross out the words that need capitals in the following sentences. Then write the capitalized forms of the words in the spaces provided. The number of spaces tells you how many corrections to make in each sentence.

1. I made an appointment to meet beverly at starbucks coffee on main street.

   _____   _____   _____

2. Between Long island and the atlantic Ocean lies a long, thin sandbar called fire island.

   _____   _____   _____   _____

3. When I'm in the supermarket checkout line, it seems as if every magazine on display has an article called "how You Can Lose Twenty pounds in two weeks."

   _____   _____   _____   _____

4. The supermarket had specials on post cereals, smithfield cold cuts, and salisbury frozen dinners.

   _____   _____   _____

5. "can't you be quiet?" I pleaded. "do you always have to talk while I'm watching general hospital on television?"

   _____   _____   _____   _____

6. On father's day, the children drove home and took their parents out to dinner at the olive garden.

   _____   _____   _____   _____

7. On memorial day, we like to picnic in washington crossing park on the delaware river.

   _____   _____   _____

8. glendale bank, where my sister Amber works, is paying for her night course, business accounting I.

   _____   _____   _____   _____

9. My father reads the *wall street journal, time* magazine, and the *bible* every night.

   _____   _____   _____

10. On thanksgiving my brother said, "let's hurry and eat so i can go watch the football game on our new sony TV."

    _____   _____   _____   _____

Review Test 2

On separate paper, do the following:

1. Write seven sentences demonstrating the seven main uses of capital letters (page 515).

2. Write eight sentences demonstrating the eight additional uses of capital letters (page 518).

Numbers and Abbreviations

Numbers

Rule 1 Spell out numbers that can be expressed in one or two words. Otherwise, use numerals—the numbers themselves.

> During the past five years, more than twenty-five barracuda have been caught in the lake.

> The parking fine was ten dollars.

> In my grandmother's attic are eighty-four pairs of old shoes.

But

> Each year about 250 baby trout are added to the lake.

> My costs after contesting a parking fine in court were $135.

> Grandmother has 382 back copies of *Reader's Digest* in her attic.

Rule 2 Be consistent when you use a series of numbers. If some numbers in a sentence or paragraph require more than two words, then use numerals throughout the selection:

> During his election campaign, State Senator Mel Grabble went to 3 county fairs, 16 parades, 45 cookouts, and 112 club dinners, and delivered the same speech 176 times.

Rule 3 Use numerals for dates, times, addresses, percentages, and parts of a book.

> The letter was dated April 3, 1872.

> My appointment was at 6:15. (*But:* Spell out numbers before *o'clock*. For example: The doctor didn't see me until seven o'clock.)

> He lives at 212 West 19th Street.

> About 20 percent of our class dropped out of school.

> One cause of the Civil War is explained in Chapter 9, page 244, of our history textbook.

Activity

1

Cross out the mistakes in numbers and write the corrections in the spaces provided.

1. Pearl Harbor was attacked on December the seventh, nineteen forty-one.

    _____   _____

2. The city council decided to install 8 new traffic lights and 30 new stop signs.

    _____   _____

3. The Memorial Day parade will start at 11:00 o'clock; 30 organizations are expected to march.

    _____   _____

www.mhhe.com/langan

Abbreviations

While abbreviations are a helpful time-saver in note taking, you should avoid most abbreviations in formal writing. Listed below are some of the few abbreviations that can be used acceptably in compositions. Note that a period is used after most abbreviations.

1. Mr., Mrs., Ms., Jr., Sr., Dr. when used with proper names:

    Mr. Tibble   Dr. Stein   Ms. O'Reilly

2. Time references:

    A.M. or a.m.   P.M. or p.m.   B.C. or A.D.   B.C.E. or C.E.

3. First or middle name in a signature:

    R. Anthony Curry   Otis T. Redding   J. Alfred Prufrock

4. Organizations and common terms known primarily by their initials:

    FBI   UN   CBS   CD   DVD

Activity

2

Cross out the words that should not be abbreviated and correct them in the spaces provided. Then compare your answers with a partner's.

1. On Mon. afternoon, Feb. 10, 2010, at five min. after two o'clock, my son was born.

    _____   _____   _____

2. For six years I lived at First Ave. and Gordon St. right next to Shore Memorial Hosp., in San Fran., Calif.

    _____   _____   _____   _____   _____

3. After we completed the chem. exam, Dr. Andrews announced she had been asked to serve as Dean of Science at Aubury U. in Ariz.

    _____   _____   _____

Review Test

Cross out the mistakes in numbers and abbreviations and correct them in the spaces provided.

1. At six forty-five P.M., the Alpha Kappa Gamma honor soc. will hold its induction ceremony.

    _____ _____

2. Stanley has a collection of *Life* mags.; it numbers two hundred and fifty-five.

    _____ _____

3. Martha has more than 200 copies of *People* mag.; she thinks they may be worth a lot of someday.

    _____ _____

4. When I was eight yrs. old, I owned three cats, two dogs, and 4 rabbits.

    _____ _____

5. Approx. half the striking workers returned to work on Nov. third, two thousand ten.

    _____ _____ _____ _____

PUNCTUATION

How does each of these signs misuse punctuation, and how could you correct the errors? Have you seen similar mistakes in signs posted on campus? on the road? in a newspaper or book?

Apostrophes

1. Larry's motorcycle
   my sister's boyfriend
   Grandmother's shotgun
   the men's room

   What is the purpose of the *'s* in the examples above?

   _____

2. They didn't mind when their dog bit people, but now
   they're leashing him because he's eating all their garden
   vegetables.

   What is the purpose of the apostrophe in *didn't, they're,*
   and *he's*?

   _____

3. I used to believe that vampires lived in the old coal bin
   of my cellar.
   The vampire's whole body recoiled when he saw the
   crucifix.

   Fred ate two baked potatoes.

   One baked potato's center was still hard.

   In each of the sentence pairs above, why is the *'s* used in
   the second sentence but not in the first?

   _____

   _____

See Appendix A for answers.

The two main uses of the apostrophe are

1. To show the omission of one or more letters in a contraction
2. To show ownership or possession

Each use is explained on the pages that follow.

Apostrophe in Contractions

A *contraction* is formed when two words are combined to make one word. An apostrophe is used to show where letters are omitted in forming the contraction. Here are two contractions:

have + not = haven't (*o* in *not* has been omitted)

I + will = I'll (*wi* in *will* has been omitted)

The following are some other common contractions:

I + am = I'm	it + is = it's
I + have = I've	it + has = it's
I + had = I'd	is + not = isn't
who + is = who's	could + not = couldn't
do + not = don't	I + would = I'd
did + not = didn't	they + are = they're

TIP: *Will* + *not* has an unusual contraction, *won't.*

Activity

1

Combine the following pairs of words into contractions. One is done for you.

1. we + are   = __we're__
2. are + not   = _____
3. you + are   = _____
4. they + have = _____
5. could + not = _____

6. should + not = _____
7. have + not   = _____
8. who + is   = _____
9. does + not   = _____
10. there + is   = _____

Working with a partner, write the contractions for the words in parentheses. One is done for you.

1. (Are not) _Aren't_ you coming with us to the concert?

2. (She is) _____ entering graduate school next year; (he will) _____ be a junior in college.

3. (There is) _____ an extra bed upstairs if (you would) _____ like to stay here for the night.

4. (They have) _____ already picked out the house they want; (it is) _____ a colonial.

5. Denise (should not) _____ complain about the cost of food if (she is) _____ not willing to grow her own by planting a backyard garden.

> **TIP:** Even though contractions are common in everyday speech and in written dialogue, it is usually best to avoid them in formal writing.

Apostrophe to Show Ownership or Possession

To show ownership or possession, we can use such words as *belongs to, possessed by, owned by,* or (most commonly) *of.*

the jacket that *belongs to* Tony

the grades *possessed by* James

the gas station *owned by* our cousin

the footprints *of* the animal

But often the quickest and easiest way to show possession is to use an apostrophe plus *s* (if the word is not a plural ending in -*s*). Thus we can say

Tony's jacket

James's grades

our cousin's gas station

the animal's footprints

Points to Remember

1. The *'s* goes with the owner or possessor (in the examples given, *Tony, James, cousin, the animal*). What follows is the person or thing possessed (in the examples given, *jacket, grades, gas station, footprints*).

2. When *'s* is handwritten in cursive script, there should always be a break between the word and the *'s*.

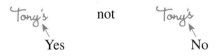

Tony's   not   Tony's
Yes   No

3. A singular word ending in *-s* (such as *James* in the earlier example) also shows possession by adding an apostrophe plus *s* (*James's*).

Activity

3

Rewrite the italicized part of each of the sentences below, using *'s* to show possession. Remember that the *'s* goes with the owner or possessor.

EXAMPLE

The toys belonging to the children filled an entire room.

The children's toys
_____

1. *The old car owned by Fred* is a classic.

_____

2. *The concentration of my grandfather* has improved because of the new medication.

_____

3. *The owner of the pit bull* was arrested after the dog attacked a child.

_____

4. *The drill of the dentist* did not hurt because he had injected my gums with Novocaine.

_____

5. *The jeep owned by Dennis* was recalled because of an engine defect.

_____

6. Is this *the hat of somebody?*

_____

7. You will probably hate *the surprise ending of the movie.*

_____

8. *The cords coming from the computer* were so tangled they looked like spaghetti.

_____

9. *The energy level possessed by the little boy* is much higher than hers.

_____

10. *The leaves of the maple tree* were turning a deep red.

_____

Add *'s* to each of the following words to make them the possessors or owners of something. Then write sentences using the words. Your sentences can be serious or playful. One is done for you.

Activity

4

1. parakeet ____*parakeet's*____ *The parakeet's cage needs cleaning.*

_____

2. mechanic _____ _____

_____

3. Lola _____ _____

_____

4. library _____ _____

_____

5. mother _____ _____

_____

Apostrophe versus Possessive Pronouns

Do not use an apostrophe with possessive pronouns. They already show ownership. Possessive pronouns include *his, hers, its, yours, ours,* and *theirs.*

Incorrect	Correct
The bookstore lost its' lease.	The bookstore lost its lease.
The racing bikes were theirs'.	The racing bikes were theirs.
The change is your's.	The change is yours.
His' problems are ours', too.	His problems are ours, too.
His' skin is more sunburned than her's.	His skin is more sunburned than hers.

Apostrophe versus Simple Plurals

When you want to make a word plural, just add *-s* at the end of the word. Do *not* add an apostrophe. For example, the plural of the word *movie* is *movies,* not *movie's* or *movies'.* Look at this sentence:

Lola adores Tony's broad shoulders, rippling muscles, and warm eyes.

The words *shoulders, muscles,* and *eyes* are simple plurals, meaning *more than one shoulder, more than one muscle, more than one eye.* The plural is shown by adding only *-s.* On the other hand, the *'s* after *Tony* shows possession—that the shoulders, muscles, and eyes belong to Tony.

Activity

5

In the space provided under each sentence, add the one apostrophe needed and explain why the other word or words ending in *-s* are simple plurals.

EXAMPLE

Karens tomato plants are almost six feet tall.

Karens: *Karen's, meaning "belonging to Karen"*

plants: *plural meaning "more than one plant"*

1. The restaurants reputation brought hungry diners from miles around.

   restaurants: _____

   diners: _____

   miles: _____

2. Marios sweater was made in Ireland by monks.

   Marios: _____

   monks: _____

3. As Tinas skill at studying increased, her grades improved.

   Tinas: _____

   grades: _____

4. After I had visited the deans office, I decided to spend more time with my books.

   deans: _____

   books: _____

5. I bought two magazines and a copy of Stephen Kings latest novel at the bookstore.

   magazines: _____

   Kings: _____

6. After six weeks without rain, the nearby streams started drying up, and the lakes water level fell sharply.

weeks: _____

streams: _____

lakes: _____

7. Rebeccas hooded red cloak makes her look like a fairy-tale character, but her heavy black boots spoil the effect.

Rebeccas: _____

boots: _____

8. When the brakes failed on Eriks truck, he narrowly avoided hitting several parked cars and two trees.

brakes: _____

Eriks: _____

cars: _____

trees: _____

9. Suddenly, the clouds opened and the skys bounty drenched the dry fields.

clouds: _____

skys: _____

fields: _____

10. My parents like Floridas winters, but they prefer to spend their summers back home in Maine.

parents: _____

Floridas: _____

winters: _____

summers: _____

Apostrophe with Plural Words Ending in -s

Plurals that end in -*s* show possession simply by adding the apostrophe (rather than an apostrophe plus *s*):

My *parents'* station wagon is ten years old.

The *students'* many complaints were ignored by the high school principal.

All the *Boy Scouts'* tents were damaged by the hailstorm.

| Activity | In each sentence, cross out the one plural word that needs an apostrophe. Then write the word correctly, with the apostrophe, in the space provided. |

6

EXAMPLE

_____*soldiers'*_____ All the ~~soldiers~~ rifles were cleaned for inspection.

1. The Smiths boat is the largest one in the marina.

_____

2. The transit workers strike has just ended.

_____

3. Two of our neighbors homes are up for sale.

_____

4. The door to the ladies room is locked.

_____

5. The horses corral needs to be repaired, for several of them have gotten loose.

_____

Review Test 1

In each sentence, cross out the two words that need apostrophes. Then write the words correctly in the spaces provided.

1. The police officers uniform was covered with mud, but she wasnt hurt.

_____   _____

2. Weve been trying for weeks to see that movie, but theres always a long line.

_____   _____

3. Alfonsos brother won last years election for class president.

_____   _____

4. The citys budget director has trouble balancing his own familys checkbook.

_____   _____

5. Taking Dianes elderly parents to church every week is one example of Pauls generous behavior.

_____   _____

6. Theres no reason to buy bottled water unless youre intent upon wasting money.

_____   _____

7. The curious child dropped his oldest sisters makeup into the bedrooms hot-air vent.

_____   _____

8. The cats babies are under my chair again; I cant find a way to keep her from bringing them near me.

_____   _____

9. Because of a family feud, Julie wasnt invited to a barbecue at her only cousins house.

_____   _____

10. Phyllis grade was the highest in the class, and Kevins grade was the lowest.

_____   _____

Review Test 2

Make the following words possessive and then use at least five of them in a not-so-serious paragraph that tells a story. In addition, use at least three contractions in the paragraph.

detective	restaurant	Angelo	student
Phoenix	sister	children	oak tree
skunk	Jay Leno	boss	Oprah Winfrey
customer	dentist	police car	yesterday
instructor	everyone	mob	Chicago

36

Quotation Marks

Introductory Activity

Read the following scene and underline all the words enclosed within quotation marks. Your instructor may also have you dramatize the scene, with one person reading the narration and two persons acting the two speaking parts—the young man and the old woman. The two speakers should imagine the scene as part of a stage play and try to make their words seem as real and true-to-life as possible.

An old woman in a Rolls-Royce was preparing to back into a parking space. Suddenly a small sports car appeared and pulled into the space. "That's what you can do when you're young and fast," the young man in the car yelled to the old woman. As he strolled away, laughing, he heard a terrible crunching sound. "What's that noise?" he said. Turning around, he saw the old woman backing repeatedly into his small car and crushing it. "You can't do that, old lady!" he yelled.

"What do you mean, I can't?" she chuckled, as metal grated against metal. "This is what you can do when you're old and rich."

1. On the basis of that passage, what is the purpose of quotation marks?

    _____

2. Do commas and periods that come after a quotation go inside or outside the quotation marks?

    _____

See Appendix A for answers.

The two main uses of quotation marks are

1. To set off the exact words of a speaker or a writer
2. To set off the titles of short works

Each use is explained on the pages that follow.

Quotation Marks to Set Off Exact Words of a Speaker or Writer

Use quotation marks when you want to show the exact words of a speaker or a writer.

"Say something tender to me," whispered Lola to Tony.

(Quotation marks set off the exact words that Lola spoke to Tony.)

Mark Twain once wrote, "The more I know about human beings, the more I like my dog."

(Quotation marks set off the exact words that Mark Twain wrote.)

"The only dumb question," the instructor said, "is the one you don't ask."

(Two pairs of quotation marks are used to enclose the instructor's exact words.)

Sharon complained, "I worked so hard on this paper. I spent two days getting information in the library and online and two days writing it. Guess what grade I got on it?"

(Note that the end quotation marks do not come until the end of Sharon's speech. Place quotation marks before the first quoted word of a speech and after the last quoted word. As long as no interruption occurs in the speech, do not use quotation marks for each new sentence.)

Complete the following statements explaining how capital letters, commas, and periods are used in quotations. Refer to the four examples as guides.

> **HINT:** In the four examples above, notice that a comma sets off the quoted part from the rest of the sentence. Also observe that commas and periods at the end of a quotation always go *inside* quotation marks.

1. Every quotation begins with a _____ letter.
2. When a quotation is split (as in the sentence above about dumb questions), the second part does not begin with a capital letter unless it is a _____ sentence.

3. _____ are used to separate the quoted part of a sentence from the rest of the sentence.

4. Commas and periods that come at the end of a quotation should go _____ the quotation marks.

The answers are *capital, new, Commas,* and *inside.*

Place quotation marks around the exact words of a speaker or writer in the sentences that follow.

1. The health-food store clerk said, Sucking on zinc lozenges can help you get over a cold.

2. How are your grades in French? my father asked.

3. An epitaph on a tombstone in Georgia reads, I told you I was sick!

4. Dave said, Let's walk faster. I think the game has already started.

5. Mark Twain once said, The man who doesn't read good books has no advantage over the man who can't.

6. The more things you read, the more things you will know, said Dr. Seuss. The more that you learn, the more places you'll go.

7. It's extremely dangerous to mix alcohol and pills, Dr. Wilson reminded us. The combination could kill you.

8. According to Nelson Mandela, Education is the great engine of personal development.

9. Be careful not to touch the fence, the guard warned. It's electrified.

10. If you judge people, said Mother Teresa, you have no time to love them.

After you complete each part of the following activity, go over answers with a partner.

1. Write a sentence in which you quote a favorite expression of someone you know. Identify the relationship of the person to you.

EXAMPLE

My father often said, "When one door closes, another opens."

_____

_____

_____

_____

_____

2. Write a quotation that contains the words *Tony asked Lola.* Write a second quotation that includes the words *Lola replied.*

_____

_____

_____

_____

_____

_____

3. Copy a sentence or two that interest you from a book or magazine. Identify the title and author of the work.

EXAMPLE

In Night Shift, Stephen King writes, "I don't like to sleep with one
leg sticking out. Because if a cool hand ever reached out from
under the bed and grasped my ankle, I might scream."

_____

_____

_____

Indirect Quotations

An *indirect quotation* is a rewording of someone else's comments, rather than a word-for-word direct quotation. The word *that* often signals an indirect quotation. Quotation marks are *not* used with indirect quotations.

Direct Quotation	Indirect Quotation
Fred said, "The distributor cap on my car is cracked." (Fred's exact spoken words are given, so quotation marks are used.)	Fred said that the distributor cap on his car was cracked. (We learn Fred's words indirectly, so no quotation marks are used.)
Sally's note to Jay read, "I'll be working late. Don't wait up for me." (The exact words that Sally wrote in the note are given, so quotation marks are used.)	Sally left a note for Jay saying she would be working late and he should not wait up for her. (We learn Sally's words indirectly, so no quotation marks are used.)

Activity

3

Rewrite the following sentences, changing words as necessary to convert the sentences into direct quotations. The first one is done for you as an example.

1. The instructor told everyone to take out a pen and sheet of paper.

    The instructor said, "Take out a pen and sheet of paper."

2. A student in the front row asked if this was a test.

    _____

3. The instructor replied that it was more of a pop quiz.

    _____

4. She claimed that anyone who had completed last night's homework would do well.

    _____

5. Another student responded that this would be easy for him.

    _____

Quotation Marks to Set Off Titles of Short Works

Titles of short works are usually set off by quotation marks. Titles of long works are underlined or put in italics. Use quotation marks around titles of short works, such as articles that appear in books, newspapers, journals, or magazines; chapters in a book; short stories; short poems; and songs. On the other hand, underline or place in italics the titles of books, magazines, newspapers, journals, plays, movies, record albums, and television shows.

Quotation Marks	Italics (or Underlining)
the chapter "So You Want War"	in the book *American Lion*
the article "Getting a Fix on Repairs"	in the newspaper the *New York Times*
the article "The Myelin Brake"	in the magazine *Science*
the essay "Lifting the Veil"	in the book *Inventing the Truth*
the story "The Night the Bed Fell"	in the book *A Thurber Carnival*
the poem "Easter, 1916"	in the book *The Yeats Reader*
the song "Bold as Love"	in the album *Continuum*
	the television show *The Daily Show*
	the movie *Gone with the Wind*

> **TIP:** In printed works, titles of books, newspapers, and so on, are always set off by italics—slanted type that looks *like this*—instead of being underlined.

Use quotation marks or underline (or italicize) as needed.

1. Whenever Gina sees the movie The Sound of Music, the song near the end, Climb Every Mountain, makes her cry.

2. Discover magazine contains an article entitled Lost Cities of the Amazon.

3. I printed out an article titled Too Much Homework? from the online version of Time to use in my sociology report.

4. Tiffany's favorite movie is Raiders of the Lost Ark, and her favorite television show is CSI: Miami.

5. Our instructor gave us a week to buy the textbook titled Personal Finance and to read the first chapter, Work and Income.

6. Every holiday season, our family watches the movie A Christmas Carol on television.

7. Looking around to make sure no one he knew saw him, Bob bought the newest National Enquirer in order to read the story called Man Explodes on Operating Table.

8. Edgar Allan Poe's short story The Murders in the Rue Morgue and his poem The Raven are in a paperback titled Great Tales and Poems of Edgar Allan Poe.

9. After Pablo bought a copy of Time magazine, he read a story entitled Stem Cell Progress and then looked for a review of the movie Avatar.

10. The night before his exam, he discovered with horror that the chapter Becoming Mature was missing from Childhood and Adolescence, the psychology text that he had bought secondhand.

Activity

4

Other Uses of Quotation Marks

1. Quotation marks are used to set off special words or phrases from the rest of a sentence:

   Many people spell the words "a lot" as *one* word, "alot," instead of correctly spelling them as two words.

   I have trouble telling the difference between "their" and "there."

> **TIP:** In printed works, *italics* are often used to set off special words or phrases. That is usually done in this book, for example.

2. Single quotation marks are used to mark off a quotation within a quotation.

   The instructor said, "Know the chapter titled 'Status Symbols' in *Adolescent Development* if you expect to pass the test."

   Susan said, "One of my favorite Mae West lines is 'I used to be Snow White, but I drifted.' "

Review Test 1

Insert quotation marks or underlining where needed in the sentences that follow.

1. Haven't you ever eaten the fruit of this tree? Eve asked Adam.

2. When her car started on the first try, Jamie said, I'm going to marry that new mechanic.

3. Take all you want, read the sign above the cafeteria salad bar, but please eat all you take.

4. After scrawling formulas all over the board with lightning speed, my math instructor was fond of asking, Any questions now?

5. Move that heap! the truck driver yelled. I'm trying to make a living here.

6. I did a summary of an article titled Aspirin and Heart Attacks in the latest issue of *Time*.

7. Writer's block is something that happens to everyone at times, the instructor explained. You simply have to keep writing to break out of it.

8. A passenger in the car ahead of Clyde threw food wrappers and empty cups out the window. That man, said Clyde to his son, is a human pig.

9. If you are working during the day, said the counselor, the best way to start college is with a night course or two.

10. I asked the professor if she would extend the research paper's deadline. Why? Do you have a heavy course load this semester? she inquired. No, I said, I'm just the world's greatest procrastinator!

Review Test 2

Look at the comic strip below and write a full description that will enable people who have not read the comic strip to visualize it clearly and appreciate its humor. Describe the setting and action in each panel, and enclose the words of the speakers in quotation marks.

© BABY BLUES PARTNERSHIP. KING FEATURES SYNDICATE

37

Commas

Commas often (though not always) signal a minor break, or pause, in a sentence. Each of the six pairs of sentences below illustrates one of the six main uses of the comma. Read each pair of sentences aloud and place a comma wherever you feel a slight pause occurs.

1. a. Frank's interests are Maria television and sports.

   b. My mother put her feet up sipped some iced tea and opened the newspaper.

2. a. Athough they are tiny insects ants are among the strongest creatures on Earth.

   b. To remove the cap of the aspirin bottle you must first press down on it.

3. a. Kitty Litter and Dredge Rivers Hollywood's leading romantic stars have made several movies together.

   b. Sarah who is my next-door neighbor just entered the hospital with an intestinal infection.

4. a. The wedding was scheduled for four o'clock but the bride changed her mind at two.

   b. Verna took three coffee breaks before lunch and then she went on a two-hour lunch break.

5. a. Lola's mother asked her "What time do you expect to get home?"

   b. "Don't bend over to pet the dog" I warned "or he'll bite you."

6. a. Roy ate seventeen hamburgers on July 29 2007 and lived to tell about it.

   b. Roy lives at 817 Cresson Street Detroit Michigan.

See Appendix A for answers.

Six Main Uses of the Comma

Commas are used mainly as follows:

1. To separate items in a series
2. To set off introductory material
3. Before and after words that interrupt the flow of thought in a sentence
4. Before two complete thoughts connected by *and, but, for, or, nor, so, yet*
5. To set off a direct quotation from the rest of a sentence
6. For certain everyday material

You may find it helpful to remember that the comma often marks a slight pause, or break, in a sentence. Read aloud the sentence examples given for each use, and listen for the minor pauses, or breaks, that are signaled by commas.

1 Comma between Items in a Series

Use commas to separate items in a series.

Do you drink tea with milk, lemon, or honey?

Today the dishwasher stopped working, the garbage bag split, and the refrigerator turned into a freezer.

The talk shows enraged him so much he did not know whether to laugh, cry, or throw up.

Reiko awoke from a restless, nightmare-filled sleep.

a. The final comma in a series is optional, but it is often used.

b. A comma is used between two descriptive words in a series only if *and* inserted between the words sounds natural. You could say:

Reiko awoke from a restless *and* nightmare-filled sleep.

But notice in the following sentence that the descriptive words do not sound natural when *and* is inserted between them. In such cases, no comma is used.

Wanda drove a shiny blue Corvette. (A shiny *and* blue Corvette doesn't sound right, so no comma is used.)

Place commas between items in a series.

1. Superman believes in truth justice and the American way.

2. The committee voted to donate $300 to the scholarship fund to reschedule the January meeting to book a band for the spring dance and to invite Professor Duncan to lecture on animal psychology in March.

Activity

1

3. Jovan had lived in three South American cities: Lima Santiago and Buenos Aires.

4. Baggy threadbare jeans feel more comfortable than pajamas to me.

5. Carmen grabbed a tiny towel bolted out of the bathroom and ran toward the ringing phone.

2 Comma after Introductory Material

Use a comma to set off introductory material.

> After punching the alarm clock with his fist, Bill turned over and went back to sleep.
>
> Looking up at the sky, I saw a man who was flying faster than a speeding bullet.
>
> Holding a baited trap, Clyde cautiously approached the gigantic mousehole.
>
> In addition, he held a broom in his hand.
>
> Also, he wore a football helmet in case a creature should leap out at his head.

a. If the introductory material is brief, the comma is sometimes omitted. In the activities here, you should use the comma.

b. A comma is also used to set off extra material at the end of a sentence. Here are two sentences where this comma rule applies:

> A sudden breeze shot through the windows, driving the stuffiness out of the room.
>
> I love to cook and eat Italian food, especially eggplant rollatini and lasagna.

Activity

2

Working with a partner, place commas after introductory material.

1. After the Civil War my ancestor opened a grocery store in Indianapolis.

2. Feeling brave and silly at the same time Tony volunteered to go onstage and help the magician.

3. While I was eating my tuna sandwich the cats circled my chair like hungry sharks.

4. Because the Antonelli children grew up near the sea they learned to swim when they were young. Even though the water is still very cold in early March the family celebrates the first day of spring with a quick dip!

5. At first putting extra hot pepper flakes on the pizza seemed like a good idea. However I felt otherwise when flames seemed about to shoot out of my mouth.

3 Comma around Words Interrupting the Flow of Thought

Use commas before and after words or phrases that interrupt the flow of thought in a sentence.

My brother, a sports nut, owns over five thousand baseball cards.

That reality show, at long last, has been canceled.

The children used the old Buick, rusted from disuse, as a backyard clubhouse.

Usually you can "hear" words that interrupt the flow of thought in a sentence. However, if you are not sure that certain words are interrupters, remove them from the sentence. If it still makes sense without the words, you know that the words are interrupters and the information they give is nonessential. Such nonessential information is set off with commas. In the sentence

Dody Thompson, who lives next door, won the javelin-throwing competition.

the words *who lives next door* are extra information, not needed to identify the subject of the sentence, *Dody Thompson.* Put commas around such nonessential information. On the other hand, in the sentence

The woman who lives next door won the javelin-throwing competition.

the words *who lives next door* supply essential information—information needed for us to identify the woman being spoken of. If the words were removed from the sentence, we would no longer know who won the competition. Commas are *not* used around such essential information.

Here is another example:

Wilson Hall, which the tornado destroyed, was ninety years old.

Here the words *which the tornado destroyed* are extra information, not needed to identify the subject of the sentence, *Wilson Hall.* Commas go around such nonessential information. On the other hand, in the sentence

The building that the tornado destroyed was ninety years old.

the words *that the tornado destroyed* are needed to identify the building. Commas are *not* used around such essential information.

As noted above, however, most of the time you will be able to "hear" words that interrupt the flow of thought in a sentence, and you will not have to think about whether the words are essential or nonessential.

Use commas to set off interrupting words.

1. During Dan's teenage years when he lived on Long Island Dan often went crabbing in the Great South Bay.

2. Dracula who had a way with women is Tony's favorite movie hero. He feels that the Wolfman on the other hand showed no class in wooing women.

3. Driving from Minneapolis to Chicago especially during a heavy snowstorm can be unnerving.

4. Mowing the grass especially when it is six inches high is my least favorite job.

5. My cousin Lucille who is wearing the black dress with the white pearls looks very stylish this evening.

4 Comma between Complete Thoughts

Use a comma between two complete thoughts connected by *and, but, for, or, nor, so, yet.*

> The wedding was scheduled for four o'clock, but the bride changed her mind at two.

> We could always tell when our instructor felt disorganized, for his shirt would not be tucked in.

> Rich has to work on Monday nights, so he always remembers to record the TV football game.

a. The comma is optional when the complete thoughts are short.

> Grace has a headache and Mark has a fever.

> Her soda was watery but she drank it anyway.

> The day was overcast so they didn't go swimming.

b. Be careful not to use a comma in sentences having *one* subject and a *double* verb. The comma is used only in sentences made up of two complete thoughts (two subjects and two verbs). In the following sentence, there is only one subject (*Kevin*) with a double verb (*will go* and *forget*). Therefore, no comma is needed:

> Kevin will go to a party tonight and forget all about tomorrow's exam.

Likewise, the following sentence has only one subject (*Rita*) and a double verb (*was* and *will work*); therefore, no comma is needed:

> Rita was a waitress at the Red Lobster last summer and probably will work there this summer.

In the following sentences, place a comma before each joining word that connects two complete thoughts (two subject-verb combinations). Do *not* place a comma within the sentences that have only one subject and a double verb; label these as "correct."

Activity

4

1. The oranges in the refrigerator were covered with blue mold and the potatoes in the cupboard felt like sponges.

2. All the pants in the shop were on sale but not a single pair was my size.

3. Martha often window-shops in the malls for hours and comes home without buying anything.

4. Martin Fizz never spent much money in bars because he ordered only carbonated drinks.

5. The whole family searched the yard inch by inch but never found Mom's missing wedding ring.

6. The mayor walked up to the podium, and she delivered the most inspiring speech of her career.

7. No one volunteered to read his or her paper out loud so the instructor called on Amber.

8. The aliens in the science fiction film visited our planet in peace but we greeted them with violence.

9. I felt like shouting at the gang of boys but didn't dare open my mouth.

10. Lenny claims that he wants to succeed in college but he has missed classes all semester.

5 Comma with Direct Quotations

Use a comma to set off a direct quotation from the rest of a sentence.

His father shouted, "Why don't you go out and get a job?"

"Our modern world has lost a sense of the sacredness of life," the speaker said.

"No," said Celia to Jerry. "I won't write your paper for you."

"Can anyone remember," wrote Emerson, "when the times were not hard and money not scarce?"

> **TIP:** Commas and periods at the end of a quotation go inside quotation marks. See also page 537.

Use commas to set off quotations from the rest of the sentence.

1. Su Lin turned to her husband and said "The man may be the head of the family, but the woman is the neck that turns the head."

2. My partner on the dance floor said "Don't be so stiff. You look as if you swallowed an umbrella."

3. The question on the anatomy test read "What human organ grows faster than any other, never stops growing, and always remains the same size?"

4. The student behind me whispered "The skin."

5. "Everyone is wise" says my eighty-year-old grandmother "until he speaks."

6 Comma with Everyday Material

Use a comma with certain everyday material.

Persons Spoken To

Tina, go to bed if you're not feeling well.

Sara, where did you put my shoes?

Are you coming with us, Owen?

Dates

March 4, 2007, is when Martha buried her third husband.

Addresses

Tony's grandparents live at 183 Roxborough Avenue, Cleveland, Ohio 44112.

> TIP: No comma is used to mark off the zip code.

Openings and Closings of Letters

Dear Santa,

Dear Ben,

Sincerely yours,

Truly yours,

> TIP: In formal letters, a colon is used after the opening: Dear Sir: *or* Dear Madam:

Numbers

The dishonest dealer turned the used car's odometer from 98,170 miles to 39,170 miles.

Place commas where needed. Compare your answers with a partner's.

1. I expected you to set a better example for the others Mike.
2. Liz with your help I passed the test.
3. The movie stars Kitty Litter and Dredge Rivers were married on September 12 2006 and lived at 3865 Sunset Boulevard Los Angeles California for one month.
4. They received 75000 congratulatory fan letters and were given movie contracts worth $3000000 in the first week of their marriage.
5. Kitty left Dredge on October 12 2006 and ran off with their marriage counselor.

Review Test 1

Insert commas where needed. In the space provided below each sentence, summarize briefly the rule that explains the use of the comma or commas.

1. The bookstore specializes in science fiction biography and mysteries.

   _____

2. After giving her lecture on stem cell research Dr. Zulak entertained questions from the audience.

   _____

3. "When will someone invent a cell phone" Lola asked "that will ring only at convenient moments?"

   _____

4. Upon the death of Queen Elizabeth I of England in 1603 James VI of Scotland became James I of England.

   _____

5. I think Roger that you had better ask someone else for your $2500 loan.

   _____

6. Hot dogs are the most common cause of choking deaths in children for a bite-size piece can easily plug up a toddler's throat.

   _____

7. Tax forms though shortened and revised every year never seem to get any simpler.

   _____

8. Sandra may decide to go to college full-time or she may start by enrolling in a couple of evening courses.

_____

9. I remember that with the terrible cruelty of children we used to make fun of the shy girl who lived on our street.

_____

10. Despite having grown up in poverty Clarence Thomas rose to become a justice of the United States Supreme Court.

_____

Review Test 2

Insert commas where needed.

1. My mother who makes the best lasagna in the world was born in Sicily.
2. "Although men have more upper-body strength" said the lecturer "women are more resistant to fatigue."
3. Many people who had had kidney transplants needed to take immune-system-suppressing drugs but that has become less common because of new medical technology.
4. Janice attended class for four hours worked at the hospital for three hours and studied at home for two hours.
5. The old soldier a member of the army that entered Berlin at the end of World War II saluted the audience as they applauded him.
6. George and Ida sat down to watch the football game with crackers sharp cheese salty pretzels and two frosty bottles of beer.
7. Although I knew exactly what was happening the solar eclipse gave me a strong feeling of anxiety.
8. The company agreed to raise a senior bus driver's salary to $42000 by January 1 2009.
9. Even though King Kong was holding her at the very top of the Empire State Building Fay Wray kept yelling at him "Let me go!"
10. Navel oranges which Margery as a little girl called belly-button oranges are her favorite fruit.

Review Test 3

On separate paper, write six sentences, each demonstrating one of the six main comma rules.

Other Punctuation Marks

38

Introductory Activity

Each of the sentences below needs one of the following punctuation marks:

;   —   -   ()   :

See if you can insert the correct mark in each sentence. Each mark should be used once.

1. The following holiday plants are poisonous and should be kept away from children and pets holly, mistletoe, and poinsettias.

2. The freeze dried remains of Annie's canary were in the clear bottle on her bookcase.

3. William Shakespeare 1564–1616 married a woman eight years his senior when he was eighteen.

4. Grooming in space is more difficult than on Earth no matter how much astronauts comb their hair, for instance, it still tends to float loosely around their heads.

5. I opened the front door, and our cat walked in proudly with a live bunny hanging from his mouth.

See Appendix A for answers.

Colon (:)

Use the colon at the end of a complete statement to introduce a list, a long quotation, or an explanation.

List

The following were my worst jobs: truck loader in an apple plant, assembler in a battery factory, and attendant in a state mental hospital.

Long Quotation

Thoreau explains in *Walden:* "I went to the woods because I wished to live deliberately, to front only the essential facts of life, and see if I could not learn what it had to teach, and not, when I came to die, discover that I had not lived."

Explanation

There are two softball leagues in our town: the fast-pitch league and the lob-pitch league.

<table>
<tr><td>**Activity**
1</td><td>Place colons where needed.

1. Three things are necessary to grow tasty tomatoes sun, rain, and patience.
2. All the signs of a coming storm were present dark skies, ominous clouds, and a rapid drop in temperature.
3. In his book *Illiterate America,* Jonathan Kozol gives startling information "Twenty-five million American adults cannot read the poison warnings on a can of pesticide, a letter from their child's teacher, or the front page of a daily paper. An additional 35 million read only at a level which is less than equal to the full survival needs of our society. Together, these 60 million people represent more than one-third of the entire adult population."</td></tr>
</table>

Semicolon (;)

The main use of the semicolon is to mark a break between two complete thoughts, as explained on page 449. Another use of the semicolon is to mark off items in a series when the items themselves contain commas. Here are some examples:

Winning prizes at the national flower show were Roberta Collins, Alabama, azaleas; Sally Hunt, Kentucky, roses; and James Weber, California, Shasta daisies.

The following books must be read for the course: *The Color Purple,* by Alice Walker; *In Our Time,* by Ernest Hemingway; and *Man's Search for Meaning,* by Victor Frankl.

Working with a partner, place semicolons where needed.

Activity 2

1. The specials at the restaurant today are eggplant Parmesan, for $16.95 black beans and rice, for $9.95 and chicken potpie, for $11.95.

2. The view of Washington's Mount Rainier was spectacular the peak was snow covered, but the lower half was covered with green forests.

3. Lola's favorite old movies are *To Catch a Thief,* starring Cary Grant and Grace Kelly *Animal Crackers,* a Marx Brothers comedy and *The Wizard of Oz,* with Judy Garland.

Dash (—)

A dash signals a pause longer than a comma but not as complete as a period. Use a dash to set off words for dramatic effect.

I didn't go out with him a second time—once was more than enough.

Some of you—I won't mention you by name—cheated on the test.

It was so windy that the VW passed him on the highway—overhead.

TIP

a. The dash can be formed on a keyboard by striking the hyphen twice (--). In handwriting, the dash is as long as two letters would be.
b. Be careful not to overuse dashes.

Place dashes where needed.

Activity 3

1. The neighbors threw loud parties that lasted long into the night often, in fact, until 2:00 or 3:00 A.M.

2. Three makes of luxury cars a Lexus, a Cadillac, and a Lincoln were the prizes in the church raffle.

3. The package finally arrived badly damaged.

Hyphen (-)

1. Use a hyphen with two or more words that act as a single unit describing a noun.

> When Jeff removed his mud-covered boots, he discovered a thumb-size hole in his sock.

> I both admire and envy her well-rounded personality.

> When the man removed his blue-tinted shades, Lonnell saw the spaced-out look in his eyes.

2. Use a hyphen to divide a word at the end of a line of writing. When you need to divide a word at the end of a line, divide it between syllables. Use your dictionary to be sure of correct syllable divisions (see also page 562).

> When Josh lifted the hood of his car, he realized one of the radiator hoses had broken.

TIP

a. Do not divide words of one syllable.

b. Do not divide a word if you can avoid doing so.

Activity

4

Place hyphens where needed.

1. A lily covered pond and a jasmine scented garden greeted us as we walked into the museum's atrium.

2. When Gwen turned on the porch light, ten legged creatures scurried every where over the crumb filled floor.

3. Will had ninety two dollars in his pocket when he left for the supermarket, and he had twenty two dollars when he got back.

Parentheses ( )

Parentheses are used to set off extra or incidental information from the rest of a sentence.

> The section of that book on the medical dangers of abortion (pages 125 to 140) is outdated.

> Yesterday at Hamburger House (my favorite place to eat), the french-fry cook asked me to go out with him.

> TIP: Do not use parentheses too often in your writing.

Add parentheses where needed.

1. Certain sections of the novel especially Chapter 5 made my heart race with suspense.
2. Leonardo da Vinci best known as the painter of the *Mona Lisa* drew plans for many inventions built several centuries after his death.
3. Did you know that Mother Teresa the nun who spent most of her life serving the poor in India was born in Macedonia?

Review Test

At the appropriate spot, place the punctuation mark shown in the margin.

; 1. Gdansk is a major Polish port it is located on a branch of the Vistula River.

— 2. There's the idiot I'd know him anywhere who dumped trash on our front lawn.

- 3. One quarter of our population people over 65 years old are eligible to get free flu shots thorough Medicare.

: 4. Ben Franklin said "If a man empties his purse into his head, no man can take it away from him. An investment in knowledge always pays the best interest."

( ) 5. One-fifth of our textbook pages 285–349 consists of footnotes and a bibliography.

SECTION 4

WORD USE

Can you find the error on the candy heart shown here? Which chapter in this section do you think might cover such an error?

39

Using the Dictionary

The dictionary is a valuable tool. To help you use it, this chapter explains essential information about dictionaries and the information they provide.

www.mhhe.com/langan

Owning Your Own Dictionaries

You can benefit greatly by owning two dictionaries. First, you should own a paperback dictionary that you can carry with you. Any of the following would be an excellent choice:

The American Heritage Dictionary, Paperback Edition

The Random House Webster's Dictionary, Paperback Edition

The Merriam-Webster Dictionary, Paperback Edition

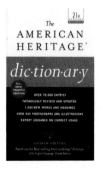
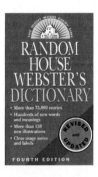
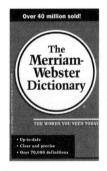

Second, you should own a desk-size, hardcover dictionary that you keep in the room where you study. All the dictionaries shown above come in hardbound versions.

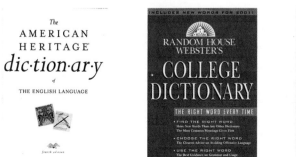
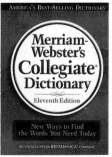

Hardbound dictionaries contain a good deal more information than the paper-back editions. For instance, a desk-size dictionary defines far more words than a paperback dictionary. And there are more definitions per word, as well. Although desk-size dictionaries cost more, they are worth the investment, because they are valuable study aids.

Dictionaries are often updated to reflect changes that occur in the language. New words come into use, and old words take on new meanings. So you should not use a dictionary that has been lying around the house for a number of years. Instead, buy yourself a new dictionary. It is easily among the best investments you will ever make.

Dictionaries on Your Computer

If you use a computer, you may have two additional ways to look up a word: online dictionaries and a dictionary that may come with your computer software.

Online Dictionaries

If your computer is connected to the Internet, you may find it easy to check words online. Here are three sites with online dictionaries:

www.merriam-webster.com

www.dictionary.com

www.yourdictionary.com

For example, if you go online to www.merriam-webster.com and type in "murder," you may see the page shown in the illustration.

By permission. From *Merriam-Webster Online Dictionary,* 2007 by Merriam-Webster, Incorporated (www.Merriam-Webster.com)

Notice the speaker icon next to the word *murder.* If you click on this icon, the word will be pronounced for you.

Often, you will also get information on *synonyms* (words with meanings similar to those of the word you have looked up) and *antonyms* (words with meanings opposite to those of the word you have looked up).

Software Dictionaries

Some word-processing programs come with a built-in dictionary. For example, if you use Microsoft Word on a Macintosh, click "Tools" and then choose "Dictionary."

Understanding a Dictionary Entry

Look at the information provided for the word *murder* in the following entry from *Random House Webster's College Dictionary:*

Spelling and syllabication

Pronunciation

Parts of speech

mur•der (mûr′dər), *n., v.,*-**dered. –der•ing. —***n.* **1.** the unlawful killing of a person, esp. when done with deliberation or premeditation or occurring during the commission of another serious crime **(first-degree murder)** or with intent but without deliberation or premeditation **(second-degree murder). 2.** something injurious, immoral, or otherwise censurable: *to get away with murder.* **3.** something extremely difficult or unpleasant: *That exam was murder!* —*v.t.* **4.** to kill by an act constituting murder. **5.** to kill or slaughter barbarously. **6.** to spoil or mar through incompetence: *The singer murdered the aria.* **7.** *Informal.* to defeat thoroughly.

Meanings

Random House Webster's College Dictionary, 2000. Published by the Random House Information Group

Spelling

The first bit of information, in the boldface (heavy-type) entry itself, is the spelling of *murder.* You probably already know the spelling of *murder,* but if you didn't, you could find it by pronouncing the syllables in the word carefully and then looking it up in the dictionary.

Use your dictionary to correct the spelling of the following words:

compatable _____   silable _____

althogh _____   troble _____

highschool _____   untill _____

Activity

1

embelish _____	fancyer _____
systimatise _____	prepostrous _____
alot _____	comotion _____
attenshun _____	Vasaline _____
wierd _____	fatel _____
laffed _____	busines _____
alright _____	jenocide _____
fony _____	poluted _____
kriterion _____	attornies _____
hetirosexual _____	chalange _____

Syllabication

The second bit of information that the dictionary gives, also in the boldface entry, is the syllabication of *murder.* Note that a dot separates the syllables.

Use your dictionary to mark the syllable divisions in the following words. Also indicate how many syllables are in each word.

j i t t e r   (_____ syllables)

m o t i v a t e   (_____ syllables)

o r a n g u t a n   (_____ syllables)

i n c o n t r o v e r t i b l e   (_____ syllables)

Noting syllable divisions will enable you to *hyphenate* a word: divide it at the end of one line of writing and complete it at the beginning of the next line. You can correctly hyphenate a word only at a syllable division, and you may have to check your dictionary to make sure of the syllable divisions.

Pronunciation

The third bit of information in the dictionary entry is the pronunciation of *murder:* (mûr′dər). You already know how to pronounce *murder,* but if you didn't, the information within the parentheses would serve as your guide. Use your dictionary to complete the following exercises that relate to pronunciation.

Vowel Sounds You will probably use the pronunciation key in your dictionary mainly as a guide to pronouncing vowel sounds (vowels are the letters *a, e, i, o,* and *u*). Here is a part of the pronunciation key in the *Random House Webster's College Dictionary:*

    a **bat**   ā **say**   e **set**   ē **bee**   i **big**

The key tells you, for example, that the sound of the short *a* is like the *a* in *bat,* the sound of the long *a* is like the *a* in *say,* and the sound of the short *e* is like the *e* in *set.*

Now look at the pronunciation key in your own dictionary. The key is probably located in the front of the dictionary or at the bottom of alternate pages. What common word in the key tells you how to pronounce each of the following sounds?

ī _____   ŭ _____

ŏ _____   ŏŏ _____

ō _____   o̅o̅ _____

(Note that a long vowel always has the sound of its own name.)

The Schwa (ə) The symbol ə looks like an upside-down *e*. It is called a *schwa,* and it stands for the unaccented sound in such words as *ago, item, easily, gallop,* and *circus.* More approximately, it stands for the sound *uh*—like the *uh* that speakers sometimes make when they hesitate. Perhaps it would help to remember that *uh,* as well as ə, could be used to represent the schwa sound.

Here are some of the many words in which the schwa sound appears: *imitation (im-uh-tā′shuhn* or *im-ə-tā′shən); elevate (el′uh-vāt* or *el′ə-vāt); horizon (huh-rī′zuhn* or *hə-rī′zən).* Open your dictionary to any page, and you will almost surely be able to find three words that make use of the schwa in the pronunciation in parentheses after the main entry.

In the spaces below, write three words that make use of the schwa, and their pronunciations.

1. _____   (_____)

2. _____   (_____)

3. _____   (_____)

Accent Marks Some words contain both a primary accent, shown by a heavy stroke (′), and a secondary accent, shown by a lighter stroke (′). For example, in the word *controversy (kon′trə vûr′se),* the stress, or accent, goes chiefly on the first syllable *(kon′),* and, to a lesser extent, on the third syllable *(vûr′).*

Use your dictionary to add stress marks to the following words:

preclude (pri klo̅o̅d)

atrophy (at rə f ē)

inveigle (in vā gəl)

ubiquitous (yo̅o̅ bik wi təs)

prognosticate (prog nos ti kāt)

2

Full Pronunciation Use your dictionary to write the full pronunciation (the information given in parentheses) for each of the following words.

1. migration _____
2. diatribe _____
3. inheritance _____
4. panacea _____
5. esophagus _____
6. independence _____
7. chronological _____
8. vicarious _____
9. quiescent _____
10. parsimony _____
11. combustible _____
12. antipathy _____
13. capricious _____
14. schizophrenia _____
15. seismological _____
16. internecine _____
17. amalgamate _____
18. quixotic _____
19. laissez-faire _____
20. antidisestablishmentarianism (This word is probably not in a paperback dictionary, but if you can say *establish* and if you break the rest of the word into individual syllables, you should be able to pronounce it.)

Now practice pronouncing each word. Use the pronunciation key in your dictionary as an aid to sounding out each syllable. Do *not* try to pronounce a word all at once; instead, work on mastering *one syllable at a time*. When you can pronounce each of the syllables in a word successfully, then say them in sequence, add the accents, and pronounce the entire word.

Parts of Speech

The next bit of information that the dictionary gives about *murder* is *n.* This abbreviation means that the meanings of *murder* as a noun will follow.

Use your dictionary if necessary to fill in the meanings of the following abbreviations:

v. = _____   sing. = _____
adj. = _____   pl. = _____

Principal Parts of Irregular Verbs

Murder is a regular verb and forms its principal parts by adding *-ed* or *-ing* to the stem of the verb. When a verb is irregular, the dictionary lists its principal parts. For example, with *give* the present tense comes first (the entry itself, *give*).

Next comes the past tense (*gave*), and then the past participle (*given*)—the form of the verb used with such helping words as *have, had,* and *was.* Then comes the present participle (*giving*)—the *-ing* form of the verb.

Look up the principal parts of the following irregular verbs and write them in the spaces provided. The first one has been done for you.

Present	Past	Past Participle	Present Participle
tear	*tore*	*torn*	*tearing*
go			
know			
steal			

Plural Forms of Irregular Nouns

The dictionary supplies the plural forms of all irregular nouns. (Regular nouns like *murder* form the plural by adding *-s* or *-es.*) Give the plurals of the following nouns. If two forms are shown, write down both.

analysis _____

dictionary _____

criterion _____

activity _____

thesis _____

Meanings

When a word has more than one meaning, the meanings are numbered in the dictionary, as with the verb *murder.* In many dictionaries, the most common meanings of a word are presented first. The introductory pages of your dictionary will explain the order in which meanings are presented.

Use the sentence context to try to explain the meaning of the underlined word in each of the following sentences. Write your definition in the space provided. Then look up and record the dictionary meaning of the word. Be sure to select the meaning that fits the word as it is used in the sentence.

Activity

3

1. In anthropology class, we studied the <u>indigenous</u> people of New Guinea.

   Your definition: _____

   Dictionary definition: _____

2. On the test, we had to put several historical events into <u>chronological</u> order.

   Your definition: _____

   Dictionary definition: _____

3. The FBI <u>squelched</u> the terrorists' plan to plant a bomb in the White House.

   Your definition: _____

   Dictionary definition: _____

4. One of the <u>cardinal</u> rules in our house was "Respect other people's privacy."

   Your definition: _____

   Dictionary definition: _____

5. A special <u>governor</u> prevents the school bus from traveling more than fifty-five miles an hour.

   Your definition: _____

   Dictionary definition: _____

Usage Labels

As a general rule, use only standard English words in your writing. If a word is not standard English (as is the case, for example, with the fourth meaning of *murder* as a verb—"to defeat thoroughly"), your dictionary will probably give it a usage label like one of the following: *informal, nonstandard, slang, vulgar, obsolete, archaic, rare.*

Look up the following words and record how your dictionary labels them. Remember that a recent hardbound desk dictionary will always be the best source of information about usage.

flunk _____

tough (meaning "unfortunate, too bad") _____

creep (meaning "an annoying person") _____

ain't _____

scam _____

Synonyms

A *synonym* is a word that is close in meaning to another word. Using synonyms helps you avoid unnecessary repetition of the same word in a paper. A paperback dictionary is not likely to give you synonyms for words, but a good desk dictionary or an online dictionary will. You might also want to own a *thesaurus,* a book that lists synonyms and *antonyms* (words approximately opposite in meaning to another word). You can also find a thesaurus online—for example, www .merriam-webster.com will give you access to a thesaurus as well as a dictionary.

Consult a desk dictionary that gives synonyms for the following words, and write the synonyms in the spaces provided.

heavy _____

escape _____

necessary _____

40

Improving Spelling

Poor spelling often results from bad habits developed in early school years. With work, you can correct such habits. If you can write your name without misspelling it, there is no reason why you can't do the same with almost any word in the English language. Following are five steps you can take to improve your spelling.

Step 1: Use the Dictionary

Get into the habit of using the dictionary (see pages 559–567). When you write a paper, allow yourself time to look up the spelling of all those words you are unsure about. Do not overlook the value of this step just because it is such a simple one. By using the dictionary, you can probably make yourself a 95 percent better speller.

Step 2: Keep a Personal Spelling List

Keep a list of words you misspell, and study these words regularly. To do this, create a chart with the headings "Incorrect Spelling," "Correct Spelling," and "Points to Remember." You can do this in a notebook or a computer file. This chart will become a personal spelling list that you can consult regularly.

To master the words on your list, do the following:

1. Write down any hint that will help you remember the spelling of a word. For example, you might want to note that *occasion* is spelled with two *c*'s and one *s,* or that *all right* is two words, not one word.

2. Study a word by looking at it, saying it, and spelling it. You may also want to write out the word one or more times, or "air-write" it with your finger in large, exaggerated motions.

3. When you have trouble spelling a long word, try to break the word into syllables and see whether you can spell each syllable. For example, *inadvertent* can be spelled easily if you can hear and spell in turn its four syllables: *in ad ver tent.* And *consternation* can be spelled easily if you hear and

spell in turn its four syllables: *con ster na tion.* Remember, then: Try to see, hear, and spell long words syllable by syllable.

4. Keep in mind that review and repeated self-testing are the keys to effective learning. When you are learning a series of words, go back after studying each new word and review all the preceding ones.

Step 3: Master Commonly Confused Words

Master the meanings and spellings of the commonly confused words on pages 578–587. Your instructor may assign twenty words at a time for you to study and may give you a series of quizzes until you have mastered the words.

Step 4: Understand Basic Spelling Rules

Explained briefly here are three rules that may improve your spelling. While exceptions sometimes occur, the rules hold true most of the time.

Rule 1: Changing y to i When a word ends in a consonant plus *y,* change *y* to *i* when you add an ending (but keep the y before *-ing*).

try + ed = tried	easy + er = easier
defy + es = defies	carry + ed = carried
ready + ness = readiness	penny + less = penniless

Rule 2: Final Silent e Drop a final *e* before an ending that starts with a vowel (the vowels are *a, e, i, o,* and *u*).

create + ive = creative	believe + able = believable
nerve + ous = nervous	share + ing = sharing

Keep the final *e* before an ending that starts with a consonant.

extreme + ly = extremely	life + less = lifeless
hope + ful = hopeful	excite + ment = excitement

Rule 3: Doubling a Final Consonant Double the final consonant of a word when all three of the following are true:

a. The word is one syllable or is accented on the last syllable.

b. The word ends in a single consonant preceded by a single vowel.

c. The ending you are adding starts with a vowel.

shop + er = shopper   thin   + est = thinnest

equip + ed = equipped   submit + ed = submitted

swim + ing = swimming   drag   + ed = dragged

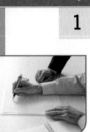

Activity

1

Working with a partner, combine the following words and endings by applying the three rules above.

1. worry   + ed   = _____

2. write   + ing = _____

3. marry   + es   = _____

4. run   + ing = _____

5. terrify + ed   = _____

6. dry   + es   = _____

7. forget + ing = _____

8. care   + ful = _____

9. control + ed   = _____

10. debate + able = _____

Step 5: Study a Basic Word List

Study the spellings of the words in the following list. They are five hundred of the words most often used in English. Your instructor may assign twenty-five or fifty words for you to study at a time and give you a series of quizzes until you have mastered the list.

Five Hundred Basic Words

ability	again	amateur	apply
absent	against	American	approach
accept	agree	among	approve
accident	all right	amount	argue
ache	almost	angry 25	around
across	a lot	animal	arrange
address	already	another	attempt
advertise	also	answer	attention
advice	although	anxious	August
after	always	appetite	automobile

Five Hundred Basic Words *(continued)*

autumn	careful 75	dear	entrance
avenue	careless	death	evening
awful	cereal	December	everything
awkward	certain	decide	examine
back	chair	deed	except
balance	change	dentist	exercise
bargain	charity	deposit	exit
beautiful	cheap	describe	expect 150
because	cheat	did	fact
become 50	cheek	died	factory
been	chicken	different	family
before	chief	dinner	far
begin	children	direction	February
being	choose	discover	few
believe	church	disease	fifteen
between	cigarette	distance	fight
bicycle	citizen	doctor 125	flower
black	city	does	forehead
blue	close	dollar	foreign
board	clothing	don't	forty
borrow	coffee	doubt	forward
bottle	collect	down	found
bottom	college	dozen	fourteen
brake	color	during	Friday
breast	come	each	friend
breathe	comfortable 100	early	from
brilliant	company	earth	gallon
brother	condition	easy	garden
building	conversation	education	general
bulletin	copy	eight	get
bureau	daily	either	good
business	danger	empty	grammar
came	daughter	English	great 175
can't	daybreak	enough	grocery

Five Hundred Basic Words *(continued)*

grow	kindergarten	men	o'clock
guess	kitchen	middle	October
half	knock	might	offer
hammer	knowledge	million	often
hand	labor	minute	old
handkerchief	laid	mistake 250	omit
happy	language	Monday	once
having	last	money	one
head	laugh	month	only
heard	learn	more	operate
heavy	led	morning	opinion
high	left	mother	opportunity
himself	leisure	mountain	optimist
hoarse	length	mouth	original
holiday	lesson 225	much	ought
home	letter	must	ounce
hospital	life	nail	overcoat
house	light	near	pain
however	listen	needle	paper
hundred	little	neither	part
hungry	loaf	never	peace
husband	loneliness	newspaper	pear 300
instead	long	nickel	pencil
intelligence 200	lose	niece	penny
interest	made	night	people
interfere	making	ninety	perfect
interrupt	many	noise	period
into	March	none	person
iron	marry	not	picture
itself	match	nothing	piece
January	matter	November 275	pillow
July	may	now	place
June	measure	number	plain
just	medicine	ocean	please

Five Hundred Basic Words (continued)

pocket	restaurant	state	though
policeman	ribbon	still	thousand
possible	ridiculous	stockings	thread
post office	right 350	straight	three
potato	said	street	through
power	same	strong	Thursday
prescription	sandwich	student	ticket
president	Saturday	studying	time
pretty	say	such	tired
probably	school	suffer	today
promise	scissors	sugar	together 425
psychology	season	suit	tomorrow
public 325	see	summer	tongue
pursue	sentence	Sunday	tonight
put	September	supper	touch
quart	service	sure	toward
quarter	seventeen	sweet	travel
quick	several	take	trouble
quiet	shoes	teach	trousers
quit	should	tear 400	truly
quite	sight	telegram	twelve
quiz	since	telephone	uncle
raise	sister	tenant	under
read	sixteenth	tenth	understand
ready	sleep	than	United States
really	smoke	Thanksgiving	until
reason	soap	that	upon
receive	soldier	theater	used
recognize	something 375	them	usual
refer	sometimes	there	valley
religion	soul	they	value
remember	soup	thing	variety
repeat	south	thirteen	vegetable
resource	stamp	this	very

Five Hundred Basic Words *(continued)*

view		Washington		whether	475	work
villain	450	watch		which		world
visitor		water		while		worth
voice		wear		white		would
vote		weather		whole		writing
wage		Wednesday		whose		written
wagon		week		wife		wrong
waist		weigh		window		year
wait		welcome		winter		yesterday
wake		well		without		yet
walk		went		woman		young
warm		were		wonder		your
warning		what		won't		you're	500

TIP: Two spelling mistakes that students often make are to write *a lot* as one word (*alot*) and to write *all right* as one word (*alright*). Do not write either *a lot* or *all right* as one word.

Vocabulary Development

41

A good vocabulary is a vital part of effective communication. A command of many words will make you a better writer, speaker, listener, and reader. Studies have shown that students with a strong vocabulary, and students who work to improve a limited vocabulary, are more successful in school. And one research study found that *a good vocabulary, more than any other factor, was common to people enjoying successful careers.* This section describes three ways of developing your word power: (1) regular reading, (2) vocabulary wordsheets, and (3) vocabulary study books. You should keep in mind from the start, however, that none of the approaches will help unless you truly decide that vocabulary development is an important goal. Only when you have this attitude can you begin doing the sustained work needed to improve your word power.

www.mhhe.com/langan

Regular Reading

Through reading a good deal, you will learn words by encountering them a number of times in a variety of sentences. Repeated exposure to a word in context will eventually make it a part of your working language.

You should develop the habit of reading a daily newspaper and one or more weekly magazines like *Time, Newsweek,* or even *People,* as well as monthly magazines suited to your interests. In addition, you should try to read some books for pleasure. This may be especially difficult at times when you also have textbook reading to do. Try, however, to redirect a regular half hour to one hour of your recreational time to reading books. Doing so, you may eventually reap the rewards of an improved vocabulary *and* discover that reading can be truly enjoyable. If you would like some recommendations, ask your instructor for a copy of the "List of Interesting Books" in the Instructor's Manual that accompanies this text.

Vocabulary Wordsheets

Vocabulary wordsheets are another means of vocabulary development. Whenever you read, you should mark off words that you want to learn. After you have accumulated a number of words, sit down with a dictionary and look up basic information about each of them. Put this information on a wordsheet like the one shown in Activity 1. Be sure also to write down a sentence in which each word appears. A word is always best learned not in a vacuum but in the context of surrounding words.

Study each word as follows. To begin with, make sure you can correctly pronounce the word and its derivations. (Pages 562–564 explain the dictionary pronunciation key that will help you pronounce each word properly.) Next, study the main meanings of the word until you can say them without looking at them. Finally, spend a moment looking at the example of the word in context. Follow the same process with the second word. Then, after testing yourself on the first and the second words, go on to the third word. After you learn each new word, remember to continue to test yourself on all the words you have studied. Repeated self-testing is a key to effective learning.

Activity	In your reading, locate four words that you would like to master. Enter them in the spaces on the vocabulary wordsheet below and fill in all the needed information. Your instructor may then check your wordsheet and perhaps give you a quick oral quiz on selected words.
1	

You may receive a standing assignment to add five words a week to a wordsheet and to study the words. Note that you can create your own wordsheets using a notebook or a computer file, or your instructor may give you copies of the wordsheet that appears below.

Vocabulary Wordsheet

1. Word: _formidable_   Pronunciation: _(fôr´ mi də bəl)_

     Meanings: _1. feared or dreaded_

     2. extremely difficult

     Other forms of the word: _formidably formidability_

     Use of the word in context: _Several formidable obstacles stand between Matt and his goal._

2. Word: _____ Pronunciation: _____

    Meanings: _____

    _____

    Other forms of the word: _____

    Use of the word in context: _____

3. Word: _____ Pronunciation: _____

    Meanings: _____

    _____

    Other forms of the word: _____

    Use of the word in context: _____

    _____

4. Word: _____ Pronunciation: _____

    Meanings: _____

    _____

    Other forms of the word: _____

    Use of the word in context: _____

    _____

5. Word: _____ Pronunciation: _____

    Meanings: _____

    _____

    Other forms of the word: _____

    Use of the word in context: _____

    _____

Vocabulary Study Books

A third way to increase your word power is to use vocabulary study books. Many vocabulary books and programs are available. The best are those that present words in one or more contexts and then provide several reinforcement activities for each word. These books will help you increase your vocabulary if you work with them on a regular basis.

42

Commonly Confused Words

Introductory Activity

Circle the five words that are misspelled in the following passage. Then see if you can write the correct spellings in the spaces provided.

You're mind and body are not as separate as you might think. Their is a lot of evidence, for instance, that if you believe a placebo (a substance with no medicine) will help you, than it will. One man is said too have recovered rapidly from an advanced case of cancer after only one dose of a drug that he believed was highly effective. Its not clear just how placebos work, but they do show how closely the mind and body are related.

1. _____

2. _____

3. _____

4. _____

5. _____

See Appendix A for answers.

Homonyms

The commonly confused words on the following pages have the same sounds but different meanings and spellings; such words are known as *homonyms*. Complete the activity for each set of homonyms, and check off and study the words that give you trouble. You may want to work in groups of two or three.

www.mhhe.com/langan

all ready   completely prepared
already   previously; before

> We were *all ready* to start the play, but the audience was still being seated.
>
> I have *already* bought the tickets.

Fill in the blanks: I am _____ for the economics examination because I have _____ studied the chapter three times.

brake   stop; the stopping device in a vehicle
break   come apart

> His car bumper has a sticker reading, "I *brake* for animals."
>
> "I am going to *break* up with Bill if he keeps seeing other women," said Rita.

Fill in the blanks: When my car's emergency _____ slipped, the car rolled back and demolished my neighbor's rose garden, which caused a _____ in our good relations with each other.

coarse   rough
course   part of a meal; a school subject; direction; certainly (as in *of course*).

> By the time the waitress served the customers the second *course* of the meal, she was aware of their *coarse* eating habits.

Fill in the blanks: Ted felt that the health instructor's humor was too _____ for his taste and was glad when he finished the _____.

hear   perceive with the ear
here   in this place

> "The salespeople act as though they don't see or *hear* me, even though I've been standing *here* for fifteen minutes," the woman complained.

Fill in the blanks: "Did you _____ about the distinguished visitor who just came into town and is staying _____ at this very hotel?"

hole   an empty spot
whole   entire

"I can't believe I ate the *whole* pizza," moaned Ralph. "I think it's going to make a *hole* in my stomach lining."

Fill in the blanks: The _____ time I was at the party I tried to conceal the _____ I had in my pants.

its   belonging to it
it's   shortened form of *it is* or *it has*

The car blew *its* transmission (the transmission belonging to it, the car).

It's (it has) been raining all week and *it's* (it is) raining now.

Fill in the blanks: _____ hot and unsanitary in the restaurant kitchen I work in, and I don't think the restaurant deserves _____ good reputation.

knew   past form of *know*
new   not old

"I had *new* wallpaper put up," said Sarah.

"I *knew* there was some reason the place looked better," said Bill.

Fill in the blanks: Lola _____ that getting her hair cut would give her face a _____ look.

know   to understand
no   a negative

"I don't *know* why my dog Fang likes to attack certain people," said Martha.

"There's *no* one thing the people have in common."

Fill in the blanks: I _____ of _____ way to tell whether that politician is honest or not.

pair   set of two
pear   fruit

"What a great *pair* of legs Tony has," said Lola to Vonnie. Tony didn't hear her, for he was feeling very sick after munching on a green *pear.*

Fill in the blanks: In his lunch box was a _____ of _____ s.

passed   went by; succeeded in; handed to
past   time before the present; beyond, as in "We worked past closing time."

> Someone *passed* him a wine bottle; it was the way he chose to forget his unhappy *past.*

Fill in the blanks: I walked _____ the instructor's office but was afraid to ask her whether or not I had _____ the test.

peace   calm
piece   part

> Nations often risk world *peace* by fighting over a *piece* of land.

Fill in the blanks: Martha did not have any _____ until she gave her dog a _____ of meat loaf.

plain   simple
plane   aircraft

> The movie star dressed in *plain* clothes and wore no makeup so she would not stand out on the *plane.*

Fill in the blanks: The game-show contestant opened the small box wrapped in _____ brown paper and found inside the keys to his own jet _____.

principal   main; a person in charge of a school
principle   law, standard, or rule

> Pete's high school *principal* had one *principal* problem: Pete. This was because there were only two *principles* in Pete's life: rest and relaxation.

Fill in the blanks: The _____ reason she dropped out of school was that she believed in the _____ of complete freedom of choice.

TIP: It might help to remember that the *e* in *principle* is also in *rule*—the meaning of *principle.*

---

right   correct; opposite of *left*
write   put words on paper

If you have the *right* course card, I'll *write* your name on the class roster.

Fill in the blanks: Eddie thinks I'm weird because I _____ with both

my _____ and my left hands.

than   used in comparisons
then   at that time

When we were kids, my friend Elaine had prettier clothes *than* I did. I really
envied her *then.*

Fill in the blanks: Marge thought she was better _____ the rest of

us, but _____ she got the lowest grade on the history test.

TIP: It might help to remember that th**e**n (with an *e*) is also a tim**e** signal.

---

their   belonging to them
there   at that place; neutral word used with verbs like *is, are, was, were, have,*
        and *had*
they're   shortened form of *they are*

Two people own that van over *there* (at that place). *They're* (they are) going
to move out of *their* apartment (the apartment belonging to them) and into
the van, in order to save money.

Fill in the blanks: _____ not going to invite us to _____ table

because _____ is no room for us to sit down.

threw   past form of *throw*
through   from one side to the other; finished

The fans *threw* so much litter onto the field that the teams could not go
through with the game.

Fill in the blanks: When Mr. Jefferson was _____ screaming about

the violence on television, he _____ the newspaper at his dog.

to   verb part, as in *to smile;* toward, as in "I'm going *to* heaven"
too   overly, as in "The pizza was *too* hot"; also, as in "The coffee was hot, *too.*"
two   the number 2

> Tony drove *to* the park *to* be alone with Lola. (The first *to* means "toward"; the second *to* is a verb part that goes with *be.*)
>
> Tony's shirt is *too* tight, *too.* (The first *too* means "overly"; the second *too* means "also.")
>
> You need *two* hands (2 hands) to handle a Whopper.

Fill in the blanks: _____ times tonight, you have been _____ ready

_____ make assumptions without asking questions first.

wear   to have on
where   in what place

> Fred wanted to *wear* his light pants on the hot day, but he didn't know *where* he had put them.

Fill in the blanks: Exactly _____ on my leg should I _____ this elastic bandage?

weather   atmospheric conditions
whether   if it happens that; in case; if

> Some people go on vacations *whether* or not the *weather* is good.

Fill in the blanks: I always ask Bill _____ or not we're going to have a

storm, for his bad knee can feel rainy _____ approaching.

whose   belonging to whom
who's   shortened form of *who is* and *who has*

> *Who's* the instructor *whose* students are complaining?

Fill in the blanks: _____ the guy _____ car I saw you in?

your   belonging to you
you're   shortened form of *you are*

> *You're* (meaning "you are") not going to the fair unless *your* brother (the brother belonging to you) goes with you.

Fill in the blanks: _____ going to have to put aside individual differences

and play together for the sake of _____ team.

Other Words Frequently Confused

Following is a list of other words that people frequently confuse. Working in groups of two or three, complete the activities for each set of words, and check off and study the words that give you trouble.

a, an Both *a* and *an* are used before other words to mean, approximately, "one."

Generally you should use *an* before words starting with a vowel (*a, e, i, o, u*):

    an ache   an experiment   an elephant   an idiot   an ox

Generally you should use *a* before words starting with a consonant (all other letters):

    a Coke   a brain   a cheat   a television   a gambler

Fill in the blanks: The women had _____ argument over _____ former boyfriend.

accept (ăk sĕpt′) receive; agree to
except (ĕk sĕpt′) exclude; but

    "I would *accept* your loan," said Bill to the bartender, "*except* that I'm not ready to pay 25 percent interest."

Fill in the blanks: _____ for the fact that she can't _____ any criticism, Lori is a good friend.

advice (ăd vīs′) noun meaning "an opinion"
advise (ăd vīz′) verb meaning "to counsel, to give advice"

    I *advise* you to take the *advice* of your friends and stop working so hard.

Fill in the blanks: I _____ you to listen carefully to any _____ you get from your boss.

affect (uh fĕkt′) verb meaning "to influence"
effect (i fĕkt′) verb meaning "to bring about something"; noun meaning "result"

    The full *effects* of marijuana and alcohol on the body are only partly known; however, both drugs clearly *affect* the brain in various ways.

Fill in the blanks: The new tax laws go into _____ next month, and they are going to _____ your income tax deductions.

among   implies three or more
between   implies only two

> We had to choose from *among* fifty shades of paint but *between* only two fabrics.

Fill in the blanks: The layoff notices distributed _____ the unhappy workers gave them a choice _____ working for another month at full pay and leaving immediately with two weeks' pay.

beside   along the side of
besides in addition to

> I was lucky I wasn't standing *beside* the car when it was hit.
> *Besides* being unattractive, these uniforms are impractical.

Fill in the blanks: _____ the alarm system hooked up to the door, our neighbors keep a gun _____ their beds.

desert (dĕz′ ərt)   stretch of dry land; (di zûrt′) to abandon one's post or duty
dessert (dĭ zûrt′)   last part of a meal

> Sweltering in the *desert,* I was tormented by the thought of an icy *dessert.*

Fill in the blanks: After their meal, they carried their _____ into the living room so that they would not miss the start of the old _____ movie about Lawrence of Arabia.

fewer   used with things that can be counted
less   refers to amount, value, or degree

> There were *fewer* than seven people in all my classes today.
> I seem to feel *less* tired when I exercise regularly.

Fill in the blanks: With _____ people able to stay home with children, today's families spend _____ time together than in the past.

loose (lo͞os)   not fastened; not tight-fitting
lose (lo͞oz)   misplace; fail to win

> Phil's belt is so *loose* that he always looks ready to *lose* his pants.

Fill in the blanks: At least once a week our neighbors _____ their dog; it's because they let him run _____.

quiet (kwī′ĭt)   peaceful
quite (kwīt)   entirely; really; rather

After a busy day, the children are now *quiet,* and their parents are *quite* tired.

Fill in the blanks: The _____ halls of the church become _____ lively during square-dance evenings.

though (thō)   despite the fact that
thought (thôt)   past form of *think*

Even *though* she worked, she *thought* she would have time to go to school.

Fill in the blanks: Yoshiko _____ she would like the job, but even _____ the pay was good, she hated the traveling involved.

Review Test 1

Underline the correct word in the parentheses. Don't try to guess. If necessary, look back at the explanations of the words.

1. The admissions (counselor, councilor) (advised, adviced) Jane to retake the entrance examination.

2. Glen felt that if he could (loose, lose) twenty pounds, the (affect, effect) on his social life might be dramatic.

3. (There, Their, They're) won't be any charge for children if (there, their, they're) accompanied by (there, their, they're) parents.

4. (Your, You're) going to have to do (a, an) better job on (your, you're) final exam if you expect to pass the (coarse, course).

5. The scene of the fire was (to, two, too) hot, so the inspectors had (to, too, two) wait at least (to, too, two) days before they could enter the building.

6. Even (though, thought) the (brakes, breaks) on my car were worn, I did not have (quiet, quite) enough money to get them replaced (right, write) away.

7. (Accept, Except) for the fact that my neighbor receives most of his mail in (plain, plane) brown wrappers, he is (know, no) stranger (than, then) anyone else in this rooming house.

8. Because the Randalls are so neat and fussy, (its, it's) hard (to, too, two) feel comfortable when (your, you're) in (their, there, they're) house.

9. (Whose, Who's) the culprit who left the paint can on the table? The paint has ruined a (knew, new) tablecloth, and (its, it's) soaked (threw, through) the linen and (affected, effected) the varnish.

10. As we (passed, past) over the river, we would never have known that there had been a forest fire here (to, too, two) years before (accept, except) for the charred tree trunks that lay (beside, besides) the banks.

Review Test 2

On a separate paper, write short sentences using the ten words shown below.

dessert	principal
its	affect
you're	past
too	through
than	knew

43 Effective Word Choice

Introductory Activity

Write a check mark beside the sentence in each pair that makes more effective use of words.

1. I flipped out when Faye broke our date. _____

   I got very angry when Faye broke our date. _____

2. Doctors as dedicated as Dr. Curtin are few and far between. _____

   Doctors as dedicated as Dr. Curtin are rare. _____

3. Yesterday I ascertained that Elena and Wes broke up. _____

   Yesterday I found out that Elena and Wes broke up. _____

Now see if you can circle the correct number in each case:

Pair (1, 2, 3) contains a sentence with slang.

Pair (1, 2, 3) contains a sentence with a cliché.

Pair (1, 2, 3) contains a sentence with a pretentious word.

See Appendix A for answers.

Choose your words carefully when you write. Always take the time to think about your word choices rather than simply using the first word that comes to mind. You want to develop the habit of selecting words that are appropriate and exact for your purposes. One way you can show sensitivity to language is by avoiding slang, clichés, and pretentious words.

Slang

We often use slang expressions when we talk because they are so vivid and colorful. However, slang is usually out of place in formal writing. Here are some examples of slang expressions:

My girlfriend *got straight* with me by saying she wanted to see other men.

Rick spent all Saturday *messing around* with his car stereo.

My boss *keeps getting on my case* for coming to work late.

My sister *cracked up* when she saw me slip on the wet grass.

The crowd was *psyched up* when the game began.

Slang expressions have a number of drawbacks: They go out of date quickly, they become tiresome if used excessively in writing, and they may communicate clearly to some readers but not to others. Also, the use of slang can be a way of evading the specific details that are often needed to make one's meaning clear in writing. For example, in "The tires on the Corvette make the car look like something else," the writer has not provided the specific details about the tires necessary for us to understand the statement clearly. In general, then, you should avoid slang in your writing. If you are in doubt about whether an expression is slang, it may help to check a recently published hardbound dictionary.

Work with a partner to rewrite the following sentences, replacing the italicized slang words with more formal ones.

Activity

1

EXAMPLE

The movie was a *real bomb,* so we *cut out* early.

The movie was terrible, so we left early.

1. My roommate told me he was going to quit school and *hit the road,* but later he admitted he was just *messing with me.*

_____

_____

2. Jason thought he would be *cool* and *flash* the *cops* who stopped him his Patrolmen's Benevolent Association card, but that didn't stop them from *nailing* him for speeding.

_____

_____

_____

3. If the instructor stops *hassling* me, I am going to *get my act together* in the course.

_____

_____

Clichés

www.mhhe.com/langan

A *cliché* is an expression that has been worn out through constant use. Some typical clichés are listed below.

Clichés	
all work and no play	saw the light
at a loss for words	short but sweet
better late than never	sigh of relief
drop in the bucket	singing the blues
easier said than done	taking a big chance
had a hard time of it	time and time again
in the nick of time	too close for comfort
in this day and age	too little, too late
it dawned on me	took a turn for the worse
it goes without saying	under the weather
last but not least	where he (she) is coming from
make ends meet	word to the wise
on top of the world	work like a dog
sad but true	

Clichés are common in speech but make your writing seem tired and stale. Also, clichés—like slang—are often a way of evading the specific details that you must work to provide in your writing. You should, then, avoid clichés and try to express your meaning in fresh, original ways.

Underline the cliché in each of the following sentences. Then substitute specific, fresh words for the trite expression.

EXAMPLE

> I passed the test <u>by the skin of my teeth</u>.
> *I barely passed the test.*

1. Hal decided not to eat anything because he was feeling under the weather.

    _____

2. Sara arrived at the train station in the nick of time.

    _____

3. Clarence was asked to make his speech short but sweet.

    _____

Pretentious Words

Some people feel they can improve their writing by using fancy, elevated words rather than simple, natural words. They use artificial and stilted language that more often obscures their meaning than communicates it clearly.

Here are some unnatural-sounding sentences:

I comprehended her statement.

While partaking of our morning meal, we engaged in an animated conversation.

I am a stranger to excessive financial sums.

Law enforcement officers directed traffic when the lights malfunctioned.

The same thoughts can be expressed more clearly and effectively by using plain, natural language, as below:

I understood what she said.

While eating breakfast, we had a lively talk.

I have never had much money.

Police officers directed traffic when the lights stopped working.

Activity

3

Cross out the pretentious words in each sentence. Then substitute clear, simple language for the artificial words.

EXAMPLE

The manager ~~reproached~~ me for my ~~tardiness~~.

The manager criticized me for being late.

1. One of Colleen's objectives in life is to accomplish a large family.

   _____

2. Upon entering our residence, we detected smoke in the atmosphere.

   _____

3. The chemistry educator asked each of the budding scholars before him not to prevaricate when explaining how everyone in the assemblage had gotten an A on the exam.

   _____

   _____

Review Test

Certain words are italicized in the following sentences. In the space provided, identify the words as *slang (S)*, *clichés (C)*, or *pretentious words (PW)*. Then rewrite the sentences, replacing the words with more effective diction.

_____ 1. The *awesome flick* we saw last night was *totally* worth the twelve *bucks* we paid to get in.

   _____

   _____

_____ 2. *Sad but true*, the only way to *climb the ladder of success* in college is to *put one's nose to the grindstone*.

   _____

_____ 3. I *ruminated over all the possibilities* and *envisioned* that I would be more *felicitous* in *academia* than *in the labor force*.

   _____

   _____

_____ 4. The victims of the car accident were shaken but *none the worse for wear.*

_____

_____

_____ 5. After *pulling an all-nighter,* my roommate *crashed* on the couch.

_____

_____

_____ 6. Be sure to *deposit* your trash in the appropriate *receptacle.*

_____

_____

_____ 7. Fred has to *work like a dog* in his advanced math class.

_____

_____

_____ 8. I work *like a dog* at a restaurant where one customer's constant complaining is *driving me up the wall.*

_____

_____

_____ 9. Everyone in our family *congregates* at Miriam's house for the annual Thanksgiving *repast.*

_____

_____

_____ 10. Carlos *totally lost it* when the clerk told him that she didn't have any blue shirts in his size.

_____

_____

44

ESL Pointers

www.mhhe.com/langan

This section covers rules that most native speakers of English take for granted but that are useful for speakers of English as a second language (ESL).

Articles

An *article* is a noun marker—it signals that a noun will follow. There are two kinds of articles: indefinite and definite. The *indefinite* articles are *a* and *an*. Use *a* before a word that begins with a consonant sound:

> **a c**arrot, **a p**ig, **a u**niform
>
> (*A* is used before *uniform* because the u in that word sounds like the consonant y plus u, not a vowel sound.)

Use *an* before a word beginning with a vowel sound:

> **an e**xcuse, **an o**nion, **an h**onor
>
> (*Honor* begins with a vowel because the *h* is silent.)

The *definite* article is *the*:

> **the** lemon, **the** fan

An article may come right before a noun:

> **a** circle, **the** summer

Or an article may be separated from the noun by words that describe the noun:

> **a** large circle, **the** long hot summer

> **TIP:** There are various other noun markers, including quantity words (*a few, many, a lot of*), numerals (*one, ten, 120*), demonstrative adjectives (*this, these*), adjectives (*my, your, our*), and possessive nouns (*Vinh's, the school's*).

Articles with Count and Noncount Nouns

To know whether to use an article with a noun and which article to use, you must recognize count and noncount nouns. (A *noun* is a word used to name something—a person, place, thing, or idea.)

Count nouns name people, places, things, or ideas that can be counted and made into plurals, such as *window, table,* and *principal* (*one window, two tables, three principals*).

Noncount nouns refer to things or ideas that cannot be counted and therefore cannot be made into plurals, such as *weather, anger,* and *happiness.* The box below lists and illustrates common types of noncount nouns.

Common Noncount Nouns

Abstractions and emotions: joy, humor, patience, mercy, curiosity

Activities: soccer, gardening, reading, writing, searching

Foods: sugar, spaghetti, fudge, chicken, lettuce

Gases and vapors: air, nitrogen, oxygen, smoke, steam

Languages and areas of study: Laotian, German, social studies, calculus, biology

Liquids: coffee, gasoline, soda, milk, water

Materials that come in bulk or mass form: lumber, soil, dust, detergent, hay

Natural occurrences: gravity, hail, snow, thunder, rust

Other things that cannot be counted: clothing, furniture, homework, machinery, money, news, transportation, work

---

The quantity of a noncount noun can be expressed with a word or words called a *qualifier,* such as *some, more, a unit of,* and so on. In the following two examples, the qualifiers are shown in *italic* type, and the noncount nouns are shown in **boldface** type.

I hear *a little* **anger** in your voice.

The pea soup had gotten thick overnight, so Kala added *more* **water** to it.

Some words can be either count or noncount nouns, depending on whether they refer to one or more individual items or to something in general:

The yearly **rains** in India are called monsoons.

(This sentence refers to individual rains; *rains* in this case is a count noun.)

Rain is something that farmers cannot live without.

(This sentence refers to rain in general; in this case, *rain* is a noncount noun.)

Using a *or* an *with Nonspecific Singular Count Nouns* Use *a* or *an* with singular nouns that are nonspecific. A noun is nonspecific when the reader doesn't know its specific identity.

A penguin cannot fly; it uses its "wings" to "fly" through the water.

(The sentence refers to any penguin, not a specific one.)

There was **a** fire today in our neighborhood.

(The reader isn't familiar with the fire. This is the first time it is mentioned.)

Using the *with Specific Nouns* In general, use *the* with all specific nouns—specific singular, plural, and noncount nouns. A noun is specific—and therefore requires the article *the*—in the following cases:

- When the noun has already been mentioned once

  There was a fire today in our neighborhood. **The** fire destroyed the Smiths' garage.

  (*The* is used with the second mention of *fire*.)

- When the noun is identified by a word or phrase in the sentence

  The lights in the bathroom do not work.

  (*Lights* is identified by the words *in the bathroom*.)

- When the noun's identity is suggested by the general context

  The coffee at Billy's Diner always tastes a week old.

  (*Coffee* is identified by the words *at Billy's Diner*.)

- When the noun names something that is unique

  Scientists warn that there is a growing hole in **the** ozone layer.

  (Earth has only one ozone layer.)

- When the noun comes after a superlative adjective (*best, biggest, wisest*)

  Many of *the* best distance runners come from East Africa.

Omitting Articles Omit articles with nonspecific plurals and nonspecific noncount nouns. Plurals and noncount nouns are nonspecific when they refer to something in general.

Lights were on all over the empty house.

Coffee should be stored in the refrigerator or freezer if possible.

Runners from Kenya, Ethiopia, and Tanzania often win world-class races.

Using *the* with Proper Nouns

Proper nouns name particular people, places, things, or ideas and are always capitalized. Most proper nouns do not require articles; those that do, however, require *the*. Following are general guidelines about when and when not to use *the*.

Do not use *the* for most singular proper nouns, including names of the following:

- *People and animals* (Rosa Parks, Skipper)
- *Continents, states, cities, streets, and parks* (Asia, North Dakota, San Diego, Rodeo Boulevard, Fairmount Park)
- *Most countries* (Thailand, Argentina, England)
- *Individual bodies of water, islands, and mountains* (Lake Tahoe, Prince Edward Island, Mount Saint Helens)

Use *the* for the following types of proper nouns:

- *Plural proper nouns* (the Jacksons, the United Arab Emirates, the Great Lakes, the Appalachian Mountains)
- *Names of large geographic areas, deserts, oceans, seas, and rivers* (the Northeast, the Gobi Desert, the Indian Ocean, the Mediterranean Sea, the Hudson River)
- *Names with the format* "the _____ of _____" (the king of Sweden, the Gulf of Aden, the University of New Hampshire)

Underline the correct form of the noun in parentheses. Compare your answers with a partner's.

Activity 1

1. (A telephone, Telephone) is found in almost every American home.
2. Franz has registered for (the, a) course in Asian history.
3. (The car, A car) Kim bought is four years old but in very good condition.
4. Dark (cloud, clouds) filled the skies over (the, a) valley.
5. My grandparents and cousins all live in (New Jersey, the New Jersey).
6. Adults should have (patience, the patience) when dealing with children.
7. My dog is afraid of (thunder, thunders).
8. Cats are known for having a great deal of (curiosity, the curiosity).
9. Through the ages, (wine, the wine) has been made out of many fruits other than grapes, such as apples and blueberries.
10. People often get lost when hiking through (Pine Barrens, the Pine Barrens), a forest in New Jersey.

Subjects and Verbs

Avoiding Repeated Subjects

In English, a particular subject can be used only once in a word group with a subject and a verb. Don't repeat a subject in the same word group by following a noun with a pronoun.

> Incorrect: My *friend she* is a wonderful cook.
>
> Correct: My **friend** is a wonderful cook.
>
> Correct: **She** is a wonderful cook.

Even when the subject and verb are separated by several words, the subject cannot be repeated in the same word group.

> Incorrect: The *flowers* that are blooming in the yard *they* are called snapdragons.
>
> Correct: The **flowers** that are blooming in the yard **are called** snapdragons.

Including Pronoun Subjects and Linking Verbs

Some languages may omit a pronoun as a subject, but in English, every sentence other than a command must have a subject. (In a command, the subject *you* is understood: [**You**] Hand in your papers now.)

> Incorrect: The party was a success. *Was* lots of fun.
>
> Correct: The party was a success. **It was** lots of fun.

Every English sentence must also have a verb, even when the meaning of the sentence is clear without the verb.

> Incorrect: Rosa's handwriting very neat.
>
> Correct: Rosa's handwriting **is** very neat.

Including *There* and *Here* at the Beginning of Sentences

Some English sentences begin with *there* or *here* plus a linking verb (usually a form of *to be: is, are,* and so on). In such sentences, the verb comes before the subject.

> **There are** oranges in the refrigerator.
>
> (The subject is the plural noun *oranges,* so the plural verb *are* is used.)
>
> **Here is** the book you wanted.
>
> (The subject is the singular noun *book,* so the singular verb *is* is used.)

In sentences like those above, remember not to omit *there* or *here*.

> Incorrect: *Are* many good reasons to quit smoking.
>
> Correct: **There are** many good reasons to quit smoking.

Not Using the Progressive Tense of Certain Verbs

The progressive tenses are made up of forms of *be* plus the *-ing* form of the main verb. They express actions or conditions still in progress at a particular time.

> Iris **will be running** for student-body president this year.

However, verbs for mental states, the senses, possession, and inclusion are normally not used in the progressive tense.

> Incorrect: **I am loving** chocolate.
>
> Correct: **I love** chocolate.
>
> Incorrect: Sonia **is having** a lovely singing voice.
>
> Correct: Sonia **has** a lovely singing voice.

Common verbs not generally used in the progressive tense are listed in the box below.

Common Verbs Not Generally Used in the Progressive

Thoughts, attitudes, and desires: agree, believe, imagine, know, like, love, prefer, think, understand, want, wish

Sense perceptions: hear, see, smell, taste

Appearances: appear, seem, look

Possession: belong, have, own, possess

Inclusion: contain, include

Using Gerunds and Infinitives after Verbs

A *gerund* is the *-ing* form of a verb that is used as a noun:

> **Complaining** is my cousin's favorite activity.
>
> (*Complaining* is the subject of the sentence.)

An *infinitive* is *to* plus the basic form of the verb (the form in which the verb is listed in the dictionary), as in **to eat.** The infinitive can function as an adverb, an adjective, or a noun.

> We were delighted **to eat** dinner on the porch.
>
> (*To eat dinner on the porch* functions as an adverb that describes the verb adjective *delighted*.)

Simon built a shelf **to hold** his DVD collection.

(*To hold his DVD collection* functions as an adjective describing the noun *shelf.*)

To have good friends is a blessing.

(*To have good friends* functions as a noun—the subject of the verb *is.*)

Some verbs can be followed by only a gerund or only an infinitive; other verbs can be followed by either. Examples are given in the following lists. There are many others; watch for them in your reading.

Verb + gerund (dislike + studying)
Verb + preposition + gerund (insist + on + paying)
Some verbs can be followed by a gerund but not by an infinitive. In many cases, there is a preposition (such as *for, in,* or *of*) between the verb and the gerund. Following are some verbs and verb-preposition combinations that can be followed by gerunds but not by infinitives.

admit	deny	look forward to
apologize for	discuss	postpone
appreciate	dislike	practice
approve of	enjoy	suspect of
avoid	feel like	talk about
be used to	finish	thank for
believe in	insist on	think about

Incorrect: Sometimes I *enjoy to eat* by myself in a restaurant.

Correct: Sometimes I **enjoy eating** by myself in a restaurant.

Incorrect: Do you *feel like to dance*?

Correct: Do you **feel like dancing**?

Verb + infinitive (agree + to leave)
Following are common verbs that can be followed by an infinitive but not by a gerund.

agree	decide	manage
arrange	expect	refuse
claim	have	wait

Incorrect: I *agreed taking* Grandma shopping this afternoon.

Correct: I **agreed to take** Grandma shopping this afternoon.

Verb + noun or pronoun + infinitive (cause + them + to flee)
Below are common verbs that are first followed by a noun or pronoun and then by an infinitive, not a gerund.

cause	force	remind
command	persuade	warn

> Incorrect: The queen *commanded the prince obeying.*
>
> Correct: The queen **commanded the prince to obey.**

Following are common verbs that can be followed either by an infinitive alone or by a noun or pronoun and an infinitive.

ask	need	want
expect	promise	would like

> Jerry **would like to join** the army.
>
> Jerry's parents **would like him to go** to college.

Verb + gerund or infinitive (begin + packing, or begin + to pack)
Following are verbs that can be followed by either a gerund or an infinitive.

begin	hate	prefer
continue	love	start

The meaning of each of the verbs above remains the same or almost the same whether a gerund or an infinitive is used.

> I prefer **eating** dinner early.
>
> I prefer **to eat** dinner early.

With the verbs below, the gerunds and the infinitives have very different meanings.

forget	remember	stop

> Nadia **stopped to put on** makeup.
>
> (She interrupted something to put on makeup.)
>
> Nadia **stopped putting on** makeup.
>
> (She discontinued putting on makeup.)

Underline the correct form in parentheses.

1. The waiter (he recited, recited) a list of dinner specials so long that I got a headache.

2. The rain seems to have stopped. (It's, Is) going to be a beautiful day.

3. (Are paints and crayons, There are paints and crayons) in that cupboard.

4. That book (contains, is containing) photos of our wedding.

5. My midterm math grade persuaded me (getting, to get) a tutor.

6. After walking in the hot sun, we (very thirsty, were very thirsty).

7. Professor Wilhelm agreed (to repeat, repeat) the lecture for students who had not been able to attend it.

8. Lucia (expects earning, expects to earn) a B in the class.

9. The pigeons on the sidewalk (pick up, they pick up) crumbs of food that people drop.

10. For lunch today I (want, am wanting) a big salad.

Adjectives

Following the Order of Adjectives in English

Adjectives describe nouns and pronouns. In English, an adjective usually comes directly before the word it describes or after a linking verb (a form of *be* or a "sense" verb such as *look, seem,* and *taste*), in which case it modifies the subject. In each of the following two sentences, the adjective is **boldfaced** and the noun it describes is *italicized.*

That is a **bright** *light.*

That *light* is **bright.**

When more than one adjective modifies the same noun, the adjectives are usually stated in a certain order, though there are often exceptions. Following is the typical order of English adjectives.

Typical Order of Adjectives in a Series

1. *An article or another noun marker:* a, an, the, Joseph's, this, three, your

2. *Opinion adjective:* exciting, plain, annoying, difficult

3. *Size:* enormous, huge, petite, tiny

4. *Shape:* circular, short, round, square

5. *Age:* newborn, recent, old, new, young
6. *Color:* pink, yellow, orange, white
7. *Nationality:* Italian, Chinese, Guatemalan, Russian
8. *Religion:* Buddhist, Catholic, Jewish, Muslim
9. *Material:* plastic, silver, cement, cotton
10. *Noun used as an adjective:* school (as in school bus), closet (as in closet shelf), birthday (as in birthday *party*)

Here are some examples of the order of adjectives:

an interesting old story

the long orange cotton dress

your elderly Hungarian cousin

Rafael's friendly little black dog

In general, use no more than two or three adjectives after the article or other noun marker. Numerous adjectives in a series can be awkward: **the lovely little old Methodist stone** church.

Using the Present and Past Participles as Adjectives

The present participle ends in *-ing*. Past participles of regular verbs end in *-ed* or *-d;* a list of the past participles of many common irregular verbs appears on pages 467–470. Both types of participles may be used as adjectives. A participle used as an adjective may come before the word it describes:

It was a **boring** *lecture.*

A participle used as an adjective may also follow a linking verb and describe the subject of the sentence:

The *lecture* was **boring.**

While both present and past participles of a particular verb may be used as adjectives, their meanings differ. Use the present participle to describe whoever or whatever causes a feeling:

a **surprising** *conversation*

(The conversation *caused* the surprise.)

Use the past participle to describe whoever or whatever experiences the feeling:

the **surprised** *waitress*

(The waitress *is surprised.*)

Here are two more sentences that illustrate the differing meanings of present and past participles.

> The horror movie was **frightening.**
>
> The audience was **frightened.**
>
> (The movie caused the fear; the audience experienced the fear.)

Following are pairs of present and past participles with similar distinctions:

annoying / annoyed	exhausting / exhausted
boring / bored	fascinating / fascinated
confusing / confused	tiring / tired
depressing / depressed	surprising / surprised
exciting / excited	

Activity

3

Underline the correct form in parentheses.

1. The (green large snake, large green snake) slithered on the lawn.
2. At the party, Julie sang a(n) (Vietnamese old, old Vietnamese) song.
3. Joanna wore a (silk blue scarf, blue silk scarf) over her beautiful red hair.
4. The long walk home from the supermarket left Mira feeling (exhausting, exhausted).
5. The constant barking of our neighbor's dog is very (annoying, annoyed).

Prepositions Used for Time and Place

In English, the use of prepositions is often not based on their common meanings, and there are many exceptions to general rules. As a result, correct use of prepositions must be learned gradually through experience. Following is a chart showing how three of the most common prepositions are used in some customary references to time and place.

Use of *On*, *In*, and *At* to Refer to Time and Place

Time

On a specific day: **on Saturday, on June 12, on your birthday**

In a part of a day: **in the morning, in the daytime** (*but* **at night**)

In a month or a year: **in November, in 1492**

> *In a period of time:* in a minute, in a couple of days, in a while
> *At a specific time:* at 10:00 A.M., at dawn, at sunset, at dinnertime
>
> Place
>
> *On a surface:* on the dresser, on the porch, on the roof
> *In a place that is enclosed:* in my bedroom, in the hallway, in the drawer
> *At a specific location:* at the pool, at the bar, at the racetrack

Underline the correct preposition in parentheses.

1. We'll resume the meeting (on, in) fifteen minutes.
2. The sailboat drifted (on, at) the quiet bay as the crew waited for the wind to return.
3. I plan to watch the game (on, in) a large TV.
4. Sonia is moving to Florida (in, at) a month.
5. The children's birthday party was held (on, at) the bowling alley.

Review Test

Underline the correct form in parentheses.

1. When I looked out the window, I was surprised by the deep (snow, snows).
2. (Is there, Is) enough room for our luggage in the trunk?
3. There are plenty of fish (in, at) the sea, Elisa told Serena, who had just broken up with her boyfriend.
4. Owls hunt (at, in) night and sleep most of the day.
5. Larry (postponed to go, postponed going) on vacation because he broke his foot.
6. My English teacher wears a (silver small, small silver) ring in his ear.
7. Marta (has, is having) a very bad cold.
8. (On, In) Valentine's Day, friends and lovers send each other affectionate cards.
9. Skinless (chicken, chickens) breasts are a food most doctors recommend because of the low fat content.
10. The customers (annoying, annoyed) by the rude waiter complained to the restaurant manager.

PRACTICE

Think of a time when practice paid off for you, and write a narrative paragraph about the experience. You may want to review Chapter 15, "Narration."

Combined Mastery Tests

45

NAME: _____

DATE: _____

SCORE
Number Correct

_____ x 5

_____%

Fragments and Run-Ons

COMBINED MASTERY TEST 1

The word groups below are numbered 1 through 20. In the space provided for each, write C if a word group is a complete sentence, write F if it is a fragment, and write RO if it is a run-on. Then correct the errors.

[1]I had a frightening dream last night, I dreamed that I was walking high up on an old railroad trestle. [2]It looked like the one I used to walk on recklessly. [3]When I was about ten years old. [4]At that height, my palms were sweating, just as they did when I was a boy. [5]I could see the ground out of the corners of my eyes, I felt a sickening, swooning sensation. [6]Suddenly, I realized there were rats below. [7]Thousands upon thousands of rats. [8]They knew I was up on the trestle, they were laughing. [9]Because they were sure they would get me. [10]Their teeth glinted in the moonlight, their red eyes were like thousands of small reflectors. [11]Which almost blinded my sight. [12]Sensing that there was something even more hideous behind me. [13]I kept moving forward. [14]Then I realized that I was coming to a gap in the trestle. [15]There was no way I could stop or go back I would have to cross over that empty gap. [16]I leaped out in despair. [17]Knowing I would never make it. [18]And felt myself falling helplessly down to the swarm of rejoicing rats. [19]I woke up bathed in sweat. [20]Half expecting to find a rat in my bed.

1. _____
2. _____
3. _____
4. _____
5. _____
6. _____
7. _____
8. _____
9. _____
10. _____
11. _____
12. _____
13. _____
14. _____
15. _____
16. _____
17. _____
18. _____
19. _____
20. _____

NAME: _____

DATE: _____

COMBINED
MASTERY TEST 2

Fragments and Run-Ons

1. _____

2. _____

3. _____

4. _____

5. _____

6. _____

7. _____

8. _____

9. _____

10. _____

11. _____

12. _____

13. _____

14. _____

15. _____

16. _____

17. _____

18. _____

19. _____

20. _____

The word groups below are numbered 1 through 20. In the space provided for each, write C if a word group is a complete sentence, write F if it is a fragment, and write RO if it is a run-on. Then correct the errors.

[1]An adequate intake of vitamins and minerals every day is essential to good health. [2]For people who don't like to take pills. [3]A good way to get needed nutrients is to plan daily menus carefully. [4]For example. [5]Green, leafy vegetables like spinach and kale contain vitamin A, maintaining healthy eyes and bones requires adequate absorption of this vitamin. [6]Which benefits the skin, as well. [7]The B vitamins can be found in a variety of foods. [8]Including eggs, lean meats, legumes, and nuts. [9]Fish, egg yolks, and liver, not to mention ordinary sunlight, are good sources of vitamin D, a nutrient that fights osteoporosis in older people, vitamin D also prevents rickets in children. [10]Vitamin C is found in fruits such as oranges, grapefruits, and tangerines. [11]It prevents scurvy and anemia, it also fights colds. [12]Green, leafy vegetables are good sources of vitamin K. [13]Which is essential to blood clotting. [14]As well as to maintaining bone mass. [15]Niacin is found in fish, peanuts, and lean meats. [16]Sometimes called vitamin B_3, it can treat diseases such as pellagra, common among chronic alcoholics, pellagra produces symptoms such as delirium, dementia, digestive problems, and amnesia. [17]While all of these vitamins are needed, minerals are needed in even greater amounts. [18]There are several macro-minerals, such as magnesium, phosphorous, sodium, and potassium. [19]Of which at least 100 mgs are needed daily. [20]Then, there are micro-minerals, among them are iron, zinc, and copper, which are required in lesser amounts.

NAME: _____

DATE: _____

Each sentence contains a mistake involving (1) standard English or irregular verb forms, (2) subject-verb agreement, or (3) consistent verb tense. Circle the letter that identifies the mistake. Then cross out the incorrect verb and write the correct form in the space provided.

_____ 1. Members of our local volunteer fire department undergoes ongoing training to keep their skills sharp.

Mistake in: a. Subject-verb agreement   b. Verb tense

_____ 2. The more the instructor explained the material and the more he wroted on the board, the more confused I got.

Mistake in: a. Irregular verb form   b. Verb tense

_____ 3. I grabbed the last carton of skim milk on the supermarket shelf, but when I checks the date on it, I realized it was not fresh.

Mistake in: a. Subject-verb agreement   b. Verb tense

_____ 4. This morning my parents argued loudly, but later they apologized to each other and embrace.

Mistake in: a. Subject-verb agreement   b. Verb tense

_____ 5. When the bell rang, Mike takes another bite of his sandwich and then prepared for class.

Mistake in: a. Irregular verb form   b. Verb tense

_____ 6. No one had stolen Ginger's keys; she had forgetted they were in her coat pocket.

Mistake in: a. Irregular verb form   b. Verb tense

_____ 7. Because I had throwed away the receipt, I couldn't return the microwave.

Mistake in: a. Irregular verb form   b. Verb tense

_____ 8. My father and uncle supports each other whenever they have an argument with their wives.

Mistake in: a. Subject-verb agreement   b. Verb tense

_____ 9. Six pines and a small oak tree grows out of the side of the cliff.

Mistake in: a. Subject-verb agreement   b. Verb tense

_____ 10. The profit earned by Bluto's sandwich shop and his wife Felicia's flower store were enough to finance a comfortable lifestyle.

Mistake in: a. Subject-verb agreement   b. Verb tense

NAME: _____

DATE: _____

**COMBINED
MASTERY TEST 4**

Verb

Each sentence contains a mistake involving (1) standard English or irregular verb forms, (2) subject-verb agreement, or (3) consistent verb tense. Circle the letter that identifies the mistake. Then cross out the incorrect verb and write the correct form in the space provided.

_____ 1. Although blood had already been drawed from the patient's arm, the doctor ordered another sample.

Mistake in: a. Irregular verb form   b. Verb tense

_____ 2. After she poured the ammonia into the bucket, Karen reels backward because the strong fumes made her eyes tear.

Mistake in: a. Subject-verb agreement   b. Verb tense

_____ 3. Flying around in space is various pieces of debris from old space satellites.

Mistake in: a. Subject-verb agreement   b. Verb tense

_____ 4. The tomatoes from our garden winned first prize at the county fair.

Mistake in: a. Irregular verb form   b. Verb tense

_____ 5. Both crying and laughing helps us get rid of tension.

Mistake in: a. Subject-verb agreement   b. Verb tense

_____ 6. Yesterday, Jan stayed at the library and completes the research for her paper.

Mistake in: a. Subject-verb agreement   b. Verb tense

_____ 7. McDonald's has selled enough hamburgers to reach to the moon.

Mistake in: a. Irregular verb form   b. Verb tense

_____ 8. When Chen peeled back the bedroom wallpaper, he discovered another layer of wallpaper and uses a steamer to get that layer off.

Mistake in: a. Subject-verb agreement   b. Verb tense

_____ 9. Rosie searched for the fifty-dollar bill she had hid somewhere in her dresser.

Mistake in: a. Irregular verb form   b. Verb tense

_____ 10. The realistic yellow tulips on the gravestone is made of a weather-resistant fabric.

Mistake in: a. Subject-verb agreement   b. Verb tense

NAME: _____

DATE: _____

Capital Letters and Punctuation

Each of the following sentences contains an error in capitalization or punctuation. Refer to the box below and write, in the space provided, the letter identifying the error. Then correct the error.

a. missing capital letter	c. missing quotation marks
b. missing apostrophe	d. missing comma

_____ 1. Andy had complete faith in his parents' willingness to help for they had come to his aid before.

_____ 2. "One of the striking differences between a cat and a lie, wrote Mark Twain, "is that a cat has only nine lives."

_____ 3. Our history professors alma mater is Princeton University.

_____ 4. Francelle wants to work for the United States environmental protection agency.

_____ 5. My parents always ask me where Im going and when I'll be home.

_____ 6. She doesn't talk about it much, but my aunt has been a member of alcoholics Anonymous for ten years.

_____ 7. Silvio had to sleep on the cold hard cement floor.

_____ 8. Whenever he gave us the keys to the car, my father would say, Watch out for the other guy."

_____ 9. If you're going to stay up late be sure to turn down the heat before going to bed.

_____ 10. I decided to have a glass of apple juice rather than order a pepsi.

NAME: _____

DATE: _____

COMBINED MASTERY TEST 6

Capital Letters and Punctuation

Each of the following sentences contains an error in capitalization or punctuation. Refer to the box below and write, in the space provided, the letter identifying the error. Then correct the error.

a. missing capital letter	c. missing quotation marks
b. missing apostrophe	d. missing comma

_____ 1. After years of dating Allen Marcy has learned to love Burger King.

_____ 2. "The diners food is always reliable," said Stan. "It's consistently bad."

_____ 3. My hometown is knoxville, tennessee.

_____ 4. "To love oneself, said Oscar Wilde, "is the beginning of a lifelong romance."

_____ 5. "The mills of God grind slowly, but they grind exceeding small" said the preacher.

_____ 6. Leslie said to the woman behind her in the theater, "will you stop talking, please?"

_____ 7. Walters arthritis is as good a predictor of the weather as the TV weather report.

_____ 8. "Before you can reach your goals," says my grandfather, you have to believe you can reach them."

_____ 9. There is little evidence that king Arthur, the legendary hero, really existed.

_____ 10. My grandfather learned to cook when he was an Army cook during World war II.

NAME: _____

DATE: _____

Word Use

Each of the following sentences contains a mistake identified in the left-hand margin. Underline the mistake and then correct it in the space provided.

Slang   1. Nicole drives the finest set of wheels in town.

_____

Wordiness   2. Truthfully, I've been wishing that the final could be postponed to a much later date sometime next week.

_____

Cliché   3. The victim, discovered the police, was as dead as a doorknob.

_____

Pretentious language   4. Harold utilizes old coffee cans to water his houseplants.

_____

Adverb error   5. The sled started slow and then picked up speed as the icy hill became steeper.

_____

Error in comparison   6. When the weather is dry, my sinuses feel more better.

_____

Confused word   7. If you neglect your friends, their likely to become former friends.

_____

Confused word   8. She's the neighbor who's dog is courting my dog.

_____

Confused word   9. If you don't put cans, jars, and newspapers on the curb for recycling, the township won't pick up you're garbage.

_____

Confused word   10. "Its not the pale moon that invites me," he sang. "Oh no, it's just the nearness of you."

_____

NAME: _____

DATE: _____

Word Use

Each of the following sentences contains a mistake identified in the left-hand margin. Underline the mistake and then correct it in the space provided.

Slang

1. After coming in to work late all last week, Sheila was canned.

   _____

Wordiness

2. At this point in time, I'm not really sure what my major will be.

   _____

Cliché

3. "The result," said the company president, "is that we need to tighten our belts."

   _____

Pretentious language

4. Dr. Philips, the veterinarian, specialized in canine and feline maladies.

   _____

Adverb error

5. The more serious I applied myself, the better my grades were.

   _____

Error in comparison

6. The respectfuller you treat people, the more likely they are to deserve your respect.

   _____

Confused word

7. The dog has lost its' flea collar.

   _____

Confused word

8. "My advise to you," said my grandmother, "is to focus on your strengths, not your fears."

   _____

Confused word

9. The principle advantage of the school cafeteria is that it's only three blocks from a Wendy's.

   _____

Confused word

10. My parents mean well, but there goals for me aren't my goals.

   _____

46

Editing Tests

The twelve editing tests in this chapter will give you practice in revising for sentence-skills mistakes. Remember that if you don't edit carefully, you run the risk of sabotaging much of the work you have put into a paper. If readers see too many surface flaws, they may assume you don't place much value on what you have to say, and they may not give your ideas a fair hearing. Revising to eliminate sentence-skills errors is a basic part of clear, effective writing.

In half of the tests, the spots where errors occur have been underlined; your job is to identify and correct each error. In the rest of the tests, you must locate as well as identify and correct the errors.

Following are hints that can help you edit the next-to-final draft of a paper for sentence-skills mistakes.

www.mhhe.com/langan

Editing Hints

1. Have at hand two essential tools: a good dictionary (see page 559) and a grammar handbook (you can use Chapter 5 and Part Five of this book).

2. Use a sheet of paper to cover your essay so that you will expose only one sentence at a time. Look for errors in grammar, spelling, and typing. It may help to read each sentence out loud. If a sentence does not read clearly and smoothly, chances are something is wrong.

3. Pay special attention to the kinds of errors you yourself tend to make. For example, if you tend to write run-ons or fragments, be especially on the lookout for those errors.

4. Proofreading symbols that may be of particular help are the following:

ℒ	omit	in the the meantime
^	insert missing letter or word	beleve
cap, lc	Add a capital (or a lowercase) letter	My persian Cat

EDITING TEST 1

Identify the five mistakes in paper format in the student paper that follows. From the box below, choose the letters that describe the five mistakes and write those letters in the spaces provided.

a. The title should not be underlined.
b. The title should not be set off in quotation marks.
c. There should not be a period at the end of a title.
d. All the major words in a title should be capitalized.
e. The title should be a phrase, not a complete sentence.
f. The first line of a paper should stand independently of the title.
g. A line should be skipped between the title and the first line of the paper.
h. The first line of a paragraph should be indented.
i. The right-hand margin should not be crowded.
j. Hyphenation should occur only between syllables.

	Writing a Successful Research Paper Requires Planning	
	This task requires three important steps: planning, planning,	
	and planning. First, determine if enough information about	
	the chosen topic can be found in the college library or	
	online. If not, choose another topic. Next, determine if the	
	topic is too broad to write about in a relatively short	
	paper. If so, limit the topic. Next, design a research plan.	
	Begin this part of the process by framing a research	
	question about the topic. For example, such a question for	
	a paper on the topic of bilingual education might be this:	
	"Is the bilingual approach the best way to mainstream	
	second-language speakers?" Next, make a preliminary list	
	of sources—books, articles, and online resources—in which	
	useful information might be found. Now, start taking notes!	

1. _____   2. _____   3. _____   4. _____   5. _____

NAME: _____

DATE: _____

Identify the sentence-skills mistakes at the underlined spots in the paragraph that follows. From the box below, choose the letter that describes each mistake and write it in the space provided. The same mistake may appear more than once.

a. fragment	d. apostrophe mistake
b. run-on	e. faulty parallelism
c. mistake in subject-verb agreement	

Looking Out for Yourself

It's sad but true: "If you don't look out for yourself, no one else will." For example, some people have a false idea about the power of a college <u>degree, they</u> think that once

₁

they <u>possesses</u> the degree, the world will be waiting on their doorstep. In fact, nobody

₂

is likely to be on their doorstep unless, through advance planning, they <u>has</u> prepared

₃

themselves for a career. <u>The kind in which good job opportunities exist.</u> Even after a

₄

person has landed a job, however, a healthy amount of self-interest is needed. People

who hide in corners or <u>with hesitation</u> to let others know about their skills <u>doesn't</u> get

₅   ₆

promotions or raises. <u>Its</u> important to take credit for a job well done, whether the job

₇

involves writing a report, <u>organized the office filing system,</u> or calming down an angry

₈

customer. Also, people should feel free to ask the boss for a raise. <u>If they work hard and

₉

really deserve it.</u> Those who look out for themselves get the <u>rewards, people</u> who depend

₁₀

on others to help them along get left behind.

1. _____ 2. _____ 3. _____ 4. _____ 5. _____

6. _____ 7. _____ 8. _____ 9. _____ 10. _____

EDITING TEST 3

Identify the sentence-skills mistakes at the underlined spots in the paragraph that follows. From the box below, choose the letter that describes each mistake and write it in the space provided. The same mistake may appear more than once.

a. fragment	e. missing comma after introductory words
b. run-on	f. mistake with quotation marks
c. mistake in verb tense	g. apostrophe mistake
d. mistake in irregular verb	

Deceptive Appearances

Appearances can be deceptive. While looking through a library window yesterday, I saw a neatly groomed woman walk by. Her clothes were skillfully <u>tailored her</u> makeup was perfect. <u>Thinking no one was looking she</u> crumpled a piece of paper in her hand. <u>And tossed it into a nearby hedge.</u> Suddenly she no longer <u>looks</u> attractive to me. On another occasion, I started talking to a person in my psychology class named Eric. Eric seemed to be a great person. He always got the class laughing with his <u>jokes, on</u> the days when Eric was absent, I think even the professor missed his lively personality. Eric asked me <u>"if I wanted to eat lunch in the cafeteria with him,"</u> and I felt happy he had <u>chose</u> me to be a friend. <u>While we were sitting in the cafeteria.</u> Eric took out an envelope with several kinds of pills inside. "Want one?" he asked. "They're uppers." I didn't want <u>one, I felt disappointed.</u> <u>Erics</u> terrific personality was the product of the pills he took.

1. _____   2. _____   3. _____   4. _____   5. _____

6. _____   7. _____   8. _____   9. _____   10. _____

NAME: _____

DATE: _____

Identify the sentence-skills mistakes at the underlined spots in the paragraph that follows. From the box below, choose the letter that describes each mistake and write it in the space provided. The same mistake may appear more than once.

a. fragment	e. apostrophe mistake
b. run-on	f. misplaced modifier
c. irregular verb mistake	g. missing quotation marks
d. missing comma after introductory words	

Corsica: a Brief History

The island of Corsica <u>lays</u> only a short distance from the southern coast of France.
₁

<u>Just north of the Italian island of Sardinia.</u> <u>Mountainous and rugged,</u> Napoleon
₂ ₃

Bonaparte, the Emperor of the French, was born on this island. Corsica is also the

setting of Alexander <u>Dumas</u> *The Corsican Brothers,* a novel about twins, who were
₄

supposed to feel each other's physical pain. <u>Early in its history</u> Corsica was occupied
₅

by the Carthaginians, the Phoenicians, the Greeks, the Etruscans, and the <u>Romans,</u>
₆

<u>becoming</u> the property of the Italian city-state of Genoa in the fourteenth century, the

island stayed in Italian hands for four hundred years. In fact, <u>existing as an independent</u>

<u>nation for a short while during the eighteenth century,</u> the official language remained
₇

Italian. That changed. <u>After the French took control 1769.</u> Genoa is said to have sold
₈

its interests in Corsica to <u>France, however,</u> Professor Cavour, my Italian teacher, once
₉

claimed that <u>"those sneaky French stole it.</u>
₁₀

1. _____ 2. _____ 3. _____ 4. _____ 5. _____

6. _____ 7. _____ 8. _____ 9. _____ 10. _____

EDITING TEST 5

Identify the sentence-skills mistakes at the underlined spots in the paragraph that follows. From the box below, choose the letter that describes each mistake and write it in the space provided. The same mistake may appear more than once.

a. fragment	e. faulty parallelism
b. run-on	f. apostrophe mistake
c. missing capital letter	g. missing quotation mark
d. mistake in subject-verb agreement	h. missing comma after introductory words

Why I Didn't Go to Church

In my boyhood years, I almost never attended church. There was an unwritten code that the guys on the corner was not to be seen in churches'. Although there was many
<u>1</u>   <u>2</u>   <u>3</u>

days when I wanted to attend a church, I felt I had no choice but to stay away. If the guys had heard I had gone to church, they would have said things like, "hey, angel, when
                                                         <u>4</u>

are you going to fly? With my group of friends, its amazing that I developed any religious
         <u>5</u>   <u>6</u>

feeling at all. Another reason for not going to church was my father. When he was around the house he told my mother, "Mike's not going to church. No boy of mine is a sissy."
     <u>7</u>

My mother and sister went to church, I sat with my father and read the Sunday paper
                               <u>8</u>

or watching television. I did not start going to church until years later. When I no longer
   <u>9</u>

hung around with the guys on the corner or let my father have power over me.
                                  <u>10</u>

1. _____ 2. _____ 3. _____ 4. _____ 5. _____

6. _____ 7. _____ 8. _____ 9. _____ 10. _____

NAME: _____

DATE: _____

Identify the sentence-skills mistakes at the underlined spots in the paragraph that follows. From the box below, choose the letter that describes each mistake and write it in the space provided. The same mistake may appear more than once.

a. fragment	e. missing quotation mark
b. run-on	f. missing comma between two complete thoughts
c. faulty parallelism	g. missing comma after introductory words
d. missing apostrophe	h. misspelled word

Billy Budd, Sailor

Herman Melville's novel *Moby Dick* is his masterpiece but the Melville book that most
¹
students know best is *Billy Budd*. The story of an innocent, handsome young sailor by that
²
name. While he is serving on the American ship *Rights of Man,* a British warship comes
alongside his and takes several American seamen prisoner, Billy is among them. After
³
serving on the British ship for only a little while the noble Billy succeeds in winning the
⁴
admiration of the British captain, Edward Vere, and that of most of the crew. Except for
John Claggart, the evil master-of-arms, whose hatred Billy has drawn for no apparent
⁵
reason. Eventually, Claggart accuses Billy of starting a mutiny, this charge is clearly untrue.
⁶
However, the master-of-arms accusation enrages the seaman, who loses his composure,
⁷
strikes Claggart, and killing him. Realizing that Claggart's accusation provoked Billy, the
⁸
captain sympathizes with the young man, but he knows he has to try Billy before a jury
on board ship. Following navel law to the letter, the jury convicts him. Shortly thereafter,
⁹
Billy is hanged, much to the regret of all those involved, but not before he utters one of
the most memorable lines in American literature: "God bless Captain Vere!
¹⁰

1. _____ 2. _____ 3. _____ 4. _____ 5. _____

6. _____ 7. _____ 8. _____ 9. _____ 10. _____

EDITING TEST 7

See if you can locate and correct the ten sentence-skills mistakes in the following passage. The mistakes are listed in the box below. As you locate each mistake, write the number of the word group containing that mistake. Use the spaces provided. Then (on separate paper) correct the mistakes.

5 fragments	_____	_____	_____	_____	_____
5 run-ons	_____	_____	_____	_____	_____

The Language Evolves

[1]Forty years ago, no one would have batted an eye over inadvertent sexism in the media, in newspapers and magazines, and on the radio and television, people used words such as "fisherman" to refer to everyone who fished. [2]"Policeman" to refer to all police officers. [3]"Postman" for anyone who carried the mail. [4]Indeed, print journalists and television broadcasters called themselves "newsmen," advertising executives were known as "ad men." [5]Even the word "mankind" was used as a blanket term to refer to the human race. [6]Despite the fact that at least half of its members were female. [7]Today the situation has changed, women figure prominently in the professions, in government, and in business. [8]As a result, more respect seems to be given them in the media. [9]In fact, many women serve as executives in the media industry itself. [10]In 1984 and in 2008, the major political parties nominated women as their vice-presidential candidates, no one doubts that someday soon a woman will run for the land's highest office. [11]Perhaps in the next presidential election. [12]As a result, the media are, more and more, granting women equal status. [13]A status that they deserve and have earned. [14]The media no longer call all fire-fighters "firemen," when referring to a non-specific doctor, lawyer, politician, scientist, or other professional, they have replaced the pronoun "he" with the more representative "he or she."

NAME: _____

DATE: _____

See if you can locate and correct the ten sentence-skills mistakes in the following passage. The mistakes are listed in the box below. As you locate each mistake, write the number of the word group containing that mistake. Use the spaces provided. Then (on separate paper) correct the mistakes.

2 fragments _____ _____	2 missing commas around an
2 missing commas between items	interrupter _____ _____
in a series _____ _____	1 apostrophe mistake _____
2 faulty parallelisms _____ _____	1 run-on _____

A Place of Fear

¹College is supposed to be a place of discovery. ²But for some students can be a place of fear. ³In the classroom for example many students are afraid of appearing dumb in front of their classmates or professors. ⁴Such students often try to hide in class by sitting in the back of the room. ⁵Avoiding eye contact with instructors. ⁶Fear prevents them from raising their hands answering questions or being part of class discussions. ⁷Fear also leads to problems outside the classroom. ⁸Worried that their peers wont like them, many college students smoke or drinking heavily to blend in with the crowd. ⁹They also try drugs or joining in hurtful pranks they may even practice unsafe sex out of fear. ¹⁰Finally, students who get into trouble are often too scared to seek help in solving their problems.

EDITING TEST 9

See if you can locate and correct the ten sentence-skills mistakes in the following passages. The mistakes are listed in the box below. As you locate each mistake, write the number of the word group containing that mistake. Use the spaces provided. Then (on separate paper) correct the mistakes.

2 fragments _____ _____	1 missing comma after
1 run-on _____	introductory words _____
1 irregular verb mistake _____	2 apostrophe mistakes _____ _____
1 missing comma between items	1 faulty parallelism _____
in a series _____	1 missing quotation mark _____

Fred's Funeral

¹Sometimes when Fred feels undervalued and depression, he likes to imagine his own funeral. ²He pictures all the people who will be there. ³He hears their hushed words sees their tears, and feels their grief. ⁴He glows with warm sadness as the minister begins a eulogy by saying, Fred Grencher was no ordinary man . . . " ⁵As the minister talks on Freds eyes grow moist. ⁶He laments his own passing and feels altogether appreciated and wonderful.

Feeding Time

⁷Recently I was at the cat house in the zoo. ⁸Right before feeding time. ⁹The tigers and lions were lying about on benches and little stands. ¹⁰Basking in the late-afternoon sun. ¹¹They seemed tame and harmless. ¹²But when the meat was brung in, a remarkable change occurred. ¹³All the cats got up and moved toward the food. ¹⁴I was suddenly aware of the rippling muscles' of their bodies and their large claws and teeth. ¹⁵They seemed three times bigger, I could feel their power.

NAME: _____

DATE: _____

See if you can locate and correct the ten sentence-skills mistakes in the following passage. The mistakes are listed in the box below. As you locate each mistake, write the number of the word group containing that mistake. Use the spaces provided. Then (on separate paper) correct the mistakes.

1 run-on _____	2 missing commas around
1 mistake in subject-verb	an interrupter _____ _____
agreement _____	1 missing comma between items
1 missing comma after	in a series _____
introductory words _____	2 apostrophe mistakes _____ _____
	2 missing quotation marks _____ _____

Walking Billboards

¹Many Americans have turned into driving, walking billboards. ²As much as we all claim to hate commercials on television we dont seem to have any qualms about turning ourselves into commercials. ³Our car bumpers for example advertise lake resorts underground caverns, and amusement parks. ⁴Also, we wear clothes marked with other peoples initials and slogans. ⁵Our fascination with the names of designers show up on the backs of our sneakers, the breast pockets of our shirts, and the right rear pockets of our blue jeans. ⁶And we wear T-shirts filled with all kinds of advertising messages. ⁷For instance, people are willing to wear shirts that read, "Dillon Construction," "Nike," or even I Got Crabs at Ed's Seafood Palace. ⁸In conclusion, we say we hate commercials, we actually pay people for the right to advertise their products.

EDITING TEST 11

See if you can locate and correct the ten sentence-skills mistakes in the following passage. The mistakes are listed in the box below. As you locate each mistake, write the number of the word group containing that mistake. Use the spaces provided. Then (on separate paper) correct the mistakes.

3 fragments _____	1 mistake in pronoun point of view _____
_____ _____	
2 run-ons _____ _____	1 dangling modifier _____
1 irregular verb mistake _____	1 missing comma between two
1 faulty parallelism _____	complete thoughts _____

Too Many Cooks

¹The problem in my college dining hall was the succession of incompetent cooks who were put in charge. ²During the time I worked there, I watched several cooks come and go. ³The first of these was Irving. ⁴He was skinny and greasy like the undercooked bacon he served for breakfast. ⁵Irving drank, by late afternoon he begun to sway as he cooked. ⁶Once, he looked at the brightly colored photograph on the orange juice machine. ⁷And asked why the TV was on. ⁸Having fired Irving, Lonnie was hired. ⁹Lonnie had a soft, round face that resembled the Pillsbury Doughboy's but he had the size and temperament of a large bear. ¹⁰He'd wave one paw and growl if you entered the freezers without his permission. ¹¹He also had poor eyesight. ¹²This problem caused him to substitute flour for sugar and using pork for beef on a regular basis. ¹³After Lonnie was fired, Enzo arrived. ¹⁴Because he had come from Italy only a year or two previously. ¹⁵He spoke little English. ¹⁶In addition, Enzo had trouble with seasoning and spices. ¹⁷His vegetables were too salty, giant bay leaves turned up in everything. ¹⁸Including the scrambled eggs. ¹⁹The cooks I worked for in the college dining hall would have made Bobby Flay go into shock.

NAME: _____

DATE: _____

See if you can locate and correct the ten sentence-skills mistakes in the following passage. The mistakes are listed in the box below. As you locate each mistake, write the number of the word group containing that mistake. Use the spaces provided. Then (on separate paper) correct the mistakes.

2 fragments _____ _____	1 missing comma between two complete thoughts _____
2 run-ons _____ _____	
1 mistake in pronoun point of view _____	1 missing quotation mark _____
1 apostrophe mistake _____	1 missing comma between items in a series _____
	1 misspelled word _____

My Ideal Date

¹Here are the ingredients for my ideal date, first of all, I would want to look as stunning as possible. ²I would be dressed in a black velvet jumpsuit. ³That would fit me like a layer of paint. ⁴My accessories would include a pair of red satin spike heels a diamond hair clip, and a full-length black mink coat. ⁵My boyfriend, Tony, would wear a sharply tailored black tuxedo, a white silk shirt, and a red bow tie. ⁶The tux would emphasize Tony's broad shoulders and narrow waist, and you would see his chest muscles under the smooth shirt fabric. ⁷Tony would pull up to my house in a long, shiney limousine, then the driver would take us to the most exclusive and glittery nightclub in Manhattan. ⁸All eyes would be on us as we entered and photographers would rush up to take our picture for *People* magazine. ⁹As we danced on the lighted floor of the club, everyone would step aside to watch us perform our moves. ¹⁰After several bottles of champagne, Tony and I would head to the observation deck of the Empire State Building. ¹¹As we gazed out over the light's of the city, Tony would hand me a small velvet box containing a fifty-carat ruby engagement ring. ¹²And ask me to marry him. ¹³I would thank Tony for a lovely evening and tell him gently, "Tony, I don't plan to marry until I'm thirty.

Sentence-Skills Achievement Test

Part 1

This test will help you measure your improvement in important sentence skills. Certain parts of the following word groups are underlined. Write *X* in the answer space if you think a mistake appears at the underlined part. Write *C* in the answer space if you think the underlined part is correct.

The headings ("Fragments," "Run-Ons," and so on) will give you clues to the mistakes to look for.

Fragments

_____ 1. After a careless driver hit my motorcycle, I decided to buy a car. At least I would have more protection against other careless drivers.

_____ 2. Because of her work with autistic children. Dr. Marie Sorrentino was awarded a National Science Foundation grant. As a result, she was able to continue her research.

_____ 3. In 1918, Francis March wrote *A History of the World War.* Which is what World War I was then called. That name changed when World War II broke out.

_____ 4. Using a magnifying glass, the little girls burned holes in the dry leaf. They then set some tissue paper on fire.

_____ 5. My brother and I seldom have fights about what to watch on television. Except with baseball games. I get bored watching baseball.

_____ 6. My roommate and I ate, talked, danced, and sang at a party the other night. Also, we played cards until 3 A.M. As a result, we both slept until noon the next day.

Run-Ons

_____ 7. The snow on most roads had been cleared off quite well, traffic was moving normally.

_____ 8. The bald eagle is also known as the American eagle, for it is the national bird of the United States.

_____ 9. I got through the interview without breaking out in a sweat, I also managed to keep my voice under control.

_____ 10. The craze for convenience in our country has gone too far. There are drive-in banks, restaurants, and even churches.

_____ 11. My most valued possession is my stoneware cooker, I can make entire meals in it at a low cost.

628

_____   12. The shopping carts outside the supermarket seemed welded together, Rita could not separate one from another.

Standard English Verbs

_____   13. I am going to borrow my father's car if he agree.

_____   14. For recreation he sets up hundreds of dominoes, and then he knocks them over.

_____   15. He stopped taking a nap after lunch because he then had trouble sleeping at night.

_____   16. There was no bread for sandwiches, so he decided to drive to the store.

Irregular Verbs

_____   17. The large pile of snow had shrank significantly after the weather got warm.

_____   18. That woman has never ran for political office before.

_____   19. They forgetted to shut the car windows; luckily it didn't rain.

_____   20. They had ate the gallon of natural vanilla ice cream in just one night.

Subject-Verb Agreement

_____   21. The children watch as the six geese, which have just landed on the meadow, waddles into the pond.

_____   22. There is two minutes left in the football game.

_____   23. He believes films that feature violence is a disgrace to our society.

_____   24. The list of books on our syllabus were not very long.

Consistent Verb Tense

_____   25. On the night of his surprise party, Alex wanted to stay home, but his sister convinced him to accompany her to the restaurant where the guests are waiting.

_____   26 Kevin eats lunch at the diner every Wednesday, but he brings a sandwich to work on the other days.

_____   27. Juan ran down the hall without looking and trips over the toy truck lying on the floor.

_____   28. Debbie enjoys riding her bike in the newly built park, which features a special path for bikers and runners.

Pronoun Agreement, Reference, and Point of View

_____ 29. The museum guides assigned to the students' tour were willing to discuss any of the exhibits <u>that you asked them about.</u>

_____ 30. We did not return to the <u>amusement park, for we</u> had to pay too much for the rides and meals.

_____ 31. Drivers should check the oil level in <u>their</u> cars every three months.

_____ 32. Someone who wastes money as much as Anton <u>puts their family's</u> financial security in jeopardy.

_____ 33. Sharon's mother was overjoyed when <u>Sharon</u> became pregnant.

_____ 34. I work at a place <u>where you have</u> to punch a time clock.

Pronoun Types

_____ 35. Giacomo and <u>him</u> plan to join the Marine Corps.

_____ 36. No one in the class is better at <u>computer programming than he.</u>

Adjectives and Adverbs

_____ 37. The little <u>girl spoke so quiet</u> I could hardly hear her.

_____ 38. Let's hope the weather doesn't get <u>any more worse.</u>

Misplaced Modifiers

_____ 39 <u>To be cooked well, people</u> should steam their vegetables.

_____ 40. <u>With a mile-wide grin,</u> Betty turned in her winning raffle ticket.

_____ 41. I bought a beautiful shirt in a local store <u>with long sleeves and French cuffs.</u>

_____ 42. I first spotted the turtle <u>playing tag on the back lawn.</u>

Dangling Modifiers

_____ 43. <u>While still a little girl,</u> her father was appointed company president.

_____ 44. <u>Running across the field,</u> I caught the baseball.

_____ 45. <u>Going down the elevator from the rooftop restaurant, a crowd</u> awaited us on the ground floor.

_____ 46. <u>Looking at my watch,</u> a taxi nearly ran me over.

Faulty Parallelism

_____ 47. The book was well written, interesting, and many instructors assigned it.

_____ 48. I put my books in a locker, changed into my gym clothes, and hurried to the yoga class.

_____ 49. Jogging, playing tennis, and a daily swim kept John from gaining back the weight he had lost.

_____ 50. In the evening I plan to write a paper, to watch a movie, and to read two chapters in my biology text.

Capital Letters

_____ 51. He thinks he's the greatest thing since italian ice cream, but he's more like frozen pizza!

_____ 52. I asked Cindy, "what time will you be leaving?"

_____ 53. On the breakfast table sat a carton of orange juice, a banana, and a bowl of cheerios cereal.

_____ 54. Mother ordered a raincoat from the catalog on Monday, and it arrived four days later.

Apostrophe

_____ 55. Marians attention was focused on the bride's gown, a Paris original.

_____ 56. He's failing the course because he doesn't have any confidence in his ability to do the work.

_____ 57. Clyde was incensed at the dentist who charged him ninety dollars to fix his son's tooth.

_____ 58. I wouldnt have attended the meeting, but the dean wanted me to share our new project with the committee.

Quotation Marks

_____ 59. In Greek mythology, Daedalus warned his son Icarus, "Don't fly too near the sun.

_____ 60. Martha said to Fred at bedtime, "Why is it that men's pajamas always have such baggy bottoms?" "You look like a circus clown in that flannel outfit."

_____ 61. The red sign on the door read, "Warning—open only in case of an emergency."

_____ 62. "I can't stand that commercial," said Sue. "Do you mind if I turn off the television?"

Comma

_____ 63. Artie attended his morning classes, ate lunch, studied for his math test, went to work, got home, and fell right to sleep.

_____ 64. Although we wanted to visit France we spent all of our vacation in Spain.

_____ 65. Power, not love or money, is what most politicians want.

_____ 66. The heel on one of Lola's shoes came off, so she spent the day walking barefoot.

_____ 67. "Thank goodness I'm almost done" I said aloud with every stroke of the broom.

_____ 68. Last night I ran into my old friend Sasha who was studying for a physics exam in the library.

Commonly Confused Words

_____ 69. The principal upon which the economist based his predictions seemed a bit strange.

_____ 70. Fortunately, I was not driving very fast when my car lost it's brakes.

_____ 71. There were many reasons that Dennis deserved the humanitarian award.

_____ 72. There are too many steps in the math formula for me to understand it.

_____ 73. The counseling center can advise you on how to prepare for an interview.

_____ 74. To many students seem to give up after getting a poor grade on one exam.

Effective Word Use

_____ 75. The teacher called to discuss Ron's social maladjustment difficulties.

_____ 76. I thought the course would be a piece of cake, but a ten-page paper was required.

_____ 77. The economy has taken a turn for the worse, but it goes without saying that it will improve soon.

_____ 78. Spike gave away his television owing to the fact that it distracted him from studying.

Part 2 (Optional)

Do Part 2 at your instructor's request. This second part of the test will provide more detailed information about your improvement in sentence skills. On a separate piece of paper, number and correct all the items you have marked with an X. For examples, see page 417. There are more than forty corrections to make in all.

Correction Symbols

Here is a list of symbols the instructor may use when marking papers. The numbers in parentheses refer to the pages that explain the skill involved.

Agr	Correct the mistake in agreement of subject and verb (475–481) or pronoun and the word the pronoun refers to (482–488).
Apos	Correct the apostrophe mistake (526–535).
Bal	Balance the parts of the sentence so they have the same (parallel) form (109–110).
Cap	Correct the mistake in capital letters (514–522).
Coh	Revise to improve coherence (87–89; 144–146).
Comma	Add a comma (544–552).
CS	Correct the comma splice (443–456).
DM	Correct the dangling modifier (502–507).
Det	Support or develop the topic more fully by adding details (58–64; 76–82).
Frag	Attach the fragment to a sentence or make it a sentence (427–442).
lc	Use a lowercase (small) letter rather than a capital (514–522).
MM	Correct the misplaced modifier (500–502).
¶	Indent for a new paragraph.
No ¶	Do not indent for a new paragraph.
Pro	Correct the pronoun mistake (482–488).
Quot	Correct the mistake in quotation marks (536–543).
R-O	Correct the run-on (443–456).
Sp	Correct the spelling error (568–574).
Trans	Supply or improve a transition (89–98).
Und	Underline or italicize (540–541).
Verb	Correct the verb or verb form (457–474).
Wordy	Omit needless words (116–118).
WW	Replace the word marked with a more accurate one (588–593).
?	Write the illegible word clearly.
/	Eliminate the word, letter, or punctuation mark so slashed.
^	Add the omitted word or words.
;/:/-/—	Add semicolon (554), colon (554); hyphen (556), or dash (555).
✓	You have something fine or good here: an expression, a detail, an idea.

Readings for Writers

What do you notice about the student in this photograph? Although surrounded by books, he seems to need only his computer. Will computers and the Internet ever replace the need for printed books? Think about this question and write a response.

Introduction to the Readings

The reading selections in Part Six will help you find topics for writing. Some of the selections provide helpful practical information. For example, you'll learn how to deal with interpersonal conflict and how to avoid being manipulated by clever ads. Other selections deal with thought-provoking aspects of contemporary life. One article, for instance, dramatizes in a vivid and painful way the tragedy that can result when teenagers drink and drive. Still other selections are devoted to a celebration of human goals and values; one essay, for example, reminds us of the power that praise and appreciation can have in our daily lives. The varied subjects should inspire lively class discussions as well as serious individual thought. The selections should also provide a continuing source of high-interest material for a wide range of writing assignments.

The selections serve another purpose as well. They will help you develop reading skills that will directly benefit you as a writer. First, through close reading, you will learn how to recognize the main idea or point of a selection and how to identify and evaluate the supporting material that develops the main idea. In your writing, you will aim to achieve the same essential structure: an overall point followed by detailed, valid support for that point. Second, close reading will help you explore a selection and its possibilities thoroughly. The more you understand about what is said in a piece, the more ideas and feelings you may have about writing on an assigned topic or a related topic of your own. A third benefit of close reading is becoming more aware of authors' stylistic devices— for example, their introductions and conclusions, their ways of presenting and developing a point, their use of transitions, their choice of language to achieve a particular tone. Recognizing these devices in other people's writing will help you enlarge your own range of writing techniques.

The Format of Each Selection

Each selection begins with a short overview that gives helpful background information. The selection is then followed by two sets of questions.

- First, there are ten reading comprehension questions to help you measure your understanding of the material. These questions involve several important reading skills: understanding vocabulary in context, recognizing a subject or topic, determining the thesis or main idea, identifying key supporting points, and making inferences. Answering the questions will enable you and your instructor to check quickly your basic understanding of a selection. More significantly, as you move from one selection to the next, you will sharpen your reading skills as well as strengthen your thinking skills—two key factors in making you a better writer.

- Following the comprehension questions are several discussion questions. In addition to dealing with content, these questions focus on structure, style, and tone.

Finally, several writing assignments accompany each selection. Many of the assignments provide guidelines on how to proceed, including suggestions for prewriting and appropriate methods of development. When writing your responses to the readings, you will have opportunities to apply all the methods of development presented in Part Two of this book.

How to Read Well: Four General Steps

Skillful reading is an important part of becoming a skillful writer. Following are four steps that will make you a better reader—both of the selections here and in your reading at large.

1 Concentrate as You Read

To improve your concentration, follow these tips. First, read in a place where you can be quiet and alone. Don't choose a spot where a TV or a video game is on or where friends or family are talking nearby. Next, sit in an upright position when you read. If your body is in a completely relaxed position, sprawled across a bed or nestled in an easy chair, your mind is also going to be completely relaxed. The light muscular tension that comes from sitting upright in a chair promotes concentration and keeps your mind ready to work. Finally, consider using your index finger (or a pen) as a pacer while you read. Lightly underline each line of print with your index finger as you read down a page. Hold your hand slightly above the page and move your finger at a speed that is a little too fast for comfort. This pacing with your index finger, like sitting upright in a chair, creates a slight physical tension that will keep your body and mind focused and alert.

2 Skim Material before You Read it

In skimming, you spend about two minutes rapidly surveying a selection, looking for important points and skipping secondary material. Follow this sequence when skimming:

- Begin by reading the overview that precedes the selection.
- Then study the title of the selection for a few moments. A good title is the shortest possible summary of a selection; it often tells you in just a few words what a selection is about.

- Next, form a basic question (or questions) out of the title. Forming questions out of the title is often a key to locating a writer's main idea—your next concern in skimming.

- Read the first two or three paragraphs and the last two or three paragraphs in the selection. Very often a writer's main idea, *if* it is directly stated, will appear in one of these paragraphs and will relate to the title.

- Finally, look quickly at the rest of the selection for other clues to important points. Are there any subheads you can relate in some way to the title? Are there any words the author has decided to emphasize by setting them off in *italic* or **boldface** type? Are there any major lists of items signaled by words such as *first, second, also, another,* and so on?

3 Read the Selection Straight Through with a Pen Nearby

Don't slow down or turn back; just aim to understand as much as you can the first time through. Place a check or star beside answers to basic questions you formed from the title, and beside other ideas that seem important. Number lists of important points 1, 2, 3, ... Circle words you don't understand. Put question marks in the margin next to passages that are unclear and that you will want to reread.

4 Work with the Material

Go back and reread passages that were not clear the first time through. Look up words that block your understanding of ideas, and write their meanings in the margin. Also, reread carefully the areas you identified as most important; doing so will enlarge your understanding of the material. Now that you have a sense of the whole, prepare a short outline of the selection by answering the following questions on a sheet of paper:

- What is the main idea?
- What key points support the main idea?
- What seem to be other important points in the selection?

By working with the material in this way, you will significantly increase your understanding of a selection. Effective reading, just like effective writing, does not happen all at once. Rather, it is a process. Often you begin with a general impression of what something means, and then, by working at it, you move to a deeper level of understanding of the material.

How to Answer the Comprehension Questions: Specific Hints

Several important reading skills are involved in the ten reading comprehension questions that follow each selection. The skills are

- Understanding vocabulary in context
- Summarizing the selection by providing a title for it
- Determining the main idea
- Recognizing key supporting details
- Making inferences

The following hints will help you apply each of these reading skills:

- *Vocabulary in context.* To decide on the meaning of an unfamiliar word, consider its context. Ask yourself, "Are there any clues in the sentence that suggest what this word means?"

- *Subject or title.* Remember that the title should accurately describe the *entire* selection. It should be neither too broad nor too narrow for the material in the selection. It should answer the question "What is this about?" as specifically as possible. Note that you may at times find it easier to do the "title" question *after* the "main idea" question.

- *Main idea.* Choose the statement that you think best expresses the main idea or thesis of the entire selection. Remember that the title will often help you focus on the main idea. Then ask yourself, "Does most of the material in the selection support this statement?" If you can answer "yes" to this question, you have found the thesis.

- *Key details.* If you were asked to give a two-minute summary of a selection, the major details are the ones you would include in that summary. To determine the key details, ask yourself, "What are the major supporting points for the thesis?"

- *Inferences.* Answer these questions by drawing on the evidence presented in the selection and on your own common sense. Ask yourself, "What reasonable judgments can I make on the basis of the information in the selection?"

In your notebook or in a computer file, keep track of your performance as you answer the ten questions for each selection. Reviewing how well you did in each case will help you understand your strengths and weaknesses.

All the Good Things

Sister Helen Mrosla

PREVIEW

Sometimes the smallest things we do have the biggest impact. A teacher's impulsive idea, designed to brighten a dull Friday-afternoon class, affected her students more than she ever dreamed. Sister Helen Mrosla's moment of classroom inspiration took on a life of its own, returning to visit her at a most unexpected time. Her account of the experience reminds us of the human heart's endless hunger for recognition and appreciation.

1 He was in the first third-grade class I taught at Saint Mary's School in Morris, Minnesota. All thirty-four of my students were dear to me, but Mark Eklund was one in a million. He was very neat in appearance but had that happy-to-be-alive attitude that made even his occasional mischievousness delightful.

2 Mark talked incessantly. I had to remind him again and again that talking without permission was not acceptable. What impressed me so much, though, was his sincere response every time I had to correct him for misbehaving—"Thank you for correcting me, Sister!" I didn't know what to make of it at first, but before long I became accustomed to hearing it many times a day.

3 One morning my patience was growing thin when Mark talked once too often, and then I made a novice teacher's mistake. I looked at him and said, "If you say one more word, I am going to tape your mouth shut!"

4 It wasn't ten seconds later when Chuck blurted out, "Mark is talking again." I hadn't asked any of the students to help me watch Mark, but since I had stated the punishment in front of the class, I had to act on it.

5 I remember the scene as if it had occurred this morning. I walked to my desk, very deliberately opened my drawer, and took out a roll of masking tape. Without saying a word, I proceeded to Mark's desk, tore off two pieces of tape and made a big X with them over his mouth. I then returned to the front of the room. As I glanced at Mark to see how he was doing, he winked at me.

That did it! I started laughing. The class cheered as I walked back to Mark's 6
desk, removed the tape, and shrugged my shoulders. His first words were, "Thank
you for correcting me, Sister."

At the end of the year I was asked to teach junior-high math. The years flew 7
by, and before I knew it Mark was in my classroom again. He was more handsome
than ever and just as polite. Since he had to listen carefully to my instruction in the
"new math," he did not talk as much in ninth grade as he had talked in the third.

One Friday, things just didn't feel right. We had worked hard on a new 8
concept all week, and I sensed that the students were frowning, frustrated with
themselves—and edgy with one another. I had to stop this crankiness before it got
out of hand. So I asked them to list the names of the other students in the room
on two sheets of paper, leaving a space after each name. Then I told them to think
of the nicest thing they could say about each of their classmates and write it down.

It took the remainder of the class period to finish the assignment, and as the 9
students left the room, each one handed me the papers. Charlie smiled. Mark
said, "Thank you for teaching me, Sister. Have a good weekend."

That Saturday, I wrote down the name of each student on a separate sheet 10
of paper, and I listed what everyone else had said about that individual.

On Monday I gave each student his or her list. Before long, the entire class 11
was smiling. "Really?" I heard whispered. "I never knew that meant anything to
anyone!" "I didn't know others liked me so much!"

No one ever mentioned those papers in class again. I never knew if the stu- 12
dents discussed them after class or with their parents, but it didn't matter. The
exercise had accomplished its purpose. The students were happy with themselves
and one another again.

That group of students moved on. Several years later, after I returned from 13
a vacation, my parents met me at the airport. As we were driving home, Mother
asked me the usual questions about the trip—the weather, my experiences in
general. There was a slight lull in the conversation. Mother gave Dad a sideways
glance and simply said, "Dad?" My father cleared his throat as he usually did
before something important. "The Eklunds called last night," he began. "Really?"
I said. "I haven't heard from them in years. I wonder how Mark is."

Dad responded quietly. "Mark was killed in Vietnam," he said. "The funeral 14
is tomorrow, and his parents would like it if you could attend." To this day I can
still point to the exact spot on I-494 where Dad told me about Mark.

I had never seen a serviceman in a military coffin before. Mark looked so 15
handsome, so mature. All I could think at that moment was, Mark, I would give
all the masking tape in the world if only you would talk to me.

The church was packed with Mark's friends. Chuck's sister sang "The Battle 16
Hymn of the Republic." Why did it have to rain on the day of the funeral? It
was difficult enough at the graveside. The pastor said the usual prayers, and the
bugler played Taps. One by one those who loved Mark took a last walk by the
coffin and sprinkled it with holy water.

I was the last one to bless the coffin. As I stood there, one of the soldiers who 17 had acted as pallbearer came up to me. "Were you Mark's math teacher?" he asked. I nodded as I continued to stare at the coffin. "Mark talked about you a lot," he said.

After the funeral, most of Mark's former classmates headed to Chuck's farm- 18 house for lunch. Mark's mother and father were there, obviously waiting for me. "We want to show you something," his father said, taking a wallet out of his pocket. "They found this on Mark when he was killed. We thought you might recognize it."

Opening the billfold, he carefully removed two worn pieces of notebook paper 19 that had obviously been taped, folded and refolded many times. I knew without looking that the papers were the ones on which I had listed all the good things each of Mark's classmates had said about him. "Thank you so much for doing that," Mark's mother said. "As you can see, Mark treasured it."

Mark's classmates started to gather 20 around us. Charlie smiled rather sheepishly and said, "I still have my list. it's in the top drawer of my desk at home." Chuck's wife said, "Chuck asked me to put his list in our wedding album." "I have mine too," Marilyn said. "It's in my diary." Then Vicki, another classmate, reached into her pocketbook, took out her wallet, and showed her worn and frazzled list to the group. "I carry this with me at all times," Vicki said without batting an eyelash. "I think we all saved our lists."

That's when I finally sat down and 21 cried. I cried for Mark and for all his friends who would never see him again.

From looking at this photograph, what can you tell about the relationship between the students and their instructor? What specific visual clues help you draw these conclusions?

www.mhhe.com/langan

READING COMPREHENSION QUESTIONS

1. The word *incessantly* in "Mark talked incessantly. I had to remind him again and again that talking without permission was not acceptable" (paragraph 2) means

   a. slowly.

   b. quietly.

   c. constantly.

   d. pleasantly.

2. The word *edgy* in "We had worked hard on a new concept all week, and I sensed that the students were frowning, frustrated with themselves—and edgy with one another. I had to stop this crankiness before it got out of hand" (paragraph 8) means

    a. funny.

    b. calm.

    c. easily annoyed.

    d. dangerous.

3. Which of the following would be the best alternative title for this selection?

    a. Talkative Mark

    b. My Life as a Teacher

    c. More Important Than I Knew

    d. A Tragic Death

4. Which sentence best expresses the main idea of the selection?

    a. Although Sister Helen sometimes scolded Mark Eklund, he appreciated her devotion to teaching.

    b. When a former student of hers died, Sister Helen discovered how important one of her assignments had been to him and his classmates.

    c. When her students were cranky one day, Sister Helen had them write down something nice about each of their classmates.

    d. A pupil whom Sister Helen was especially fond of was tragically killed while serving in Vietnam.

5. Upon reading their lists for the first time, Sister Helen's students

    a. were silent and embarrassed.

    b. were disappointed.

    c. pretended to think the lists were stupid, although they really liked them.

    d. smiled and seemed pleased.

6. In the days after the assignment to write down something nice about one another,

    a. students didn't mention the assignment again.

    b. students often brought their lists to school.

    c. Sister Helen received calls from several parents complaining about the assignment.

    d. Sister Helen decided to repeat the assignment in every one of her classes.

7. According to Vicki,
   a. Mark was the only student to have saved his list.
   b. Vicki and Mark were the only students to have saved their lists.
   c. Vicki, Mark, Charlie, Chuck, and Marilyn were the only students to have saved their lists.
   d. all the students had saved their lists.

8. The author implies that
   a. she was surprised to learn how much the lists had meant to her students.
   b. Mark's parents were jealous of his affection for Sister Helen.
   c. Mark's death shattered her faith in God.
   d. Mark's classmates had not stayed in touch with one another over the years.

9. *True or false?* _____ The author implies that Mark had gotten married.

10. We can conclude that when Sister Helen was a third-grade teacher, she
    a. was usually short-tempered and irritable.
    b. wasn't always sure how to discipline her students.
    c. didn't expect Mark to do well in school.
    d. had no sense of humor.

DISCUSSION QUESTIONS

About Content

1. What did Sister Helen hope to accomplish by asking her students to list nice things about one another?

2. At least some students were surprised by the good things others wrote about them. What does this tell us about how we see ourselves and how we communicate our views of others?

3. "All the Good Things" has literally traveled around the world. Not only has it been reprinted in numerous publications, but many readers have sent it out over the Internet for others to read. Why do you think so many people love this story? Why do they want to share it with others?

About Structure

4. This selection is organized according to time. What three separate time periods does it cover? What paragraphs are included in the first time period? The second? The third?

5. Paragraph 8 includes a cause-and-effect structure. What part of the paragraph is devoted to the cause? What part is devoted to the effect? What transition word signals the break between the cause and the effect?

6. What does the title "All the Good Things" mean? Is this a good title for the essay? Why or why not?

About Style and Tone

7. Sister Helen is willing to let her readers see her weaknesses as well as her strengths. Find a place in the selection in which the author shows herself as less than perfect.

8. What does Sister Helen accomplish by beginning her essay with the word "he"? What does that unusual beginning tell the reader?

9. How does Sister Helen feel about her students? Find evidence that backs up your opinion.

10. Sister Helen comments on Mark's "happy-to-be-alive" attitude. What support does she provide that makes us understand what Mark was like?

WRITING ASSIGNMENTS

www.mhhe.com/langan

Assignment 1: Writing a Paragraph

Early in her story, Sister Helen refers to a "teacher's mistake" that forced her to punish a student in front of the class. Write a paragraph about a time you gave in to pressure to do something because others around you expected it. Explain what the situation was, what happened, and how you felt afterward. Here are two sample topic sentences:

> Even though I knew it was wrong, I went along with some friends who shoplifted at the mall.

> Just because my friends did, I made fun of a kid in my study hall who was a slow learner.

Assignment 2: Writing a Paragraph

Sister Helen's students kept their lists for many years. What souvenir of the past have you kept for a long time? Why? Bring your souvenir to class and describe it to a partner. Write a paragraph describing the souvenir, how you got it, and what it means to you. Begin with a topic sentence such as this:

> I've kept a green ribbon in one of my dresser drawers for over ten years because it reminds me of an experience I treasure.

Assignment 3: Writing an Essay

It's easy to forget to let others know how much they have helped us. Only after one of the students died did Sister Helen learn how important the list of positive comments had been to her class. Write an essay about someone to whom you are grateful and explain what that person has done for you. In your thesis statement, introduce the person and describe his or her relationship to you. Also include a general statement of what that person has done for you. Your thesis statement can be similar to any of these:

My brother Roy has been an important part of my life.

My best friend Ginger helped me through a major crisis.

Mrs. Morrison, my seventh-grade English teacher, taught me a lesson for which I will always be grateful.

Use freewriting to help you find interesting details to support your thesis statement. You may find two or three separate incidents to write about, each in a paragraph of its own. Or you may find it best to use several paragraphs to give a detailed narrative of one incident or two or three related events. (Note how Sister Helen uses several separate "scenes" to tell her story.) Whatever your approach, use some dialogue to enliven key parts of your essay. (Review the reading to see how Sister Helen uses dialogue throughout her essay.)

Alternatively, write an essay about three people to whom you are grateful. In that case, each paragraph of the body of your essay would deal with one of those people. The thesis statement in such an essay might be similar to this:

There are three people who have made a big difference in my life.

Rowing the Bus
Paul Logan

PREVIEW

There is a well-known saying that goes something like this: All that is necessary in order for evil to triumph is for good people to do nothing. Even young people are forced to face cruel behavior and to decide how they will respond to it. In this essay, Paul Logan looks back at a period of schoolyard cruelty in which he was both a victim and a participant. With unflinching honesty, he describes his behavior then and how it helped to shape the person he has become.

When I was in elementary school, some older kids made me row the bus. Row- 1
ing meant that on the way to school I had to sit in the dirty bus aisle littered with
paper, gum wads, and spitballs. Then I had to simulate the motion of rowing while
the kids around me laughed and chanted, "Row, row, row the bus." I was forced to
do this by a group of bullies who spent most of their time picking on me.

I was the perfect target for them. I was small. I had no father. And my 2
mother, though she worked hard to support me, was unable to afford clothes and
sneakers that were "cool." Instead she dressed me in outfits that we got from
"the bags"—hand-me-downs given as donations to a local church.

Each Wednesday, she'd bring several bags of clothes to the house and pull 3
out musty, wrinkled shirts and worn bell-bottom pants that other families no
longer wanted. I knew that people were kind to give things to us, but I hated
wearing clothes that might have been donated by my classmates. Each time I
wore something from the bags, I feared that the other kids might recognize
something that was once theirs.

Besides my outdated clothes, I wore thick glasses, had crossed eyes, and 4
spoke with a persistent lisp. For whatever reason, I had never learned to say the
"s" sound properly, and I pronounced words that began with "th" as if they began
with a "d." In addition, because of my severely crossed eyes, I lacked the hand
and eye coordination necessary to hit or catch flying objects.

As a result, footballs, baseballs, soccer balls and basketballs became my 5
enemies. I knew, before I stepped onto the field or court, that I would do something clumsy or foolish and that everyone would laugh at me. I feared humiliation so much that I became skillful at feigning illnesses to get out of gym class.
Eventually I learned how to give myself low-grade fevers so the nurse would
write me an excuse. It worked for a while, until the gym teachers caught on.
When I did have to play, I was always the last one chosen to be on any team.
In fact, team captains did everything in their power to make their opponents get
stuck with me. When the unlucky team captain was forced to call my name, I
would trudge over to the team, knowing that no one there liked or wanted me.
For four years, from second through fifth grade, I prayed nightly for God to give
me school days in which I would not be insulted, embarrassed, or made to feel
ashamed.

I thought my prayers were answered when my mother decided to move dur- 6
ing the summer before sixth grade. The move meant that I got to start sixth grade
in a different school, a place where I had no reputation. Although the older kids
laughed and snorted at me as soon as I got on my new bus—they couldn't miss
my thick glasses and strange clothes—I soon discovered that there was another
kid who received the brunt of their insults. His name was George, and everyone
made fun of him. The kids taunted him because he was skinny; they belittled
him because he had acne that pocked and blotched his face; and they teased him
because his voice was squeaky. During my first gym class at my new school, I
wasn't the last one chosen for kickball; George was.

George tried hard to be friends with me, coming up to me in the cafeteria 7 on the first day of school. "Hi. My name's George. Can I sit with you?" he asked with a peculiar squeakiness that made each word high-pitched and raspy. As I nodded for him to sit down, I noticed an uncomfortable silence in the cafeteria as many of the students who had mocked George's clumsy gait during gym class began watching the two of us and whispering among themselves. By letting him sit with me, I had violated an unspoken law of school, a sinister code of childhood that demands there must always be someone to pick on. I began to realize two things. If I befriended George, I would soon receive the same treatment that I had gotten at my old school. If I stayed away from him, I might actually have a chance to escape being at the bottom.

Within days, the kids started taunting us whenever we were together. "Who's 8 your new little buddy, Georgie?" In the hallways, groups of students began mumbling about me just loud enough for me to hear, "Look, it's George's ugly boyfriend." On the bus rides to and from school, wads of paper and wet chewing gum were tossed at me by the bigger, older kids in the back of the bus.

It became clear that my friendship with George was going to cause me several 9 more years of misery at my new school. I decided to stop being friends with George. In class and at lunch, I spent less and less time with him. Sometimes I told him I was too busy to talk; other times I acted distracted and gave one-word responses to whatever he said. Our classmates, sensing that they had created a rift between George and me, intensified their attacks on him. Each day, George grew more desperate as he realized that the one person who could prevent him from being completely isolated was closing him off. I knew that I shouldn't avoid him, that he was feeling the same way I felt for so long, but I was so afraid that my life would become the hell it had been in my old school that I continued to ignore him.

Then, at recess one day, the meanest kid in the school, Chris, decided he 10 had had enough of George. He vowed that he was going to beat up George and anyone else who claimed to be his friend. A mob of kids formed and came after me. Chris led the way and cornered me near our school's swing sets. He grabbed me by my shirt and raised his fist over my head. A huge gathering of kids surrounded us, urging him to beat me up, chanting "Go, Chris, go!"

"You're Georgie's new little boyfriend, aren't you?" he yelled. The hot blast 11 of his breath carried droplets of his spit into my face. In a complete betrayal of the only kid who was nice to me, I denied George's friendship.

"No, I'm not George's friend. I don't like him. He's stupid," I blurted out. 12 Several kids snickered and mumbled under their breath. Chris stared at me for a few seconds and then threw me to the ground.

"Wimp. Where's George?" he demanded, standing over me. Someone pointed 13 to George sitting alone on top of the monkey bars about thirty yards from where we were. He was watching me. Chris and his followers sprinted over to George and yanked him off the bars to the ground. Although the mob quickly encircled them, I could still see the two of them at the center of the crowd, looking at each other. George seemed stoic, staring straight through Chris. I heard the familiar chant of "Go, Chris, go!" and watched as his fists began slamming into George's head and body. His face bloodied and his nose broken, George crumpled to the ground and sobbed without even throwing a punch. The mob cheered with pleasure and darted off into the playground to avoid an approaching teacher.

14 Chris was suspended, and after a few days, George came back to school. I wanted to talk to him, to ask him how he was, to apologize for leaving him alone and for not trying to stop him from getting hurt. But I couldn't go near him. Filled with shame for denying George and angered by my own cowardice, I never spoke to him again.

15 Several months later, without telling any students, George transferred to another school. Once in a while, in those last weeks before he left, I caught him watching me as I sat with the rest of the kids in the cafeteria. He never yelled at me or expressed anger, disappointment, or even sadness. Instead he just looked at me.

16 In the years that followed, George's silent stare remained with me. It was there in eighth grade when I saw a gang of popular kids beat up a sixth-grader because, they said, he was "ugly and stupid." It was there my first year in high school, when I saw a group of older kids steal another freshman's clothes and throw them into the showers. It was there a year later, when I watched several seniors press a wad of chewing gum into the hair of a new girl on the bus. Each time that I witnessed another awkward, uncomfortable, scared kid being tormented, I thought of George, and gradually his haunting stare began to speak to me. No longer silent, it told me that every child who is picked on and taunted deserves better, that no one—no matter how big, strong, attractive, or popular—has the right to abuse another person.

17 Finally, in my junior year when a loudmouthed, pink-skinned bully named Donald began picking on two freshmen on the bus, I could no longer deny George. Donald was crumpling a large wad of paper and preparing to bounce it off the back of the head of one of the young students when I interrupted him.

18 "Leave them alone, Don," I said. By then I was six inches taller and, after two years of high-school wrestling, thirty pounds heavier than I had been in my freshman year. Though Donald was still two years older than me, he wasn't much bigger. He stopped what he was doing, squinted, and stared at me.

19 "What's your problem, Paul?"

20 I felt the way I had many years earlier on the playground when I watched the mob of kids begin to surround George.

21 "Just leave them alone. They aren't bothering you," I responded quietly.

22 "What's it to you?" he challenged. A glimpse of my own past, of rowing the bus, of being mocked for my clothes, my lisp, my glasses, and my absent father flashed in my mind.

23 "Just don't mess with them. That's all I am saying, Don." My fingertips were tingling. The bus was silent. He got up from his seat and leaned over me, and I rose from my seat to face him. For a minute, both of us just stood there, without a word, staring.

"I'm just playing with them, Paul," he said, chuckling. "You don't have to 24 go psycho on me or anything." Then he shook his head, slapped me firmly on the chest with the back of his hand, and sat down. But he never threw that wad of paper. For the rest of the year, whenever I was on the bus, Don and the other troublemakers were noticeably quiet.

Although it has been years since my days on the playground and the school 25 bus, George's look still haunts me. Today, I see it on the faces of a few scared kids at my sister's school—she is in fifth grade. Or once in a while I'll catch a glimpse of someone like George on the evening news, in a story about a child who brought a gun to school to stop the kids from picking on him, or in a feature about a teen-ager who killed herself because everyone teased her. In each school, in almost every classroom, there is a George with a stricken face, hoping that someone nearby will be strong enough to be kind—despite what the crowd says—and brave enough to stand up against people who attack, tease, or hurt those who are vulnerable.

If asked about their behavior, I'm sure the bullies would say, "What's it to 26 you? It's just a joke. It's nothing." But to George and me, and everyone else who has been humiliated or laughed at or spat on, it is everything. No one should have to row the bus.

READING COMPREHENSION QUESTIONS

1. The word *simulate* in "Then I had to simulate the motion of rowing while the kids around me laughed and chanted, 'Row, row, row the bus'" (paragraph 1) means
   a. sing.
   b. ignore.
   c. imitate.
   d. release.

2. The word *rift* in "I decided to stop being friends with George. . . . Our classmates, sensing that they had created a rift between George and me, intensified their attacks on him" (paragraph 9) means
   a. friendship.
   b. agreement.
   c. break.
   d. joke.

3. Which of the following would be the best alternative title for this selection?
   a. A Sixth-Grade Adventure
   b. Children's Fears
   c. Dealing with Cruelty
   d. The Trouble with Busing

4. Which sentence best expresses the main idea of the selection?

   a. Although Paul Logan was the target of other students' abuse when he was a young boy, their attacks stopped as he grew taller and stronger.

   b. When Logan moved to a different school, he discovered that another student, George, was the target of more bullying than he was.

   c. Logan's experience of being bullied and his shame at how he treated George eventually made him speak up for someone else who was teased.

   d. Logan is ashamed that he did not stand up for George when George was being attacked by a bully on the playground.

5. When Chris attacked George, George reacted by

   a. fighting back hard.

   b. shouting for Logan to help him.

   c. running away.

   d. accepting the beating.

6. Logan finally found the courage to stand up for abused students when he saw

   a. Donald about to throw paper at a younger student.

   b. older kids throwing a freshman's clothes into the shower.

   c. seniors putting bubble gum in a new student's hair.

   d. a gang beating up a sixth-grader whom they disliked.

7. *True or false?*_____ After Logan confronted Donald on the bus, Donald began picking on Logan as well.

8. *True or false?* _____ The author suggests that his mother did not care very much about him.

9. The author implies that, when he started sixth grade at a new school,

   a. he became fairly popular.

   b. he decided to try out for athletic teams.

   c. he was relieved to find a kid who was more unpopular than he.

   d. he was frequently beaten up.

10. We can conclude that

   a. the kids who picked on George later regretted what they had done.

   b. George and the author eventually talked together about their experience in sixth grade.

   c. the author thinks kids today are kinder than they were when he was in sixth grade.

   d. the author is a more compassionate person now because of his experience with George.

DISCUSSION QUESTIONS

About Content

1. Logan describes a number of incidents involving students' cruelty to other students. Find at least three such events. What do they seem to have in common? Judging from such incidents, what purpose does cruel teasing seem to serve?

2. Throughout the essay, Paul Logan talks about cruel but ordinary school behavior. But in paragraph 25, he briefly mentions two extreme and tragic consequences of such cruelty. What are those consequences, and why do you think he introduces them? What is he implying?

About Structure

3. Below, write three time transitions Logan uses to advance his narration.

   _____   _____   _____

4. Logan describes the gradual change within him that finally results in his standing up for a student who is being abused. Where in the narrative does Logan show how internal changes may be taking place within him? Where in the narrative does he show that his reaction to witnessing bullying has changed?

5. Paul Logan titled his selection "Rowing the Bus." Yet very little of the essay actually deals with the incident the title describes. Why do you think Logan chose that title? In groups of two or three, come up with alternative titles and discuss why they would or would not be effective.

About Style and Tone

6. Give examples of how Logan appeals to our senses in paragraphs 1–4.

   Sight _____

   Smell _____

   Hearing _____

7. What is Logan's attitude toward himself regarding his treatment of George? Find three phrases that reveal his attitude and write them on a separate piece of paper.

WRITING ASSIGNMENTS

Assignment 1: Writing a Paragraph

Logan writes, " In each school, in almost every classroom, there is a George with a stricken face." Think of a person who filled the role of George in one of your classes. Then write a descriptive paragraph about that person, explaining why he or she was a target and what form the teasing took. Be sure to include a description of your own thoughts and actions regarding the student who was teased. Your topic sentence might be something like one of these:

A girl in my fifth-grade class was a lot like George in "Rowing the Bus."

Like Paul Logan, I suffered greatly in elementary school from being bullied.

Try to include details that appeal to two or three of the senses.

Assignment 2: Writing a Paragraph

Paul Logan feared that his life at his new school would be made miserable if he continued being friends with George. So he ended the friendship, even though he felt ashamed of doing so. Think of a time when you have wanted to do the right thing but felt that the price would be too high. Maybe you knew a friend was doing something dishonest and wanted him to stop but were afraid of losing his friendship. Or perhaps you pretended to forget a promise you had made because you decided it was too difficult to keep. Write a paragraph describing the choice you made and how you felt about yourself afterward.

Assignment 3: Writing an Essay

Logan provides many vivid descriptions of incidents in which bullies attack other students. Reread these descriptions, and consider what they teach you about the nature of bullies and bullying. Then write an essay that supports the following main idea:

Bullies seem to share certain qualities.

Identify two or three qualities; then discuss each in a separate paragraph. You may use two or three of the following as the topic sentences for your supporting paragraphs, or come up with your own supporting points:

Bullies are cowardly.

Bullies make themselves feel big by making other people feel small.

Bullies cannot feel very good about themselves.

Bullies are feared but not respected.

Bullies act cruelly in order to get attention.

Develop each supporting point with one or more anecdotes or ideas from any of the following: your own experience, your understanding of human nature, and "Rowing the Bus."

The Scholarship Jacket

Marta Salinas

| PREVIEW |

All of us have suffered disappointments and moments when we have felt we've been treated unfairly. In "The Scholarship Jacket," originally published in *Growing Up Chicana: An Anthology*, Marta Salinas writes about one such moment in her childhood in southern Texas. By focusing on an award that school authorities decided she should not receive, Salinas shows us the pain of discrimination as well as the need for inner strength.

The small Texas school that I attended carried out a tradition every year during the eighth-grade graduation: a beautiful jacket in gold and green, the school colors, was awarded to the class valedictorian, the student who had maintained the highest grades for eight years. The scholarship jacket had a big gold *S* on the left front side, and the winner's name was written in gold letters on the pocket. 1

My oldest sister, Rosie, had won the jacket a few years back, and I fully expected to win also. I was fourteen and in the eighth grade. I had been a straight-A student since the first grade, and the last year I had looked forward to owning that jacket. My father was a farm laborer who couldn't earn enough money to feed eight children, so when I was six I was given to my grandparents to raise. We couldn't participate in sports at school because there were registration fees, uniform costs, and trips out of town; so even though we were quite agile and athletic, there would never be a sports school jacket for us. This one, the scholarship jacket, was our only chance. 2

In May, close to graduation, spring fever struck, and no one paid any attention to class; instead we stared out the windows and at each other, wanting to speed up the last few weeks of school. I despaired every time I looked in the mirror. Pencil-thin, with not a curve anywhere, I was called "Beanpole" and "String Bean," and I knew that's what I looked like. A flat chest, no hips, and a brain, that's what I had. That really isn't much for a fourteen-year-old to work with, I thought, as I absent-mindedly wandered from my history class to the gym. Another hour of sweating during basketball and displaying my toothpick legs was coming up. Then I remembered my P.E. shorts were still in a bag under my desk where I'd forgotten them. I had to walk all the way back and get them. Coach Thompson was a real bear if anyone wasn't dressed for P.E. She had said I was a good forward and once she even tried to talk Grandma into letting me join the team. Grandma, of course, said no. 3

I was almost back at my classroom door when I heard angry voices and 4 arguing. I stopped. I didn't mean to eavesdrop; I just hesitated, not knowing what to do. I needed those shorts and I was going to be late, but I didn't want to interrupt an argument between my teachers. I recognized the voices: Mr. Schmidt, my history teacher; and Mr. Boone, my math teacher. They seemed to be arguing about me. I couldn't believe it. I still remember the shock that rooted me flat against the wall as if I were trying to blend in with the graffiti written there.

"I refuse to do it! I don't care who her father is; her grades don't even begin 5 to compare to Martha's. I won't lie or falsify records. Martha has a straight-A-plus average and you know it." That was Mr. Schmidt, and he sounded very angry. Mr. Boone's voice sounded calm and quiet.

"Look, Joann's father is not only on the Board, he owns the only store in 6 town; we could say it was a close tie and—"

The pounding in my ears drowned out the rest of the words, only a word here 7 and there filtered through. ". . . Martha is Mexican . . . resign . . . won't do it. . . ." Mr. Schmidt came rushing out, and luckily for me went down the opposite way toward the auditorium, so he didn't see me. Shaking, I waited a few minutes and then went in and grabbed my bag and fled from the room. Mr. Boone looked up when I came in but didn't say anything. To this day I don't remember if I got in trouble in P.E. for being late or how I made it through the rest of the afternoon. I went home very sad and cried into my pillow that night so Grandmother wouldn't hear me. It seemed a cruel coincidence that I had overheard that conversation.

The next day when the principal called me into his office, I knew what it 8 would be about. He looked uncomfortable and unhappy. I decided I wasn't going to make it any easier for him, so I looked him straight in the eye. He looked away and fidgeted with the papers on his desk.

"Martha," he said, "there's been a change in policy this year regarding the 9 scholarship jacket. As you know, it has always been free." He cleared his throat and continued. "This year the Board decided to charge fifteen dollars—which still won't cover the complete cost of the jacket."

I stared at him in shock and a small sound of dismay escaped my throat. I 10 hadn't expected this. He still avoided looking in my eyes.

"So if you are unable to pay the fifteen dollars for the jacket, it will be given 11 to the next one in line."

Standing with all the dignity I could muster, I said, "I'll speak to my grand- 12 father about it, sir, and let you know tomorrow." I cried on the walk home from the bus stop. The dirt road was a quarter of a mile from the highway, so by the time I got home, my eyes were red and puffy.

"Where's Grandpa?" I asked Grandma, looking down at the floor so she wouldn't 13 ask me why I'd been crying. She was sewing on a quilt and didn't look up.

"I think he's out back working in the bean field." 14

I went outside and looked out at the fields. There he was. I could see him 15 walking between the rows, his body bent over the little plants, hoe in hand. I walked slowly out to him, trying to think how I could best ask him for the money. There was a cool breeze blowing and a sweet smell of mesquite in the air, but I didn't appreciate it. I kicked at a dirt clod. I wanted that jacket so much. It was more than just being a valedictorian and giving a little thank-you speech for the jacket on graduation night. It represented eight years of hard work and expectation. I knew I had to be honest with Grandpa; it was my only chance. He saw me and looked up.

He waited for me to speak. I cleared my throat nervously and clasped my 16 hands behind my back so he wouldn't see them shaking. "Grandpa, I have a big favor to ask you," I said in Spanish, the only language he knew. He still waited silently. I tried again. "Grandpa, this year the principal said the scholarship jacket is not going to be free. It's going to cost fifteen dollars and I have to take the money in tomorrow, otherwise it'll be given to someone else." The last words came out in an eager rush. Grandpa straightened up tiredly and leaned his chin on the hoe handle. He looked out over the field that was filled with the tiny green bean plants. I waited, desperately hoping he'd say I could have the money.

He turned to me and asked quietly, "What does a scholarship jacket mean?" 17

I answered quickly; maybe there was a chance. "It means you've earned it 18 by having the highest grades for eight years and that's why they're giving it to you." Too late I realized the significance of my words. Grandpa knew that I understood it was not a matter of money. It wasn't that. He went back to hoeing the weeds that sprang up between the delicate little bean plants. It was a time-consuming job; sometimes the small shoots were right next to each other. Finally he spoke again.

"Then if you pay for it, Marta, it's not a scholarship jacket, is it? Tell your 19 principal I will not pay the fifteen dollars."

I walked back to the house and locked myself in the bathroom for a long 20 time. I was angry with Grandfather even though I knew he was right, and I was angry with the Board, whoever they were. Why did they have to change the rules just when it was my turn to win the jacket?

It was a very sad and withdrawn girl who dragged into the principal's office 21 the next day. This time he did look me in the eyes.

"What did your grandfather say?" 22

I sat very straight in my chair. 23

"He said to tell you he won't pay the fifteen dollars." 24

The principal muttered something I couldn't understand under his breath, 25 and walked over to the window. He stood looking out at something outside. He looked bigger than usual when he stood up; he was a tall, gaunt man with gray hair, and I watched the back of his head while I waited for him to speak.

"Why?" he finally asked. "Your grandfather has the money. Doesn't he own 26 a small bean farm?"

I looked at him, forcing my eyes to stay dry. "He said if I had to pay for it, 27 then it wouldn't be a scholarship jacket," I said and stood up to leave. "I guess you'll just have to give it to Joann." I hadn't meant to say that; it had just slipped out. I was almost to the door when he stopped me.

"Martha—wait."   28

I turned and looked at him, waiting. What did he want now? I could feel my   29 heart pounding. Something bitter and vile-tasting was coming up in my mouth; I was afraid I was going to be sick. I didn't need any sympathy speeches. He sighed loudly and went back to his big desk. He looked at me, biting his lip, as if thinking.

"OK, damn it. We'll make an exception in your case. I'll tell the Board,   30 you'll get your jacket."

I could hardly believe it. I spoke in a trembling rush. "Oh, thank you, sir!"   31 Suddenly I felt great. I didn't know about adrenaline in those days, but I knew something was pumping through me, making me feel as tall as the sky. I wanted to yell, jump, run the mile, do something. I ran out so I could cry in the hall where there was no one to see me. At the end of the day, Mr. Schmidt winked at me and said, "I hear you're getting a scholarship jacket this year."

His face looked as happy and innocent as a baby's, but I knew better. With-   32 out answering I gave him a quick hug and ran to the bus. I cried on the walk home again, but this time because I was so happy. I couldn't wait to tell Grandpa and ran straight to the field. I joined him in the row where he was working and without saying anything I crouched down and started pulling up the weeds with my hands. Grandpa worked alongside me for a few minutes, but he didn't ask what had happened. After I had a little pile of weeds between the rows, I stood up and faced him.

"The principal said he's making an exception for me, Grandpa, and I'm getting   33 the jacket after all. That's after I told him what you said."

Grandpa didn't say anything; he just gave me a pat on the shoulder and a   34 smile. He pulled out the crumpled red handkerchief that he always carried in his back pocket and wiped the sweat off his forehead.

"Better go see if your grandmother needs any help with supper."   35

I gave him a big grin. He didn't fool me. I skipped and ran back to the house   36 whistling some silly tune.

READING COMPREHENSION QUESTIONS

www.mhhe.com/langan

1. The word *falsify* in "I won't lie or falsify records. Martha has a straight-A-plus average and you know it" (paragraph 5) means
   a. make untrue.
   b. write down.
   c. keep track of.
   d. sort alphabetically.

2. The word *dismay* in "I stared at him in shock and a small sound of dismay escaped my throat. I hadn't expected this" (paragraph 10) means

  a. joy.

  b. comfort.

  c. relief.

  d. disappointment.

3. Which sentence best expresses the central point of the selection?

  a. It is more important to be smart than good-looking or athletic.

  b. People who are willing to pay for an award deserve it more than people who are not.

  c. By refusing to give in to discrimination, the author finally received the award she had earned.

  d. Always do what the adults in your family say, even if you don't agree.

4. Which sentence best expresses the main idea of paragraph 2?

  a. Marta wanted to win the scholarship jacket to be like her sister Rosie.

  b. The scholarship jacket was especially important to Marta because she was unable to earn a jacket in any other way.

  c. The scholarship jacket was better than a sports school jacket.

  d. Marta resented her parents for sending her to live with her grandparents.

5. Which sentence best expresses the main idea of paragraph 7?

  a. Marta was shocked and saddened by the conversation she overheard.

  b. Marta didn't want her grandmother to know she was crying.

  c. Mr. Schmidt didn't see Marta when he rushed out of the room.

  d. Marta didn't hear every word of Mr. Schmidt's and Mr. Boone's conversation.

6. Marta was raised by her grandparents because

  a. she wanted to learn to speak Spanish.

  b. her father did not earn enough money to feed all his children.

  c. she wanted to learn about farming.

  d. her parents died when she was six.

7. *True or false?* _____ Marta was called by a different name at school.

8. We can infer from paragraph 8 that the principal was "uncomfortable and unhappy" because

  a. the students had not been paying attention in class during the last few weeks before graduation.

  b. his office was very hot.

  c. he was ashamed to tell Marta that she had to pay fifteen dollars for a jacket that she had earned.

  d. Mr. Boone and Mr. Schmidt were fighting in the hallway.

9. The author implies that the Board members were not going to give Marta the scholarship jacket because

    a. she was late for P.E. class.

    b. they wanted to award the jacket to the daughter of an important local citizen.

    c. another student had better grades.

    d. they didn't think it was fair to have two members of the same family win the jacket.

10. *True or false?* _____ The author implies that the Board's new policy to require a fee for the scholarship jacket was an act of discrimination.

DISCUSSION QUESTIONS

About Content

1. Why was winning the scholarship jacket so important to Marta?

2. What seemed to be the meaning of the argument between Mr. Schmidt and Mr. Boone?

3. After Marta's grandfather asks her what the scholarship jacket is, the author writes, " 'It means you've earned it by having the highest grades for eight years and that's why they're giving it to you.' Too late I realized the significance of my words" (paragraph 18). What is the significance of her words?

About Structure

4. Why do you think Salinas begins her essay with a detailed description of the scholarship jacket? How does her description contribute to our interest in her story?

5. At what point does Salinas stop providing background information and start giving a time-ordered narration of a particular event in her life?

6. In the course of the essay, Salinas rides an emotional roller-coaster. Find and write here three words or phrases she uses to describe her different emotional states:

_____   _____   _____

About Style and Tone

7. As you read the essay, what impression do you form of Salinas's grandfather? What kind of man does he seem to be? What details does Salinas provide in order to create that impression?

8. In paragraph 12, Salinas writes, "Standing with all the dignity I could muster, I said, 'I'll speak to my grandfather about it, sir, and let you know tomorrow.'" What other evidence does Salinas give us that her dignity is important to her?

WRITING ASSIGNMENTS

Assignment 1: Writing a Paragraph

Write a paragraph about a time when you experienced or witnessed an injustice. Describe the circumstances surrounding the incident and why you think the people involved acted as they did. In your paragraph, describe how you felt at the time and any effect the incident has had on you. Your topic sentence could be something like one of the following:

> I was angry when my supervisor promoted his nephew even though I was more qualified.

> A friend of mine recently got into trouble with authorities even though he was innocent of any wrongdoing.

Assignment 2: Writing a Paragraph

Marta stresses again and again how important the scholarship jacket was to her and how hard she worked to win it. In groups of two or three, discuss something you each worked hard to achieve when you were younger. Then write a paragraph about that experience. How long did you work toward that goal? How did you feel when you finally succeeded? Or write about not achieving the goal. How did you cope with the disappointment? What did you learn from the experience?

Assignment 3: Writing an Essay

This story contains several examples of authority figures—specifically, the two teachers, the principal, and Marta's grandfather. Write an essay describing three qualities that you think an authority figure should possess. Such qualities might include honesty, fairness, compassion, and knowledge.

In the body of your essay, devote each supporting paragraph to one of those qualities. Within each paragraph, give an example or examples of how an authority figure in your life has demonstrated that quality.

You may write about three different authority figures who have demonstrated those three qualities to you. Alternatively, one authority figure may have demonstrated all three.

Your thesis statement might be similar to one of these:

> My older brother, my grandmother, and my football coach have been models of admirable behavior for me.

> My older brother's honesty, courage, and kindness to others have set a valuable example for me.

Joe Davis: A Cool Man
Beth Johnson

PREVIEW

Drugs and guns, crime and drugs, drugs and lies, liquor and drugs. If there was one constant in Joe Davis's life, it was drugs, the substances that ruled his existence. Personal tragedy was not enough to turn him off the path leading to the brink of self-destruction. Finally Joe was faced with a moment of decision. The choice he made has opened doors into a world that the old Joe barely knew existed.

Joe Davis was the coolest fourteen-year-old he'd ever seen.   1

He went to school when he felt like it. He hung out with a wild crowd. He 2 started drinking some wine, smoking some marijuana. "Nobody could tell me anything," he says today. "I thought the sun rose and set on me." There were rules at home, but Joe didn't do rules. So he moved in with his grandmother.

Joe Davis was the coolest sixteen-year-old he'd ever seen.   3

Joe's parents gave up on his schooling and signed him out of the tenth grade. 4 Joe went to work in his dad's body shop, but that didn't last long. There were rules there, too, and Joe didn't do rules. By the time he was in his mid-teens, Joe was taking pills that got him high, and he was even using cocaine. He was also smoking marijuana all the time and drinking booze all the time.

Joe Davis was the coolest twenty-five-year-old he'd ever seen.   5

He was living with a woman almost twice his age. The situation wasn't great, 6 but she paid the bills, and certainly Joe couldn't pay them. He had his habit to support, which by now had grown to include heroin. Sometimes he'd work at a low-level job, if someone else found it for him. He might work long enough to get a paycheck and then spend it all at once. Other times he'd be caught stealing and get fired first. A more challenging job was not an option, even if he had bothered to look for one. He couldn't put words together to form a sentence, unless the sentence was about drugs. Filling out an application was difficult. He wasn't a strong reader. He couldn't do much with numbers. Since his drug habit had to be paid for, he started to steal. He stole first from his parents, then from his sister. Then he stole from the families of people he knew. But eventually the people he knew wouldn't let him into their houses, since they knew he'd steal from them. So he got a gun and began holding people up. He chose elderly people and others who weren't likely to fight back. The holdups kept him in drug money, but things at home were getting worse. His woman's teenage daughter was getting out of line. Joe decided it was up to him to discipline her. The girl didn't like it. She told her boyfriend. One day, the boyfriend called Joe out of the house.

Bang. 7

Joe Davis was in the street, his nose in the dirt. His mind was still cloudy from 8 his most recent high, but he knew something was terribly wrong with his legs. He couldn't move them; he couldn't even feel them. His mother came out of her house nearby and ran to him. As he heard her screams, he imagined what she was seeing. Her oldest child, her first baby, her bright boy who could have been and done anything, was lying in the gutter, a junkie with a .22 caliber bullet lodged in his spine.

The next time Joe's head cleared, he was in a hospital bed, blinking up at his 9 parents as they stared helplessly at him. The doctors had done all they could; Joe would live, to everyone's surprise. But he was a paraplegic—paralyzed from his chest down. It was done. It was over. It was written in stone. He would not walk again. He would not be able to control his bladder or bowels. He would not be able to make love as he did before. He would not be able to hold people up, then hurry away.

Joe spent the next eight months being moved between several Philadelphia 10 hospitals, where he was shown the ropes of life as a paraplegic. Officially he was being "rehabilitated"—restored to a productive life. There was just one problem: Joe. "To be rehabilitated, you must have been habilitated first," he says today. "That wasn't me." During his stay in the hospitals, he found ways to get high every day.

Finally Joe was released from the hospital. He returned in his wheelchair to 11 the house he'd been living in when he was shot. He needed someone to take care of him, and his woman friend was still willing. His drug habit was as strong as ever, but his days as a stickup man were over. So he started selling drugs. Business was good. The money came in fast, and his own drug use accelerated even faster.

A wheelchair-bound junkie doesn't pay much attention to his health or clean- 12 liness. Eventually Joe developed his first bedsore: a deep, rotting wound that ate into his flesh, overwhelming him with its foul odor. He was admitted to Magee Rehabilitation Hospital, where he spent six months on his stomach while the ghastly wound slowly healed. Again, he spent his time in the hospital using drugs. This time his drug use did not go unnoticed. Soon before he was scheduled to be discharged, hospital officials kicked him out. He returned to his friend's house and his business. But then the police raided the house. They took the drugs; they took the money; they took the guns.

"I really went downhill then," says Joe. With no drugs and no money to get 13 drugs, life held little meaning. He began fighting with the woman he was living with. "When you're in the state I was in, you don't know how to be nice to anybody," he says. Finally she kicked him out of the house. When his parents took him in, Joe did a little selling from their house, trying to keep it low-key, out of sight, so they wouldn't notice. He laughs at the notion today. "I thought I could control junkies and tell them, 'Business only during certain hours.'" Joe got high when his monthly Social Security check came, high when he'd make a purchase for someone else and get a little something for himself, high when a visitor would share drugs with him. It wasn't much of a life. "There I was," he says, "a junkie with no education, no job, no friends, no means of supporting myself. And now I had a spinal cord injury."

Then came October 25, 1988. Joe had just filled a prescription for pills to 14 control his muscle spasms. Three hundred of the powerful muscle relaxants were there for the taking. He swallowed them all.

"It wasn't the spinal cord injury that did it," he says. "It was the addiction." 15

Joe tried hard to die, but it didn't work. His sister heard him choking and called 16 for help. He was rushed to the hospital, where he lay in a coma for four days.

Joe has trouble finding the words to describe what happened next. 17

"I had . . . a spiritual awakening, for lack of any better term," he says. "My 18 soul had been cleansed. I knew my life could be better. And from that day to this, I have chosen not to get high."

Drugs, he says, "are not even a temptation. That life is a thing that happened 19 to someone else."

Joe knew he wanted to turn himself around, but he needed help in knowing where 20 to start. He enrolled in Magee Hospital's vocational rehabilitation program. For six weeks, he immersed himself in discussions, tests, and exercises to help him determine the kind of work he might be suited for. The day he finished the rehab program, a nurse at Magee told him about a receptionist's job in the spinal cord injury unit at Thomas Jefferson Hospital. He went straight to the hospital and met Lorraine Buchanan, coordinator of the unit. "I told her where I was and where I wanted to go," Joe says. "I told her, 'If you give me a job, I will never disappoint you. I'll quit first if I see I can't live up to it.'" She gave him the job. The wheelchair-bound junkie, the man who'd never been able to hold a job, the drug-dependent stickup man who "couldn't put two words together to make a sentence" was now the first face, the first voice that patients encountered when they entered the spinal cord unit. "I'd never talked to people like that," says Joe, shaking his head. "I had absolutely no back-ground. But Lorraine and the others, they taught me to speak. Taught me to greet people. Taught me to handle the phone." How did he do in his role as a receptionist? A huge smile breaks across Joe's face as he answers, "Excellent."

Soon, his personal life also took a very positive turn. A month after Joe 21 started his job, he was riding a city bus to work. A woman recovering from knee surgery was in another seat. The two smiled, but didn't speak.

A week later, Joe spotted the woman again. The bus driver sensed something 22 was going on and encouraged Joe to approach her. Her name was Terri. She was a receptionist in a law office. On their first date, Joe laid his cards on the table. He told her his story. He also told her he was looking to get married. "That about scared her away," Joe recalls. "She said she wasn't interested in marriage. I asked, 'Well, suppose you did meet someone you cared about who cared about you and treated you well. Would you still be opposed to the idea of marriage?' She said no, she would consider it then. I said, 'Well, that's all I ask.'"

Four months later, as the two sat over dinner in a restaurant, Joe handed Terri 23 a box tied with a ribbon. Inside was a smaller box. Then a smaller box, and a smaller one still. Ten boxes in all. Inside the smallest was an engagement ring. After another six months, the two were married in the law office where Terri works. Since then, she has been Joe's constant source of support, encouragement, and love.

After Joe had started work at Jefferson Hospital, he talked with his supervisor, 24 Lorraine, about his dreams of moving on to something bigger, more challenging. She encouraged him to try college. He had taken and passed the high school general equivalency diploma (GED) exam years before, almost as a joke, when he was recovering from his bedsores at Magee. Now he enrolled in a university mathematics course. He didn't do well. "I wasn't ready," Joe says. "I'd been out of school seventeen years. I dropped out." Before he could let discouragement overwhelm him, he enrolled at Community College of Philadelphia (CCP), where he signed up for basic math and English courses. He worked hard, sharpening study skills he had never developed in his earlier school days. Next he took courses toward an associate's degree in mental health and social services, along with a certificate in addiction studies. Five years later, he graduated from CCP, the first member of his family ever to earn a college degree. He went on to receive a bachelor's degree in mental health from Hahnemann University in Philadelphia and then a master of social work from the University of Pennsylvania.

Today, Joe is the coordinator of "Think First," a violence and injury preven- 25 tion program operated by Magee Rehabilitation Hospital, where he also serves as a case manager for patients with spinal cord injuries. Once a month, he and two other men with such injuries speak to a group of first-time offenders who were arrested for driving under the influence of drugs or alcohol. He talks with government officials about passing stricter gun legislation and installing injury-prevention programs in public schools, and he visits local schools to describe the lessons of his life with students there. In every contact with every individual, Joe has one goal: to ensure the safety and well-being of young people.

At a presentation at a disciplinary school outside of Philadelphia, Joe gazes 26 with quiet authority at the unruly crowd of teenagers. He begins to speak, telling them about speedballs and guns, fast money and bedsores, even about the leg bag that collects his urine. At first, the kids snort with laughter at his honesty. When they laugh, he waits patiently, then goes on. Gradually the room grows quieter as Joe tells them of his life and then asks them about theirs. "What's important to you? What are your goals?" he says. "I'm still in school because when I was young, I chose the dead-end route many of you are on. But now I'm doing what I have to do to get where I want to go. What are you doing?"

He tells them more, about broken dreams, about his parents' grief, about the 27 former friends who turned away from him when he was no longer a source of drugs. He tells them of the continuing struggle to regain the trust of people he once abused. He tells them about the desire that consumes him now, the desire to make his community a better place to live. His wish is that no young man or woman should have to walk the path he's walked in order to value the precious gift of life. The teenagers are now silent. They look at this broad-shouldered black man in his wheelchair, his head and beard close-shaven, a gold ring in his ear. His hushed words settle among them like gentle drops of cleansing rain. "What are you doing? Where are you going?" he asks them. "Think about it. Think about me."

Joe Davis is the coolest forty-eight-year-old you've ever seen.   28

READING COMPREHENSION QUESTIONS

1. The word *immersed* in "For six weeks, he immersed himself in discussions, tests, and exercises to help him determine the kind of work he might be suited for" (paragraph 20) means
   a. totally ignored.
   b. greatly angered.
   c. deeply involved.
   d. often harmed.

2. Which sentence best expresses the central point of the selection?
   a. Most people cannot improve their lives once they turn to drugs and crime.
   b. Joe Davis overcame a life of drugs and crime and a disability to lead a rich, meaningful life.
   c. The rules set by Joe Davis's parents caused him to leave home and continue a life of drugs and crime.
   d. Joe Davis's friends turned away from him once they learned he was no longer a source of drugs.

3. A main idea may cover more than one paragraph. Which sentence best expresses the main idea of paragraphs 21–23?
   a. First sentence of paragraph 21
   b. Second sentence of paragraph 21
   c. First sentence of paragraph 22
   d. First sentence of paragraph 23

4. Which sentence best expresses the main idea of paragraph 24?
   a. It was difficult for Joe to do college work after being out of school for so many years.
   b. Lorraine Buchanan encouraged Joe to go to college.
   c. Joe's determination enabled him to overcome a lack of academic preparation and eventually succeed in college.
   d. If students would stay in high school and work hard, they would not have to go to the trouble of getting a high school GED.

www.mhhe.com/langan

5. Joe Davis quit high school
    a. when he was fourteen.
    b. when he got a good job at a hospital.
    c. when he was in the tenth grade.
    d. after he was shot.

6. Joe tried to kill himself by
    a. swallowing muscle-relaxant pills.
    b. shooting himself.
    c. overdosing on heroin.
    d. not eating or drinking.

7. According to the selection, Joe first met his wife
    a. in the hospital, where she was a nurse.
    b. on a city bus, where they were both passengers.
    c. on the job, where she was also a receptionist.
    d. at Community College of Philadelphia, where she was also a student.

8. Joe decided to stop using drugs
    a. when he met his future wife.
    b. right after he was shot.
    c. when he awoke after a suicide attempt.
    d. when he was hired as a receptionist.

9. We can conclude from paragraph 26 that
    a. Joe is willing to reveal very personal information about himself in order to reach young people with his story.
    b. Joe was angry at the Philadelphia students who laughed at parts of his story.
    c. Joe is glad he did not go to college directly from high school.
    d. Joe is still trying to figure out what his life goals are.

10. When the author writes, "Joe Davis was the coolest fourteen- (or sixteen- or twenty-five-) year-old he'd ever seen," she is actually expressing
    a. her approval of the way Joe was living then.
    b. her envy of Joe's status in the community.
    c. her mistaken opinion of Joe at these stages in his life.
    d. Joe's mistaken opinion of himself at these stages in his life.

DISCUSSION QUESTIONS

About Content

1. When speaking of his suicide attempt, Joe said, "It wasn't the spinal cord injury that did it. It was the addiction" (paragraph 15). What do you think Joe meant? Why does he blame his addiction, rather than his disability, for his decision to try to end his life?

2. Why do you think the students Joe spoke to laughed as he shared personal details of his life? Why did they later quiet down? What effect do you think his presentation had on these students?

3. Joe wants young people to learn the lessons he has learned without having to experience his hardships. What lessons have you learned in your life that you would like to pass on to others?

About Structure

4. Paragraphs 1, 3, 5, and 28 are very similar. In what important way is paragraph 28 different from the others? What do you think Johnson is suggesting by introducing that difference?

5. Johnson tells the story of Joe's shooting briefly, in paragraphs 6–8. She could have chosen to go into much more detail about that part of the story. For instance, she could have described any previous relationship between Joe and the young man who shot him, or what happened to the shooter afterward. Why do you think she chose not to concentrate on those details? How would the story have been different if she had focused on them?

6. In paragraphs 21–23, Johnson condenses an important year in Joe's life into three paragraphs. Locate and write below three of the many transitions that are used as part of the time order in those paragraphs.

   _____   _____   _____

About Style and Tone

7. In paragraph 12, Johnson describes Joe's poor physical condition. She could have simply written, "Joe developed a serious bedsore." Instead she writes, "Eventually Joe developed his first bedsore: a deep, rotting wound that ate into his flesh, overwhelming him with its foul odor." Why do you think she provided such graphic detail? What is the effect on the reader?

8. How do you think Johnson feels about Joe Davis? What hints lead you to that conclusion? Work with a partner to find and list support for it.

WRITING ASSIGNMENTS

Assignment 1: Writing a Paragraph

Like Joe Davis, many of us have learned painful lessons from life. And like him, we wish we could pass those lessons on to young people to save them from making the same mistakes.

Write a one-paragraph letter to a young person you know. In it, use your experience to pass on a lesson you wish he or she would learn. Begin with a topic sentence in which you state the lesson you'd like to teach, as in these examples:

> My own humiliating experience taught me that shoplifting is a very bad idea.

> I learned the hard way that abandoning your friends for the "cool" crowd will backfire on you.

> The sad experience of a friend has taught me that teenage girls should not give in to their boyfriends' pressure for sex.

> Dropping out of high school may seem like a great idea, but what happened to my brother should convince you otherwise.

Your letter should describe in detail the lesson you learned and how you learned it. Exchange letters with a partner and help each other to revise and edit.

Assignment 2: Writing a Paragraph

Although Joe's parents loved him, they weren't able to stop him from using drugs, skipping school, and doing other self-destructive things. Think of a time that you have seen someone you cared about doing something you thought was bad for him or her. What did you do? What did you want to do?

Write a paragraph in which you describe the situation and how you responded. Make sure to answer the following questions:

> What was the person doing?

> Why was I concerned about him or her?

> Did I feel there was anything I could do?

> Did I take any action?

> How did the situation finally turn out?

Assignment 3: Writing an Essay

1. One of Joe's goals is to regain the trust of the friends and family members he abused during his earlier life. Have you ever given a second chance to someone who treated you poorly? Write an essay about what happened. You could begin with a thesis statement something like this: "Although my closest friend betrayed my trust, I decided to give him another chance."

You could then go on to structure the rest of your essay in this way:

- In your first supporting paragraph, explain what the person did to lose your trust. Maybe it was an obviously hurtful action, like physically harming you or stealing from you. Or perhaps it was something more subtle, like insulting or embarrassing you.

- In your second supporting paragraph, explain why you decided to give the person another chance.

- In your third supporting paragraph, tell what happened as a result of your giving the person a second chance. Did he or she treat you better this time? Or did the bad treatment start over again?

- In your concluding paragraph, provide some final thoughts about what you learned from the experience.

Alternatively, write an essay about a time that you were given a second chance by someone whose trust you had abused. Follow the same pattern of development.

The Fist, the Clay, and the Rock
Donald Holland

PREVIEW

In this narrative, Donald Holland recalls a high school teacher's inspiring question: *If the world were a fist, would you rather be a rock or a ball of clay?* Emphasizing the power of knowledge in the classroom and beyond, Mr. Gery encouraged his students to become rocks—strong, resilient learners.

The best teacher I ever had was Mr. Gery, who taught 12th grade English. 1 He started his class with us by placing on the front desk a large mound of clay and, next to it, a rock about the size of a tennis ball. That got our attention quickly, and the class quieted down and waited for him to talk.

Mr. Gery looked at us and smiled and said, "If there were a pill I could give 2 you that would help you learn, and help you want to learn, I would pass it out right now. But there is no magic pill. Everything is up to you."

Then Mr. Gery held up his fist and kind of shook it at us. Some of us looked 3 at each other. *What's going on?* we all thought. Mr. Gery continued: "I'd like you to imagine something for me. Imagine that my fist is the real world—not the sheltered world of this school but the real world. Imagine that my fist is everything that can happen to you out in the real world."

Then he reached down and pointed to the ball of clay and also the rock. He 4 said, "Now imagine that you're either this lump of clay or you're the rock. Got that?" He smiled at us, and we waited to see what he was going to do.

He went on, "Let's say you're this ball of clay, and you're just sitting around 5 minding your own business and then out of nowhere here's what happens." He made a fist again and he smashed his fist into the ball of clay, which quickly turned into a half-flattened lump.

He looked at us, still smiling. "If the real world comes along and takes a 6 swing at you, you're likely to get squashed. And you know what, the real world will come along and take a swing at you. You're going to take some heavy hits. Maybe you already have taken some heavy hits. Chances are that there are more down the road. So if you don't want to get squashed, you're better off if you're not a piece of clay.

"Now let's say you're the rock and the real world comes along and takes a 7 swing at you. What will happen if I smash my fist into this rock?" The answer was obvious. Nothing would happen to the rock. It would take the blow and not be changed.

He continued, "So what would you like to be, people, the clay or the rock? 8 And what's my point? What am I trying to say to you?"

Someone raised their hand and said, "We should all be rocks. It's bad news 9 to be clay." And some of us laughed, though a bit uneasily.

Mr. Gery went on. "OK, you all want to be rocks, don't you? Now my ques- 10 tion is, 'How do you get to be a rock? How do you make yourself strong, like the rock, so that you won't be crushed and beaten up even if you take a lot of hits?'"

We didn't have an answer right away and he went on, "You know I can't be 11 a fairy godmother. I can't pull out a wand and say, 'Thanks for wanting to be a rock. I hereby wave my wand and make you a rock.' That's not the way life works. The only way to become a rock is to go out and make yourself a rock.

"Imagine you're a fighter getting ready for a match. You go to the gym, and 12 maybe when you start you're flabby. Your whole body is flab and it's soft like the clay. To make your body hard like a rock, you've got to train.

"Now if you want to train and become hard like the rock, I can help you. 13 You need to develop skills, and you need to acquire knowledge. Skills will make you strong, and knowledge is power. It's my job to help you with language skills. I'll help you train to become a better reader. I'll help you train to be a better writer. But you know, I'm just a trainer. I can't make you be a fighter.

"All I can do is tell you that you need to make yourself a fighter. You need 14 to become a rock. Because you don't want to be flabby when the real world comes along and takes a crack at you. Don't spend the semester just being Mr. Cool Man or Ms. Designer Jeans or Mr. or Ms. Sex Symbol of the class. Be someone. Be someone."

He then smashed that wad of clay one more time, and the thud of his fist 15 broke the silence and then created more silence. He sure had our total attention.

"At the end of the semester, some of you are going to leave here, and you're 16 still going to be clay. You're going to be the kind of person that life can smush around, and that's sad. But some of you, maybe a lot of you, are going to be rocks. I want you to be a rock. Go for it. And when this comes"—and he held up his fist—"you'll be ready."

And then Mr. Gery segued into talking about the course. But his demonstra- 17 tion stayed with most of us. And as the semester unfolded, he would call back his vivid images. When someone would not hand in a paper and make a lame excuse, he would say, "Whatever you say, Mr. Clay." Or "Whatever you say, Ms. Clay." Or if someone would forget their book, or not study for a test, or not do a reading assignment, he would say, "Of course, Mr. Clay." Sometimes we would get into it also and call out, "Hey, Clayman."

Mr. Gery worked us very hard, but he was not a mean person. We all knew he 18 was a kind man who wanted us to become strong. It was obvious he wanted us to do well. By the end of the semester, he had to call very few of us Mr. or Ms. Clay.

READING COMPREHENSION QUESTIONS

www.mhhe.com/langan

1. The word *squashed* in "If the real world comes along and takes a swing at you, you're likely to get squashed. And you know what, the real world will come along and take a swing at you" (paragraph 6) means
   a. upset.
   b. ignored.
   c. crushed.
   d. excited.

2. The words *segued into* in "And then Mr. Gery segued into talking about the course. But his demonstration stayed with most of us" (paragraph 17) mean
   a. stopped.
   b. transitioned.
   c. gave up.
   d. anticipated.

3. Which of the following would be the best alternative title for this selection?
   a. Mr. Gery's English Class
   b. Life's Heavy Hits
   c. Training to Be a Fighter in Life
   d. Mr. Clayman

4. Which sentence best expresses the main idea of the selection?

    a. The students in Mr. Gery's class experienced difficulties in their lives.

    b. Mr. Gery's job was to transform his students into fighters.

    c. Mr. Gery's students were the only ones who could make themselves strong.

    d. Although Mr. Gery worked his students very hard, he was a kind man.

5. The students in Mr. Gery's twelfth-grade English class wanted to be

    a. clay.

    b. fists.

    c. rocks.

    d. teachers.

6. *True or false?* _____ Mr. Gery promised all his students that they would be rocks at the end of the semester.

7. When Mr. Gery smashed his fist into the mound of clay for a second time, his students

    a. remained silent.

    b. laughed uneasily.

    c. shouted "Mr. Clayman."

    d. looked bored.

8. When the author writes, "The best teacher I ever had was Mr. Gery," we can conclude that Mr. Gery

    a. was an easy teacher.

    b. made English fun and exciting.

    c. taught the author a meaningful lesson.

    d. taught the author to be a better writer.

9. When Mr. Gery asked his students if they wanted to be the clay or the rock (paragraph 8), we can infer that

    a. he did not know what they would say.

    b. he knew that they wanted to be the rock.

    c. he thought that some of them wanted to be the clay.

    d. his students already knew how to be the rock.

10. When Mr. Gery called a student "Mr. Clay" or "Ms. Clay" (paragraph 17), we can infer that

    a. he was disgusted with the student.

    b. he hoped to embarrass the student.

    c. he forgot the student's name.

    d. he wanted the student to do better.

DISCUSSION QUESTIONS

About Content

1. Why did the author mention several times that Mr. Gery smiled at his students throughout his entire demonstration? How would his students have responded if Mr. Gery scowled?

2. What do you think Mr. Gery meant when he told his students, "Everything is up to you" (paragraph 2)? Do you feel this way about learning? About life?

3. Do you know anyone who is like a flattened lump of clay? Do you know anyone who is strong like a well-trained fighter? What factors determine a person's fate?

About Structure

4. The author uses narration to illustrate his main point. Below, write three time transitions he uses to advance his narration.

_____   _____   _____

5. The author uses dialogue to recount what Mr. Gery told his class about the fist, the clay, and the rock but does not use dialogue to tell his readers what Mr. Gery said about the course (paragraph 17). Why do you think the author chose this narrative strategy?

About Style and Tone

6. Is the author just telling his readers about his twelfth-grade English teacher, or is the author hoping to inspire his readers to do something?

7. What do you think Mr. Gery's attitude toward those students who "already have taken some heavy hits" is (paragraph 6)? What does he offer these students?

WRITING ASSIGNMENTS

www.mhhe.com/langan

Assignment 1: Writing a Paragraph

Write a paragraph about an influential teacher in your life. Perhaps you had a very inspiring teacher who challenged you to try your best, or you had a teacher who took the time to learn about what was happening in your life outside the classroom. Provide plenty of detail to let your readers know why you consider this teacher so influential. Your topic sentence may begin like this:

The teacher who inspired me to _____.

Assignment 2: Writing a Paragraph

Mr. Gery tells his students, "All I can do is tell you that you need to make yourself a fighter" (paragraph 14). Do you know a person who took some "heavy hits" but remained hard like a rock, someone who didn't want to be flabby when the real world came along and took a crack at him or her? Write a paragraph describing how this person trained and made him- or herself a fighter. Introduce that person in your topic sentence, as in these examples:

> My older brother was born without the ability to hear, but through hard work and a positive attitude he did well in school, played sports, and graduated from Gallaudet University.

> Although my best friend was involved in a very abusive relationship, she left her abuser, sought counseling, and today volunteers at a women's shelter.

Then give several specific examples of the person's efforts. Conclude by providing a prediction for this person's future.

Assignment 3: Writing an Essay

Mr. Gery tells his students that some of them will leave his class as lumps of clay and some will leave as rocks. Those who are clay will get smashed around, but those who are rocks will be ready for life. Write an essay in which you compare a "clay" person and a "rock" person. Perhaps you know someone who is addicted to alcohol but refuses to recognize the problem and someone who attends Alcoholics Anonymous and is living a sober life. Develop your essay by describing each person in detail. You can present your details point by point or one side at a time (see pages 229–230). Share your rough draft with a partner to get and give feedback for revision. Refer to the checklist on the inside back cover.

What Good Families Are Doing Right
Dolores Curran

> **PREVIEW**
>
> It isn't easy to be a successful parent these days. Pressured by the conflicting demands of home and workplace, confused by changing moral standards, and drowned out by the constant barrage of new media, today's parents seem to be facing impossible odds in their struggle to raise healthy families. Yet some parents manage to "do it all"—and even remain on speaking terms with their children. How do they do it? Dolores Curran's survey offers some significant suggestions; her article could serve as a recipe for a successful family.

I have worked with families for fifteen years, conducting hundreds of semi- 1
nars, workshops, and classes on parenting, and I meet good families all the time.
They're fairly easy to recognize. Good families have a kind of visible strength.
They expect problems and work together to find solutions, applying common
sense and trying new methods to meet new needs. And they share a common
shortcoming—they can tell me in a minute what's wrong with them, but they
aren't sure what's right with them. Many healthy families with whom I work, in
fact, protest at being called *healthy.* They don't think they are. The professionals
who work with them do.

To prepare the book on which this article is based, I asked respected workers 2
in the fields of education, religion, health, family counseling, and voluntary organizations to identify a list of possible traits of a healthy family. Together we
isolated fifty-six such traits, and I sent this list to five hundred professionals who
regularly work with families—teachers, doctors, principals, members of the clergy,
scout directors, YMCA leaders, family counselors, social workers—asking them
to pick the fifteen qualities they most commonly found in healthy families.

While all of these traits are important, the one most often cited as central to 3
close family life is communication: The healthy family knows how to talk—and
how to listen.

"Without communication you don't know one another," wrote one family 4
counselor. "If you don't know one another, you don't care about one another,
and that's what the family is all about."

"The most familiar complaint I hear from wives I counsel is 'He won't talk 5
to me' and 'He doesn't listen to me,'" said a pastoral marriage counselor. "And
when I share this complaint with their husbands, they don't hear *me,* either."

"We have kids in classes whose families are so robotized by television that 6
they don't know one another," said a fifth-grade teacher.

Professional counselors are not the only ones to recognize the need. The 7
phenomenal growth of communication groups such as Parent Effectiveness Training, Parent Awareness, Marriage Encounter, Couple Communication, and literally
hundreds of others tells us that the need for effective communication—the sharing of deepest feelings—is felt by many.

Healthy families have also recognized this need, and they have, either instinc- 8
tively or consciously, developed methods of meeting it. They know that conflicts
are to be expected, that we all become angry and frustrated and discouraged.
And they know how to reveal those feelings—good and bad—to each other.
Honest communication isn't always easy. But when it's working well, there are
certain recognizable signs or symptoms, what I call the hallmarks of the successfully communicating family.

The Family Exhibits a Strong Relationship between the Parents

According to Dr. Jerry M. Lewis—author of a significant work on families, *No* 9
Single Thread—healthy spouses complement, rather than dominate, each other.

Either husband or wife could be the leader, depending on the circumstances. In the unhealthy families he studied, the dominant spouse had to hide feelings of weakness while the submissive spouse feared being put down if he or she exposed a weakness.

Children in the healthy family have no question about which parent is boss. 10 Both parents are. If children are asked who is boss, they're likely to respond, "Sometimes Mom, sometimes Dad." And, in a wonderful statement, Dr. Lewis adds, "If you ask if they're comfortable with this, they look at you as if you're crazy—as if there's no other way it ought to be."

My survey respondents echo Dr. Lewis. One wrote, "The healthiest families 11 I know are ones in which the mother and father have a strong, loving relationship. This seems to flow over to the children and even beyond the home. It seems to breed security in the children and, in turn, fosters the ability to take risks, to reach out to others, to search for their own answers, become independent and develop a good self-image."

The Family Has Control over Television

Television has been maligned, praised, damned, cherished, and even thrown out. 12 It has more influence on children's values than anything else except their parents. Over and over, when I'm invited to help families mend their communication ruptures, I hear "But we have no time for this." These families have literally turned their "family-together" time over to television. Even those who control the quality of programs watched and set "homework-first" regulations feel reluctant to intrude upon the individual's right to spend his or her spare time in front of the set. Many families avoid clashes over program selection by furnishing a set for each family member. One of the women who was most desperate to establish a better sense of communication in her family confided to me that they owned nine sets. Nine sets for seven people!

Whether the breakdown in family communication leads to excessive viewing 13 or whether too much television breaks into family lives, we don't know. But we do know that we can become out of one another's reach when we're in front of a TV set. The term *television widow* is not humorous to thousands whose spouses are absent even when they're there. One woman remarked, "I can't get worried about whether there's life after death. I'd be satisfied with life after dinner."

In family-communication workshops, I ask families to make a list of phrases 14 they most commonly hear in their home. One parent was aghast to discover that his family's most familiar comments were "What's on?" and "Move." In families like this one, communication isn't hostile—it's just missing.

But television doesn't have to be a villain. A 1980 Gallup Poll found that 15 the public sees great potential for television as a positive force. It can be a tremendous device for initiating discussion on subjects that may not come up elsewhere, subjects such as sexuality, corporate ethics, sportsmanship, and marital fidelity.

Even very bad programs offer material for values clarification if family mem- 16
bers view them together. My sixteen-year-old son and his father recently watched
a program in which hazardous driving was part of the hero's characterization. At
one point, my son turned to his dad and asked, "Is that possible to do with that
kind of truck?"

"I don't know," replied my husband, "but it sure is dumb. If that load shifted 17
. . ." With that, they launched into a discussion on the responsibility of drivers
that didn't have to originate as a parental lecture. Furthermore, as the discussion
became more engrossing to them, they turned the sound down so that they could
continue their conversation.

Parents frequently report similar experiences; in fact, this use of television 18
was recommended in the widely publicized 1972 Surgeon General's report as
the most effective form of television gatekeeping by parents. Instead of turning
off the set, parents should view programs with their children and make moral
judgments and initiate discussion. Talking about the problems and attitudes of a
TV family can be a lively, nonthreatening way to risk sharing real fears, hopes,
and dreams.

The Family Listens and Responds

"My parents say they want me to come to them with problems, but when I do, 19
either they're busy or they only half-listen and keep on doing what they were
doing—like shaving or making a grocery list. If a friend of theirs came over to
talk, they'd stop, be polite, and listen," said one of the children quoted in a *Christian Science Monitor* interview by Ann McCarroll. This child put his finger on
the most difficult problem of communicating in families: the inability to listen.

It is usually easier to react than to respond. When we react, we reflect our 20
own experiences and feelings; when we respond, we get into the other person's
feelings. For example:

Tom, age seventeen: "I don't know if I want to go to college. I don't think
I'd do very well there."

Father: "Nonsense. Of course you'll do well."

That's reacting. This father is cutting off communication. He's refusing either 21
to hear the boy's fears or to consider his feelings, possibly because he can't
accept the idea that his son might not attend college. Here's another way of
handling the same situation:

Tom: "I don't know if I want to go to college. I don't think I'd do very well
there."

Father: "Why not?"

Tom: "Because I'm not that smart."

Father: "Yeah, that's scary. I worried about that, too."

Tom: "Did you ever come close to flunking out?"

Father: "No, but I worried a lot before I went because I thought college would be full of brains. Once I got there, I found out that most of the kids were just like me."

This father has responded rather than reacted to his son's fears. First, he 22 searched for the reason behind his son's lack of confidence and found it was fear of academic ability (it could have been fear of leaving home, of a new environment, of peer pressure, or of any of a number of things); second, he accepted the fear as legitimate; third, he empathized by admitting to having the same fear when he was Tom's age; and, finally, he explained why his, not Tom's, fears turned out to be groundless. He did all this without denigrating or lecturing.

And that's tough for parents to do. Often we don't want to hear our children's 23 fears, because those fears frighten us; or we don't want to pay attention to their dreams because their dreams aren't what we have in mind for them. Parents who deny such feelings will allow only surface conversation. It's fine as long as a child says, "School was OK today," but when she says, "I'm scared of boys," the parents are uncomfortable. They don't want her to be afraid of boys, but since they don't quite know what to say, they react with a pleasant "Oh, you'll outgrow it." She probably will, but what she needs at the moment is someone to hear and understand her pain.

In Ann McCarroll's interviews, she talked to one fifteen-year-old boy who 24 said he had *"some* mother. Each morning she sits with me while I eat breakfast. We talk about anything and everything. She isn't refined or elegant or educated. She's a terrible housekeeper. But she's interested in everything I do, and she always listens to me—even if she's busy or tired."

That's the kind of listening found in families that experience real communi- 25 cation. Answers to the routine question "How was your day?" are heard with the eyes and heart as well as the ears. Nuances are picked up and questions are asked, although problems are not necessarily solved. Members of a family who really listen to one another instinctively know that if people listen to you, they are interested in you. And that's enough for most of us.

The Family Recognizes Unspoken Messages

Much of our communication—especially our communication of feelings—is 26 nonverbal. Dr. Lewis defines *empathy* as "someone responding to you in such a way that you feel deeply understood." He says, "There is probably no more important dimension in all of human relationships than the capacity for empathy. And healthy families teach empathy." Their members are allowed to be mad, glad, and sad. There's no crime in being in a bad mood, nor is there betrayal in being happy while someone else is feeling moody. The family recognizes that bad days and good days attack everyone at different times.

Nonverbal expressions of love, too, are the best way to show children that 27 parents love each other. A spouse reaching for the other's hand, a wink, a squeeze on the shoulder, a "How's-your-back-this-morning?" a meaningful glance across the room—all these tell children how their parents feel about each other.

The most destructive nonverbal communication in marriage is silence. Silence 28 can mean lack of interest, hostility, denigration, boredom, or outright war. On the part of a teen or preteen, silence usually indicates pain, sometimes very deep pain. The sad irony discovered by so many family therapists is that parents who seek professional help when a teenager becomes silent have often denied the child any other way of communicating. And although they won't permit their children to become angry or to reveal doubts or to share depression, they do worry about the withdrawal that results. Rarely do they see any connection between the two.

Healthy families use signs, symbols, body language, smiles, and other ges- 29 tures to express caring and love. They deal with silence and withdrawal in a positive, open way. Communication doesn't mean just talking or listening; it includes all the clues to a person's feelings—his bearing, her expression, their resignation. Family members don't have to say, "I'm hurting," or, "I'm in need." A quick glance tells that. And they have developed ways of responding that indicate caring and love, whether or not there's an immediate solution to the pain.

The Family Encourages Individual Feelings and Independent Thinking

Close families encourage the emergence of individual personalities through open 30 sharing of thoughts and feelings. Unhealthy families tend to be less open, less accepting of differences among members. The family must be Republican, or Bronco supporters, or gun-control advocates, and woe to the individual who says, "Yes, but . . . ."

Instead of finding differing opinions threatening, the healthy family finds 31 them exhilarating. It is exciting to witness such a family discussing politics, sports, or the world. Members freely say, "I don't agree with you," without risking ridicule or rebuke. They say, "I think it's wrong . . ." immediately after Dad says, "I think it's right . . ."; and Dad listens and responds.

Give-and-take gives children practice in articulating their thoughts at home 32 so that eventually they'll feel confident outside the home. What may seem to be verbal rambling by preteens during a family conversation is a prelude to sorting out their thinking and putting words to their thoughts.

Rigid families don't understand the dynamics of give-and-take. Some label 33 it disrespectful and argumentative; others find it confusing. Dr. John Meeks, medical director of the Psychiatric Institute of Montgomery County, Maryland, claims that argument is a way of life with normally developing adolescents. "In early adolescence they'll argue with parents about anything at all; as they grow older, the quantity of argument decreases but the quality increases." According to Dr. Meeks, arguing is something adolescents need to do. If the argument doesn't become too bitter, they have a good chance to test their own beliefs and feelings. "Incidentally," says Meeks, "parents can expect to 'lose' most of these arguments, because adolescents are not fettered by logic or even reality." Nor are they likely to be polite. Learning how to disagree respectfully is a difficult task, but good families work at it.

Encouraging individual feelings and thoughts, of course, in no way presumes 34 that parents permit their children to do whatever they want. There's a great difference between permitting a son to express an opinion on marijuana and allowing him to use it. That his opinion conflicts with his parents' opinion is OK as long as his parents make sure he knows their thinking on the subject. Whether he admits it or not, he's likely at least to consider their ideas if he respects them.

Permitting teenagers to sort out their feelings and thoughts in open discus- 35 sions at home gives them valuable experience in dealing with a bewildering array of situations they may encounter when they leave home. Cutting off discussion of behavior unacceptable to us, on the other hand, makes our young people feel guilty for even thinking about values contrary to ours and ends up making those values more attractive to them.

The Family Recognizes Turn-Off Words and Put-Down Phrases

Some families deliberately use hurtful language in their daily communication. 36 "What did you do all day around here?" can be a red flag to a woman who has spent her day on household tasks that don't show unless they're not done. "If only we had enough money" can be a rebuke to a husband who is working as hard as he can to provide for the family. "Flunk any tests today, John?" only discourages a child who may be having trouble in school.

Close families seem to recognize that a comment made in jest can be insult- 37 ing. A father in one of my groups confided that he could tease his wife about everything but her skiing. "I don't know why she's so sensitive about that, but I back off on it. I can say anything I want to about her cooking, her appearance, her mothering—whatever. But not her skiing."

One of my favorite exercises with families is to ask them to reflect upon 38 phrases they most like to hear and those they least like to hear. Recently, I invited seventy-five fourth- and fifth-graders to submit the words they most like to hear from their mothers. Here are the five big winners:

"I love you."

"Yes."

"Time to eat."

"You can go."

"You can stay up late."

And on the children's list of what they least like to hear from one another 39 are the following:

"I'm telling."

"Mom says!"

"I know something you don't know."

"You think you're so big."

"Just see if I ever let you use my bike again."

It can be worthwhile for a family to list the phrases members like most and 40 least to hear, and post them. Often parents aren't even aware of the reaction of their children to certain routine comments. Or keep a record of the comments heard most often over a period of a week or two. It can provide good clues to the level of family sensitivity. If the list has a lot of "shut ups" and "stop its," that family needs to pay more attention to its relationships, especially the role that communication plays in them.

The Family Interrupts, but Equally

When Dr. Jerry M. Lewis began to study the healthy family, he and his staff 41 videotaped families in the process of problem solving. The family was given a question, such as "What's the main thing wrong with your family?" Answers varied, but what was most significant was what the family actually did: who took control, how individuals responded or reacted, what were the put-downs, and whether some members were entitled to speak more than others.

The researchers found that healthy families expected everyone to speak 42 openly about feelings. Nobody was urged to hold back. In addition, these family members interrupted one another repeatedly, but no one person was interrupted more than anyone else.

Manners, particularly polite conversational techniques, are not hallmarks of 43 the communicating family. This should make many parents feel better about their family's dinner conversation. One father reported to me that at their table people had to take a number to finish a sentence. Finishing sentences, however, doesn't seem all that important in the communicating family. Members aren't sensitive to being interrupted, either. The intensity and spontaneity of the exchange are more important than propriety in conversation.

The Family Develops a Pattern of Reconciliation

"We know how to break up," one man said, "but who ever teaches us to make 44 up?" Survey respondents indicated that there is indeed a pattern of reconciliation in healthy families that is missing in others. "It usually isn't a kiss-and-make-up situation," explained one family therapist, "but there are certain rituals developed over a long period of time that indicate it's time to get well again. Between husband and wife, it might be a concessionary phrase to which the other is expected to respond in kind. Within a family, it might be that the person who stomps off to his or her room voluntarily reenters the family circle, where something is said to make him or her welcome."

When I asked several families how they knew a fight had ended, I got 45 remarkably similar answers from individuals questioned separately. "We all come out of our rooms," responded every member of one family. Three members of another family said, "Mom says, 'Anybody want a Pepsi?' " One five-year-old scratched his head and furrowed his forehead after I asked him how he knew the family fight was over. Finally, he said, "Well, Daddy gives a great big yawn and says, 'Well . . .' " This scene is easy to visualize, as one parent decides that the unpleasantness needs to end and it's time to end the fighting and to pull together again as a family.

Why have we neglected the important art of reconciling? "Because we have 46 pretended that good families don't fight," says one therapist. "They do. It's essential to fight for good health in the family. It gets things out into the open. But we need to learn to put ourselves back together—and many families never learn this."

Close families know how to time divisive and emotional issues that may 47 cause friction. They don't bring up potentially explosive subjects right before they go out, for example, or before bedtime. They tend to schedule discussions rather than allow a matter to explode, and thus they keep a large measure of control over the atmosphere in which they will fight and reconcile. Good families know that they need enough time to discuss issues heatedly, rationally, and completely—and enough time to reconcile. "You've got to solve it right there," said one father. "Don't let it go on and on. It just causes more problems. Then when it's solved, let it be. No nagging, no remembering."

The Family Fosters Table Time and Conversation

Traditionally, the dinner table has been a symbol of socialization. It's probably 48 the one time each day that parents and children are assured of uninterrupted time with one another.

Therapists frequently call upon a patient's memory of the family table during 49 childhood in order to determine the degree of communication and interaction there was in the patient's early life. Some patients recall nothing. Mealtime was either so unpleasant or so unimpressive that they have blocked it out of their memories. Therapists say that there is a relationship between the love in a home and life around the family table. It is to the table that love or discord eventually comes.

But we are spending less table time together. Fast-food dining, even within 50 the home, is becoming a way of life for too many of us. Work schedules, individual organized activities, and television all limit the quantity and quality of mealtime interaction. In an informal study conducted by a church group,

68 percent of the families interviewed in three congregations saw nothing wrong with watching television while eating.

Families who do a good job of communicating tend to make the dinner meal 51 an important part of their day. A number of respondents indicated that adults in the healthiest families refuse dinner business meetings as a matter of principle and discourage their children from sports activities that cut into mealtime hours. "We know which of our swimmers will or won't practice at dinnertime," said a coach, with mixed admiration. "Some parents never allow their children to miss dinners. Some don't care at all." These families pay close attention to the number of times they'll be able to be together in a week, and they rearrange schedules to be sure of spending this time together.

The family that wants to improve communication should look closely at its 52 attitudes toward the family table. Are family table time and conversation important? Is table time open and friendly or warlike and sullen? Is it conducive to sharing more than food—does it encourage the sharing of ideas, feelings, and family intimacies?

We all need to talk to one another. We need to know we're loved and appre- 53 ciated and respected. We want to share our intimacies, not just physical intimacies but all the intimacies in our lives. Communication is the most important element of family life because it is basic to loving relationships. It is the energy that fuels the caring, giving, sharing, and affirming. Without genuine sharing of ourselves, we cannot know one another's needs and fears. Good communication is what makes all the rest of it work.

Based on the traits that Curran describes in her essay, are either of the families pictured here "successful" families? What is it about the family's appearance and interaction with one another that lets you know this? In what ways is the "successful" family different from the other family pictured? Considering these questions and the essay you've just read, write a paragraph in which you contrast the two families pictured here.

READING COMPREHENSION QUESTIONS

1. The word *aghast* in "One parent was aghast to discover that his family's most familiar comments were 'What's on?' and 'Move'" (paragraph 14) means
   a. horrified.
   b. satisfied.
   c. curious.
   d. amused.

2. The word *engrossing* in "as the discussion became more engrossing to them, they turned the sound down so that they could continue their conversation" (paragraph 17) means
   a. disgusting.
   b. intellectual.
   c. foolish.
   d. interesting.

3. Which of the following would be the best alternative title for this selection?
   a. Successful Communication
   b. How to Solve Family Conflicts
   c. Characteristics of Families
   d. Hallmarks of the Communicating Family

4. Which sentence best expresses the article's main point?
   a. Television can and often does destroy family life.
   b. More American families are unhappy than ever before.
   c. A number of qualities mark the healthy and communicating family.
   d. Strong families encourage independent thinking.

5. *True or false?* _____ According to the article, healthy families have no use for television.

6. Healthy families
   a. never find it hard to communicate.
   b. have no conflicts with each other.
   c. know how to reveal their feelings.
   d. permit one of the parents to make all final decisions.

7. The author has found that good families frequently make a point of being together
    a. in the mornings.
    b. after school.
    c. during dinner.
    d. before bedtime.

8. *True or false?* _____ The article implies that the most troublesome nonverbal signal is silence.

9. The article implies that
    a. verbal messages are always more accurate than nonverbal ones.
    b. in strong families, parents practice tolerance of thoughts and feelings.
    c. parents must avoid arguing with their adolescent children.
    d. parents should prevent their children from watching television.

10. From the article, we can conclude that
    a. a weak marital relationship often results in a weak family.
    b. children should not witness a disagreement between parents.
    c. children who grow up in healthy families learn not to interrupt other family members.
    d. parents always find it easier to respond to their children than to react to them.

DISCUSSION QUESTIONS

About Content

1. What are the nine hallmarks of a successfully communicating family? Which of the nine do you feel are most important?

2. How do good parents control television? How do they make television a positive force instead of a negative one?

3. In paragraph 20, the author says, "It is usually easier to react than to respond." What is the difference between the two terms *react* and *respond*?

4. Why, according to Curran, is a "pattern of reconciliation" (paragraph 44) crucial to good family life? Besides those patterns mentioned in the essay, can you describe a reconciliation pattern you have developed with friends or family?

About Structure

5. What is the thesis of the selection? Write here the number of the paragraph in which it is stated: _____

6. What purpose is achieved by Curran's introduction (paragraphs 1–2)? Why is a reader likely to feel that her article will be reliable and worthwhile?

7. Curran frequently uses dialogue or quotations from unnamed parents or children as the basis for her examples. The conversation related in paragraphs 16–17 is one instance. Find three other dialogues used to illustrate points in the essay and write the numbers below:

   Paragraph(s) _____

   Paragraph(s) _____

   Paragraph(s) _____

About Style and Tone

8. Curran enlivens the essay by using some interesting and humorous remarks from parents, children, and counselors. One is the witty comment in paragraph 5 from a marriage counselor: "And when I share this complaint with their husbands, they don't hear *me*, either." Find two other places where the author keeps your interest by using humorous or enjoyable quotations, and write the numbers of the paragraphs here:

   _____   _____

WRITING ASSIGNMENTS

www.mhhe.com/langan

Assignment 1: Writing a Paragraph

Write a definition paragraph on the hallmarks of a *bad* family. Your topic sentence might be "A bad family is one that is _____, _____, and _____." To get started, you should first reread the features of a good family explained in the selection. Doing so will help you think about what qualities are found in a bad family. Prepare a list of as many bad qualities as you can think of. Then go through the list and decide on the qualities that seem most characteristic of a bad family.

Assignment 2: Writing a Paragraph

Curran tells us five phrases that some children say they most like to hear from their mothers (paragraph 38). When you were younger, what statement or action of one of your parents (or another adult) would make you especially happy—or sad? Write a paragraph that begins with a topic sentence like one of the following:

A passing comment my grandfather once made really devastated me.

When I was growing up, there were several typical ways my mother treated me that always made me sad.

A critical remark by my fifth-grade teacher was the low point of my life.

My mother has always had several lines that make her children feel very pleased.

You may want to write a narrative that describes in detail the particular time and place of a statement or action. Or you may want to provide three or so examples of statements or actions and their effect on you.

To get started, make up two long lists of childhood memories involving adults—happy memories and sad memories. Then decide which memory or memories you could most vividly describe in a paragraph. Remember that your goal is to help your readers see for themselves why a particular time was sad or happy for you.

Assignment 3: Writing an Essay

In light of Curran's description of what healthy families do right, examine your own family. Which of Curran's traits of communicative families fit your family? Write an essay pointing out three things that your family is doing right in creating a communicative climate for its members. Or, if you feel your family could work harder at communicating, write the essay about three specific ways your family could improve. In either case, choose three of Curran's nine "hallmarks of the successfully communicating family" and show how they do or do not apply to your family.

In your introductory paragraph, include a thesis statement as well as a plan of development that lists the three traits you will talk about. Then present these traits in turn in three supporting paragraphs. Develop each paragraph by giving specific examples of conversations, arguments, behavior patterns, and so on, that illustrate how your family communicates. Finally, conclude your essay with a summarizing sentence or two and a final thought about your subject.

To get ideas flowing, draw a picture of your family, and consider what the word *family* means to you. In groups of two or three, share your pictures and definitions, discussing how your family communicates. Compare and contrast your experiences with "successful" communication.

Do It Better

Ben Carson, M.D., with Cecil Murphey

PREVIEW

If you suspect that you are now as "smart" as you'll ever be, then read this selection. Taken from the book *Think Big*, it is about Dr. Ben Carson, who was sure he was "the dumbest kid in the class" when he was in fifth grade. Carson tells how he turned his life totally around from what was a path of failure. Today he is a famous neurosurgeon at the Johns Hopkins University Children's Center in Baltimore, Maryland.

"Benjamin, is this your report card?" my mother asked as she picked up the 1 folded white card from the table.

"Uh, yeah," I said, trying to sound casual. Too ashamed to hand it to her, I had 2 dropped it on the table, hoping that she wouldn't notice until after I went to bed.

It was the first report card I had received from Higgins Elementary School 3 since we had moved back from Boston to Detroit, only a few months earlier.

I had been in the fifth grade not even two weeks before everyone considered 4 me the dumbest kid in the class and frequently made jokes about me. Before long I too began to feel as though I really was the most stupid kid in fifth grade. Despite Mother's frequently saying, "You're smart, Bennie. You can do anything you want to do," I did not believe her.

No one else in school thought I was smart, either. 5

Now, as Mother examined my report card, she asked, "What's this grade in 6 reading?" (Her tone of voice told me that I was in trouble.) Although I was embarrassed, I did not think too much about it. Mother knew that I wasn't doing well in math, but she did not know I was doing so poorly in every subject.

While she slowly read my report card, reading everything one word at a time, 7 I hurried into my room and started to get ready for bed. A few minutes later, Mother came into my bedroom.

"Benjamin," she said, "are these your grades?" She held the card in front of 8
me as if I hadn't seen it before.

"Oh, yeah, but you know, it doesn't mean much." 9

"No, that's not true, Bennie. It means a lot." 10

"Just a report card." 11

"But it's more than that." 12

Knowing I was in for it now, I prepared to listen, yet I was not all that 13
interested. I did not like school very much and there was no reason why I should.
Inasmuch as I was the dumbest kid in the class, what did I have to look forward
to? The others laughed at me and made jokes about me every day.

"Education is the only way you're ever going to escape poverty," she said. 14
"It's the only way you're ever going to get ahead in life and be successful. Do
you understand that?"

"Yes, Mother," I mumbled. 15

"If you keep on getting these kinds of grades you're going to spend the rest 16
of your life on skid row, or at best sweeping floors in a factory. That's not the kind
of life that I want for you. That's not the kind of life that God wants for you."

I hung my head, genuinely ashamed. My mother had been raising me and 17
my older brother, Curtis, by herself. Having only a third-grade education herself,
she knew the value of what she did not have. Daily she drummed into Curtis
and me that we had to do our best in school.

"You're just not living up to your potential," she said. "I've got two mighty 18
smart boys and I know they can do better."

I had done my best—at least I had when I first started at Higgins Elementary 19
School. How could I do much when I did not understand anything going on in
our class?

In Boston we had attended a parochial school, but I hadn't learned much 20
because of a teacher who seemed more interested in talking to another female
teacher than in teaching us. Possibly, this teacher was not solely to blame—perhaps
I wasn't emotionally able to learn much. My parents had separated just before we
went to Boston, when I was eight years old. I loved both my mother and father
and went through considerable trauma over their separating. For months afterward,
I kept thinking that my parents would get back together, that my daddy would
come home again the way he used to, and that we could be the same old family
again—but he never came back. Consequently, we moved to Boston and lived with
Aunt Jean and Uncle William Avery in a tenement building for two years until
Mother had saved enough money to bring us back to Detroit.

Mother kept shaking the report card at me as she sat on the side of my bed. 21
"You have to work harder. You have to use that good brain that God gave you,
Bennie. Do you understand that?"

"Yes, Mother." Each time she paused, I would dutifully say those words. 22

"I work among rich people, people who are educated," she said. "I watch 23
how they act, and I know they can do anything they want to do. And so can

you." She put her arm on my shoulder. "Bennie, you can do anything they can do—only you can do it better!"

Mother had said those words before. Often. At the time, they did not mean 24 much to me. Why should they? I really believed that I was the dumbest kid in fifth grade, but of course, I never told her that.

"I just don't know what to do about you boys," she said. "I'm going to talk 25 to God about you and Curtis." She paused, stared into space, then said (more to herself than to me), "I need the Lord's guidance on what to do. You just can't bring in any more report cards like this."

As far as I was concerned, the report card matter was over.   26

The next day was like the previous ones—just another bad day in school, 27 another day of being laughed at because I did not get a single problem right in arithmetic and couldn't get any words right on the spelling test. As soon as I came home from school, I changed into play clothes and ran outside. Most of the boys my age played softball, or the game I liked best, "Tip the Top."

We played Tip the Top by placing a bottle cap on one of the sidewalk cracks. 28 Then taking a ball—any kind that bounced—we'd stand on a line and take turns throwing the ball at the bottle top, trying to flip it over. Whoever succeeded got two points. If anyone actually moved the cap more than a few inches, he won five points. Ten points came if he flipped it into the air and it landed on the other side.

When it grew dark or we got tired, Curtis and I would finally go inside and 29 watch TV. The set stayed on until we went to bed. Because Mother worked long hours, she was never home until just before we went to bed. Sometimes I would awaken when I heard her unlocking the door.

Two evenings after the incident with the report card, Mother came home 30 about an hour before our bedtime. Curtis and I were sprawled out, watching TV. She walked across the room, snapped off the set, and faced both of us. "Boys," she said, "you're wasting too much of your time in front of that television. You don't get an education from staring at television all the time."

Before either of us could make a protest, she told us that she had been pray- 31 ing for wisdom. "The Lord's told me what to do," she said. "So from now on, you will not watch television, except for two preselected programs each week."

"Just *two* programs?" I could hardly believe she would say such a terrible 32 thing. "That's not—"

"And *only* after you've done your homework. Furthermore, you don't play 33 outside after school, either, until you've done all your homework."

"Everybody else plays outside right after school," I said, unable to think of 34 anything except how bad it would be if I couldn't play with my friends. "I won't have any friends if I stay in the house all the time—"

"That may be," Mother said, "but everybody else is not going to be as suc- 35 cessful as you are—"

"But, Mother—"   36

"This is what we're going to do. I asked God for wisdom, and this is the 37 answer I got."

I tried to offer several other arguments, but Mother was firm. I glanced at 38 Curtis, expecting him to speak up, but he did not say anything. He lay on the floor, staring at his feet.

"Don't worry about everybody else. The whole world is full of 'everybody 39 else,' you know that? But only a few make a significant achievement."

The loss of TV and play time was bad enough. I got up off the floor, feeling 40 as if everything was against me. Mother wasn't going to let me play with my friends, and there would be no more television—almost none, anyway. She was stopping me from having any fun in life.

"And that isn't all," she said. "Come back, Bennie."   41

I turned around, wondering what else there could be.   42

"In addition," she said, "to doing your homework, you have to read two 43 books from the library each week. Every single week."

"Two books? Two?" Even though I was in fifth grade, I had never read a 44 whole book in my life.

"Yes, two. When you finish reading them, you must write me a book report 45 just like you do at school. You're not living up to your potential, so I'm going to see that you do."

Usually Curtis, who was two years older, was the more rebellious. But this time 46 he seemed to grasp the wisdom of what Mother said. He did not say one word.

She stared at Curtis. "You understand?"   47

He nodded.   48

"Bennie, is it clear?"   49

"Yes, Mother." I agreed to do what Mother told me—it wouldn't have 50 occurred to me not to obey—but I did not like it. Mother was being unfair and demanding more of us than other parents did.

The following day was Thursday. After school, Curtis and I walked to the 51 local branch of the library. I did not like it much, but then I had not spent that much time in any library.

We both wandered around a little in the children's section, not having any 52 idea about how to select books or which books we wanted to check out.

The librarian came over to us and asked if she could help. We explained that 53 both of us wanted to check out two books.

"What kind of books would you like to read?" the librarian asked.   54

"Animals," I said after thinking about it. "Something about animals."   55

"I'm sure we have several that you'd like." She led me over to a section of 56 books. She left me and guided Curtis to another section of the room. I flipped through the row of books until I found two that looked easy enough for me to read. One of them, *Chip, the Dam Builder*—about a beaver—was the first one I had ever checked out. As soon as I got home, I started to read it. It was the first book I ever read all the way through even though it took me two nights. Reluctantly I admitted afterward to Mother that I really had liked reading about Chip.

Within a month I could find my way around the children's section like 57 someone who had gone there all his life. By then the library staff knew

Curtis and me and the kind of books we chose. They often made suggestions. "Here's a delightful book about a squirrel," I remember one of them telling me.

As she told me part of the story, I tried to appear indifferent, but as soon as 58
she handed it to me, I opened the book and started to read.

Best of all, we became favorites of the librarians. When new books came in 59
that they thought either of us would enjoy, they held them for us. Soon I became
fascinated as I realized that the library had so many books—and about so many
different subjects.

After the book about the beaver, I chose others about animals—all types of 60
animals. I read every animal story I could get my hands on. I read books about
wolves, wild dogs, several about squirrels, and a variety of animals that lived in
other countries. Once I had gone through the animal books, I started reading
about plants, then minerals, and finally rocks.

My reading books about rocks was the first time the information ever became 61
practical to me. We lived near the railroad tracks, and when Curtis and I took
the route to school that crossed by the tracks, I began paying attention to the
crushed rock that I noticed between the ties.

As I continued to read more about rocks, I would walk along the tracks, 62
searching for different kinds of stones, and then see if I could identify them.

Often I would take a book with me to make sure that I had labeled each 63
stone correctly.

"Agate," I said as I threw the stone. Curtis got tired of my picking up stones 64
and identifying them, but I did not care because I kept finding new stones all
the time. Soon it became my favorite game to walk along the tracks and identify
the varieties of stones. Although I did not realize it, within a very short period
of time, I was actually becoming an expert on rocks.

Two things happened in the second half of fifth grade that convinced me of 65
the importance of reading books.

First, our teacher, Mrs. Williamson, had a spelling bee every Friday after- 66
noon. We'd go through all the words we'd had so far that year. Sometimes she
also called out words that we were supposed to have learned in fourth grade.
Without fail, I always went down on the first word.

One Friday, though, Bobby Farmer, whom everyone acknowledged as the 67
smartest kid in our class, had to spell "agriculture" as his final word. As soon
as the teacher pronounced his word, I thought, *I can spell that word.* Just the
day before, I had learned it from reading one of my library books. I spelled it
under my breath, and it was just the way Bobby spelled it.

If I can spell "agriculture," I'll bet I can learn to spell any other word in 68
the world. I'll bet I can learn to spell better than Bobby Farmer.

Just that single word, "agriculture," was enough to give me hope.   69

The following week, a second thing happened that forever changed my life. 70
When Mr. Jaeck, the science teacher, was teaching us about volcanoes, he held

up an object that looked like a piece of black, glass-like rock. "Does anybody know what this is? What does it have to do with volcanoes?"

Immediately, because of my reading, I recognized the stone. I waited, but 71 none of my classmates raised their hands. I thought, *This is strange. Not even the smart kids are raising their hands.* I raised my hand.

"Yes, Benjamin," he said. 72

I heard snickers around me. The other kids probably thought it was a joke, 73 or that I was going to say something stupid.

"Obsidian," I said. 74

"That's right!" He tried not to look startled, but it was obvious he hadn't 75 expected me to give the correct answer.

"That's obsidian," I said, "and it's formed by the supercooling of lava when 76 it hits the water." Once I had their attention and realized I knew information no other student had learned, I began to tell them everything I knew about the subject of obsidian, lava, lava flow, supercooling, and compacting of the elements.

When I finally paused, a voice behind me whispered, "Is that Bennie Carson?" 77

"You're absolutely correct," Mr. Jaeck said and he smiled at me. If he had 78 announced that I'd won a million-dollar lottery, I couldn't have been more pleased and excited.

"Benjamin, that's absolutely, absolutely right," he repeated with enthusiasm 79 in his voice. He turned to the others and said, "That is wonderful! Class, this is a tremendous piece of information Benjamin has just given us. I'm very proud to hear him say this."

For a few moments, I tasted the thrill of achievement. I recall thinking, *Wow,* 80 *look at them. They're all looking at me with admiration. Me, the dummy! The one everybody thinks is stupid. They're looking at me to see if this is really me speaking.*

Maybe, though, it was I who was the most astonished one in the class. Although 81 I had been reading two books a week because Mother told me to, I had not realized how much knowledge I was accumulating. True, I had learned to enjoy reading, but until then I hadn't realized how it connected with my schoolwork. That day—for the first time—I realized that Mother had been right. Reading is the way out of ignorance, and the road to achievement. I did not have to be the class dummy anymore.

For the next few days, I felt like a hero at school. The jokes about me 82 stopped. The kids started to listen to me. *I'm starting to have fun with this stuff.*

As my grades improved in every subject, I asked myself, "Ben, is there any 83 reason you can't be the smartest kid in the class? If you can learn about obsidian, you can learn about social studies and geography and math and science and everything."

That single moment of triumph pushed me to want to read more. From then 84 on, it was as though I could not read enough books. Whenever anyone looked for me after school, they could usually find me in my bedroom—curled up, reading a library book—for a long time, the only thing I wanted to do. I had stopped caring about the TV programs I was missing; I no longer cared about playing Tip the Top or baseball anymore. I just wanted to read.

In a year and a half—by the middle of sixth grade—I had moved to the top 85 of the class.

READING COMPREHENSION QUESTIONS

1. The word *trauma* in "I loved both my mother and father and went through considerable trauma over their separating. For months afterward, I kept thinking that my parents would get back together, . . . but he never came back" (paragraph 20) means
   a. love.
   b. knowledge.
   c. distance.
   d. suffering.

2. The word *acknowledged* in "One Friday, though, Bobby Farmer, whom everyone acknowledged as the smartest kid in our class, had to spell 'agriculture' as his final word" (paragraph 67) means
   a. denied.
   b. recognized.
   c. forgot.
   d. interrupted.

3. Which of the following would be the best alternative title for this selection?
   a. The Importance of Fifth Grade
   b. The Role of Parents in Education
   c. The Day I Surprised My Science Teacher
   d. Reading Changed My Life

4. Which sentence best expresses the main idea of this selection?
   a. Children who grow up in single-parent homes may spend large amounts of time home alone.
   b. Because of parental guidance that led to a love of reading, the author was able to go from academic failure to success.
   c. Most children do not take school very seriously, and they suffer as a result.
   d. Today's young people watch too much television.

5. Bennie's mother
   a. was not a religious person.
   b. spoke to Bennie's teacher about Bennie's poor report card.

   c. had only a third-grade education.

   d. had little contact with educated people.

6. To get her sons to do better in school, Mrs. Carson insisted that they

   a. stop watching TV.

   b. finish their homework before playing.

   c. read one library book every month.

   d. all of the above.

7. *True or false?* _____ Bennie's first experience with a library book was discouraging.

8. We can conclude that Bennie Carson believed he was dumb because

   a. in Boston he had not learned much.

   b. other students laughed at him.

   c. he had done his best when he first started at Higgins Elementary School, but still got poor grades.

   d. all of the above.

9. We can conclude that the author's mother believed

   a. education leads to success.

   b. her sons needed to be forced to live up to their potential.

   c. socializing was less important for her sons than a good education.

   d. all of the above.

10. From paragraphs 70–80, we can infer that

   a. Bennie thought his classmates were stupid because they did not know about obsidian.

   b. Mr. Jaeck knew less about rocks than Bennie did.

   c. this was the first time Bennie had answered a difficult question correctly in class.

   d. Mr. Jaeck thought that Bennie had taken too much class time explaining about obsidian.

DISCUSSION QUESTIONS

About Content

1. How do you think considering himself the "dumbest kid in class" affected Bennie's schoolwork?

2. The author recalls his failure in the classroom as an eight-year-old child by writing, "perhaps I wasn't emotionally able to learn much" (paragraph 20).

Why does he make this statement? What do you think parents and schools can do to help children through difficult times?

3. How did Mrs. Carson encourage Bennie to make school—particularly reading—a priority in his life? What effect did her efforts have on Bennie's academic performance and self-esteem?

4. As a child, Carson began to feel confident about his own abilities when he followed his mother's guidelines. How might Mrs. Carson's methods help adult students build up their own self-confidence and motivation?

About Structure

5. What is the main order in which the details of this selection are organized— time order or listing order? Locate and write below three of the many transitions that are used as part of that time order or listing order.

_____   _____   _____

6. In paragraph 65, Carson states, "Two things happened in the second half of fifth grade that convinced me of the importance of reading books." What two transitions does Carson use in later paragraphs to help readers recognize those two events? Write those two transitions here:

_____   _____

About Style and Tone

7. Instead of describing his mother, Carson reveals her character through specific details of her actions and words. Find one paragraph in which this technique is used, and write its number here: _____. What does this paragraph tell us about Mrs. Carson?

8. Why do you suppose Carson italicizes sentences in paragraphs 67, 68, 71, 80, and 82? What purpose do the italicized sentences serve?

www.mhhe.com/langan

WRITING ASSIGNMENTS

Assignment 1: Writing a Paragraph

The reading tells about some of Carson's most important school experiences, both positive and negative. Write a paragraph about one of your most important experiences in school. To select an event to write about, consider the following questions and discuss them in groups of two or three:

Which teachers or events in school influenced how I felt about myself?

What specific incidents stand out in my mind as I think back to elementary school?

To get started, you might use freewriting to help you remember and record the details. Then begin your draft with a topic sentence similar to one of the following:

A seemingly small experience in elementary school encouraged me greatly.

If not for my sixth-grade teacher, I would not be where I am today.

My tenth-grade English class was a turning point in my life.

Use concrete details—actions, comments, reactions, and so on—to help your readers see what happened.

Assignment 2: Writing a Paragraph

Reading helped Bennie, and it can do a lot for adults, too. Most of us, however, don't have someone around to make us do a certain amount of personal reading every week. In addition, many of us don't have as much free time as Bennie and Curtis had. How can adults find time to read more? Write a paragraph listing several ways adults can add more reading to their lives.

To get started, simply write down as many ways as you can think of—in any order. Here is an example of a prewriting list for this paper:

Situations in which adults can find extra time to read:
  Riding to and from work or school
  In bed at night before turning off the light
  While eating breakfast or lunch
  Instead of watching some TV
  In the library

Feel free to use items from the list above, but see if you can add at least one or two of your own points as well. Use descriptions and examples to emphasize and dramatize your supporting details.

Assignment 3: Writing an Essay

Mrs. Carson discovered an effective way to boost her children's achievement and self-confidence. There are other ways as well. Write an essay whose thesis statement is "There are several ways parents can help children live up to their potential." Then, in the following paragraphs, explain and illustrate two or three methods parents can use. In choosing material for your supporting paragraphs, you might consider some of these areas, or think of others on your own:

Assigning regular household "chores" and rewarding a good job

Encouraging kids to join an organization that fosters achievement: Scouts, Little League, religious group, or neighborhood service club

Going to parent-teacher conferences at school and then working more closely with children's teachers—knowing when assignments are due, and so on

Giving a child some responsibility for an enjoyable family activity, such as choosing decorations or food for a birthday party

Setting up a "Wall of Fame" in the home where children's artwork, successful schoolwork, and so on, can be displayed

Setting guidelines (as Mrs. Carson did) for use of leisure time, homework time, and the like

Draw on examples from your own experiences or from someone else's—including those of a classmate or Bennie Carson, if you like.

Anxiety: Challenge by Another Name
James Lincoln Collier

PREVIEW

What is your basis for making personal decisions? Do you aim to rock the boat as little as possible, choosing the easy, familiar path? There is comfort in sticking with what is safe and well known, just as there is comfort in eating bland mashed potatoes. But James Lincoln Collier, author of numerous articles and books, decided soon after leaving college not to live a mashed-potato sort of life. In this essay, first published in *Reader's Digest,* he tells how he learned to recognize the marks of a potentially exciting, growth-inducing experience, to set aside his anxiety, and to dive in.

Between my sophomore and junior years at college, a chance came up for me to spend the summer vacation working on a ranch in Argentina. My roommate's father was in the cattle business, and he wanted Ted to see something of it. Ted said he would go if he could take a friend, and he chose me. 1

The idea of spending two months on the fabled Argentine pampas was exciting. Then I began having second thoughts. I had never been very far from New England, and I had been homesick my first weeks at college. What would it be like in a strange country? What about the language? And besides, I had promised 2 to teach my younger brother to sail that summer. The more I thought about it, the more the prospect daunted me. I began waking up nights in a sweat.

In the end I turned down the proposition. As soon as Ted asked somebody 3 else to go, I began kicking myself. A couple of weeks later I went home to my old summer job, unpacking cartons at the local supermarket, feeling very low. I had turned down something I wanted to do because I was scared, and I had ended up feeling depressed. I stayed that way for a long time. And it didn't help when I went back to college in the fall to discover that Ted and his friend had had a terrific time.

In the long run that unhappy summer taught me a valuable lesson out of 4 which I developed a rule for myself: *do what makes you anxious, don't do what makes you depressed.*

I am not, of course, talking about severe states of anxiety or depression, 5 which require medical attention. What I mean is that kind of anxiety we call stage fright, butterflies in the stomach, a case of nerves—the feelings we have at a job interview, when we're giving a big party, when we have to make an important presentation at the office. And the kind of depression I am referring to is that downhearted feeling of the blues, when we don't seem to be interested in anything, when we can't get going and seem to have no energy.

I was confronted by this sort of situation toward the end of my senior year. 6 As graduation approached, I began to think about taking a crack at making my living as a writer. But one of my professors was urging me to apply to graduate school and aim at a teaching career.

I wavered. The idea of trying to live by writing was scary—a lot more scary 7 than spending a summer on the pampas, I thought. Back and forth I went, making my decision, unmaking it. Suddenly, I realized that every time I gave up the idea of writing, that sinking feeling went through me; it gave me the blues.

The thought of graduate school wasn't what depressed me. It was giving up 8 on what deep in my gut I really wanted to do. Right then I learned another lesson. To avoid that kind of depression meant, inevitably, having to endure a certain amount of worry and concern.

The great Danish philosopher Søren Kierkegaard believed that anxiety always 9 arises when we confront the possibility of our own development. It seems to be a rule of life that you can't advance without getting that old, familiar, jittery feeling.

Even as children we discover this when we try to expand ourselves by, say, 10 learning to ride a bike or going out for the school play. Later in life we get butterflies when we think about having that first child, or uprooting the family from the old hometown to find a better opportunity halfway across the country. Anytime, it seems, that we set out aggressively to get something we want, we meet up with anxiety. And it's going to be our traveling companion, at least part of the way, in any new venture.

When I first began writing magazine articles, I was frequently required to 11 interview big names—people like Richard Burton, Joan Rivers, sex authority

William Masters, baseball great Dizzy Dean. Before each interview I would get butterflies and my hands would shake.

At the time, I was doing some writing about music. And one person I par- 12 ticularly admired was the great composer Duke Ellington. On stage and on television, he seemed the very model of the confident, sophisticated man of the world. Then I learned that Ellington still got stage fright. If the highly honored Duke Ellington, who had appeared on the bandstand some ten thousand times over thirty years, had anxiety attacks, who was I to think I could avoid them?

I went on doing those frightening interviews, and one day, as I was getting 13 onto a plane for Washington to interview columnist Joseph Alsop, I suddenly realized to my astonishment that I was looking forward to the meeting. What had happened to those butterflies?

Well, in truth, they were still there, but there were fewer of them. I had 14 benefited, I discovered, from a process psychologists call "extinction." If you put an individual in an anxiety-provoking situation often enough, he will eventually learn that there isn't anything to be worried about.

Which brings us to a corollary to my basic rule: *you'll never eliminate anxi-* 15 *ety by avoiding the things that caused it.* I remember how my son Jeff was when I first began to teach him to swim at the lake cottage where we spent our summer vacations. He resisted, and when I got him into the water he sank and sputtered and wanted to quit. But I was insistent. And by summer's end he was splashing around like a puppy. He had "extinguished" his anxiety the only way he could— by confronting it.

The problem, of course, is that it is one thing to urge somebody else to take 16 on those anxiety-producing challenges; it is quite another to get ourselves to do it.

Some years ago I was offered a writing assignment that would require three 17 months of travel through Europe. I had been abroad a couple of times on the usual "If it's Tuesday this must be Belgium"*trips, but I hardly could claim to know my way around the continent. Moreover, my knowledge of foreign languages was limited to a little college French.

I hesitated. How would I, unable to speak the language, totally unfamiliar 18 with local geography or transportation systems, set up interviews and do research? It seemed impossible, and with considerable regret I sat down to write a letter begging off. Halfway through, a thought—which I subsequently made into another corollary to my basic rule—ran through my mind: *you can't learn if you don't try.* So I accepted the assignment.

There were some bad moments. But by the time I had finished the trip I was 19 an experienced traveler. And ever since, I have never hesitated to head for even the most exotic of places, without guides or even advance bookings, confident that somehow I will manage.

---

*Reference to a film comedy about a group of American tourists who visited too many European countries in too little time.

The point is that the new, the different, is almost by definition scary. But 20
each time you try something, you learn, and as the learning piles up, the world
opens to you.

I've made parachute jumps, learned to ski at forty, flown up the Rhine in a 21
balloon. And I know I'm going to go on doing such things. It's not because I'm
braver or more daring than others. I'm not. But I don't let the butterflies stop
me from doing what I want. Accept anxiety as another name for challenge, and
you can accomplish wonders.

READING COMPREHENSION QUESTIONS

1. The word *daunted* in "The more I thought about [going to Argentina], the
   more the prospect daunted me. I began waking up nights in a sweat"
   (paragraph 2) means

   a. encouraged.
   b. interested.
   c. discouraged.
   d. amused.

2. The word *corollary* in "Which brings us to a corollary to my basic rule:
   you'll never eliminate anxiety by avoiding the things that caused it"
   (paragraph 15) means

   a. an idea that follows from another idea.
   b. an idea based on a falsehood.
   c. an idea that creates anxiety.
   d. an idea passed on from one generation to another.

3. Which of the following would be the best alternative title for this selection?

   a. A Poor Decision
   b. Don't Let Anxiety Stop You
   c. Becoming a Writer
   d. The Courage to Travel

4. Which sentence best expresses the main idea of the selection?

   a. The butterflies-in-the-stomach type of anxiety differs greatly from severe
      states of anxiety or depression.
   b. Taking on a job assignment that required traveling helped the author get
      over his anxiety.
   c. People learn and grow by confronting, not backing away from, situations
      that make them anxious.
   d. Anxiety is a predictable part of life that can be dealt with in positive ways.

5. When a college friend invited the writer to go with him to Argentina, the writer
   a. turned down the invitation.
   b. accepted eagerly.
   c. was very anxious about the idea but went anyway.
   d. did not believe his friend was serious.

6. *True or false?* _____ As graduation approached, Collier's professor urged him to try to make his living as a writer.

7. *True or false?* _____ The philosopher Søren Kierkegaard believed that anxiety occurs when we face the possibility of our own development.

8. *Extinction* is the term psychologists use for
   a. the inborn tendency to avoid situations that make one feel very anxious.
   b. a person's gradual loss of confidence.
   c. the natural development of a child's abilities.
   d. the process of losing one's fear by continuing to face the anxiety-inspiring situation.

9. The author implies that
   a. it was lucky he didn't take the summer job in Argentina.
   b. his son never got over his fear of the water.
   c. Duke Ellington's facing stage fright inspired him.
   d. one has to be more daring than most people to overcome anxiety.

10. The author implies that
    a. anxiety may be a signal that one has an opportunity to grow.
    b. he considers his three-month trip to Europe a failure.
    c. facing what makes him anxious has eliminated all depression from his life.
    d. he no longer has anxiety about new experiences.

DISCUSSION QUESTIONS

About Content

1. Collier developed the rule "Do what makes you anxious, don't do what makes you depressed" (paragraph 4). How does he distinguish between feeling anxious and feeling depressed?

2. With a partner, discuss the following questions, and then share your ideas with the whole class: In what way does Collier believe that anxiety is positive? How, according to him, can we eventually overcome our fears? Have you ever gone ahead and done something that made you anxious? How did it turn out?

About Structure

3. Collier provides a rule and two corollary rules that describe his attitude toward challenge and anxiety. Below, write the location of that rule and its corollaries.

   Collier's rule: paragraph _____

   First corollary: paragraph _____

   Second corollary: paragraph _____

   How does Collier emphasize the rule and its corollaries?

4. Collier uses several personal examples in his essay. Find three instances of these examples and explain how each helps Collier develop his main point.

About Style and Tone

5. In paragraph 3, Collier describes the aftermath of his decision not to go to Argentina. He could have just written, "I worked that summer." Instead he writes, "I went home to my old summer job, unpacking cartons at the local supermarket." Why do you think he provides that bit of detail about his job? What is the effect on the reader?

6. Authors often use testimony by authorities to support their points. Where in Collier's essay does he use such support? What do you think it adds to his piece?

7. In the last sentence of paragraph 10, Collier refers to anxiety as a "traveling companion." Why do you think he uses that image? What does it convey about his view of anxiety?

8. Is Collier just telling about a lesson he has learned for himself, or is he encouraging his readers to do something? How can you tell?

WRITING ASSIGNMENTS

www.mhhe.com/langan

Assignment 1: Writing a Paragraph

Collier explains how his life experiences made him view the term *anxiety* in a new way. Write a paragraph in which you explain how a personal experience of yours has given new meaning to a particular term. Following are some terms you might consider for this assignment:

Failure	Homesickness
Friendship	Maturity
Goals	Success

Here are two sample topic sentences for this assignment:

> I used to think of failure as something terrible, but thanks to a helpful boss, I now think of it as an opportunity to learn.

> The word *creativity* has taken on a new meaning for me ever since I became interested in dancing.

Assignment 2: Writing a Paragraph

The second corollary to Collier's rule is "You can't learn if you don't try" (paragraph 18). Write a paragraph using this idea as your main idea. Support it with your own experience, someone else's experience, or both. One way of developing this point is to compare two approaches to a challenge: One person may have backed away from a frightening opportunity while another person decided to take on the challenge. Or you could write about a time when you learned something useful by daring to give a new experience a try. In that case, you might discuss your reluctance to take on the new experience, the difficulties you encountered, and your eventual success. In your conclusion, include a final thought about the value of what was learned.

Listing a few skills you have learned will help you decide on the experience you wish to write about. To get you started, below is a list of things adults often need to go to some trouble to learn.

Driving with a stick shift

Taking useful lecture notes

Knowing how to do well on a job interview

Asking someone out on a date

Making a speech

Standing up for your rights

Assignment 3: Writing an Essay

Collier describes three rules he follows when facing anxiety. In an essay, write about one or more rules, or guidelines, that you have developed for yourself through experience. If you decide to discuss two or three such guidelines, mention or refer to them in your introductory paragraph. Then go on to discuss each in one or more paragraphs of its own. Include at least one experience that led you to develop a given guideline, and tell how it has helped you at other times in your life. You might end with a brief summary and an explanation of how the guidelines as a group have helped. If you decide to focus on one rule, include at least two or three experiences that help to illustrate your point.

To prepare for this assignment, spend some time freewriting about the rules or guidelines you have set up for yourself. Continue writing until you feel you have a central idea for which you have plenty of interesting support. Then organize that support into a scratch outline, such as this one:

Thesis: I have one rule that keeps me from staying in a rut—Don't let the size of a challenge deter you; instead, aim for it by making plans and taking steps.

Topic sentence 1: I began to think about my rule one summer in high school when a friend got the type of summer job that I had only been thinking about.

Topic sentence 2: After high school, I began to live up to my rule when I aimed for a business career and entered college.

Topic sentence 3: My rule is also responsible for my having the wonderful boyfriend (*or* girlfriend *or* spouse *or* job) I now have.

Let's Really Reform Our Schools
Anita Garland

> ### PREVIEW
>
> A few years ago, the National Commission on Excellence in Education published *A Nation at Risk,* in which commission members described what they saw as a "rising tide of mediocrity" in our schools. Other studies have pointed to students' poor achievement in science, math, communication, and critical thinking. What can our schools do to improve students' performance? Anita Garland has several radical ideas, which she explains in this selection. As you read it, think about whether or not you agree with her points.

American high schools are in trouble. No, that's not strong enough. American 1 high schools are disasters. "Good" schools today are only a rite of passage for American kids, where the pressure to look fashionable and act cool outweighs any concern for learning. And "bad" schools—heaven help us—are havens for the vicious and corrupt. There, metal detectors and security guards wage a losing battle against the criminals that prowl the halls.

Desperate illnesses require desperate remedies. And our public schools are 2 desperately ill. What is needed is no meek, fainthearted attempt at "curriculum revision" or "student-centered learning." We need to completely restructure our thinking about what schools are and what we expect of the students who attend them.

The first change needed to save our schools is the most fundamental one. 3
Not only must we stop *forcing* everyone to attend school; we must stop *allowing*
the attendance of so-called students who are not interested in studying. Mandatory school attendance is based upon the idea that every American has a right to
basic education. But as the old saying goes, your rights stop where the next guy's
begin. A student who sincerely wants an education, regardless of his or her
mental or physical ability, should be welcome in any school in this country. But
"students" who deliberately interfere with other students' ability to learn, teachers' ability to teach, and administrators' ability to maintain order should be
denied a place in the classroom. They do not want an education. And they should
not be allowed to mark time within school walls, waiting to be handed their
meaningless diplomas while they make it harder for everyone around them to
either provide or receive a quality education.

By requiring troublemakers to attend school, we have made it impossible to 4
deal with them in any effective way. They have little to fear in terms of punishment. Suspension from school for a few days doesn't improve their behavior.
After all, they don't want to be in school anyway. For that matter, mandatory
attendance is, in many cases, nothing but a bad joke. Many chronic troublemakers are absent so often that it is virtually impossible for them to learn anything.
And when they *are* in school, they are busy shaking down other students for
their lunch money or jewelry. If we permanently banned such punks from school,
educators could turn their attention away from the troublemakers and toward
those students who realize that school is a serious place for serious learning.

You may ask, "What will become of these young people who aren't in school?" 5
But consider this: What is becoming of them now? They are not being educated.
They are merely names on the school records. They are passed from grade to
grade, learning nothing, making teachers and fellow students miserable. Finally
they are bumped off the conveyor belt at the end of twelfth grade, oftentimes
barely literate, and passed into society as "high school graduates." Yes, there would
be a need for alternative solutions for these young people. Let the best thinkers
of our country come up with some ideas. But in the meanwhile, don't allow our
schools to serve as a holding tank for people who don't want to be there.

Once our schools have been returned to the control of teachers and genuine 6
students, we could concentrate on smaller but equally meaningful reforms. A
good place to start would be requiring students to wear school uniforms. There
would be cries of horror from the fashion slaves, but the change would benefit
everyone. If students wore uniforms, think of the mental energy that could be
redirected into more productive channels. No longer would young girls feel the
need to spend their evenings laying out coordinated clothing, anxiously trying to
create just the right look. The daily fashion show that currently absorbs so much
of students' attention would come to a halt. Kids from modest backgrounds could
stand out because of their personalities and intelligence, rather than being tagged
as losers because they can't wear the season's hottest sneakers or jeans. Affluent

kids might learn they have something to offer the world other than a fashion statement. Parents would be relieved of the pressure to deal with their offspring's constant demands for wardrobe additions.

Next, let's move to the cafeteria. What's for lunch today? How about a Milky 7 Way bar, a bag of Fritos, a Coke, and just to round out the meal with a vegetable, maybe some french fries. And then back to the classroom for a few hours of intense mental activity, fueled on fat, salt, and sugar. What a joke! School is an institution of education, and that education should be continued as students sit down to eat. Here's a perfect opportunity to teach a whole generation of Americans about nutrition, and we are blowing it. School cafeterias, of all places, should demonstrate how a healthful, low-fat, well-balanced diet produces healthy, energetic, mentally alert people. Instead, we allow school cafeterias to dispense the same junk food that kids could buy in any mall. Overhaul the cafeterias! Out with the candy, soda, chips, and fries! In with the salads, whole grains, fruits, and vegetables!

Turning our attention away from what goes on during school hours, let's 8 consider what happens after the final bell rings. Some school-sponsored activities are all to the good. Bands and choirs, foreign-language field trips, chess or skiing or drama clubs are sensible parts of an extracurricular plan. They bring together kids with similar interests to develop their talents and leadership ability. But other common school activities are not the business of education. The prime example of inappropriate school activity is in competitive sports between schools.

Intramural sports are great. Students need an outlet for their energies, and 9 friendly competition against one's classmates on the basketball court or baseball diamond is fun and physically beneficial. But the wholesome fun of sports is quickly ruined by the competitive team system. School athletes quickly become the campus idols, encouraged to look down on classmates with less physical ability. Schools concentrate enormous amounts of time, money, and attention upon their teams, driving home the point that competitive sports are the *really* important part of school. Students are herded into gymnasiums for "pep rallies" that whip up adoration of the chosen few and encourage hatred of rival schools. Boys' teams are supplied with squads of cheerleading girls . . . let's not even get into what the subliminal message is *there*. If communities feel they must have competitive sports, let local businesses or even professional teams organize and fund the programs. But school budgets and time should be spent on programs that benefit more than an elite few.

Another school-related activity that should get the ax is the fluff-headed, 10 money-eating, misery-inducing event known as the prom. How in the world did the schools of America get involved in this showcase of excess? Proms have to be the epitome of everything that is wrong, tasteless, misdirected, inappropriate, and just plain sad about the way we bring up our young people. Instead of simply letting the kids put on a dance, we've turned the prom into a bloated nightmare that ruins young people's budgets, their self-image, and even their lives. The pressure to show up at the prom with the best-looking date, in the most expensive clothes, wearing the most exotic flowers, riding in the most extravagant form of transportation, dominates the thinking of many students for months before the prom itself. Students cling to doomed, even abusive romantic relationships rather than risk being dateless for this night of nights. They lose any concept of meaningful values as they implore their parents for more, more, more money to throw into the jaws of the prom god. The adult trappings of the prom— the slinky dresses, emphasis on romance, slow dancing, nightclub atmosphere— all encourage kids to engage in behavior that can have tragic consequences. Who knows how many unplanned pregnancies and alcohol-related accidents can be directly attributed to the pressures of prom night? And yet, not going to the prom seems a fate worse than death to many young people—because of all the hype about the "wonder" and "romance" of it all. Schools are not in the business of providing wonder and romance, and it's high time we remembered that.

We have lost track of the purpose of our schools. They are not intended to be   11 centers for fun, entertainment, and social climbing. They are supposed to be institutions for learning and hard work. Let's institute the changes suggested here—plus dozens more—without apology, and get American schools back to business.

www.mhhe.com/langan

READING COMPREHENSION QUESTIONS

1. The word *affluent* in "Kids from modest backgrounds could stand out because of their personalities and intelligence. . . . Affluent kids might learn they have something to offer the world other than a fashion statement" (paragraph 6) means
   a. intelligent.
   b. troubled.
   c. wealthy.
   d. poor.

2. The word *implore* in "They lose any concept of meaningful values as they implore their parents for more, more, more money to throw into the jaws of the prom god" (paragraph 10) means
   a. beg.
   b. ignore.
   c. pay.
   d. obey.

3. Which of the following would be the best alternative title for this selection?
   a. America's Youth
   b. Education of the Future
   c. Social Problems of Today's Students
   d. Changes Needed in the American School System

4. Which sentence best expresses the main idea of the selection?

    a. Excesses such as the prom and competitive sports should be eliminated from school budgets.

    b. Major changes are needed to make American schools real centers of learning.

    c. Attendance must be voluntary in our schools.

    d. The best thinkers of our country must come up with ideas on how to improve our schools.

5. Garland believes that mandatory attendance at school

    a. gives all students an equal chance at getting an education.

    b. allows troublemakers to disrupt learning.

    c. is cruel to those who don't really want to be there.

    d. helps teachers maintain control of their classes.

6. Garland is against school-sponsored competitive sports because she believes that

    a. exercise and teamwork should not have a role in school.

    b. they overemphasize the importance of sports and athletes.

    c. school property should not be used in any way after school hours.

    d. they take away from professional sports.

7. We can infer that Garland believes

    a. teens should not have dances.

    b. proms promote unwholesome values.

    c. teens should avoid romantic relationships.

    d. proms are even worse than mandatory education.

8. The author clearly implies that troublemakers

    a. are not intelligent.

    b. really do want to be in school.

    c. should be placed in separate classes.

    d. don't mind being suspended from school.

9. *True or false?* _____ We can conclude that the author feels that teachers and genuine students have lost control of our schools.

10. The essay suggests that the author would also oppose

    a. school plays.

    b. serving milk products in school cafeterias.

    c. the selection of homecoming queens.

    d. stylish school uniforms.

DISCUSSION QUESTIONS

About Content

1. What reforms does Garland suggest in her essay? Think back to your high school days. Which of the reforms that Garland suggests do you think might have been most useful at your high school?

2. Garland's idea of voluntary school attendance directly contradicts the "stay in school" campaigns. Do you agree with her idea? What do you think might become of students who choose not to attend school?

3. At the end of her essay, Garland writes, "Let's institute the changes suggested here—plus dozens more." What other changes do you think Garland may have in mind? What are some reforms you think might improve schools?

About Structure

4. The thesis of this essay can be found in the introduction, which is made up of the first two paragraphs. Find the thesis statement and write it here:

_____

_____

5. The first point on Garland's list of reforms is the elimination of mandatory (that is, required) education. Then she goes on to discuss other reforms. Find the transition sentence that signals that she is leaving the discussion about mandatory education and going on to other needed changes. Write that sentence here:

_____

_____

6. What are two transitional words that Garland uses to introduce two of the other reforms?

_____   _____

About Style and Tone

7. Garland uses some colorful images to communicate her ideas. For instance, in paragraph 5 she writes, "Finally [the troublemakers] are bumped off the conveyor belt at the end of twelfth grade, oftentimes barely literate, and passed into society as 'high school graduates.'" What does the image of a conveyor belt imply about schools and about the troublemakers? What do the quotation marks around *high school graduates* imply?

8. What do the italicized words in the following three colorful images from the essay imply about today's schools and students?

. . . don't allow our schools to serve as a *holding tank* for people who don't want to be there. (paragraph 5)

A good place to start would be requiring students to wear school uniforms. There would be cries of horror from the *fashion slaves* . . . (paragraph 6)

Students are *herded* into gymnasiums for "pep rallies" that whip up adoration of the chosen few . . . (paragraph 9)

9. To convey her points, does the author use a formal, straightforward tone or an informal, impassioned tone? Give examples from the essay to support your answer.

WRITING ASSIGNMENTS

www.mhhe.com/langan

Assignment 1: Writing a Paragraph

Write a persuasive paragraph in which you agree or disagree with one of Garland's suggested reforms. Your topic sentence may be something simple and direct, like these:

I strongly agree with Garland's point that attendance should be voluntary in our high schools.

I disagree with Garland's point that high school students should be required to wear uniforms.

Alternatively, you may want to develop your own paragraph calling for reform in some other area of American life. Your topic sentence might be like one of the following:

We need to make radical changes in our treatment of homeless people.

Strong new steps must be taken to control the sale of guns in our country.

Major changes are needed to keep television from dominating the lives of our children.

Assignment 2: Writing a Paragraph

If troublemakers were excluded from schools, what would become of those troublemakers? Write a paragraph in which you suggest two or three types of programs that troublemakers could be assigned to. Explain why each program would be beneficial to the troublemakers themselves and to society in general. You might want to include in your paragraph one or more of the following:

Apprentice programs

Special neighborhood schools for troublemakers

Reform schools

Work-placement programs

Community service programs

Assignment 3: Writing an Essay

Garland suggests ways to make schools "institutions for learning and hard work" (paragraph 11). She wants to get rid of anything that greatly distracts students from their education, such as having to deal with troublemakers, overemphasis on fashion, and interschool athletics. When you were in high school, what tended most to divert your attention from learning? Write an essay explaining in full detail the three things that interfered most with your high school education. You may include any of Garland's points, but present details that apply specifically to you. Organize your essay by using emphatic order—in other words, save whatever interfered most with your education for the last supporting paragraph.

It is helpful to write a sentence outline for this kind of essay. Here, for example, is one writer's outline for an essay titled "Obstacles to My High School Education."

Thesis: There were three main things that interfered with my high school education.

Topic sentence 1: Concern about my appearance took up too much of my time and energy.

  a. Since I was concerned about my looking good, I spent too much time shopping for clothes.
  b. In order to afford the clothes, I worked twenty hours a week, drastically reducing my study time.
  c. Spending even more time on clothes, I fussed every evening over what I would wear to school the next day.

Topic sentence 2: Cheerleading was another major obstacle to my academic progress in high school.

  a. I spent many hours practicing in order to make the cheerleading squad.
  b. Once I made the squad, I had to spend even more time practicing and then attending games.
  c. Once when I didn't make the squad, I was so depressed for a while that I couldn't study, and this had serious consequences.

Topic sentence 3: The main thing that interfered with my high school education was my family situation.

  a. Even when I had time to study, I often found it impossible to do so at home, since my parents often had fights that were noisy and upsetting.

b. My parents showed little interest in my schoolwork, giving me little reason to work hard for my classes.

c. When I was in eleventh grade, my parents divorced; this was a major distraction for me for a long time.

To round off your essay with a conclusion, you may simply want to restate your thesis and main supporting points. After you finish a first draft, swap essays with a classmate and share revision advice; use the checklist on the inside back cover to guide your critique.

How They Get You to Do That
Janny Scott

PREVIEW

So you think you're sailing along in life, making decisions based on your own preferences? Not likely! Janny Scott brings together the findings of several researchers to show how advertisers, charitable organizations, politicians, employers, and even your friends get you to say "yes" when you should have said "no"—or, at least, "Let me think about that."

1   The woman in the supermarket in a white coat tenders a free sample of "lite" cheese. A car salesman suggests that prices won't stay low for long. Even a penny will help, pleads the door-to-door solicitor. Sale ends Sunday! Will work for food.

2   The average American exists amid a perpetual torrent of propaganda. Everyone, it sometimes seems, is trying to make up someone else's mind. If it isn't an athletic shoe company, it's a politician, a panhandler, a pitchman, a boss, a billboard company, a spouse.

3   The weapons of influence they are wielding are more sophisticated than ever, researchers say. And they are aimed at a vulnerable target—people with less and less time to consider increasingly complex issues.

4   As a result, some experts in the field have begun warning the public, tipping people off to precisely how "the art of compliance" works. Some critics have taken to arguing for new government controls on one pervasive form of persuasion—political advertising.

The persuasion problem is "the essential dilemma of modern democracy," 5 argue social psychologists Anthony Pratkanis and Elliot Aronson, the authors of *Age of Propaganda: The Everyday Use and Abuse of Persuasion.*

As the two psychologists see it, American society values free speech and 6 public discussion, but people no longer have the time or inclination to pay attention. Mindless propaganda flourishes, they say; thoughtful persuasion fades away.

The problem stems from what Pratkanis and Aronson call our "message- 7 dense environment." The average television viewer sees nearly 38,000 commercials a year, they say. "The average home receives . . . [numerous] pieces of junk mail annually and . . . [countless calls] from telemarketing firms."

Bumper stickers, billboards and posters litter the public consciousness. Ath- 8 letic events and jazz festivals carry corporate labels. As direct selling proliferates, workers patrol their offices during lunch breaks, peddling chocolate and Tupperware to friends.

Meanwhile, information of other sorts multiplies exponentially. Technology 9 serves up ever-increasing quantities of data on every imaginable subject, from home security to health. With more and more information available, people have less and less time to digest it.

"It's becoming harder and harder to think in a considered way about any- 10 thing," said Robert Cialdini, a persuasion researcher at Arizona State University in Tempe. "More and more, we are going to be deciding on the basis of less and less information."

Persuasion is a democratic society's chosen method for decision making and 11 dispute resolution. But the flood of persuasive messages in recent years has changed the nature of persuasion. Lengthy arguments have been supplanted by slogans and logos. In a world teeming with propaganda, those in the business of influencing others put a premium on effective shortcuts.

Most people, psychologists say, are easily seduced by such shortcuts. Humans 12 are "cognitive misers," always looking to conserve attention and mental energy— leaving themselves at the mercy of anyone who has figured out which shortcuts work.

The task of figuring out shortcuts has been embraced by advertising agen- 13 cies, market researchers, and millions of salespeople. The public, meanwhile, remains in the dark, ignorant of even the simplest principles of social influence.

As a result, laypeople underestimate their susceptibility to persuasion, psy- 14 chologists say. They imagine their actions are dictated simply by personal preferences. Unaware of the techniques being used against them, they are often unwittingly outgunned.

As Cialdini tells it, the most powerful tactics work like jujitsu: They draw 15 their strength from deep-seated, unconscious psychological rules. The clever "compliance professional" deliberately triggers these "hidden stores of influence" to elicit a predictable response.

One such rule, for example, is that people are more likely to comply with a 16 request if a reason—no matter how silly—is given. To prove that point, one researcher tested different ways of asking people in line at a copying machine to let her cut the line.

When the researcher asked simply, "Excuse me, I have five pages. May I use 17 the Xerox machine?" only 60 percent of those asked complied. But when she added nothing more than "because I have to make some copies," nearly every one agreed.

The simple addition of "because" unleashed an automatic response, even 18 though "because" was followed by an irrelevant reason, Cialdini said. By asking the favor in that way, the researcher dramatically increased the likelihood of getting what she wanted.

Cialdini and others say much of human behavior is mechanical. Automatic 19 responses are efficient when time and attention are short. For that reason, many techniques of persuasion are designed and tested for their ability to trigger those automatic responses.

"These appeals persuade not through the give-and-take of argument and 20 debate," Pratkanis and Aronson have written. ". . . They often appeal to our deepest fears and most irrational hopes, while they make use of our most simplistic beliefs."

Life insurance agents use fear to sell policies, Pratkanis and Aronson say. 21 Parents use fear to convince their children to come home on time. Political leaders use fear to build support for going to war—for example, comparing a foreign leader to Adolf Hitler.

As many researchers see it, people respond to persuasion in one of two ways: 22 If an issue they care about is involved, they may pay close attention to the arguments; if they don't care, they pay less attention and are more likely to be influenced by simple cues.

Their level of attention depends on motivation and the time available. As 23 David Boninger, a UCLA psychologist, puts it, "If you don't have the time or motivation, or both, you will pay attention to more peripheral cues, like how nice somebody looks."

Cialdini, a dapper man with a flat Midwestern accent, describes himself as 24 an inveterate sucker. From an early age, he said recently, he had wondered what made him say yes in many cases when the answer, had he thought about it, should have been no.

So in the early 1980s, he became "a spy in the wars of influence." He took 25 a sabbatical and, over a three-year period, enrolled in dozens of sales training programs, learning firsthand the tricks of selling insurance, cars, vacuum cleaners, encyclopedias, and more.

He learned how to sell portrait photography over the telephone. He took a 26 job as a busboy in a restaurant, observing the waiters. He worked in fund-raising, advertising, and public relations. And he interviewed cult recruiters and members of bunco squads.

By the time it was over, Cialdini had witnessed hundreds of tactics. But he 27 found that the most effective ones were rooted in six principles. Most are not new, but they are being used today with greater sophistication on people whose fast-paced lifestyle has lowered their defenses.

Reciprocity. People have been trained to believe that a favor must be repaid in kind, 28 even if the original favor was not requested. The cultural pressure to return a favor is so intense that people go along rather than suffer the feeling of being indebted.

Politicians have learned that favors are repaid with votes. Stores offer free 29 samples—not just to show off a product. Charity organizations ship personalized address labels to potential contributors. Others accost pedestrians, planting paper flowers in their lapels.

Commitment and Consistency. People tend to feel they should be consistent— 30 even when being consistent no longer makes sense. While consistency is easy, comfortable, and generally advantageous, Cialdini says, "mindless consistency" can be exploited.

Take the "foot in the door technique." One person gets another to agree to a 31 small commitment, like a down payment or signing a petition. Studies show that it then becomes much easier to get the person to comply with a much larger request.

Another example Cialdini cites is the "lowball tactic" in car sales. Offered 32 a low price for a car, the potential customer agrees. Then at the last minute, the sales manager finds a supposed error. The price is increased. But customers tend to go along nevertheless.

Social Validation. People often decide what is correct on the basis of what other 33 people think. Studies show that is true for behavior. Hence, sitcom laugh tracks, tip jars "salted" with a bartender's cash, long lines outside nightclubs, testimonials, and "man on the street" ads.

Tapping the power of social validation is especially effective under certain 34 conditions: When people are in doubt, they will look to others as a guide; and when they view those others as similar to themselves, they are more likely to follow their lead.

Liking. People prefer to comply with requests from people they know and like. 35 Charities recruit people to canvass their friends and neighbors. Colleges get alumni to raise money from classmates. Sales training programs include grooming tips.

According to Cialdini, liking can be based on any of a number of factors. 36 Good-looking people tend to be credited with traits like talent and intelligence. People also tend to like people who are similar to themselves in personality, background, and lifestyle.

Authority. People defer to authority. Society trains them to do so, and in many 37 situations deference is beneficial. Unfortunately, obedience is often automatic, leaving people vulnerable to exploitation by compliance professionals, Cialdini says.

As an example, he cites the famous ad campaign that capitalized on actor 38 Robert Young's role as Dr. Marcus Welby, Jr., to tout the alleged health benefits of Sanka decaffeinated coffee.

An authority, according to Cialdini, need not be a true authority. The trap- 39 pings of authority may suffice. Con artists have long recognized the persuasive power of titles like doctor or judge, fancy business suits, and expensive cars.

Scarcity. Products and opportunities seem more valuable when the supply is 40 limited.

As a result, professional persuaders emphasize that "supplies are limited." Sales 41 end Sunday and movies have limited engagements—diverting attention from whether the item is desirable to the threat of losing the chance to experience it at all.

The use of influence, Cialdini says, is ubiquitous. 42

Take the classic appeal by a child of a parent's sense of consistency: "But 43 you said . . ." And the parent's resort to authority: "Because I said so." In addition, nearly everyone invokes the opinions of like-minded others—for social validation—in vying to win a point.

One area in which persuasive tactics are especially controversial is political 44 advertising—particularly negative advertising. Alarmed that attack ads might be alienating voters, some critics have begun calling for stricter limits on political ads.

In Washington, legislation pending in Congress would, among other things, 45 force candidates to identify themselves at the end of their commercials. In that way, they might be forced to take responsibility for the ads' contents and be unable to hide behind campaign committees.

"In general, people accept the notion that for the sale of products at least, 46 there are socially accepted norms of advertising," said Lloyd Morrisett, president of the Markle Foundation, which supports research in communications and information technology.

"But when those same techniques are applied to the political process—where 47 we are judging not a product but a person, and where there is ample room for distortion of the record or falsification in some cases—there begins to be more concern," he said.

On an individual level, some psychologists offer tips for self-protection. 48

- Pay attention to your emotions, says Pratkanis, an associate professor of 49 psychology at UC Santa Cruz: "If you start to feel guilty or patriotic, try to figure out why." In consumer transactions, beware of feelings of inferiority and the sense that you don't measure up unless you have a certain product.

- Be on the lookout for automatic responses, Cialdini says. Beware 50 foolish consistency. Check other people's responses against objective facts. Be skeptical of authority, and look out for unwarranted liking for any "compliance professionals."

Since the publication of his most recent book, *Influence: The New Psychol-* 51
ogy of Modern Persuasion, Cialdini has begun researching a new book on ethical uses of influence in business—addressing, among other things, how to instruct
salespeople and other "influence agents" to use persuasion in ways that help,
rather than hurt, society.

"If influence agents don't police themselves, society will have to step in to 52
regulate . . . the way information is presented in commercial and political set-
tings," Cialdini said. "And that's a can of worms that I don't think anybody wants
to get into."

Have you ever been persuaded by negative advertising? Why do you think attack
ads, like the one pictured here, are so effective?

READING COMPREHENSION QUESTIONS

1. The word *wielding* in "The weapons of influence they are wielding are more
   sophisticated than ever" (paragraph 3) means
   a. handling effectively.
   b. giving up.
   c. looking for.
   d. demanding.

2. The word *peripheral* in "As David Boninger . . . puts it, 'If you don't have the time or motivation, or both, you will pay attention to more peripheral cues, like how nice somebody looks'" (paragraph 23) means

   a. important.

   b. dependable.

   c. minor.

   d. attractive.

3. Which of the following would be the best alternative title for this selection?

   a. Automatic Human Responses

   b. Our Deepest Fears

   c. The Loss of Thoughtful Discussion

   d. Compliance Techniques

4. Which sentence best expresses the selection's main point?

   a. Americans are bombarded by various compliance techniques, the dangers of which can be overcome through understanding and legislation.

   b. Fearful of the effects of political attack ads, critics are calling for strict limits on such ads.

   c. With more and more messages demanding our attention, we find it harder and harder to consider any one subject really thoughtfully.

   d. The persuasion researcher Robert Cialdini spent a three-year sabbatical learning the tricks taught in dozens of sales training programs.

5. *True or false?* _____ According to the article, most laypeople think they are more susceptible to persuasion than they really are.

6. According to the article, parents persuade their children to come home on time by appealing to the children's sense of

   a. fair play.

   b. guilt.

   c. humor.

   d. fear.

7. When a visitor walks out of a hotel and a young man runs up, helps the visitor with his luggage, hails a cab, and then expects a tip, the young man is depending on which principle of persuasion?

   a. reciprocity

   b. commitment and consistency

   c. social validation

   d. liking

8. An inference that can be drawn from paragraph 49 is that
   a. Anthony Pratkanis is not a patriotic person.
   b. one compliance technique involves appealing to the consumer's patriotism.
   c. people using compliance techniques never want consumers to feel inferior.
   d. consumers pay too much attention to their own emotions.

9. One can infer from the selection that
   a. the actor Robert Young was well known for his love of coffee.
   b. Sanka is demonstrably better for one's health than other coffees.
   c. the actor Robert Young was also a physician in real life.
   d. the TV character Marcus Welby Jr. was trustworthy and authoritative.

10. We can conclude that to resist persuasive tactics, a person must
   a. buy fewer products.
   b. take time to question and analyze.
   c. remain patriotic.
   d. avoid propaganda.

DISCUSSION QUESTIONS

About Content

1. What unusual method did Robert Cialdini apply to learn more about compliance techniques? Were you surprised by any of the ways he used his time during that three-year period? Have you ever been employed in a position in which you used one or more compliance techniques?

2. What are the six principles that Cialdini identifies as being behind many persuasion tactics? Describe an incident in which you were subjected to persuasion based on one or more of these principles.

3. In paragraph 16, we learn that "people are more likely to comply with a request if a reason—no matter how silly—is given." Do you find that to be true? Have you complied with requests that, when you thought about them later, were backed up with silly or weak reasons? Describe such an incident. Why do you think such requests work?

4. In paragraphs 44–47, the author discusses persuasive tactics in political advertising. Why might researchers view the use of such tactics in this area as "especially controversial"? Discuss this issue in groups of two or three, taking into consideration the question of "attack ads" (see page 718).

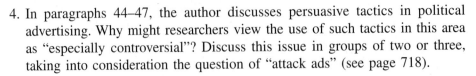

About Structure

5. What is the effect of Janny Scott's introduction to the essay (paragraphs 1–2)? On the basis of that introduction, why is a reader likely to feel that the selection will be worth his or her time?

6. Which of the following best describes the conclusion of the selection?
   a. It just stops.
   b. It restates the main point of the selection.
   c. It focuses on possible future occurrences.
   d. It presents a point of view that is the opposite of views in the body of the selection.

   Is this conclusion effective? Why or why not?

About Style and Tone

7. Why might Robert Cialdini have identified himself to the author as an "inveterate sucker"? How does that self-description affect how you regard Cialdini and what he has to say?

8. The author writes, "People defer to authority. Society trains them to do so; and in many situations deference is beneficial" (paragraph 37). Where does the author himself use the power of authority to support his own points? In what situations would you consider authority to be beneficial?

WRITING ASSIGNMENTS

www.mhhe.com/langan

Assignment 1: Writing a Paragraph

According to the article, "laypeople underestimate their susceptibility to persuasion. . . . They imagine their actions are dictated simply by personal preferences. Unaware of the techniques being used against them, they are often unwittingly outgunned" (paragraph 14). After having read the selection, do you believe that statement is true of you? Write a paragraph in which you either agree with or argue against the statement. Provide clear, specific examples of ways in which you are or are not influenced by persuasion.

Your topic sentence might be like either of these:

After reading "How They Get You to Do That," I recognize that I am more influenced by forms of persuasion than I previously thought.

Many people may "underestimate their susceptibility to persuasion," but I am not one of those people.

Assignment 2: Writing a Paragraph

Think of an advertisement—on TV, or on the Internet, in print, or on a billboard—that you have found especially memorable. Write a paragraph in which you describe it. Provide specific details that make your reader understand why you remember it so vividly. Conclude your paragraph by indicating whether or not the advertisement persuaded you to buy or do what it was promoting.

Assignment 3: Writing an Essay

Robert Cialdini identifies "social validation" as a strong persuasion technique. Social validation involves people's need to do what they hope will get approval from the crowd, rather than thinking for themselves. The essay provides several examples of social validation, such as laughing along with a laugh track and getting in a long line to go to a nightclub.

Choose a person you know for whom the need for social validation is very strong. Write an essay about that person and how the need for social validation has impacted several areas of his or her life. Develop each paragraph with colorful, persuasive examples of the person's behavior. (You may wish to write about an invented person, in which case, feel free to use humorous exaggeration to make your points.)

Here is a possible outline for such an essay:

Thesis statement: My cousin Nina has a very strong need for social validation.

Topic sentence 1: Instead of choosing friends because of their inner qualities, Nina chooses them on the basis of their popularity.

Topic sentence 2: Nina's wardrobe has to be made up of the newest and most popular styles.

Topic sentence 3: Instead of having any real opinions of her own, Nina adopts her most popular friend's point of view as her own.

End your essay with a look into the future of a person whose life is ruled by the need for social validation.

Alternatively, write about the most independent thinker you know, someone who tends to do things his or her way without worrying much about what others say.

Managing Conflicts in Relationships
Rudolph F. Verderber

PREVIEW

How do you handle the conflicts in your life? Do you get angry? Do you give in? Whatever your methods, you will probably recognize them in this excerpt from the widely used textbook *Communicate!* (8th ed.), by Rudolph F. Verderber.

Conflicts include clashes over facts and definitions ("Charley was the first 1 one to talk." "No, it was Mark." or "Your mother is a battle-ax." "What do you mean, a 'battle-ax'?"); over values ("Bringing home pencils and pens from work is not stealing." "Of course it is." or "The idea that you have to be married to have sex is completely outdated." "No, it isn't."); and, perhaps the most difficult to deal with, over ego involvement ("Listen, I've been a football fan for thirty years; I ought to know what good defense is." "Well, you may be a fan, but that doesn't make you an expert.").

Although many people view conflict as bad (and, to be sure, conflict situa- 2 tions are likely to make us anxious and uneasy), it is inevitable in any significant relationship. Moreover, conflict is sometimes useful in that it forces us to make choices; to resolve honest differences; and to test the relative merits of our attitudes, behaviors, needs, and goals. Now let's consider methods of dealing with conflict.

Methods of Dealing with Conflict

Left to their own devices, people engage in many behaviors, both negative and 3 positive, to cope with or manage their conflicts. The various methods of dealing with conflict can be grouped into five major patterns: withdrawal, surrender, aggression, persuasion, and problem-solving discussion. Let's consider each of these methods in turn.

Withdrawal One of the most common, and certainly one of the easiest, ways 4 to deal with conflict is to withdraw. When people *withdraw*, they physically or psychologically remove themselves from the situation.

Physical withdrawal is, of course, easiest to identify. Suppose Eduardo and 5 Justina get into a conversation about Eduardo's smoking. Justina says, "Eduardo,

I thought you told me that whether you stopped smoking completely or not, you weren't going to smoke around the house. Now here you are lighting up!" Eduardo may withdraw physically by saying "I don't want to talk about it" and going to the basement to finish a project he was working on.

Psychological withdrawal may be less noticeable but is every bit as common. 6 Using the same example, when Justina begins to talk about Eduardo's smoking in the house, Eduardo may sit quietly in his chair looking at Justina, but all the time she speaks he is thinking about the poker game he will be going to the next evening.

Besides being quite common, both kinds of withdrawal are basically nega- 7 tive. Why? Because they neither eliminate nor attempt to manage the conflict. As researchers Roloff and Cloven note, "Relational partners who avoid conflicts have more difficulty resolving disputes." In the case of the physical withdrawal, Justina may follow Eduardo to the basement, where the conflict will be resumed; if not, the conflict will undoubtedly resurface later—and will probably be intensified—when Justina and Eduardo try to resolve another, unrelated issue. In the case of the psychological withdrawal, Justina may force Eduardo to address the smoking issue, or she may go along with Eduardo's ignoring it but harbor a resentment that may negatively affect their relationship.

Another reason why withdrawal is negative is that it results in what Cloven 8 and Roloff call "mulling behavior." By *mulling* they mean thinking about or stewing over an actual or perceived problem until the participants perceive the conflict as more severe and begin engaging in blaming behavior. Thus, in many cases, not confronting the problem when it occurs only makes it more difficult to deal with in the long run.

Nevertheless, conflicts do occasionally go away if left alone. There appear 9 to be two sets of circumstances in which withdrawal may work. First, when the withdrawal represents temporary disengagement for the purpose of letting the heat of the conflict subside, it can be an effective technique for managing conflict. Consider this example: Bill and Margaret begin to argue over inviting Bill's mother for Thanksgiving dinner. During the conversation, Margaret begins to get angry about what her mother-in-law said to her recently about the way she and Bill are raising their daughter. Margaret says, "Hold it a minute; let me make a pot of coffee. We can both relax a bit, and then we'll talk about this some more." A few minutes later, having calmed down, she returns, ready to approach the conflict more objectively. Margaret's action is not true withdrawal; it's not meant as a means of avoiding confrontation. Rather, it provides a cooling-off period that will probably benefit them both.

The second set of circumstances in which withdrawal may work is when a 10 conflict occurs between people who communicate infrequently. Consider Josh and Mario, who work in the same office. At two office gatherings, they have gotten into arguments about whether the company really cares about its employees. At the next office gathering, Mario avoids sitting near Josh. Again, this form of withdrawal serves as a means of avoiding conflict rather than contributing to it. In this case, Mario judges that it simply isn't that important to resolve the disagreement. It is fair to say that not every conflict needs to be resolved. Withdrawal is a negative pattern only when it is a person's major way of managing conflict.

Surrender A second method of managing conflict is to surrender. As you might 11 suspect, *surrender* means giving in immediately to avoid conflict. Although altering a personal position in order to accommodate another can be positive when it's done in the spirit of cooperation, using surrender as a primary coping strategy is unhealthy.

Some people are so upset by the prospect of conflict that they will do any- 12 thing to avoid it. For instance, Juan and Mariana are discussing their vacation plans. Juan would like just the two of them to go, but Mariana has talked with two of their friends who will be vacationing the same week about going together. After Juan mentions that he'd like the two of them to go alone, Mariana says, "But I think it would be fun to go with another couple, don't you?" Juan replies, "OK, whatever you want." Even though Juan really wants the two of them to go alone, rather than describe his feelings or give reasons for his position, he gives in to avoid conflict.

Habitual surrender is a negative way of dealing with conflict for at least two 13 reasons. First, decisions should be made on their merits, not to avoid conflict. If one person gives in, there is no testing of the decision—no one knows what would really be best. Second, surrender can be infuriating to the other person. When Mariana tells Juan what she thinks, she probably wants Juan to see her way as the best. But if Juan simply surrenders, Mariana might believe that Juan still dislikes her plan but is playing the martyr. And his unwillingness to present his reasons could lead to even more conflict.

The contention that surrender is a negative way of dealing with conflict 14 should be qualified to the extent that it reflects a Western cultural perspective. In some cultures, surrendering is a perfectly legitimate way of dealing with conflict. In Japanese culture, for instance, it is thought to be more humble and face-saving to surrender than to risk losing respect through conflict.

Aggression A third method of dealing with conflict is through aggression. 15 *Aggression* entails the use of physical or psychological coercion to get one's way. Through aggression, people attempt to force others to accept their ideas or wishes, thereby emerging as "victors" in conflicts.

Aggression seldom improves a relationship, however. Rather, aggression is 16 an emotional reaction to conflict. Thought is short-circuited, and the person lashes out physically or verbally. People who use aggression are concerned not with the merits of an issue but only with who is bigger, who can talk louder, who can act nastier, or who can force the other to give in. With either physical or verbal aggression, conflict is escalated or obscured but not managed.

Persuasion A fourth method of managing conflict is by persuasion. *Persuasion* 17
is the attempt to change either the attitude or the behavior of another person
in order to seek accommodation. At times during the discussion of an issue,
one party may try to persuade the other that a particular action is the right one.
Suppose that at one point in their discussion about buying a car, Sheila says,
"Don't we need a lot of room?" Kevin might reply, "Enough to get us into the
car together, but I don't see why we need more than that." Sheila and Kevin
are now approaching a conflict situation. At this point, Sheila might say, "Kevin,
we are constantly complaining about the lack of room in our present car.
Remember last month when you were upset because we couldn't even get our
two suitcases into the trunk and we had to put one of them in the backseat?
And how many times have we been embarrassed when we couldn't drive our
car with friends because the backseat is too small for even two normal-sized
people?" Statements like these represent an attempt at resolving the conflict
through persuasion.

When persuasion is open and reasonable, it can be a positive means of 18
resolving conflict. However, persuasion can also degenerate into manipulation,
as when a person says, "You know, if you back me on this, I could see to it that
you get a few more of the good accounts, and if you don't, well . . ." Although
persuasive efforts may fuel a conflict, if that persuasion has a solid logical base,
it is at least possible that the persuasion will resolve the conflict.

Discussion A fifth method of dealing with conflict is *problem-solving discussion*— 19
the verbal weighing and considering of the pros and cons of the issues in conflict.
Discussion is the most desirable means of dealing with conflict in a relationship
because it provides for open consideration of issues and because it preserves
equality. Resolving conflict through discussion is often difficult to accomplish,
however, because it requires all parties involved to cooperate: The participants
must be objective in their presentation of issues, honest in stating their feelings
and beliefs, and open to the solution that proves to be most satisfactory and in
the best interests of those involved.

Problem-solving discussion includes defining and analyzing the problem, 20
suggesting possible solutions, selecting the solution that best fits the analysis,
and working to implement the decision. In everyday situations, all five steps
are not always considered completely, nor are they necessarily considered in
the order given. But when two people perceive a conflict emerging, they need
to be willing to step back from the conflict and proceed systematically toward
a solution.

Does this process sound too idealized? Or impracticable? Discussion is dif- 21
ficult, but when two people commit themselves to trying, chances are that they
will discover that through discussion they arrive at solutions that meet both their
needs and do so in a way that maintains their relationship.

READING COMPREHENSION QUESTIONS

1. The word *harbor* in "Justina may force Eduardo to address the smoking issue, or she may go along with Eduardo's ignoring it but harbor a resentment that may negatively affect their relationship" (paragraph 7) means
   a. hold on to.
   b. avoid.
   c. give up.
   d. pretend.

2. The word *accommodate* in "Although altering a personal position in order to accommodate another can be positive when it's done in the spirit of cooperation . . ." (paragraph 11) means
   a. to disagree with.
   b. to adjust to.
   c. to agree with.
   d. to insult.

3. Which sentence best expresses the main point of the selection?
   a. Many people have a negative view of conflict.
   b. There are five main ways, both positive and negative, with which people deal with conflict.
   c. Conflicts can force people to make choices and to test their attitudes, actions, needs, and aims.
   d. It is better not to intensify or hide conflict.

4. The main idea of paragraphs 9–10 can be found in the
   a. second sentence of paragraph 9.
   b. third sentence of paragraph 9.
   c. first sentence of paragraph 10.
   d. second sentence of paragraph 10.

5. From the reading, we can infer that the author believes that
   a. withdrawal never works.
   b. whether or not surrender is generally a good way to manage conflict is related to one's cultural perspective.
   c. aggression is an attempt to change either the attitude or the behavior of another person in order to seek accommodation.
   d. discussion is the easiest way of dealing with conflict in a relationship.

6. What is the relationship between the following two sentences: "When persuasion is open and reasonable, it can be a positive means of resolving conflict. However, persuasion can also degenerate into manipulation . . ." (paragraph 18)?

    a. comparison

    b. contrast

    c. cause and effect

    d. illustration

7. Three of the following sentences are supporting details for an argument. Which of the sentences expresses the point of those supporting details?

    a. People who use aggression are concerned not with the merits of an issue but only with who can force the other person to give in.

    b. Aggression usually harms a relationship.

    c. In aggression, thought is short-circuited and the person lashes out physically or verbally.

    d. With either physical or verbal aggression, conflict is escalated or obscured but not managed.

8. We can infer that the author of this selection

    a. believes that conflict should be avoided at all costs.

    b. feels that conflict is the best way to strengthen a relationship.

    c. feels that conflict can be positive if handled appropriately.

    d. believes that withdrawal is never an appropriate method of dealing with conflict.

9. *True or false?* _____ In healthy relationships, conflict can always be avoided.

10. *True or false?* _____ One reason that discussion is effective in resolving conflicts is that it preserves equality.

DISCUSSION QUESTIONS

About Content

1. Which of Verderber's five methods of dealing with conflict do you—or do people you know—typically use? Give examples.

2. Why do you think Verderber regards discussion as "the most desirable means of dealing with conflict in a relationship" (paragraph 19)? And why might he feel that discussion "is often difficult to accomplish" (paragraph 19)?

3. Verderber writes that conflict is sometimes useful because it forces us to make choices and test attitudes. When in your life has conflict been a good thing? What did you learn from it?

4. Suggest ways that someone you know could be encouraged to deal effectively with his or her specific conflict.

5. Why does Verdeber believe that withdrawing from a conflict rarely results in a long-term resolution?

About Structure

6. What technique explained in Chapter 18 of this textbook does Verderber use to introduce this material?

7. Why does Verderber use subheadings?

About Style and Tone

8. What method does the author use most often to define concepts such as "psychological withdrawal" and "surrender"?

9. How would your describe the author's tone (his attitude toward his subject)?

   a. emotional

   b. objective and fair

   c. cold and withdrawn

   d. excited

WRITING ASSIGNMENTS

www.mhhe.com/langan

Assignment 1: Writing a Paragraph

Think of a person you know whom you would define as one of the following: a withdrawer, a surrenderer, an aggressor, or a persuader. Write a paragraph in which you describe this person and his or her approach to dealing with conflict. Include at least one specific example of his or her behavior. Here are two sample topic sentences like the one you might use.

Henry's approach to problem-solving is sometimes too aggressive.

Alicia is afraid of personal conflict and usually lets her husband and children get their way.

Assignment 2: Writing a Paragraph

What advice would you give to Eduardo and Justina, the couple in the reading who are in conflict about Eduardo's smoking? What do you think Eduardo should do? What should Justina do? Write a paragraph advising the couple on how to handle their problem.

Assignment 3: Writing an Essay

When have you and another person had an important conflict that you needed to deal with? (To be "important," the conflict need not be earth-shattering, just a conflict you were unwilling to ignore.) Write an essay that describes the nature of the conflict, and then take the reader through the process that occurred as you and the other person dealt with it. Use transitional words such as *first, next,* and *finally* to help the reader follow the action. In the final paragraph, provide a conclusion that states how satisfied or dissatisfied you felt about the process or that explains what you learned from this experience. Here are two sample thesis statements like the one you might use.

> I know now that Melissa had manipulated me when she convinced me to let her submit one of my English papers as her own.

> Being aggressive is not the best way to fight a traffic ticket.

"Extra Large," Please
Diane Urbina

PREVIEW

Why are so many kids today overweight or even obese? According to Diane Urbina, the number-one culprit is junk food, which is available anytime, any-where—and in ever-increasing portion sizes. Urbina argues that schools, fast-food restaurants, and the media have a responsibility to raise awareness about nutrition and save people of all ages from a public-health disaster.

School lunches have always come in for criticism. When I was a kid, we 1 complained about "mystery meat" and "leftover surprise casserole." Half a canned pear in a shaky nest of Jell-O didn't do much to excite our tastebuds. I hid my share of limp green beans under my napkin, the better to escape the eagle eye of lunchroom monitors who encouraged us to eat our soggy, overcooked vegetables.

But the cafeteria lunches were there, and so we ate them. (Most of them. 2 OK, I hid the gooey tapioca pudding, too.) I think we accepted the idea that being delicious was not the point. The meals were reasonably nutritious and they fueled our young bodies for the mental and physical demands of the day. In my case, that demand included walking a quarter-mile to and from school, enjoying three recesses a day, and taking part in gym class a couple of times a week. After-school hours, at least when the weather was good, were spent outdoors playing kickball or tag with neighbor kids.

I can imagine you wondering, "Who cares?" I don't blame you. My mem- 3 ories of schooldays in northern Indiana thirty-some years ago aren't all that fascinating even to me. And yet I think you should care, because of one fact I haven't mentioned yet. When I was a kid and looked around at other kids my age, I saw all kinds of differences. There were tall ones and short ones and black and white and brown ones, rude ones and polite ones, popular ones and geeky ones, athletic ones and uncoordinated ones. But you know what? There weren't many heavy ones. The few there were stood out because they were unusual. I think that if you had asked me at the time, I would have told you that kids are just naturally skinny.

Flash forward to the present. Walk down any city street in America. Sit in a 4 mall and watch the people stream by. You don't need to be a rocket scientist to notice something's changed. Whether you call them big-boned, chubby, husky, or plus-sized, kids are heavy, lots of them. If your own eyes don't convince you, here are the statistics: Since 1980, the number of American kids who are dangerously overweight has tripled. More than 16 percent of our children—that's 1 in 6—qualify as "obese." Hordes of them are developing diet-related diabetes, a disease that used to be seen almost always in adults. When California's students grades 5 through 12 were given a basic fitness test, almost 8 out of 10 failed.

Part of the problem is that many kids don't have good opportunities to exer- 5 cise. They live in neighborhoods without sidewalks or paths where they can walk, bike, or skate safely. Drug activity and violent crime may make playing outside dangerous. They can reach their schools only by car or bus. Many of those schools are so short of money they've scrapped their physical-fitness classes. Too few communities have athletic programs in place.

Electronic entertainment also plays a role in the current state of affairs. Kids 6 used to go outside to play with other kids because it was more fun than sitting around the house. Today, kids who sit around the house have access to dozens of cable TV channels, the Internet, DVD players, and a dizzying assortment of video games.

Still another cause is the lack of parental supervision. When I was a kid, 7 most of us had a mom or an older sibling at home telling us to get off our butts and go outside. (The alternative was often to stay inside and do chores. We chose to go out and play.) Now, most American families have two working parents. For most of the daylight hours, those parents just aren't around to encourage their kids to get some exercise. A related problem is that parents who can't be home much may feel guilty about it. One way of relieving that guilt is to buy Junior the game system of his dreams and a nice wide-screen TV to play it on.

These are all complicated problems whose solutions are equally complicated. 8 But there is one cause of the fattening of America's kids that can be dealt with more easily. And that cause is the enormous influence that fast-food restaurants and other sources of calorie-laden junk have gained over America's kids.

I'm no health nut. I like an occasional Quarter Pounder as well as the next 9 mom. There is no quicker way to my kids' hearts than to bring home a newly released DVD, a large pepperoni pie and a bag of Chicken McNuggets. But in our home, an evening featuring extra mozzarella and bottles of 7-Up is a once-in-a-while treat—sort of a guilty pleasure.

To many of today's kids, fast food is not a treat—it's their daily diet. Their normal dinnertime equals McDonald's, Pizza Hut, Domino's, Burger King, Taco Bell, or Kentucky Fried Chicken, all washed down with Pepsi. And increasingly, lunchtime at school means those foods too. About 20 percent of our nation's schools have sold chain restaurants the right to put their food items on the lunch line. Many schools also allow candy and soft-drink vending machines on their campuses. The National Soft Drink Association reports that 60 percent of public and private middle schools and high schools make sodas available for purchase. 10

Believe me, when I was a kid, if the lunchline had offered me a couple of slices of double-crust stuffed pepperoni-sausage pizza instead of a Turkey Submarine, I would have said yes before you could say the words "clogged arteries." And when I needed a mid-afternoon pick-me-up, I would have gladly traded a handful of change for a Coke and a Snickers bar. 11

And then I would have gone back into algebra class and spent the hour bouncing between a sugar high and a fat-induced coma. 12

Stopping off at Taco Bell for an occasional Seven-Layer Burrito is one thing. But when fast foods become the staple of young people's diets, it's the kids who become Whoppers. And it has become the staple for many. According to researchers at Children's Hospital Boston, during any given week, three out of four children eat a fast-food meal one or more times a day. The beverages they chug down are a problem, too. The U.S. Department of Agriculture says that every day, the average adolescent drinks enough soda and fruit beverages to equal the sugar content of 50 chocolate-chip cookies. 13

The problem isn't only that burgers, fries, and sodas aren't nutritious to begin with—although they aren't. What has made the situation much worse is the increasingly huge portions sold by fast-food restaurants. Back when McDonald's began business, its standard meal consisted of a hamburger, two ounces of French fries, and a 12-ounce Coke. That meal provided 590 calories. But today's customers don't have to be satisfied with such modest portions. For very little more money, diners can end up with a quarter-pound burger, extra-large fries, and extra-large cup of Coke that add up to 1,550 calories. A whole generation of kids is growing up believing that this massive shot of fat, sugar, and sodium equals a "normal portion." As a result, they're becoming extra large themselves. 14

As kids sit down to watch the after-school and Saturday-morning shows designed for them, they aren't just taking in the programs themselves. They're seeing at least an hour of commercials for every five hours of programming. On Saturday mornings, nine out of 10 of those commercials are for sugary cereals, fast foods, and other non-nutritious junk. Many of the commercials are tied in with popular toys or beloved cartoon characters or movies aimed at children. Watching those commercials makes the kids hungry—or at least they think they're hungry. (Thanks to all the factors mentioned here, many children can no 15

Who is the intended audience of this advertisement? How do you know? The ad may be effective, but considering Urbina's point in her essay, is it socially responsible? Why or why not?

longer tell if they're genuinely hungry or not. They've been programmed to eat for many reasons other than hunger.) So they snack as they sit in front of the TV set. Then at mealtime, they beg to go out for more junk food. And they get bigger, and bigger, and bigger.

There is no overnight solution 16 to the problem of American children's increasing weight and decreasing level of physical fitness. But can anything be done? To begin with, fast-food meals and junk-food vending machines should be banned from schools. Our education system should be helping children acquire good nutritional habits, not assisting them in committing slow nutritional suicide.

In addition, commercials for 17 junk food should be banned from TV during children's viewing time, specifically Saturday mornings.

And finally, fast-food restau- 18 rants should be required to do what tobacco companies—another manufacturer of products known to harm people's health—have to do. They should display in their restaurants, and in their TV and print ads as well, clear nutritional information about their products. For instance, a young woman at Burger King who was considering ordering a Double Whopper with Cheese, a king-size order of fries and a king-size Dr. Pepper could read something like this:

Your meal will provide 2030 calories, 860 of those calories from fat. 19

Your recommended daily intake is 2000 calories, with no more than 600 of 20 *those calories coming from fat.*

At a glance, then, the customer could see that in one fast-food meal, she was 21 taking in more calories and fat than she should consume in an entire day.

Overweight kids today become overweight adults tomorrow. Overweight 22 adults are at increased risk for heart disease, diabetes, stroke, and cancer. Schools, fast-food restaurants, and the media are contributing to a public-health disaster in the making. Anything that can be done to decrease the role junk food plays in kids' lives needs to be done, and done quickly.

READING COMPREHENSION QUESTIONS

1. The word *hordes* in "More than 16 percent of our children—that's 1 in 6— qualify as 'obese.' Hordes of them are developing diet-related diabetes, a disease that used to be seen almost always in adults" (paragraph 4) means
   a. few.
   b. many.
   c. hardly any.
   d. a handful.

2. The word *complicated* in "These are all complicated problems whose solutions are equally complicated" (paragraph 8) means
   a. simple.
   b. interesting.
   c. complex.
   d. easy.

3. Which of the following would be the best alternative title for this selection?
   a. Healthy School Lunches
   b. Solving Childhood Obesity
   c. The Dangers of Childhood Obesity
   d. Too Much of a Junk Thing

4. Which sentence best expresses the central idea of the selection?
   a. Electronic entertainment is responsible for childhood obesity.
   b. More physical-fitness classes are needed to solve childhood obesity.
   c. We need to reduce the role that junk food plays in children's lives and help children acquire good nutritional habits.
   d. School lunches are much more nutritious than junk food.

5. According to the author, which of the following does *not* contribute to childhood obesity?
   a. Electronic entertainment
   b. Fewer opportunities to exercise
   c. Occasional fast-food treats
   d. Lack of parental supervision

6. *True or false?* _____ Today, 1 in 6 children in America qualifies as "obese."

7. The author argues that fast-food restaurant chains should be required to
   a. provide nutritional information about their products.
   b. reduce the portion sizes of their products.
   c. use healthier ingredients in their products.
   d. reduce the amount of saturated fats contained in their products.

8. Many public and private middle schools and high schools
   a. provide students with healthy lunch options.
   b. refuse to allow candy vending machines on their campuses.
   c. make soft drinks available for purchase.
   d. refuse to offer items from fast-food restaurant chains.

9. From the article, we can infer that the author
   a. believes her readers are genuinely concerned about her topic.
   b. is trying to convince her readers about the importance of her topic.
   c. is trying to encourage her readers to lobby for school lunch reform.
   d. believes that the solution to childhood obesity is simple.

10. When the author suggests that fast-food restaurants should be required to display nutritional information about their products, she is assuming that
    a. many of the items will exceed the recommended daily intake of calories.
    b. the tobacco companies will also display information about their products.
    c. fast-food restaurants will feel pressured to offer healthier menu items.
    d. people will then choose to eat more wisely.

DISCUSSION QUESTIONS

About Content

1. In paragraph 3, the author says to her readers, "I can imagine you wondering, 'Who cares?'" Does she blame her readers? Why does she think they should care?

2. Do you feel that the author's solutions in paragraphs 16–18 will solve "the problem of American children's increasing weight and decreasing level of physical fitness"? With a partner, discuss what other solutions are needed to counteract this problem.

3. How might the author revise her essay to appeal directly to children and teenagers? What might she say to them? What might convince them to change their eating habits?

About Structure

4. What patterns of development does the author use in her essay? Explain.

5. The author uses *addition words* to signal added ideas. Locate and write three of these words:

   _____   _____   _____

6. The author uses the first-person approach, which relies on her own experiences. Do you feel that she is credible? What details does she include in her essay to convince us of her trustworthiness?

About Style and Tone

7. In paragraph 1, the author recounts her experiences eating school lunches. She could have simply written, "I ate casseroles, canned fruits, and cooked vegetables." Instead she writes, "Half a canned pear in a shaky nest of Jell-O didn't do much to excite our tastebuds. I hid my share of limp green beans under my napkin, the better to escape the eagle eye of lunchroom monitors who encouraged us to eat our soggy, overcooked vegetables." Why do you think she provides such vivid details? What is the effect on her readers?

8. The author uses statistics as well as personal experiences. Find three places in the selection where statistics are cited:

   Paragraph _____

   Paragraph _____

   Paragraph _____

   What do statistics accomplish that anecdotes cannot?

9. What are a few words that the author would probably use to describe the people who are responsible for fast-food marketing? Find evidence in the selection to support your opinion.

WRITING ASSIGNMENTS

www.mhhe.com/langan

Assignment 1: Writing a Paragraph

Diane Urbina discusses why 1 in 6 children in our country is considered obese. Choose one of the problems she identifies, such as lack of opportunities for children to exercise, and write a paragraph in which you discuss what could be done to help solve the problem. Following are a few possible topic sentences for this assignment:

> Children would have more opportunities to exercise if the government would allocate funds to build playgrounds, fields, and basketball courts.

> Parents should spend time with their children doing physical activities, such as riding bikes, going for hikes, or swimming at the neighborhood pool.

Assignment 2: Writing a Paragraph

What did you learn from the selection, or what do you already know, about obesity that might influence your own future? Write a paragraph in which you list three or four ways in which you could minimize or avoid some of the problems often faced by those struggling with their weight. For instance, you may decide to do whatever you can to remain as healthy as possible throughout your life. That might involve taking daily walks, eating less junk food, and cooking more nutritious meals. Your topic sentence might simply be "There are three important ways in which I hope to avoid some of the problems often faced by those struggling with obesity."

Assignment 3: Writing an Essay Using Internet Research

As Diane Urbina discovered while doing her research, when California's students in grades 5 through 12 were given a basic fitness test, almost 80 percent failed (paragraph 4). What can people—students, parents, teachers, administrators, and community members—do to change these statistics and help produce more physically active students? Use the Internet to see what some experts have suggested. Then write an essay on three ways to promote physical fitness.

   To start your research, use the very helpful search engine Google (www.google.com). Try one of the following phrases or some related phrase:

physical fitness and children

exercise and children

The Most Hateful Words

Amy Tan

PREVIEW

For years, a painful exchange with her mother lay like a heavy stone on Amy Tan's heart. In the following essay, Tan, author of best-selling novels including *The Joy Luck Club* and *The Kitchen God's Wife*, tells the story of how that weight was finally lifted. This essay is from her memoir, *The Opposite of Fate*.

The most hateful words I have ever said to another human being were to 1 my mother. I was sixteen at the time. They rose from the storm in my chest and I let them fall in a fury of hailstones: "I hate you. I wish I were dead. . . ."

I waited for her to collapse, stricken by what I had just said. She was still 2 standing upright, her chin tilted, her lips stretched in a crazy smile. "Okay, maybe I die too," she said between huffs. "Then I no longer be your mother!" We had many similar exchanges. Sometimes she actually tried to kill herself by running into the street, holding a knife to her throat. She too had storms in her chest. And what she aimed at me was as fast and deadly as a lightning bolt.

For days after our arguments, she would not speak to me. She tormented me, 3 acted as if she had no feelings for me whatsoever. I was lost to her. And because of that, I lost, battle after battle, all of them: the times she criticized me, humiliated me in front of others, forbade me to do this or that without even listening to one good reason why it should be the other way. I swore to myself I would never forget these injustices. I would store them, harden my heart, make myself as impenetrable as she was.

I remember this now, because I am also remembering another time, just a 4 few years ago. I was forty-seven, had become a different person by then, had become a fiction writer, someone who uses memory and imagination. In fact, I was writing a story about a girl and her mother, when the phone rang.

It was my mother, and this surprised me. Had someone helped her make the 5 call? For a few years now, she had been losing her mind through Alzheimer's disease. Early on, she forgot to lock her door. Then she forgot where she lived. She forgot who many people were and what they had meant to her. Lately, she could no longer remember many of her worries and sorrows.

"Amy-ah," she said, and she began to speak quickly in Chinese. "Something 6 is wrong with my mind. I think I'm going crazy."

I caught my breath. Usually she could barely speak more than two words at 7 a time. "Don't worry," I started to say.

"It's true," she went on. "I feel like I can't remember many things. I can't 8 remember what I did yesterday. I can't remember what happened a long time ago, what I did to you. . . ." She spoke as a drowning person might if she had bobbed to the surface with the force of will to live, only to see how far she had already drifted, how impossibly far she was from the shore.

She spoke frantically: "I know I did something to hurt you." 9

"You didn't," I said. "Don't worry." 10

"I did terrible things. But now I can't remember what. . . . And I just want 11 to tell you . . . I hope you can forget, just as I've forgotten."

I tried to laugh so she would not notice the cracks in my voice. "Really, 12 don't worry."

"Okay, I just wanted you to know." 13

After we hung up, I cried, both happy and sad. I was again that sixteen-year- 14 old, but the storm in my chest was gone.

My mother died six months later. By then she had bequeathed to me her 15 most healing words, as open and eternal as a clear blue sky. Together we knew in our hearts what we should remember, what we can forget.

READING COMPREHENSION QUESTIONS

1. The word *stricken* in "I waited for her to collapse, *stricken* by what I had just said" (paragraph 2) means
   a. wounded.
   b. amused.
   c. annoyed.
   d. bored.

2. The word *bequeathed* in "By then she had *bequeathed* to me her most healing words, those that are as open and eternal as a clear blue sky" (paragraph 15) means
   a. denied.
   b. sold.
   c. given.
   d. cursed.

www.mhhe.com/langan

3. Which sentence best expresses the central idea of the selection?
   a. Because of Alzheimer's disease, the author's mother forgot harsh words the two of them had said to each other.
   b. Amy Tan had a difficult relationship with her mother that worsened over the years.
   c. Years after a painful childhood with her mother, Amy Tan was able to realize peace and forgiveness.
   d. Despite her Alzheimer's disease, Amy Tan's mother was able to apologize to her daughter for hurting her.

4. Which sentence best expresses the main idea of paragraphs 1–2?
   a. Amy Tan's mother was sometimes suicidal.
   b. Amy Tan wanted to use words to hurt her mother.
   c. It is not unusual for teenagers and their parents to argue.
   d. Amy Tan and her mother had a very hurtful relationship.

5. Which sentence best expresses the main idea of paragraphs 8–9?
   a. The author's mother was deeply disturbed by the thought that she had hurt her daughter.
   b. Alzheimer's disease causes people to become confused and unable to remember things clearly.
   c. The author's mother could not even remember what she had done the day before.
   d. The author's mother had changed very little from what she was like when Tan was a child.

6. After arguing with her daughter, the author's mother
   a. would say nice things about her to others.
   b. would immediately forget they had argued.
   c. would refuse to speak to her.
   d. would apologize.

7. When she was a girl, the author swore that she
   a. would never forget her mother's harsh words.
   b. would never be like her mother.
   c. would publicly embarrass her mother by writing about her.
   d. would never have children.

8. The first sign that the author's mother had Alzheimer's disease was
   a. forgetting where she lived.
   b. being able to speak only two or three words at a time.
   c. forgetting people's identities.
   d. forgetting to lock her door.

9. We can infer from paragraph 2 that
   a. the author wished her mother were dead.
   b. the author immediately felt guilty for the way she had spoken to her mother.
   c. the author's mother was emotionally unstable.
   d. the author's mother was physically abusive.

10. The author implies, in paragraphs 9–15, that
    a. she was pleased by her mother's sense of guilt.
    b. her love and pity for her mother were stronger than her anger.
    c. she did not recall what her mother was talking about.
    d. she was annoyed by her mother's confusion.

DISCUSSION QUESTIONS

About Content

1. How would you describe Amy Tan's mother? What kind of mother does she appear to have been?

2. In the discussion at the end of the essay, Tan chooses to keep her emotions hidden from her mother. Why do you think she does this?

3. What does Tan mean by her last line, "Together we knew in our hearts what we should remember, what we can forget."

About Structure

4. Tan makes effective use of parallel structure in writing her story. What are two examples of parallelism that help make her sentences clear and easy to read?

5. Tan begins her essay from the point of view of a sixteen-year-old girl but finishes it from the perspective of a woman in her late forties. Where in the essay does Tan make the transition between those two perspectives? What words does she use to signal the change?

6. Paragraph 5 describes a sequence of events, and the writer uses several transition words to signal time relationships. Locate three of those transitions and write them here:

_____   _____   _____

About Style and Tone

7. What effect does Tan achieve by using so many direct quotations?

8. Tan uses images of the weather throughout her essay. Find three instances in which Tan mentions weather and list them below. What does she accomplish with this technique?

_____   _____   _____

WRITING ASSIGNMENTS

Assignment 1: Writing a Paragraph

www.mhhe.com/langan

Despite being an adult, Tan recalls feeling like a sixteen-year-old girl again when she speaks to her mother. Think about something in your life that has the power to reconnect you to a vivid memory. Write a paragraph in which you describe your memory and the trigger that "takes you back" to it. Begin your paragraph with a topic sentence that makes it clear what you are going to discuss. Then provide specific details so that readers can understand your memory. Here are sample topic sentences.

Whenever I see swings, I remember the day in second grade when I got into my first fistfight.

The smell of cotton candy takes me back to the day my grandfather took me to my first baseball game.

I can't pass St. Joseph's Hospital without remembering the day, ten years ago, when my brother was shot.

Assignment 2: Writing a Paragraph

In this essay, we see that Tan's relationship with her mother was very complicated. Who is a person with whom you have a complex relationship—maybe a relationship you'd describe as "love-hate" or "difficult"? Write a paragraph about that relationship. Be sure to give examples or details to show readers why you have such difficulties with this person.

Your topic sentence should introduce the person you plan to discuss. For example:

To me, my mother in-law is one of the most difficult people in the world. (*Or,* My mother-in-law and I have contrasting points of view on several issues.)

While I respect my boss, he is simply a very difficult person.

Even though I love my sister, I can't stand to be around her.

Be sure to provide specific examples or details to help your reader understand why the relationship is so difficult for you. For example, if you decide to write about your boss, you will want to describe specific behaviors that show why you consider him or her difficult.

Assignment 3: Writing an Essay

Like Tan's mother, most of us have at some time done something we wish we could undo. If you had a chance to revisit your past and change one of your actions, what would it be? Write an essay describing something you would like to undo.

In your first paragraph, introduce exactly what you did. Here are three thesis statements that students might have written:

I wish I could undo the night I decided to drive my car while I was drunk.

If I could undo any moment in my life, it would be the day I decided to drop out of high school.

One moment from my life I would like to change is the time I picked on an unpopular kid in sixth grade.

Be sure to provide details and, if appropriate, actual words that were spoken, so that your readers can "see and hear" what happened. Once you've described the moment that you wish to take back, write three reasons why you feel the way you do. Below is a scratch outline for the first topic.

I wish I could undo the night I decided to drive my car while I was drunk.

1. Caused an accident that hurt others.

2. Lost my license, my car, and my job.

3. Affected the way others treat me.

To write an effective essay, you will need to provide specific details explaining each reason you identify. For instance, to support the third reason above, you might describe new feelings of guilt and anger you have about yourself as well as provide examples of how individual people now treat you differently. To end your essay, you might describe what you would do today if you could replay what happened.

Share a draft of your essay with a classmate, and offer to critique his or her paper as well. Use the Four Bases checklist on the inside back cover to help you revise.

Group Pressure
Rodney Stark

PREVIEW

We've all experienced group pressure at one time or another, but how much do we really know about how that phenomenon affects us? The following selection from the college textbook *Sociology* (3rd ed.) by Rodney Stark, will give you a fascinating view of this common behavioral situation.

It is self-evident that people tend to conform to the expectations and reactions 1
of others around them. But what are the limits of group pressure? Can group pressure cause us to deny the obvious, even physical evidence?

Over thirty-five years ago, Solomon Asch performed the most famous exper- 2
imental test of the power of group pressure to produce conformity. Since then his study has been repeated many times, with many variations confirming his original results. Perhaps the best way to understand what Asch discovered is to pretend that you are a subject in his experiment.

You have agreed to take part in an experiment on visual perception. Upon 3
arriving at the laboratory, you are given the seventh in a line of eight chairs. Other students taking part in the experiment sit in each of the other chairs. At the front of the room the experimenter stands by a covered easel. He explains that he wants you to judge the length of lines in a series of comparisons. He will place two decks of large cards upon the easel. One card will display a single vertical line. The other card will display three vertical lines, each of a different length. He wants each of you to decide which of the three lines on one card is the same length as the single line on the other card. To prepare you for the task, he displays a practice card. You see the correct line easily, for the other lines are noticeably different from the comparison line.

The experiment begins. The first comparison is just as easy as the practice 4
comparison. One of the three lines is obviously the same length as the comparison line, while the other two are very different. Each of the eight persons answers in turn, with you answering seventh. Everyone answers correctly. On the second pair of cards, the right answer is just as easy to spot, and again all eight subjects are correct. You begin to suspect that the experiment is going to be a big bore.

Then comes the third pair. The judgment is just as easy as before. But the 5
first person somehow picks a line that is obviously wrong. You smile. Then the

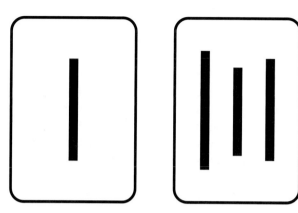

second person also picks the same obviously wrong line. What's going on? Then the third, fourth, fifth, and sixth subjects answer the same way. It's your turn. You know without doubt that you are right, yet six people have confidently given the wrong answer. You are no longer bored. Instead, you are a bit confused, but you go ahead and choose the line you are sure is right. Then the last person picks the same wrong line everyone else has chosen.

A new pair is unveiled, and the same thing happens again. All the others 6 pick an obviously wrong line. The experimenter remains matter-of-fact, not commenting on right or wrong answers but just marking down what people pick. Should you stick it out? Should you go along? Maybe something's wrong with the light or with your angle of vision. Your difficulty lasts for eighteen pairs of cards. On twelve of them, all the others picked a line you knew was incorrect.

When the experiment is over, the experimenter turns to you with a smile and 7 begins to explain. You were the only subject in the experiment. The other seven people were stooges paid by Professor Asch to answer exactly the way they did. The aim of the experiment was to see if social pressure could cause you to reject the evidence of your own eyes and conform.

In his first experiment, Asch tested fifty people in this situation. Almost a 8 third of them went along with the group and gave the wrong answer at least half of the time. Another 40 percent yielded to the group some of the time, but less than half of the time. Only 25 percent refused to yield at all. Those who yielded to group pressure were more likely to do so as the experiment progressed. Nearly everyone withstood the group the first several times, but as they continued to find themselves at odds with the group, most subjects began to weaken. Many shifted in their chairs, trying to get a different line of vision. Some blushed. Finally, 75 percent of them began to go along at least a few times.

The effects of group pressure were also revealed in the behavior of those 9 who steadfastly refused to accept the group's misjudgments. Some of these people became increasingly uneasy and apologetic. One subject began to whisper to his neighbor, "Can't help it, that's the one," and later, "I always disagree—darn it!" Other subjects who refused to yield dealt with the stress of the situation by giving each nonconforming response in a progressively louder voice and by casting challenging looks at the others. In a recent replication of the Asch study, one subject loudly insulted the other seven students whenever they made a wrong choice. One retort was "What funny farm did you turkeys grow up on, huh?"

The Asch experiment shows that a high number of people will conform even   10 in a weak group situation. They were required merely to disagree with strangers, not with their friends, and the costs of deviance were limited to about half an hour of disapproval from people they hardly knew. Furthermore, subjects were not faced with a difficult judgment—they could easily see the correct response. Little wonder, then, that we are inclined to go along with our friends when the stakes are much higher and we cannot even be certain that we are right.

www.mhhe.com/langan

READING COMPREHENSION QUESTIONS

1. The word *stooges* in "The other seven people were stooges paid by Professor Asch to answer exactly the way they did" (paragraph 7) means
   a. comedians.
   b. people who played a role.
   c. true subjects in an experiment.
   d. educators.

2. The word *replication* in "In a recent replication of the Asch study, one subject loudly insulted the other seven students . . . " (paragraph 9) means
   a. memory.
   b. repeat.
   c. image.
   d. prediction.

3. Which of the following is the topic of the selection?
   a. visual perception
   b. Solomon Asch
   c. Asch's experiment on group pressure
   d. stooges in an experiment

4. Which sentence from the reading comes closest to expressing the main idea of the selection?
   a. "Upon arriving at the laboratory, you are given the seventh in a line of eight chairs."
   b. "The experimenter remains matter-of-fact, not commenting on right or wrong answers but just marking down what people pick."

c. "In his first experiment, Asch tested fifty people in this situation."

d. "The Asch experiment shows that a high number of people will conform even in a weak group situation."

5. In Solomon Asch's experiment, when does the subject realize that he or she is the subject?

a. soon after the experiment begins.

b. during the experiment.

c. after the experiment ends.

d. never.

6. Most of the people Professor Asch tested

a. refused to yield to group pressure.

b. yielded to group pressure immediately.

c. yielded to group pressure eventually.

d. got angry because other members of the group gave incorrect answers.

7. What percentage of the subjects in the experiment refused to conform?

a. 33

b. 50

c. 25

d. 75

8. The author implies that

a. the power of group pressure is limited.

b. Asch's findings are not supported by other research.

c. group pressure makes people deny what they know to be true.

d. group pressure can be easily withstood.

9. We can conclude from this essay that people react to group pressure

a. in ways that are similar.

b. in many different ways.

c. by conforming almost immediately.

d. by conforming only when threatened.

10. We can infer that, during the experiment, many of Asch's subjects became

a. bored.

b. violent.

c. excited.

d. insecure.

DISCUSSION QUESTIONS

About Content

1. Were you at all surprised by the results of Solomon Asch's experiment? If you had been one of the subjects, do you think you would have stuck to your answers, or would you have gone along with the group? Why?

2. What reasons might the subjects in the Asch experiment have had for eventually giving in and accepting the group's wrong answers?

3. Stark refers to the Asch experiment as a "weak group situation," one in which the group is made up of strangers and the stakes are not very high. What might a "strong group situation" be? Give examples.

4. Have you ever been in a situation when you wanted to resist group pressure? What was the situation, and why did you want to resist? What could you have done to resist?

About Structure

5. What technique explained in Chapter 18 of this book does Stark use to introduce the essay?

6. Why does Stark address the reader directly by using "you"?

About Style and Tone

7. What effect does including direct quotations in paragraph 9 have in helping Stark achieve his purpose?

8. Should what Stark says in the last paragraph be placed earlier in the essay? Explain why or why not.

WRITING ASSIGNMENTS

www.mhhe.com/langan

Assignment 1: Writing a Paragraph

Have you had the following experience? From conversation with a friend, you believe you know his or her opinion on some matter. But when the two of you are with a larger group, you hear the friend agree with the general group opinion, even though it is different from the opinion he or she held before. The opinion might be about something unimportant, such as the quality of a new movie or TV show. Or it may be about something more important, such as whether or not someone is likable. Write a description of that experience. An opening statement for this paper might be something like this one:

> Group pressure caused _____ to change his (her) opinion about someone new at school.

Assignment 2: Writing a Paragraph

The "lines on the card" experiment gives just a hint of the kind of pressure that group opinion can bring to bear on an individual. What bigger, more important examples of group pressure can you think of? They might be ones occurring in your family, in your town, in your school, in your city, in the country, or in the world. Write a paragraph in which you describe one or more examples that you believe show group pressure on individual behavior. Here are a few topics to consider writing about:

- Making fun of a particular student

- Racial problems in a school or city

- The use of drugs or alcohol within a group of friends

- Being part of a gang

- Being a fan of a sports team

As you describe someone's behavior, be sure to include details that help show group pressure.

Assignment 3: Writing an Essay

The Stark essay explains an experiment done to determine how peer pressure exerted by strangers can affect someone. However, the author believes that pressure from friends is often much stronger and, therefore, might make someone give in quicker than the subjects in the experiment did. Do you agree? Write an essay in which you discuss three examples of peer pressure on someone to do things he or she really didn't want to do. Take these examples from your own experiences or from those of people you know well. Try answering questions such as the following when you draft your essay:

- Who was the source of the pressure?

- How did he, she, or they exert this pressure?

- How did the person being pressured feel (angry, anxious, fearful, uncomfortable, etc.)?

- What were the effects of the subject's giving in to—or resisting—the pressure?

In the Beginning
Roxanne Black

PREVIEW

For most of us, "health" is an either-or concept. Either we're sick or we're well. Either we're OK or we're not. But for people with chronic illness, the situation is different. There are good days and bad days, advances and setbacks. But like a shadow, the illness is always there. As a young teenager, Roxanne Black began learning the realities of chronic illness. This excerpt is taken from her autobiography, *Unexpected Blessings: Finding Hope and Healing in the Face of Illness.*

1 I sat at my bedroom window in my wheelchair, watching my high school rowing team pull away from the shore, eight friends smiling and waving as they moved into the choppy water. Not long ago, I'd been one of them.

2 I loved everything about rowing, the feeling of freedom, the teamwork, the sense of strength and accomplishment. When I rowed, I was at peace and forgot about my problems. Not that I'd had many then. In most ways, I was a typical New Jersey teenager, a shy high school freshman who lived with her mother in a small row house that overlooked Lake's Bay. My mother and I didn't have two dimes to rub together, but with that view from our windows, we considered ourselves rich.

3 It was after rowing one afternoon that I had the first inkling that something might be wrong with me—a sharp stab of back pain that took my breath away.

4 "What's the matter?" my mother asked when she saw me wincing.

5 "I don't know," I said, stretching. "I guess I strained a muscle."

6 By evening, the pain was excruciating. My mother filled a hot bath with Epsom salts, and later gave me a heating pad. I took a couple of Tylenol and decided I'd stay away from crew practice for a few days. In my young life, this had been the antidote for any ailment. Eventually everything passed, given time and a little rest.

7 But not this time. Instead of decreasing, the pain grew so intense that I could barely sit up in bed the next morning.

8 My mother took one look at me and said, "I'm taking you to the doctor."

9 But by the time we arrived at the office, the pain had subsided and the doctor advised that we simply continue with the heating pad and baths.

Two days later, I developed chest pains that by evening were so acute I could 10 barely breathe. Now I was beginning to worry.

This time the doctor prescribed antibiotics, thinking I might have an infec- 11 tion. The pains intensified over the next few days; then they too vanished.

This pattern of new symptoms that appeared, intensified, then vanished con- 12 tinued with an itchy red rash, which covered my body. After it mysteriously disappeared, my ankles swelled so severely that I was unable to fit into any of my shoes.

Although the doctor tracked my reports, took bloodwork, and examined me 13 closely, he couldn't figure out what was wrong. My symptoms were elusive; it was hard to pin them down.

Finally he referred me to a specialist. By the day of my appointment, all my 14 symptoms had subsided except for my swollen ankles. My mother and I arrived at his office, expecting this new doctor would prescribe another medication for what was probably an allergic reaction.

Although I'd never seen this doctor's face before, his cool, sober demeanor 15 as we walked in gave me a sense of foreboding.

After a routine examination, he studied my bloodwork, then touched my 16 ankles, which were so full of fluid they could be molded like lumps of clay.

Then he looked up and a strange word floated from his mouth. Lupus. I saw 17 it, like in a cartoon caption, odd and ominous, hanging in the air.

The word meant nothing to me, but my mother's reaction did; she covered 18 her face with her hands. In her work as a nurse, she'd spent years caring for patients with chronic illness. As I watched her sniff and take out a Kleenex, it hit me that this must be serious, something that Tylenol and bed rest weren't going to solve.

My health had always been part of my identity, something I was as certain 19 of as my strong legs and pumping heart. Now I was being told baffling facts about kidney function, inflammation, and antibodies.

But when the doctor said I was to be admitted to a children's hospital in 20 Philadelphia the following day for testing, I realized a chapter of my life was abruptly ending and a new one was about to start.

When I returned home, I looked up *lupus* in our medical dictionary: a chronic 21 autoimmune disease, potentially debilitating and sometimes fatal, that was first discovered in the Middle Ages. The illness follows an unpredictable course, with episodes of activity, called flares, alternating with periods of remission. During a flare, the immune system attacks the body's cells and tissue, resulting in inflammation and tissue damage.

The words "sometimes fatal" stood out to me, as if they were written in blood. 22 Just as harrowing were the lists of possible manifestations: dermatological, musculoskeletal, hematological, renal, hepatic, pulmonary. What else was there?

How had this ancient disease that only affected one in many hundreds in the 23 United States ended up in Atlantic City, residing in a teenager like me?

For that, there was no answer. 24

"There's always one moment in childhood when the door opens and lets the 25 future in," Graham Greene wrote. I don't know if most people remember that moment, but I do.

At the children's hospital, I shared a room with a three-year-old girl with a 26 winsome face and shiny black hair cut in a bob. She was so vibrant and lively, I assumed she was someone's daughter or sister, until I glimpsed a tiny hospital ID bracelet on her wrist.

Her name was Michelle, and we bonded from the moment we met. She 27 brought a herd of plastic ponies to my bedside, and we brushed their manes and made up stories.

"Why's she here?" I asked when her parents arrived, looking drawn and 28 worried.

"She has a hole in her heart," her mother told me. "She's having open-heart 29 surgery tomorrow."

A steady stream of doctors arrived to talk to Michelle's parents. I heard the 30 terse murmur of their voices behind the curtain that separated our room. Through it all, Michelle dashed between the beds, oblivious to the drama around her. She was so vital and energetic, it was hard to believe that anything serious was wrong with her.

I'd never known a sick child before, and now I was in a hospital full of 31 them. It seemed unnatural seeing toddlers on IV's, babies on ventilators, adolescents with leg braces, struggling to walk. A parade of pediatric malfunction passed my door, children smashed in motor accidents, suffering from muscular dystrophy and leukemia. This alternate world had existed all along, behind my formerly sunny, innocent life.

The next day I was to find out the results of my kidney biopsy, and Michelle 32 was headed to surgery. Before she left, she walked over and hugged me so tightly that I could smell the baby shampoo in her hair. Then she solemnly handed me a drawing she'd made of a house, a girl, and a tree.

"This is you, isn't it?"   33

She nodded.   34

"Well it's beautiful, thanks. I'll see you later."   35

I waited all day for them to bring Michelle back, trying to distract myself 36 by reading and crocheting, but it was no use. Breakfast came and went, then lunch, and still there was no sign of her.

Early in the evening, I was talking on the pay phone in the hallway when 37 an alarm sounded, and doctors began running down the hall from all directions. A woman's voice intoned a code over the loudspeakers, a foreign babble.

As I hung up, I saw two new figures running down the hallway. Their fea- 38 tures grew terribly familiar as they approached. It was Michelle's parents, their faces smeared with tears, heading in the same direction as the doctors.

My mother came out and hurried me back into the room. When she shut the 39 door, I stood there, looking at Michelle's bed, at the picture on the table she had drawn for me. I took out a little prayer book I'd brought along and began a prayer, infusing it with all the love and intention I could muster. A long terrible female scream pierced the silence.

A young floor nurse walked in a short while later. Her sad face was state- 40 ment enough, but then she told us. Michelle hadn't made it. She'd suffered a heart attack and died.

So there it was, and I had to face it: Life wasn't fair. Prayers weren't always 41 answered. The young and innocent could be lost. The door had swung open, and I had been pushed through to the other side.

READING COMPREHENSION QUESTIONS

www.mhhe.com/langan

1. The word *antidote* in "In my young life, this had been the antidote for any ailment" (paragraph 6) means
   a. poison.
   b. cause.
   c. symptom.
   d. remedy.

2. The word *debilitating* in "When I returned home, I looked up *lupus* in our medical dictionary: a chronic, autoimmune disease potentially debilitating and sometimes fatal . . ." (paragraph 21) means
   a. painful.
   b. incurable.
   c. incapacitating.
   d. serious.

3. Which of the following would be the best alternative title for this selection?
   a. Lupus
   b. Farewell to Rowing
   c. A Health Crisis
   d. Another World

4. Which sentence best expresses the main idea of the selection?
   a. "When I rowed, I was at peace and forgot my problems."
   b. "My symptoms were elusive; I couldn't pin them down."
   c. "So here it was, and I had to face it: Life wasn't fair."
   d. "The illness follows an unpredictable course, with episodes of activity called flares, alternating with periods of remission."

5. The writer and her mother
   a. lived in the city.
   b. lived in suburban Maryland.
   c. lived in a house overlooking a bay.
   d. were about to move to New Jersey.

6. *True or false* _____ Michelle, the child Black met in the hospital, also suffered from lupus.

7. *True or false* _____ The writer's disease was diagnosed quickly by her doctors.

8. From what the author says, we can conclude that Michelle
   a. looked very ill.
   b. showed no signs that she was ill.
   c. was an annoying roommate.
   d. was another patient's sister.

9. The author implies that she
   a. was baffled about how she had contracted lupus.
   b. felt sure that the doctors could cure her illness.
   c. wasn't particularly religious.
   d. had little faith in doctors.

10. We can infer that the writer
    a. had been around sick children before.
    b. felt great anxiety and sorrow about what happened to Michelle.
    c. wasn't worried about Michelle.
    d. saw no connection between her own situation and Michelle's.

DISCUSSION QUESTIONS

About Content

1. What signals did Roxanne get from her mother and her doctor that she had a serious disease?

2. According to this essay, when was the disease lupus first identified?

3. Why did the author enjoy rowing so much?

4. What accounts for Roxanne's mother's immediate reaction to hearing that her daughter had lupus?

About Structure

5. What in the introduction to this essay captures the attention of readers and gets them to read on?

6. In what part of the essay does the author's thesis appear, and why did the author choose to place it there?

About Style and Tone

7. Paragraph 25 contains a quotation from the novelist Graham Greene. How does this quotation help the author achieve her purpose?

8. Reread paragraphs 18 and 19. What words are used in these paragraphs to maintain coherence?

WRITING ASSIGNMENTS

www.mhhe.com/langan

Assignment 1: Writing a Paragraph

The diagnosis of lupus marked the beginning of a new chapter in Black's life. Similarly, most people look at certain events in their lives as marking a division between "how things used to be" and "how they are now." Such incidents might be a move to a new town, a divorce, the death of a loved one, a change in schools, or the birth of a child. Write a paragraph about one such incident in your life. Explain in what ways your life was changed by that incident.

Here are two sample topic sentences like the one you might use:

The birth of my son drastically altered my social life.

Working as a supermarket cashier last summer changed my attitude about the value of higher education.

Assignment 2: Writing a Paragraph

After Black was diagnosed with lupus, she naturally learned a great deal about the illness and its effects. What is a topic that you know more about than the average person because of some situation in your life? Maybe you know a lot about cars because your dad is a mechanic. Maybe you know about sign language because you have a deaf friend. Maybe you know about Puerto Rican food because your grandmother cooks it. Write a paragraph about that topic and explain how you know about it.

Assignment 3: Writing an Essay

At the end of this essay, Black writes, "So there it was, and I had to face it: Life wasn't fair." In your opinion, is life fair? Why or why not? Write an essay explaining your answer. Provide three examples or develop three reasons supporting your belief that life is or is not fair.

From Father to Son, Last Words to Live by
Dana Canedy

PREVIEW

On October 14, 2006, Dana Canedy's fiancé, First Sgt. Charles Monroe King, died in combat in Baghdad; their son Jordan was only seven months old. Before Charles was deployed to Iraq, he began recording a journal—a blend of stories from his life and pieces of advice—for Jordan. In this essay, Canedy, a *New York Times* editor, describes the acute pain of losing her son's father and seeks comfort in the words he left behind.

He drew pictures of himself with angel wings. He left a set of his dog tags 1 on a nightstand in my Manhattan apartment. He bought a tiny blue sweat suit for our baby to wear home from the hospital.

Then he began to write what would become a 200-page journal for our son, 2 in case he did not make it back from the desert in Iraq.

For months before my fiancé, First Sgt. Charles Monroe King, kissed my 3 swollen stomach and said goodbye, he had been preparing for the beginning of the life we had created and for the end of his own.

He boarded a plane in December 2005 with two missions, really—to lead 4 his young soldiers in combat and to prepare our boy for a life without him.

Dear son, Charles wrote on the last page of the journal, "I hope this book 5 is somewhat helpful to you. Please forgive me for the poor handwriting and grammar. I tried to finish this book before I was deployed to Iraq. It has to be something special to you. I've been writing it in the states, Kuwait and Iraq."

The journal will have to speak for Charles now. He was killed Oct. 14 when 6 an improvised explosive device detonated near his armored vehicle in Baghdad. Charles, 48, had been assigned to the Army's First Battalion, 67th Armored Regiment, Fourth Infantry Division, based in Fort Hood, Tex. He was a month from completing his tour of duty.

For our son's first Christmas, Charles had hoped to take him on a carriage 7 ride through Central Park. Instead, Jordan, now 9 months old, and I snuggled under a blanket in a horse-drawn buggy. The driver seemed puzzled about why I was riding alone with a baby and crying on Christmas Day. I told him.

"No charge," he said at the end of the ride, an act of kindness in a city that 8 can magnify loneliness.

On paper, Charles revealed himself in a way he rarely did in person. He thought hard about what to say to a son who would have no memory of him. Even if Jordan will never hear the cadence of his father's voice, he will know the wisdom of his words. 9

Never be ashamed to cry. No man is too good to get on his knee and humble himself to God. Follow your heart and look for the strength of a woman. 10

Charles tried to anticipate questions in the years to come. Favorite team? I am a diehard Cleveland Browns fan. Favorite meal? Chicken, fried or baked, candied yams, collard greens and cornbread. Childhood chores? Shoveling snow and cutting grass. First kiss? Eighth grade. 11

In neat block letters, he wrote about faith and failure, heartache and hope. He offered tips on how to behave on a date and where to hide money on vacation. Rainy days have their pleasures, he noted: Every now and then you get lucky and catch a rainbow. 12

Charles mailed the book to me in July, after one of his soldiers was killed and he had recovered the body from a tank. The journal was incomplete, but the horror of the young man's death shook Charles so deeply that he wanted to send it even though he had more to say. He finished it when he came home on a two-week leave in August to meet Jordan, then 5 months old. He was so intoxicated by love for his son that he barely slept, instead keeping vigil over the baby. 13

I can fill in some of the blanks left for Jordan about his father. When we met in my hometown of Radcliff, Ky., near Fort Knox, I did not consider Charles my type at first. He was bashful, a homebody and got his news from television rather than newspapers (heresy, since I'm a *New York Times* editor). 14

But he won me over. One day a couple of years ago, I pulled out a list of the traits I wanted in a husband and realized that Charles had almost all of them. He rose early to begin each day with prayers and a list of goals that he ticked off as he accomplished them. He was meticulous, even insisting on doing my ironing because he deemed my wrinkle-removing skills deficient. His rock-hard warrior's body made him appear tough, but he had a tender heart. 15

He doted on Christina, now 16, his daughter from a marriage that ended in divorce. He made her blush when he showed her a tattoo with her name on his arm. Toward women, he displayed an old-fashioned chivalry, something he expected of our son. Remember who taught you to speak, to walk and to be a gentleman, he wrote to Jordan in his journal. These are your first teachers, my little prince. Protect them, embrace them and always treat them like a queen. 16

Though as a black man he sometimes felt the sting of discrimination, Charles betrayed no bitterness. It's not fair to judge someone by the color of their skin, where they're raised or their religious beliefs, he wrote. Appreciate people for who they are and learn from their differences. 17

He had his faults, of course. Charles could be moody, easily wounded and infuriatingly quiet, especially during an argument. And at times, I felt, he put the military ahead of family. 18

He had enlisted in 1987, drawn by the discipline and challenges. Charles **19** had other options—he was a gifted artist who had trained at the *Art Institute of Chicago*—but felt fulfilled as a soldier, something I respected but never really understood. He had a chest full of medals and a fierce devotion to his men.

He taught the youngest, barely out of high school, to balance their checkbooks, **20** counseled them about girlfriends and sometimes bailed them out of jail. When he was home in August, I had a baby shower for him. One guest recently reminded me that he had spent much of the evening worrying about his troops back in Iraq.

Charles knew the perils of war. During the months before he went away and **21** the days he returned on leave, we talked often about what might happen. In his journal, he wrote about the loss of fellow soldiers. Still, I could not bear to answer when Charles turned to me one day and asked, "You don't think I'm coming back, do you?" We never said aloud that the fear that he might not return was why we decided to have a child before we planned a wedding, rather than risk never having the chance.

But Charles missed Jordan's birth because he refused to take a leave from **22** Iraq until all of his soldiers had gone home first, a decision that hurt me at first. And he volunteered for the mission on which he died, a military official told his sister, Gail T. King. Although he was not required to join the resupply convoy in Baghdad, he believed that his soldiers needed someone experienced with them. "He would say, 'My boys are out there, I've got to go check on my boys,'" said First Sgt. Arenteanis A. Jenkins, Charles's roommate in Iraq.

In my grief, that decision haunts me. Charles's father faults himself for not **23** begging his son to avoid taking unnecessary risks. But he acknowledges that it would not have made a difference. "He was a born leader," said his father, Charlie J. King. "And he believed what he was doing was right."

Back in April, after a roadside bombing remarkably similar to that which **24** would claim him, Charles wrote about death and duty.

The 18th was a long, solemn night, he wrote in Jordan's journal. We had a **25** memorial for two soldiers who were killed by an improvised explosive device. None of my soldiers went to the memorial. Their excuse was that they didn't want to go because it was depressing. I told them it was selfish of them not to pay their respects to two men who were selfless in giving their lives for their country.

Things may not always be easy or pleasant for you, that's life, but always **26** pay your respects for the way people lived and what they stood for. It's the honorable thing to do.

When Jordan is old enough to ask how his father died, I will tell him of **27** Charles's courage and assure him of Charles's love. And I will try to comfort him with his father's words.

God blessed me above all I could imagine, Charles wrote in the journal. I **28** have no regrets, serving your country is great.

He had tucked a message to me in the front of Jordan's journal. This is the let- **29** ter every soldier should write, he said. For us, life will move on through Jordan. He will be an extension of us and hopefully everything that we stand for. . . . I would like to see him grow up to be a man, but only God knows what the future holds.

READING COMPREHENSION QUESTIONS

1. The word *meticulous* in "He was meticulous, even insisting on doing my ironing because he deemed my wrinkle-removing skills deficient" (paragraph 15) means
   a. sloppy.
   b. careful and precise.
   c. generous and warm.
   d. careless.

2. The word *chivalry* in "Toward women, he displayed an old-fashioned chivalry, something he expected of our son. Remember who taught you to speak, to walk and to be a gentleman, he wrote to Jordan in his journal" (paragraph 16) means
   a. politeness.
   b. outlook.
   c. rudeness.
   d. attitude.

3. Which of the following would be the best alternative title for this selection?
   a. A Soldier's Letter
   b. Jordan's Early Years
   c. A Father's Gift to His Son
   d. Charles's Military Experience

4. Which sentence best expresses the main idea of the selection?
   a. Charles Monroe King writes about his experiences as a soldier in Iraq.
   b. Charles Monroe King provides his son Jordan with personal proverbs.
   c. Both Jordan's father, Charles Monroe King, and Jordan's mother, Dana Canedy, provide their son with words to live by.
   d. Dana Canedy writes an article for the *New York Times* about her fiancé's love for their son, Jordan.

5. Charles Monroe King was killed
   a. a month after starting his tour of duty in Iraq.
   b. a month before taking leave to visit Jordan for the first time.
   c. a month before completing his tour of duty in Iraq.
   d. a month after witnessing a roadside bombing that killed two of his soldiers.

6. *True or false?* _____ Charles's father begged his son to avoid taking unnecessary risks by joining a resupply convoy in Baghdad.

7. Charles and his fiancé first met in

    a. Radcliff, Kentucky.

    b. New York, New York.

    c. Cleveland, Ohio

    d. Chicago, Illinois.

8. Which of the following did Charles *not* write in his journal?

    a. Always be ashamed to cry.

    b. It's not fair to judge someone by the color of their skin.

    c. Every now and then you get lucky and catch a rainbow.

    d. Always pay your respects for the way people lived and what they stood for.

9. Charles wrote in his journal, "Follow your heart and look for the strength of a woman" (paragraph 10). From this passage, we can infer that he

    a. did not trust his mind.

    b. felt that women were stronger than men.

    c. felt that men were stronger than women.

    d. was sincere and respected women.

10. The author writes, "And at times, I felt, he put the military ahead of family" (paragraph 18). After reading the entire selection, we can infer that she

    a. never forgave Charles for putting the military ahead of his family.

    b. should have begged Charles not to sign up for the dangerous convoy mission.

    c. understood Charles's duty to his country.

    d. did not understand why Charles could not put his family ahead of the military.

DISCUSSION QUESTIONS

About Content

1. What did Charles hope to accomplish by writing the journal? Do you feel that he was successful? What does the author, Charles's fiancée, hope to accomplish by writing her article and publishing it in the *New York Times*?

2. The author writes that "on paper, Charles revealed himself in a way he rarely did in person" (paragraph 9). Why do you think this occurred?

3. What are some words of wisdom that you received from your parents or family members? What words do you have to inspire others?

About Structure

4. What patterns of development does the author use in her essay? Explain.

5. The author uses several time transition words to signal time relationships. Find three of these time words, and write them here:

    _____   _____

6. In paragraphs 22 and 23, the author includes information told to her by people other than Charles, such as his sister and his roommate in Iraq. Why do you think she chose this narrative strategy?

About Style and Tone

7. In paragraphs 1 and 2, the author does not indicate whom the pronoun "he" refers to: "He drew pictures of himself with angel wings. He left a set of his dog tags on a nightstand in my Manhattan apartment. He bought a tiny blue sweat suit for our baby to wear home from the hospital. Then he began to write what would become a 200-page journal for our son, in case he did not make it back from the desert in Iraq." Why do you think she waited until the third paragraph to provide a pronoun reference?

8. How do you think the author feels about America's military involvement in Iraq? Find evidence in the selection to support your opinion.

WRITING ASSIGNMENTS

www.mhhe.com/langan

Assignment 1: Writing a Paragraph

Author Dana Canedy weaves excerpts from her fiancé Charles's journal into her own essay about him. Write a paragraph about a person in your life whom you care about—such as a relative, a spouse, or a close friend—but whom you recognize has "faults, of course" (paragraph 18). Perhaps you enjoy this person's company but are annoyed by her grumbling. Or you admire the person's work ethic but find his flirting uncomfortable. In your topic sentence, state both sides of your feelings, as in the following sample topic statement:

> While Jim is a terrific supervisor, he sometimes flirts too much with the office staff.

Then fully describe one side of your subject's personality before you begin describing the other. Throughout the paragraph, illustrate your point with specific revealing comments and incidents.

Before you begin writing, describe your subject to a partner. Ask which supporting details seem most interesting and most relevant to the topic.

Assignment 2: Writing a Paragraph

Describe a person you know who has managed to positively touch the lives of nearly everyone around him or her. Divide your paragraph into three sections. These sections could be about *individuals* the person has impacted, such as any of these:

A grandchild

A former student

A coworker

Assignment 3: Writing an Essay

Charles Monroe King was a person who did not judge others by the color of their skin, where they were raised, or their religious beliefs, perhaps because, as his fiancé pointed out, he "sometimes felt the sting of discrimination" (paragraph 17). Write an essay about how it feels to be discriminated against. Select several specific instances in your life when you felt that someone was judging you unfairly. In your essay, devote each supporting paragraph to one such anecdote, describing what happened and how you responded.

A Drunken Ride, a Tragic Aftermath
Theresa Conroy and Christine M. Johnson

> ### PREVIEW
>
> Have you ever sat behind the wheel of your car after drinking? Have you ever assured yourself, "I haven't had too much. I'm still in control"? If you have, you're not alone. The large number of arrests for drunk driving proves that plenty of drivers who have been drinking thought they were capable of getting home safely. After all, who would get into a car with the intention of killing himself or herself or others? Yet killing is exactly what many drunk drivers do. If all drivers could read the following selection—a newspaper report on one tragic accident—perhaps the frequent cautions about drinking and driving would have more impact. Read the article and see if you agree.

When Tyson Baxter awoke after that drunken, tragic night—with a bloodied 1
head, broken arm, and battered face—he knew that he had killed his friends.

"I knew everyone had died," Baxter, eighteen, recalled. "I knew it before 2
anybody told me. Somehow, I knew."

Baxter was talking about the night of Friday, September 13, the night he and 3
seven friends piled into his Chevrolet Blazer after a beer-drinking party. On
Street Road in Upper Southampton, he lost control, rear-ended a car, and smashed
into two telephone poles. The Blazer's cab top shattered, and the truck spun
several times, ejecting all but one passenger.

Four young men were killed.   4

Tests would show that Baxter and the four youths who died were legally 5
intoxicated.

Baxter says he thinks about his dead friends on many sleepless nights at the 6
Abraxas Drug and Alcohol Rehabilitation Center near Pittsburgh, where, on
December 20, he was sentenced to be held after being found delinquent on
charges of vehicular homicide.

"I drove them where they wanted to go, and I was responsible for their lives," 7
Baxter said recently from the center, where he is undergoing psychological treatment. "I had the keys in my hand, and I blew it."

The story of September 13 is a story about the kind of horrors that drinking 8
and driving is spawning among high school students almost everywhere, . . .
about parents who lost their children in a flash and have filled the emptiness with
hatred, . . . about a youth whose life is burdened with grief and guilt because he
happened to be behind the wheel.

It is a story that the Baxter family and the dead boys' parents agreed to tell 9
in the hope that it would inspire high school students to remain sober during this
week of graduation festivities—a week that customarily includes a ritual night
of drunkenness.

It is a story of the times.   10

The evening of September 13 began in high spirits as Baxter, behind the wheel 11
of his gold Blazer, picked up seven high school chums for a drinking party for
William Tennent High School students and graduates at the home of a classmate.
Using false identification, according to police, the boys purchased one six-pack
of beer each from a Warminster Township bar.

The unchaperoned party, attended by about fifty teenagers, ended about 12
10:30 P.M. when someone knocked over and broke a glass china cabinet. Baxter and his friends decided to head for a fast-food restaurant. As Baxter turned
onto Street Road, he was trailed by a line of cars carrying other partygoers.

Baxter recalled that several passengers were swaying and rocking the high- 13
suspension vehicle. Police were unable to determine the vehicle's exact speed,
but, on the basis of the accounts of witnesses, they estimated it at fifty-five miles
per hour—ten miles per hour over the limit.

"I thought I was in control," Baxter said. "I wasn't driving like a nut; I was 14
just . . . driving. There was a bunch of noise, just a bunch of noise. The truck
was really bouncing.

"I remember passing two [cars]. That's the last I remember. I remember a 15 big flash, and that's it."

Killed in that flash were: Morris "Marty" Freedenberg, sixteen, who landed 16 near a telephone pole about thirty feet from the truck, his face ripped from his skull; Robert Schweiss, eighteen, a Bucks County Community College student, whose internal organs were crushed when he hit the pavement about thirty feet from the truck; Brian Ball, seventeen, who landed near Schweiss, his six-foot-seven-inch frame stretched three inches when his spine was severed; and Christopher Avram, seventeen, a premedical student at Temple University, who landed near the curb about ten feet from the truck.

Michael Serratore, eighteen, was thrown fifteen feet from the truck and 17 landed on the lawn of the CHI Institute with his right leg shattered. Baxter, who sailed about ten feet after crashing through the windshield of the Blazer, lost consciousness after hitting the street near the center lane. About five yards away, Paul Gee Jr., eighteen, lapsed into a coma from severe head injuries.

John Gahan, seventeen, the only passenger left in the Blazer, suffered a 18 broken ankle.

Brett Walker, seventeen, one of several Tennent students who saw the carnage 19 after the accident, would recall later in a speech to fellow students: "I ran over [to the scene]. These were the kids I would go out with every weekend.

"My one friend [Freedenberg], I couldn't even tell it was him except for his 20 eyes. He had real big, blue eyes. He was torn apart so bad . . . ."

Francis Schweiss was waiting up for his son, Robert, when he received a tele- 21 phone call from his daughter, Lisa. She was already at Warminster General Hospital.

"She said Robbie and his friends were in a bad accident and Robbie was not 22 here" at the hospital, Schweiss said. "I got in my car with my wife; we went to the scene of the accident."

There, police officers told Francis and Frances Schweiss that several boys 23 had been killed and that the bodies, as well as survivors, had been taken to Warminster General Hospital.

"My head was frying by then," Francis Schweiss said. "I can't even describe 24 it. I almost knew the worst was to be. I felt as though I were living a nightmare. I thought, 'I'll wake up. This just can't be.'"

In the emergency room, Francis Schweiss recalled, nurses and doctors were 25 scrambling to aid the injured and identify the dead—a difficult task because some bodies were disfigured and because all the boys had been carrying fake drivers' licenses.

A police officer from Upper Southampton was trying to question friends of 26 the dead and injured—many of whom were sobbing and screaming—in an attempt to match clothing with identities.

When the phone rang in the Freedenberg home, Robert Sr. and his wife, Bobbi, 27 had just gone upstairs to bed; their son Robert Jr. was downstairs watching a movie on television.

Bobbi Freedenberg and her son picked up the receiver at the same time. It 28 was from Warminster General. . . . There had been a bad accident. . . . The family should get to the hospital quickly.

Outside the morgue about twenty minutes later, a deputy county coroner told 29 Rob Jr., twenty-two, that his brother was dead and severely disfigured; Rob decided to spare his parents additional grief by identifying the body himself.

Freedenberg was led into a cinder-block room containing large drawers 30 resembling filing cabinets. In one of the drawers was his brother, Marty, identifiable only by his new high-top sneakers.

"It was kind of like being taken through a nightmare," Rob Jr. said. "That's 31 something I think about every night before I go to sleep. That's hell. . . . That whole night is what hell is all about for me."

As was his custom, Morris Ball started calling the parents of his son's friends 32 after Brian missed his 11:00 P.M. curfew.

The first call was to the Baxters' house, where the Baxters' sixteen-year-old 33 daughter, Amber, told him about the accident.

At the hospital, Morris Ball demanded that doctors and nurses take him to 34 his son. The hospital staff had been unable to identify Brian—until Ball told them that his son wore size fourteen shoes.

Brian Ball was in the morgue. Lower left drawer.   35

"He was six foot seven, but after the accident he measured six foot ten, 36 because of what happened to him," Ball said. "He had a severed spinal cord at the neck. His buttocks were practically ripped off, but he was lying down and we couldn't see that. He was peaceful and asleep.

"He was my son and my baby. I just can't believe it sometimes. I still can't 37 believe it. I still wait for him to come home."

Lynne Pancoast had just finished watching the 11:00 P.M. news and was curled 38 up in her bed dozing with a book in her lap when the doorbell rang. She assumed that one of her sons had forgotten his key, and she went downstairs to let him in.

A police light was flashing through the window and reflecting against her 39 living room wall; Pancoast thought that there must be a fire in the neighborhood and that the police were evacuating homes.

Instead, police officers told her there had been a serious accident involving 40 her son, Christopher Avram, and that she should go to the emergency room at Warminster General.

At the hospital she was taken to an empty room and told that her son was dead. 41

Patricia Baxter was asleep when a Warminster police officer came to the house 42 and informed her that her son had been in an accident.

At the hospital, she could not immediately recognize her own son lying on a 43 bed in the emergency room. His brown eyes were swollen shut, and his straight brown hair was matted with blood that had poured from a deep gash in his forehead.

While she was staring at his battered face, a police officer rushed into the 44 room and pushed her onto the floor—protection against the hysterical father of a dead youth who was racing through the halls, proclaiming that he had a gun and shouting, "Where is she? I'm going to kill her. I'm going to kill him. I'm going to kill his mother."

The man, who did not have a gun, was subdued by a Warminster police 45 officer and was not charged.

Amid the commotion, Robert Baxter, a Lower Southampton highway patrol 46 officer, arrived at the hospital and found his wife and son.

"When he came into the room, he kept going like this," Patricia Baxter said, 47 holding up four fingers. At first, she said, she did not understand that her husband was signaling that four boys had been killed in the accident.

After Tyson regained consciousness, his father told him about the deaths.   48

"All I can remember is just tensing up and just saying something," Tyson 49 Baxter said. "I can remember saying, 'I know.'

"I can remember going nuts."   50

In the days after the accident, as the dead were buried in services that Tyson 51 Baxter was barred by the parents of the victims from attending, Baxter's parents waited for him to react to the tragedy and release his grief.

"In the hospital he was nonresponsive," Patricia Baxter said. "He was home 52 for a month, and he was nonresponsive.

"We never used to do this, but we would be upstairs and listen to see if Ty 53 responded when his friends came to visit," she said. "But the boy would be silent. That's the grief that I felt. The other kids showed a reaction. My son didn't."

Baxter said, however, that he felt grief from the first, that he would cry in 54 the quiet darkness of his hospital room and, later, alone in the darkness of his bedroom. During the day, he said, he blocked his emotions.

"It was *just* at night. I thought about it all the time. It's still like that."   55

At his parents' urging, Baxter returned to school on September 30.   56

"I don't remember a thing," he said of his return. "I just remember walking 57 around. I didn't say anything to anybody. It didn't really sink in."

Lynne Pancoast, the mother of Chris Avram, thought it was wrong for 58 Baxter to be in school, and wrong that her other son, Joel, a junior at William Tennent, had to walk through the school halls and pass the boy who "killed his brother."

Morris Ball said he was appalled that Baxter "went to a football game while 59 my son lay buried in a grave."

Some William Tennent students said they were uncertain about how they should 60 treat Baxter. Several said they went out of their way to treat him normally, others said they tried to avoid him, and others declined to be interviewed on the subject.

The tragedy unified the senior class, according to the school principal, Kenneth 61 Kastle. He said that after the accident, many students who were friends of the victims joined the school's Students Against Driving Drunk chapter.

Matthew Weintraub, seventeen, a basketball player who witnessed the bloody 62 accident scene, wrote to President Reagan and detailed the grief among the student body. He said, however, that he experienced a catharsis after reading the letter at a student assembly and, as a result, did not mail it.

"And after we got over the initial shock of the news, we felt as though we 63 owed somebody something," Weintraub wrote. "It could have been us and maybe we could have stopped it, and now it's too late. . . .

"We took these impressions with us as we then visited our friends who had 64 been lucky enough to live. One of them was responsible for the accident; he was the driver. He would forever hold the deaths of four young men on his conscience. Compared with our own feelings of guilt, [we] could not begin to fathom this boy's emotions. He looked as if he had a heavy weight upon his head and it would remain there forever."

About three weeks after the accident, Senator H. Craig Lewis (D., Bucks) 65 launched a series of public forums to formulate bills targeting underage drinking. Proposals developed through the meetings include outlawing alcohol ads on radio and television, requiring police to notify parents of underage drinkers, and creating a tamperproof driver's license.

The parents of players on William Tennent's 1985–1986 boys' basketball team, 66 which lost Ball and Baxter because of the accident, formed the Caring Parents of William Tennent High School Students to help dissuade students from drinking.

Several William Tennent students, interviewed on the condition that their 67 names not be published, said that, because of the accident, they would not drive after drinking during senior week, which will be held in Wildwood, N.J., after graduation June 13.

But they scoffed at the suggestion that they curtail their drinking during the 68 celebrations.

"We just walk [after driving to Wildwood]," said one youth. "Stagger is more 69 like it."

"What else are we going to do, go out roller skating?" an eighteen-year-old 70 student asked.

"You telling us we're not going to drink?" one boy asked. "We're going to 71 drink very heavily. I want to come home retarded. That's senior week. I'm going to drink every day. Everybody's going to drink every day."

Tyson Baxter sat at the front table of the Bucks County courtroom on Decem- 72 ber 20, his arm in a sling, his head lowered, and his eyes dry. He faced twenty counts of vehicular homicide, four counts of involuntary manslaughter, and two counts of driving under the influence of alcohol.

Patricia Ball said she told the closed hearing that "it was Tyson Baxter who 73 killed our son. They used the car as a weapon. We know they killed our children as if it were a gun. They killed our son.

"I really could have felt justice [was served] if Tyson Baxter was the only 74 one who died in that car," she said in an interview, "because he didn't take care of our boys."

Police officers testified before Bucks County President Judge Isaac S. Garb 75 that tests revealed that the blood-alcohol levels of Baxter and the four dead boys were above the 0.10 percent limit used in Pennsylvania to establish intoxication.

Baxter's blood-alcohol level was 0.14 percent, Ball's 0.19 percent, Schweiss's 76 0.11 percent, Avram's 0.12 percent, and Freedenberg's 0.38 percent. Baxter's level indicated that he had had eight or nine drinks—enough to cause abnormal bodily functions such as exaggerated gestures and to impair his mental faculties, according to the police report.

After the case was presented, Garb invited family members of the dead teens 77 to speak.

In a nine-page statement, Bobbi Freedenberg urged Garb to render a decision 78 that would "punish, rehabilitate, and deter others from this act."

The parents asked Garb to give Baxter the maximum sentence, to prohibit 79 him from graduating, and to incarcerate him before Christmas Day. (Although he will not attend formal ceremonies, Baxter will receive a diploma from William Tennent this week.)

After hearing from the parents, Garb called Baxter to the stand.   80

"I just said that all I could say was, 'I'm sorry; I know I'm totally responsible 81 for what happened,'" Baxter recalled. "It wasn't long, but it was to the point."

Garb found Baxter delinquent and sentenced him to a stay at Abraxas Reha- 82 bilitation Center—for an unspecified period beginning December 23—and community service upon his return. Baxter's driver's license was suspended by the judge for an unspecified period, and he was placed under Garb's jurisdiction until age twenty-one.

Baxter is one of fifty-two Pennsylvania youths found responsible for fatal 83 drunken-driving accidents in the state in 1985.

Reflecting on the hearing, Morris Ball said there was no legal punishment 84 that would have satisfied his longings.

"They can't bring my son back," he said, "and they can't kill Tyson Baxter." 85

Grief has forged friendships among the dead boys' parents, all of whom blame 86 Tyson Baxter for their sons' deaths. Every month they meet at each other's homes, but they seldom talk about the accident.

Several have joined support groups to help them deal with their losses. Some 87 said they feel comfortable only with other parents whose children are dead.

Bobbi Freedenberg said her attitude had worsened with the passage of time. 88 "It seems as if it just gets harder," she said. "It seems to get worse."

Freedenberg, Schweiss, and Pancoast said they talk publicly about their sons' 89 deaths in hopes that the experience will help deter other teenagers from drunken driving.

Schweiss speaks each month to the Warminster Youth Aid Panel—a group 90 of teenagers who, through drug use, alcohol abuse, or minor offenses, have run afoul of the law.

"When I talk to the teens, I bring a picture of Robbie and pass it along to 91 everyone," Schweiss said, wiping the tears from his cheeks. "I say, 'He was with us last year.' I get emotional and I cry. . . .

"But I know that my son helps me. I firmly believe that every time I speak, 92 he's right on my shoulder."

When Pancoast speaks to a group of area high school students, she drapes 93 her son's football jersey over the podium and displays his graduation picture.

"Every time I speak to a group, I make them go through the whole thing 94 vicariously," Pancoast said. "It's helpful to get out and talk to kids. It sort of helps keep Chris alive. . . . When you talk, you don't think."

At Abraxas, Baxter attended high school classes until Friday. He is one of three 95 youths there who supervise fellow residents, who keep track of residents' whereabouts, attendance at programs, and adherence to the center's rules and regulations.

Established in Pittsburgh in 1973, the Abraxas Foundation provides an alter- 96 native to imprisonment for offenders between sixteen and twenty-five years old whose drug and alcohol use has led them to commit crimes.

Licensed and partially subsidized by the Pennsylvania Department of Health, 97 the program includes work experience, high school education, and prevocational training. Counselors conduct individual therapy sessions, and the residents engage in peer-group confrontational therapy sessions.

Baxter said his personality had changed from an "egotistical, arrogant" teen- 98 ager to someone who is "mellow" and mature.

"I don't have quite the chip on my shoulder. I don't really have a right to 99 be cocky anymore," he said.

Baxter said not a day went by that he didn't remember his dead friends.   100

"I don't get sad. I just get thinking about them," he said. "Pictures pop 101 into my mind. A tree or something reminds me of the time. . . . Sometimes I laugh. . . . Then I go to my room and reevaluate it like a nut," he said.

Baxter said his deepest longing was to stand beside the graves of his four 102 friends.

More than anything, Baxter said, he wants to say good-bye.   103

"I just feel it's something I *have* to do, . . . just to talk," Baxter said, avert- 104 ing his eyes to hide welling tears. "Deep down I think I'll be hit with it when I see the graves. I know they're gone, but they're not gone."

READING COMPREHENSION QUESTIONS

1. The word *fathom* in "Compared with our own feelings of guilt, [we] could not begin to fathom this boy's emotions" (paragraph 64) means
    a. choose.
    b. understand.
    c. mistake.
    d. protest.

2. The word *dissuade* in "The parents . . . formed the Caring Parents of William Tennent High School Students to help dissuade students from drinking" (paragraph 66) means
    a. discourage.
    b. delay.
    c. organize.
    d. frighten.

3. Which of the following would be the best alternative title for this selection?
    a. The Night of September 13
    b. A Fatal Mistake: Teenage Drinking and Driving
    c. The Agony of Parents
    d. High School Drinking Problems

4. Which sentence best expresses the main idea of the selection?
    a. Teenagers must understand the dangers and consequences of drinking and driving.
    b. Tyson Baxter was too drunk to drive that night.
    c. The Abraxas Foundation is a model alternative program to imprisonment for teenagers.
    d. Teenagers are drinking more than ever before.

5. The hospital had trouble identifying the boys because
    a. officials could not find their families.
    b. the boys all had false licenses and some of their bodies were mutilated.
    c. there weren't enough staff members on duty at the hospital that night.
    d. everyone was withholding information.

6. Tyson Baxter feels that
    a. the judge's sentence was unfair.
    b. he will never graduate from high school.
    c. he is responsible for the whole accident.
    d. he should not be blamed for the accident.

7. *True or false?* _____ Because of the accident, all the seniors promised that they would not drink during senior week.

8. The authors imply that the parents of the dead boys felt that
   a. Tyson should not be punished.
   b. their boys shared no blame for the accident.
   c. Tyson should have come to the boys' funerals.
   d. Tyson should be allowed to attend graduation.

9. The authors imply that most of the parents' anger has been toward
   a. school officials.
   b. Senator H. Craig Lewis.
   c. their local police.
   d. Tyson Baxter.

10. The authors imply that Tyson
   a. behaved normally after the accident.
   b. will always have a problem with alcohol.
   c. no longer thinks about his dead friends.
   d. is benefiting from his time at Abraxas.

DISCUSSION QUESTIONS

About Content

1. Why do the authors call their narrative "a story of the times"?

2. Exactly why did four teenagers die in the accident? To what extent were their deaths the driver's fault? Their own fault? Society's fault?

3. What effect has the accident had on other Tennent students? In view of the tragedy, can you explain the reluctance of the Tennent students to give up drinking during "senior week"?

4. How would you describe the attitude of Tyson Baxter after the accident? How would you characterize the attitude of the parents? Whose attitude, if any, seems more appropriate under the circumstances?

About Structure

5. The lead paragraphs in a newspaper article such as this one are supposed to answer questions known as the *five W's:* who, what, where, when, and why.

   Which paragraphs in the article answer these questions? _____

6. The authors *do not* use transitional words to move from one section of their article to the next. How, then, do they manage to keep their narrative organized and clear?

About Style and Tone

7. Why do the authors use so many direct quotations in their account of the accident? How do these quotations add to the effectiveness of the article?

8. What seems to be the authors' attitude toward Tyson Baxter at the end of the piece? Why do you think they end with Tyson's desire to visit his dead friends' graves? What would have been the effect of ending with Lynne Pancoast's words in paragraph 94?

WRITING ASSIGNMENTS

Assignment 1: Writing a Paragraph

While drunk drivers are of all ages, a large percentage of them are young. Write a paragraph explaining what you think would be one or more *effective* ways of dramatizing to young people the dangers of drunk driving. Keep in mind that the young are being cautioned all the time, and that some of the warnings are so familiar that they probably don't have any impact.

What kind of caution or cautions would make young people take notice? Develop one approach in great detail or suggest several approaches for demonstrating the dangers of drunk driving to the young.

Assignment 2: Writing a Paragraph

Tyson Baxter's friends might still be alive if Baxter had not been drunk when he drove. But there is another way the deaths could have been avoided—the boys might have refused to get into the car. Such a refusal would not have been easy; one does not, after all, want to embarrass a person who has given you a ride to some event. But sometimes it may be absolutely necessary to make such a refusal. In groups of two or three, discuss various ways to turn down a ride from a driver who may be drunk. Then write a paragraph suggesting one or more strategies.

Assignment 3: Writing an Essay

A number of letters to the editor followed the appearance of "A Drunken Ride, a Tragic Aftermath." Here are some of them:

> To the Editor:
> I am deeply concerned by the June 8 article, "A Drunken Ride, a Tragic Aftermath," not because of the tragedy it unfolds, but because of the tragedy that is occurring as a result.

It is an injustice on the part of the parents whose children died to blame Tyson Baxter so vehemently for those deaths. (I lost my best friend in a similar accident eight years ago, and I haven't forgotten the pain or the need to blame.) All the youths were legally intoxicated. None of them refused to go with Mr. Baxter, and I submit that he did not force them to ride with him.

Yes, Mr. Baxter is guilty of drunk driving, but I would like the other parents to replace Mr. Baxter with their sons and their cars and ask themselves again where the blame lies.

Tyson Baxter did not have the intent to kill, and his car was not the weapon. All these boys were Mr. Baxter's friends. The weapon used to kill them was alcohol, and in a way each boy used it on himself.

If we are to assign blame, it goes far beyond one drunk eighteen-year-old. The answer lies in our society and its laws—laws about drinking and driving, and laws of parenting, friendship, and responsibility. Why, for instance, didn't the other youths call someone to come get them, or call a taxi, rather than choose to take that fatal ride?

These parents should be angry and they should fight against drunk driving by making people aware. But they shouldn't continue to destroy the life of one boy whose punishment is the fact that he survived.

Elizabeth Bowen
Philadelphia

To the Editor:

I could not believe the attitude of the parents of the boys who were killed in the accident described in the June 8 article "A Drunken Ride, a Tragic Aftermath." Would they really feel that justice was done if Tyson Baxter were dead, too?

Tyson Baxter is not the only guilty person. All the boys who got into the vehicle were guilty, as well as all the kids at the party who let them go. Did any of the parents question their children earlier that fateful night as to who would be the "designated driver" (or did they think their sons would never go out drinking)?

How would those parents feel if their son happened to be the one behind the wheel?

I do not want to lessen the fact that Tyson Baxter was guilty (a guilt he readily admits to and will carry with him for a lifetime). However, should he have to carry his own guilt and be burdened with everyone else's guilt as well?

Andrea D. Colantti
Philadelphia

To the Editor:

Reading the June 8 article about the tragic aftermath of the drunken-driving accident in which high school students were killed and injured, I was aware of a major missing element. That element is the role of individual responsibility.

While we cannot control everything that happens to us, we can still manage many of the events of our lives. Individual responsibility operates at two levels. First is the accountability each person has for his own actions. To drink, or not to drink. To drink to excess, or to remain sober. To ride with someone who has been drinking, or to find another ride.

Second is the responsibility to confront those who are drinking or using drugs and planning to drive. To talk to them about their alcohol or drug consumption, to take their keys, call a cab, or do whatever else a friend would do.

The toughest, most punitive laws will not prevent people from drinking and driving, nor will they rectify the results of an accident. The only things we can actually control are our personal choices and our responses.

Don't drink and drive. Don't ride with those that do. Use your resources to stop those who try.

Gregory A. Gast
Willow Grove

To the Editor:

After reading the June 8 article about the tragic accident involving the students from William Tennent High School, my heart goes out to the parents of the boys who lost their lives. I know I can't begin to understand the loss they feel. However, even more so, my heart goes out to them for their inability to forgive the driver and their ability to wish him dead.

I certainly am not condoning drunk driving; in fact, I feel the law should be tougher.

But how can they be so quick to judge and hate this boy, when all their sons were also legally drunk, some more so than the driver, and any one of them could have easily been the driver himself? They all got into the car knowingly drunk and were noisily rocking the vehicle. They were all teenagers, out for a night of fun, never thinking of the consequences of drunk driving.

I would view this differently had the four dead boys been in another car, sober, and hit by a drunk driver. However, when you knowingly enter a car driven by someone who is drunk and are drunk yourself, you are responsible for what happens to you.

Tyson Baxter, the driver, needs rehabilitation and counseling. He will live with this for the rest of his life. The parents of the four boys who died need to learn about God, who is forgiving, and apply that forgiveness to a boy who desperately needs it. He could have easily been one of their sons.

Debbie Jones
Wilmington

These letters make apparent a difference of opinion about how severely Tyson Baxter should be punished. Write an essay in which, in an introductory paragraph, you advance your judgment about the appropriate punishment for Tyson Baxter. Then provide three supporting paragraphs in which you argue and defend your opinion. You may use or add to ideas stated in the article or the letters, but think through the ideas yourself and put them into your own words.

Assignment 4: Writing an Essay Using Internet Research

The tragic deaths of Tyson Baxter's four friends highlight the problem of drinking and driving. What can be done to get drunken drivers off the road? Use the Internet to research the topic. Then write an essay that explains three ways to get intoxicated drivers off the road. These could include ways to prevent people from drinking and driving in the first place, or ways to keep a person convicted of drunken driving from doing it again.

To begin your research, use the very helpful search engine Google (www .google.com). Try one of the following phrases or some related phrase:

keeping drunk drivers off the road

drunk drivers and prevention

successful prevention programs for drunk driving

As you proceed, you'll develop a sense of how to "track down" and focus a topic by adding more information to your search words and phrases.

Answers to Sentence-Skills Diagnostic Test and Introductory Activities

PREVIEW

The Appendix provides answers for the Sentence-Skills Diagnostic Test on pages 412–417 and for the Introductory Activities in Part Five.

SENTENCE-SKILLS DIAGNOSTIC TEST *(pages 412–417)*

Fragments
1. X
2. C
3. X
4. X
5. C
6. X

Run-Ons
7. C
8. X
9. X
10. X
11. C
12. X

Standard English Verbs
13. C
14. C
15. X
16. X

Irregular Verbs
17. X
18. C
19. C
20. X

Subject-Verb Agreement
21. X
22. X
23. C
24. X

Consistent Verb Tense
25. X
26. C
27. C
28. X

Pronoun Agreement, Reference, and Point of View
29. X
30. C
31. X
32. C
33. X
34. C

Pronoun Types
35. X
36. C

Adjectives and Adverbs
37. X
38. X

Misplaced Modifiers
39. X
40. C
41. X
42. X

Dangling Modifiers
43. C
44. X
45. C
46. X

Faulty Parallelism
47. X
48. C
49. X
50. C

Capital Letters
51. X
52. X
53. C
54. X

Apostrophe
55. C
56. X
57. C
58. X

Quotation Marks
59. C
60. X
61. X
62. C

Comma
63. X
64. X
65. C
66. X
67. C
68. X

Commonly Confused Words
69. X
70. X
71. C
72. X
73. X
74. C

Effective Word Use
75. X
76. X
77. X
78. X

INTRODUCTORY ACTIVITIES

Fragments (page 427)

1. thought
2. subject
3. verb
4. subject

Run-Ons (page 443)

1. period
2. *but*
3. semicolon
4. *when*

Standard English Verbs (page 457)

enjoyed . . . enjoys; started . . . starts; cooked . . . cooks

1. past . . . -*ed*
2. present . . . -*s*

Irregular Verbs (page 466)

1. crawled, crawled (regular)
2. brought, brought (irregular)
3. used, used (regular)
4. did, done (irregular)
5. gave, given (irregular)
6. laughed, laughed (regular)
7. went, gone (irregular)
8. scared, scared (regular)
9. dressed, dressed (regular)
10. saw, seen (irregular)

Subject-Verb Agreement (page 475)

The second sentence in each pair is correct.

Pronoun Agreement and Reference (page 482)

The second sentence in each pair is correct.

Misplaced and Dangling Modifiers (page 500)

1. *Intended:* On their wedding day, Clyde and Charlotte decided to have two children.
   Unintended: Clyde and Charlotte decided to have two children who would appear on their wedding day.
2. *Intended:* The students who failed the test no longer like the math instructor.
   Unintended: The math instructor failed the test.
3. *Intended:* My dog sat with me as I smoked a pipe.
   Unintended: My dog smoked a pipe.
4. *Intended:* He was busy talking on a cell phone.
   Unintended: His car was talking on a cell phone.

Capital Letters (page 514)

All the answers to questions 1 through 13 should be in capital letters.
14. The   15. I   16. That

Apostrophes (page 527)

1. The purpose of the ‘*s* is to show possession (Larry owns the motorcycle, the boyfriend belongs to the sister, Grandmother owns the shotgun, the room belongs to the men).
2. The purpose of the apostrophe is to show the omission of one or more letters in a contraction—two words shortened to form one word.
3. In each of the second sentences, the ‘*s* shows possession: the body of the vampire; the center of the baked potato. In each of the first sentences, the *s* is used to form a simple plural: more than one vampire; more than one potato.

Quotation Marks *(page 536)*

1. The purpose of quotation marks is to set off the exact words of a speaker. (The words that the young man actually spoke aloud are set off with quotation marks, as are the words that the old woman spoke aloud.)
2. Commas and periods go inside quotation marks.

Commas *(page 544)*

1. a. Frank's interests are Maria, television, and sports.
   b. My mother put her feet up, sipped some iced tea, and opened the newspaper.
2. a. Although they are tiny insects, ants are among the strongest creatures on Earth.
   b. To remove the cap of the aspirin bottle, you must first press down on it.
3. a. Kitty Litter and Dredge Rivers, Hollywood's leading romantic stars, have made several movies together.
   b. Sarah, who is my next-door neighbor, just entered the hospital with an intestinal infection.
4. a. The wedding was scheduled for four o'clock, but the bride changed her mind at two.
   b. Verna took three coffee breaks before lunch, and then she went on a two-hour lunch break.
5. a. Lola's mother asked her, "What time do you expect to get home?"
   b. "Don't bend over to pat the dog," I warned, "or he'll bite you."
6. a. Roy ate seventeen hamburgers on July 29, 2007, and lived to tell about it.
   b. Roy lives at 817 Cresson Street, Detroit, Michigan.

Other Punctuation Marks *(page 553)*

1. pets: holly
2. freeze-dried
3. Shakespeare (1564–1616)
4. Earth; no
5. proudly—with

Commonly Confused Words *(page 578)*

1. Your
2. There
3. then
4. to
5. It's

Effective Word Choice *(page 588)*

1. "Flipped out" is slang.
2. "Few and far between" is a cliché.
3. "Ascertained" is a pretentious word.

Credits

Text Credits

Page 640 "All the Good Things" by Sister Helen P. Mrosla, O.S.F. Originally published in *Proteus,* Spring 1991. Reprinted by permission as edited and published by *Reader's Digest* in October, 1991; **654** "The Scholarship Jacket," by Marta Salinas from *Nosotros: Latina Literature Today* by Maria del Carmen Boza, Beverly Silva, and Carmen Valle (eds.). Copyright © 1986 by Bilingual Press, Arizona State University, Tempe, AZ.; **661** "Joe Davis: A Cool Man" by Beth Johnson. Copyright © Beth Johnson. Reprinted with permission. Beth Johnson lives in Lederach, Pennsylvania; **669** "The Fist, The Clay, and The Rock" by Donald Holland. Reprinted by permission of the author; **674** "What Good Families are Doing Right" by Dolores Curran. Reprinted from *McCall's,* March 1983. Reprinted by permission of Dolores Curran, author and parent-educator; **688** "Do it Better!" Excerpt from *Think Big* by Benjamin Carson, MD with Cecil Murphey. Copyright © 1992 by Benjamin Carson, M.D. Used by permission of Zondervan Publishing; **698** "Anxiety: Challenge by Another Name" by James Lincoln Collier. Originally published by *Reader's Digest,* December 1986. Reprinted by permission of the author; **705** "Let's Really Reform Our Schools" by Anita Garland. Copyright © 1994. Reprinted by permission of the author; **713** "How They Get You to Do That" by Janny Scott. Originally published in the *Los Angeles Times,* July 23, 1992. Copyright 1992, Los Angeles Times. Reprinted by permission; **723** Excerpt from VERDERBER, *Communicate!,* 8E. ©1996 Wadsworth, a part of Cengage Learning, Inc. Reproduced by permission. www.cengage.com/permissions; **730** "Extra Large, Please" by Diane Urbina. Reprinted by permission of the author; **738** "The Most Hateful Words" from *The Opposite of Fate* by Amy Tan. Copyright 2003 by Amy Tan. First appeared in *The New Yorker.* Reprinted by permission of the author and the Sandra Dijkstra Literary Agency; **744** "Group Pressure" from STARK, *Sociology,* 3E. © 1989 Wadsworth, a part of Cengage Learning, Inc. Reproduced by permission. www.cengage.com/permissions; **750** "In the Beginning" from *Unexpected Blessings* by Roxanne Black, copyright © 2008 by Roxanne Black. Used by permission of Avery Publishing, an imprint of Penguin Group (USA); **756** "From Father to Son, Last Words to Live by" by Dana Canedy. Copyright © 2007 by The New York Times Co. Used by permission and protected by the Copyright Laws of the United States. The printing, copying, redistribution, or retransmission of the Material without express written permission is prohibited; **762** "A Drunken Ride, A Tragic Aftermath" by Theresa Conroy and Christine M. Johnson, reprinted from *The Philadelphia Inquirer.* Copyright © 1986 The Philadelphia Inquirer. Reprinted by permission.

Photo Credits

Part 1 Opener © Getty Images/Digital Vision; **Chapter 1 Opener** © Stockbyte/Getty Images; **12** © Jeff Greenberg/PhotoEdit; **CO 2** © Asia Images Group/Getty Images; **CO 3** © BananaStock/PunchStock; **85** © Thomas Northcut/Getty Images; **CO 4** © PhotoAlto/Sigrid Olsson/Getty Images; **CO 5** © Bill Pugliano/Getty Images; **CO 6** © Jupiterimages/Getty Images; **Part 2 Opener** © Royalty-Free/Corbis; **CO 7** © Hill Street Studios/Getty Images; **CO 8** © Zia Soleil/Getty Images; **190** © PhotoAlto/Alamy; **203** © David Young Wolff/ Photo Edit; **204** © Corbis; **CO 10** USGS photo by Don Becker; **218** © PhotoSpin, Inc/Alamy; **224** © Stephanie Carter/Photodisc; **CO 11** © Bob Daemmrich/The Image Works; **228** © Premium Stock/Imagestate; **239** (left): © ABC/Photofest; **239** (right): © IPS Co., Ltd./Beateworks/Corbis; **CO 12** © Bob Daemmrich/The Image Works; **254** © Jose Luis Pelaez, Inc./Corbis; **259** © Steve Prezant/Corbis; **CO 13** © Steve Jennings/WireImage/

Index